AN

EXPOSITION

OF THE

THIRTY-NINE ARTICLES

OF THE

CHURCH OF ENGLAND:

BY

GILBERT, BISHOP OF SARUM.

WITH

AN APPENDIX

CONTAINING THE AUGSBURG CONFESSION, CREED OF POPE PIUS IV., &c.

REVISED AND CORRECTED,

WITH COPIOUS NOTES, AND ADDITIONAL REFERENCES,

BY THE

REV. JAMES R. PAGE, A.M.

OF QUEEN'S COLLEGE, CAMBRIDGE, MINISTER OF CARLISLE CHAPEL, LAMBETH.

LONDON:

PRINTED FOR SCOTT, WEBSTER, AND GEARY,

36, CHARTERHOUSE SQUARE.

1837.

LONDON:
PRINTED BY A. SWEETING, BARTLETT'S BUILDINGS, HOLBORN.

TO THE MOST REVEREND FATHER IN GOD,

WILLIAM HOWLEY, D.D.,

LORD ARCHBISHOP OF CANTERBURY,

&c., &c., &c.

My Lord,

I should only transgress the bounds of propriety, and do violence to your Grace's feelings, were I to trespass upon you with a tedious or complimentary address.

I cannot, however, but say, that, in availing myself of your Grace's kind and condescending permission, it is to me a cause of much thankfulness and sincere gratification to dedicate this volume to your Grace, not alone because of the high station in which Providence has placed you, but also because I believe that the merits of Bishop Burnet's 'Exposition of the Thirty-nine Articles' are well known to, and duly appreciated by, your Grace.

My earnest desire, My Lord, has been to make this valuable work still more useful to the church of England. Should my efforts be even in the least degree successful, I shall, I

DEDICATION.

am persuaded, have done something towards the attainment of an object near to your Grace's heart.

That 'the great Shepherd and Bishop of souls' may abundantly bless your Grace here, and crown you with glory hereafter, is the prayer of

Your Grace's

Most obedient and obliged humble Servant,

JAMES R. PAGE.

London, Dec. 1836.

EDITOR'S PREFACE.

It has been justly observed by a great master of nature,

'The evil that men do lives after them:
'The good is oft interred with their bones.'

But with the man who serves God in his generation it is far otherwise; for, while his manifold infirmities vanish away like the morning cloud, his 'work of faith and labour of love' linger behind, and by them 'he, being dead, yet speaketh.' The marble and brass are employed—but employed in vain —to perpetuate the memory of that man of whom it may be said, 'he did no good among his people;' while the unassuming work of the other lives to be valued by each succeeding generation. Thus it was, and thus it has been, with our Author. He laboured for his Redeemer; 'was a man subject to like passions as we are;' encountered no small share of reviling and calumny: but his failings are gone—the tongue of insult has long since been silent in the grave; while his writings have erected for him a monument which can never moulder away, so long as that church, of which he was so bright an ornament, shall exist. Indeed, his fame is not bounded by the circle of his own church, or his own country. But it is not our present business to treat of these subjects; neither to enter into any comparison between the several writings of that great man. The Editor's observations must be confined to that book, with which (however unworthy) he has the honour of being connected. Of that volume he can safely say, that, although some alterations for the better might be made in its style and arrangement, take it 'for all in all,' it is a splendid work. And were the writer to add his own experience he would say, that the more it is explored the more valuable instruction it will bestow. Our Author was a man of great mind and extensive learning; and, as is common to such men, imagined that his readers were likely to know as much as himself: therefore, he did not so fully develope some subjects and arguments as, in condescension to the weakness of others, he should have done. Hence we find some most important points so buried in his work, that the student must first learn them by taking a more extensive course of reading; but then he is at once delighted and surprised to discover, on renewing his acquaintance with Burnet, that what has been gleaned in the choicest gardens of theology, had merely escaped his observation when he first read the 'Exposition of the Thirty-nine Articles.'

Bishop Burnet had long felt the want of such a volume as that which he has supplied. This, together with the solicitations of the Queen, archbishop Tillotson, and other distinguished individuals, and the great influx of popish priests, who were actively engaged in calumniating the doctrine of our church, induced the Bishop to commence the work, which was carefully revised by Tillotson and Stillingfleet; and, when complete, dedicated to William III. But we must allow the Bishop to give his own interesting account:—

'I published this year (1699) an Exposition of the Thirty-nine Articles of Religion: it seemed a work much wanted, and it was justly to be wondered at, that none of our divines had attempted any such performance, in a way suitable to the dignity of the subject: for some slight analyses of them are not worth either mentioning or reading. It was a work that required study and labour, and laid a man open to many attacks; this made some of my friends advise me against publishing it; in compliance with them, I kept it five years by me, after I had finished it: but I was now prevailed on by the Archbishop, and many of my own order, besides a great many others, to delay the publishing it no longer. It seemed a proper addition to the History of the Reformation, to explain and prove the doctrine which was then established. I was moved first by the late Queen, and pressed by the late Archbishop, to write it: I can appeal to the Searcher of all hearts, that I wrote it with great sincerity and a good intention; and with all the application and care I was capable of. I did then expect, what I have since met with, that malicious men would employ both their industry and ill-nature to find matter for censure and cavils; but though there have been some books writ on purpose against it, and many in sermons and other treatises have occasionally reflected, with great severity, upon several passages in it, yet this has been done with so little justice or reason, that I am not yet convinced, that there is one single period or expression that is justly remarked on, or that can give me any occasion either to retract, or so much as to explain any one part of that whole work; which I was very ready to have done, if I had seen cause for it. There was another reason that seemed to determine me to the publishing it at this time. Upon the peace of Ryswick, a great swarm of priests came over to England; not only those whom the Revolution had frighted away, but many more new men, who appeared in many places with great insolence; and it was said that they boasted of the favour and protection of which they were assured.'

Some of those arguments which influenced the good Bishop might now be urged, were any apology required for sending forth a new edition of such a work. There may however be some apology necessary for *this* edition: but we trust that, when the following brief outline is examined, those who might be disposed to censure any interference with Bishop Burnet will be satisfied; and that, when they have learned that Burnet is still before them, they will be pleased to accept the humble industry of the Editor.

In the first place, the Author's text has been preserved with strict fidelity; indeed, in some places, where the Editor felt it almost necessary to make some alteration, he, upon consulting the earlier editions, and observing the reading similar, left the words as he found them.

2d. The references to the fathers, councils, and other authorities, have been almost universally verified; and, in many instances, corrected, and so enlarged as to render them easy of access to the student.

3d. A large number of scripture references have been added. In different parts of his work, Bishop Burnet lays down propositions without giving the scriptures by which they may be proved. Thus, in Art. VI. p. 92, our Author states two propositions—God's command to put in writing what he had revealed; and the end contemplated—the guarding against the uncertainty of tradition. Again, in pp. 97, 98, there are several distinct propositions—that the Old Testament was read in the hearing of the women and children—that all appeals were made to the law and prophets—that the greatest questions were decided by the written word. Burnet appears to have assumed that all his readers could, without delay, produce the scriptures in proof of these positions. The Editor has, however, added references in these and all other instances where they might be considered not merely additions, but also improvements.

4th. The canons and decrees of councils, and other documents of importance, referred to, have been given in the original, and from the most authentic sources—the places where they are to be found being specified.

5th. Copious notes have been added, containing, besides other information, notices of the principal heretics and persons of note, with an accurate account of their opinions: also extracts, chiefly from the works of the most distinguished divines of the sixteenth and seventeenth centuries, opening and illustrating the chief points in controversy between us and the church of Rome. In an Appendix has also been given the Confession of Augsburg, and Creed of pope Pius IV. in the English and original tongues; and, in the original only, the Canons and Rubric of the Mass.

Indices of Texts of Scripture, and of the matter contained in the Notes, have also been given, together with a list of Authors quoted in the Editor's portion of the volume.

In fine, the Editor's design has been to make, as far as was possible within such a compass, this great work what he humbly hopes it may be found—a manual for the theological student.

The Editor has, in conclusion, but to request the kind indulgence of the public; and to hope that his readers will be more anxious to discover some good, than to seek out faults, in his work. He would now commit the result of his labours to the great HEAD of the church, with sincere prayer that He would be pleased to pardon its imperfections, and to accept and bless it to the promotion of His own glory.

JAMES R. PAGE, A. M.

London, Dec. 1836.

TO THE

KING.

SIR,

THE title of *Defender of the Faith*, the noblest of all those which belong to this imperial crown, that has received a new lustre by Your MAJESTY's carrying it, is that which You have so gloriously acquired, that if Your MAJESTY had not found it among them, what You have done must have secured it to Yourself by the best of all claims. We should be as much ashamed not to give it to Your MAJESTY, as we were to give it to those who had been fatally led into the design of overturning that, which has been beyond all the examples in history preserved and hitherto maintained by Your MAJESTY.

The Reformation had its greatest support and strength from the crown of England; while two of Your renowned ancestors were the chief defenders of it in foreign parts. The blood of England mixing so happily with theirs, in your royal person, seemed to give the world a sure prognostic of what might be looked for from so great a conjunction. Your MAJESTY has outdone all expectations; and has brought matters to a state far beyond all our hopes.

But amidst the laurels that adorn You, and those applauses that do every where follow You, suffer me, GREAT SIR, in all humility to tell You, that your work is not yet done, nor your glory complete, till You have employed that power which God has put in your hands, and before which nothing has been able hitherto to stand, in the supporting and securing this Church, in the bearing down Infidelity and Impiety, in the healing the wounds and breaches that are made among those who do in common profess this faith, but are unhappily disjointed and divided by some differences that are of less importance: and, above all things, in the raising the power and efficacy of this religion, by a suitable reformation of our lives and manners.

EPISTLE DEDICATORY.

How much soever men's hearts are out of the reach of human authority, yet their lives, and all outward appearances, are governed by the example and influences of their Sovereigns.

The effectual pursuing of these designs, as it is the greatest of all those glories of which mortals are capable; so it seems to be the only thing that is now wanting, to finish the brightest and perfectest character that will be in history.

It was in order to the promoting these ends, that I undertook this work; which I do now most humbly lay before Your MAJESTY, with the profoundest respect and submission.

May God preserve Your MAJESTY, till You have gloriously finished what You have so wonderfully carried on. All that You have hitherto set about, how small soever the beginnings and hopes were, has succeeded in your hands, to the amazement of the whole world: the most desperate face of affairs has been able to give You no stop.

Your MAJESTY seems born under an ascendant of Providence; and therefore, how low soever all our hopes are, either of raising the power of religion, or of uniting those who profess it; yet we have been taught to despair of nothing that is once undertaken by Your MAJESTY.

This will secure to You the blessing of the present and of all succeeding ages, and a full reward in that glorious and immortal state that is before You: to which, that Your MAJESTY may have a sure, though a late admittance, is the daily and most earnest prayer of,

May it please Your MAJESTY,
Your Majesty's most loyal,
most obedient, and most
devoted subject and servant,

GI. SARUM, C. G.

PREFACE.

It has been often reckoned among the things that were wanting, that we had not a full and clear explanation of the Thirty-nine Articles, which are the sum of our doctrine, and the confession of our faith. The modesty of some, and the caution of others, may have obliged them to let alone an undertaking, that might seem too assuming for any man to venture on, without a command from those who had authority to give it. It has been likewise often suggested, that those Articles seemed to be so plain a transcript of St. Austin's doctrine, in those much disputed points, concerning the *decrees* of *God*, and the *efficacy* of *grace*, that they were not expounded by our divines for that very reason; since the far greater number of them is believed to be now of a different opinion.

I should have kept within the same bounds, if I had not been first moved to undertake this work by that *great prelate*, who then sat at the helm: and after that, determined in it by a command that was sacred to me by respect, as well as by duty. Our late primate lived long enough to see the design finished. He read it over with an exactness that was peculiar to him. He employed some weeks wholly in perusing it, and he corrected it with a care that descended even to the smallest matters; and was such as he thought became the importance of this work. And when that was done, he returned it to me with a letter, that, as it was the last I ever had from him, so it gave the whole such a character, that how much soever that might raise its value with true judges, yet in decency it must be suppressed by me, as being far beyond what any performance of mine could deserve. He gave so favourable an account of it to our late blessed queen, that she was pleased to tell me, she would find leisure to read it: and the last time that I was admitted to the honour of waiting on her, she commanded me to bring it to her. But she was soon after that carried to the source, to the *fountain of life*, in whose *light* she now sees both *light* and truth. So great a breach as was then made upon all our hopes put a stop upon this, as well as upon much greater designs.

This work has lain by me ever since: but has been often not only reviewed by myself, but by much better judges. The late most learned bishop of Worcester read it very carefully. He marked every thing in it that he thought needed a review;

and his censure was in all points submitted to. He expressed himself so well pleased with it to myself, and to some others, that I do not think it becomes me to repeat what he said of it. Both the most reverend archbishops, with several of the bishops, and a great many learned divines, have also read it. I must, indeed, on many accounts own, that they may be inclined to favour me too much, and to be too partial to me; yet they looked upon this work as a thing of that importance, that I have reason to believe they read it over severely: and if some small corrections may be taken for an indication that they saw no occasion for greater ones, I had this likewise from several of them.

Yet after all these approbations, and many repeated desires to me to publish it, I do not pretend to impose this upon the reader as the work of authority. For even our *most reverend metropolitans* read it only as private divines, without so severe a canvassing of all particulars as must have been expected, if this had been intended to pass for an authorized work under a public stamp. Therefore my design in giving this relation of the motives that led me first to compose, and now to publish this, is only to justify myself, both in the one and in the other, and to shew that I was not led by any presumption of my own, or with any design to dictate to others.

In the next place I will give an account of the method in which I executed this design. When I was a professor of divinity thirty years ago, I was then obliged to run over a great many of the systems and bodies of divinity that were writ by the chief men of the several divisions of Christendom. I found many things among them that I could not like: the stiffness of method, the many dark terms, the niceties of logic, the artificial definitions, the heaviness as well as the sharpness of style, and the diffusive length of them, disgusted me: I thought the whole might well be brought into less compass, and be made shorter and more clear, less laboured, and more simple. I thought many controversies might be cut off, some being only disputes about words, and founded on mistakes; and others being about matters of little consequence, in which errors are less criminal, and so they may be more easily borne with. This set me then on composing a great work in divinity: but I stayed not long enough in that station to go through above the half of it. I entered upon the same design again, but in another method, during my stay at London, in the privacy that I then enjoyed, after I had finished the history of our Reformation. These were advantages which made this performance much the easier to me: and perhaps the late archbishop might, from what he knew of the progress I had made in them, judge me the more proper for this undertaking. For after I have said so much to justify my own engaging in such a work, I think I ought to say all I can to justify, or at least to excuse, his making choice of me for it.

PREFACE.

When I had resolved to try what I could do in this method, of following the thread of our Articles, I considered, that as I was to explain the Articles of this church, so I ought to examine the writings of the chief divines that lived either at the time in which they were prepared, or soon after it. When I was about the history of our Reformation, I had laid out for all the books that had been writ within the time comprehended in that period: and I was confirmed in my having succeeded well in that collection, by a printed catalogue, that was put out by one Mansel, in the end of queen Elizabeth's reign, of all the books that had been printed from the time that printing-presses were first set up in England to that year. This I had from the present lord archbishop of York; and I saw by it, that very few books had escaped my search. Those that I had not fallen on were not writ by men of name, nor upon important subjects. I resolved, in order to this work, to bring my inquiry further down.

The first, and indeed the much best writer of queen Elizabeth's time, was bishop Jewel; the lasting honour of the see in which the providence of God has put me, as well as of the age in which he lived; who had so great share in all that was done then, particularly in compiling the second book of Homilies, that I had great reason to look on his works as a very sure commentary on our Articles, as far as they led me. From him I carried down my search through Reynolds, Humphreys, Whitaker, and the other great men of that time.

Our divines were much diverted in the end of that reign from better inquiries, by the *disciplinarian controversies;* and though what Whitgift and Hooker writ on those heads was much better than all that came after them; yet they neither satisfied those against whom they writ, nor stopped the writings of their own side. But as waters gush in when the banks are once broken, so the breach that these had made proved fruitful. Parties were formed, secular interests were grafted upon them, and new quarrels followed those that first began the dispute. The contests in Holland concerning *predestination* drew on another scene of contention among us as well as them, which was managed with great heat. Here was matter for angry men to fight it out, till they themselves and the whole nation grew weary of it. The question about the morality of the Fourth Commandment was an unhappy incident that raised a new strife. The controversies with the church of Rome were for a long while much laid down. The archbishop of Spalata's* works had appeared with great pomp in

---

* Marcus Antonius De Dominis, first a Jesuit, afterwards archbishop of Spalata. He visited England for the purpose of reconciling the Protestants and papists; to further this end he wrote a book, entitled 'De Republica Ecclesiastica.' He embraced the Protestant faith, 'and afforded,' says Hume, 'great triumph to the nation by their gaining so considerable a proselyte from the papists. But the mortification followed soon after: the archbishop, though advanced to some ecclesiastical preferments, received not enough to gratify his ambition.' He retracted his protest against

king James's time, and they drew the observation of the learned world much after them; though his unhappy relapse, and fatal catastrophe, made them be less read afterwards than they well deserved to have been.

When the progress of the house of Austria began to give their neighbours great apprehensions, so that the Protestant religion seemed to come under a very thick cloud, and upon that jealousies began to arise at home, in king Charles's reign, this gave occasion to two of the best books that we yet have: the one set out by archbishop Laud, writ with great learning, judgment, and exactness; the other by Chillingworth, writ with so clear a thread of reason, and in so lively a style, that it was justly reckoned the best book that had been writ in our language. It was about the nicest point in popery, that by which they had made the most proselytes, and that had once imposed on himself, concerning the infallibility of the church, and the motives of credibility.

Soon after that, we fell into the confusions of *civil war*, in which our divines suffered so much, that, while they were put on their own defence against those that had broke the peace of the church and state, few books were written, but on those subjects that were then in debate among ourselves, concerning the government of the church, and our liturgy and ceremonies. The disputes about the decrees of God were again managed with a new heat. There were also great abstractions set on foot in those times concerning *justification by faith*, and these were both so subtile, and did seem to have such a tendency not only to *antinomianism*, but to a *libertine* course of life, that many books were writ on those subjects. That noble work of the Polyglot Bible, together with the collection of the critics, set our divines much on the study of the scriptures, and the oriental tongues, in which Dr. Pocock and Dr. Lightfoot were singularly eminent. In all Dr. Hammond's writings, one sees great learning and solid judgment; a just temper in managing controversies; and, above all, a spirit of true and primitive piety, with great application to the right understanding of the scriptures, and the directing of all to practice. Bishop Pearson on the Creed, as far as it goes, is the perfectest work we have. His learning was profound and exact, his method good, and his style clear: he was equally happy both in the force of his arguments, and in the plainness of his expressions.

Upon the restoration of the royal family, and the church, the first scene of writing was naturally laid in the late times,

---

popery, and returned to Rome. There it appears that his opinions were changed again, for he wrote letters to England expressive of regret at the step he had taken. Some of these were intercepted, and led to his imprisonment by command of Pope Urban VIII. He died in confinement in the year 1625. Hume styles him, 'the famous Antonio De Dominis, no despicable philosopher;' and according to Cave, he was the author of the first philosophical account of the rainbow.—[ED.]

and with relation to conformity. But we quickly saw that popery was a restless thing, and was the standing enemy of our church: so soon as that shewed itself, then our divines returned to those controversies, in which no man bare a greater share, and succeeded in it with more honour, than bishop Stillingfleet, both in his vindication of archbishop Laud, and in the long continued dispute concerning the *idolatry* of the *church of Rome*. When the dangers of popery came nearer us, and became sensible to all persons, then a great number of our divines engaged in those controversies. They writ short and plain, and yet brought together, in a great variety of small tracts, the substance of all that was contained in the large volumes, writ both by our own divines and by foreigners. There was in these a solidity of argument, mixed with an agreeableness in the way of writing, that both pleased and edified the nation; and did very much confound, and at last silence, the few and weak writers that were of the Romish side. The inequality that was in this contest was too visible to be denied; and therefore they, who set it first on foot, let it fall: for they had other methods to which they trusted more, than to that unsuccessful one of writing. In those treatises, the substance of all our former books is so fully contained, and so well delivered, that in them the doctrines of our church, as to all controverted points, are both clearly and copiously set forth.

The perusing of all this was a large field: and yet I thought it became me to examine all with a due measure of exactness. I have taken what pains I could to digest every thing in the clearest method, and in the shortest compass, into which I could possibly bring it. So that in what I have done, I am, as to the far greatest part, rather an historian and a collector of what others have writ, than an author myself. This I have performed faithfully, and I hope with some measure of diligence and exactness; yet if, in such a variety, some important matters are forgot, and if others are mistaken, I am so far from reckoning it an injury to have those discovered, that I will gladly receive any advices of that kind: I will consider them carefully, and make the best use of them I can, for the undeceiving of others, as soon as I am convinced that I have misled them.

If men seek for truth in the meekness of Christ, they will follow this method in those private and brotherly practices recommended to us by our Saviour. But for those that are contentious, and do not obey the truth, I shall very little regard any opposition that may come from them. I had no other design in this work, but first to find out the truth myself, and then to help others to find it out. If I succeed to any degree in this design, I will bless God for it: and if I fail in it, I will bear it with the humility and patience that becomes me. But as soon as I see a better work of this kind,

PREFACE.

I shall be among the first of those who shall recommend that, and disparage this.

There is no part of this whole work, in which I have laboured with more care, and have writ in a more uncommon method, than concerning *predestination*. For, as my small reading had carried me further in that controversy than in any other whatsoever, both with relation to ancients and moderns, and to the most esteemed books in all the different parties; so I weighed the Article with that impartial care that I thought became me; and have taken a method, which is, for aught I know, new, of stating the arguments of all sides with so much fairness, that those, who knew my own opinion in this point, have owned to me, that they could not discover it by any thing that I had written. They were inclined to think that I was of another mind than they took me to be, when they read my arguings of that side. I have not, in the explanation of that Article, told what my own opinion was; yet here I think it may be fitting to own, that I follow the doctrine of the Greek church, from which St. Austin departed, and formed a new system. After this declaration, I may now appeal both to St. Austin's disciples, and to the Calvinists, whether I have not stated both their opinions and arguments, not only with truth and candour, but with all possible advantages.

One reason, among others, that led me to follow the method I have pursued in this controversy, is to offer at the best means I can for bringing men to a better understanding of one another, and to a mutual forbearance in these matters. This is at present the chief point in difference between the Lutherans and the Calvinists. Expedients for bringing them to an union in these heads are projects that can never have any good effect: men whose opinions are so different, can never be brought to an agreement: and the settling on some equivocal formularies, will never lay the contention that has arisen concerning them: the only possible way of a sound and lasting reconciliation is, to possess both parties with a sense of the force of the arguments that lie on the other side; that they may see they are no way contemptible; but are such as may prevail on wise and good men. Here is a foundation laid for charity: and if to this, men would add a just sense of the difficulties in their own side, and consider that the ill consequences drawn from opinions are not to be charged on all that hold them, unless they do likewise own those consequences; then it would be more easy to agree on some general propositions, by which those ill consequences might be condemned, and the doctrine in general settled; leaving it free to the men of the different systems to adhere to their own opinions; but withal obliging them to judge charitably and favourably of others, and to maintain communion with them, notwithstanding that diversity.

It is a good step even to the bringing men over to an opinion, to persuade them to think well of those who hold it. This goes as it were half way; and if it is not possible to bring men quite to think as we do, yet a great deal is done both towards that, and towards the healing those wounds in which the church lies a bleeding, when they come to join in the same communion, and in such acts of worship as do agree with their different persuasions. For as in the sacrament of the eucharist, both Lutherans and Calvinists agreeing in the same devotions and acts of worship, a mere point of speculation concerning the manner in which Christ is present, ought not to divide those who agree in every thing else that relates to the sacrament: every one may in that be left to the freedom of his own thoughts, since neither opinion has any influence on practice, or on any part either of public worship or of secret devotion.

Upon the same account it may be also suggested, that when all parties acknowledge that God is the sovereign Lord of the universe; that he governs it by a providence, from which nothing is hid, and to which nothing can resist; and that he is likewise holy and just, true and faithful, merciful and gracious, in all his ways; those who agree about all this, should not differ, though they cannot fall into the same methods of reconciling these together. And if they do all agree to bless God for all the good that they either do or receive, and to accuse themselves for all the ill that they either do or suffer: if they agree that they ought to be humble, and to mistrust their own strength, to pray earnestly to God for assistance, and to depend on him, to trust to him, and likewise to employ their own faculties with all possible care and diligence, in the cleansing their hearts, and governing their words and actions; here the great truths of both sides are safe; every thing that has an influence on practice is agreed on; though neither side can meet in the same ways of joining all these together.

In the church of Rome the difference is really the same between St. Austin's disciples and the followers of Molina; and yet, how much soever they may differ and dispute in the schools, their worship being the same, they do all join in it. We of this church are very happy in this respect; we have all along been much divided, and once almost broken to pieces, while we disputed concerning these matters: but now we are much happier; for though we know one another's opinions, we live not only united in the same worship, but in great friendship and love with those of other persuasions. And the boldness of some among us, who have reflected in sermons, or otherwise, on those who hold Calvin's system, has been much blamed, and often censured by those who, though they hold the same opinions with them, yet are both more charitable in their thoughts, and more discreet in their expressions.

But till the Lutherans abate of their rigidity in censuring the opinions of the Calvinists, as charging God with all those blasphemous consequences that they think follow the doctrine of absolute decrees; and till the Calvinists, in Holland, Switzerland, and Geneva, abate also of theirs, in charging the others as enemies to the grace of God, and as guilty of those consequences that they think follow the doctrine of conditionate decrees, it is not possible to see that much wished for agreement come to any good effect.

He who believes that an ill consequence is justly drawn from any opinion, is in the right, when he is by that determined against it. But because he thinks he sees that the consequence is clear, and cannot be avoided; he ought not for that to judge so ill of those who hold the opinion, but declare at the same time, that they abhor the consequence; that they prevaricate in that declaration; and that they both see the consequence, and own it; though for decency's sake they disclaim it. He ought rather to think, that either they do not see the consequence, but satisfy themselves with some of those distinctions, with which it is avoided; or, that though they do see it, yet they look on that only as an objection, which indeed they cannot well answer. They may think that a point of doctrine may be proved by such convincing arguments, that they may be bound to believe it, though there lie objections against it which they cannot avoid, and consequences seem to follow on it which they abhor, and are sure cannot be true, though they cannot clear the matter so well as they wish they could do. In that case, when a man is inclined by strong arguments to an opinion, against which he sees difficulties which he cannot resolve, he ought either to suspend his assent; or, if he sees a superiority of argument of one side, he may be determined by that, though he cannot satisfy even himself in the objections that are against it: in that case he ought to reflect on the weakness and defects of his faculties, which cannot rise up to full and comprehensive ideas of things, especially in that which relates to the attributes of God, and to his counsels or acts. If men can be brought once to apprehend this rightly, it may make propositions for peace and union hopeful and practicable; and till they are brought to this, all such propositions may well be laid aside; for men's minds are not yet prepared for that which can only reconcile this difference, and heal this breach.

I shall conclude this Preface with a reply, that a very eminent divine among the Lutherans in Germany made to me, when I was pressing this matter of union with the Calvinists upon him, with all the topics with which I could urge it, as necessary upon many accounts, and more particularly with relation to the present state of affairs. He said, he wondered much to see a divine of the church of England press that so much on him, when we, notwithstanding the danger we were then in (it was in the year 1686), could not agree our differences. They differed about important matters, concerning the attributes of God, and his providence; concerning the guilt of sin, whether it was to be charged on God, or on the sinner; and whether men ought to make good use of their faculties, or if they ought to trust entirely to an irresistible grace? These were matters of great moment: but, he said, we in England differed only about forms of government and worship, and about things that were of their own nature indifferent; and yet we had been quarrelling about these for above an hundred years; and we were not yet grown wiser by all the mischief that this had done us, and by the imminent danger we were then in. He concluded, Let the church of England heal her own breaches, and then all the rest of the reformed churches will with great respect admit of her mediation to heal theirs. I will not presume to tell how I answered this: but I pray God to enlighten and direct all men, that they may consider well how it ought to be answered.

ARTICULI RELIGIONIS

Anno 1562.

The Articles of our Church were at the same time prepared both in Latin and English; so that both are equally authentical: it is therefore proper to give them here in Latin, since the English of them is only inserted in the following work. This is the more necessary, because many of the collations, set down at the end of the introduction, relate to the Latin text.

ARTICULI de quibus convenit inter Archiepiscopos et Episcopos utriusque Provinciæ, et Clerum Universum in Synodo, Londini, Anno 1562. secundum computationem Ecclesiæ Anglicanæ, ad tollendam opinionum dissentionem, et consensum in vera Religione firmandum. Editi Authoritate serenissimæ Reginæ. Londini, apud Johannem Day, 1571.

I. *De fide in sacro-sanctam Trinitatem.*

UNUS est vivus et verus Deus, æternus, incorporeus, impartibilis, impassibilis, immensæ potentiæ, sapientiæ ac bonitatis, creator et conservator omnium, tum visibilium, tum invisibilium. Et in unitate hujus divinæ naturæ tres sunt personæ, ejusdem essentiæ, potentiæ ac æternitatis, Pater, Filius, et Spiritus sanctus.

II. *De verbo, sive Filio Dei, qui verus homo factus est.*

FILIUS, qui est verbum patris, ab æterno a patre genitus, verus et æternus Deus, ac patri consubstantialis, in utero beatæ virginis, ex illius substantia naturam humanam assumpsit: ita ut duæ naturæ, divina et humana, integre atque perfecte in unitate personæ fuerint inseparabiliter conjunctæ, ex quibus est unus Christus, verus Deus et verus homo, qui vere passus est, crucifixus, mortuus, et sepultus, ut patrem nobis reconciliaret, essetque hostia, non tantum pro culpa originis, verum etiam pro omnibus actualibus hominum peccatis.

III. *De descensu Christi ad Inferos.*

QUEMADMODUM Christus pro nobis mortuus est, et sepultus, ita est etiam credendus ad Inferos descendisse.

ARTICULI

IV. De resurrectione Christi.

CHRISTUS vere a mortuis resurrexit, suumque corpus cum carne, ossibus, omnibusque ad integritatem humanæ naturæ pertinentibus, recepit: cum quibus in cœlum ascendit, ibique residet, quoad extremo die ad judicandos homines reversurus sit.

V. De Spiritu sancto.

SPIRITUS sanctus, a patre et filio procedens, ejusdem est cum patre et filio essentiæ, majestatis, et gloriæ, verus ac æternus Deus.

VI. De divinis Scripturis, quod sufficiant ad salutem.

SCRIPTURA sacra continet omnia, quæ ad salutem sunt necessaria, ita ut quicquid in ea nec legitur, neque inde probari potest, non sit a quoquam exigendum, ut tanquam articulus fidei credatur, aut ad salutis necessitatem requiri putetur.

Sacræ Scripturæ nomine, eos Canonicos libros veteris et novi Testamenti intelligimus, de quorum authoritate, in ecclesia nunquam dubitatum est.

De nominibus et numero librorum sacræ Canonicæ Scripturæ veteris Testamenti.

Genesis.	Prior liber Paralipom.
Exodus.	Secundus liber Paralipom.
Leviticus.	Primus liber Esdræ.
Numeri.	Secundus liber Esdræ.
Deuteron.	Liber Hester.
Josuæ.	Liber Job.
Judicum.	Psalmi.
Ruth.	Proverbia.
Prior liber Samuelis.	Ecclesiastes vel Concionator.
Secundus liber Samuelis.	Cantica Solomonis.
Prior liber Regum.	IV Prophetæ Majores.
Secundus liber Regum.	XII Prophetæ Minores.

Alios autem libros (at ait Hieronymus) legit quidem Ecclesia, ad exempla vitæ, et formandos mores: illos tamen ad dogmata confirmanda non adhibet, ut sunt

Tertius liber Esdræ.	Baruch propheta.
Quartus liber Esdræ.	Canticum trium puerorum.
Liber Tobiæ.	Historia Susannæ.
Liber Judith.	De Bel et Dracone.
Reliquum libri Hester.	Oratio Manassis.
Liber Sapientiæ.	Prior liber Machabeorum.
Liber Jesu filii Sirach.	Secundus liber Machabeorum.

Novi Testamenti omnes libros (ut vulgo recepti sunt) recipimus, et habemus pro Canonicis.

VII. *De veteri Testamento.*

TESTAMENTUM vetus novo contrarium non est, quandoquidem tam in veteri, quam in novo, per Christum, qui unicus est Mediator Dei et hominum, Deus et homo, æterna vita humano generi est proposita. Quare male sentiunt, qui veteres tantum in promissiones temporarias sperasse confingunt. Quanquam lex a Deo data per Mosen (quoad cæremonias et ritus) Christianos non astringat, neque civilia ejus præcepta in aliqua republica necessario recipi debeant, nihilominus tamen ab obedientia mandatorum (quæ moralia vocantur) nullus (quantumvis Christianus) est solutus.

VIII. *De tribus Symbolis.*

SYMBOLA tria, Nicænum, Athanasii, et quod vulgo Apostolorum appellatur, omnino recipienda sunt, et credenda, nam firmissimis Scripturarum testimoniis probari possunt.

IX. *De peccato originali.*

PECCATUM originis non est (ut fabulantur Pelagiani) in imitatione Adami situm, sed est vitium, et depravatio naturæ, cujuslibet hominis ex Adamo naturaliter propagati: qua fit, ut ab originali justitia quam longissime distet, ad malum sua natura propendeat, et caro semper adversus spiritum concupiscat, unde in unoquoque nascentium, iram Dei atque damnationem meretur. Manet etiam in renatis hæc naturæ depravatio. Qua fit, ut affectus carnis, Græce φρόνημα σαρκὸς, (quod alii sapientiam, alii sensum, alii affectum, alii studium carnis interpretantur,) legi Dei non subjiciatur. Et quanquam renatis et credentibus nulla propter Christum est condemnatio, peccati tamen in sese rationem habere concupiscentiam, fatetur Apostolus.

X. *De libero arbitrio.*

EA est hominis post lapsum Adæ conditio, ut sese naturalibus suis viribus, et bonis operibus, ad fidem et invocationem Dei convertere ac præparare non possit. Quare absque gratia Dei (quæ per Christum est) nos præveniente, ut velimus, et cooperante, dum volumus, ad pietatis opera facienda, quæ Deo grata sunt et accepta, nihil valemus.

XI. *De hominis justificatione.*

TANTUM propter meritum Domini ac Servatoris nostri Jesu Christi, per fidem, non propter opera, et merita nostra, justi coram Deo reputamur. Quare sola fide nos justificari doctrina est saluberrima, ac consolationis plenissima, ut in homilia de justificatione hominis fusius explicatur.

XII. *De bonis operibus.*

BONA opera, quæ sunt fructus fidei, et justificatos sequuntur, quanquam peccata nostra expiare, et divini judicii severitatem ferre non possunt; Deo tamen grata sunt, et accepta in Christo, atque ex vera et viva fide necessario profluunt, ut plane ex illis, æque fides viva cognosci possit, atque arbor ex fructu judicari.

XIII. De operibus ante justificationem.

OPERA quæ fiunt ante gratiam Christi, et spiritus ejus afflatum, cum ex fide Jesu Christi non prodeant, minime Deo grata sunt, neque gratiam (ut multi vocant) de congruo merentur. Immo cum non sunt facta ut Deus illa fieri voluit et præcepit, peccati rationem habere non dubitamus.

XIV. De operibus supererogationis.

OPERA quæ supererogationis appellant, non possunt sine arrogantia et impietate prædicari. Nam illis declarant homines, non tantum se Deo reddere, quæ tenentur, sed plus in ejus gratiam facere, quam deberent, cum aperte Christus dicat; Cum feceritis omnia quæcunque præcepta sunt vobis, dicite, Servi inutiles sumus.

XV. De Christo, qui solus est sine peccato.

CHRISTUS in nostræ naturæ veritate, per omnia similis factus est nobis, excepto peccato, a quo prorsus erat immunis, tum in carne, tum in spiritu. Venit ut agnus, absque macula, qui mundi peccata per immolationem sui semel factam tolleret, et peccatum (ut inquit Johannes) in eo non erat: sed nos reliqui etiam baptizati, et in Christo regenerati, in multis tamen offendimus omnes. Et si dixerimus, quod peccatum non habemus, nos ipsos seducimus, et veritas in nobis non est.

XVI. De peccato post Baptismum.

NON omne peccatum mortale post Baptismum voluntarie perpetratum, est peccatum in Spiritum sanctum, et irremissibile. Proinde lapsis a Baptismo in peccata, locus pœnitentiæ non est negandus. Post acceptum Spiritum sanctum possumus a gratia data recedere, atque peccare, denuoque per gratiam Dei resurgere, ac resipiscere; ideoque illi damnandi sunt, qui se, quamdiu hic vivant, amplius non posse peccare affirmant, aut vere resipiscentibus veniæ locum denegant.

XVII. De prædestinatione et electione.

PRÆDESTINATIO ad vitam, est æternum Dei propositum, quo ante jacta mundi fundamenta, suo consilio, nobis quidem occulto, constanter decrevit, eos quos in Christo elegit ex hominum genere, a maledicto et exitio liberare, atque (ut vasa in honorem efficta) per Christum, ad æternam salutem adducere. Unde qui tam præclaro Dei beneficio sunt donati, illi spiritu ejus, opportuno tempore operante, secundum propositum ejus vocantur, vocationi per gratiam parent, justificantur gratis, adoptantur in filios Dei, unigeniti ejus Jesu Christi imagini efficiuntur conformes, in bonis operibus sancte ambulant, et demum ex Dei misericordia pertingunt ad sempiternam felicitatem.

Quemadmodum prædestinationis et electionis nostræ in Christo pia consideratio, dulcis, suavis, et ineffabilis consolationis plena est vere piis, et his qui sentiunt in se vim spiritus Christi, facta carnis, et membra, quæ adhuc sunt super terram, mortificantem, animumque ad cœlestia et superna rapientem; tum quia fidem nostram de æterna salute consequenda per Christum plurimum stabilit atque confirmat, tum quia amorem nostrum in Deum vehementer accendit: ita hominibus curiosis, carnalibus, et Spiritu Christi destitutis, ob oculos perpetuo versari prædestinationis Dei sententiam, perniciosissimum est præcipitium, unde illos diabolus protrudit, vel in desperationem, vel in æque perniciosam impurissimæ vitæ securitatem; deinde promissiones divinas sic amplecti oportet, ut nobis in sacris literis generaliter propositæ sunt, et Dei voluntas in nostris actionibus ea sequenda est, quam in verbo Dei habemus, diserte revelatam.

XVIII. *De speranda æterna salute tantum in nomine Christi.*

SUNT et illi anathematizandi, qui dicere audent unumquemque in lege aut secta quam profitetur esse servandum, modo juxta illam et lumen naturæ accurate vixerit, cum sacræ literæ tantum Jesu Christi nomen prædicent, in quo salvos fieri homines oporteat.

XIX. *De Ecclesia.*

ECCLESIA Christi visibilis est cœtus fidelium, in quo verbum Dei purum prædicatur, et sacramenta, quoad ea quæ necessario exigantur, juxta Christi institutum recte administrantur. Sicut erravit ecclesia Hierosolymitana, Alexandrina, et Antiochena; ita et erravit Ecclesia Romana, non solum quoad agenda, et cæremoniarum ritus, verum in his etiam quæ credenda sunt.

XX. *De Ecclesiæ authoritate.*

HABET Ecclesia ritus sive cæremonias statuendi jus, et in fidei controversiis authoritatem; quamvis ecclesiæ non licet quicquam instituere, quod verbo Dei scripto adversetur, nec unum scripturæ locum sic exponere potest, ut alteri contradicat. Quare licet Ecclesia sit divinorum librorum testis et conservatrix, attamen ut adversus eos nihil decernere, ita præter illos nihil credendum de necessitate salutis debet obtrudere.

XXI. *De authoritate Conciliorum generalium.*

GENERALIA Concilia sine jussu et voluntate Principum

congregari non possunt; et ubi convenerint, quia ex hominibus constant, qui non omnes spiritu et verbo Dei reguntur, et errare possunt, et interdum errarunt etiam in his quæ ad Deum pertinent; ideoque quæ ab illis constituuntur, ut ad salutem necessaria, neque robur habent, neque authoritatem, nisi ostendi possint e sacris literis esse desumpta.

XXII. *De Purgatorio.*

DOCTRINA Romanensium de purgatorio, de indulgentiis, de veneratione, et adoratione, tum imaginum, tum reliquiarum, nec non de invocatione sanctorum, res est futilis, inaniter conficta, et nullis Scripturarum testimoniis innititur: immo verbo Dei contradicit.

XXIII. *De ministrando in Ecclesia.*

NON licet cuiquam sumere sibi munus publice prædicandi, aut administrandi Sacramenta in Ecclesia, nisi prius fuerit ad hæc obeunda legitime vocatus et missus. Atque illos legitime vocatos et missos existimare debemus, qui per homines, quibus potestas vocandi ministros, atque mittendi in vineam Domini, publice concessa est in Ecclesia, cooptati fuerint, et adsciti in hoc opus.

XXIV. *De loquendo in Ecclesia lingua quam populus intelligit.*

LINGUA populo non intellecta, publicas in Ecclesia preces peragere, aut Sacramenta administrare, verbo Dei, et primitivæ Ecclesiæ consuetudini plane repugnat.

XXV. *De Sacramentis.*

SACRAMENTA a Christo instituta, non tantum sunt notæ professionis Christianorum, sed certa quædam potius testimonia, et efficacia signa gratiæ atque bonæ in nos voluntatis Dei, per quæ invisibiliter ipse in nos operatur, nostramque fidem in se non solum excitat, verum etiam confirmat.

Duo a Christo Domino nostro in Evangelio instituta sunt Sacramenta: scilicet, Baptismus, et Cœna Domini.

Quinque illa vulgo nominata Sacramenta, scilicet, confirmatio, pœnitentia, ordo, matrimonium, et extrema unctio, pro Sacramentis Evangelicis habenda non sunt, ut quæ, partim a prava Apostolorum imitatione profluxerunt, partim vitæ status sunt in Scripturis quidem probati: sed sacramentorum eandem cum Baptismo et Cœna Domini rationem non habentes, ut quæ signum aliquod visibile, seu cæremoniam, a Deo institutam, non habeant.

Sacramenta non in hoc instituta sunt a Christo ut spectarentur, aut circumferrentur, sed ut rite illis uteremur, et in his duntaxat qui digne percipiunt salutarem habent effectum: Qui vero indigne percipiunt, damnationem (ut inquit Paulus) sibi ipsis acquirunt.

XXVI. *De vi institutionum divinarum, quod eam non tollat malitia Ministrorum.*

QUAMVIS in Ecclesia visibili, bonis mali semper sunt admixti, atque interdum ministerio verbi et Sacramentorum administrationi præsint; tamen cum non suo, sed Christi nomine agant, ejusque mandato et authoritate ministrent, illorum ministerio uti licet, cum in verbo Dei audiendo, tum in Sacramentis percipiendis. Neque per illorum malitiam effectus institutorum Christi tollitur, aut gratia donorum Dei minuitur, quoad eos qui fide et rite sibi oblata percipiunt, quæ propter institutionem Christi et promissionem efficacia sunt, licet per malos administrentur.

Ad Ecclesiæ tamen disciplinam pertinet, ut in malos ministros inquiratur, accusenturque ab his, qui eorum flagitia noverint, atque tandem justo convicti judicio deponantur.

XXVII. *De Baptismo.*

BAPTISMUS non est tantum professionis signum, ac discriminis nota, qua Christiani a non Christianis discernantur, sed etiam est signum regenerationis per quod, tanquam per instrumentum, recte baptismum suscipientes, Ecclesiæ inseruntur, promissiones de remissione peccatorum, atque adoptione nostra in filios Dei per Spiritum sanctum visibiliter obsignantur, fides confirmatur, et vi divinæ invocationis gratia augetur.

Baptismus parvulorum omnino in Ecclesia retinendus est, ut qui cum Christi institutione optime congruat.

XXVIII. *De Cœna Domini.*

CŒNA Domini non est tantum signum mutuæ benevolentiæ Christianorum inter sese, verum potius est Sacramentum nostræ per mortem Christi redemptionis.

Atque adeo, rite, digne, et cum fide sumentibus, panis quem frangimus est communicatio corporis Christi: similiter poculum benedictionis est communicatio sanguinis Christi.

Panis et vini transubstantiatio in Eucharistia ex sacris literis probari non potest. Sed apertis Scripturæ verbis adversatur, Sacramenti naturam evertit, et multarum superstitionum dedit occasionem.

Corpus Christi datur, accipitur, et manducatur in Cœna, tantum cœlesti et spirituali ratione. Medium autem, quo corpus Christi accipitur et manducatur in Cœna, fides est.

Sacramentum Eucharistiæ ex institutione Christi non servabatur, circumferebatur, elevabatur, nec adorabatur.

XXIX. *De manducatione corporis Christi, et impios illud non manducare.*

IMPII, et fide viva destituti, licet carnaliter et visibiliter (ut Augustinus loquitur) corporis et sanguinis Christi Sacramentum dentibus premant, nullo tamen modo Christi participes efficiuntur. Sed potius tantæ rei Sacramentum, seu Symbolum, ad judicium sibi manducant et bibunt.

XXX. *De utraque specie.*

CALIX Domini laicis non est denegandus, utraque enim pars Dominici Sacramenti, ex Christi institutione et præcepto, omnibus Christianis ex æquo administrari debet.

XXXI. *De unica Christi oblatione in cruce perfecta.*

OBLATIO Christi semel facta, perfecta est redemptio, propitiatio et satisfactio pro omnibus peccatis totius mundi, tam originalibus, quam actualibus; neque præter illam unicam est ulla alia pro peccatis expiatio: unde missarum sacrificia, quibus vulgo dicebatur, sacerdotem offerre Christum in remissionem pœnæ, aut culpæ, pro vivis et defunctis, blasphema figmenta sunt, et perniciosæ imposturæ.

XXXII. *De conjugio Sacerdotum.*

EPISCOPIS, presbyteris, et diaconis nullo mandato divino præceptum est, ut aut cœlibatum voveant, aut a matrimonio abstineant. Licet igitur etiam illis, ut cæteris omnibus Christianis, ubi hoc ad pietatem magis facere judicaverint, pro suo arbitratu matrimonium contrahere.

XXXIII. *De excommunicatis vitandis.*

QUI per publicam Ecclesiæ denunciationem rite ab unitate Ecclesiæ præcisus est, et excommunicatus, is ab universa fidelium multitudine (donec per pœnitentiam publice reconciliatus fuerit arbitrio judicis competentis) habendus est tanquam ethnicus et publicanus.

XXXIV. *De traditionibus Ecclesiasticis.*

TRADITIONES atque cæremonias easdem, non omnino necessarium est esse ubique, aut prorsus consimiles. Nam ut variæ semper fuerunt, et mutari possunt, pro regionum, temporum, et morum diversitate, modo nihil contra verbum Dei instituatur.

Traditiones, et cæremonias ecclesiasticas, quæ cum verbo Dei non pugnant, et sunt authoritate publica institutæ atque probatæ, quisquis privato consilio volens, et data opera, publice violaverit, is ut qui peccat in publicum ordinem Ecclesiæ, quique lædit authoritatem Magistratus, et qui infirmorum fratrum conscientias vulnerat, publice, ut cæteri timeant, arguendus est.

Quælibet Ecclesia particularis, sive nationalis, authoritatem habet instituendi, mutandi, aut abrogandi cæremonias, aut ritus ecclesiasticos, humana tantum authoritate institutos, modo omnia ad ædificationem fiant.

XXXV. De Homiliis.

TOMUS secundus Homiliarum, quarum singulos titulos huic articulo subjunximus, continet piam et salutarem doctrinam, et his temporibus necessariam, non minus quam prior tomus Homiliarum, quæ editæ sunt tempore Edwardi sexti: Itaque eas in Ecclesiis per ministros diligenter, et clare, ut a populo intelligi possint, recitandas esse judicavimus.

De nominibus Homiliarum.

Of the right Use of the Church.
Against peril of Idolatry.
Of repairing and keeping clean of Churches.
Of good Works.
First, of Fasting.
Against Gluttony and Drunkenness.
Against Excess in Apparel.
Of Prayer.
Of the place and time of Prayer.
That common Prayers and Sacraments ought to be ministered in a known Tongue.
Of the reverent Estimation of God's Word.
Of Alms-doing.
Of the Nativity of Christ.
Of the Passion of Christ.
Of the Resurrection of Christ.
Of the worthy receiving of the Sacrament of the Body and Blood of Christ.
Of the Gifts of the Holy Ghost.
Of the Rogation-Days.
Of the state of Matrimony.
Of Repentance.
Against Idleness.
Against Rebellion.

XXXVI. De Episcoporum et Ministrorum consecratione.

LIBELLUS de consecratione Archiepiscoporum, et Episcoporum, et de ordinatione Presbyterorum et Diaconorum, editus nuper temporibus Edwardi VI. et authoritate Parliamenti illis ipsis temporibus confirmatus, omnia ad ejusmodi consecrationem et ordinationem necessaria continet, et nihil habet, quod ex se sit, aut superstitiosum, aut impium: itaque quicunque juxta ritus illius libri consecrati aut ordinati sunt, ab anno secundo prædicti regis Edwardi, usque ad hoc tempus, aut in posterum juxta eosdem ritus consecrabuntur, aut ordinabuntur, rite atque ordine, atque legitime statuimus esse, et fore consecratos et ordinatos.

XXXVII. De civilibus Magistratibus.

REGIA Majestas in hoc Angliæ regno, ac cæteris ejus dominiis, summam habet potestatem, ad quam omnium statuum hujus regni, sive illi ecclesiastici sint, sive civiles, in omnibus causis, suprema gubernatio pertinet, et nulli externæ jurisdictioni est subjecta, nec esse debet.

Cum Regiæ Majestati summam gubernationem tribuimus, quibus titulis intelligimus animos, quorundam calumniatorum offendi, non damus Regibus nostris, aut verbi Dei, aut Sacramentorum administrationem, quod etiam Injunctiones ab Elizabetha Regina nostra, nuper editæ, apertissime testantur: sed eam tantum prærogativam, quam in sacris Scripturis a Deo ipso, omnibus piis Principibus, videmus semper fuisse attributam: hoc est, ut omnes status atque ordines fidei suæ a Deo commissos, sive illi ecclesiastici sint, sive civiles, in officio contineant, et contumaces ac delinquentes gladio civili coerceant.

Romanus pontifex nullam habet jurisdictionem in hoc regno Angliæ.

Leges regni possunt Christianos, propter capitalia et gravia crimina, morte punire.

Christianis licet, ex mandato magistratus, arma portare, et justa bella administrare.

XXXVIII. *De illicita bonorum communicatione.*

FACULTATES et bona Christianorum non sunt communia, quoad jus et possessionem, (ut quidam Anabaptistæ falso jactant,) debet tamen quisque de his quæ possidet, pro facultatum ratione, pauperibus eleemosynas benigne distribuere.

XXXIX. *De jurejurando.*

QUEMADMODUM juramentum vanum et temerarium a Domino nostro Jesu Christo, et Apostolo ejus Jacobo, Christianis hominibus interdictum esse fatemur: ita Christianorum religionem minime prohibere censemus, quin jubente magistratu in causa fidei et charitatis jurare liceat, modo id fiat juxta Prophetæ doctrinam, in justitia, in judicio, et veritate.

Confirmatio Articulorum.

HIC liber antedictorum Articulorum jam denuo approbatus est, per assensum et consensum Serenissimæ Reginæ Elizabethæ Dominæ nostræ, Dei gratia Angliæ, Franciæ, et Hiberniæ Reginæ, defensoris fidei, &c. retinendus, et per totum regnum Angliæ exequendus. Qui Articuli et lecti sunt, et denuo confirmati subscriptione D. Archiepiscopi et Episcoporum superioris domus, et totius Cleri inferioris domus, in Convocatione, Anno Domini 1571.

CONTENTS.

INTRODUCTION, page 1.
Heresies gave the rise to larger Articles, ib.
A form of doctrine settled by the apostles, 2.
Bishops sent round them a declaration of their faith, ib.
These were afterwards enlarged, 3.
This done at the council of Nice, ib.
Many wild sects at the beginning of the Reformation, 4.
And many complying papists put them on framing this collection, 5.
The Articles set out at first by the king's authority, 7.
A question whether they are only Articles of peace or doctrine, ib.
They bind the consciences of the clergy, ib.
The laity only bound to peace by them, ib.
The subscription to them imports an assent to them, and not only an acquiescing in them, 9.
But the Articles may have different senses; and if the words will bear them, there is no prevarication in subscribing them so, 10.
This illustrated in the third Article, ib.
The various readings of the Articles collated with the MSS., 11.
An account of those various readings, 17.

ARTICLE 1.
That there is a God, proved by the consent of mankind, 19.
Obj. 1. Some nations do not believe a Deity. This is answered, 20.
Obj. 2. It is not the same belief among them all. This is answered, 21.
The visible world proves a Deity, ib.
Time nor number cannot be eternal nor infinite, 22.
Moral arguments to prove that the world had a beginning, 23.
Such a regular frame could not be fortuitous, 24.
Objection from the production of insects answered, ib.
Argument from miracles well attested, 25.
Argument from the idea of God examined, ib.
God is eternal, and necessarily exists, 26.
The unity of the Deity, 27.
God is without body, 28.
Outward manifestations only to declare his presence and authority, 29.
No successive acts in God, 30.
Question concerning God's immanent acts, ib.
God has no passions, 31.
Phrases in scripture of these explained, ib.
Some thoughts concerning the power and wisdom of God, 32.
True ideas of the goodness of God, 33.
Of creation and annihilation, 35.

Of the providence of God, 36.
Objections against it answered, ib.
Whether God does immediately produce all things, 38.
Thought and liberty not proper to matter, 39.
Whether beasts think, or are only machines, 40.
How bodies and spirits are united, ib.
The doctrine of the Trinity, 42.
Whether revealed in the Old Testament, or not, 43.
The doctrine stated, ib.
Argument from the form of Baptism, 44.
Other arguments for it, 45.
This was received in the first ages of Christianity, 47.
Some attempt to the stating true ideas of God, 48.

ART. II.
Christ, how the Son of God, 51.
Argument from the beginning of St. John's Gospel, 52.
Reflections on the state of the world at that time, 53.
Arguments from the Epistle to the Philippians, 54.
Other arguments complicated, 56.
Argument from adoration due to him, 57.
The silence of the Jews proves this was not then thought to be idolatry by them, 58.
Argument from the Epistle to the Hebrews, 59.
God and man in Christ made one person, 61.
An account of Nestorius's doctrine, 63.
Christ was to us an expiatory sacrifice, 65.
An account of expiatory sacrifices, ib.
The agonies of Christ explained, 67.

ART. III.
Ruffin first published this in the Creed, 69.
Several senses put on this Article, 70.
A local descent into hell, ib.
What may be the true sense of the Article, 72.

ART. IV.
The proof of Christ's resurrection, 73.
The Jews in that time did not disprove it, 75.
Several proofs of the incredibility of a forgery in this matter, ib.
The nature and proof of a miracle, 77.
What must be ascribed to good or evil spirits, ib.
The apostles could not be imposed on, 78.
Nor could they have imposed on the world, 79.
Of Christ's ascension, 80.
Curiosity in these matters taxed, ib.
The authority with which Christ is now vested, 82.

ART. V.
The senses of the word, *Holy Ghost*, 84.
It stands oft for a person, ib.
Curiosities to be avoided about procession, 85.
The Holy Ghost is truly God, 87.

ART. VI.
The controversy about oral tradition, 92.
That was soon corrupted, 93.
Guarded against by revelation, 94.
Tradition corrupted among the Jews, ib.
The scripture appealed to by Christ and the apostles, 95.
What is well proved from scripture, 97.
Objections from the darkness of scripture answered, ib.
No sure guard against error, nor against sin, 99.
The proof of the canon of the scripture, 100.
Particularly of the New Testament, 101.
These books were early received, 105.
The canon of the Old Testament proved, ib.
Concerning the Pentateuch, 107.
Objections against the Old Testament answered, 108.

CONTENTS.   xxix

Concerning the various readings, 109.
The nature and degrees of inspiration, 110.
Concerning the historical parts of scripture, 111.
Concerning the reasonings in scripture, 112.
Of the Apocryphal books, 113.

ART. VII.

No difference between the Old and New Testament, 116.
Proofs in the Old Testament of the Messias, 117.
In the prophets; chiefly in Daniel, 121.
The proofs all summed up, ib.
Objections of the Jews answered, 122.
The hopes of another life in the Old Testament, 124.
Our Saviour proved the resurrection from the words to Moses, 125.
Expiation of sin in the old dispensation, 126.
Sins then expiated by the blood of Christ, 127.
Of the rites and ceremonies among the Jews, 128.
Of their judiciary laws, 129.
Of the moral law, 130.
The principles of morality, 131.
Of idolatry, ib.
Concerning the Sabbath, 132.
Of the second table, 133.
Of not coveting what is our neighbour's, 134.

ART. VIII.

Concerning the Creed of Athanasius, 135.
And the condemning clauses in it, 136.
Of the Apostles' Creed, 137.

ART. IX.

Different opinions concerning original sin, 140.
All men liable to death by it, ib.
A corruption spread through the whole race of Adam, 141.
Of the state of innocence, 143.
Of the effects of Adam's fall, 144.
God's justice vindicated, 145.
Of the imputation of Adam's sin, ib.

St. Austin's doctrine in this point, 146.
This is opposed by many others, 148.
Both sides pretend their doctrines agree with the Article, 150.

ART. X.

The true notion of liberty, 152.
The feebleness of our present state, 154.
Inward assistances promised in the new covenant, 155.
The effect that these have on men, 156.
Concerning preventing-grace, 157.
Of its being efficacious or universal, 158.

ART. XI.

Concerning justification, 160.
Concerning faith, 162.
The difference between the church of England and the church of Rome in this point, 164.
The conditions upon which men are justified, 168.
The use to be made of this doctrine, 169.

ART. XII.

The necessity of holiness, 170.
Concerning merit, 172.
Of the defects of good works, ib.

ART. XIII.

Actions in themselves good, yet may be sins in him who does them, 174.
Of the seventh chapter to the Romans, 175.
This is not a total incapacity, 176.

ART. XIV.

Of the great extent of our duty, 177.
No counsels of perfection, 178.
Many duties which do not bind at all times, 179.
It is not possible for man to supererogate, 180.
Objections against this answered ib.
The steps by which that doctrine prevailed, 182.

ART. XV.

Christ's spotless holiness, 184.

Of the imperfections of the best of men, 185.

ART. XVI.

Concerning mortal and venial sin, 187.

Of the sin against the Holy Ghost, 188.

Of the pardon of sin after baptism, 189.

That as God forgives, the church ought also to forgive, ib.

Concerning apostacy, and sin unto death, 191.

ART. XVII.

The state of the question, 193.

The doctrine of the supralapsarians and sublapsarians, 194.

The doctrine of the remonstrants and the Socinians, 195.

This is a controversy that arises out of natural religion, ib.

The history of this controversy both in ancient and modern times, 196.

The arguments of the supralapsarians, 204.

The arguments of the sublapsarians, 212.

The arguments of the remonstrants, 213.

They affirm a certain prescience, 217.

The Socinians' plea, 221.

General reflections on the whole matter, ib.

The advantages and disadvantages of both sides, and the faults of both, 223.

In what both do agree, 224.

The sense of the Article, 225.

The cautions added to it, 226.

Passages in the Liturgy explained, 227.

ART. XVIII.

Philosophers thought men might be saved in all religions, 228.

So do the Mahometans, ib.

None are saved but by Christ, 229.

Whether some may not be saved by him, who never heard of him, 230.

None are in covenant with God, but through the knowledge of Christ, 231.

But for others, we cannot judge of the extent of the mercies of God, 231.

Curiosity is to be restrained, ib.

ART. XIX.

We ought not to believe that any are infallible, without good authority, 234.

Just prejudices against some who pretend to it, 235.

No miracles brought to prove this, 236.

Proofs brought from scripture, 238.

Things to be supposed previous to these, ib.

A circle is not to be admitted, 239.

The notes given of the true church, ib.

These are examined, 240.

And whether they do agree to the church of Rome, 241.

The truth of doctrine must be first settled, ib.

A society that has a true baptism, is a true church, 242.

Sacraments are not annulled by every corruption, 244.

We own the baptism and orders given in the church of Rome, ib.

And yet justify our separating from them, 245.

Objections against private judging, ib.

Our reasons are given us for that end, 246.

Our minds are free as our wills are, 247.

The church is still visible, but not infallible, 248.

Of the pope's infallibility, 250.

That was not pretended to in the first ages, 251.

The dignity of sees rose from the cities, ib.

Popes have fallen into heresy, ib.

Their ambition and forgeries, 252.

Their cruelty, ib.

The power of deposing princes claimed by them as given them by God, 254.

This was not a corruption only of discipline, but of doctrine, 255

Arguments for the pope's infallibility, 256.
No foundation for it in the New Testament, 257.
St. Peter never claimed it, 258.
Christ's words to him explained, 259.
Of the keys of the kingdom of heaven, ib.
Of binding and loosing, 260.

ART. XX.
Of church-power in rituals, 263.
The practice of the Jewish church, 264.
Changes in these sometimes necessary, 265.
The practice of the Apostles, 266.
Subjects must obey in lawful things, 267.
But superiors must not impose too much, ib.
The church has authority, though not infallible, 268.
Great respect due to her decisions, 269.
But no absolute submission, ib.
The church is the depository of the scriptures, 270.
The church of Rome run in a circle, ib.

ART. XXI.
Councils cannot be called, but by the consent of princes, 272.
The first were called by the Roman emperors, ib.
Afterwards the popes called them, 273.
Then some councils thought on methods to fix their meeting, 274.
What makes a council to be general, 275.
What numbers are necessary, ib.
How must they be cited, ib.
No rules given in scripture concerning their constitution, 275.
Nazianzen's complaints of councils, 276.
Councils have been contrary to one another, ib.
Disorders and intrigues in councils, ib.
They judge not by inspiration, 277.

The churches may examine their proceedings, and judge of them, 277.
Concerning the pope's bull confirming them, ib.
They have an authority, but not absolute, ib.
Nor do they need the pope's bulls, ib.
The several churches know their traditions best, 278.
The fathers do argue for the truth of the decisions, but not from their authority, 279.
No prospect of another general council, ib.
Popes are jealous of them, ib.
And the world expects little from them, ib.
Concerning the words, 'Tell the church,' 280.
How the church is the pillar and ground of truth, ib.
Christ's promise, 'I am with you alway, even to the end of the world,' 281.
Of that, 'It seemed good to the Holy Ghost, and to us,' ib.
Some general councils have erred, 282.

ART. XXII.
The doctrine of purgatory, 285.
Sins once pardoned are not punished, 286.
Unless with chastisements in this life, 287.
No state of satisfaction after death, 288.
No mention made of that in scripture, 289.
But it is plain to the contrary, ib.
Different opinions among the ancients, ib.
The original of purgatory, 291.
A passage in Maccabees considered, ib.
A passage in the Epistle to the Corinthians considered, 293.
The progress of the belief of purgatory, 294.
Prayers for the dead among the ancients, ib.
Endowments for redeeming out of purgatory, 296.

Whether these ought to be sacred, or not, 297.
The doctrine of pardons and indulgences, 298.
It is only the excusing from penance, 300.
No foundation for it in scripture, ib.
General rules concerning idolatry, 301.
Of the idolatry of heathens, 302.
Laws given to the Jews against it, ib.
The expostulations of the prophets, 303.
Concerning the golden calf, 304.
And the calves at Dan and Bethel, ib.
The apostles opposed all idolatry, 305.
St. Paul at Athens, and to the Romans, 306.
The sense of the primitive fathers upon it, 307.
The first use of images among Christians, ib.
Pictures in churches for instruction, 309.
Were afterwards worshipped, ib.
Contests about that, ib.
Images of the Deity and Trinity, 310.
On what the worship of images terminates, 311.
The due worship settled by the council at Trent, 312.
Images consecrated, and how, 313.
Arguments for worshipping them answered, 314.
Arguments against the use or worship of images, ib.
The worship of relics, 315.
The progress of superstition, 316.
A due regard to the bodies of martyrs, ib.
No warrant for this in scripture, 317.
Hezekiah broke the brazen serpent, ib.
The memorable passage concerning the body of St. Polycarp, ib.
Fables and forgeries prevailed, 318.

The souls of the martyrs believed to hover about their tombs, 319.
Nothing of this kind objected to the first Christians, 320.
Disputes between Vigilantius and St. Jerome, ib.
No invocation of saints in the Old Testament, 322.
The invocating angels condemned in the New Testament, 323.
No saints invocated, Christ only, ib.
No mention of this in the three first ages, 324.
In the fourth, martyrs were invocated, 325.
The progress that this made, 326.
Scandalous offices in the church of Rome, ib.
Arguments against this invocation, 327.
An apology for those who began it, ib.
The scandal given by it, 329.
Arguments for it answered, 330.
Whether the saints see all things in God, ib.
This no part of the communion of saints, 331.
Prayers ought to be directed only to God, ib.
Revealed religion designed to deliver the world from idolatry, 332.

ART. XXIII.

A succession of pastors ought to be in the church, 333.
This was settled by the Apostles, 334.
And must continue to the end of the world, ib.
It was settled in the first age of the church, 335.
The danger of men's taking to themselves this authority without a due vocation, 336.
The difference between means of salvation, and precepts for order's sake, ib.
What is lawful authority, 337.
What may be done upon extraordinary occasions, 338.
Necessity is above rules of order, ib.

CONTENTS.

The high priests in our Saviour's time, 339.
Baptism by women, 340.

ART. XXIV.
The chief end of worshipping God, 341.
The practice of the Jews, 342.
Rules given by the Apostles, ib.
The practice of the church, 343.
Arguments for worship in an unknown tongue answered, 344.

ART. XXV.
Difference between sacraments and rites, 347.
Sacraments do not imprint a character, ib.
But are not mere ceremonies, 349.
What is necessary to constitute a sacrament, ib.
That applied to baptism, 350.
And to the eucharist, 351.
No mention of seven sacraments before Peter Lombard, ib.
Confirmation, no sacrament, ib.
How practised among us, 352.
The use of chrism in it is new, 353.
Oil early used in Christian rituals, ib.
Bishops only consecrated the chrism, 354.
In the Greek church presbyters applied it, ib.
This used in the western church, but condemned by the popes, ib.
Disputes concerning confirmation, 355.
Concerning penance, ib.
The true notion of repentance, 356.
Confession not the matter of a sacrament, 357.
The use of confession, ib.
The priest's pardon ministerial, 358.
And restrained within bounds, 360.
Auricular confession not necessary, 361.
Not commanded in the New Testament, ib.
The beginnings of it in the church, 362.
Many canons about penance, 363.
Confession forbid at Constantinople.
The ancient discipline slackened, 364.
Confession may be advised, but not commanded, 365.
The good and bad effects it may have, ib.
Of contrition and attrition, 366.
The ill effects of the doctrine of attrition, 367.
Of doing the penance or satisfaction, 368.
Concerning sorrow for sin, ib.
Of the ill effects of hasty absolution, 369.
Of fasting and prayer, ib.
Of the form, 'I absolve thee,' 370.
Of holy orders, 371.
Of the ancient form of ordinations, 372.
Of delivering the vessel, 373.
Orders no sacrament, ib.
Whether bishops and priests are of the same order, 374.
Of marriage, ib.
It can be no sacrament, 375.
Intention not necessary, ib.
How marriage is called a mystery or sacrament, 376.
Marriage dissolved by adultery, 377.
The practice of the church in this matter, 378.
Of extreme unction, ib.
St. James's words explained, 379.
Oil much used in ancient rituals, 381.
Pope Innocent's Epistle considered, ib.
Anointing used in order to recovery, 383.
Afterwards as the sacrament of the dying, ib.
The sacraments are to be used, 384.
And to be received worthily, ib.

ART. XXVI.
Sacraments are not effectual as prayers are, 386.
Of the doctrine of intention, 388.

The ill consequences of it, 388.
Of a just severity in discipline, 389.
Particularly towards the clergy, 390.

ART. XXVII.

Concerning St. John's Baptism, 391.
The Jews used baptism, ib.
The Christian baptism, 392.
The difference between it and St. John's, 393.
The necessity of baptism, 394.
It is a precept but not a mean of salvation, ib.
Baptism unites us to the church, 395.
It also saves us, ib.
St. Peter's words explained, 396.
St. Austin's doctrine of baptism, ib.
Baptism is a federal stipulation, 397.
In what sense it was of more value to preach than to baptize, 398.
Of infant baptism, ib.
It is grounded on the law of nature, 399.
And the law of Moses, and warranted in the New Testament, ib.
In what sense children can be holy, 400.
It is also very expedient, 401.

ART. XXVIII.

The change made in this Article in queen Elizabeth's time, 402.
The explanation of our doctrine, 403.
Of the rituals in the passover, ib.
Of the words, 'This is my body,' 404.
And, 'This cup is the new testament in my blood,' 405.
Of the horror the Jews had at blood, ib.
In what sense only the disciples could understand our Saviour's words, 406.
The discourse (John vi.) explained, 407.
It can only be understood spiritually, 408.

Bold figures much understood in the East, 409.
A plain thing needs no great proof, 410.
Of unworthy receivers, and the effect of that sin, 411.
Of the effects of worthy receiving, 412.
Of federal symbols, ib.
Of the communion of the body and blood of Christ, 413.
Of the like phrases in scripture, 414.
Of our sense of the phrase *real presence*, ib.
Transubstantiation explained, 415.
Of the words of consecration, 416.
Of the consequences of transubstantiation, 418.
The grounds upon which it was believed, 419.
This is contrary to the testimony of all our faculties, both sense and reason, ib.
We can be sure of nothing, if our senses do deceive us, 420.
The objection from believing mysteries, answered, 421.
The end of all miracles considered, 422.
Our doctrine of a mystical presence is confessed by those of the church of Rome, 423.
St. Austin's rule about figures, ib.
Presumptions concerning the belief of the ancients in this matter, 424.
They had not that philosophy which this doctrine has forced on the church of Rome, ib.
This was not objected by heathens, 427.
No heresies or disputes arose upon this, as they did on all other points, ib.
Many new rituals unknown to them, have sprung out of this doctrine, 428.
In particular, the adoring the sacrament, 429.
Prayers in the masses of the saints inconsistent with it, ib.
They believed the elements were bread and wine after consecration, ib.

Many authorities brought for this, 430.
Eutychians said, Christ's humanity was swallowed of his divinity, 431.
The fathers argue against this from the doctrine of the eucharist, ib.
The force of that argument explained, 432.
The fathers say our bodies are nourished by the sacrament, 433.
They call it the type, sign, and figure, of the body and blood of Christ, 434.
The prayer of consecration calls it so, 436.
That compared with the prayer in the Missal, ib.
The progress of the doctrine of the corporal presence, 437.
Reflection on the ages in which it grew, ib.
The occasion on which it was advanced in the eastern church, 439.
Paschase Radbert taught it first, 440.
But many wrote against him, ib.
Afterwards Berengarius opposed it, 442.
The schoolmen descanted on it, 443.
Philosophy was corrupted to support it, ib.
Concerning consubstantiation, 444.
It is an opinion that may be borne with, ib.
The adoration of the eucharist is idolatry, 445.
The plea against that considered, ib.
Christ is not to be worshipped, though present, 447.
Concerning reserving the sacrament, ib.
Concerning the elevation of it, 448.

ART. XXIX.

The wicked do not receive Christ, 450.

The doctrine of the fathers in this point, 451.
More particularly St. Austin's, ib.

ART. XXX.

The chalice was given to all, 452.
Not to the disciples as priests, 453.
The breaking of bread explained, ib.
Sacraments must be given according to the institution, ib.
No arguments from ill consequences to be admitted, unless in cases of necessity, 454.
Concomitance a new notion, ib.
Universal practice for giving the chalice, 455.
The case of the Aquarii, ib.
The first beginning of taking away the cup, 456.
The decree of the council of Constance, 457.

ART. XXXI.

The term *sacrifice* of a large signification, 459.
The primitive Christians denied that they had any sacrifices, ib.
The eucharist has no virtue, but as it is a communion, 460.
Strictly speaking there is only one Priest and one Sacrifice in the Christian religion, 461.
The fathers did not think the eucharist was a propitiatory sacrifice, 463.
But call it a sacrifice in a larger sense, ib.
Masses without a communion not known then, 464.
None might be at mass, who did not communicate, ib.
The importance of the controversies concerning the eucharist, 465.

ART. XXII.

No divine law against a married clergy, 467.
Neither in the Old or New Testament, but the contrary, 468.

The church has not power to make a perpetual law against it, 470.
The ill consequences of such a law, ib.
No such law in the first ages, 471.
When the laws for the celibate began, 472.
The practice of the church not uniform in it, ib.
The progress of these laws in England, ib.
The good and the bad of celibate balanced, 473.
It is not lawful to make vows in this matter, 474.
Nor do they bind when made, 475.
Oaths ill made are worse to be kept, ib.

ART. XXXIII.

A temper to be observed in church-discipline, 477.
The necessity of keeping it up, ib.
Extremes in this to be avoided, 478.
Concerning the delivering any to Satan, 479.
The importance of an anathema, 480.
Of the effect of church-censures, ib.
What it is when they are wrong applied, 481.
The causeless jealousy of church-power, ib.
How the laity was once taken into the exercise of it, 482.
The pastors of the church have authority, ib.
Defects in this no just cause of separation, 484.
All these brought in by popery, ib.
A correction of them intended at the Reformation, ib.

ART. XXXIV.

The obligation to obey canons and laws, 485.

The great sin of schism and disobedience, 486.
The true notion of scandal, 487.
The fear of giving scandal no warrant to break established laws, 488.
Human laws are not unalterable, ib.
The respect due to ancient canons, ib.
The corruptions of the canon law, 489.
Great varieties in rituals, 490.
Every church is a complete body, ib.

ART. XXXV.

The occasion of compiling the Homilies, 491.
We are not bound to every thing in them, 492.
But only to the doctrine, ib.
This illustrated in the charge of idolatry, ib.
What is meant by their being necessary for those times, ib.

ART. XXXVI.

The occasion of this Article, 494.
An explanation of the words, 'Receive ye the Holy Ghost,' 495.

ART. XXXVII.

Queen Elizabeth's injunction concerning the supremacy, 497.
The pope's universal jurisdiction not warranted by any of the laws of Christ, 498.
Nor acknowledged in the first ages, 499.
Begun on the occasion of the Arian controversy, 500.
Contested in many places, ib.
The progress that it made, 501.
The patriarchal authority founded on the division of the Roman empire, sunk with it, 502.
The power exercised by the kings of Judah in religious matters, ib.
That is founded on scriptures, 503.

CONTENTS.

Practised in all ages, 503.
And particularly in England, 504.
Methods used by popish princes to keep the ecclesiastical authority under the civil, 505.
The temporal power is over all persons, ib.
And in all causes, ib.
The importance of the term *head*, 507.
The necessity of capital punishments, ib.
The measure of these, 508.
The lawfulness of war, 509.
Our Saviour's words explained, 510.
In what cases war is just, 511.
Warranted by the laws of God, ib.
How a subject may serve in an unlawful war, 511.

ART. XXXVIII.

Concerning property and charity, 513.
The proportion of charity to the poor, 414.

ART. XXXIX.

The lawfulness of oaths proved, 515.
From natural religion and the scriptures, ib.
The form of swearing among the Jews, 516.
Our Saviour's words and St. James's against all swearing explained, 517.
When oaths may be lawfully taken, 518.

AN

EXPOSITION

OF THE

ARTICLES

OF

THE CHURCH OF ENGLAND.

Articles whereupon it was agreed by the Archbishops and Bishops of both provinces and the whole Cleargie, in the Convocation holden at London in the Yeare of our Lorde GOD 1562, according to the Computation of the Church of Englande, for the avoiding of the Diversities of Opinions, and for the stablishing of Consent touching true Religion. Put forth by the Queen's Authoritie.

THE title of these articles leads me to consider, 1st, The time, the occasion, and the design of compiling them. 2dly, the authority that is stamped upon them both by church and state, and the obligation that lies upon all of our communion to assent to them, and more particularly the importance of the subscription to which the clergy are obliged. As to the first, it may seem somewhat strange to see such a collection of tenets made the standard of the doctrine of a church that is deservedly valued by reason of her moderation: this seems to be a departing from the simplicity of the first ages, which yet we pretend to set up for a pattern. Among them, the owning the belief of the creeds then received was thought sufficient: and, when some heresies had occasioned a great enlargement to be made in the creeds, the third general council thought fit to set a bar against all farther additions; and yet all those creeds, one of which goes far beyond the Ephesine standard, make but one article of the thirty-nine of which this book consists. Many of these do also relate to subtile and abstruse points, in which it is not easy to form a clear judgment; and much less can it be convenient to impose so great a collection of tenets upon a whole church, to excommunicate such as affirm any of them to be erroneous, and to reject those from the service of the church who cannot assent to every one of these. The negative Articles of No infallibility, No supremacy in the pope, No transubstantiation, No purgatory, and the like, give

THE INTRODUCTION.

yet a farther colour to exceptions; since it may seem that it was enough not to have mentioned these, which implies a tacit rejecting of them. It may, therefore, appear to be too rigorous to require a positive condemning of those points: for, a very high degree of certainty is required, to affirm a negative proposition.

In order to the explaining this matter, it is to be confessed, that, in the beginnings of Christianity, the declaration that was required even of a bishop's faith was conceived in very general terms. There was a form settled very early in most churches: this St. Paul, in one place, calls 'the form of doctrine that was delivered;' in another place, 'the form of sound words,' which those, who were fixed by the apostles in particular churches, had received from them. These words of his do import a standard, or *fixed formulary*, by which all doctrines were to be examined. Some have inferred from them, that the apostles delivered that creed, which goes under their name, every where in the same form of words. But there is great reason to doubt of this, since the first apologists for Christianity, when they deliver a short abstract of the Christian faith, do all vary from one another, both as to the order and as to the words themselves; which they would not have done, if the churches had all received one settled form from the apostles. They would all have used the same words, and neither more nor less. It is more probable, that in every church there was a *form* settled, which was delivered to it by some apostle, or companion of the apostles, with some variation: of which at this distance of time, considering how defective the history of the first ages of Christianity is, it is not possible, nor very necessary for us to be able to give a clear account. For instance; in the whole extent or neighbourhood of the Roman empire, it was at first of great use to have this in every Christian's mouth, that our Saviour *suffered under Pontius Pilate;* because this fixed the time, and carried in it an appeal to records and evidences, that might then have been searched for. But if this religion went at first far to the *eastward*, beyond all commerce with the Romans, there is not that reason to think that this should have been a part of the shortest form of this doctrine; it being enough that it was related in the gospel. These forms of the several churches were preserved with that sacred respect that was due to them: this was esteemed the *depositum* or trust of a church, which was chiefly committed to the keeping of the bishop. In the first ages, in which the bishops or clergy of the several churches could not meet together in synods to examine the doctrine of every new bishop, the method, upon which the circumstances of those ages put them, was this: the new bishop sent round him, and chiefly to the bishops of the more eminent sees, the profession of his faith, according

Marginal references: Rom. vi. 17. 1 Tim. iv. 6. vi. 3. 2 Tim. i. 13.

to the form that was fixed in his church: and when the neighbouring bishops were satisfied in this, they held communion with him, and not only owned him for a bishop, but maintained such a commerce with him as the state of that time did admit of.

But as some heresies sprung up, there were enlargements made in several churches, for the condemning those, and for excluding such as held them, from their communion. The council of Nice examined many of those creeds, and out of them they put their creed in a fuller form. The addition made by the council of Constantinople was put into the creeds of some particular churches, several years before that council met. So that though it received its authority from that council, yet they rather confirmed an article which they found in the creeds of some churches, than made a new one. It had been an invaluable blessing, if the Christian religion had been kept in its first simplicity. The council of Ephesus took care that the creed, by which men profess their Christianity, should receive no new additions, but be fixed according to the Constantinopolitan standard; yet they made decrees in points of faith, and the following councils went on in their steps, adding still new decrees, with anathematisms against the contrary doctrines; and declaring the assertors of them to be under an *anathema*, that is, under a very heavy curse of being totally excluded from their communion, and even from the communion of Jesus Christ. And whereas the new bishops had formerly only declared their faith, they were then required, besides that, to declare, that they received such councils, and rejected such doctrines, together with such as favoured them; who were sometimes mentioned by name. This increased daily. We have a full account of the special declaration that a bishop was obliged to make, in the first canon of that which passed for the fourth council of Carthage. But while, by reason of new emergencies, this was swelling to a vast bulk, general and more implicit formularies came to be used, the bishops declaring that they received and would observe all the decrees and traditions of holy councils and fathers. And the papacy coming afterwards to carry every thing before it, a formal oath, that had many loose and indefinite words in it, which were very large and comprehensive, was added to all the declarations that had been formerly established. The enlargements of creeds were at first occasioned by the prevarications of heretics; who having put senses favouring their opinions, to the simpler terms in which the first creeds were proposed, therefore it was thought necessary to add more express words. And this was absolutely necessary as to some points; for it being necessary to shew that the Christian religion did not bring in that idolatry which it condemned in heathens, it was also necessary to state this matter so, that it should appear that they worshipped no creature; but that the Person to whom all agreed to pay divine adoration was truly God: and it being found that an equivocation was used in all other words except that of the *same substance*, they judged it necessary to fix on it, besides some other words that they at first brought in, but which were afterwards corrupted by the glosses that were put on them. At all times it is very necessary to free the Christian religion from the imputations of idolatry; but this was never so necessary, as when Christianity was engaged in such a struggle with paganism: and since the main article then in dispute with the heathens was idolatry, and the lawfulness of worshipping any besides the great and eternal God, it was of the last importance to the Christian cause, to take care that the heathens might have no reason to believe that they worshipped a creature. There was therefore just reason given to secure this main point, and to put an end to equivocation, by establishing a term, which, by the confession of all parties, did not admit of any. It had been a great blessing to the church, if a stop had been put here; and that those nice descantings, that were afterwards so much pursued, had been more effectually discouraged than they were. But men ever were and ever will be men. Factions were formed and interests were set up. Heretics had shewed so much dissimulation when they were low, and so much cruelty when they prevailed, that it was thought necessary to secure the church from the disturbances that they might give them: and thus it grew to be a rule to enlarge the doctrines and decisions of the church. So that in stating the doctrines of this church so copiously, our reformers followed a method that had been used in a course of many ages.

There were, besides this common practice, two particular circumstances in that time, that made this seem to be the more necessary. One was, that at the breaking out of that light, there sprang up with it many impious and extravagant sects, which broke out into most violent excesses. This was no extraordinary thing, for we find the like happened upon the first spreading of the gospel; many detestable sects grew up with it, which tended not a little to the defaming of Christianity, and the obstructing its progress. I shall not examine what influence evil spirits might have both in the one and the other: but one visible occasion of it was, that by the first preaching of the gospel, as also upon the opening the reformation, an inquiry into the matters of religion being then the subject of men's studies and discourses, many men of warm and ill-governed imaginations, presuming on their own talents, and being desirous to signalize themselves, and to have a name in the world, went beyond their depth in study, without the necessary degrees of knowledge, and the yet more necessary dispositions of mind for arriving at a right understanding of divine matters. This happening soon after the reformation was first set on foot, those, whose corruptions were struck at by it, and who both hated and persecuted it on that account, did not fail to lay hold of and to improve the advantage which these sects gave them. They said, that the sectaries had only spoke out what the rest thought; and at last they held to this, that all sects were the natural consequences of the reformation, and of shaking off the doctrine of the infallibility of the church. To stop those calumnies, the Protestants of Germany prepared that confession of their faith which they offered to the diet at Augsburg,* and which carries its name. And, after their example, all the other churches, which separated from the Roman communion, published the confessions of their faith, both to declare their doctrine for the instruction of their own members, and for covering them from the slanders of their adversaries.

Another reason that the first reformers had for their descending into so many particulars, and for all these negatives that are in their confessions, was this: they had smarted long under the tyranny of popery, and so they had reason to secure themselves from it, and from all those who were leavened with it. They here in England had seen how many had complied with every alteration both in king Henry and king Edward's reign, who not only declared themselves to have been all the while papists, but became bloody persecutors in queen Mary's reign: therefore it was necessary to keep all such out of their body, that they might not secretly undermine and betray it. Now since the church of Rome owns all that is positive in our doctrine, there could be no discrimination made, but by condemning the most important of those additions, that they have

* This celebrated confession was dictated by Luther, and drawn up by Melancthon. It contains twenty-eight chapters. Twenty-one of which set forth the opinions of the Protestants; the other seven the errors and superstitions of the church of Rome. Dr. Mosheim gives the following most interesting account of the presentation of this confession, and of its effect upon the diet:—
'Charles V. arrived at Augsburg the 15th of June, 1530, and on the twentieth day of the same month the diet was opened. As it was unanimously agreed, that the affairs of religion should be brought upon the carpet before the deliberations relating to the intended war with the Turks, the Protestant members of this great assembly received from the emperor a formal permission to present to the diet, on the 25th of June, an account of their religious principles and tenets. In consequence of this Christian Bayer, chancellor of Saxony, read, in the German language, in presence of the emperor and the assembled princes, the famous confession which has been since distinguished by the denomination of the Confession of Augsburg. The princes heard it with the deepest attention and recollection of mind; it confirmed some in the principles they had embraced, surprised others, and many, who, before this time, had little or no idea of the religious sentiments of Luther, were now not only convinced of their innocence, but were, moreover, delighted with their purity and simplicity. The copies of this confession, which after being read, were delivered to the emperor, were signed and subscribed by John, elector of Saxony, by four princes of the empire, George, marquis of Brandenburg, Ernest, duke of Lunenburg, Philip, landgrave of Hesse, Wolfgang, prince of Anhalt, and by the imperial cities of Nuremberg and Reutlingen, who all thereby solemnly declared their assent to the doctrines contained in it.'—See the confession of Augsburg, in APPENDIX A.—[ED.]

brought into the Christian religion, in express words: and though in matters of fact, or in theories of nature, it is not safe to affirm a negative, because it is seldom possible to prove it; yet the fundamental article, upon which the whole reformation and this our church depends, is this, that the whole doctrines of the Christian religion are contained in the Scripture, and that therefore we are to admit no article as a part of it till it is proved from scripture. This being laid down, and well made out, it is not at all unreasonable to affirm a negative upon an examination of all those places of scripture that are brought for any doctrine, and that seem to favour it, if they are found not at all to support it, but to bear a different, and sometimes a contrary sense, to that which is offered to be proved by them. So there is no weight in this cavil, which looks plausible to such as cannot distinguish common matters from points of faith. This may serve in general to justify the largeness and the particularities of this confession of our faith. There were some steps made to it in king Henry's time, in a large book that was then published under the title of *The Necessary Erudition*, that was a treatise set forth to instruct the nation. Many of the errors of popery were laid open and condemned in it: but none were obliged to assent to it, or to subscribe it. After that, the worship was reformed, as being that which pressed most; and in that a foundation was laid for the articles that came quickly after it. How or by whom they were prepared, we do not certainly know; by the remains of that time it appears, that, in the alterations that were made, there was great precaution used, such as matters of that nature required, questions were framed relating to them, these were given about to many bishops and divines, who gave in their several answers that were collated and examined very maturely: all sides had a free and fair hearing before conclusions were made.

In the fermentation, that was working over the whole nation at that time, it was not possible that a thing of that nature could have passed by the methods that are more necessary in regular times: and therefore they could not be offered at first to synods or convocations. The corruptions complained of were so beneficial to the whole body of the clergy, that it is justly to be wondered at that so great a number was prevailed with to concur in reforming them: but, without a miracle, they could not have been agreed to by the major part. They were prepared, as is most probable, by Cranmer and Ridley, and published by the regal authority. Not as if our kings had pretended to an authority to judge in points of faith, or to decide controversies: but as every private man must choose for himself, and believe according to the convictions of his reason and conscience (which is to be examined and proved in its proper place), so every prince or legislative power must give the public sanction and authority according to his own persuasion; this makes indeed such a sanction to become a law, but does not alter the nature of things, nor oblige the consciences of the subjects, unless they come under the same persuasions. Such laws have indeed the operation of all other laws; but the doctrines authorized by them have no more truth than they had before without any such publication. Thus the part that our princes had in the reformation was only this, that they, being satisfied with the grounds on which it went, received it themselves, and enacted it for their people. And this is so plain and just a consequence of that liberty which every man has of believing and acting according to his own convictions, that when this is well made out, there can be no colour to question the other. It was also remarkable, that the law, which stood first in Justinian's code, was an edict of Theodosius's; who, finding the Roman empire under great distractions by the diversity of opinions in matter of religion, did appoint that doctrine to be held which was received by Damasus bishop of Rome, and Peter bishop of Alexandria; such an edict as that, being put in so conspicuous a part of the *law*, was a full and soon observed precedent for our princes to act according to it.

The next thing to be examined is the use of the Articles, and the importance of the subscriptions of the clergy to them. Some have thought that they are only *Articles of Union and Peace;* that they are a standard of *doctrine* not to be contradicted, or disputed; that the sons of the church are only bound to acquiesce silently to them; and that the subscription binds only to a general compromise upon those Articles, that so there may be no disputing nor wrangling about them. By this means they reckon, that, though a man should differ in his opinion from that which appears to be the clear sense of any of the Articles; yet he may with a good conscience subscribe them, if the Article appears to him to be of such a nature, that, though he thinks it wrong, yet it seems not to be of that consequence, but that it may be borne with, and not contradicted. I shall not now examine whether it were more fit for leaving men to the due freedom of their thoughts, that the subscription did run no higher, it being in many cases a great hardship to exclude some very deserving persons from the service of the church, by requiring a subscription to so many particulars, concerning some of which they are not fully satisfied. I am only now to consider what is the importance of the subscriptions now required among us, and not what might be reasonably wished that it should be.

As to the laity, and the whole body of the people, certainly to them these are only the articles of church-communion; so that every person who does not think that there is some proposition in them that is erroneous to so high a degree, that he cannot hold communion with such as hold it, may and is obliged to continue in our communion: for certainly there may be many opinions held in matters of religion, which a man may believe to be false, and yet may esteem them to be of so little importance to the chief design of religion, that he may well hold communion with those whom he thinks to be so mistaken. Here a necessary distinction is to be remembered between articles of faith and articles of doctrine: the one are held necessary to salvation, the other are only believed to be true; that is, to be revealed in the scriptures, which is a sufficient ground for esteeming them true. *Articles of faith* are doctrines that are so necessary to salvation, that without believing them there is not a fœderal right to the covenant of grace: these are not many, and in the establishment of any doctrine for such, it is necessary both to prove it from scripture, and to prove its being necessary to salvation, as a mean settled by the covenant of grace in order to it. We ought not indeed to hold communion with such as make doctrines, that we believe not to be true, to pass for articles of faith; though we may hold communion with such as do think them true, without stamping so high an authority upon them. To give one instance of this in an undeniable particular. In the days of the apostles there were Judaizers of two sorts: some thought the Jewish nation was still obliged to observe the Mosaical law; but others went farther, and thought that such an observation was indispensably necessary to salvation. Both these opinions were wrong, but the one was tolerable, and the other was intolerable, because it pretended to make that, a necessary condition of salvation, which God had not commanded. The apostles complied with the Judaizers of the first sort, as 'they became all things to all men, that so they might gain some' of every sort of men: yet they declared openly against the other, and said, that if men were *circumcised*, or were willing to come under such a yoke, *Christ profited them nothing;* and upon that supposition he had *died in vain.* From this plain precedent we see what a difference we ought to make between errors in doctrinal matters, and the imposing them as articles of faith. We may live in communion with those who hold errors of the one sort, but must not with those of the other. This also shews the tyranny of that church, which has imposed the belief of every one of her doctrines on the consciences of her votaries, under the highest pains of anathemas, and as articles of faith. But whatever those at Trent did, this church very carefully avoided the laying that weight upon even those doctrines which she receives as true; and therefore though she drew up a large form of doctrine, yet to all her lay-sons this is only a standard of what she teaches, and they are no more to them

1 Cor. ix. 19—23.

than articles of church-communion. The citations that are brought from those two great primates, Laud and Bramhall, go no farther than this: they do not seem to relate to the clergy that subscribe them, but to the laity and body of the people. The people, who do only join in communion with us, may well continue to do so, though they may not be fully satisfied with every proposition in them: unless they should think that they struck against any of the articles, or foundations of faith; and, as they truly observe, there is a great difference to be observed in this particular between the imperious spirit of the church of Rome, and the modest freedom which ours allows.

But I come, in the next place, to consider what the clergy is bound to by their subscriptions. The meaning of every subscription is to be taken from the design of the imposer, and from the words of the subscription itself. The title of the Articles bears, that they were agreed upon in convocation, *for the avoiding of diversities of Opinions, and for the stablishing consent touching true Religion.* Where it is evident, that a *consent in opinion* is designed. If we in the next place consider the declaration that the church has made in the canons, we shall find, that though by the 5th canon, which relates to the whole body of the people, such are only declared to be excommunicated *ipso facto,* who shall affirm any of the Articles to be *erroneous,* or such as he may not with a good conscience subscribe to; yet the 36th canon is express for the clergy, requiring them to subscribe *willingly,* and *ex animo;* and *acknowledge all and every article to be agreeable to the word of God:* upon which canon it is that the form of the subscription runs in these words, which seem expressly to declare a man's own opinion, and not a bare consent to an article of peace, or an engagement to silence and submission. The statute of the 13th of queen Elizabeth, cap. 12, which gives the legal authority to our requiring subscriptions, in order to a man's being capable of a benefice, requires that every clergyman should read the Articles in the church, with a declaration of his *unfeigned assent to them.* These things make it appear very plain, that the subscriptions of the clergy must be considered as a declaration of their own opinion, and not as a bare obligation to silence. There arose in king James the First's reign great and warm disputes concerning the decrees of God, and those other points that were settled in Holland by the synod of Dort against the Remonstrants; divines of both sides among us appealed to the Articles, and pretended they were favourable to them: for though the first appearance of them seems to favour the doctrine of absolute decrees, and the irresistibility of grace; yet there are many expressions that have another face, and so those of the other persuasion pleaded for themselves from these. Upon this a royal declaration was set forth, in which, after mention is made of *those* disputes, *and that the men of all sides did take the Articles to be for them, order is given for stopping those disputes for the future; and for shutting them in God's promises as they be generally set forth in the holy scriptures, and the general meaning of the Articles of the* Church of England, *according to them; and that no man thereafter should put his own sense or comment to be the meaning of the Article, but should take it in the literal and grammatical sense.* In this there has been such a general acquiescing, that the fierceness of these disputes has gone off, while men have been left to subscribe the Articles according to their literal and grammatical sense. From which two things are to be inferred: the one is, that the subscription does import an assent to the Article; and the other is, that an Article being conceived in such general words, that it can admit of different literal and grammatical senses, even when the senses given are plainly contrary one to another, yet both may subscribe the Article with a good conscience, and without any equivocation. To make this more sensible, I shall give an instance of it in an Article concerning which there is no dispute at present.

The third Article concerning Christ's *descent into hell* is capable of three different senses, and all three are both literal and grammatical. The first is, that Christ descended locally into hell, and preached to the *spirits there in prison;* and this has one great advantage on its side, that those who first prepared the Articles in king Edward's time were of this opinion; for they made it a part of it, by adding in the Article those words of St. Peter as the proof or explanation of it. Now, though that period was left out in queen Elizabeth's time, yet, no declaration was made against it; so that this sense was once in possession, and was never expressly rejected: besides that, it has great support from the authority of many fathers, who understood the *descent into hell* according to this explanation. A second sense, of which that Article is capable, is, that by *hell* is meant the *grave,* according to the signification of the original word in the Hebrew; and this is supported by the words of *Christ's descending into the lower parts of the earth;* as also by this, that several creeds, that have this Article, have not that of Christ's being buried; and some, that mention his burial, have not this of his *descent into hell.* A third sense is, that by hell, according to the signification of the Greek word, is to be meant the place or region of spirits separated from their bodies: so that by Christ's *descent into hell* is only to be meant, that his soul was really and entirely disunited from his body, not lying dead in it as in an apoplectical fit, not hovering about it, but that it was translated into the seats of departed souls. All these three senses differ very much from one another, and yet they are all senses that are literal and grammatical; so that in which of these soever a man conceives the Article, he may subscribe it, and he does no way prevaricate in so doing. If men would therefore understand all the other Articles in the same largeness, and with the same equity, there would not be that occasion given for unjust censure that there has been. Where then the Articles are conceived in large and general words, and have not more special and restrained terms in them, we ought to take that for a sure indication, that the church does not intend to tie men up too severely to particular opinions, but that she leaves all to such a liberty as is agreeable with the purity of the faith.

And this seems sufficient to explain the title of the Articles, and the subscriptions that are required of the clergy to them.

The last thing to be settled is the true reading of the Articles; for, there being some small diversity between the printed editions and the manuscripts that were signed by both houses of convocation, I have desired the assistance both of Dr. Green, the present worthy Master of Corpus Christi college in Cambridge, and of some of the learned Fellows of that body; that they would give themselves the trouble to collate the printed editions, and their manuscripts, with such a scrupulous exactness as becomes a matter of this importance: which they were pleased to do very minutely. I will set down both the collations as they were transmitted to me; beginning with that which I had from the Fellows four years ago.

ARTICLE III.

Of the going down of Christ into hell.

These words, said to be left out, are found in the original Articles, signed by the chief clergy of both provinces, now extant in the manuscript libraries of C. C. C. C. in the book called Synodalia: *but distinguished from the rest with lines of* minium: *which lines plainly appear to have been done afterwards, because the leaves and lines of the original are exactly numbered at the end; which number without these lines were manifestly false.*

As Christ died for us, and was buried; so also it is to be believed, that he went down into hell. [" for his body lay in the grave " till his resurrection; but his " soul, being separate from his " body, remained with the spirits " which were detained in prison; " that is to say, in hell, and " there preached unto them."]

THE INTRODUCTION.

ARTICLE VI.

In the original these words only are found, Testamentum vetus novo contrarium non est, quandoquidem, &c.

The Old Testament is not to be rejected as if it were contrary to the New, but to be retained. Forasmuch as, &c.

ARTICLE IX.

The Latin of the original is, Et quanquam renatis et credentibus nulla propter Christum est condemnatio.

And although there is no condemnation to them that believe, and are baptized, &c.

ARTICLE X.

Of Grace.

This article is not found in the original.

The grace of Christ, or the Holy Ghost, which is given by him, doth, &c.

ARTICLE XVI.

Blasphemy against the Holy Ghost.

This is not found.

The blasphemy against the Holy Ghost is then committed, when, &c.

ARTICLE XIX.

This is not found.

All men are bound to keep the precepts of the moral law, although the law given from God, &c.

ARTICLE XX.

Of the authority of the church.

This Article agrees with the original; but these words, The church hath power to decree rites and ceremonies, and authority in controversies of faith, *supposed to begin the Article, are not found in any part thereof.*

It is not lawful for the church to ordain any thing that is contrary to God's words written, &c.

ARTICLE XXVI.

Of the sacraments.

In the fourteenth line of this Article, immediately after these words, (But yet have not like nature with Baptism and the Lord's Supper) *follows,* quomodo nec pœnitentia, *which, being marked underneath with* minium, *is left out in the translation.*

Sacraments ordained of Christ, &c.

*This Article agrees with the original, as far as these words, (*𝔞𝔫𝔡 𝔥𝔞𝔱𝔥 𝔤𝔦𝔟𝔢𝔫 𝔬𝔠𝔠𝔞𝔰𝔦𝔬𝔫 𝔱𝔬 𝔪𝔞𝔫𝔶 𝔰𝔲𝔭𝔢𝔯𝔰𝔱𝔦𝔱𝔦𝔬𝔫𝔰*) *where follows,* Christus in cœlum ascendens, corpori suo immortalitatem dedit, naturam non abstulit, humanæ enim naturæ veritatem (juxta scripturas) perpetuo retinet, quam uno et definito loco esse, et non in multa vel omnia simul loca diffundi oportet; quum igitur Christus in cœlum sublatus, ibi usque ad finem sæculi sit permansurus, atque inde, non aliunde (ut loquitur Augustinus) venturus sit, ad judicandum vivos et mortuos, non debet quisquam fidelium, carnis et ejus et sanguinis realem, et corporalem (ut loquuntur) presentiam in Eucharistia vel credere vel profiteri. *These words are marked and scrawled over with minium, and the words immediately following* (corpus tamen Christi datur, accipitur, et manducatur in cœna, tantum cœlesti et spirituali ratione) *are inserted · in a different hand just before them, in a line and a half left void; which plainly appears to be done afterwards, by reason the same hand has altered the first number of lines, and, for* viginti quatuor, *made* quatuordecim.

ARTICLE XXIX.
Of the Lord's Supper.
𝔈𝔥𝔢 𝔖𝔲𝔭𝔭𝔢𝔯 𝔬𝔣 𝔱𝔥𝔢 𝔏𝔬𝔯𝔡 𝔦𝔰 not only a sign of, &c.

The three last Articles, viz. the 39*th, Of the Resurrection of the Dead; the* 40*th, that the Souls of men do neither perish with their bodies* (neque otiosi dormiant *is added in the original); and the* 42*d, that all shall not be saved at last, are found in the original, distinguished only with a marginal line of* minium: *but the* 41*st, Of the* Millenarians, *is wholly left out.*

The number of Articles does not exactly agree, by reason some are inserted, which are found only in king Edward's Articles, but none are wanting that are found in the original.

Corpus Christi Col. *Feb.* 4*th,* 1695-6.

UPON examination we judge these to be all the material differences, that are unobserved, between the original manuscripts and the B. of Salisbury's printed copy. *Witness our hands,*

Jo. *Jaggard,*
Rob. *Mosse,*   Fellows of the said college.
Will. *Lunn,*

After I had procured this, I was desirous likewise to have the printed editions collated with the second publication of the articles in the year 1571; in which the convocation reviewed those of 1562, and made some small alterations: and these were very lately procured for me by my reverend friend, Dr. Green, which I will set down as he was pleased to communicate them to me.

THE INTRODUCTION.

[*Note,* MS. *stands for* Manuscript, *and* Pr. *for* Print.]

Art. 1. MS. and true God, and he is everlasting, without body.
Pr. *and true God, everlasting, without body.*
Art. 2. MS. but also for all actual sins of men.
Pr. *but also for actual sins of men.*
Art. 3. MS. so also it is to be believed.
Pr. *so also is it to be believed.*
Art. 4. MS. Christ did truly arise again.
Pr. *Christ did truly rise again.*
MS. until he return to judge all men at the last day.
Pr. *until he return to judge men at the last day.*
Art. 6. MS. to be believed as an article of the faith.
Pr. *to be believed as an article of faith.*
MS. requisite as necessary to salvation.
Pr. *requisite or necessary to salvation.*
MS. in the name of holy scripture.
Pr. *in the name of the holy scripture.*
MS. but yet doth it not apply.
Pr. *but yet doth not apply.*
MS. Baruch.
Pr. *Baruch the prophet.*
MS. and account them for canonical.
Pr. *and account them canonical.*
Art. 8. MS. by most certain warranties of holy scripture
Pr. *by most certain warrant of holy scripture.*
Art. 9. MS. but it is the fault.
Pr. *but is the fault.*
MS. whereby man is very far gone from his original righteousness.
Pr. *whereby man is far gone from original righteousness.*
MS. in them that be regenerated.
Pr. *in them that are regenerated.*

Art. De Gratia, *non habetur in* MS.

Art. 10. MS. a good will and working in us.
Pr. *a good will and working with us.*
Art. 14. MS. cannot be taught without arrogancy and impiety.
Pr. *cannot be taught without arrogancy and iniquity.*
MS. we be unprofitable servants.
Pr. *we are unprofitable servants.*
Art. 15. MS. sin only except.
Pr. *sin only excepted.*
MS. to be the Lamb without spot.
Pr. *to be a Lamb without spot.*

THE INTRODUCTION.

    MS. but we the rest, although baptized, and born again in Christ, yet we all offend.
    Pr. *but all we the rest, although baptized, and if born in Christ, yet offend.*

    Art. *De Blasphemia in Sp. Sanct. non est in MS.*

Art. 16. *MS.* wherefore the place for penitence.
    Pr. *wherefore the grant of repentance.*
Art. 17. *MS.* so excellent a benefit of God given unto them, be called according.
    Pr. *so excellent a benefit of God, be called according.*
    MS. as because it doth fervently kindle their love.
    Pr. *as because it doth frequently kindle their love.*

    Art. *Omnes obligantur, &c. non est in MS.*

Art. 18. *MS.* to frame his life according to the law and the light of nature.
    Pr. *to frame his life according to that law, and the light of nature.*
Art. 19. *MS.* congregation of faithful men in the which the pure Word.
    Pr. *congregation of faithful men in which the pure Word.*
Art. 20. *MS.* the church hath power to decree rites or ceremonies, and authority in controversies of faith. And yet.
    These words are not in the original MS.
    MS. ought it not to enforce any thing.
    Pr. *it ought not to enforce any thing.*
Art. 21. *MS.* and when they be gathered together (forasmuch.
    Pr. *and when they be gathered (forasmuch.*
Art. 22. *MS.* is a fond thing vainly invented.
    Pr. *is a fond thing vainly feigned.*
Art. 24. *MS.* in a tongue not understanded of the people.
    Pr. *in a tongue not understood of the people.*
Art. 25. *MS.* and effectual signs of grace and God's goodwill towards us.
    Pr. *and effectual signs of grace and God's will towards us.*
    MS. and extream annoyling.
    Pr. *and extream unction.*
Art. 26. *MS.* in their own name, but do minister by Christ's commission and authority.
    Pr. *in their own name, but in Christ's, and do minister by his commission and authority.*

THE INTRODUCTION.

        MS. and in the receiving of the Sacraments.
        Pr. and in the receiving the Sacraments.
        MS. and rightly receive the Sacraments.
        Pr. and rightly do receive the Sacraments.
Art. 27. *MS.* from others that be not christned, but is also a sign.
        Pr. from others that be not christned, but it is also a sign.
        MS. forgiveness of sin, and of our adoption.
        Pr. forgiveness of sin, of our adoption.
Art. 28. *MS.* to have amongst themselves.
        Pr. to have among themselves.   partaking
        MS. the bread which we break is a communion of the body of Christ.
        Pr. the bread which we break is a partaking of the body of Christ.   partaking
        MS. and likewise the cup of blessing is a communion of the blood of Christ.
        Pr. and likewise the cup of blessing is a partaking of the blood of Christ.
        MS. or the change of the substance of bread and wine into the substance of Christ's body and blood cannot be proved by holy writ, but is repugnant.
        Pr. or the change of the substance of bread and wine in the supper of the Lord cannot be proved by holy writ, but it is repugnant.
        MS. but the mean whereby the body of Christ is received.
        Pr. and the mean whereby the body of Christ is received.
        MS. lifted up or worshipped.
        Pr. lifted up and worshipped.
Art. 31. *MS.* is the perfect redemption.
        Pr. is that perfect redemption.
        MS. to have remission of pain or guilt were forged fables.
        Pr. to have remission of pain and guilt were blasphemous fables.
Art. 33. *MS.* that hath authority thereto.
        Pr. that hath authority thereunto.
Art. 34. *MS.* diversity of countries, times, and men's manners.
        Pr. diversity of countries and men's manners.
        MS. and be ordained and appointed by common authority.
        Pr. and be ordained and approved by common authority.
        MS. the consciences of the weak brethren.
        Pr. the consciences of weak brethren.

Art. 35. *MS.* of homilies, the titles whereof we have joined under this article, do contain.
Pr. *of homilies, the several titles whereof we have joined under this article, doth contain.*
MS. wholesome doctrine, and necessary for this time, as doth the former book which was set forth.
Pr. *wholesome doctrine, necessary for these times, as doth the former book of homilies which were set forth.*
MS. and therefore are to be read in our churches by the ministers, diligently, plainly, and distinctly, that they may be understanded of the people.
Pr. *and therefore we judge them to be read in churches by the ministers, diligently and distinctly, that they may be understood of the people.*
MS. ministred in a tongue known.
Pr. *ministred in a known tongue.*

Art. De Libro Precationum, &c. non est in *MS.*

Art. 36. *MS.* in the time of the most noble K. Edward the Sixth.
Pr. *in the time of Edward the Sixth.*
MS. superstitious or ungodly.
Pr. *superstitious and ungodly.*
Art. 37. *MS.* whether they be ecclesiastical or not.
Pr. *whether they be ecclesiastical or civil.*
MS. the minds of some slanderous folks to be offended.
Pr. *The minds of some dangerous folks to be offended.*
MS. we give not to our princes.
Pr. *we give not our princes.*
MS. or of sacraments.
Pr. *or of the sacraments.*
MS. the injunctions also lately set forth.
Pr. *the injunctions also set forth.*
MS. and serve in the wars.
Pr. *and serve in lawful wars.*
Art. 38. *MS.* every man oughteth of such things.
Pr. *every man ought of such things.*

Art. 39. Edw. VI. *et qui sequuntur, non sunt in MS.*

We th' archbishops and bishops of either province of this realm of England, lawfully gathered together in this provincial synod holden at London, with continuations and prorogations of the same, do receive, profess and acknowledge the xxxviii *Articles before written in* xix *pages going before, to contain true and sound doctrine, and do approve and ratify the same by the subscription of our hands the* xi[th] *day of* May *in the year of our Lord* 1571, *and in the year of the reign of our sovereign lady* Elizabeth *by the grace of God of* England, France, *and* Ireland, *queen, defender of the faith,* &c. *the thirteenth.*

    Matthue Cantuar.   N. Bangor.
    Rob. Winton.   Ri. Cicestren.
    Jo. Heref.   Thom. Lincoln.
    Richarde Ely.   Wilhelmus Exon.
    Nic. Wigorn.
    Jo. Sarisburien.
    Edm. Roffen.

From these diversities a great difficulty will naturally arise about this whole matter. The manuscripts of Corpus Christi are without doubt originals.

The hands of the subscribers are well known; they belonged to archbishop Parker, and were left by him to that college, and they are signed with a particular care; for at the end of them there is not only a sum of the number of the pages, but of the lines in every page. And though this was the work only of the convocation of the province of Canterbury; yet the archbishop of York, with the bishops of Duresme and Chester, subscribed them likewise, and they were also subscribed by the whole lower house. But we are not sure that the like care was used in the convocation, anno 1571; for the Articles are only subscribed by the archbishop of Canterbury, and ten bishops of his province; nor does the subscription of the lower house appear. These Articles were first printed in the year 1563, conform to the present impressions which are still in use among us. So the alterations were then made while the thing was fresh and well known, therefore no fraud nor artifice is to be suspected, since some objections would have been then made, especially by the great party of the complying papists, who then continued in the church: they would not have failed to have made much use of this, and to have taken great advantages from it, if there had been any occasion or colour for it; and yet nothing of this kind was then done.

One alteration of more importance was made in the year 1571. Those words of the 20th Article, *The church hath power to decree rites or ceremonies, and authority in controversies of faith,* were left out both in the manuscripts, and in the printed editions, but were afterwards restored according to the Articles printed anno 1563. I cannot find out in what year they were again put in the printed copies. They appear in two several impressions in queen Elizabeth's time, which are in my hands; it passes commonly that it was done by archbishop Laud; and his enemies laid this upon him among other things, that he had corrupted the doctrine of this church by this addition; but he cleared himself of that, as well he might, and, in a speech in the star-chamber, appealed to the original, and affirmed these words were in it.

The true account of this difficulty is this. When the Articles were first settled, they were subscribed by both houses upon paper; but, that being done, they were afterward ingrossed in parchment, and made up in form to remain as records. Now, in all such bodies, many alterations are often made after a minute or first draught is agreed on, before the matter is brought to full perfection; so these alterations, as most of them are small and inconsiderable, were made between the time that they were first subscribed, and the last voting of them. But the original records, which, if extant, would have cleared the whole matter, having been burnt in the fire of London, it is not possible to appeal to them; yet what has been proposed may serve, I hope, fully to clear the difficulty.

I now go to consider the Articles themselves.

ARTICLE I.

Of Faith in the Holy Trinity.

There is but one living and true God, everlasting, without body, parts or passions, of infinite power, wisdom, and goodness, the maker and preserver of all things both visible and invisible; and in the unity of this Godhead there be three Persons of one substance, power, and eternity, the Father, the Son, and the Holy Ghost.

THE natural order of things required, that the first of all articles in religion should be concerning the being and attributes of God: for all other doctrines arise out of this. But the title appropriates this to the holy Trinity; because that is the only part of the Article which peculiarly belongs to the Christian religion; since the rest is founded on the principles of natural religion.

There are six heads to be treated of, in order to the full opening of all that is contained in this Article.

1. That there is a God.
2. That there is but one God.
3. Negatively, That this God hath neither body, parts, nor passions.

ART. I.

4. Positively, That he is of infinite power, wisdom, and goodness.

5. That he at first created, and does still preserve all things, not only what is material and visible, but also what is spiritual and invisible.

6. The Trinity is here asserted.

These being all points of the highest consequence, it is very necessary to state them as clearly, and to prove them as fully, as may be.

The first is, *That there is a God.* This is a proposition, which in all ages has been so universally received and believed, some very few instances being only assigned of such as either have denied or doubted of it, that the very consent of so many ages and nations, of such different tempers and languages, so vastly remote from one another, has been long esteemed a good argument, to prove that either there is somewhat in the nature of man, that by a secret sort of instinct does dictate this to him: or that all mankind has descended from one common stock, and that this belief has passed down from the first man to all his posterity. If the more polite nations had only received this, some might suggest, that wise men had introduced it as a mean to govern human society, and to keep it in order: or, if only the more barbarous had received this, it might be thought to be the effect of their fear, and their ignorance: but, since all sorts, as well as all ages, of men have received it, this alone goes a great way to assure us of the being of a God.

To this two things are objected, first, That some nations, such as Soldania, Formosa, and some in America, have been discovered in these last ages, that seem to acknowledge no Deity. But to this, two things are to be opposed: 1st, That those who first discovered these countries, and have given that account of them, did not know them enough, nor understand their language so perfectly as was necessary to enable them to comprehend all their opinions: and this is the more probable, because others, that have writ after them, assure us that they are not without all sense of religion, which the first discoverers had too hastily affirmed: some prints of religion begin to be observed among those of Soldania, though it is certainly one of the most degenerated of all nations. But a second answer to this is, That those nations, of whom these reports are given out, are so extremely sunk from all that is wise or regular, great and good in human nature, so rude and untractable, and so incapable of arts and discipline, that if the reports concerning them are to be believed, and if that weakens the argument from the common consent of mankind of the one hand, it strengthens it on another; while it appears that human nature, when it wants this impression, it wants with it all that is great or orderly in it, and shews a brutality almost as low and base as is that of beasts. Some men are born without some of their senses, and others without the use of reason and memory;

and yet those exceptions do not prove that the imperfections of such persons are not irregularities against the common course of things: the monstrousness, as well as the miseries, of persons so unhappily born tend to recommend more effectually the perfection of human nature. So, if these nations, which are supposed to be without the belief of a God, are such a low and degenerated piece of human nature, that some have doubted whether they are a perfect race of men or not, this does not derogate from, but rather confirms, the force of this argument, from the general consent of all nations.

A second exception to this argument is, That men have not agreed in the same notions concerning the Deity: some believing two gods, a good and a bad, that are in a perpetual contest together: others holding a vast number of gods, either all equal or subaltern to one another: and some believing God to be a corporeal being, and that the sun, moon, and stars, and a great many other beings, are gods: since then, though all may acknowledge a Deity in general, they are yet subdivided into so many different conceits about it, no argument can be drawn from this supposed consent, which is not so great in reality as it seems to be. But, in answer to this, we must observe, that the constant sense of mankind agreeing in this, that there is a superior Being that governs the world, shews that this fixed persuasion has a deep root, though, the weakness of several nations being practised upon by designing men, they have in many things corrupted this notion of God. That might have arisen from the tradition of some true doctrines vitiated in the conveyance. Spirits made by God to govern the world by the order and under the direction of the Supreme Mind, might easily come to be looked on as subordinate deities: some evil and lapsed spirits might in a course of some ages pass for evil gods. The apparitions of the Deity under some figures might make these figures to be adored: and God being considered as the supreme Light, this might lead men to worship the sun as his chief vehicle: and so by degrees he might pass for the supreme God. Thus it is easy to trace up these mistakes to what may justly be supposed to be their first source and rise. But still the foundation of them all was a firm belief of a superior nature that governed the world. Mankind agreeing in that, an occasion was thereby given to bad and designing men to graft upon it such other tenets as might feed superstition and idolatry, and furnish the managers of those impostures with advantages to raise their own authority. But, how various soever the several ages and nations of the world may have been as to their more special opinions and rites, yet the general idea of a God remained still unaltered, even amidst all the changes that have happened in the particular forms and doctrines of religion.

Another argument for the being of God is taken from the visible world, in which there is a vast variety of beings

ART. I.

curiously framed, and that seem designed for great and noble ends. In these we see clear characters of God's eternal power and wisdom. And that is thus to be made out. It is certain, that nothing could give being to itself; so the things which we see either had their being from all eternity: or were made in time: and either they were from all eternity in the same state, and under the same revolutions of the heavens, as they are at present: or they fell into the order and method, in which they do now roll, by some happy chance, out of which all the beauty and usefulness of the creation did arise. But, if all these suppositions are manifestly false, then it will remain, that if things neither were from all eternity as they now are, nor fell into their present state by chance, then there is a superior Essence that gave them being, and that moulded them as we see they now are. The first branch of this, that they were not as now they are from all eternity, is to be proved by two sorts of arguments; the one intrinsical, by demonstrating this to be impossible; the other moral, by shewing that it is not at all credible. As to the first, it is to be considered, that a successive duration made up of parts, which is called time, and is measured by a successive rotation of the heavens, cannot possibly be eternal. For if there were eternal revolutions of Saturn in his course of thirty years, and eternal revolutions of days as well as years, of minutes as well as hours, then the one must be as infinite as the other; so that the one must be equal to the other, both being infinite; and yet the latter are some millions of times more than the other, which is impossible. Further; of every past duration, as this is true, that once it was present; so this is true, that once it was to come; this being a necessary affection of every thing that exists in time: if then all past durations were all once future, or to be, then we cannot conceive such a succession of durations eternal, since once every one of them was to come. Nor can all this, or any part of it, be turned against us, who believe that some beings are immortal, and shall never cease to be; for all those future durations have never actually been, but are still produced of new, and so continued in being. This argument may seem to be too subtile, and it will require some attention of mind to observe and discover the force of it; but, after we have turned it over and over again, it will be found to be a true demonstration. The chief objection that lies against it is, that, in the opinion of those who deny that there are any indivisible points of matter, and that believe that matter is infinitely divisible, it is not absurd to say, that one infinite is more than another: for the smallest crum of matter is infinite, as well as the whole globe of the earth: and, therefore, the revolutions of Saturn may be infinite, as well as the revolutions of days, though the one be vastly more numerous than the other. But there is this difference betwixt the succession of time, and the composition of matter; that those, who deny indivisibles, say that no one point can be assigned: for, if ART. points could be assigned or numbered, it is certain that they I. could not be infinite; for an infinite number seems to be a contradiction: but, if the series of mankind were infinite, since this is visibly divided into single individuals, as the units in that series, then here arises an infinite number composed of units or individuals that can be assigned. The same is to be said of minutes, hours, days, and years: nor can it be said with equal reason, that every portion of time is divisible to infinity, as well as every parcel of matter. It seems evident, that there is a present time; and that past, present, and to come, cannot be said to be true of any thing all at once: therefore the objection against the assigning points in matter does not overthrow the truth of this argument. But if it is thought that this is rather a sleight of metaphysics that entangles one, than a plain and full conviction, let us turn next to such reasonings as are more obvious, and that are more easily apprehended.

The other moral arguments are more sensible as well as they are of a more complicated nature; and proceed thus: The history of all nations, of all governments, arts, sciences, and even instituted religions, the peopling of nations, the progress of commerce and of colonies, are plain indications of the novelty of the world; no sort of trace remaining, by which we can believe it to be ancienter than the books of Moses represent it to be. For, though some nations, such as the Egyptians and the Chineses, have boasted of a much greater antiquity, yet it is plain, we hear of no series of history for all those ages; so that what they had relating to them, if it is not wholly a fiction, might have been only in astronomical tables, which may be easily run backwards as well as forward. The very few eclipses which Ptolemy could hear of is a remarkable instance of the novelty of history; since the observing such an extraordinary accident in the heavens, in so pure an air, where the sun was not only observed, but adored, must have been one of the first effects of learning or industry. All these characters of the novelty of the world have been so well considered by Lucretius, and other atheists, that they gave up the point, and thought it evident that this present frame of things had certainly a beginning.

The solution that those men, who found themselves driven from this of the world's being eternal, have given to this difficulty, by saying that all things have run by chance into the combinations and channels in which we see nature run, is so absurd, that it looks like men who are resolved to believe any thing, how absurd soever, rather than to acknowledge religion. For what a strange conceit is it, to think that chance could settle on such a regular and useful frame of things, and continue so fixed and stable in it, and that chance could do so

ART. I.

much at once, and should do nothing ever since! The constancy of the celestial motions; the obliquity of the zodiac, by which different seasons are assigned to different climates; the divisions of this globe into sea and land, into hills and vales; the productions of the earth, whether latent, such as mines, minerals, and other fossils; or visible, such as grass, grain, herbs, flowers, shrubs, and trees; the small beginnings, and the curious compositions of them: the variety and curious structure of insects; the disposition of the bodies of perfecter animals; and, above all, the fabric of the body of man, especially the curious discoveries that anatomy and microscopes have given us; the strange beginning and progress of those; the wonders that occur in every organ of sense, and the amazing structure and use of the brain, are all such things, so artificial, and yet so regular, and so exactly shaped and fitted for their several uses, that he, who can believe all this to be chance, seems to have brought his mind to digest any absurdity.

That all men should resemble one another in the main things, and yet that every man should have a peculiar look, voice, and way of writing, is necessary to maintain order and distinction in society: by these we know men, if we either see them, hear them speak in the dark, or receive any writing from them at a distance; without these, the whole commerce of life would be one continued course of mistake and confusion. This, I say, is such an indication of wisdom, that it looks like a violence to nature to think it can be otherwise.

The only colour, that has supported this monstrous conceit, that things arise out of chance, is, that it has long passed current in the world, that great varieties of insects do arise out of corrupted matter. They argue, that, if the sun's shining on a dunghill can give life to such swarms of curious creatures, it is but a little more extraordinary, to think that animals and men might have been formed out of well-disposed matter, under a peculiar aspect of the heavens. But the exacter observations, that have been made in this age by the help of glasses, have put an end to this answer, which is the best that Lucretius and other atheists found to rest in. It is now fully made out, that the production of all insects whatsoever is in the way of generation: heat and corruption do only hatch those eggs that insects leave to a prodigious quantity every where. So that this, which is the only specious thing in the whole plea for atheism, is now given up by the universal consent of all the inquirers into nature.

And now to bring the force of this long argument to a head: If this world was neither from all eternity in the state in which it is at present, nor could fall into it by chance or accident, then it must follow that it was put into the state in which we now see it by a Being of vast power and wisdom. This is the great and solid argument on which religion rests;

and it receives a vast accession of strength from this, that we plainly see matter has not motion in or of itself: every part of it is at quiet till it is put in motion that is not natural to it; for many parts of matter fall into a state of rest and quiet; so that motion must be put in them by some impulse or other. Matter, after it has passed through the highest refinings and rectifyings possible, becomes only more capable of motion than it was before; but still it is a passive principle, and must be put in motion by some other being. This has appeared so necessary even to those who have tried their utmost force to make God as little needful as possible in the structure of the universe, that they have yet been forced to own, that there must have been once a vast motion given to matter by the Supreme Mind.

A third argument for the being of a God is, that, upon some great occasions, and before a vast number of witnesses, some persons have wrought miracles: that is, they have put nature out of its course, by some words or signs, that of themselves could not produce those extraordinary effects: and therefore such persons were assisted by a power superior to the course of nature; and by consequence there is such a Being, and that is God. To this the atheists do first say, that we do not know the secret virtues that are in nature: the loadstone and opium produce wonderful effects: therefore, unless we knew the whole extent of nature, we cannot define what is supernatural and miraculous, and what is not so. But, though we cannot tell how far nature may go, yet of some things we may, without hesitation, say, they are beyond natural powers. Such were the wonders that Moses wrought in Egypt and in the wilderness, by the speaking a few words, or the stretching out of a rod. We are sure these could not by any natural efficiency produce those wonders. And the like is to be said of the miracles of Christ, particularly of his raising the dead to life again, and of his own resurrection. These we are sure did not arise out of natural causes. The next thing atheists say to this, is, to dispute the truth of the facts: but of that I shall treat in another place, when the authority of revealed religion comes to be proved from those facts. All that is necessary to be added here, is, that if facts, that are plainly supernatural, are proved to have been really done, then here is another clear and full argument, to prove a Being superior to nature, that can dispose of it at pleasure: and that Being must either be God, or some other invisible being that has a strength superior to the settled course of nature. And if invisible beings, superior to nature, whether good or bad, are once acknowledged, a great step is made to the proof of the Supreme Being.

There is another famed argument taken from the idea of God; which is laid thus: that, because one frames a notion of infinite perfection, therefore there must be such a Being, from whom that notion is conveyed to us. This argument is also managed by other methods, to give us a demonstration of the being of a God. I am unwilling to say any thing to derogate from any argument that is brought to prove this conclusion; but, when he, who insists on this, lays all other arguments aside, or at least slights them as not strong enough to prove the point, this naturally gives jealousy, when all those reasons, that had for so many ages been considered as solid proofs, are neglected, as if this only could amount to a demonstration. But, besides, this is an argument that cannot be offered by any to another person, for his conviction; since, if he denies that he has any such idea, he is without the reach of the argument. And if a man will say that any such idea, which he may raise in himself, is only an aggregate that he makes of all those perfections, of which he can form a thought, which he lays together, separating from them every imperfection that he observes to be often mixed with some of those perfections: if, I say, a man will affirm this, I do not see that the inference from any such thought that he has formed within himself, can have any great force to persuade him that there is any such Being. Upon the whole, it seems to be fully proved, that there is a Being that is superior to matter, and that gave both being and order to it, and to all other things. This may serve to prove the being of a God. It is fit in the next place to consider, with all humble modesty, what thoughts we can, or ought to have of the Deity.

That Supreme Being must have its essence of itself necessarily and eternally; for it is impossible that any thing can give itself being; so it must be eternal. And, though eternity in a succession of determinate durations was proved to be impossible, yet it is certain that something must be eternal; either matter, or a Being superior to it, that has not a duration defined by succession, but is a simple essence, and eternally was, is, and shall be, the same. There is nothing contradictory to itself in this notion: it is indeed above our capacity to form a clear thought of it; but it is plain it must be so, and that this is only a defect in our nature and capacity, that we cannot distinctly apprehend that which is so far above us. Such a Being must have also necessary existence in its notion; for whatsoever is infinitely perfect must necessarily exist; since we plainly perceive that necessary existence is a perfection, and that contingent existence is an imperfection, which supposes a being that is produced by another, and that depends upon it: and, as this superior Being did exist from all eternity, so it is impossible, it should cease to be; since nothing that once has actually a being can ever cease to be, but by an act of a superior Being annihilating it. But there being nothing superior to the Deity, it is impossible that it should ever cease to be: what was self-existent from all eternity, must also be so to all eternity; and it is as impossible that a simple essence can annihilate itself, as that it can make itself.

So much concerning the first and capital article of all religion, the existence and being of a God; which ought not to be proved by any authorities from scripture, unless from the recitals that are given in it concerning miracles, as was already hinted at. But as to the authority of such passages in scripture, which affirm that there is a God, it is to be considered, that before we can be bound to submit to them, we must believe three propositions antecedent to that; 1. That there is a God. 2. That all his words are true. 3. That these are his words. What, therefore, must be believed before we acknowledge the scriptures cannot be proved out of them. It is then a strange assertion, to say, that the being of a God cannot be proved by the light of nature, but must be proved by the scriptures; since our being assured that there is a God is the first principle upon which the authority of the scriptures depends.

The second proposition in the Article is, That *there is but one God*. As to this, the common argument, by which it is proved, is the order of the world; from whence it is inferred, that there cannot be more gods than one, since, where there are more than one, there must happen diversity and confusion. This is by some thought to be no good reason; for if there are more gods, that is, more beings infinitely perfect, they will always think the same thing, and be knit together with an entire love. It is true, in things of a moral nature, this must so happen: for beings infinitely perfect must ever agree. But in physical things, capable of no morality, as in creating the world sooner or later, and the different systems of beings, with a thousand other things that have no moral goodness in them, different beings infinitely perfect might have different thoughts. So this argument seems still of great force to prove the unity of the Deity. The other argument from reason, to prove the unity of God, is from the notion of a Being infinitely perfect. For a superiority over all other beings comes so naturally into the idea of infinite perfection, that we cannot separate it from it. A Being therefore, that has not all other beings inferior and subordinate to it, cannot be infinitely perfect; whence it is evident, that there is but one God. But, besides all this, the unity of God seems to be so frequently and so plainly asserted in the scripture, that we see it was the chief design of the whole Old Testament, both of Moses and the prophets, to establish it, in opposition to the false opinions of the heathen concerning a diversity of gods. This is often repeated in the most solemn words, as, ** 'Hear, O Israel; the Lord our God is one Deut.vi.4.

* שמע ישראל יהוה אלהינו יהוה אחד ' Hear, Israel, Jehovah, our God, is one Jehovah.' On this passage the Jews lay great stress; and it is one

28   AN EXPOSITION OF

ART. God.' It is the first of the Ten Commandments, 'Thou
1.   shalt have no other gods but me.' And all things in heaven
Isa. xliv. 6. and earth are often said to be made by this one God. Nega-
8.   tive words are also often used, 'There is none other God but
      one: besides me there is none else, and I know no other':*
      the going after other gods is reckoned the highest and the
John xvii. most unpardonable act of idolatry. The New Testament goes
3.   on in the same strain. Christ speaks of the only *true God*,
Mat. iv. 10. and that he alone ought to be worshipped and served; all the
1 Cor. viii.
5, 6. apostles do frequently affirm the same thing: they make the
      believing of one God, in opposition to the many Gods of the
      heathens, the chief article of the Christian religion; and they
Eph. iv. 4, lay down this as the chief ground of our obligation to mutual
5, 6. love and union among ourselves, That 'there is one God, one
      Lord, one faith, one baptism.' Now, since we are sure that
      there is but one Messias, and one doctrine delivered by him,
      it will clearly follow that there must be but one God.

So the unity of the Divine Essence is clearly proved both from the order and government of the world, from the idea of infinite perfection, and from those express declarations that are made concerning it in the scriptures; which last is a full proof to all such as own and submit to them.

The third head in this Article is that which is negatively expressed, that *God is without body, parts, or passions*. In general, all these are so plainly contrary to the ideas of infinite perfection, and they appear so evidently to be imperfections, that this part of the Article will need little explanation. We do plainly perceive that our bodies are clogs to our minds; and all the use, that even the purest sort of body, in an estate conceived to be glorified, can be of to a mind, is to be an instrument of local motion, or to be a repository of ideas for memory and imagination: but God, who is every where, and is one pure and simple act, can have no such use for a body. A mind dwelling in a body is in many respects superior to it; yet in some respects is under it. We, who feel how an act of our mind can so direct the motions of our body that a thought sets our limbs and joints a going, can, from thence, conceive how that the whole extent of matter should receive such motions as the acts of the Supreme Mind give it; but yet not as a body united to it, or that the Deity either needs such a body, or can receive any trouble from it. Thus far the apprehension of the thing is very plainly made

---

of the four passages which they write on their phylacteries. On the word Elohim, Simeon Ben Joachi says, ' Come and see the mystery of the word Elohim : there are three degrees, and each degree is by itself alone, and yet they are all one, and joined together in one, and are not divided from each other.'—*Bagster's Comprehensive Bible.—Note on the passage.* —[ED.]

* The passage stands thus in Isa. xliv. 6. 'Thus saith the Lord, the King of Israel, and his redeemer the Lord of Hosts; I *am* the first and I *am* the last; and beside me *there is* no God.' These titles are in the New Testament given to the Lord Jesus Christ, Rev. i. 8, 11—13, 17, 18. and xxii. 12, 13, 16.—[ED.]

out to us. Our thoughts put some parts of our body in a present motion, when the organization is regular, and all the parts are exact, and when there is no obstruction in those vessels or passages, through which that heat and those spirits, do pass, that cause the motion. We do in this perceive, that a thought does command matter; but our minds are limited to our bodies, and these do not obey them, but as they are in an exact disposition and a fitness to be so moved. Now these are plain imperfections; but, removing them from God, we can from thence apprehend that all the matter in the universe may be so entirely subject to the Divine Mind, that it shall move and be whatsoever and wheresoever he will have it to be. This is that which all men do agree in.

ART. 1.

But many of the philosophers thought that matter, though it was moved and moulded by God at his pleasure, yet was not made by him, but was self-existent, and was a passive principle, but coexistent to the Deity, which they thought was the active principle: from whence some have thought, that the belief of two gods, one good and another bad, did spring: though others imagine that the belief of a bad god did arise from the corruption of that tradition concerning fallen angels, as was before suggested. The philosophers could not apprehend that things could be made out of nothing, and therefore they believed that matter was co-eternal with God. But it is as hard to apprehend how a mind, by its thought, should give motion to matter, as how it should give it being. A being not made by God is not so easily conceivable to be under the acts of his mind, as that which is made by him. This conceit plainly destroys infinite perfection, which cannot be in God, if all beings are not from him, and under his authority; besides that, successive duration has been already proved inconsistent with eternity. This opinion of the world's being a body to God, as the mind that dwells in it, and actuates it, is the foundation of atheism: for if it be once thought that God can do nothing without such a body, then, as this destroys the idea of infinite perfection, so it makes way to this conceit, that since matter is visible, and God invisible, there is no other God, but the vast extent of the universe. It is true, God has often shewed himself in visible appearances; but that was only his putting a special quantity of matter into such motions, as should give a great and astonishing idea of his nature, from that appearance: which was both the effect of his power, and the symbol of his presence. And thus what glorious representations soever were made either on mount Sinai, or in the pillar of the cloud, and cloud of glory, those were no indications of God's having a body; but were only manifestations, suited to beget such thoughts in the minds of men, that dwelt in bodies, as might lay the principles and foundations of religion deep in them. The language of the scriptures speaks to

ART. I. the capacities of men, and even of rude men in dark times, in which most of the Scriptures were writ: but, though God is spoke of as having a face, eyes, ears, a smelling, hands and feet, and as coming down to view things on earth, all this is expressed after the manner of men, and is to be understood in a way suitable to a pure spirit. For the great care that was used, even under the most imperfect state of revelation, to keep men from framing any image or similitude of the Deity, shewed that it was far from the meaning of those expressions, that God had an organized body. These do therefore signify only the several varieties of Providence. When God was pleased with a nation, his *face* was said to *shine* upon it; for so a man looks towards those whom he loves. The particular care he takes of them, and the answering their prayers, is expressed by figures borrowed from *eyes* and *ears:* the peculiar dispensations of rewards and punishments are expressed by his *hands;* and the exactness of his justice and *wisdom* is expressed by *coming down* to view the state of human affairs. Thus it is clear that God has no body: nor has he *parts*, for we can apprehend no parts but of a body: so, since it is certain that God has no body, he can have *no parts:* something like parts does indeed belong to spirits, which are their thoughts distinct from their being, and they have a succession of them, and do oft change them. But infinite perfection excludes this from the idea of God; successive thoughts, as well as successive duration, seem inconsistent both with eternity, and with infinite perfection. Therefore the essence of God is one perfect thought, in which he both views and wills all things: and though his transient acts that pass out of the divine essence, such as creation, providence, and miracles, are done in a succession of time; yet his immanent acts, his knowledge and his decrees, are one with his essence. Distinct thoughts are plainly an imperfection, and argue a progress in knowledge, and a deliberation in council, which carry defect and infirmity in them. To conceive how this is in God is far above our capacity: who, though we feel our imperfection in successive acts, yet cannot apprehend how all things can be both seen and determined by one single thought. But the divine Essence being so infinitely above us, it is no wonder if we can frame no distinct act concerning its knowledge or will.

There is indeed a vast difficulty that arises here; for those acts of God are supposed free; so that they might have been otherwise than we see they are: and then it is not easy to imagine how they should be one with the divine Essence, to which necessary existence does certainly belong. It cannot be said that those acts are necessary, and could not be otherwise: for, since all God's transient acts are the certain effects of his immanent ones, if the immanent ones are necessary, then the transient must be so likewise, and so every thing must be necessary: a chain of necessary fate must run through the whole order of things; and God himself then is no free being, but acts by a necessity of nature. This some have thought was no absurdity: God is necessarily just, true, and good, not by any extrinsic necessity, for that would import an outward limitation, which destroys the idea of God; but by an intrinsic necessity that arises from his own infinite perfection. Some have from hence thought that, since God acts by infinite wisdom and goodness, things could not have been otherwise than they are: for what is infinitely wise or good cannot be altered, or made either better or worse. But this seems on the other hand very hard to conceive: for it would follow from thence, that God could neither have made the world sooner nor later, nor any other way than now it is: nor could he have done any one thing otherwise than as it is done. This seems to establish fate, and to destroy industry and all prayers and endeavours. Thus there are such great difficulties on all hands in this matter that it is much the wisest and safest course to adore what is above our apprehensions, rather than to inquire too curiously, or determine too boldly in it. It is certain that God acts both freely and perfectly: nor is he a Being subject to change, or to new acts; but *he is what he is*, both infinite and incomprehensible: we can neither apprehend how he made, nor how he executes his decrees. So we must leave this difficulty, without pretending that we can explain it, or answer the objections that arise against all the several ways by which divines have endeavoured to resolve it.

The third thing under the head I now consider is, God's being *without passions*. That will be soon explained. Passion is an agitation that supposes a succession of thoughts, together with a trouble for what is past, and a fear of missing what is aimed at. It arises out of a heat of mind, and produces a vehemence of action. Now all these are such manifest imperfections, that it does plainly appear they cannot consist with infinite perfection. Yet after all this, there are several passions, such as *anger, fury, jealousy*, and *revenge, bowels of mercy, compassion* and *pity, joy* and *sorrow*, that are ascribed to God in the common forms of speech, that occur often in scripture, as was formerly observed, with relation to those figures that are taken from the parts of a human body. Passion produces a vehemence of action: so, when there is in the providences of God such a vehemence as, according to the manner of men, would import a passion, then that passion is ascribed to God: when he punishes men for sin, he is said to be *angry:* when he does that by severe and redoubled strokes, he is said to be full of *fury and revenge:* when he punishes for idolatry, or any dishonour done himself, he is said to be *jealous:* when he changes the course of his proceedings, he is said to *repent:* when his dispensations of providence are very gentle, and his judgments come slowly from him, he is said to have *bowels*. And thus all the varieties of Providence come to be expressed by all that variety of passions, which among men might give occasion to such a variety of proceeding.

The fourth head in this article is concerning the *power, wisdom, and goodness* of God, that he is *infinite* in them. If he can give being to things that are not, and can also give all the possibilities of motion, size, and shape, to beings that do exist, here is power without bounds. A power of creating must be infinite, since nothing can resist it. If some things are in their own nature impossible, that does not arise from the want of power in God, which extends to every thing that is possible. But that, which is supposed to be impossible of its own nature, cannot actually be: otherwise a thing might both be and not be; and it is perceptible to every man that this is impossible. It is not want of power in God, that he cannot lie nor sin: it is the infinite purity of the Divine nature that makes this impossible, by reason of his infinite perfection. Nor is it a want of power in God, that the truth of propositions concerning things that are past, as that yesterday once was, is unalterable. Among impossibilities, one is, to take from any being that which is essential to it. God can annihilate every being at his pleasure; for, as he gave being with a thought, so he can destroy it with another: and this does fully assert the infinite power of God. But if he has made beings with such peculiar essences, as that matter must be extended and impenetrable, and that it is capable of peculiar surfaces and other modes, which are only its different sizes and shapes, then matter cannot be, and yet not be, extended; nor can these modes subsist, if the matter of which they are the modes is withdrawn. The infinite power of God is fully believed by those who acknowledge both his power of creating and annihilating; together with a power of disposing of the whole creation, according to the possibilities of every part or individual of it; though they cannot conceive a possibility of separating the essential properties of any being from itself; that is to say, that it may both be, and not be, at the same time; since an essential property is that which cannot be without that substance to which it belongs.

The wisdom of God consists first in his seeing all the possibilities of things, and then in his knowing all things that either are, or ever were, or shall be: the former is called the knowledge of simple *intelligence* or *apprehension*; the other is called the knowledge of *vision*. The one arises from the perfection of the divine Essence, by which he apprehends whatever is possible; the other arises from his own decrees, in which the whole order of things is fixed. But besides these two ideas that we can frame of the knowledge of God, some have imagined a third knowledge, which, because it is of a middle order betwixt *intelligence* and *vision*, they have called a *middle knowledge;* which is the knowing certainly how, according to all the possibilities of circumstances in which free agents might be put, they should choose and act. Some have thought that this was a vain and needless conceit; and that it is impossible that such knowledge should be certain, or more than conjectural; and, since conjecture implies doubt, it is an imperfect act, and so does not become a Being of infinite perfection. But others have thought that the infinite perfection of the divine Mind must go so far as to foresee certainly what free creatures are to do; since upon this foresight only they imagine that the justice or goodness of God in his providence can be made out or defended. It seemed fit to mention this upon the present occasion; but it will be then proper to inquire more carefully about it, when the article of *predestination* is explained.

It is necessary to state the idea of the goodness of God most carefully; for we naturally enough frame great and just ideas of power and wisdom; but we easily fall into false conceits of goodness. This is that of all the divine perfections in which we are the most concerned, and so we ought to be the most careful to frame true ideas of it: it is also that, of all God's attributes, of which the scriptures speak most copiously. Infinite goodness is a tendency to communicate the divine perfections to all created beings, according to their several capacities. God is original goodness, all perfect and happy in himself, acting and seeing every thing in a perfect light; and he having made rational beings capable of some degrees of his light, purity, and perfection, the first and primary act of goodness is to propose to them such means as may raise them to these, to furnish them with them, to move them oft to them, to accept and to assist their sincere endeavours after them. A second act of goodness, which is but in order to the first, is to pity those miseries into which men fall, as long as there is any principle or possibility left in them of their becoming good; to pardon all such sins as men have committed, who turn to the purposes of becoming seriously good, and to pass by all the frailties and errors of those who are truly and upon the main good, though surprise and strong temptations prove often too hard for them. These two give us as full an idea as we can have of perfect goodness; whose first aim must be the making us good, and like to that original goodness: pity and pardon coming in but in a subsidiary way, to carry on the main design of making men truly good. Therefore the chief act and design of goodness is the making us truly good; and, when any person falls below that possibility, he is no more the object of pity or pardon, because he is no more capable of becoming good. Pardon is offered on design to make us really good; so it is not to be sought for, nor rested in, but in order to a farther end, which is the reforming our natures, and the making us partakers of the divine nature. We are not therefore to frame ideas of a feeble goodness in God, that yields to importunate cries, or that melts at a vast degree of misery. Tenderness in human nature is a great ornament and perfection, necessary to dispose us to much benignity and mercy: but, in the common administration of justice, this tenderness must be restrained; otherwise it would slacken the rigour of punishment too much, which might dissolve the order and peace of human societies. But since we cannot see into the truth of men's hearts, a charitable disposition and a compassionate temper are necessary to make men sociable and kind, gentle and humane. God, who sees our hearts, and is ever assisting all our endeavours to become truly good, needs not this tenderness, nor is he indeed capable of it; for, after all its beauty with relation to the state wherein we are now put, yet, in itself it implies imperfection. Nor can the miseries and howlings of wicked beings, after all the seeds and possibilities of goodness are utterly extinguished in them, give any pity to the divine Being. These are no longer the object of the primary act of his goodness, and therefore they cannot come under its secondary acts. It is of such great consequence to settle this notion right in our minds, that it well deserves to be so copiously opened; since we now see in what respects God's goodness is without bounds, and infinite; that is, it reaches to all men, after all sins whatsoever, as long as they are capable of becoming good. It is not a limitation of the divine goodness to say, that some men and some states are beyond it; no more than it is a limitation of his power to say, that he cannot sin, or cannot do impossibilities: for a goodness, towards persons not capable of becoming good, is a goodness that does not agree with the infinite purity and holiness of God. It is such a goodness, that if it were proposed to the world, it would encourage men to live in sin, and to think that a few acts of homage offered to God, perhaps in our last extremities, could so far please him, as to bribe and corrupt him.

This is that which makes idolatry so great a sin, so often forbid by God, and so severely punished, not only as it is injurious to the majesty of God, but because it corrupts the ideas or notions of God. Those ideas rightly formed are the basis upon which all religion is built. The seeds and principles of a new and godlike nature spring up in us as we form ourselves upon the true ideas or notions of God. Therefore, when God is proposed to be adored by us under a visible shape or image, all the acts of religion offered to it are only so many pieces of pageantry, and end in the flatterings and the magnifyings of it with much pomp, cruelty, or lasciviousness, according to the different genius of several nations. So the forming a false notion of the goodness of God, as a tenderness that is to be overcome with importunities and howlings, and other submissions, and not to be gained only by becoming like him, is a capital and fundamental error in religion.

The next branch of this article is, God's *creating and preserving of all things;* and that both material substances, which are visible, and immaterial and spiritual substances, which are invisible. God's creating all things has been already made out. If matter could neither be eternal, nor give itself a being, then it must have its being from God. Creating does naturally import infinite power; for that power is clearly without bounds, that can make things out of nothing: a bounded power, which can only shape and mould matter, must suppose it to have a being, before it can work upon it. We cannot indeed form a distinct thought of creation, for we cannot apprehend what nothing is. The nearest approach we can bring ourselves to a true idea of this, is, the considering our own thoughts; especially our ideas of mathematical proportions, and the other affections of bodies: those ideas are the modes of a spiritual substance; and there is no likeness nor resemblance between them and the modes of material substances, which are only the occasions of our having those ideas, and not in any wise the matter out of which they are formed. Here seems to be a sort of beings brought out of nothing; but, after all, this is vastly below creation, and is only a faint resemblance of it.

With the power of creating we must also join that of annihilating, which is equal to it, and must necessarily be supposed to be in God, because we plainly perceive it to be a perfection. The recalling into nothing a being brought out of nothing, is a necessary consequence of infinite power, when it thinks fit so to exert itself. There is a common notion in the world, that things would fall back into nothing of themselves, if they were not preserved by the same infinite Power that made them: but without question it is an act of the same infinite Power to reduce a being to nothing, that it is to bring a being out of nothing: so whatever has once a being, must of its nature continue still to be, without any new causality or influence. This must be acknowledged, unless it can be said, that a tendency to annihilation is the consequent of a created being. But as this would make the preservation of the world to be a continued violence to a natural tendency that is in all things; so there is no more reason to imagine that beings have a tendency to annihilation, than that nothing had a tendency to creation. It is absurd to think that any thing can have a tendency to that which is essentially opposite to itself, and is destructive of it.

The preservation of things is the keeping the frame of nature, and the order of the universe, in such a state as is suitable to the purposes of the supreme Mind. It is true, natural

ART.
I.
agents must ever keep the course in which they are once put; and the great heavenly orbs, as well as all smaller motions, must ever have rolled on in one constant channel, when they were once put into it; so in this respect it may seem that conservation by a special act is not necessary. But we perceive a freedom in our own natures, and a power that our minds have, not only to move our own bodies, but by them, and by the help of such engines as we can invent, we make a vast change in this earth from what it would be, if it were left unwrought. In a course of some ages, the whole world, by the natural progress of things, would be a forest: both earth and air are very much different from what they would be, if men were not free agents, and did not cultivate the earth, and thereby purify the air. The working of mines, minerals, and other fossils, makes also a great change in its bowels; it gives vent to some damps which might much affect the air, and it frees the earth from earthquakes. Thus the industry of man has in many respects changed both earth and air very sensibly from what it would have been, if the world had not those inhabitants in it. Nor do we know what natural force other spirits inhabiting in or about it, or at least using subtiler bodies, may have, or in what influences or operations they may exert that force on material substances. Upon all these accounts it is, that the world could not be preserved in a constant and regular state, if the supreme Mind had not a direction both of men's wills and actions, and of the course of nature: for, unless it is thought that man is really no free agent, but acts in a chain as certainly as other natural agents do, it must be acknowledged, that by the interposition of men's minds, together with their power over matter, the course of the first motion that was given to the universe is so changed, that if there is not a constant providence, the frame of nature must go out of the channel into which God did at first put it. The order of things on this earth takes a great turn from the wind, both as to the fruitfulness of the earth, and to the operations on the sea, and has likewise a great influence on the purity of the air, and, by consequence, on men's good or ill health; and the wind, or the agitation of the air, turns so often and so quick, that it seems to be the great instrument of Providence, upon which an unconceivable variety of things does naturally depend. I do not deny, but that it may be said, that all those changes in the air arise from certain and mechanical, though to us unknown, causes; which may be supported from this, that between the tropics, where the influence of the heavenly bodies is stronger, the wind and weather are more regular; though even that admits of great exceptions: yet it has been the common sense of mankind, that, besides the natural causes of the alterations in the air, they are under a particular influence and direction of Providence: and it is in itself highly probable, to say no more

of it. This may either be managed immediately by the acts of the divine Mind, to which nature readily obeys, or by some subaltern mind, or angel, which may have as natural an efficiency over an extent of matter proportioned to its capacity, as a man has over his own body, and over that compass of matter that is within his reach. Which way soever God governs the world, and what influence soever he has over men's minds, we are sure that the governing and preserving his own workmanship is so plainly a perfection, that it must belong to a Being infinitely perfect: and there is such a chain in things, those of the greatest consequence arising often from small and inconsiderable ones, that we cannot imagine a Providence, unless we believe every thing to be within its care and view.

The only difficulty that has been made in apprehending this has arisen from the narrowness of men's minds, who have measured God rather by their own measure and capacity, than by that of infinite perfection, which, as soon as it is considered, will put an end to all farther doubtings about it. When we perceive that a vast number of objects enter in at our eye by a very small passage, and yet are so little jumbled in that crowd, that they open themselves regularly, though there is no great space for that neither; and that they give us a distinct apprehension of many objects that lie before us, some even at a vast distance from us, both of their nature, colour, and size; and by a secret geometry, from the angles that they make in our eye, we judge of the distance of all objects both from us, and from one another. If to this we add the vast number of figures that we receive and retain long and with great order in our brains, which we easily fetch up either in our thoughts or in our discourses, we shall find it less difficult to apprehend how an infinite mind should have the universal view of all things ever present before it. It is true, we do not so easily conceive how free minds are under this Providence, as how natural agents should always move at its direction. But we perceive that one mind can work upon another. A man raises a sound of words, which carry such signs of his inward thoughts, that, by this motion in the air, another man's ear is so struck upon that thereby an impression is made upon his brain, by which he not only conceives what the other man's thought was, but is very powerfully inclined to consent to it, and to concur with it. All this is a great way about, and could not be easily apprehended by us, if we had not a clear and constant perception of it. Now since all this is brought about by a motion upon our brains, according to the force with which we are more or less affected, it is very reasonable for us to apprehend that the supreme Mind can, besides many other ways to us less known, put such motions in our brain, as may give us all such thoughts

ART.
I.

as it intends to impress upon us, in as strong and effectual a manner as may fully answer all its purposes.

The great objection that lies against the power and the goodness of Providence, from all that evil that is in the world, which God is either not willing or not able to hinder, will be more properly considered in another place; at present it is enough in general to observe, that God's providence must carry on every thing according to its nature; and since he has made some free beings capable of thought, and of good and evil, we must believe, that, as the course of nature is not oft put out of its channel, unless when some extraordinary thing is to be done, in order to some great end, so, in the government of free agents, they must be generally left to their liberty, and not put too oft off their bias: this is a hint to resolve that difficulty by, concerning all the moral evil, which is, generally speaking, the occasion of most of the physical evil that is in the world. A providence thus settled, that extends itself to all things both natural and free, is necessary to preserve religion, to engage us to prayers, praises, and to a dependence on it, and a submission to it. Some have thought it was necessary to carry this farther, and so they make God to be the first and immediate cause of every action or motion. This some modern writers have taken from the schools, and have dressed it in new phrases of general laws, particular wills, and occasional causes; and so they express or explain God's producing every motion that is in matter, and his raising every sensation, and, by the same parity of reason, every cogitation in minds: this they think arises out of the idea of infinite perfection, and fully answers these words of the scriptures, that 'in God we live, move, and have our being.' To others all this seems first unnecessary; for, if God has made matter capable of motion, and capable of receiving it from the stroke or impulse that another piece of matter gives it, this comes as truly from God, as if he did immediately give every motion by an act of his own will. It seems more suitable to the beauty of his workmanship, to think that he has so framed things that they hold on in that course in which he has put them, than to make him perpetually produce every new motion. And the bringing God immediately into every thing, may, by an odd reverse of effects, make the world think that every thing is done as much without him, as others are apt to imagine that every thing is done by him. And though it is true that we cannot distinctly apprehend how a motion in our brain should raise such a thought as answers to it in our minds; yet it seems more reasonable to think that God has put us under such an order of being from which that does naturally follow, than that he himself should interpose in every thought. The difficulty of apprehending how a thing is done, can be no prejudice to the belief of it, when we have the infinite power of God in our thoughts, who may be as easily conceived to have once for all put us in a method of receiving such sensations, by a general law or course of nature, as to give us new ones at every minute. But the greatest difficulty against this is, that it makes God the first physical cause of all the evil that is in the world: which, as it is contrary to his nature, so, it absolutely destroys all liberty; and this puts an end to all the distinctions between good and evil, and consequently to all religion. And as for those large expressions that are brought from scripture, every word in scripture is not to be stretched to the utmost physical sense to which it can be carried: it is enough if a sense is given to it, that agrees to the scope of it: which is fully answered by acknowledging, that the power and providence of God is over all things, and that it directs every thing to wise and good ends, from which nothing is hid, by which nothing is forgot, and to which nothing can resist. This scheme of providence fully agrees with the notion of a Being infinitely perfect, and with all that the scriptures affirm concerning it; and it lays down a firm foundation for all the acts and exercises of religion.

As to the power and providence of God with relation to invisible beings, we plainly perceive that there is in us a principle capable of thought and liberty, of which, by all that appears to us, matter is not at all capable: after its utmost refinings by fires and furnaces, it is still passive, and has no self-motion, much less thought, in it. Thought seems plainly to arise from a single principle, that has no parts, and is quite another thing than the motion of one subtile piece of matter upon another can be supposed to be. If thought is only motion, then no part of us thinks, but as it is in motion; so that only the moving particles, or rather their surfaces, that strike upon one another, do think: but such a motion must end quickly in the dissipation and evaporation of the whole thinking substance; nor can any of the quiescent parts have any perception of such thoughts, or any reflection upon them. And to say that matter may have other affections unknown to us besides motion, by which it may think, is to affirm a thing without any sort of reason: it is rather a flying from an argument, than an answering it: no man has any reason to affirm this, nor can he have any. And besides, all our cogitations of immaterial things, proportions, and numbers, do plainly shew that we have a being in us distinct from matter, that rises above it, and commands it: we perceive we have a freedom of moving and acting at pleasure. All these things give us a clear perception of a being that is in us distinct from matter, of which we are not able to form a complete idea: we having only four perceptions of its nature and operations. 1. That it thinks. 2. That it has an inward power of choice. 3. That by its will it can move and command the body. And, 4. That it is in a close and entire union with it, that it has a

ART. I.
dependence on it, as to many of its acts, as well as an authority over it in many other things. Such a being that has no parts must be immortal in its nature, for every single being is immortal. It is only the union of parts that is capable of being dissolved; that which has no parts is indissoluble. To this two objections are made: one is, that beasts seem to have both thought and freedom, though in a lower order: if then matter can be capable of this in any degree how low soever, a higher rectification of matter may be capable of a higher degree of it. It is therefore certain, that either beasts have no thought or liberty at all, and are only pieces of finely organized matter, capable of many subtile motions, that come to them from objects without them, but that they have no sensation nor thought at all about them: or, since how prettily soever some may have dressed up this notion, it is that which human nature cannot receive or bear; there being such evident indications of even high degrees of reason among the beasts; it is more reasonable to imagine, that there may be spirits of a lower order in beasts, that have in them a capacity of thinking and choosing; but that so entirely under the impressions of matter, that they are not capable of that largeness, either of thought or liberty, that is necessary to make them capable of good or evil, of rewards and punishments; and that therefore they may be perpetually rolling about from one body to another. Another objection to the belief of an immaterial substance in us is, that we feel it depends so entirely on the fabric and state of the brain, that a disorder, a vapour, or humour in it, defaces all our thoughts, our memory, and imagination; and, since we find that which we call *mind* sinks so low upon a disorder of the body, it may be reasonable to believe, that it evaporates, and is quite dissipated, upon the dissolution of our bodies: so that the soul is nothing but the livelier parts of the blood, called the animal spirits. In answer to this, we know that those animal spirits are of such an evanid and subtile nature, that they are in a perpetual waste, new ones always succeeding as the former go off: but we perceive at the same time that our soul is a stable and permanent being, by the steadiness of its acts and thoughts; we being for many years plainly the same beings, and therefore our souls cannot be such a loose and evaporating substance as those spirits are. The spirits are indeed the inward organs of the mind, for memory, speech, and bodily motion; and, as these flatten or are wasted, the mind is less able to act: as when the eye or any other organ of sense is weakened, the sensations grow feeble on that side: and as a man is less able to work, when all those instruments he makes use of are blunted; so the mind may sink upon a decay or disorder in those spirits, and yet be of a nature wholly different from them. How a mind should work on matter, cannot, I confess, be clearly comprehended. It cannot be denied by any that

is not a direct atheist, that the thoughts of the supreme Mind give impressions and motions to matter. So our thoughts may give a motion, or the determination of motion, to matter, and yet rise from substances wholly different from it. Nor is it inconceivable, that the supreme Mind should have put our minds likewise under such a subordination to some material motions, that out of them peculiar thoughts should arise in us. And though this union is that which we cannot distinctly conceive; yet there is no difficulty in it, equal to that of our imagining that matter can think or move itself. We perceive that we ourselves and the rest of mankind have thinking principles within us; so from thence it is easy enough to us to apprehend, that there may be other thinking beings, which either have no bodies at all, but act purely as intellectual substances: or, if they have bodies, that they are so subtilized as to be capable of a vast quickness of motion, such in proportion as we perceive to be in our animal spirits, which in the minute that our minds command them, are raising motions in the remotest parts of our bodies. Such bodies may also be so thin as to be invisible to us; and as among men some are good and some bad, and of the bad some seem to be determinedly, and, as to all appearance, incurably bad; so there may have been a time and state of liberty, in which those spirits were left to their choice, whether they would continue in their innocency, or fall from it; and such as continued might be for ever fixed in that state, or exalted to higher degrees in it: and such as fell from it might fall irrecoverably into a state of utter apostacy from God, and of rebellion against him. There is nothing in this theory that is incredible: therefore, if the scriptures have told us any thing concerning it, we have no reason to be prejudiced against them upon that account: besides that, there are innumerable histories in many several countries and ages of the world, of extraordinary apparitions, and other unaccountable performances, that could only have been done by invisible powers. Many of those are so well attested, that it argues a strange pitch of obstinacy, to refuse to believe a matter of fact when it is well vouched, and when there is nothing in reason to oppose it, but an unwillingness to believe invisible beings. It is true, this is an argument in which a fabulous humour will go far, and in which some are so credulous as to swallow down every thing; therefore all wise men ought to suspend their belief, and not to go too fast: but when things are so undeniably attested, that there is no reason to question the exactness or the credit of the witnesses, it argues a mind unreasonably prepossessed to reject all such evidence.

All those invisible beings were created by God, and are not to be considered as emanations or rays of his essence, which was a gross conceit of such philosophers as fancied that

ART. I.

the Deity had parts. They are beings created by him, and are capable of passing through various scenes, in bodies more or less refined. In this life the state of our minds receives vast alterations from the state of our bodies, which ripen gradually: and after they are come to their full growth, they cannot hold in that condition long, but sink down much faster than they grew up; some humours or diseases discomposing the brain, which is the seat of the mind, so entirely, that it cannot serve it, at least so far as to reflex acts. So in the next state it is possible that we may at first be in a less perfect condition by reason of this, that we may have a less perfect body, to which we may be united between our death and the general resurrection; and there may be a time, in which we may receive a vast addition and exaltation in that state by the raising up of our former bodies, and the reuniting us to them, which may give us a greater compass, and a higher elevation.

These things are only proposed as suppositions, that have no absurdity in them: so that, if they should happen to be the parts of a revealed religion, there is no reason to doubt of it, or to reject it, on such an account.

The last branch of this article is the assertion of that great doctrine of the Christian religion concerning the Trinity, or three Persons in one divine essence. It is a vain attempt to go about to prove this by reason: for it must be confessed, that we should have had no cause to have thought of any such thing, if the scriptures had not revealed it to us. There are indeed prints of a very ancient tradition in the world, of three in the Deity;* called the *Word*, or the *Wisdom*, and the *Spirit*, or the *Love*, besides the fountain of both these, God: this was believed by those from whom the most ancient phi-

---

* Doctor Buchanan, in his Christian Researches in Asia, observes, that the chief and distinguishing doctrines of the Scripture—the Trinity in Unity; the incarnation of the Deity; a vicarious atonement for sin; and the influence of the Divine Spirit on the mind of man—are held by the eastern nations, though in gross ignorance respecting the only living and true God. Of the Trinity he writes:

'The Hindoos believe in one God, Brahma; and yet they represent him as subsisting in three persons; and they worship one or other of these persons in every part of India. And what proves distinctly that they hold this doctrine is, that their most ancient representation of the Deity is formed of *one* body and *three* faces. The most remarkable of these is that at the caves of Elephanta, in an island near Bombay. The author visited it in the year 1808; nor has he seen any work of art in the east, which he contemplated with greater wonder: whether considered with respect to its colossal size, its great antiquity, the beauty of the sculpture, or the excellence of the preservation. From causes which cannot now be known, the Hindoos have long since ceased to worship at this temple. Each of the faces of the Triad is about five feet in length. The whole of the statue and the spacious temple which contains it, is cut out of the solid rock of the mountain. The Hindoos assign to these works an immense antiquity, and attribute the workmanship to the Gods. The temple of Elephanta is certainly one of the wonders of the world, and is, perhaps, a grander effort of the ingenuity of man, than the pyramids of Egypt. Whence then have the Hindoos derived the idea of a Triune God? It should seem as if they had heard of the ELOHIM of Revelation in the first chapter of Genesis—"Let us make man."'—[ED.]

losophers had their doctrines. The author of the Book of Wisdom, Philo, and the Chaldee paraphrasts, have many things that shew that they had received those traditions from the former ages; but it is not so easy to determine what gave the first rise to them.

It has been much argued, whether this was revealed in the Old Testament or not; some from the plural termination of *Elohim*, which is joined to singular verbs, and from that of the Lord raining fire from the Lord upon Sodom (*Jehovah* from *Jehovah*); from the description of the Wisdom of God in the 8th of the Proverbs, as a Person with God from all eternity; and from the mention that is often made of the Spirit, as well as the Word of God that came to the prophets; they have, I say, from all these places, and some others, concluded, that this is contained in the Old Testament. Others have doubted of this, and have said that the name *Elohim*, though of a plural termination, being often joined to a singular verb, makes it reasonable to think it was a singular: which, by somewhat peculiar to that language, might be of a plural termination. Nor have they thought that since angels carry the name of God, when they went on special deputations from him, the angels being called *Jehovah* could be very confidently urged: that sublime description of the *Wisdom* of God in the Proverbs seems not to them to be a full proof in this matter: for the Wisdom there mentioned seems to be the Wisdom of creation and providence, which is not personal, but belongs to the essence; nor do they think that those places in the Old Testament, in which mention is made of the *Word*, or of the *Spirit* of God, can settle this point; for these may only signify God's revealing himself to his prophets. Therefore, whatever secret tradition the Jews might have had among them concerning this, from whom perhaps the Greeks might have also had it; yet many do not pretend to prove this from passages in the Old Testament alone: though the expositions given to some of them in the New Testament prove to us, who acknowledge it, what was the true meaning of those passages; yet, take the Old Testament in itself without the New, and it must be confessed that it will not be easy to prove this article from it.

But there are very full and clear proofs of it in the New Testament; and they had need be both full and clear, before a doctrine of this nature can be pretended to be proved by them. In order to the making this mystery to be more distinctly intelligible, different methods have been taken. By *one Substance* many do understand a numerical or individual unity of substance; and by *three Persons* they understand three distinct subsistences in that essence. It is not pretended by these, that we can give a distinct idea of *Person* or *Subsistence*, only they hold it imports a real diversity in one from another, and even such a diversity from the substance

ART. I. of the Deity itself, that some things belong to the Person which do not belong to the Substance: for the Substance neither begets nor is begotten; neither breathes, nor proceeds. If this carries in it something that is not agreeable to our notions, nor like any thing that we can apprehend, to this it is said, that, if God has revealed that in the scripture which is thus expressed, we are bound to believe it, though we can frame no clear apprehension about it. God's eternity, his being all one single act, his creating and preserving all things, and his being every where, are things that are absolute riddles to us: we cannot bring our minds to conceive them, and yet we must believe that they are so; because we see much greater absurdities must follow upon our conceiving that they should be otherwise. So if God has declared this inexplicable thing concerning himself to us, we are bound to believe it, though we cannot have any clear idea how it truly is. For there appear as strange and unanswerable difficulties in many other things, which yet we know to be true; so if we are once well assured that God has revealed his doctrine to us, we must silence all objections against it, and believe it: reckoning that our not understanding it, as it is in itself, makes the difficulties seem to be much greater than otherwise they would appear to be, if we had light enough about it, or were capable of forming a more perfect idea of it while we are in this depressed state.

Others give another view of this matter, that is not indeed so hard to be apprehended: but that has an objection against it, that seems as great a prejudice against it, as the difficulty of apprehending the other way is against that: it is this; they do hold that there are three Minds; that the first of these three, who is from that called the Father, did from all eternity by an emanation of essence beget the Son, and by another emanation that was from eternity likewise, and was as essential to him as the former, both the first and the second, did jointly breathe forth the Spirit; and that these are three distinct Minds, every one being God, as much as the other: only the Father is the fountain, and is only self-originated. All this is in a good degree intelligible: but it seems hard to reconcile it both with the idea of unity, which seems to belong to a Being of infinite perfection; and with the many express declarations that are made in the scriptures concerning the unity of God. Instead of going farther into explanations of that which is certainly very far beyond all our apprehensions, and that ought therefore to be let alone, I shall now consider what declarations are made in the scripture concerning this point.

The first and the chief is in that charge and commission which our Saviour gave to his apostles to go and make disciples to him among all nations, 'baptizing them in the name of the Father, the Son, and the Holy Ghost.' By *name* is meant either an authority derived to them, in the virtue of which all nations were to be baptized: or that the persons so baptized are dedicated to the *Father, Son,* and *Holy Ghost.* Either of these senses, as it proves them all to be *Persons,* so it sets them in an equality, in a thing that can only belong to the *divine Nature.* Baptism is the receiving men from a state of sin and wrath, into a state of favour, and into the rights of the sons of God, and the hopes of eternal happiness, and a calling them by the name of God. These are things that can only be offered and assured to men in the name of the great and eternal God; and therefore, since, without any distinction or note of inequality, they are all three set together as Persons in whose name this is to be done, they must be all three the true God; otherwise it looks like a just prejudice against our Saviour, and his whole gospel, that by his express direction the first entrance to it, which gives the visible and fœderal right to those great blessings that are offered by it, or their initiation into it, should be in the name of two created beings, (if the one can be called properly so much as a being, according to their hypothesis,) and that even in an equality with the supreme and increated Being. The plainness of this charge, and the great occasion upon which it was given, makes this an argument of such force and evidence, that it may justly determine the whole matter.

A second argument is taken from this, that we find St. Paul begins or ends most of his Epistles with a salutation in the form of a wish, which is indeed a prayer, or a benediction, in the name of those who are so invocated; in which he wishes the churches 'grace, mercy, and peace, from God the Father and the Lord Jesus Christ;'* which is an invocation of Christ, in conjunction with the Father, for the greatest blessings of favour and mercy: that is a strange strain, if he was only a creature; which yet is delivered without any mitigation or softening in the most remarkable parts of his Epistles. This is carried farther in the conclusion of the Second Epistle to the Corinthians; 'The grace of the Lord Jesus Christ, the love of God, and the fellowship of the Holy Ghost, be with you.' It is true this is expressed as a wish, and not in the nature of a prayer, as the common salutations are: but here three great blessings are wished to them as from three fountains, which imports that they are three different Persons, and yet equal: for, though in order the Father is first, and is generally put first, yet, here Christ is named, which seems to be a strange reversing of things, if they are not equal as to their essence or substance. It is true the second is not named here, *the Father,* as elsewhere, but only *God;* yet, since he is

ART. 1.

Matt. xxviii. 19.

2 Cor. xiii. 14.

---

* Rom. i. 7.   Rom. xvi. 20, 24.   1 Cor. xvi. 23.   1 Cor. i. 3.   2 Cor. i. 2.
Gal. i. 3.   Gal. vi. 18.   Eph. i. 2.   Eph. vi. 23.   Phil. i. 2.   Phil. iv. 23.
Col. i. 2.   1 Thess. i. 1.   1 Thess. v. 28.   2 Thess. i. 2.   2 Thess. iii. 18.
1 Tim. i. 2.   2 Tim. i. 2.   Tit. i. 4.   Philem. 3. 25.   2 John i. 3.

ART. I.

mentioned as distinct from Christ and the Holy Ghost, it must be understood of the *Father*; for, when the *Father* is named with *Christ*, sometimes he is called *God* simply, and sometimes *God the Father*.

This argument from the threefold salutation appears yet stronger in the words in which St. John addresses himself to the seven churches in the beginning of the Revelations:

Rev. i. 4, 5.
'Grace and peace from him which is, which was, and which is to come; and from the seven spirits which are before his throne; and from Jesus Christ.' By the *seven spirits* must be meant one or more persons, since he wishes or declares *grace and peace* from them: now either this must be meant of angels, or of the Holy Ghost. There are no where prayers made, or blessings given, in the name of angels: this were indeed a worshipping them; against which there are express authorities, not only in the other books of the New Testament, but in this book in particular. Nor can it be imagined that angels could have been named before *Jesus Christ*: so then it remains, that, *seven* being a number that imports both variety and perfection, and that was the sacred number among the Jews, this is a mystical expression, which is no extraordinary thing in a book that is all over mysterious; and it imports one Person from whom all that variety of gifts, administrations, and operations, that were then in the church did flow; and this is the *Holy Ghost*. But as to his being put in order before Christ, as upon the supposition of an equality, the going out of the common order is no great matter; so since there was to come after this a full period that concerned Christ, it might be a natural way of writing to name him last. Against all this it is objected, that the designation that is given to the first of these in a circumlocution that imports eternity, shews that the great God, and not the person of the Father, is to be meant: but then how could St. John, writing to the churches, wish them grace and peace from the other two? A few verses after this, the same description of eternal duration is given to Christ, and is a strong proof of his eternity, and, by consequence, of his divinity: so what is brought so soon after as a character of the eternity of the Son, may be also here used to denote the eternal Father. These are the chief places in which the Trinity is mentioned all together.

I do not insist on that contested passage of St. John's

1 John v. 7.
Epistle; there are great doubtings made about it; the main ground of doubting being the silence of the Fathers, who never made use of it in the disputes with the Arians and Macedonians. There are very considerable things urged, on the other hand, to support the authority of that passage; yet I think it is safer to build upon sure and indisputable grounds: so I leave it to be maintained by others who are more fully persuaded of its being authentical. There is no

need of it. This matter is capable of a very full proof, whether that passage is believed to be a part of the canon, or not.

It is no small confirmation of the truth of this doctrine, that we are certain it was universally received over the whole Christian church long before there was either a Christian prince to support it by his authority, or a council to establish it by consent: and, indeed, the council of Nice did nothing but declare what was the faith of the Christian church, with the addition only of the word *consubstantial:* for, if all the other words of the Creed settled at Nice are acknowledged to be true, that of the three Persons being of one substance will follow from thence by a just consequence. We know, both by what Tertullian and Novatian writ, what was the faith both of the Roman and the African churches. From Irenæus we gather the faith both of the Gallican and the Asiatic churches. And the whole proceedings in the case of Samosatenus,* that was the solemnest business that passed while the church was under oppression and persecution, give us the most convincing proof possible, not only of the faith of the eastern churches at that time, but of their zeal likewise in watching against every breach that was made in so sacred a part of their trust and *depositum.*

These things have been fully opened and enlarged on by

* Paulus Samosatenus, who flourished in the latter end of the third century, succeeded Demetrianus in the see of Antioch. He was at first poor, but amassed very considerable wealth by his corrupt practices, by his oppression of the brethren, by his using his patronage to advance his own interests;—thus turning godliness into gain. He was, besides, a man of very immoral character, and lived in such a manner as proved him totally unfit to govern in the church of God. He endeavoured to revive the heresy of Artemon, 'which affirmed Christ to be a mere man,' but after his incarnation, by his improvement of the wisdom and power which were imparted to him, to have been made God. Eusebius quotes from a volume, written in his day to confute this 'blasphemous untruth,' the following in reply to the daring assertion of these men, that the apostles and early fathers taught this heresy unto the time of Victor, thirteenth bishop of Rome: ' This peradventure might seem to have some likelihood of truth, if it were not oppugned first by all the holy Scriptures, next by the books of sundry men long before the time of Victor, which they published against the Gentiles, and in confutation of the heretical opinions of their time. I mean Justin Miltiades, Tatian, and Clemens, with many others, in all which works Christ is preached and published to be God. Who knoweth not that the works of Irenæus, Melito, and all other Christians, do confess Christ to be both God and man?'

A Synod was held at Antioch which was attended by many distinguished bishops, who there 'met with the rotten sheep which corrupted the flock of Christ.' Samosatenus endeavoured to conceal his opinions, but his 'blasphemy against Christ' was laid open by many, and especially by Malchion, a very eloquent man, a moderator in moral discipline in the school of Antioch, and who, for his sincere faith in Christ, was advanced to the ministry. Paul was condemned, and a letter (from which some of the above is taken) was written to Dionysius and Maximus, bishops of Rome and Alexandria, and 'to all our fellow bishops, elders, and deacons, throughout the world, and to the whole universal and Catholic church under heaven,' in which the character of Paul is given at some length. Paul was deposed by the Synod, but refused to surrender the church or house until an edict was obtained from the emperor to expel him. He was succeeded by Domnus, the son of Demetrianus, Paul's predecessor, a man adorned with those gifts required in a bishop.—[Ed.]

ART. I.

others, to whom the reader is referred; I shall only desire him to make this reflection on the state of Christianity at that time; the disputes that were then to be managed with the heathens, against the deifying or worshipping of men, and those extravagant fables concerning the genealogies of their heroes and gods, must have obliged the Christians rather to have silenced and suppressed the doctrine of the Trinity, than to have owned and published it: so that nothing but their being assured that it was a necessary and fundamental article of their faith, could have led them to own it in so public a manner; since the advantages that the heathen would have taken from it, must be too visible not to be soon observed. The heathens retorted upon them their doctrine of a man's being a God, and of God's having a Son; and every one who engaged in this controversy framed such answers to these objections as he thought he could best maintain. This, as it gave the rise to the errors which some brought into the church, so it furnishes us with a copious proof of the common sense of the Christians of those ages, who all agreed in general to the doctrine, though they had many different, and some very erroneous ways of explaining it among them.

I now come to the special proofs concerning each of the three Persons: but, there being other articles relating to the Son and the Holy Ghost, the proofs of these two will belong more properly to the explanation of those articles; therefore all that belongs to this article is to prove that the Father is truly God; but that needs not be much insisted on, for there is no dispute about it: none deny that he is God; many think that he is so truly God, that there is no other that can be called God besides him, unless it be in a larger sense of the word: and, therefore, I will here conclude all that seems necessary to be said on this first article; on which if I have dwelt the longer, it was because the stating the idea of God right being the fundamental article of all religion, and the key into every part of it, this was to be done with all the fulness and clearness possible.

In a word, to recapitulate a little what has been said; the liveliest way of framing an idea of God is to consider our own souls, which are said to be made after the *image of God*. An attentive reflection on what we perceive in ourselves, will carry us farther than any other thing whatsoever, to form just and true thoughts of God. We perceive what thought is, but, with that, we do also perceive the advantage of such an easy thought as arises out of a sensation, such as seeing or hearing, which gives us no trouble: we think, without any trouble, of many of the objects that we see all at once, or so near all at once, that the progression from one object to another is scarce perceptible; but the labour of study and of pursuing consequences wearies us, though the pleasure or the vanity of having found them out compensates for the pain they gave us, and sets men on to new inquiries. We perceive in ourselves a love of truth, and a vexation when we see we are in error, or are in the dark: and we feel that we act the most perfectly, when we act upon the clearest views of truth, and in the strictest pursuance of it; and the more present and regular, the more calm and steady, that our thoughts of all things are, that lie in our compass to know, present, past, or to come, we do plainly perceive that we do thereby become perfecter and happier beings. Now out of all this we can easily rise up in our thoughts to an idea of a mind that sees all things by a clear and full intuition, without the possibility of being mistaken, and that ever acts in that light, upon the surest prospect, and with the perfectest reason; and that does therefore always rejoice in every thing it does, and has a constant perception of all truth ever present to it. This idea does so genuinely arise from what we perceive both of the perfections and the imperfections of our own minds, that a very little reflection will help us to form it to a very high degree.

The perception also that we have of goodness, of a desire to make others good, and of the pleasure of effecting it; of the joy of making any one wiser or better, of making any one's life easy, and of raising his mind higher, will also help us in the forming of our ideas of God. But in this we meet with much difficulty and disappointment. So this leads us to apprehend how diffusive of itself infinite goodness must needs be; and what is the eternal joy that infinite love has, in bringing so many to that exalted state of endless happiness. We do also feel a power, issuing from us by a thought, that sets our bodies in motion; the varieties in our thoughts create a vast variety in the state of our bodies; but with this, as that power is limited to our own bodies; so it is often checked by disorders in them, and the soul suffers a great deal from those painful sensations that its union with the body subjects it to. From hence we can easily apprehend how the Supreme Mind can by a thought set matter into what motions it will, all matter being constantly subject to such impressions as the acts of the Divine Mind give it. This absolute dominion over all matter makes it to move, and shapes it according to the acts of that Mind; and matter has no power, by any irregularity it falls into, to resist those impressions which do immediately command and govern it; nor can it throw any uneasy sensations into that perfect Being.

This conduces also to give us a distinct idea of miracles. All matter is uniform: and it is only the variety of its motions and texture that makes all the variety that is in the world. Now, as the acts of the Eternal Mind gave matter its first motion, and put it into that course that we do now call

ART. I.

the course of nature, so another act of the same Mind can either suspend, stop, or change that course at pleasure, as he who throws a bowl may stop it in its course, or throw it back if he will; this being only the altering that impulse which himself gave: so, if one act of the infinite Mind puts things in a regular course, another act interposed may change that at pleasure. And thus with relation to God, miracles are no more difficult than any other act of Providence: they are only more amazing to us, because they are less ordinary, and go out of the common and regular course of things. By all this it appears how far the observation of what we perceive concerning ourselves may carry us to form livelier and clearer thoughts of God.

So much may suffice upon the first article.

ARTICLE II.

Of the Word or Son of God, which was made very Man.

The Son, which is the Word of the Father, begotten from Everlasting of the Father; the very and eternal God, of one Substance with the Father, took Man's Nature in the Womb of the Blessed Virgin of her Substance; so that two whole and perfect Natures, that is, the Godhead and Manhood, were joined together in one Person; never to be divided: whereof is one Christ, very God and very Man: who truly suffered, was dead and buried, to reconcile his Father to us, and to be a Sacrifice not only for Original Guilt, but also for actual Sins of Men.

THERE are in this article five heads to be explained.
I. That the Son or Word is of the same substance with the Father, begotten of him from all eternity.
II. That he took man's nature upon him in the womb of the blessed virgin, and of her substance.
III. That the two natures of the Godhead and manhood, both still perfect, were in him joined in one person never to be divided.
IV. That Christ truly suffered, was crucified, dead, and buried.
V. That he was our sacrifice to reconcile the Father to us, and that not only for original guilt, but for actual sins.

The first of these leads me to prosecute what was begun in the former article: and to prove, that the *Son* or *Word*, was from all eternity begotten of the same substance with the *Father*. It is here to be noted, that Christ is, in two respects, the *Son*, and *the only-begotten Son of God*. The one is, as he was man; the miraculous overshadowing of the blessed Virgin by the Holy Ghost having, without the ordinary course of nature, formed the first beginnings of Christ's human body in the womb of the Virgin. Thus, that miracle being instead of a natural begetting, he may, in that respect, be called the *begotten*, and *the only-begotten Son of God*. The other sense is, that the *Word*, or the divine Person, was in, and of, the substance of the Father, and so was truly God. It is also to be considered, that by the word *one substance* is to be understood that this second Person is not a creature of a pure and excellent nature, like God, holy and perfect, as we are called to be; but is truly God, as the *Father* is. *Begetting* is a term that naturally signifies the relation between the *Father* and the *Son*; but, what it strictly signifies here is not possible for us to understand, till we

ART. II.

comprehend this whole matter: nor can we be able to assign a reason why the emanation of the *Son*, and not that of the *Holy Ghost* likewise, is called *begetting*. In this we use the scripture terms, but must confess we cannot frame a distinct apprehension of that which is so far above us. This *begetting* was from all eternity: if it had been in time, the *Son* and Holy Ghost must have been creatures; but, if they are truly God, they must be eternal, and not produced by having a being given them, but educed of a substance that was eternal, and from which they did eternally spring. All these are the natural consequences of the main article that is now to be proved; and, when it is once proved clearly from scripture, these do follow by a natural and necessary deduction.

John i. 1, 2, 3.

The first and great proof of this is taken from the words with which St. John begins his Gospel.* 'In the beginning was the Word, and the Word was with God, and the Word was God; the same was in the beginning with God. All things were made by him, and without him was not any thing made that was made.' Here it is to be observed, that these words are set down here, before St. John comes to speak of Christ's being made in our nature: this passage belongs to another precedent being that he had. The *beginning* also here is set to import, that it was before creation or time: now a duration before time is eternal. So this *beginning* can be no other than that duration which was before *all things that were made*. It is also plainly said, over and over again, that *all things were made* by this *Word*. A power to create must be infinite; for, it is certain, that a power which can give being is without bounds. And, although the word *make* may seem capable of a larger sense, yet, as in other places of the New Testament, the stricter word *create* is used and applied to Christ, as the

Colos. i. 16.

'Maker of all things in heaven and earth, visible and invisible;' so the word *make* is used through the Old Testament for

Isai. xl. 26, 28. xliv. 24. xlv. 5, &c. xlviii. 12. 13. li. 12, 13. Jer. x. 1--16. Acts iv. 24, 25.

create; so that God's *making the heaven and the earth* is the character frequently given of him to distinguish him from idols and false gods. And of this *Word* it is likewise said, that *he was with God*, and *was God*. These words seem very plain, and the place where they are put by St. John, in the front of his Gospel, as it were an inscription upon it, or an introduction to it, makes it very evident, that he, who of all the writers of the New Testament has the greatest plainness and simplicity of style, would not have put words here, such as were not to be understood in a plain and literal signification, without any key to lead us to any other sense of them. This had been to lay a stone of stumbling in the very threshold; particularly to the Jews, who were apt to cavil at Christianity, and were particularly jealous of every thing that savoured of idolatry, or of the plurality of gods. And upon this occasion

---

* For a full and critical examination of this passage, see Pearson on the Creed, page 177, Dobson's Edition.

I desire one thing to be observed, with relation to all those ART.
subtile expositions which those who oppose this doctrine put II.
upon many of those places by which we prove it; that they
represent the apostles as magnifying Christ in words that at
first sound seem to import his being the true God; and yet
they hold that in all these they had another sense, and a reserve of some other interpretation, of which their words were
capable. But can this be thought fair dealing? Does it look
like honest men to write thus; not to say, men inspired in
what they preached and writ? and not rather like impostors,
to use so many sublime and lofty expressions concerning
Christ as God, if all these must be taken down to so low a
sense, as to signify only that he was miraculously formed, and
endued with an extraordinary power of miracles, and an
authority to deliver a new religion to the world; and that he
was, in consideration of his exemplary death which he underwent so patiently, raised up from the grave, and had divine
honours conferred upon him. In such an hypothesis as this,
the world going in so naturally to the excessive magnifying,
and even the deifying of wonderful men, it had been necessary
to have prevented any such mistakes, and to have guarded
against the belief of them rather than to have used a continued
strain of expressions, that seem to carry men violently into
them, and that can hardly, nay very hardly, be softened by all
the skill of critics, to bear any other sense. It is to be considered farther, that, when St. John writ his Gospel, there
were three sorts of men particularly to be considered. The
Jews, who could bear nothing that savoured of idolatry; so
no stumbling-block was to be laid in their way, to give them
deeper prejudices against Christianity. Next to these were
the Gentiles; who, having worshipped a variety of gods, were
not to be indulged in any thing that might seem to favour their
polytheism. In fact, we find particular caution used, in the
New Testament, against the worshipping angels or saints. Matt. iv.
How can it therefore be imagined, that words would have been 10. Colos.
used, that, in the plain signification that did arise out of the Acts x. 25.
first hearing of them, imported that a man was God, if this 26. xiv. 14,
had not been strictly true? The apostles ought, and must, 15. Rev.
have used a particular care to have avoided all such expres- xxii. 8, 9.
sions, if they had not been literally true. The third sort of
men in St. John's time were those, of whom intimation is
frequently given through all the Epistles, who were then
endeavouring to corrupt the purity of the Christian doctrine,
and to accommodate it so, both to the Jew and to the Gentile, as to avoid the cross and persecution upon the account
of it. Church-history, and the earliest writers after St. John,
assure us, that Ebion* and Cerinthus* denied the divinity of

---

* Whence the Ebionites derived their name is uncertain. According to some
they were so called from the founder of their sect, Ebion. Eusebius states that
they were "called Ebionites, *i. e.* poor men, for they were poor and abject, in

Christ, and asserted that he was a mere man. Controversy naturally carries men to speak exactly; and, among human writers, those who let things fall more carelessly from their pens, when they apprehend no danger or difficulty, are more correct both in their thoughts and in their expressions, when things are disputed; therefore, if we should have no other regard to St. John, but as an ordinary, cautious, and careful man, we must believe that he weighed all his words in that point, which was then the matter in question; and to clear which, we have good ground to believe, both from the testimony of ancient writers, and from the method that he pursues quite through it all, that he writ his Gospel; and that, therefore, every part of it, but this beginning of it more signally, was writ, and is to be understood, in the sense which the words naturally import; that the *Word which took flesh*, and assumed the human nature, had a being *before the worlds were made*, and that this *Word was God*, and *made the world*.

Another eminent proof of this is in St. Paul's Epistle to the Philippians; in which, when he is exhorting Christians to humility, he gives an argument for it from our Saviour's example. He begins with the dignity of his person, expressed thus; 'that he was in the form of God, and that he thought it no robbery to be equal with God:' then his humi-

---

delivering the doctrine concerning Christ.' They judged him 'a simple and a common man; and for his forwardness of manners found justified only as man, and born of Mary and her husband.' They thought that the observance of the law was necessary, ' as though salvation were not by faith alone in Christ, and corresponding conversation of life.' Others of the same name, according to Eusebius, avoided the absurdity of their speeches; not denying the Lord to have been born of the Virgin, and the Holy Ghost; yet, when called on to confess him to be God, the Word and Wisdom before his incarnation, they fell into the same sin with their companions. They contended for the 'corporal observation of the law;' rejected the epistles of the apostle Paul, and accused him of having fallen from the law. They used a gospel of their own, indiscriminately called the gospel of the Nazarines or Hebrews, about which there have been many disputes amongst the learned. They observed the Jewish Sabbaths and other ceremonies, only they observed *Sunday*, in like manner as the Christians, in remembrance of the resurrection of Christ. They are generally placed among the heretics of the apostolic age; 'yet (remarks Dr. Mosheim) they really belong to the second century, which was the earliest period of their existence as a sect.'

Cerinthus was a Jew, who attempted to form a new system, by a combination of the doctrines of Christ with the opinions and errors of the Jews and Gnostics. He taught the necessity of circumcision, and that the Prophets and law were given by angels, and that the world was made by them. He maintained that Jesus was not born of a virgin, which he affirmed to be impossible, but of Mary and Joseph—that Jesus was not Christ, but that Christ came upon him in the form of a dove—that Jesus suffered and rose again, but not Christ; for Christ, he said, fled away from him before his passion. He taught that the kingdom of Christ should become earthly —that after the resurrection, Christ should reign over us on earth one thousand years. He lusted, saith Eusebius, after the satisfying of the belly with meat, drink, and marriage; to which he added, holy days, oblations, and slaughter for sacrifices. Such was the millenium which he held out to his followers. Irenæus relates, on the authority of Polycarp, that St. John having gone to a public bath, and hearing that Cerinthus was there, returned hastily, saying, ' Let us speedily go hence, lest the bath come to ruin, wherein Cerinthus, the enemy of the truth, batheth himself.' ' So zealous (remarks Eusebius) were the apostles and their disciples, that they communicated not even in word with the corrupters of the truth.'—[ED.]

liation comes, that he 'made himself of no reputation, but took on him the form of a servant,' (the same word with that used in the former verse:) after which follows his exaltation, and a *name* or authority *above every name* or authority is said to be given him; so that 'all in heaven, earth, and under the earth (which seems to import angels, men, and devils), should bow at his name, and confess that he is the Lord.' Now, in this progress that is made in these words, it is plain that the dignity of Christ's person is represented as antecedent both to his humiliation and to his exaltation. It was that which put the value on his humiliation, as his humiliation was rewarded by his exaltation. This dignity is expressed first, that he was in *the form of God*, before he humbled himself: he was certainly in the *form of a servant*, that is, really a servant, as other servants are; he was obedient to his parents, he was under the authority both of the Romans, of Herod, and of the sanhedrim: therefore since his being really a servant is expressed by his being in *the form of a servant*, his being in *the form of God* must also import that he was truly *God*. But the following words, that *he thought it not robbery to be equal*, or *be held equal* (for so the word may be rendered) *with God*, carry such a natural signification of his being neither a made nor subordinate *God*, and that his divinity is neither precarious nor by concession, that fuller words cannot be devised for expressing an entire equality. Those who deny this are aware of it, and therefore they have put another sense on the words, *in the form of God*. They think, that they signify his appearing in the world, as one sent in the name of God, representing him, working miracles, and delivering a law in his name: and the words rendered, *he thought it no robbery*, they render, he did not *catch at*, or *vehemently desire to be held in equal honour with God*. And some authorities are found, in eloquent Greek authors, who use the words rendered, *he thought it not robbery*, in a figurative sense, for the earnestness of desire, or the pursuing after a thing greedily, as robbers do for their prey. This rendering represents St. Paul as treating so sacred a point in the figures of a high and seldom used rhetoric, which, one would think, ought to have been expressed more exactly. But, if even this sense is allowed, it will make a strange period, and a very odd sort of an argument, to enforce humility upon us, because Christ, though working miracles, did not desire, or snatch at, divine adorations, in an equality with God. The sin of Lucifer, and the cause of his fall, is commonly believed to be his desire to be equal to God; and yet this seems to be such an extravagant piece of pride, that it is scarce possible to think that even the sublimest of created beings should be capable of it. To be next to God seems to be the utmost height to which even the diabolical pride could aspire: so that here, by the sense which the Socinians put on those words, they will import,

ART.
II.

that we are persuaded to be humble from the example of Christ, who did not affect an equality with God! the bare repeating of this seems so fully to expose and overthrow it, that I think it is not necessary to say more upon this place.

The next head of proof is made up of more particulars. All the names, the operations, and even the attributes, of God, are in full and plain words given to Christ. He is called God; his blood is said to be *the blood of God; God is said to have laid down his life for us;* Christ is called the *true God,* the *great God,* the *Lord of glory,* the *King of kings,* and *the Lord of lords;* and, more particularly, the name Jehovah is ascribed to him in the same word in which the LXX interpreters had translated it throughout the whole Old Testament. So that this constant uniformity of style between the Greek of the New, and that translation of the Old Testament which was then received, and was of great authority among the Jews, and was yet of more authority among the first Christians, is an argument that carries such a weight with it, that this alone may serve to determine the matter. The creating, the preserving, and the governing, of all things, is also ascribed to Christ in a variety of places, but most remarkably, when it is said, that 'by him were all created, that are in heaven and that are in earth, visible and invisible, whether they be thrones, or dominions, or principalities, or powers: all things were created by him, and for him: and he is before all things, and by him all things consist.' He is said to have 'known what was in man, to have known men's secret thoughts, and to have known all things:' that 'as the Father was known of none but of the Son, so none knew the Son but the Father.' He ' pardons sin, sends the Spirit, gives grace and eternal life, and he shall raise the dead at the last day.' When all these things are laid together in that variety of expressions, in which they lie scattered in the New Testament, it is not possible to retain any reverence for those books, if we imagine that they are writ in a style so full of approaches to the deifying of a mere man, that, without a very critical studying of languages and phrases, it is not possible to understand them otherwise. Idolatry, and a plurality of gods, seem to be the main things that the scriptures warn us against; and yet here is a pursued thread of passages and discourses, that do naturally lead a man to think that Christ is the *true God,* who yet, according to these men, only acted in his name, and has now a high honour put on him by him.

Acts xx. 28.
1 John iii. 16.
1 John v. 20.
Tit. ii. 13.
Jam. ii. 1.
Rev. i. 8.
Rev. xix. 16.

Col. i. 16, 17.
John ii. 25.
Matt. xi. 27.
Matt. ix. 6.
John xv. 26.
John xiv. 13.
John v. 25, 26.
John vi. 39, 40.

This carries me to another argument to prove that the *Word* that was *made flesh* was truly God. Nothing but the true God can be the proper object of adoration. This is one of those truths that seems almost so evident, that it needs not to be proved. Adoration is the humble prostration of ourselves before God, in acts that own our dependence upon him, both for our being, and for all the blessings that we do either enjoy or hope for, and also in earnest prayers to him for the continuance of these to us. This is testified by such outward gestures and actions as are most proper to express our humility and submission to God: all this has so clear and so inseparable a relation to the only true God, as its proper object, that it is scarce possible to apprehend how it should be separated from him, and given to any other. And, as this seems evident from the nature of things, so it is not possible to imagine how any thing could have been prohibited in more express and positive, and in more frequently-repeated words, and longer reasonings, than the offering of divine worship, or any part of it, to creatures. The chief design of the Mosaical religion was to banish all idolatry and polytheism out of the minds of the Jews, and to possess them with the idea of one God, and of one object of worship. The reasons upon which those prohibitions are founded are universal; which are, the unity of God's essence, and his jealousy in not giving his honour to another. It is not said that they should not worship any as God, till they had a precept or declaration for it. There is no reserve for any such time; but they are plainly forbid to worship any but the great God, because he was one, and was jealous of his glory. The New Testament is writ in the same strain: Christ, when tempted of the Devil, answered, 'Thou shalt worship the Lord thy God, and him only shalt thou serve.' The apostles charged all idolaters 'to forsake those idols and to serve the living God.' The angel refused St. John's worship, commanding him to 'worship God'. The Christian faith does, in every particular, raise the ideas of God and of religion to a much greater purity and sublimity than the Mosaical dispensation had done; so it is not to be imagined, that in the chief design of revealed religion, which was the bringing men from idolatry to the worship of one God, it should make such a breach, and extend it to a creature. All this seems fully to prove the first proposition of this argument, that God is the only proper object of adoration. The next is, that Christ is proposed in the New Testament as the object of divine worship. I do not in proof of this urge the instances of those who fell down at Christ's feet and worshipped him, while he was on earth: for it may be well answered to that, that, a prophet was worshipped with the civil respect of falling down before him, among the Jews; as appears in the history of Elijah and Elisha: nor does it appear that those who worshipped Christ had any apprehension of his being God; they only considered him as the Messias, or as some eminent prophet. But the mention that St. Luke makes in his Gospel, of the disciples worshipping Christ at his ascension, comes more home to this matter. All those salutations in the beginning and conclusion of the Epistles, in which 'grace, mercy, and peace' are wished 'from God the Father, and the Lord Jesus Christ,' are implied invocations of him. It is also plain,

ART. II.

Matt. iv. 10.
Acts xiv. 15.
Acts xvii. 29.
1 Thess. i. 9.
Rev. xix. 10.

Luke xxiv. 52.

ART. II.

2 Cor. xii. 8, 9.
Phil. ii. 10.
Heb. i. 6.
Rev. v. 8.
to the end.

that it was to him that St. Paul *prayed,* when he was under the temptations of the Devil, as they are commonly understood; 'Every knee must bow to him: the angels of God worship him:' *all the hosts in heaven* are represented in St. John's visions as falling down prostrate before him, and worshipping him *as they worship the Father.* He is proposed as the object of our faith, hope, and love; as the Person whom we are to obey, to pray to, and to praise; so that every act of worship, both external and internal, is directed to him as to its proper object. But the instance of all others, that is the clearest in this point, is in the last words of St. Stephen, who was the first martyr, and whose martyrdom is so particularly related by St. Luke: he then in his last minutes saw Christ *at the right hand of God;* and in his last breath he worshipped him in two short prayers, that are, upon the matter, the same with those in which our blessed Saviour worshipped his Father

Acts vii. 59, 60.

on the cross; 'Lord Jesus, receive my spirit: Lord, lay not this sin to their charge.' From this it seems very evident, that, if Christ was not the true God, and equal to the Father, then this proto-martyr died in two acts that seem not only idolatrous, but also blasphemous; since he worshipped Christ in the same acts in which Christ had worshipped his Father. It is certain, from all this deduction of particulars, that his human nature cannot be worshipped; therefore there must be another nature in him, to which divine worship is due, and on the account of which he is to be worshipped.

It is plain, that when this religion was first published, together with these duties in it as a part of it, the Jews, though implacably set against it, yet never accused it of idolatry; though that charge, of all others, had served their purposes the best who intended to blacken and blast it. Nothing would have been so well heard, and so easily apprehended, as a just prejudice against it, as this. The argument would have appeared as strong as it was plain: and as the Jews could not be ignorant of the acts of the Christian worship, when so many fell back to them from it who were offended at other parts of it: so they had the books, in which it was contained, in their hands. Notwithstanding all which, we have all possible reason to believe that, this objection against it was never made by any of them, in the first age of Christianity: upon all which, I say, it is not to be imagined that they could have been silent on this head, if a mere man had been thus proposed among the Christians as the object of divine worship. The silence of the apostles, in not mentioning nor answering this, is such a proof of the silence of the Jews, that it would indeed disparage all their writings, if we could think, that, while they mentioned and answered the other prejudices of the Jews, which in comparison to this are small and inconsiderable matters, they should have passed over this, which must have been the greatest and the plausiblest of them all, if it was one at all. Therefore, as the silence of the apostles is a clear proof that the Jews were silent also, and did not object this; and since their silence could neither flow from their ignorance, nor their undervaluing of this religion; it seems to be certain, that the first opening of the Christian doctrine did not carry any thing in it that could be called the worshipping of a creature. It follows from hence, that the Jews must have understood this part of our religion in such a manner as agreed with their former ideas. So we must examine these: they had this settled among them, that God dwelt in the cloud of glory, and that, by virtue of that inhabitation, divine worship was paid to God as dwelling in the cloud; that it was called *God, God's Throne, his Holiness, his Face, and the Light of his Countenance*: they went up to the temple to worship God, as dwelling there *bodily*, that is substantially, so *bodily* sometimes signifies, or in a corporeal appearance. This seems to have been a Person that was truly God, and yet was distinct from that which appeared and spake to Moses; for this seems to be the importance of these words: 'Behold, I send an angel before thee to keep thee in the way, and to bring thee to the place which I have prepared: beware of him, and obey his voice, provoke him not; for he will not pardon your transgressions: for my name is in him.' These words do plainly import a person to whom they belong; and yet they are a pitch far above the angelical dignity. So that angel must here be understood, in a large sense, for one sent of God; and it can admit of no sense so properly, as, that the eternal Word, which dwelt afterwards in the man Christ Jesus, dwelt then in that cloud of glory. It was also one of the prophecies received by the Jews, 'that the glory of the second temple was to exceed the glory of the first.' The chief character of the glory of the first was that inhabitation of the divine presence among them; from hence it follows, that such an inhabitation of God in a creature, by which that creature was not only called God, but that adoration was due to it upon that account, was a notion that could not have scandalized the Jews, and was indeed the only notion that agreed with their former ideas, and that could have been received by them without difficulty or opposition. This is a strong inducement to believe that this great article of our religion was at that time delivered and understood in that sense.

If the *Son* or *Word* is truly God, he must be from all eternity, and must also be of the same substance with the Father, otherwise he could not be God; since a God of another substance, or of another duration, is a contradiction.

The last argument that I shall offer is taken from the beginning of the Epistle to the Hebrews: to the apprehending the force of which, this must be premised, that all those who acknowledge that Christ ought to be honoured and wor-

AN EXPOSITION OF

ART II.

shipped as the Father, must say that this is due to him either because he is truly God : or because he is a person of such a high and exalted dignity, that God has, upon the consideration of that, appointed him to be so worshipped. Now this second notion may fall under another distinction; that either he was of a very sublime order by nature, as some angelical being, that though he was created, yet had this high privilege bestowed upon him: or that he was a prophet illuminated and authorized in so particular a manner beyond all others, that, out of a regard to that, he was exalted to this honour of being to be worshipped. One of these must be chosen by all who do not believe him to be truly God: and indeed one of these was the Arian,* as the other is the Socinian,† hypo-

---

* Arius, a Presbyter of Alexandria, a 'man very skilful in the subtilties of sophistical logic,' and remarkable for his eloquence, arose in the beginning of the fourth century. He entered the field of controversy against his bishop, Alexander of Alexandria, who, in his discourses, treated the doctrine of the Trinity, and of the unity in the Trinity, 'somewhat too curiously.' Arius suspected Alexander of an intention to revive the heresy of Sabellius (who maintained that the three persons in the Trinity were one, but differed from his master Naetus in that Sabellius did not allege that the Father suffered), and opposed him with much zeal, and too much of the spirit of contention. His opposition led into the opposite extreme, and he laid down his doctrine thus:—' If the Father begat the Son, then had the Son, which was begotten, a beginning of essence; hereby it is maintained that there was a time when the Son was not, and consequently that he had his essence of nothing.' From this it appears that he separated the Son from the Father. He held the Son to be the highest of beings whom the Father had created, and by whom he made the worlds—consequently inferior to the Father, not only as touching his manhood, but also as to his godhead. The first general Council was summoned and assembled at Nice, in the year 325, in consequence of the manner in which this destructive heresy spread throughout the empire. At that famous council was this antichristian heresy condemned; and a creed drawn up, and afterwards at the Council of Constantinople adopted and enlarged, which is held by, and read in the communion service of, the Church of England. Arius was excommunicated, and died at Constantinople, according to the testimony of Socrates Scholasticus, a most wretched death.—[ED.]

† 'The Socinians are said to have derived this denomination from the illustrious family of the Sozzini, which flourished a long time at Sienna in Tuscany, and produced several great and eminent men, and among others Lælius and Faustus Socinus, who are commonly supposed to have been the founders of this sect. The former was the son of Marianus, a famous lawyer, and was himself a man of uncommon genius and learning ; to which he added, as his very enemies are obliged to acknowledge, the lustre of a virtuous life, and of unblemished manners. Being forced to leave his country, in the year 1547, on account of the disgust he had conceived against popery, he travelled through France, England, Holland, Germany, and Poland, in order to examine the religious sentiments of those who had thrown off the yoke of Rome, and thus at length to come at the truth. After this he settled at Zurich, where he died in the year 1562, before he had arrived at the fortieth year of his age. His mild and gentle disposition rendered him averse from whatever had the air of contention and discord. He adopted the Helvetic confession of faith, and professed himself a member of the church of Switzerland ; but this did not engage him to conceal entirely the doubts he had formed in relation to certain points of religion, and which he communicated, in effect, by letter, to some learned men, whose judgment he respected, and in whose friendship he could confide. His sentiments were indeed propagated, in a more public manner, after his death ; since Faustus, his nephew and his heir, is supposed to have drawn from the papers he left behind him that religious system upon which the sect of the Socinians was founded.

'It is, however, to be observed, that this denomination does not always convey the same idea, since it is susceptible of different significations, and is, in effect, used sometimes in a more strict and proper, and at others in a more improper and

thesis. For how much soever the Arians might exalt him in words, yet if they believed him to be a creature made in time, so that once he was not; all that they said of him can amount to no more, but that he was a creature of a spiritual nature; and this is plainly the notion which the scripture gives us of angels. Artemon, Samosatenus, Photinus, and the Socinians in our days, consider our Saviour as a great prophet and lawgiver, and into this they resolve his dignity. In opposition to both these, that Epistle begins with expressions that are the more severe, because they are negative, which are to be understood more strictly than positive words. Christ is not only preferred to angels, but is set in opposition to them, as one of another order of beings. 'Made so much better than angels, as he hath by inheritance obtained a more excellent name than they. For unto which of the angels said he at any time, Thou art my Son, this day have I begotten thee? When he bringeth in the first begotten into the world, he saith, And let all the angels of God worship him. Of the angels he saith, Who maketh his angels spirits, and his ministers a flame of fire. But unto the Son he saith, Thy throne, O God, is for ever and ever. And, Thou, Lord, in the beginning hast laid the foundation of the earth: and the heavens are the works of thy hands. Thou art the same, and thy years shall not fail. But to which of the angels said he at any time, Sit on my right hand, till I make thine enemies thy footstool? Are they not all ministering spirits, sent forth to minister for them who shall be heirs of salvation?'

ART. II.

Heb. i. 4,
5,
6,
7,
8,
10,
12,
13,
14.

---

extensive sense. For, according to the usual manner of speaking, all are termed Socinians whose sentiments bear a certain affinity to the system of Socinus; and they are more especially ranked in that class, who either boldly deny, or artfully explain away, the doctrines that assert the Divine nature of Christ, and a Trinity of persons in the Godhead. But, in a strict and proper sense, they only are deemed the members of this sect who embrace wholly, or with a few exceptions, the form of theological doctrine which Faustus Socinus either drew up himself, or received from his uncle, and delivered to the Unitarian brethren, or Socinians, in Poland and Transylvania.

'The sum of their theology is as follows:—"God, who is infinitely more perfect than man, though of a similar nature in some respects, exerted an act of that power by which he governs all things; in consequence of which an extraordinary person was born of the Virgin Mary. That person was Jesus Christ, whom God first translated to heaven by that portion of his divine power which is called the Holy Ghost; and having instructed him fully there in the knowledge of his will, counsels, and designs, sent him again into this sublunary world, to promulgate to mankind a new rule of life, more excellent than that under which they had formerly lived, to propagate divine truth by his ministry, and to confirm it by his death.

'"Those who obey the voice of this Divine Teacher (and this obedience is in the power of every one whose will and inclination leads that way), shall one day be clothed with new bodies, and inhabit eternally those blessed regions, where God himself immediately resides. Such, on the contrary, as are disobedient and rebellious shall undergo most terrible and exquisite torments, which shall be succeeded by annihilation, or the total extinction of their being."

'The whole system of Socinianism, when stripped of the embellishments and commentaries with which it has been loaded and disguised by its doctors, is really reducible to the few propositions now mentioned.' *Mosheim*.—[ED.]

ART. II.

Chap. ii. 16.

Chap. iii. 1.

This opposition is likewise carried on through the whole second chapter; one passage in it being most express to shew both that his nature had a subsistence before his incarnation, and that it was not of an angelical order of beings, since he 'took not on him the nature of angels, but the seed of Abraham.' Thus, in a great variety of expressions, the conceit of Christ's being of an angelical nature is very fully condemned. From that the writer goes next to the notion of his being to be honoured, because he was an eminent prophet; on which he enters with a very solemn preface, inviting them to 'consider the apostle and high-priest of our profession:' then he compares Moses to him, as to the point of being 'faithful to him who had appointed him.' But how eminent soever Moses was above all other prophets, and how harshly soever it must have sounded to the Jews to have stated the difference in terms so distant as that of a *servant* and a *son*, of *one who built the house*, and *of the house itself*; yet we see the apostle does not only prefer Christ to Moses, but puts him in another order and rank; which could not be done according to the Socinian hypothesis. From all which this conclusion naturally follows,—that if Christ is to be worshipped, and that this honour belongs to him neither as an angel, nor as a prophet, that then it is due to him because he is truly God.

The second branch of this article is, that he *took man's nature upon him in the womb of the blessed Virgin, and of her substance*. This will not need any long or laboured proof, since the texts of scripture are so express that nothing but wild extravagance can withstand them. Christ was in all things like unto us, except his miraculous conception by the Virgin: he was the son of Abraham and of David. But among the frantic humours that appeared at the Reformation, some, in opposition to the superstition of the church of Rome, studied to derogate as much from the blessed Virgin on the one hand, as she had been over-exalted on the other: so they said, that Christ had only gone through her. But this impiety sunk so soon, that it is needless to say any thing more to refute it.

The third branch of the Article is, that *these two natures were joined in one Person, never to be divided*. What a person is that results from a close conjunction of two natures, we can only judge of by considering man, in whom there is a material and a spiritual nature joined together. They are two natures as different as any we can apprehend among all created beings; yet these make but one man. The matter of which the body is composed does not subsist by itself, is not under all those laws of motion to which it would be subject, if it were mere inanimated matter; but, by the indwelling and actuation of the soul, it has another spring within it, and has another course of operations. According to this, then, to

THE XXXIX ARTICLES. 63

subsist by another is when a being is acting according to its ART. II.
natural properties, but yet in a constant dependance upon
another being; so our bodies subsist by the subsistence of
our souls. This may help us to apprehend how that as the
body is still a body, and operates as a body, though it subsists by the indwelling and actuation of the soul; so in the
person of Jesus Christ the human nature was entire, and still
acted according to its own character; yet there was such an
union and inhabitation of the eternal Word in it, that there did
arise out of that a communication of names and characters, as
we find in the scriptures. A man is called tall, fair, and
healthy, from the state of his body; and learned, wise, and
good, from the qualities of his mind: so Christ is called
holy, harmless, and undefiled; is said to have died, risen, and
ascended up into heaven, with relation to his human nature:
he is also said to be in 'the form of God, to have created all Phil. ii. 6.
things, to be the brightness of the Father's glory, and the Heb. i. 3.
express image of his person,' with relation to his divine
nature. The ideas that we have of what is material, and
what is spiritual, lead us to distinguish in a man those descriptions that belong to his body from those that belong to
his mind; so the different apprehensions that we have of
what is created and uncreated must be our thread to guide us
into the resolution of those various expressions that occur in
the scriptures concerning Christ.

The design of the definition, that was made by the church
concerning Christ's having one person, was chiefly to distinguish the nature of the *indwelling* of the Godhead in him
from all prophetical inspirations. The Mosaical degree of
prophecy was in many respects superior to that of all the
subsequent prophets: yet the difference is stated between
Christ and Moses, in terms that import things quite of another nature; the one being mentioned as a servant, the
other as the Son that built the house. It is not said that
God appeared to Christ, or that he spoke to him; but God
was ever with him, and in him; and while 'the Word was John i. 14.
made flesh,' yet still 'his glory was as the glory of the only- Isai. vi. 1,
begotten Son of God.' The glory that Isaiah saw, was called John xii.
his glory; and on the other hand, God is said to have pur- 41.
chased his church with his own blood. If Nestorius,* in Acts xx. 28.

---

* Nestorius, a man of some learning and much eloquence, but of a very arrogant and overbearing disposition, was a native of Germany, and a Presbyter of Antioch. On the death of Sisinius, bishop of Constantinople, he was sent for by the emperor Theodosius, and appointed to that see. He so persecuted the Arians, that they destroyed by fire their own churches, rather than suffer them to fall into his hands. But although so zealous against heresy and heretics, yet he does not appear to have been much influenced by the truth which he professed to uphold. He brought with him from Antioch a certain Presbyter, named Anastasius, who declaimed much against the use of the term θεοτοκος as applied to the Virgin Mary, and contended that she ought to be called the Mother of Christ, and not the Mother of God. Nestorius warmly espoused the cause of Anastasius; and was accused of maintaining that in Christ the divine was superadded to the human

opposing this, meant only, as some think it appears by many citations out of him, that the blessed Virgin was not to be called simply *the Mother of God,* but *the Mother of him that was God;* and if that of making two persons in Christ was only fastened on him as a consequence, we are not at all concerned in the matter of fact, whether Nestorius was misunderstood and hardly used, or not; but the doctrine here asserted is plain in the scriptures, that, though the human nature in Christ acted still according to its proper character, and had a peculiar will, yet, there was such a constant presence, indwelling, and actuation on it from the eternal *Word,* as did constitute both human and divine nature one *Person.* As these are thus so entirely united, so they are never to be separated. Christ is now exalted to the highest degrees of glory and honour; and the characters of *blessing, honour,* and *glory,* are represented, in St. John's visions, as offered 'to the Lamb for ever and ever.' It is true, St. Paul speaks as if Christ's mediatory office and kingdom were to cease after the day of judgment, and that then he was to deliver up all to the Father. For though, when the full number of the elect shall be gathered, the full end of his death will be attained; and when these saints shall be glorified with him and by him, his office as Mediator will naturally come to an end; yet his own personal glory shall never cease: and if every saint shall inherit an everlasting kingdom, much more shall he who has merited all that to them, and has conferred it on them, be for ever possessed of his glory.

The fourth branch of the Article is concerning the truth of Christ's crucifixion, his death and burial. The matter of fact concerning the death of Christ is denied by no Christian; the Jews do all acknowledge it; the first enemies to Christianity did all believe this, and reproached his followers with it. This was that which all Christians gloried in and avowed; so that no question was made of his death, except by a small number called *Docetæ,* who were not esteemed Christians, till Mahomet denied it in his Alcoran, who pretends that he was withdrawn, and that a Jew was crucified in his stead. But this corruption of the history of the gospel came too late afterwards, to have any shadow of credit due to it; nor was there any sort of proof offered to support it. So this

---

nature. He was cited before the third general Council held at Ephesus, A.D. 431, or, according to some, 434. Here, writes Socrates, he spoke as follows:—'I verily will not consent to call him God who grew to man's estate by two months, and three months, and so forth: therefore I wash my hands from your blood; and from henceforth I will no more come into your company.' When he saw the consequences of this speech in the disorder which such sentiments created, he made a recantation, which, not being considered sincere, was not received. He was therefore condemned, deposed, and banished, by order of the council, which decreed—'That Christ was one divine person, in whom two natures were most closely and intimately united, but without being mixed or confounded together.' Nestorius died in Oasis, the place of his banishment, and after his death his followers divided into different parties.—[ED.]

doctrine concerning the death of Christ is to be received as an unquestionable truth. There is no part of the gospel writ with so copious a particularity, as the history of his sufferings and death; as there was indeed no part of the gospel so important as this is.

ART. II.

The fifth branch of the Article is, that he was a *true sacrifice to reconcile the Father to us, and that not only for original, but for actual sins.* The notion of an expiatory sacrifice, which was then, when the New Testament was writ, well understood all the world over, both by Jew and Gentile, was this, that the sin of one person was transferred on a man or beast, who was upon that devoted and offered up to God, and suffered in the room of the offending person; and by this oblation, the punishment of the sin being laid on the sacrifice, an expiation was made for sin, and the sinner was believed to be reconciled to God.* This, as appears through the whole book of Leviticus, was the design and effect of the *sin* and *tresspass offerings* among the Jews, and more particularly of the goat that was offered up for the sins of the whole people on the day of atonement. This was a piece of religion well known both to Jew and Gentile, that had a great many phrases belonging to it, such as the sacrifices being offered *for*, or *instead* of, *sin*, and *in the name*, or on the account, of the sinner; *its bearing of* sin, and *becoming* sin, or the *sin-offering*; its being the *reconciliation*, the *atonement*, and the *redemption*, of the sinner, by which the sin was no more *imputed*, but *forgiven*, and for

Levit. xvi.

---

* 'Of the several sacrifices under the law, that one, which seems most exactly to illustrate the sacrifice of Christ, and which is expressly compared with it by the writer to the Hebrews, is that which was offered for the whole assembly on the solemn anniversary of expiation. The circumstances of this ceremony, whereby atonement was to be made for the sins of the whole Jewish people, seem so strikingly significant, that they deserve a particular detail. On the day appointed for this general expiation, the priest is commanded to offer a bullock and a goat, as sin-offerings, the one for himself, and the other for the people: and, having sprinkled the blood of these in due form before the mercy-seat, to lead forth a second goat, denominated the scape-goat: and, after laying both his hands upon the head of the scape-goat, and confessing over him all the iniquities of the people, *to put them upon the head of the goat*, and to send the animal thus bearing the sins of the people away into the wilderness: in this manner expressing, by an action which cannot be misunderstood, that the atonement, which it is directly affirmed was to be effected by the sacrifice of the sin-offering, consisted in removing from the people their iniquities by a symbolical translation to the animal. For it is to be remarked, that the ceremony of the scape-goat is not a *distinct* one; it is the continuation of the process, and is evidently the concluding part, and symbolical consummation, of the sin-offering. So that the transfer of the iniquities of the people upon the head of the scape-goat, and the bearing them away to the wilderness, manifestly imply, that the atonement effected by the sacrifice of the sin-offering consisted in the transfer and consequent removal of those iniquities. What, then, are we taught to infer from this ceremony?—That, as the atonement under the law, or expiation of the legal transgressions, was represented as a translation of those transgressions, in the act of sacrifice in which the animal was slain, and the people thereby cleansed from their legal impurities, and released from the penalties which had been incurred; so, the great atonement for the sins of mankind was to be effected by the sacrifice of Christ, undergoing, for the restoration of men to the favour of God, that death, which had been denounced against sin; and which he suffered in like manner as if the sins of men had been *actually* transferred to him, as those of the congregation had been *symbolically* transferred to the sin-offering of the people.' *Magee.*—[Ed.]

F

ART.
II.

which the sinner was *accepted*. When therefore this whole set of phrases, in its utmost extent, is very often, and in a great variety, applied to the death of Christ, it is not possible for us to preserve any reverence for the New Testament, or the writers of it, so far as to think them even honest men, not to say inspired men, if we can imagine, that in so sacred and important a matter they could exceed so much as to represent that to be our sacrifice which is not truly so: this is a point which will not bear figures and amplifications; it must be treated of strictly, and with a just exactness of expression. Christ is called the

John i. 29.
1 Pet. ii. 24.
2 Cor. v. 21.
Matt. xx. 28.
Rom. iii. 25.
1 John ii. 2.
Eph. i. 7.
Col. i. 14, 20, 21, 22.
Heb. ix. 11, 12, 13, 14.
Heb. ix. 26, 28.
Heb. x. 10, 12, 14, 19, 29.
Heb. xiii. 12, 20.

'Lamb of God that taketh away the sins of the world;' he is said 'to have borne our sins in his own body; to have been made sin for us;' it is said, that 'he gave his life a ransom for many;' that 'he was the propitiation for the sins of the whole world;' and that 'we have redemption through his blood, even the remission of our sins.' It is said, that 'he hath reconciled us to his Father in his cross, and in the body of his flesh through death:' that he by 'his own blood entered in once into the holy place, having obtained eternal redemption for us:' that 'once in the end of the world hath he appeared to put away sin, by the sacrifice of himself:' that 'he was once offered to bear the sins of many:' that 'we are sanctified by the offering of the body of Christ once for all:' and that, 'after he had offered one sacrifice for sin, he sat down for ever on the right hand of God.' It is said, that 'we enter into the holiest by the blood of Christ, that is the blood of the new covenant, by which we are sanctified:' that 'he hath sanctified the people with his own blood: and was the great shepherd of his people, through the blood of the

1 Pet. i.19.
1 Pet. ii. 24.
1 Pet. iii. 18.

everlasting covenant:' that 'we are redeemed with the precious blood of Christ, as of a lamb without blemish and without spot;' and, that 'Christ suffered once for sins, the just for the unjust, that he might bring us to God.' In these, and in a great many more passages that lie spread in all the parts of the New Testament, it is as plain, as words can make any thing, that the death of Christ is proposed to us as our sacrifice and reconciliation, our atonement and redemption. So it is not possible for any man that considers all this, to imagine, that Christ's death was only a confirmation of his gospel, a pattern of a holy and patient suffering of death, and a necessary preparation to his resurrection; by which he gave us a clear proof of a resurrection, and by consequence of eternal life, as by his doctrine he had shewed us the way to it. By this all the high commendations of his death amount only to this, that he by dying has given a vast credit and authority to his gospel, which was the powerfullest mean possible to redeem us from sin, and to reconcile us to God: but this is so contrary to the whole design of the New Testament, and to the true importance of that great variety of phrases, in which this matter is set out, that, at this rate of expounding scripture, we can never know what we may build upon, especially when the great importance of this thing, and of our having right notions concerning it, is well considered. St. Paul does, in his Epistle to the Romans, state an opposition between the death of Christ, and the sin of Adam; the ill effects of the one being removed by the other: but he plainly carries the death of Christ much farther than that it had only healed the wound that was given by Adam's sin; 'for as the judgment was of one (sin) to condemnation, the free gift is of many offences to justification.' But, in the other places of the New Testament, Christ's death is set forth so fully, as a propitiation for the sins of the whole world, that it is a very false way of arguing to infer, that because in one place that is set in opposition to Adam's sin, that therefore the virtue of it was to go no farther than to take away that sin. It has indeed removed that, but it has done a great deal more besides.

ART. II.

Rom. v. 12, to the end.

Thus it is plain that Christ's death was our sacrifice: the meaning of which is this; that God, intending to reconcile the world to himself, and to encourage sinners to repent and turn to him, thought fit to offer the pardon of sin, together with the other blessings of his gospel, in such a way as should demonstrate both the guilt of sin, and his hatred of it; and yet with that, his love of sinners, and his compassions towards them. A free pardon without a sacrifice had not been so agreeable neither to the majesty of the great Governor of the world, nor the authority of his laws, nor so proper a method to oblige men to that strictness and holiness of life that he designed to bring them to: and therefore he thought fit to offer his pardon, and those other blessings, through a Mediator, who was to deliver to the world this new and holy rule of life, and to confirm it by his own unblemished life: and in conclusion, when the rage of wicked men, who hated him for the holiness both of his life and of his doctrine, did work them up into such a fury as to pursue him to a most violent and ignominious death, he, in compliance with the secret design of his Father, did not only go through that dismal series of sufferings, with the most entire resignation to his Father's will, and with the highest charity possible towards those who were his most unjust and malicious murderers; but he at the same time underwent great agonies in his mind; which struck him with such an amazement and sorrow even to the death, that upon it he did sweat great drops of blood, and on the cross he felt a withdrawing of those comforts, that till then had ever supported him, when he cried out, 'My God, my God, why hast thou forsaken me?' It is not easy for us to apprehend in what that agony consisted: for we understand only the agonies of pain, or of conscience, which last arise out of the horror of guilt, or the apprehension of the wrath of God. It is indeed certain, that he who had no sin could have no such horror in him; and yet it is as certain, that he could not be

Isai. liii. 10.
Acts ii. 23.
Rev. xiii. 8.

F 2

ART. II.

put into such an agony only through the apprehension and fear of that violent death, which he was to suffer next day: therefore we ought to conclude, that there was an inward suffering in his mind, as well as an outward visible one in his body. We cannot distinctly apprehend what that was, since he was sure both of his own spotless innocence, and of his Father's unchangeable love to him. We can only imagine a vast sense of the heinousness of sin, and a deep indignation at the dishonour done to God by it, a melting apprehension of the corruption and miseries of mankind by reason of sin, together with a never-before-felt withdrawing of those consolations that had always filled his soul. But what might be farther in his agony, and in his last dereliction, we cannot distinctly apprehend; only this we perceive, that our minds are capable of great pain as well as our bodies are. Deep horror, with an inconsolable sharpness of thought, is a very intolerable thing. Notwithstanding the bodily or substantial indwelling of the fulness of the Godhead in him, yet he was capable of feeling vast pain in his *body*: so that he might become a complete sacrifice, and that we might have from his sufferings a very full and amazing apprehension of the guilt of sin; all those emanations of joy, with which the indwelling of the *eternal Word* had ever till then filled his soul, might then, when he needed them most, be quite withdrawn, and he be left merely to the firmness of his faith, to his patient resignation to the will of his heavenly Father, and to his willing readiness of drinking up that cup which his Father had put in his hand to drink.

There remains but one thing to be remembered here, though it will come to be more specially explained, when other Articles are to be opened; which is, that this reconciliation, which is made by the death of Christ, between God and man, is not absolute and without conditions. He has established the covenant, and has performed all that was incumbent on him, as both the priest and the sacrifice, to do and to suffer; and he offers this to the world, that it may be closed with by them, on the terms on which it is proposed; and if they do not accept of it upon these conditions, and perform what is enjoined them, they can have no share in it.

ARTICLE III.

Of the going down of Christ into Hell.

As Christ died for us and was buried, so also is it to be believed that he went down into Hell.

This was much fuller when the Articles were at first prepared and published in king Edward's reign; for these words were added to it, 'That the body of Christ lay in the grave until his resurrection; but his spirit, which he gave up, was with the spirits which were detained in prison, or in hell, and preached to them, as the place in St. Peter testifieth.' Thus a determined sense was put upon this Article, which is now left more at large, and is conceived in words of a more general signification. In order to the explaining this, it is to be premised, that the article in the Creed, of Christ's *descent into hell*, is mentioned by no writer before Ruffin,* who in the beginning of the fifth century does indeed speak of it: but he tells us, that it was neither in the symbol of the Roman, nor of the Oriental churches; and that he found it in the symbol of his own church at Aquileia. But as there was no other article in that symbol that related to Christ's burial, so the words which he gives us, *descendit ad inferna*, 'he descended to the lower parts,' do very naturally signify *burial*, according to these words of St. Paul, 'he ascended; what is it, but that he also descended first to the lower parts of the earth?' And Ruffin himself understood these words in that sense. Eph. iv. 9.

None of the fathers in the first ages, neither Irenæus, Tertullian, Clemens, nor Origen, in the short abstracts that they give us of the Christian faith, mention any thing like this and in all that great variety of Creeds, that was proposed by the many councils that met in the fourth century, this is not in any one of them, except in that which was agreed to at Arimini, and was pretended, though falsely, to have been made at Sirmium: in that it is set down in a Greek word that does exactly answer Ruffin's *inferna*, καταχθόνια: and it stood there instead of *buried*. When it was put in the Creed that carries Athanasius's name, though made in the sixth or seventh century, the word was changed to Ἅιδης, or Hell: but yet it seems to have been understood to signify Christ's burial, there

---

* 'Ruffinus, a Presbyter of Aquileia, is famous on account of his Latin translations of Origen, and other Greek writers—his commentaries on several passages of the Holy Scriptures, and his bitter contest with Jerome. He would have obtained a very honourable place among the Latin writers of this century (the 4th), had it not been his misfortune to have had the powerful and foul-mouthed Jerome for his adversary.'—*Mosheim.* Ruffinus first published the Apostles' creed, as the creed of the church of Aquileia.—[Ed.]

being no other word put for it in that Creed. Afterwards it was put into the symbol of the western church: that was done at first in the words in which Ruffin had expressed it, as appears by some ancient copies of Creeds which were published by the great primate Usher.

We are next to consider what the importance of these words in themselves is; for it is plain that the use of them in the Creed is not very ancient nor universal. We have a most unquestionable authority for this, that our Saviour's *soul was in hell*. In the Acts of the Apostles, St. Peter, in the first sermon that was preached after the wonderful effusion of the Spirit at Pentecost, applies these words of David concerning 'God's not leaving his soul in hell, nor suffering his Holy One to see corruption,' to the resurrection of Christ. Now since, in the composition of a man, there is a body and a spirit, and since it is plain that the raising of Christ on the third day was before that his body in the course of nature was corrupted; the other branch seems to relate to his *soul;* though it is not to be denied, but that in the Old Testament *soul* in some places stands for a *dead body*. But if that were the sense of the word, there would be no opposition in the two parts of this period; the one will be only a redundant repetition of the other: therefore it is much more natural to think that this other branch concerning Christ's soul being left in *hell*, must relate to that which we commonly understand by soul. If then his *soul was not to be left in hell,* then from thence it plainly follows that once it was in *hell,* and, by consequence, that Christ's soul descended into *hell.*

Some very modern writers have thought that this is to be understood figuratively of the wrath of God due for sin, which Christ bore in his soul, besides the torments that he suffered in his body: and they think that these are here mentioned by themselves, after the enumeration of the several steps of his bodily sufferings: and this being equal to the torments of *hell*, as it is that which delivers us from them, might in a large way of expression be called *a descending into hell*. But as neither the word *descend,* nor *hell,* are to be found in any other place of scripture in this sense, nor in any of the ancients, among whom the signification of this phrase is more likely to be found than among moderns; so this being put after *buried,* it plainly shews that it belongs to a period subsequent to his burial: there is therefore no regard to be had to this notion.

Others have thought, that by Christ's *descent into hell* is to be understood his continuing in the state of the dead for some time: but there is no ground for this conceit neither, these words being to be found in no author in that signification.

Many of the fathers thought, that Christ's soul went locally into *hell*, and preached to some of the *spirits* there in *prison;* that there he *triumphed over Satan,* and *spoiled him,* and carried some souls with him into glory. But the account that the scriptures give us of the exaltation of Christ begins it always at his resurrection: nor can it be imagined, that so memorable a transaction as this would have been passed over by the three first evangelists, and least of all by St. John, who coming after the rest, and designing to supply what was wanting in them, and intending particularly to magnify the glory of Christ, could not have passed over so wonderful an instance of it. We have no reason to think, that such a matter would have been only insinuated in general words, and not have been plainly related. The triumph of Christ over principalities and powers is ascribed by St. Paul to his cross, and was the effect and result of his death. The place of St. Peter seems to relate to the preaching to the *Gentile* world, by virtue of that inspiration that was derived from Christ; which was therefore called *his Spirit;* and the *spirits in prison* were the *Gentiles*, who were shut up in idolatry as *in prison*, and so were under the power of the 'prince of the power of the air,' who is called 'the god of this world;' that is, of the *Gentile* world: it being one of the ends for which Christ was anointed of his Father, 'to open the prisons to them that were bound.' So then, though there is no harm in this opinion, yet it not being founded on any part of the history of the gospel, and it being supported only by passages that may well bear another sense, we may lay it aside, notwithstanding the reverence we bear to those that asserted it; and that the rather, because the first fathers that were next the source say nothing of it.

ART. III.

Col. ii. 14, 15.

Eph. ii. 2. 2 Cor. iv. 4. Is. lxi. 1.

Another conceit has had a great course among some of the latest fathers and the schoolmen: they have fancied that there was a place to which they have given a peculiar name, *Limbus Patrum*, a sort of a partition in hell, where all the good men of the old dispensation, that had died before Christ, were detained; and they hold that our Saviour went thither, and emptied that place, carrying all the souls that were in it with him to heaven. Of this the scriptures say nothing; not a word either of the patriarchs going thither, or of Christ's delivering them out of it: and though there are not in the Old Testament express declarations and promises made concerning a future state, 'Christ having brought life and immortality to light through his gospel;' yet all the hints given of it shew that they looked for an immediate admission to blessedness after death. So David, 'Thou wilt shew me the path of life: in thy presence is fulness of joy, and at thy right hand are pleasures for evermore. Thou shalt guide me here by thy counsel, and afterwards receive me to glory.' Isaiah says, that 'the righteous when they die enter into peace.' In the New Testament there is not a hint given of this; for though some passages may seem to favour Christ's delivering some souls out of *hell*, yet there is nothing that by any management can be brought to look this way.

Ps. xvi. 11. Acts ii. 31. Ps. lxxiii. 24. Is. lvii. 2.

There is another sense of which these words [*descended into*

ART. III.

See Bishop Pearson on the Creed.

Luke xxiii. 43, 46.

hell] are capable: by *hell* may be meant the invisible place to which departed souls are carried after death: for, though the Greek word so rendered does now commonly stand for the place of the damned, and for many ages has been so understood, yet, at the time of writing the New Testament, it was among Greek authors used indifferently for the place of all departed souls, whether good or bad; and by it were meant the invisible regions where those spirits were lodged: so, if these words are taken in this large sense, we have in them a clear and literal account of our Saviour's *soul* descending into *hell;* it imports that he was not only dead in a more common acceptation, as it is usual to say a man is dead, when there appear no signs of life in him; and that he was not as in a deep ecstasy or fit that seemed death, but that he was truly dead; that his soul was neither in his body, nor hovering about it, ascending and descending upon it, as some of the Jews fancied souls did for some time after death; but that his soul was really removed out of his body, and carried to those unseen regions of departed spirits, among whom it continued till his resurrection. That the regions of the blessed were known then to the Jews by the name of *Paradise*, as hell was known by the name of *Gehenna*, is very clear from Christ's last words, 'To-day thou shalt be with me in Paradise;' and 'Into thy hands do I commend my spirit.' This is a plain and full account of a good sense that may be well put on the words; though, after all, it is still to be remembered, that, in the first Creeds that have this article, that of Christ's burial not being mentioned in them, it follows from thence, as well as from Ruffin's own sense of it, that they understood this only of Christ's burial.

ARTICLE IV.

Of the Resurrection of Christ.

Christ did truly rise again from Death, and took again his Body, with Flesh, Bones, and all things appertaining to the Perfection of Man's Nature, wherewith he ascended into Heaven, and there sitteth, until he return to judge all Men at the Last Day.

THERE are four branches of this Article: the first is concerning the truth of Christ's resurrection. The second concerning the completeness of it: that he took to him again his whole body. The third is concerning his ascension and continuance in heaven. And the fourth is concerning his returning to judge all men at the last day. These things are all so expressly affirmed, and that in so particular a manner, in the New Testament, that if the authority of that book is once well proved, little doubting will remain concerning them.

It is punctually told in it, that the body of Christ was laid in the sepulchre: that a stone was laid to the mouth of it: that it was rolled away, and upon that Christ arose and left the death-clothes behind him: that those who viewed the sepulchre, saw no body there: that in the same body Christ shewed himself to his disciples, so that they all knew him; he talked with them, and they did eat and drink with him, and he made Thomas feel to the print of the nails and spear. It is as plainly told, that the apostles looked on, and saw him ascend up to heaven, and that a cloud received him out of their sight. It is also said very plainly, that he shall come again at the last day, and judge all men both the quick and the dead. So that if the truth of the gospel is once fully proved, it will not be necessary to insist long upon the special proof of these particulars: somewhat will only be necessary to be said in explanation of them.

The gospel was first preached, and soon after put in writing; in which these particulars are not only delivered, but are set forth with many circumstances relating to them. The credit of the whole is put on that issue concerning the truth of Christ's resurrection; so that the overthrowing the truth of that was the overturning the whole gospel, and struck at the credit of it all. This was transacted as well as first published at Jerusalem, where the enemies of it had all possible advantages in their hands; their interest was deeply concerned, as well as their malice was much kindled at it. They had both power and wealth in their hands, as well as credit and authority among the people. The Romans left them at full liberty,

ART. IV.

as they did the other nations whom they conquered, to order their own concerns as they pleased. And even the Romans themselves began quickly to hate and persecute the Christians: they became the objects of popular fury, as Tacitus tells us. The Romans looked upon Christ as one that set on the Jews to those tumults that were then so common among them, as Suetonius affirms: which shews both how ignorant they were of the doctrine of Christ, and how much they were prejudiced against it. Yet this gospel did spread itself, and was believed by great multitudes both at Jerusalem and in all Judea; and from thence it was propagated in a very few years to a great many remote countries.

Among all Christians the article of the resurrection and ascension of Christ was always looked on as the capital one upon which all the rest depended. This was attested by a considerable number of men, against whose credit no objection was made; who affirmed, that they all had seen him, and conversed frequently with him after his resurrection; that they saw him ascend up into heaven; and that, according to a promise he had made them, they had received extraordinary powers from him to work miracles in his name, and to speak in divers languages. This last was a most amazing character of a supernatural power lodged with them, and was a thing of such a nature, that it must have been evident to every man whether it was true or false: so that the apostles relating this so positively, and making such frequent appeals to it, that way of proceeding carries a strong and undeniable evidence of truth in it. These wonders were gathered together in a book, and published in the very time in which they were transacted: the 'Acts of the Apostles' were writ two years after St. Paul was carried prisoner to Rome; and St. Luke begins that book with the mention of the gospel that he had formerly writ, as that gospel begins with the mention of some other gospels that were writ before it. Almost all the Epistles speak of the temple of Jerusalem as yet in being; of the Jews as then in peace and prosperity, hating and persecuting the Christians every where: they do also frequently intimate the assurance they had of a great deliverance that was to happen quickly to the Christians, and of terrible judgments that were to be poured out on the Jews; which was soon after that accomplished in the most signal manner of any thing that is recorded in history.

These things do clearly prove that all the writings of the New Testament were both composed and published in the age in which that matter was transacted. The Jews, who from all the places of their dispersion went frequently to Jerusalem, to keep the great festivities of their religion there, had occasion often to examine upon the place the truth of the resurrection and ascension of Christ, and of the effusion of the Holy Ghost: yet, even in that infancy of Christianity, in which it had so little visible strength, no proof was so much as ever pretended in opposition to those great and essential points; which being matters of fact, and related with a great variety of circumstances, had been easily confuted, if there had been any ground for it. The great darkness at the time of Christ's death, the rending the vail of the temple in two, as well as what was more public, the renting of the rocks at his death: his being laid in a new sepulchre, and a watch being set about it; and the watchmen reporting, that while they slept, the body of Christ was carried away: the apostles breaking out all of the sudden into that variety of tongues on Pentecost; the miracles that they wrought, and the proceedings of the sanhedrim with them; were all things so publicly done, that as the discovery of falsehood in any one of these was in the power of the Jews, if any such was, so that alone had most effectually destroyed the credit of this religion, and stopped its progress.

The writings of the New Testament were at that time no secrets, they were in all men's hands, and were copied out freely by every one that desired it. We find within a hundred years after that time, both by the Epistle of the church of Smyrna, by Justin, and Irenæus, not to mention Clemens of Rome, who lived in that time, or Ignatius and Polycarp, who lived very near it, that the authority of these writings was early received and submitted to; that they were much read, and well known; and that they began very soon to be read at the meetings of the Christians for worship, and were esteemed by the several churches as the great trust and *depositum* that was lodged with them. So that though, by the negligence of copiers, some small variations might happen among some of the copies, yet as they do all agree in the main, and most signally in those particulars that are mentioned in this article; so it was not possible for any that should have had the wickedness to set about it, to have corrupted the New Testament by any additions or alterations; it being so early spread into so many hands, and that in so many different places.

When all this matter is laid together, it appears to have as full an evidence to support it, as any matter of fact can possibly have. The narration gave great scope to a variety of inquiries; it raised much disputing, opposition, and persecution; and yet nothing was ever pretended to be proved that could subvert its credit: great multitudes received this doctrine, and died for it in the age in which the matters of fact, upon which its credit was built, were well attested, and in which the truth or falsehood of them might have been easily known; which it is reasonable to believe that all men would carefully examine, before they embraced and assented to that which was likely to draw on them sufferings that would probably end in death. Those who did spread this doctrine, as well as those who first received it, had no interest beside that of truth to engage them to it. They could expect neither wealth nor greatness from it: they were obliged to travel much, and to labour hard; to wrestle through great difficulties, and to endure many indignities. They saw others die on the account of it, and had reason to look for the like usage themselves.

The doctrine that they preached related either to the facts concerning the person of Christ, or to the rules of life which they delivered. These were all pure, just, and good; they tended to settle the world upon the foundations of truth and sincerity, and that sublime pitch of righteousness, of doing as they would be done by; they tended to make men sober and temperate, chaste and modest, meek and humble, merciful and charitable; so that from thence there was no colour given for suspecting any fraud or design in it. The worship of God in this religion was pure and simple, free from cost or pomp, from theatrical shows, as well as idolatrous rites, and had in it all possible characters becoming the purity of the Supreme Mind. When therefore so much concurs to give credit to a religion, there ought to be evident proofs brought to the contrary, before it can be disbelieved or rejected. So many men forsaking the religion in which they were born and bred, which has always a strong influence even upon the greatest minds; and there being so many particular prejudices both upon Jews and Gentiles, by the opinions in which they had been bred, and the impressions which had gone deep in them, it could be no slight matter that could overcome all that.

The Jews expected a conqueror for their Messias, who should have raised both the honour of their law and their nation, and so were much possessed against one of a mean appearance; and when they saw that their law was to be superseded, and that the Gentiles were to be brought into equal privileges with themselves, they could not but be deeply prejudiced both against the person and doctrine of Christ.

The philosophers despised divine inspiration, and secret assistances, and had an ill opinion of miracles; and the herd among the Gentiles were so accustomed to pomp and show in their religious performances, that they must have nauseated the Christian simplicity, and the corruption of their morals must have made them uneasy at a religion of so much strictness. All sorts of men lay under very strong prejudices against this religion; nor was there any one article or branch of it, that flattered any of the interests, appetites, passions, or vanities of men, but all was very much to the contrary. They were warned to prepare for trials and crosses, and, in particular, for a severe and fiery trial that was speedily to come upon them.

There was nothing of the way or manner of impostors that

THE XXXIX ARTICLES.

appeared in the methods in which the gospel was propagated. When the apostles saw that some were endeavouring to lessen them and their authority, they took no fawning ways: they neither flattered nor spared those churches that were under their care: they charged them home with their faults, and asserted their own character in a strain that shewed they were afraid of no discoveries. They appealed to the miracles that they had wrought, and to those gifts and divine virtues of which they were not only possessed themselves, but which were by their ministry conferred on others. The 'demonstration of the Spirit,' or inspiration that was in them, appeared in the *power*, that is, in the miracles which accompanied it, and those they wrought openly in the sight of many witnesses. An uncontested miracle is the fullest evidence that can be given of a divine commission.

ART. IV.

1 Cor. ii. 4.

A miracle is a work that exceeds all the known powers of nature, and that carries in it plain characters of a power superior to any human power. We cannot indeed fix the bounds of the powers of nature; but yet we can plainly apprehend what must be beyond them. For instance, we do not know what secret virtues there may be in plants and minerals; but we do know that bare words can have no natural virtue in them to cure diseases, much less to raise the dead: we know not what force imagination or credulity may have in critical diseases; but we know that a dead man has no imagination: we know also, that blindness, deafness, and an inveterate palsy, cannot be cured by conceit: therefore such miracles as the giving sight to a man born blind, speech to the deaf and dumb, and strength to the paralytic; but most of all, the giving life to the dead, and that not only to persons laid out as dead, but to one that was carried out to be buried, and to another that had been four days dead, and in his grave; all this was done with a bare word, without any sort of external application: this, I say, as it is clearly above the force of imagination, so it is beyond the powers of nature.

These things were not done in the dark, nor in the presence of a few, in whom a particular confidence was put; but in full day-light, and in the sight of great numbers, enemies as well as friends, and some of those enemies were both the most enraged, and the most capable of making all possible exceptions to what was done. Such were the rulers of the synagogues, and the Pharisees in our Saviour's time: and yet they could neither deny the facts, nor pretend that there was any deceit or jugglery in them. We have in this all possible reason to conclude, that both the things were truly done as they are related, and that no just exception was, or could be, made to them.

If it is pretended, that those wonderful things were done by the power of an evil spirit, that does both acknowledge the truth of the relation, and also its being supernatural.

ART IV.

This answer, taken from the power of evil spirits, is sometimes to be made use of, when extraordinary things are well attested, and urged in proof of that which upon other reasons we are assured is false. It is certain, that as we have a great power over vast quantities of gross and heavy matter, which by the motion of a very subtile body, our animal spirits, we can master and manage: so angels, good or bad, may, by virtue of subtile bodies, in which they may dwell, or which upon occasion they may assume, do many things vastly above either our force to do, or our imagination to apprehend how it is done by them. Therefore an action, that exceeds all the known powers of nature, may yet be done by an evil spirit that is in rebellion against its Maker, and that designs to impose upon us by such a mighty performance. But then the measure, by which we must judge of this, is by considering what is the end or design driven at in such a wonderful work: if it is a good one, if it tends to reform the manners of men, and to bring them off from magic, idolatry, and superstition, to the worship of one pure and eternal Mind; and if it tends to reform their actions, as well as their speculations and their worship; to turn them from immorality, falsehood, and malice, to a pure, a sincere, and a mild temper; if it tends to regulate society, as well as to perfect the nature and faculties of every single man; then we may well conclude, that no evil spirit can so far depart from its own nature, as to join its forces, and co-operate in such a design: for then, the kingdom of Satan could not stand, if he were thus divided against himself;' according to what our Saviour said, when this was objected against the miracles that he wrought.

Matt. xii. 25, 26.

These are all the general considerations that concur to prove the truth of the history of the gospel, of which the resurrection and ascension of Christ are the two main articles; for they, being well proved, give authority to all the rest. As to the resurrection in particular, it is certain the apostles could not be deceived in that matter: they saw Christ frequently after he rose from the dead; they met him once with a great company of five hundred with them: they heard him talk and argue with them; he opened the scriptures to them with so peculiar an energy, that they felt their hearts set on fire, even when they did not yet perceive that it was he himself: they did not at first either look for his resurrection, nor believe those who reported him risen: they made all due inquiry, and some of them went beyond all reasonable bounds in their doubting: so far were they from an easy and soon-imposed-on credulity. His sufferings and their own fears had so amazed them, that they were contriving how to separate and disperse themselves when he at first appeared to them. Men so full of fear, and so far from all hope, are not apt to be easy in believing. So it must be concluded, that either the account which the apostles gave the world of Christ's resurrection is true: or they were gross impostors; since it is clear, that the circumstances and numbers, mentioned in that history, shew there could be no deception in it. And it is as little possible to conceive that there could be any imposture in it: for, not to repeat again what has been already said, that they were under no temptations to set about any such deceit, but very much to the contrary; and that there is no reason to think they were either bad enough to enter upon such a design, or capable and skilful enough to manage it; they being many of them illiterate fishermen of Galilee, who had no acquaintance at Jerusalem to furnish them with that which might be necessary for executing such a contrivance: the circumstances of that transaction are to be well examined, and then it will appear that no number of bold and dexterous men, furnished with all advantages whatsoever, could have effected this matter.

ART. IV.

Great numbers had been engaged in the procuring our Saviour to be crucified: the whole sanhedrim, besides multitudes of the people, who upon all occasions are easily drawn in to engage in tumultuary commotions: all these were concerned to examine the event of this matter. He was buried in a new sepulchre lately hewed out of a rock, so that there was no coming at it by any secret ways: a watch was set: and all this at a time in which the full-moon gave a great light all the night long: and Jerusalem being very full of people who were then there in great numbers to keep the passover, that being the second night of so vast a rendezvous, it is reasonable to think that great numbers were walking in the fields, or at least might be so, some later, and some earlier. Now, if an imposture was to be set about, the guard was to be frighted or mastered, which could not be done without giving the alarm, and that must have quickly brought a multitude upon them. Christ's body must have been disposed of: some other tomb was to be looked for to lodge it in: the wounds that were in it would have made it to be soon known if found.

Here a bold attempt was to be undertaken, by a company of poor irresolute men, who must trust one another entirely, otherways they knew all might soon be discovered. One of their number had betrayed Christ a few days before; another had forsworn him, and all had forsaken him; and yet these men are supposed all of the sudden so firm in themselves, and so sure of one another, as to venture on the most daring thing that was ever undertaken by men, when not a circumstance could ever be found out to fix upon them the least suspicion. The priests and the Pharisees must be thought a strange stupid sort of creatures, if they did not examine where the apostles were all that night: besides many other particulars, which might have been a thread to lead them into strict inquiries, unless it was because they believed the report that the watch had brought them of Christ's rising again. When they had this certain reason to believe it, and yet resolved to oppose it, the only thing they could do was to seem to neglect the matter, and only to decry it in general as an imposture, without going into particulars; which certainly they would not have done, if they themselves had not been but too sure of the truth of it.

When all this is laid together, it is the most unreasonable thing imaginable to think that there was an imposture in this matter, when no colour nor shadow of it ever appeared, and when all the circumstances, and not only probabilities, but even moral possibilities, are so full to the contrary.

The ascension of Christ has not indeed so full a proof: nor is it capable of it, neither does it need it; for the resurrection, well proved, makes that very credible. For this we have only the testimony of the apostles, who did all attest that they saw it, being all together in an open field: when Christ was walking and discoursing with them, and when he was blessing them, he was parted from them: they saw him ascend, till a cloud received him, and took him out of their sight. And then two angels appeared to them, and assured them that 'he should come again in like manner as they had seen him ascend.' Here is a very particular relation, with many circumstances in it, in which it was not possible for the apostles to be mistaken; so that, there being no reason to suspect their credit, this rests upon that authority. But ten days after, it received a much clearer proof; when the Holy Ghost was poured out on them in so visible a manner, and with most remarkable effects. Immediately upon it they spoke with divers tongues, and wrought many miracles, and all in the name of Christ. They did often and solemnly disclaim their doing any of those wonderful things by any power of their own: they owned that all they had or did was derived to them from Jesus of Nazareth, of whose resurrection and ascension they were appointed to be the witnesses.

Christ's coming again to judge the world at the last day is so often affirmed by himself in the gospel, and is so frequently mentioned in the writings of his apostles, that this is a main part of his doctrine; so that his resurrection, ascension, together with the effusion of the Holy Ghost, having in general proved his mission, and his whole doctrine, this is also proved by them. Enough seems to be said in proof of all the parts of this Article; it remains only that somewhat should be added in explanation of them.

As to the resurrection, it is to little purpose to inquire, whether our Saviour's body was kept all the while in a complete organization, that so by this miracle it might be preserved in a natural state, for his soul to re-enter it: or whether by the course of nature the vast number of the inward conveyances that were in the body were stopped;

and if all of a sudden, when the time of the resurrection came, all was again put in a vital state, fit to be animated by his soul. There must have been a miracle either way: so it is to little purpose to inquire into it. The former, though a continued miracle, yet seems to agree more fully to these words, 'Thou wilt not suffer thy Holy One to see corruption.' It is to as little purpose to inquire how our Saviour's new body was supplied with blood, since he had lost the greatest part of it on the cross: whether that was again by the power of God brought back into his veins; or whether, as he himself had formerly said, that 'man lives not by bread alone, but by every word that proceeds out of the mouth of God,' blood was supplied by miracle: or whether his body, that was then of the nature of a glorified body, though yet on earth, needed the supplies of blood to furnish new spirits for serving the natural functions; he eating and drinking so seldom, that we may well believe it was done rather to satisfy his apostles, than to answer the necessities of nature; these are curiosities that signify so little, if we could certainly resolve them, that it is to no purpose to inquire about them, since we cannot know what to determine in them. This in general is certain, that the same soul returned back to the same body; so that the same man who died, rose again; and that is our faith. We need not trouble ourselves with inquiring how to make out the three days of Christ's being in the grave; days stand, in the common acceptation, for a portion of a day. We know the Jews were very exact to the rest on the sabbath, so the body was without question laid in the grave before the sun-set on Friday; so that was the first day; the sabbath was a complete one; and a good part of the third day, that is, the night, with which the Jews began to count the day, was over before he was raised up.

As for his stay on earth forty days, we cannot pretend to give an account of it; whether his body was passing through a slow and physical purification, to be meet for ascending; or whether he intended to keep a proportion between his gospel and the law of Moses; that as he suffered at the time of their killing the passover, so the effusion of the Holy Ghost was fixed for Pentecost, and that therefore he would stay on earth till that time was near, not to put his apostles upon too long an expectation without his presence; which might be necessary to animate them, till they should be endued with power from on high. As to the manner of his ascension, it is also questioned whether the body of Christ, as it ascended, was so wonderfully changed, as to put on the subtilty and purity of an ethereal body; or whether it retains still the same form in heaven that it had on earth; or if it put on a new one: it is more probable that it did; and that the wonderful glory that appeared in his countenance and whole person at his transfiguration, was a manifestation of

ART. IV.

Ps. xvi. 10.

Deut. viii. 3.
Matt. iv. 4.

that more permanent glory, to which it was to be afterwards exalted. It seems probable from what St. Paul says, ('that flesh and blood shall not inherit the kingdom of God,' which relates to our glorified bodies, when 'we shall bear the image of the second and the heavenly Adam,') that Christ's body has no more the modifications of flesh and blood in it; and that the glory of the celestial body is of another nature and texture than that of the terrestrial. It is easily imagined how this may be, and yet the body to be numerically the same: for, all matter being uniform, and capable of all sort of motion, and by consequence of being either much grosser or much purer, the same portion of matter that made a thick and heavy body here on earth, may be put into that purity and fineness as to be no longer a fit inhabitant of this earth, or to breathe this air, but to be meet to be transplanted into ethereal regions.

Christ as he went up into heaven, so he had the whole government of this world put into his hands, and the whole ministry of angels put under his command, even in his human nature. So that 'all things are now in subjection to him.' All power and authority is derived from him, and he does whatsoever he pleases both in heaven and earth. 'In him all fulness dwells.' And as, the Mosaical tabernacle being filled with glory, the emanations of it did by the *Urim* and *Thummim* enlighten and direct that people, so, out of that fulness, that dwelt bodily in Christ, there is a constant emanation of his grace and spirit descending on his church. He does also intercede for us at his Father's right hand, where he is preparing a place for us. The meaning of all which is this, that as he is vested with an unconceivably high degree of glory, even as man, so the merit of his death is still fresh and entire; and in the virtue of that, the sins of all that come to God through him, claiming to his death as to their sacrifice, and obeying his gospel, are pardoned, and they are 'sealed by his Spirit until the day of redemption.' In conclusion, when all God's design with this world is accomplished, it shall be set on fire, and all the great parts of which it is composed, as of elements, shall be melted and burnt down; and then when by that fire probably the portions of matter, which was in the bodies of all who have lived upon earth, shall be so far refined and fixed, as to become both incorruptible and immortal, then they shall be made meet for the souls that formerly animated them, to re-enter every one into his own body, which shall be then so moulded as to be a habitation fit to give it everlasting joy or everlasting torment. Then shall Christ appear visibly in some very conspicuous place in the clouds of heaven, where every eye shall see him: he shall appear in his 'own glory,' that is, in his human glorified body: he shall appear in the 'glory of his angels,' having vast numbers of these about him, attending on him:

but, which is above all, he shall appear in 'his Father's glory;' that is, there shall be then a most wonderful manifestation of the eternal Godhead dwelling in him; and then shall he pass a final sentence upon all that ever lived upon earth, according to all that they have done in the body, whether it be good or bad. The righteous shall ascend as he did, and shall meet him in the clouds, and be for ever with him; and the wicked shall sink into a state of darkness and misery, of unspeakable horror of mind, and everlasting pain and torment.

ART. IV.

Luke ix. 26.
Rom. xiv. 10—12.
Matt. xxv. 31—46.
2 Cor. v. 10.
1 Thes. iv. 17.
Dan. xii. 2.
Matt. xxv. 46.

ARTICLE V.

Of the Holy Ghost.

The Holy Ghost proceeding from the Father and the Son, is of one Substance, Majesty, and Glory, with the Father and the Son, very and eternal God.

IN order to the explaining this Article, we must consider, first, the importance of the term *Spirit*, or *Holy Spirit*; secondly, his *procession* from the *Father* and the *Son*; and, thirdly, that he is truly God, of the same *substance* with the *Father* and the *Son*. Spirit signifies wind or breath, and in the Old Testament it stands frequently in that sense: the Spirit of God, or wind of God, stands sometimes for a high and strong wind; but more frequently it signifies a secret impression made by God on the mind of a prophet: so that the *Spirit of God* and *the spirit of prophecy* are set in opposition to the vain imaginations, the false pretences, or the diabolical illusions, of those who assumed to themselves the name and the authority of a prophet, without a true mission from God. But when God made representations either in a dream or in an ecstasy to any person, or imprinted a sense of his will on their minds, together with such necessary characters as gave it proof and authority, this was an illapse from God, as a breathing from him on the soul of the prophet.

In the New Testament this word *Holy Ghost* stands most commonly for that wonderful effusion of those miraculous virtues that was poured out at *Pentecost* on the apostles; by which their spirits were not only exalted with extraordinary degrees of zeal and courage, of authority and utterance, but they were furnished with the gifts of tongues and of miracles. And besides that first and great effusion, several Christians received particular talents and inspirations, which are most commonly expressed by the word *Spirit* or *inspiration*. Those inward assistances, by which the frame and temper of men's minds are changed and renewed, are likewise called *the Spirit*, or *the Holy Spirit*, or *Holy Ghost*. So Christ said to Nicodemus, that 'except a man was born of water and of the Spirit, he cannot see the kingdom of God;' and that his 'heavenly Father would give the Holy Spirit to every one that asked him.' By these it is plain, that extraordinary or miraculous inspirations are not meant, for these are not every Christian's portion; there is no question made of all this.

The main question is, whether by *Spirit*, or *Holy Spirit*, we are to understand one person, that is the fountain of all those gifts and operations; or whether by *one Spirit* is only to be meant the power of God flowing out and shewing itself in many wonderful operations. The adversaries of the Trinity will have the *Spirit*, or *Holy Spirit*, to signify no person, but only the divine gifts or operations. But in opposition to this it is plain, that in our Saviour's last and long discourse to his disciples, in which he promised to send them his Spirit, he calls him *another Comforter*, to be sent in his stead, or to supply his absence; and the whole tenor of the discourse runs on him as a *person:* 'He shall abide with you: he shall guide you into all truth; and shew you things to come. He shall bring all things into your remembrance: he shall convince the world of sin, of righteousness, and of judgment.' In all these places he is so plainly spoken of, not as a quality or operation, but as a person; and that without any key or rule to understand the words otherwise, that this alone may serve to determine the matter now in dispute. Christ's commission to *preach* and *baptize* in the name of *the Father, the Son,* and *the Holy Ghost,* does plainly make him a person, since it cannot be said that we are to be called by the name of a virtue or operation. St. Paul does also, in a long discourse upon the diversity of gifts, administrations, and operations, ascribe them all to *one Spirit,* as their author and fountain: of whom he speaks as of a person, distributing these in order to several ends, and in different measures. He speaks of the Spirit's 'searching all things,' of his 'interceding for us,' of our 'grieving the Spirit, by which we are sealed.' This is the language used concerning a person, not a quality. 'All these,' says he, 'worketh that one and the self-same Spirit, dividing to every man severally as he will.' Now it is not to be conceived, how that both our Saviour and his apostles should use the phrase of a person so constantly in speaking of the *Spirit,* and should so critically and in the way of argument pursue that strain, if he is not a person: they not only insist on it, and repeat it frequently, but they draw an argument from it for union and love, and for mutual condescension and sympathy. Upon all these grounds it is evident, that the *Holy Spirit* is in the scripture proposed to us as a person, under whose economy all the various gifts, administrations, and operations, that are in the church, are put.

The second particular relating to this Article is, the *procession* of this *Spirit* from the *Father* and the *Son.* The word *procession,* or, as the schoolmen term it, *spiration,* is only made use of in order to the naming this relation of the *Spirit* to the *Father* and *Son,* in such a manner as may best answer the sense of the word *Spirit:* for it must be confessed that we can frame no explicit idea of this matter: and therefore we must speak of it either strictly in scripture words, or in such words as arise out of them, and that have the same signification with them. It is therefore a vain attempt of the schoolmen to undertake to give a reason why the second person is said to

ART. V.

John xiv. 16, 26.

John xvi. 8—13.

1 Cor. xii. 4, 8, 9, 11, 13.

1 Cor. ii. 10.
Rom. viii. 26.
Eph. iv. 30.

ART. V.

be *generated*, and so is called *Son*, and the third to *proceed*, and so is called *Spirit*. All these subtilties can have no foundation, and signify nothing towards the clearing this matter, which is rather darkened than cleared by a pretended illustration. In a word, as we should never have believed this mystery, if the scripture had not revealed it to us, so we understand nothing concerning it, besides what is contained in the scriptures: and therefore, if in any thing, we must think soberly upon those subjects. The scriptures call the second, *Son*, and the third, *Spirit*; so generation and procession are words that may well be used, but they are words concerning which we can form no distinct conception. We only use them because they belong to the words *Son* and *Spirit*. The *Spirit*, in things that we do understand, is somewhat that proceeds, and the Son is a person begotten; we therefore, believing that the Holy Ghost is a *person*, apply the word *procession* to the manner of his emanation from the Father; though at the same time we must acknowledge that we have no distinct thought concerning it. So much in general concerning *procession*. It has been much controverted whether the *Holy Spirit* proceeds from the *Father* only, or from the *Father* and the *Son*.

In the first disputes concerning the divinity of the *Holy Ghost* with the Macedonians, who denied it, there was no other contest but whether he was truly God or not. When that was settled by the council of Constantinople, it was made a part of the Creed; but it was only said that he *proceeded* from the *Father*: and the council of Ephesus soon after that fixed on that Creed, decreeing that no additions should be made to it: yet about the end of the sixth century, in the western church an addition was made to the article, by which the Holy Ghost was affirmed to *proceed from the Son*, as well as from the Father. And when the eastern and western churches, in the ninth century, fell into an humour of quarrelling upon the account of jurisdiction, after some time of anger, in which they seem to be searching for matter to reproach one another with, they found out this difference: the Greeks reproached the Latins for thus adding to the faith, and corrupting the ancient symbol, and that contrary to the decree of a general council. The Latins, on the other hand, charged them for detracting from the dignity of the *Son*: and this became the chief point in controversy between them.

Here was certainly a very unhappy dispute; inconsiderable in its original, but fatal in its consequences. We of this church, though we abhor the cruelty of condemning the eastern churches for such a difference, yet do receive the Creed according to the usage of the western churches: and therefore, though we do not pretend to explain what *procession* is, we believe according to the Article, that the *Holy Ghost proceeds* both from the *Father* and the *Son*: because in that discourse of our Saviour's that contains the promise of the *Spirit*, and that long description of him as a *person*, Christ not only says, that 'the Father will send the Spirit in his name,' but adds, that 'he will send the Spirit;' and though he says next, 'who proceedeth from the Father,' yet since he sends him, and that he was to supply his room, and to act in his name, this implies a relation, and a sort of subordination in the *Spirit* to the *Son*. This may serve to justify our adhering to the Creeds, as they had been for many ages received in the western church: but we are far from thinking that this proof is so full and explicit, as to justify our separating from any church, or condemning it, that should stick exactly to the first Creeds, and reject this addition.

ART. V.

John xiv. 26.
John xv. 26.

The third branch of the Article is, that this Holy Ghost or person, thus proceeding, is truly God, of the same substance with the Father and the Son. That he is God, was formerly proved by those passages in which the whole Trinity in all the three persons is affirmed: but besides that, 'the lying to the Holy Ghost' by Ananias and Sapphira, is said to be 'a lying not unto men, but to God:' his being called 'another Comforter; his teaching all things; his guiding into all truth; his telling things to come; his searching all things, even the deep things of God;' his being called 'the Spirit of the Lord,' in opposition to 'the spirit of a man; his making intercession for us; his changing us into the same image with Christ,' are all such plain characters of his being *God*, that those who deny that, are well aware of this, that, if it is once proved that he is a person, it will follow that he must be God; therefore all that was said to prove him a *person* is here to be remembered as a proof that he is truly God. So that though there is not such a variety of proofs for this, as there was for the divinity of the *Son*, yet the proof of it is plain and clear. And from what was said upon the first Article concerning the unity of God, it is also certain, that if he is *God*, he must be *of one substance, majesty, and glory, with the Father and the Son.*

Acts v. 34.
John xiv. 16, 26. xvi. 13.
1 Cor. ii. 10, 11.
Rom. viii. 26.
2 Cor. iii. 17, 18.

ARTICLE VI.

Of the Sufficiency of Holy Scriptures for Salvation.

Holy Scripture containeth all things necessary to Salvation: so that whatsoever is not read therein, nor may be proved thereby, is not to be required of any Man, that it should be believed as an Article of Faith, or to be thought requisite or necessary to Salvation. In the name of the Holy Scripture we do understand those Canonical Books of the Old and New Testament, of whose Authority was never any doubt in the Church.

Of the Names and Number of the Canonical Books.

Genesis	The First Book of *Chronicles*
Exodus	The Second Book of *Chronicles*
Leviticus	The First Book of *Esdras*
Numbers	The Second Book of *Esdras*
Deuteronomy	The Book of *Esther*
Joshua	The Book of *Job*
Judges	The *Psalms*
Ruth	The *Proverbs*
The First Book of *Samuel*	*Ecclesiastes* or Preacher
The Second Book of *Samuel*	*Cantica* or Song of *Solomon*
The First Book of *Kings*	Four Prophets the greater
The Second Book of *Kings*	Twelve Prophets the less.

And the other Books (as Hierom saith) the Church doth read for Example of Life, and Instruction of Manners; but yet it doth not apply them to establish any Doctrine. Such are these following:

The Third Book of *Esdras*	*Baruch* the Prophet
The Fourth Book of *Esdras*	The Song of the Three Children
The Book of *Tobias*	The History of *Susanna*
The Book of *Judith*	Of *Bel* and *the Dragon*
The rest of the Book of *Esther*	The Prayer of *Manasses*
The Book of *Wisdom*	The First Book of *Maccabees*
Jesus the Son of *Syrach*	The Second Book of *Maccabees.*

All the Books of the New Testament as they are commonly received, we do receive, and account them Canonical.*

---

* The following is the new canon of scripture first set forth by the council of Trent, and afterwards confirmed and declared necessary to be received, with other articles of faith, by the bull of Pope Pius IV., A.D. 1564.

' Sacrosancta œcumenica et generalis tridentina synodus, in Spiritu Sancto legitime congregata, præsidentibus in ea eisdem tribus apostolicæ sedis legatis, hoc sibi perpetuo ante oculos proponens, ut sublatis erroribus, puritas ipsa evangelii in ecclesia conservetur quod promissum ante prophetas in scripturas sanctis, Dominus noster Jesus Christus Dei Filius, proprio ore primum promulgavit: deinde per suos apos-

THE XXXIX ARTICLES. 89

IN this Article there are two important heads, and to each of ART.
them a proper consequence does belong. The first is, that the VI.
holy scriptures do contain all things necessary to salvation:
the negative consequence that ariseth out of that is, that no
article that is not either read in it, or that may not be proved
by it, is to be required to be believed as an article of faith, or
to be thought necessary to salvation. The second is, the
settling the canon of the scripture both of the Old and New
Testament; and the consequence that arises out of that is, the
rejecting the books commonly called *Apocryphal,* which, though
they may be read by the church *for example of life, and instruction of manners,* yet are no part of the canon, nor is any doctrine to be established by them.*

---

tolos tanquam fontem omnis et salutaris veritatis, et morum disciplinæ, omni creaturæ prædicari jussit: perspiciensque hanc veritatem et disciplinam contineri in libris scriptis, et sine scripto traditionibus, quæ ipsius Christi ore ab apostolis acceptæ, aut ab ipsis apostolis, Spiritu sancto dictante, quasi per manus traditæ, ad nos usque pervenerunt; orthodoxorum patrum exempla secuta, omnes libros tam veteris quam novi Testamenti, cum utriusque unus Deus sit auctor, necnon traditiones ipsas, tum ad fidem, tum ad mores pertinentes, tanquam vel ore tenus a Christo, vel a Spiritu sancto dictatas, et continua successione in ecclesia catholica conservatas, pari pietatis affectu ac reverentia suscipit, et veneratur. Sacrorum vero librorum indicem huic decreto adscribendum censuit; ne cui dubitatio suboriri possit, quinam suit, qui ab ipsa synodo suscipiuntur. Sunt vero infra scripti; Testamenti veteris, quinque Moysi, id est, Genesis, Exodus, Leviticus, Numeri, Deuteronomium: Josue, Judicum, Ruth, quatuor Regum, duo Paralipomenon, Esdræ primus et secundus qui dicitur Nehemias; Tobias, Judith, Esther, Job, Psalterium Davidicum centum quinquaginta psalmorum, Parabolæ, Ecclesiastes, Canticum canticorum, Sapientia, Ecclesiasticus, Isaias, Jeremias cum Baruch, Ezechiel, Daniel; duodecim prophetæ minores, id est, Osea, Joel, Amos, Abdias, Jonas, Michæas, Nahum, Habacuc, Sophonias, Aggæus, Zacharias, Malachias; duo Machabæorum, primus et secundus. Testamenti novi, quatuor Evangelia, secundum Matthæum, Marcum, Lucam et Joannum, Actus Apostolorum a Luca evangelista conscripti: quatuordecim Epistolæ Pauli apostoli, ad Romanos, duæ ad Corinthios, ad Galatas, ad Ephesios, ad Philippenses, ad Colossenses, duæ ad Thessalonicenses, duæ ad Timotheum, ad Titum, ad Philemonem, ad Hebræos: Petri apostoli duæ, Joannis apostoli tres, Jacobi apostoli una, Judæ apostoli una, et Apocalypsis Joannis apostoli. Si quis autem libros ipsos integros cum omnibus suis partibus, prout in ecclesia catholica legi consueverunt, et in veteri vulgata Latina editione habentur, pro sacris et canonicis non susceperit, et traditiones prædictas sciens et prudens contempserit; anathema sit.'—*Conc. Trid. Sess. iv.*

'Cætera item omnia a sacris canonibus, et œcumenicis conciliis, ac præcipue a sacrosancta Tridentina synodo tradita, definita, et declarata, indubitanter recipio atque profiteor; simulque contraria omnia, atque hæreses, quascumque ab ecclesia damnatas, rejectas, et anathematizatas, ego pariter damno, rejicio et anathematizo. Hanc veram catholicam fidem extra quam nemo salvus esse potest, quam in præsenti sponte profiteor et veraciter teneo, eamdem integram et inviolatam usque ad extremum vitæ spiritum constantissime, Deo adjuvante, retinere et confiteri, atque a meis subditis, vel illis quorum cura ad me in munere meo spectabit, teneri, doceri, et prædicari, quantum in me erit, curaturum, ego idem N. spondeo, voveo, ac juro. Sic me Deus adjuvet et hæc sancta Dei Evangelia.' *Bulla Pii IV. sup. form jur. prof. fid.*—[ED.]

* The books not admitted into the canon of scripture were called Apocryphal—a word derived from ἀποκρύπτω, 'to hide,' because of their not being submitted to public inspection as the inspired books were: or, according to others, from ἀπὸ τῆς κρύπτης, because they were not admitted into the ark, the place where the canonical books were deposited.

'Concerning the books that belong to the New Testament, there is not any difference between us and other churches about them. For though some few particular and private persons have both of late and heretofore, either out of their error

AN EXPOSITION OF

ART.
VI.

After the main foundations of religion in general, in the belief of a God, or more specially of the Christian religion in the doctrine of the Trinity, and of the death, resurrection, and ascension of Christ, are laid down; the next point to be settled is, what is *the rule of this faith,* where is it to be found, and with whom is it lodged? The church of Rome and we do both agree, that the scriptures are of divine inspiration: those of that communion acknowledge, that every thing which is contained in scripture is true, and comes from God; but they add to this, that the books of the New Testament

---

rejected, or out of their curiosity (more than befitted them) debated, the canonical authority of the Epistle of St. Paul to the Hebrews, the Epistle of St. James, the Second Epistle of St. Peter, the Second and Third of St. John, the Epistle of St. Jude, and the Apocalypse, besides some other lesser parts of the gospels; yet can it never be shewed, that any entire church, nor that any national or provincial council, nor that any multitude of men in their confessions or catechisms, or other such public writings, have rejected them, or made any doubt of them at all. Indeed, Luther, and some certain men that lived with him in Germany (no great number nor party of them), were other whiles of that mind, that the Epistle of St. James, &c., might be called into question, whether they were canonical, or no; but afterwards they amended their judgment, and persisted no longer in that error, wherein some others of the Latin church (but never any considerable number or eminent persons there) had been involved before them. And at this day all the churches of Christendom are at one accord for the books of the New Testament. But for the Old Testament they are not so. For herein the canon of the council at Trent hath made the Roman church to differ both from *itself* (considered as it was in former ages) and from all other churches besides, by adding to the old Canon (strictly and properly so taken) six entire books which were never in it before, that is to say, Tobit, Ecclesiasticus, Wisdom, Judith, the First and the Second of the Maccabees, together with certain other pieces of Baruch, Esther, and Daniel; all which before the time of this new council (where the Pope and his partisans, both in this and in many other divine matters besides, took a most enormous liberty to define what they pleased) were wont to be severed, even among themselves, from the true canonical scriptures. To the body whereof they have now not only annexed them, and made the one to be of equal authority with the other, but they have likewise added this above all, That whosoever shall not receive them, as they do, and believe them to be as good canonical scriptures as the rest (that is, all equally inspired by God, and delivered over to his church for such, ever since they were first written), must undergo the curse of their unhallowed sentence, and be made incapable of eternal salvation. The capacity and assured hope whereof, though (thanks be to God) it never was, nor never will be, in their power to take from us, yet have they laid their most unchristian anathema upon all other churches and persons of the world, and excluded them from all possibility of being saved, unless their new decree in this particular, and the Pope's new creed in this and many other particulars (as unsound and as false as this), be first received and believed for the true articles of our Christian faith. By which their unsufferable and inexcusable determination in that council, they have given the world sufficient cause to reject the council, if there were no other reasons to be brought against it (as many and very many other there be) but this alone—that herein against the common faith, and the catholic canon of the church of God, they have gone about to bind all men's consciences to theirs, and given no more faith or reverence to the true and infallible scriptures of God, than they do to other additional books and writings of men.

'For the whole current of antiquity runs against them. And the universal church of Christ, as well under the Old as the New Testament, did never so receive these books, which are now by us termed Apocryphal; nor ever acknowledged them to be of the same order, authority, or reverence, with the rest, which both they and we call strictly and properly canonical.

'In proof whereof we shall here recite the testimony of the church in every age concerning the canon of the Old Testament, and the books that belong thereunto. Where the question will not be. First, Whether those Apocryphal books either have been heretofore, or may still be, read in the church, for the better instruction and

were occasionally written, and not with the design of making them the full rule of faith, but that many things were delivered orally by the apostles, which, if they are faithfully transmitted to us, are to be received by us with the same submission and respect that we pay to their writings: and they also believe, that these traditions are conveyed down infallibly to us, and that to distinguish betwixt true and false doctrines and traditions, there must be an infallible authority lodged by Christ with his church. We, on the contrary, affirm that the scriptures are a complete *rule of faith*,* and

---

edifying of the people in many good precepts of life: Second, Nor whether they may be joined together in one common volume with the Bible, and comprehended under the general name of Holy Scripture, as that name is largely and improperly taken: Third, Nor whether the moral rules, and profitable histories and examples, therein contained, may be set forth and cited in a sermon or other treatise of religion: Fourth, Nor whether the ancient fathers thought these books (at least many passages in them) worthy of their particular consideration both for the elucidation of divers places in the Old Testament, and for the better enabling of them to get a more perfect understanding of the ecclesiastical story: Fifth, Nor yet, whether, in the very articles of faith, some certain sayings that are found in those books (agreeable herein to the others that are canonical) may not be brought for the more abundant explaining and clearing of them. For all this we grant, and to all these purposes there may be good use made of an apocryphal book. But the question only is, whether all or any of those books be purely, positively, and simply divine scripture, or to all purposes, and in all senses, sacred and canonical, so as that they may be said (or ever were so accounted) to be of the same equal and sovereign authority with the rest, for the establishing and determining of any matter of faith, or controversies in religion, no less than the true and undoubted canonical books of scripture themselves.'—*Cosin.*

Bishop Cosin, then, in his unanswerable 'Scholastical history of the canon of scripture,' brings forward the testimonies of every age to the sixteenth century in support of ours, and consequently against the new canon of the church of Rome.

The reader may on this important article consult with much advantage Sir H. Lynde, who proves that 'the entire canon of scriptures which we profess (without the apocryphal additions) is confirmed by pregnant testimonies in all ages, from the first to the sixteenth, and most of them acknowledged by the Romanists themselves.' And also answers 'our adversaries' pretences, from the authorities of fathers, and councils, to prove the Apocryphal books canonical.' *Via Devia,* sections v. and vi.—[ED.]

* When the holy scriptures are called the rule of faith, we are to understand, the rule whereby to judge of controversies in matters of faith—the rule whereby that which is according to the faith may be made manifest, and heresy detected. The rule is one thing: that whereby we decide what is, or is not, according to the rule, another. The question of the judge must therefore be ever considered apart from that of the rule itself. ' Every man,' observes Chillingworth, ' is to judge for himself with the judgment of discretion, and to choose either his religion first, and then his church, as we say; or, as you say (addressing the Romanist), his church first, and then his religion.' To exclude men from exercising their reason would make their faith in the first place irrational, because they could have no reason to believe; and in the second place, 'altogether uncertain, and its object may as well be a falsehood, as a truth; because if I have no reason why I believe it true, then I have no certainty, but it may be false; for the only certainty I can have that my belief is not false, is because I have rational grounds to evidence it true, which when removed, what certainty can I have that I do not err?' Besides, when any man embraces the communion of the papal church, he has reason for so doing, or he has not. If he has not, then his belief is 'irrational, uncertain, and absurd: if he hath, then he believes the Romish church infallible, because his reason judgeth it to be so; and so the church is beholden to the judgment of his private reason for his belief of her infallibility.' If it be objected by the Romanists, that reason is not a sure guide, we again answer with Whitby:—' Can you conduct me to a surer guide than reason? Yes, you will answer, to the church. But if my reason,

ART. VI.

that the whole Christian religion is contained in them, and no where else; and although we make great use of tradition, especially that which is most ancient and nearest the source, to help us to a clear understanding of the scriptures; yet as to matters of faith we reject all oral tradition, as an incompetent mean of conveying down doctrines to us, and we refuse to receive any doctrine, that is not either expressly contained in scripture, or clearly proved from it.

Ex. xvii. 14. xxiv. 4.
Deu. xxvii. 8. xxxi. 9, 19, 22, 24—26.
Jos. xxiv. 26.
Is. viii. 1. xxx. 8.
Jer. xxxvi. 2, 28—32.
Hab. ii. 2.
Luk. i. 3, 4.
John xx. 31.
2 Pet. i. 15, 16.
Rev. i. 11, 19. xxi. 5.

In order to the opening and proving of this, it is to be considered, what God's design, in first ordering Moses, and after him all inspired persons, to put things in writing, could be: it could be no other than to free the world from the uncertainties and impostures of *oral tradition*. All mankind being derived from one common source, it seems it was much easier in the first ages of the world to preserve the tradition pure, than it could possibly be afterwards: there were only a few things then to be delivered concerning God; as, that he was one spiritual Being, that he had created all things, that he alone was to be worshipped and served; the rest relating

---

being fallible, may misguide me, why may it not when it conducts me to the church; especially as you yourselves profess to believe the church's infallibility upon prudential motives?' The judge then is the same in both churches, and must be kept quite distinct from the rule itself. Hence is evident the folly of Romanists, who, when they would assail our rule of faith, spend all their time in exposing the errors and absurdities into which men's private fancies have carried them: whereas such errors arise from men making something else, their own private spirit or their traditions, to be either a substitute for, or supplement to, the only unerring rule—the written word of God.†

The rule to which all questions of religion must be brought is the *lex scripta*—the written word; 'and if this word,' observes Chillingworth, 'be sufficient to inform us what is the faith, it must of necessity be sufficient to teach us what is heresy; seeing heresy is nothing but a manifest deviation from, and an opposition to, the faith. That which is straight will plainly teach us what is crooked; and one contrary cannot but manifest the other.' But if the scriptures be not the rule, how then shall 'the notes of the church,' which the Romanist is bound to examine before he can join or remain in his own communion, be determined? And if the scriptures be a sufficient rule whereby to try these, why not so for the trying of other questions—why not of all? The scriptures then are not the judge, but only a sufficient rule for those to judge by who believe them to be the word of God.

This distinction is all-important—indeed, the observance of it is indispensable in this controversy. By thus keeping questions, which have no necessary connexion, in their proper place, the champions of the papal system are at once deprived of the use of those weapons, which they have sometimes wielded with so much apparent success against Protestants; while they themselves are involved in inextricable difficulties if compelled to attack the sufficiency and completeness of the scriptures as a rule whereby to determine questions of religion; for how shall the question of the church be determined but by that rule which we adopt—the written word? Thus in the chief of questions are they compelled to have recourse to our rule.

In order to fully understand this point, the reader must study Chillingworth, chap. ii. '*Scripture the only rule whereby to judge of controversies.*'—ED.

---

† The reader will see this particular point ably handled by Bishop Taylor—'*Of the sufficiency of the Holy Scriptures to salvation.*'

to the history of the world, and chiefly of the first man that was made in it. There were also great advantages on the side of *oral tradition;* the first men were very long-lived, and they saw their own families spread extremely, so that they had on their side both the authority which long life always has, particularly concerning matters of fact, and the credit that parents have naturally with their own children, to secure tradition. Two persons might have conveyed it down from Adam to Abraham; Methuselah lived above three hundred years while Adam was yet alive, and Sem was almost a hundred when he died, and he lived much above a hundred years in the same time with Abraham, according to the Hebrew. Here is a great period of time filled up by two or three persons: and yet in that time the tradition of those very few things in which religion was then comprehended, was so universally and entirely corrupted, that it was necessary to correct it by immediate revelation to Abraham: God intending to have a peculiar people to himself out of his posterity, commanded him to forsake his kindred and country, that he might not be corrupted with an idolatry, that we have reason to believe was then but beginning among them. We are sure his nephew Laban was an idolater: and the danger of mixing with the rest of mankind was then so great, that God ordered a mark to be made on the bodies of all descended from him, to be the *seal of the covenant,* and the badge and cognizance of his posterity: by that distinction, and by their living in a wandering and unfixed manner, they were preserved for some time from idolatry; God intending afterwards to settle them in an instituted religion. But though the beginnings of it, I mean the promulgation of the law on mount Sinai, was one of the most amazing things that ever happened, and the fittest to be orally conveyed down, the law being very short, and the circumstances in the delivery of it most astonishing; and though there were many rites and several festivities, appointed chiefly for the carrying down the memory of it; though there was also in that dispensation the greatest advantage imaginable for securing this tradition, all the main acts of their religion being to be performed in one place, and by men of one tribe and family; as they were also all the inhabitants of a small tract of ground, of one language, and by their constitutions obliged to maintain a constant commerce among themselves: they having farther a continuance of signal characters of God's miraculous presence among them, such as the operation of the water of jealousy, the plenty of the sixth year to supply them all the sabbatical year, and till the harvest of the following year: together with a succession of prophets that followed one another, either in a constant course, or at least soon after one another; but above all, the presence of God which appeared in the cloud of glory, and in those answers that were given by the *Urim* and

ART. VI.

Gen. xii. 1.
Jos. xxiv. 2, 3.

Gen. xxxi. 19, 30.

ART. VI.

Ex. xxv. 22. xxix. 42.
1 Sa. xxiii. 9—12.
Ex. xxiv. 12.

Thummim; all which must be confessed to be advantages on the side of tradition, vastly beyond any that can be pretended to have been in the Christian church; yet notwithstanding all these, God commanded Moses to write all their law, as the Ten Commandments were, by the immediate power or finger of God, writ on tables of stone. When all this is laid together and well considered, it will appear that God by a particular economy intended them to secure revealed religion from the doubtfulness and uncertainties of oral tradition.

It is much more reasonable to believe, that the Christian religion, which was to be spread to many remote regions, among whom there could be little communication, should have been fixed in its first beginnings by putting it in writing, and not left to the looseness of reports and stories. We do plainly see, that though the methods of knowing and communicating truth are now surer and better fixed than they have been in most of the ages which have passed since the beginnings of this religion; yet in every matter of fact such additions are daily made, as it happens to be reported, and every point of doctrine is so variously stated, that if religion had not a more assured bottom than tradition, it could not have that credit paid to it that it ought to have. If we had no greater certainty for religion than report, we could not believe it very firmly, nor venture upon it: so in order to the giving this doctrine such authority as is necessary for attaining the great ends proposed in it, the conveyance of it must be clear and unquestionable; otherwise as it would grow to be much mixed with fable, so it would come to be looked on as all a fable. Since then oral tradition, when it had the utmost advantages possible of its side, failed so much in the conveyance both of natural religion, and of the Mosaical, we see that it cannot be relied on as a certain method of preserving the truths of revealed religion.

In our Saviour's time, tradition was set up on many occasions against him, but he never submitted to it: on the contrary he reproached the Jews with this, that they had made

Matt. xv. 3, 6, 9.

'the laws of God of no effect by their traditions;' and he told them, that they 'worshipped God in vain, when they taught for doctrines the commandments of men.' In all his disputes with the Pharisees, he appealed to Moses and the prophets; he bade them 'search the scriptures; for in them,' said he,

John v. 39.

'ye think ye have eternal life, and they testify of me.' *Ye think* is, by the phraseology of that time, a word that does not refer to any particular *conceit* of theirs; but imports, that as they *thought,* so in them they had *eternal life.* Our Saviour justifies himself and his doctrine often by words of scripture, but never once by tradition. We see plainly, that in our Saviour's time the tradition of the resurrection was so doubtful among the Jews, that the Sadducees, a formed party among them, did openly deny it. The authority of tradition had likewise imposed two very mischievous errors upon the strictest sect of the Jews that adhered the most firmly to it: the one was, that they understood the prophecies concerning the Messias sitting on the 'throne of David' literally: they thought that, in imitation of David, he was not only to free his own country from a foreign yoke, but that he was to subdue, as David had done, all the neighbouring nations. This was to them a stone of stumbling, and a rock of offence; so their adhering to their traditions proved their ruin in all respects. The other error, to which the authority of tradition led them, was their preferring the rituals of their religion to the moral precepts that it contained: this not only corrupted their own manners, while they thought that an exactness of performing, and a zeal in asserting, not only the ritual precepts that Moses gave their fathers, but those additions to them which they had from tradition, that were accounted hedges about the law: that this, I say, might well excuse or atone for the most heinous violations of the rules of justice and mercy: but this had yet another worse effect upon them, while it possessed them with such prejudices against our Saviour and his apostles, when they came to see that they set no value on those practices that were recommended by tradition, and that they preferred pure and sublime morals even to Mosaical ceremonies themselves, and set the Gentiles at liberty from those observances. So that the ruin of the Jews, their rejecting the Messias, and their persecuting his followers, arose chiefly from this principle that had got in among them, of believing tradition, and of being guided by it.

The apostles, in all their disputes with the Jews, make their appeals constantly to the scriptures; they set a high character on those of Berea for examining them, and comparing the doctrine that they preached with them. In the Epistles to the Romans, Galatians, and Hebrews, in which they pursue a thread of argument, with relation to the prejudices that the Jews had taken up against Christianity, they never once argue from tradition, but always from the scriptures; they do not pretend only to disparage modern tradition, and to set up that which was more ancient: they make no such distinction, but hold close to the scriptures. When St. Paul sets out the advantages that Timothy had by a religious education, he mentions this, 'that of a child he had known the holy scriptures, which were able to make him wise unto salvation, through faith which is in Christ Jesus:' that is, the belief of the Christian religion was a key to give him a right understanding of the Old Testament; and upon this occasion St. Paul adds, 'all scripture (that is, the whole Old Testament) is given by divine inspiration;' or (as others render the words) 'all the divinely inspired scripture is profitable for doctrine, for reproof, for correction, for instruction in righteousness, that the man of God may be perfect, throughly furnished unto all good works.' The New Testament was writ on the same design with the Old; that, as St. Luke expresses it, 'we might know the certainty of those things wherein we have been instructed: These things were written,' saith St. John, 'that ye might believe that Jesus is the Christ, the Son of God, and that believing ye might have life through his name.' When St. Peter knew by a special revelation that he was near his end, he writ his Second Epistle, that they might have that as a mean of keeping 'those things always in remembrance after his death.' Nor do the apostles give us any hints of their having left any thing with the church, to be conveyed down by an oral tradition, which they themselves had not put in writing: they do sometimes refer themselves to such things as they had delivered to particular churches; but by tradition in the apostles' days, and for some ages after, it is very clear, that they meant only the conveyance of the faith, and not any unwritten doctrines: they reckoned the faith was a sacred *depositum* which was committed to them; and that was to be preserved pure among them. But it were very easy to shew in the continued succession of all the first Christian writers, that they still appealed to the scriptures, that they argued from them, that they condemned all doctrines that were not contained in them; and when at any time they brought human authorities to justify their opinions or expressions, they contented themselves with a very few, and those very late, authorities: so that their design in vouching them seems to be rather to clear themselves from the imputation of having innovated any thing in the doctrine, or in the ways of expressing it, than that they thought those authorities were necessary to prove them by. For in that case they must have taken a great deal more pains than they did, to have followed up, and proved, the tradition much higher than they went.

We do also plainly see that such traditions as were not founded on scripture were easily corrupted, and on that account were laid aside by the succeeding ages. Such were the opinion of Christ's reign on earth for a thousand years; the saints not seeing God till the resurrection; the necessity of giving infants the eucharist; the divine inspiration of the seventy interpreters; besides some more important matters, which in respect to those times are not to be too much descanted upon. It is also plain, that the Gnostics, the Valentinians, and other heretics, began very early to set up a pretension to a tradition delivered by the apostles to some particular persons, as a key for understanding the secret meanings that might be in scripture; in opposition to which, both Irenæus, Tertullian, and others, make use of two sorts of arguments: the one is the authority of the scripture itself, by which they confuted their errors; the other is a point of fact, that there was no such tradition. In asserting this, they appeal to those churches which had been founded by the apostles, and in which a succession of bishops had been continued down. They say, in these we must search for apostolical tradition. This was not said by them as if they had designed to establish tradition, as an authority distinct from, or equal to, the scriptures: but only to shew the falsehood of that pretence of the heretics, and that there was no such tradition for their heresies as they gave out.

ART. VI.

When this whole matter is considered in all its parts, such as, 1st, That nothing is to be believed as an article of faith, unless it appears to have been revealed by God. 2dly, That oral tradition appears, both from the nature of man, and the experience of former times, to be an incompetent conveyer of truth. 3dly, That some books were written for the conveyance of those matters, which have been in all ages carefully preserved and esteemed sacred. 4thly, That the writers of the first ages do always argue from, and appeal to, these books: and, 5thly, That what they have said without authority from them has been rejected in succeeding ages; the truth of this branch of our article is fully made out.

If what is contained in the scripture in express words is the object of our faith, then it will follow, that whatsoever may be proved from thence, by a just and lawful consequence, is also to be believed. Men may indeed err in framing these consequences and deductions, they may mistake or stretch them too far: but though there is much sophistry in the world, yet there is also true logic, and a certain thread of reasoning. And the sense of every proposition being the same, whether expressed always in the same or in different words; then whatsoever appears to be clearly the sense of any place of scripture, is an object of faith, though it should be otherwise expressed than as it is in scripture, and every just inference from it must be as true as the proposition itself is: therefore it is a vain cavil to ask express words of scripture for every article. That was the method of all the ancient heretics: Christ and his apostles argued from the words and passages in the Old Testament, to prove such things as agreed with the true sense of them, and so did all the fathers; and therefore so may we do.

The great objection to this is, that the scriptures are dark, that the same place is capable of different senses, the literal and the mystical: and therefore, since we cannot understand the true sense of the scripture, we must not argue from it, but seek for an interpreter of it, on whom we may depend. All sects argue from thence, and fancy that they find their tenets in it: and therefore this can be no sure way of finding out sacred truth, since so many do err that follow it. In answer to this, it is to be considered, that the Old Testament was delivered to the whole nation of the Jews; that Moses was read in the synagogue, in the hearing of the women and children; that whole nation was to take their doctrine and rules from it: all appeals were made to the law and to the prophets among

Deut. vi. 3, 6—9. xi. 18—21. xxxi. 11— 13. Jos. viii. 32—35.

H

ART.
VI.

2 Ki. xxiii.
2, 21, 24.
Ne. viii. 1
—8, 18.
Is. viii. 20.
xxxiv. 16.
Matt. ii. 4
—6.
Luk. iv. 16
—21. vii.
19—23.
xxiv. 25—
27.
Acts xvii.
2, 3. xviii.
28. xxviii.
23.

them: and though the prophecies of the Old Testament were in their style and whole contexture dark, and hard to be understood; yet when so great a question as this, Who was the true Messias? came to be examined, the proofs urged for it were passages in the Old Testament. Now the question was, how these were to be understood? No appeal was here made to tradition, or to church-authority, but only by the enemies of our Saviour. Whereas he and his disciples urge these passages in their true sense, and in the consequences that arose out of them. They did in that appeal to the rational faculties of those to whom they spoke. The Christian religion was at first delivered to poor and simple multitudes, who were both illiterate and weak: the Epistles, which are by much the hardest to be understood of the whole New Testament, were addressed to the whole churches, to all the *faithful* or *saints;* that is, to all the Christians in those churches. These were afterwards read in all their assemblies. Upon this it may reasonably be asked, were these writings clear in that age, or were they not? If they were not, it is unaccountable why they were addressed to the whole body, and how they came to be received and entertained as they were. It is the end of speech and writing, to make things to be understood; and it is not supposable, that men inspired by the Holy Ghost either could not or would not express themselves so as that they should be clearly understood. It is also to be observed, that the new dispensation is opposed to the old, as light is to darkness, an open face to a vailed, and substance to shadows. Since then the Old Testament was so clear, that David, both in the 19th, and most copiously in the 119th Psalm, sets out very fully the light which the laws of God gave them in that darker state, we have much more reason to conclude, that the new dispensation should be much brighter. If there was no need of a certain expounder of scripture then, there is much less now. Nor is there any provision made in the new for a sure guide; no intimations are given where to find one: from all which we may conclude, that the books of the New Testament were clear in those days, and might well be understood by those to whom they were at first addressed. If they were clear to them, they may be likewise clear to us: for though we have not a full history of that time, or of the phrases and customs, and particular opinions, of that age, yet the vast industry of the succeeding ages, of these two last in particular, has made such discoveries, besides the other collateral advantages which learning and a niceness in reasoning has given us, that we may justly reckon, that though some hints in the Epistles, which relate to the particulars of that time, may be so lost, that we can at best but make conjectures about them; yet, upon the whole matter, we may well understand all that is necessary to salvation in the scripture.

We may indeed fall into mistakes as well as into sins;

and into errors of ignorance, as well as into sins of ignorance. God has dealt with our understandings as he hath dealt with our wills: he proposes our duty to us, with strong motives to obedience; he promises us inward assistances, and accepts of our sincere endeavours; and yet this does not hinder many from perishing eternally, and others from falling into great sins, and so running great danger of eternal damnation; and all this is because God has left our wills free, and does not constrain us to be good. He deals with our understandings in the same manner; he has set his will and the knowledge of salvation before us, in writings that are framed in a simple and plain style, in a language that was then common, and is still well understood, that were at first designed for common use; they are soon read, and it must be confessed that a great part of them is very clear: so we have reason to conclude, that if a man reads these carefully and with an honest mind; if he prays to God to direct him, and follows sincerely what he apprehends to be true, and practises diligently those duties that do unquestionably appear to be bound upon him by them, that then he shall find out enough to save his soul; and that such mistakes as lie still upon him, shall either be cleared up to him by some happy providence, or shall be forgiven him by that infinite mercy, to which his sincerity and diligence is well known. That bad men should fall into grievous errors, is no more strange, than that they should commit heinous sins: and the errors of good men, in which they are neither wilful nor insolent, will certainly be forgiven, as well as their sins of infirmity. Therefore all the ill use that is made of the scripture, and all the errors that are pretended to be proved by it, do not weaken its authority or clearness. This does only shew us the danger of studying them with a biassed or corrupted mind, of reading them too carelessly, of being too curious in going farther than as they open matters to us; and in being too implicit in adhering to our education, or in submitting to the dictates of others.

So far I have explained the first branch of this Article. The consequence that arises out of it is so clear, that it needs not be proved: *That therefore nothing ought to be esteemed an article of faith, but what may be found in it, or proved from it.* If this is our rule, our entire and only rule, then such doctrines as are not in it ought to be rejected; and any church that adds to the Christian religion, is erroneous for making such additions, and becomes tyrannical if she imposes them upon all her members, and requires positive declarations, subscriptions, and oaths, concerning them. In so doing she forces such as cannot have communion with her, but by affirming what they believe to be false, to withdraw from that which cannot be had without departing from the truth. So all the additions of the five sacraments—of the invocation of angels and saints; of the worshipping of images, crosses, and relics; of the corporal presence in the eucharist; of the sacrifice offered in it for the dead as well as for the living; together with the adoration offered to it; with a great many more—are certainly errors, unless they can be proved from scripture; and they are intolerable errors, if as the scripture is express in opposition to them, so they defile the worship of Christians with idolatry: but they become yet most intolerable, if they are imposed upon all that are in that communion, and if creeds or oaths in which they are affirmed are required of all in their communion. Here is the main ground of justifying our forming ourselves into a distinct body from the Roman church, and therefore it is well to be considered.* The farther discussing of this will come properly in, when other particulars come to be examined.

From hence I go to the second branch of this Article, which gives us the canon of the scripture. Here I shall begin with the New Testament; for though in order the Old Testament is before the New, yet the proof of the one being more distinctly made out by the concurring testimonies of other writers, than can possibly be pretended for the other, and the New giving an authority to the Old by asserting it so

---

* This question of separation is ably unfolded in the following extract:—

'If therefore the church of Rome did thrust the Protestants from her communion, for doing nothing but what became them as members of the catholic church, then that must be the schismatical party, and not the Protestants. For, supposing any church (though pretending to be never so catholic) doth restrain her communion within such narrow and unjust bounds, that she declares such excommunicate, who do not approve all such errors in doctrine, and corruptions in practice, which the communion of such a church may be liable to, the cause of that division which follows, falls upon that church which exacts these conditions from the members of her communion: that is, when the errors and corruptions are such as are dangerous to salvation. For in this case, that church hath first divided herself from the catholic church; for, the communion of that lying open and free to all, upon the necessary conditions of Christian communion, whatever church takes upon her to limit and enclose the bounds of the catholic, becomes thereby divided from the communion of the catholic church: and all such who disown such an unjust enclosure, do not so much divide from the communion of that church so enclosing, as return to the communion of the primitive and universal church. The catholic church therefore lies open and free, like a common field to all inhabitants; now if any particular number of these inhabitants should agree together, to enclose part of it, without consent of the rest, and not to admit any others to their right of common, without consenting to it, which of these two parties, those who deny to yield their consent, or such who deny their rights if they will not, are guilty of the violation of the public and common rights of the place? Now, this is plainly the case between the church of Rome and ours; the communion of the catholic church lies open to all such who own the fundamentals of Christian faith, and are willing to join in the profession of them: now to these your church adds many particular doctrines, which have no foundation in scripture, or the consent of the primitive church—these, and many superstitious practices, are enjoined by her as conditions of her communion, so that all those are debarred any right of communion with her, who will not approve of them; by which it appears your church is guilty of the first violation of the union of the catholic; and whatever number of men are deprived of your communion, for not consenting to your usurpations, do not divide themselves from you any farther than you have first separated yourselves from the catholic church. And when your church by this act is already separated from the communion of the catholic church, the disowning of those things wherein your church is become schismatical cannot certainly be any culpable separation. For, whatever is so, must be from a church so far as it is catholic; but in our case it is from a church so far only as it is not catholic, i.e.

expressly, I shall therefore prove first the canon of the New Testament. I will not urge that of the testimony of the Spirit, which many have had recourse to: this is only an argument to him that feels it, if it is one at all; and therefore it proves nothing to another person: besides the utmost that with reason can be made of this is, that a good man feeling the very powerful effects of the Christian religion on his own heart, in the reforming his nature, and the calming his conscience, together with those comforts that arise out of it, is convinced in general of the whole of Christianity, by the happy effects that it has upon his own mind: but it does not from this appear how he should know that such books and such passages in them should come from a divine original, or that he should be able to distinguish what is genuine in them from what is spurious. To come therefore to such arguments as may be well insisted upon and maintained.

The canon of the new Testament, as we now have it, is fully proved from the quotations out of the books of the New Testament by the writers of the first and second centuries; such as Clemens, Ignatius, Justin, Irenæus, and several

---

so far as it hath divided herself from the belief and communion of the universal church. . . . .
 ' For which we must farther consider, that although nothing separates a church properly from the catholic, but what is contrary to the being of it; yet a church may separate herself from the communion of the catholic, by taking upon her to make such things the necessary conditions of her communion, which never were the conditions of communion with the catholic church. As for instance, though we should grant, adoration of the eucharist, invocation of saints, and veneration of images, to be only superstitious practices taken up without sufficient grounds in the church; yet since it appears that the communion of the catholic church was free for many hundred years, without approving or using these things; that church which shall not only publicly use, but enjoin, such things upon pain of excommunication from the church, doth, as much as in her lies, draw the bounds of catholic communion within herself, and so divides herself from the true catholic church. For whatever confines must likewise divide the church; for by that confinement a separation is made between the part confined, and the other, which separation must be made by the party so limiting Christian communion. As it was the case of the Donatists, who were therefore justly charged with schism, because they confined the catholic church within their own bounds: and if any other church doth the same which they did, it must be liable to the same charge which they were. The sum of this discourse is, that the being of the catholic church lies in essentials; that for a particular church to disagree from all other particular churches in some extrinsical and accidental things, is not to separate from the catholic church so as to cease to be a church; but still whatever church makes such extrinsical things the necessary conditions of communion, so as to cast men out of the church who yield not to them, is schismatical in so doing; for it thereby divides itself from the catholic church; and the separation from it is so far from being schism, that being cast out of the church on these terms only returns them to the communion of the catholic church. On which grounds it will appear that yours is the schismatical church, and not ours. For although, before this imposing humour came into particular churches, schism was defined by the fathers, and others, to be a voluntary departure out of the church, yet that cannot in reason be understood of any particular, but the true catholic church; for not only persons but churches may depart from the catholic church; and in such cases, not those who depart from the communion of such churches, but those churches which departed from the catholic, are guilty of the schism.'—*Stillingfleet.*
 The reader ought also to consult Chillingworth, chap. v. '*Separation of Protestants from the church of Rome, not guilty of schism.*'—[ED.]

others. Papias, who conversed with the disciples of the apostles, is cited by Eusebius in confirmation of St. Matthew's Gospel, which he says was writ by him in Hebrew: he is also cited to prove that St. Mark writ his Gospel from St. Peter's preaching; which is also confirmed by Clemens of Alexandria; not to mention later writers. Irenæus says St. Luke writ his Gospel according to St. Paul's preaching; which is supported by some words in St. Paul's Epistles that relate to passages in that Gospel: yet certainly he had likewise other vouchers; those 'who from the beginning were eye-witnesses and ministers of the word;' though the whole might receive its full authority from St. Paul's approbation. St. John writ later than the other three; so the testimonies concerning his Gospel are the fullest and the most particular. Irenæus has laboured the proof of this matter with much care and attention: he lived within a hundred years of St. John, and knew Polycarp that was one of his disciples: after him come Tertullian and Origen, who speak very copiously of the four Gospels; and from them all the ecclesiastical writers have without any doubting or controversy acknowledged and cited them, without the least shadow of any opposition, except what was made by Marcion and the Manichees.

Next to these authorities we appeal to the catalogues of the books of the New Testament, that are given us in the third and fourth centuries by Origen, a man of great industry, and that had examined the state of many churches; by St. Athanasius, by the council of Laodicea and Carthage; and after these we have a constant succession of testimonies, that do deliver these as the canon universally received. All this laid together does fully prove this point; and that the more clearly, when these particulars are considered. 1st, That the books of the New Testament were read in all their churches, and at all their assemblies, so that this was a point in which it was not easy for men to mistake. 2dly, That this was so near the fountain, that the originals themselves of the apostles were no doubt so long preserved. 3dly, That both the Jews, as appears from Justin Martyr, and the Gentiles, as appears by Celsus, knew that these were the books in which the faith of the Christians was contained. 4thly, That some question was made touching some of them, because there was not that clear or general knowledge concerning them, that there was concerning the others; yet upon fuller inquiry all acquiesced in them. No doubt was ever made about thirteen of St. Paul's Epistles; because there were particular churches or persons, to whom the originals of them were directed: but the strain and design of that to the Hebrews being to remove their prejudices, that high one, which they had taken up against St. Paul as an enemy to their nation, was to be kept out of view, that it might not blast the good effects which were intended by it; yet it is cited oftener than once by Clemens of Rome:

and though the ignorance of many of the Roman church, who thought that some passages in it favoured the severity of the Novatians, that cut off apostates from the hopes of repentance, made them question it, of which mention is made both by Origen, Eusebius, and Jerome, who frequently affirm, that the Latin church, or the Roman, did not receive it; yet Athanasius reckons both this and the seven general Epistles among the canonical writings. Cyril of Jerusalem, who had occasion to be well informed about it, says, that he delivers his catalogue from the church, as she had received it from the apostles, the ancient bishops, and the governors of the church; and reckons up in it both the seven general Epistles, and the fourteen of St. Paul. So does Ruffin, and so do the councils of Laodicea and Carthage;[b] the canons of the former being received into the body of the *Canons*[b] of the *Universal Church*. Irenæus, Origen, and Clemens of Alexandria,[c] cite the Epistle to the Hebrews frequently. Some question was made of the Epistle of St. James, the Second of St. Peter, the Second and Third of St. John, and St. Jude's Epistle. But both Clemens of Rome,[d] Ignatius, and Origen, cite St. James's Epistle; Eusebius[e] says it was known to most, and read in most Christian churches: the like is testified by St. Jerome.[f] St. Peter's Second Epistle is cited by Origen and Firmilian;[g] and Eusebius[h] says it was held very useful even by those who held it not canonical; but since the First Epistle was never questioned by any, the Second that carries so many characters of its genuineness, such as St. Peter's name at the head of it, the mention of the transfiguration, and of his being an eye-witness of it, are evident proofs of its being writ by him. The Second and Third Epistles of St. John are cited by Irenæus, Clemens and Dennis of Alexandria, and by Tertullian.[i] The Epistle of St. Jude is also cited by Tertullian.* Some of those general Epistles were not addressed to any particular body, or church, that might have preserved the originals of them, but were sent about in the nature of circular letters; so that it is no wonder if they were not received so early, and with such an unanimity, as we find concerning the four Gospels, the Acts of the Apostles, and thirteen of St. Paul's Epistles. These, being first fixed upon

ART. VI.

Orig. Ep. ad African.
Orig. Exh. ad Martyr.
Euseb.His. lib.vi.c.14.
Hieron.Ep. ad Dardan.
Cyr.Catec. iv.

---

[a] Apud Hieron.
[b] Can. 60. Can. 47.
[c] Iren. l. iii. c. 38. Orig. l. iii. et vii. cont. Cels. Dial. con. Marc. et Ep. ad Afric. Clem. Alex. Strom. lib. ii.—iv. et vi.
[d] Ignat. Ep. ad Eph. Orig. Hom. 13. in Gones.
[e] Eus. Hist. l. ii. c. 23. l. iii. c. 25.
[f] Hieron. Pref. in Ep. Jac.
[g] Orig. cont. Marcion. Firmil. inter Epist. Cyprian. Ep. 75. p. 226. Oxon. 1682.
[h] Eus. Hist. l. iii. c. 3.
[i] Iren. l. i. c. 13. Clem. Alex. Strom. 2. Tertul. de Carne Chr. c. 24. Eus. Hist. l. vi. c. 25. Tertul. de cultu fœm.
* The reader will find these writers quoted at length in 'Lardner's Credibility,' &c.—[ED.]

by an unquestioned and undisputed tradition, made that here was a standard once ascertained to judge the better of the rest: so when the matter was strictly examined, so near the fountain that it was very possible and easy to find out the certainty of it, then in the beginning of the fourth century the canon was settled, and universally agreed to. The style and matter of the Revelation, as well as the designation of *Divine* given to the author of it, gave occasion to many questions about it: Clemens of Rome cites it as a prophetical book:* Justin Martyr says it was writ by John, one of Christ's twelve apostles; Irenæus calls it the Revelation of St. John, the disciple of our Lord, writ almost in our own age, in the end of Domitian's reign. Melito writ upon it: Theophilus of Antioch, Hippolytus, Clemens and Dennis of Alexandria, Tertullian, Cyprian, and Origen, do cite it. And thus the canon of the New Testament seems to be fully made out by the concurrent testimony of the several churches immediately after the apostolical time.

[Marginal references: Clem. in Ep. ad Cor. Justin.con. Tryphon. Iren. l. v. c. xxiii. & xxv. Eus. Hist. l. iv. c. 24, 26. l. v. c. 18. l. vii. c. 25.]

Here it is to be observed, that a great difference is to made between all this and the oral tradition of a doctrine, in which there is nothing fixed or permanent, so that the whole is only report carried about and handed down. Whereas here is a book, that was only to be copied out and read publicly, and by all persons, between which the difference is so vast, that it is as little possible to imagine how the one should continue pure, as how the other should come to be corrupted. There was never a book of which we have that reason to be assured that it is genuine, that we have here. There happened to be constant disputes among Christians from the second century downward, concerning some of the most important parts of this doctrine; and by both sides these books were appealed to: and though there might be some variations in readings and translations, yet no question was made concerning the canon, or the authenticalness of the books themselves; unless it were by the Manichees, who came indeed to be called Christians, by a very enlarged way of speaking; since it is justly strange how men who said that the Author of the universe, and of the Mosaical dispensation, was an evil God; and who held that there were two supreme Gods, a good and an evil one; how such men, I say, could be called Christians.

---

* This citation of the book of Revelation by Clemens of Rome is not noticed by Lardner, Paley, or Mr. Horne in his 'Introduction,' &c. Tomline says, 'The earliest author now extant, who mentions this book, is Justin Martyr, who lived about sixty years after it was written, and he ascribes it to St. John.' Mr. Horne, however, following Lardner, mentions Hermas, Ignatius, and Polycarp, who lived before the time of Justin Martyr, as having referred to this book. We have taken some pains to discover Burnet's grounds for his statement respecting Clemens of Rome, and think it probable that the following is the passage from Clemens which he had in view, and which appears to be a reference to Rev. xxii. 12 : ' For from him are all things; and thus he speaks to us beforehand: "Behold the Lord cometh, and his reward is before his face, to render to every man according to his work." '—[Ed.]

The authority of those books is not derived from any judgment that the church made concerning them; but from this, that it was known that they were writ, either by men who were themselves the apostles of Christ, or by those who were their assistants and companions, at whose order, or under whose direction and approbation, it was known that they were written and published. These books were received and known for such, in the very apostolical age itself; so that many of the apostolical men, such as Ignatius and Polycarp, lived long enough to see the canon generally received and settled. The suffering and depressed state of the first Christians was also such, that as there is no reason to suspect them of imposture, so it is not at all credible that an imposture of this kind could have passed upon all the Christian churches. A man in a corner might have forged the Sibylline oracles, or some other pieces which were not to be generally used; and they might have appeared soon after, and credit might have been given too easily to a book or writing of that kind: but it cannot be imagined, that in an age in which the belief of this doctrine brought men under great troubles, and in which miracles and other extraordinary gifts were long continued in the church, that, I say, either false books could have been so early obtruded on the church as true, or that true books could have been so vitiated as to lose their original purity, while they were so universally read and used; and that so soon; or that the writers of that very age and of the next should have been so generally and so grossly imposed upon, as to have cited spurious writings for true. These are things that could not be believed in the histories or records of any nation: though the value that the Christians set upon these books, and the constant use they made of them, reading a parcel of them every Lord's day, make this much less supposable in the Christian religion, than it could be in any other sort of history or record whatsoever. The early spreading of the Christian religion to so many remote countries and provinces, the many copies of these books that lay in countries so remote, the many translations of them that were quickly made, do all concur to make the impossibility of any such imposture the more sensible. Thus the canon of the New Testament is fixed upon clear and sure grounds.

From thence, without any farther proof, we may be convinced of the canon of the Old Testament. Christ does frequently cite Moses and the prophets; he appeals to them; and though he charged the Jews of that time, chiefly their teachers and rulers, with many disorders and faults, yet he never once so much as insinuated that they had corrupted their law, or other sacred books; which, if true, had been the greatest of all those abuses that they had put upon the people. Our Saviour cited their books according to the translation that was then in credit and common use amongst them. When

ART. VI.

Luke xxiv. 25—27.

Luke xxiv. 44.

Rom. iii. 2.

2 Tim. iii. 15.

one asked him which was the great commandment, he answered, 'How readest thou?' And he proved the chief things relating to himself, his death and resurrection, from the prophecies that had gone before; which ought to have been fulfilled in him: he also cites the Old Testament, by a threefold division of the 'law of Moses, the Prophets, and the Psalms;' according to the three orders of books into which the Jews had divided it. The *Psalms*, which was the first among the holy writings, being set for that whole volume, St. Paul says, that 'to the Jews were committed the oracles of God:' he reckons that among the chief of their privileges, but he never blames them for being unfaithful in this trust; and it is certain that the Jews have not corrupted the chief of those passages that are urged against them to prove Jesus to have been the Christ. So that the Old Testament, at least the translation of the LXX interpreters, which was in common use and in high esteem among the Jews in our Saviour's time, was, as to the main, faithful and uncorrupted. This might be farther urged from what St. Paul says concerning those scriptures which Timothy had learned of a child; these could be no other than the books of the Old Testament. Thus if the writings of the New Testament are acknowledged to be of divine authority, the full testimony, that they give to the books of the Old Testament, does sufficiently prove their authority and genuineness likewise. But to carry this matter yet farther:

Moses wrought such miracles both in Egypt, in passing through the Red Sea, and in the wilderness, that, if these are acknowledged to be true, there can be no question made of his being sent of God, and authorized by him to deliver his will to the Jewish nation. The relation given of those miracles represents them to be such in themselves, and to have been acted so publicly, that it cannot be pretended they were tricks, or that some bold asserters gained a credit to them by affirming them. They were so publicly transacted, that the relations given of them are either downright fables: or they were clear and uncontested characters of a prophet authorized of God. Nor is the relation of them made with any of those arts that are almost necessary to impostors. The Jewish nation is all along represented as froward and disobedient, apt to murmur and rebel. The laws it contains, as to the political part, are calculated to advance both justice and compassion, to awaken industry, and yet to repress avarice. Liberty and authority are duly tempered; the moral part is pure, and suitable to human nature, though with some imperfections and tolerances which were connived at, but yet regulated: and for the religious part, idolatry, magic, and all human sacrifices, were put away by it. When we consider what remains are left us of the idolatry of the Egyptians, and what was afterward among the Greeks and Romans, who were polite and well constituted as to their civil laws and rules, and may be

esteemed the most refined pieces of heathenism, we do find a ART.
simplicity and purity, a majesty and gravity, a modesty with VI.
a decency, in the Jewish rituals, to which the others can in no
sort be compared.

In the books of Moses, no design for himself appears; his
posterity were but in the crowd, Levites without any character
of distinction; and he spares neither himself nor his brother,
when there was occasion to mention their faults, no more than
he does the rest of his countrymen. It is to be farther considered, that the laws and policy appointed by Moses settled
many rules and rights that must have perpetuated the remembrance of them. The land was to be divided by lot, and every
share was to descend in an inheritance; the frequent assemblies at Jerusalem on the three great festivals, the sabbaths,
the new moons, the sabbatical year, and the great jubilee, the
law of the double tithe, the sacrifices of so many different
kinds, the distinctions of meats, the prohibition of eating blood,
together with many other particulars, were all founded upon
it. Now let it be a little considered, whether the foundation
of all this, I mean the five books of Moses, could be a forgery
or not. If the Pentateuch was delivered by Moses himself to
the Jews, and received by them as the rule both of their religion and policy, then it is not possible to conceive, but that
the recital of all that is contained from the book of Exodus to
the end of Deuteronomy was known by them to be true; and
this establishes the credit of the whole. But if this is not
admitted, then let it be considered in what time it can possibly
be supposed that this imposture could have appeared. There
is a continued series of books of their history, that goes down
to the Babylonish captivity; so if there was an imposture of
this sort set on foot in that time, all that history must have
been made upon it, and an account must have been given of
the discovery of those books; otherwise the imposture must
have been too weak to have gained credit. Whereas, on the
contrary, the whole thread of their history represents these
books to have been always amongst them.

The discovery made in the reign of Josias cannot be supposed to be of this sort; since how much disorder soever the
long and wicked reign of Manasses might have brought them
under, and what havoc soever might have been made of the
writings that were held sacred among them, yet it was impossible that a series of forged laws and histories could have been
put upon them; of which there was still a continued memory
preserved among them; and that they could be brought to
believe that a book and a law full of so much history, and of
so many various and unusual rites founded upon it, had been
held sacred among them for many ages; if it was but a new
invention. Therefore this is an extravagant conceit: so that 2 Chron.
the book, that was then found in the temple, was either the xxxiv. 14.
original of the law written by Moses's own hand; for so the

ART. VI.

Ch. xxvi. 16. to the end of Deut. Deu. xxviii. from 36. to the end.

words may be rendered: or it may be understood of some of the last chapters of Deuteronomy, which seem by the tenor of them to have been at first a book by themselves, though afterwards joined to the rest of Deuteronomy; and in the collection that Josias was making, these might be wanting at first; and in these there are such severe threatenings, that it was no wonder if a heart so tender as Josias's was very much affected at the reading them.

Upon the whole matter, there is no period in the whole history of the Jews, to which any suspicion of such an imposture can be fastened before the Babylonish captivity: so it must be laid either upon the times of the captivity, or soon after their return out of it. Now, not to observe that men in such circumstances are seldom capable of things of that nature, can it be imagined that a series of books, that run through many ages, could have been framed so particularly, and yet so exactly, that nothing in any concurrent history could ever be brought to disprove any part of it? That such a thing could pass in so short a time upon a whole nation, while so many men remembered, or might well remember, what they had been before the captivity, if they had not all known that it was true, is a most inconceivable thing. These books were so far from being disputed, though we see their neighbours the Samaritans were inclined enough to contest every thing with them, that all acquiesced in them, and in that second beginning of their being a state, as it is opened in the books of Esdras and Nehemiah, and in Daniel, and the three prophets of the second temple, all the other books were received among them without dispute: and their law was in such high esteem, that about two hundred years after that, the king of Egypt did with much entreaty, and at a vast charge, procure a translation of it to be made in Greek.

The Jewish nation, as they live much within themselves, where it is safe for them to profess their religion, so they have had the divine authority of their books so deeply infused into them from age to age, that now above sixteen hundred years, though it is not possible for them to practise the main parts of their religion, and though they suffer much for professing it, yet they do still adhere to it, and practise as much of it as they can by the law itself, which ties the chief performances of that religion to one determinate place. This is a firmness which has never yet appeared in any other religion besides the Jewish and the Christian: for all the several shapes of heathenism have often changed, and they all went off as soon as the government that supported them fell, and that another came in its place. Whereas these have subsisted long, not only without the support of the civil power, but under many severe persecutions: which is at least a good moral argument to prove, that these religions had another foundation, and a deeper root, than any other religion could ever pretend to. Yet,

after all, it is not to be denied, but that in the collection that
was made of the books of the Old Testament after the captivity, by Ezra and others, or after that burning of many of the
books of their law under Antiochus Epiphanes, mentioned in
the book of Maccabees, that some disorder might happen;
that there might be such regard had to some copies, as not to
alter some manifest faults that were in them, but that, instead
of that, they might have marked on the margin that which
was the true reading; and a superstitious conceit might have
afterwards crept in, and continued in after-ages, of a mystery
in that matter, upon their first letting these faults continue in
the text with the marginal annotation of the correction of them.
There might be also other marginal annotations of the modern
names of places set against the ancient ones, to guide the
reader's judgment; and afterwards the modern name might
have been writ instead of the ancient one. These are things
that might naturally enough happen; and will serve to resolve
many objections against the texts of the Old Testament. All
the numbers of persons as well as of years might also have been
writ in numerical letters, though afterwards they came all to
be set down in words at large: and while they were in letters,
as some might have been worn out, and lost in ancient copies,
so others were, by the resemblance of some letters, very like
to be mistaken: nor could men's memories serve them so well
to correct mistakes in numbers as in other matters. This may
shew a way to reconcile many seeming differences between
the accounts that are variously stated in some of the books of
the Bible, and between the Hebrew and the Septuagint. In
these matters our church has made no decision; and so divines are left to a just freedom in them.

In general, we may safely rely upon the care and providence
of God, and the industry of men, who are naturally apt to
preserve things of that kind entire, which are highly valued
among them. And therefore we conclude, that the books of
the Old Testament are preserved pure down to us, as to all
those things for which they were written; that is, in every
thing that is either an object of faith, or a rule of life; and as to
lesser matters which visibly have no relation to either of these,
there is no reason to think that every copier was so divinely
guided that no small error might surprise him. In fact, we
know that there are many various readings, which might have
arisen from the haste and carelessness of copiers, from their
guessing wrong that which appeared doubtful or imperfect in
the copy, and from a superstitious adhering to some apparent
faults, when they found them in copies of a venerable antiquity.
But when all those various readings are compared together, it
appears that as they are inconsiderable, so they do not concern our faith nor our morals; the setting which right was the
main end of revelation. The most important diversity relates
to chronology: but the account of time, especially in the first

ages, is of no consequence to our believing right, or to our living well: and therefore, if some errors or mistakes should appear to be among those different readings, these give no just cause to doubt of the whole. And indeed, considering the many ages through which those books have passed, we have much more reason to wonder, that they are brought down to us so entire, and so manifestly genuine in all their main and important parts, than that we should see some prints of the frailty of those who copied and preserved them.

It remains only upon this head to consider what inspiration and an inspired book is, and how far that matter is to be carried. When we talk with one another, a noise is made in the air that strikes with such vibrations on the ears of others, that, by the motion thereby made on the brain of another, we do convey our thoughts to another person: so that the impression made on the brain is that which communicates our thoughts to another. By this we can easily apprehend how God may make such impressions on men's brains, as may convey to them such things as he intends to make known to them.

This is the general notion of inspiration: in which the manner and degree of the impression may make it at the least as certain that the motion comes from God, as a man may be certain that such a thing was told him by such a person, and not by any other. Now there may be different degrees both of the objects that are revealed, and of the manner of the revelation. To some it may be given in charge to deliver rules and laws to men: and because that ought to be expressed in plain words without pomp or ornament, therefore upon such occasions the imagination is not to be much agitated; but the impression must be made so naked, that the understanding may clearly apprehend it; and by consequence that it may be plainly expressed. In others, the design may be only to employ them in order to the awakening men to observe a law already received and owned; that must be done with such pompous visions of judgments coming upon the violation of those laws, as may very much alarm those to whom they are sent: both the representations and the expressions must be fitted to excite men, to terrify, and so to reform them. Now because the imagination, whether when we are transported in our thoughts being awake, or in dreams, is capable of having those scenes acted upon it, and of being so excited by them, as to utter them with pompous figures, and in a due rapidity; this is another way of inspiration that is strictly called *prophecy* in the Old Testament. A great deal of the style used in this must relate to the particulars of the time to which it belongs: many allusions, hints, and forms of speech, must be used, that are lively and proverbial; which cannot be understood, unless we had all those concurrent helps which are lost even in the next age, if not preserved in books, and so they must be quite lost after many ages are past, when no other memorials are left of the time in which they were transacted. This must needs make the far greater part of all the prophetic writings to be very dark to us; not to insist upon the peculiar genius of the language in which the prophets wrote, and on the common customs of those climates and nations to this day, that are very different from our own.

A third degree of inspiration might be, when there were no discoveries of future events to be made: but good and holy men were to be inwardly excited by God to compose such poems, hymns, and discourses, as should be of great use both to give men clearer and fuller apprehensions of divine things, and also insensibly to charm them with a pleasant and exalted way of treating them. And if the providence of God should so order them in the management of their composures, that it may afterwards appear that predictions were intermixed with them; yet they are not to be called prophets, unless God had revealed to them the mystical intent of such predictions: so that though the Spirit of God prophesied in them, yet they themselves not understanding it, are not to be accounted prophets. Of this last sort are the books of the Psalms, Job, Proverbs, Ecclesiastes, &c.

According to the different order of these inspirations was the Old Testament divided into three volumes. The inspiration of the New Testament is all to be reduced to the first sort, except the Revelation, which is purely and strictly prophetical. The other parts of the New Testament are writ after a softer and clearer illumination, and in a style suitable to it. Now because enthusiasts and impostors may falsely pretend to divine commissions and inspirations, it is necessary (both for the undeceiving of those who may be misled by a hot and ungoverned imagination, and for giving such an authority to men truly inspired, as may distinguish them from false pretenders) that the man thus inspired should have some evident sign or other, either some miraculous action that is visibly beyond the powers of nature, or some particular discovery of somewhat that is to come, which must be so expressed, that the accomplishment of it may shew it to be beyond the conjectures of the most sagacious: by one or both of those a man must prove, and the world must be convinced, that he is sent and directed by God. And if such men deliver their message in writing, we must receive such writings as sacred and inspired.

In these writings some parts are historical, some doctrinal, and some elenchtical or argumentative. As to the historical part, it is certain that whatsoever is delivered to us, as a matter truly transacted, must be indeed so: but it is not necessary, when discourses are reported, that the individual words should be set down just as they were said; it is enough if the effect of them is reported: nor is it necessary that the order of time should be strictly observed, or that all the conjunctions in such relation should be understood severely according to their grammatical meaning. It is visible that all the sacred writers write in a diversity of style, according to their different tempers, and to the various impressions that were made upon them. In that the inspiration left them to the use of their faculties, and to their previous customs and habits: the design of revelation, as to this part of its subject, is only to give such representations of matters of fact, as may both work upon and guide our belief; but the order of time, and the strict words, having no influence that way, the writers might dispose them, and express them, variously, and yet all be exactly true. For the conjunctive particles do rather import that one passage comes to be related after another, than that it was really transacted after it.

As to the doctrinal parts, that is, the rules of life, which these books set before us, or the propositions that are offered to us in them, we must entirely acquiesce in these, as in the voice of God, who speaks to us by the means of a person, whom he, by his authorizing him in so wonderful a manner, obliges us to hear and believe. But when these writers come to explain or argue, they use many figures that were well known in that age: but because the signification of a figure is to be taken from common use, and not to be carried to the utmost extent that the words themselves will bear, we must therefore inquire, as much as we can, into the manner and phraseology of the time in which such persons lived, which with relation to the New Testament will lead us far: and by this we ought to govern the extent and importance of these figures.

As to their arguings, we are farther to consider, that sometimes they argue upon certain grounds, and at other times they go upon principles, acknowledged and received by those with whom they dealt. It ought never to be made the only way of proving a thing, to found it upon the concessions of those with whom we deal; yet when a thing is once truly proved, it is a just and usual way of confirming it, or at least of silencing those who oppose it, to shew that it follows naturally from those opinions and principles that are received among them. Since therefore the Jews had, at the time of the writing of the New Testament, a peculiar way of expounding many prophecies and passages in the Old Testament, it was a very proper way to convince them, to allege many places according to their key and methods of exposition. Therefore, when divine writers argue upon any point, we are always bound to believe the conclusions that their reasonings end in, as parts of divine revelation: but we are not bound to be able to make out, or even to assent to, all the premises made use of by them in their whole extent; unless it appears

THE XXXIX ARTICLES. 113

plainly that they affirm the premises as expressly as they do ART.
the conclusions proved by them.   VI.

And thus far I have laid down such a scheme concerning
inspiration and inspired writings, as will afford, to such as
apprehend it aright, a solution to most of these difficulties
with which we are urged on the account of some passages in the
sacred writings. The laying down a scheme that asserts an immediate inspiration which goes to the style, and to every tittle,
and that denies any error to have crept *into any of the copies*,
as it seems on the one hand to raise the honour of the scriptures very highly, so it lies open, on the other hand, to
great difficulties, which seem insuperable in that hypothesis;
whereas a middle way, as it settles the divine inspiration of
these writings, and their being continued down genuine and
unvitiated to us, as to all that, for which we can only suppose
that inspiration was given; so it helps us more easily out of
all difficulties, by yielding that which serves to answer them,
without weakening the authority of the whole.

I come in the last place to examine the negative consequence that arises out of this head, which excludes those
books commonly called apocryphal, that are here rejected,
from being a part of the canon: and this will be easily made
out. The chief reason that presses us Christians to acknowledge the Old Testament is the testimony that Christ and his
apostles gave to those books, as they were then received by
the Jewish church; to whom ' were committed the oracles of
God.' Now it is not so much as pretended, that ever these
books were received among the Jews, or were so much as
known to them. None of the writers of the New Testament
cite or mention them; neither Philo nor Josephus speaks of
them. Josephus on the contrary says, they had only twenty-
two books that deserved belief, but that those which were
written after the time of Artaxerxes were not of equal credit
with the rest: and that in that period they had no prophets
at all. The Christian church was for some ages an utter
stranger to those books. Melito, bishop of Sardis, being desired by Onesimus to give him a perfect catalogue of the
books of the Old Testament, took a journey on purpose to
the east, to examine this matter at its source: and having, as
he says, made an exact inquiry, he sent him the names of
them just as we receive the canon; of which Eusebius says, Eus. Hist.
that he has preserved it, because it contained all those books l. iv. c. 26.
which the church owned. Origen gives us the same catalogue
according to the tradition of the Jews, who divided the Old In Psal. i.
Testament into twenty-two books, according to the letters of
their alphabet. Athanasius reckons them up in the same In Synop.
manner to be twenty-two, and he more distinctly says, 'that In Ep.
he delivered those, as they had received them by tradition, pasch.
and as they were received by the whole church of Christ,
because some presumed to mix apocryphal books with the

I

ART. VI.

Catech. 4.

Can. 95, and 60.

Can. 47.

divine scriptures: and therefore he was set on it by the orthodox brethren, in order to declare the canonical books delivered as such by tradition, and believed to be of divine inspiration. It is true,' he adds, 'that besides these there were other books which were not put into the canon, but yet were appointed by the fathers to be read by those who first come to be instructed in the way of piety: and then he reckons up most of the apocryphal books.' Here is the first mention we find of them, as indeed it is very probable they were made at Alexandria, by some of those Jews who lived there in great numbers. Both Hilary and Cyril of Jerusalem give us the same catalogue of the books of the Old Testament, and affirm, that they delivered them thus according to the tradition of the ancients. Cyril says, that all other books are to be put in a second order. Gregory Nazianzen reckons up the twenty-two books, and adds that none besides them are genuine. The words that are in the Article are repeated by St. Jerome in several of his prefaces. And that which should determine this whole matter is, that the council of Laodicea by an express canon delivers the catalogue of the canonical books as we do, decreeing that these only should be read in the church. Now the canons of this council were afterwards received into the code of the canons of the universal church; so that here we have the concurring sense of the whole church of God in this matter.

It is true, the book of the Revelation not being reckoned in it, this may be urged to detract from its authority: but it was already proved, that that book was received much earlier into the canon of the scriptures, so the design of this canon being to establish the authority of those books that were to be read in the church, the darkness of the Apocalypse making it appear reasonable not to read it publicly, that may be the reason why it is not mentioned in it, as well as in some later catalogues.

Here we have four centuries clear for our canon, in exclusion to all additions. It were easy to carry this much farther down, and to shew that these books were never by any express definition received into the canon till it was done at Trent: and that in all the ages of the church, even after they came to be much esteemed, there were divers writers, and those generally the most learned of their time, who denied them to be a part of the canon. At first many writings were read in the churches, that were in high reputation both for the sake of the authors, and of the contents of them, though they were never looked on as a part of the canon: such were Clemens's Epistle, the books of Hermas, the Acts of the Martyrs, besides several other things which were read in particular churches. And among these the apocryphal books came also to be read, as containing some valuable books of instruction, besides several fragments of the Jewish history,

which were perhaps too easily believed to be true. These ART.
therefore being usually read, they came to be reckoned among VI.
canonical scriptures: for this is the reason assigned in the
third council of Carthage for calling them canonical, because
they had received them from their fathers as books that were
to be read in churches: and the word *canonical* was by some
in those ages used in a large sense, in opposition to spurious;
so that it signified no more than that they were genuine. So
much depends upon this Article, that it seemed necessary to
dwell fully upon it, and to state it clearly.

It remains only to observe the diversity between the Articles now established, and those set forth by king Edward. In the latter there was not a catalogue given of the books of scripture, nor was there any distinction stated between the canonical and the apocryphal books. In those there is likewise a paragraph, or rather a parenthesis, added after the words *proved thereby*, in these words, *Although sometimes it may be admitted by God's faithful people as pious, and conducing unto order and decency:* which are now left out, because the authority of the church as to matters of order and decency, which was only intended to be asserted by this period, is more fully explained and stated in the 35th Article.

ARTICLE VII.

Of the Old Testament.

The Old Testament is not contrary to the New: for both in the Old and New Testament everlasting Life is offered to Mankind by Christ, who is the only Mediator between God and Man, being both God and Man. Wherefore they are not to be heard which feign that the Old Fathers did look only for Transitory Promises.

Although the Law given from God by Moses, as touching Ceremonies and Rites, do not bind Christian Men, nor the Civil Precepts thereof ought of necessity to be received in any Commonwealth, yet notwithstanding no Christian Man whatsoever is free from the Obedience of the Commandments which are called Moral.

THIS Article is made up of the sixth and the nineteenth of king Edward's Articles laid together: only the nineteenth of king Edward's has these words after *moral: Wherefore they are not to be heard, which teach that the holy scriptures were given to none but to the weak; and brag continually of the Spirit, by which they do pretend that all whatsoever they preach is suggested to them; though manifestly contrary to the holy scriptures.* This whole Article relates to the Antinomians, as these last words were added by reason of the extravagance of some enthusiasts at that time; but that madness having ceased in queen Elizabeth's time, it seems it was thought that there was no more occasion for those words.

There are four heads that do belong to this Article: First, that the Old Testament is not contrary to the New. Secondly, that Christ was the Mediator in both dispensations, so that salvation was offered in both by him. Thirdly, that the ceremonial and the judiciary precepts in the law of Moses do not bind Christians. Fourthly, that the moral law does still bind all Christians.

To the first of these the Manichees of old, who fancied that there was a bad as well as a good God, thought that these two great principles were in a perpetual struggle; and they believed the old dispensation was under the bad one, which was taken away by the new, that is the work of the good God. But they who held such monstrous tenets must needs reject the whole New Testament, or very much corrupt it: since there is nothing plainer, than that the prophets of the Old foretold the New with approbation; and the writers of the New prove both their commission and their doctrine from passages of the Old Testament. This therefore could not be affirmed without rejecting many of the books that we own, and corrupting the rest. So this deserves no more to be considered.

ART. VII.

Upon this occasion it will be no improper digression, to consider what revelation those under the Mosaical law, or that lived before it, had of the Messias: this is an important matter: it is a great confirmation of the truth of the Christian religion, as it will furnish us with proper arguments against the Jews. It is certain they have long had, and still have, an expectation of a Messias. Now the characters and predictions concerning this person must have been fulfilled long ago: or the prophecies will be found to be false: and if they do meet and were accomplished in our Saviour's person, and if no other person could ever pretend to this, then that which is undertaken to be proved will be fully performed. The first promise to Adam after his sin, speaks of an enmity between the seed of the serpent and the seed of the woman: 'It shall bruise thy head, and thou shalt bruise his heel.' The one might hurt the other in some lesser instances, but the other was to have an entire victory at last; which is plainly signified by the figures of bruising the heel, and bruising the head, which was to be performed by one who was to bear this character of being the woman's seed. The next promise was made to Abraham, 'In thee shall all the families of the earth be blessed:' this was lodged in his seed or posterity, upon his being ready to offer up his son Isaac: that promise was renewed to Isaac, and after him to Jacob: when he was dying, it was lodged by him in the tribe of Judah, when he prophesied, that 'the sceptre should not depart from Judah, nor the lawgiver from between his feet, till Shiloh should come; and the gathering of the people,' that is, of the Gentiles, 'was to be to him.' It is certain the ten tribes were lost in their captivity, whereas the tribe of Judah was brought back, and continued to be a political body under their own laws, till a breach was made upon that by the Romans first reducing them to the form of a province, and soon after that destroying them utterly: so that either that prediction was not accomplished: or the *Shiloh*, the *Sent*, to whom the Gentiles were to be gathered, came before they lost their sceptre and laws.

Gen. iii. 15.

Gen. xii. 3. Gen. xxii. 18. Gen. xxvi. 24. Gen. xxviii. 14. Gen. xlix. 10.

Moses told the people of Israel, that God 'was to raise up among them a prophet like unto him, to whom they ought to hearken,' otherwise God would 'require it of them.' The character of Moses was, that he was a lawgiver, and the author of an entire body of instituted religion; so they were to look for such a one. Balaam prophesied darkly of one whom he saw as at a great distance from his own time; and he spoke of a 'Star that should come out of Jacob, and a sceptre out of Israel:' some memorial of which was probably preserved among the Arabians. In the book of Psalms there are many

Deut. xviii. 15.

Num. xxiv. 17.

ART.
VII

things said of David, which seem capable of a much auguster sense than can be pretended to be answered by any thing that befell himself. What is said in the 2d, the 16th, the 22d, the 45th, the 102d, and the 110th Psalms, affords us copious instances of this. Passages in these Psalms must be stretched by figures that go very high, to think they were all fulfilled in David or Solomon: but in their literal and largest sense they were accomplished in Christ, to whom God said, 'Thou art my son, this day have I begotten thee.' In him that was verified, 'Thou wilt not leave my soul in hell, neither wilt thou suffer thy Holy One to see corruption. His hands and his feet were pierced, and lots were cast upon his vesture.' Of him it may be strictly said, 'Thy throne, O God, is for ever and ever.' To him that belonged, 'The Lord said unto my Lord, Sit thou on my right hand, till I make thine enemies thy footstool.' And, 'The Lord sware and will not repent, Thou art a priest for ever after the order of Melchisedeck.'

The prophets gave yet more express predictions concerning the Messias. Isaiah did quiet the fears of Ahaz, and of the

Isa. vii. 14. house of David, by saying, 'The Lord himself shall give you a sign, Behold, a virgin shall conceive and bear a son.' It was certainly no sign for one that was a *virgin*, to conceive afterwards and bear a son; therefore the *sign* or extraordinary thing here promised as a signal pledge of God's care of the house of David, must lie in this, that one still remaining a *virgin* should conceive and bear a son; not to insist upon the strict signification of the word in the original. The same

Isa. xi. 1, 2. prophet did also foretell, that as this Messias, or the *Branch*, should spring from the stem of Jesse, so also he was to be

Ver. 10. full of the Spirit of the Lord; and 'that the Gentiles should seek to him.' In another place he enumerates many of the miracles that should be done by him: he was to give sight to

Isa. xxxv. 5, 6. the blind, make the deaf to hear, the lame to walk. He does further set forth his character; not that of a warrior or con-

Isa. xlii. 1—4. queror; on the contrary, 'He was not to cry nor strive, nor break the bruised reed, or quench the smoking flax; he was to bring forth judgment to the Gentiles, and the isles were to

Isa. liii. wait for his law.' There is a whole chapter in the same prophet, setting forth the mean appearance that the Messias was to make, the contempt he was to fall under, and the sufferings he was to bear; and that for the sins of others, which were to be laid on him; so that his soul or life was to be made an *offering for sin*, in reward of which he was to be highly exalted.

Isa. lxi. In another place his mission is set forth, not in the strains of war, or of conquest, but of preaching to the poor, setting the prisoners free as in a year of jubilee, and comforting the afflicted and such as mourned. In the two last chapters of that prophet mention is made more particularly of the Gentiles that were to be called by him, and the *isles that were afar off*, out of whom God was to take some *for priests and Levites:*

which shewed plainly, that a new dispensation was to be opened by him, in which the Gentiles were to be *priests and Levites*, which could not be done while the Mosaical law stood, that had tied these functions to the tribe of Levi, and to the house of Aaron. Jeremy renewed the promise to the house of David, of 'a king that should reign and prosper; in whose days Judah and Israel were to dwell safely, whose name was to be, The Lord our Righteousness.' It is certain this promise was never literally accomplished; and therefore recourse must be had to a mystical sense. The same prophet gives a large account of a 'new covenant that God was to make with the house of Israel, not according to the covenant that he made with their fathers, when he brought them out of Egypt.' We have also two characters given of that covenant: one is, that God 'would put his law in their inward parts, and write it in their hearts;' that he would be their God, and that they should all be taught of him: the other is, 'that he would forgive their iniquities, and remember their sin no more.' One of these is in opposition to their law, that consisted chiefly in rituals, and had no promises of inward assistances; and the other is in opposition to the limited pardon that was offered, in that dispensation, on the condition of the many sacrifices that they were required to offer. There is a prediction to the same purpose in Ezekiel. Joel prophesied of an extraordinary effusion of the Spirit of God on great numbers of persons, old and young, that was to happen before the great and terrible day of the Lord, that is, before the final destruction of Jerusalem. Micah, after he had foretold several things of the dispensation of the Messiah, says that he was to come out of Bethlehem Ephratah. Haggai encouraged those who were troubled at the meanness of the temple, which they had raised after their return out of the captivity. It had neither the outward glory in its fabric that Solomon's temple had, nor the more real glory of the ark, with the *tables of the Law;* of *fire from heaven on the altar;* of a *succession of prophets;* of the *Urim and Thummim,* and the *cloud* between the cherubims; which last, strictly speaking, was the glory; all which had been in Solomon's temple, but were wanting in that. In opposition to this, the prophet, in the name of God, promised that he would in a 'little while shake the heavens and the earth,' and 'shake all nations;' words that import some surprising and great change; upon which the 'desire of all nations should come, and God would fill the house with his glory;' and 'the glory of this latter house should exceed the glory of the former, for in that place God would give peace.' Here is a plain prophecy, that this temple was to have a glory, not only equal but superior to the glory of Solomon's temple: these words are too august to be believed to have been accomplished, when Herod rebuilt the temple with much magnificence; for that was nothing in comparison of the real glory, of the symbols

ART. VII.

Jer. xxiii. 5.

Jer. xxxi. 31—34

Ezek. xxxvi. 25, &c.
Joel ii. 28, &c.
Micah v. 2.
Hag. ii. 6 —9.

ART. VII.

Zech. ix. 9.

Mal. iii. 1, 3.

of the presence of God, that were wanting in it. This cannot answer the words, that the *desire of all nations* was to come, and that God would *give peace* in that place. So that either this prophecy was never fulfilled: or somewhat must be assigned during the second temple, that will answer those solemn expressions, which are plainly applicable to our Saviour, who was the expectation of the *Gentiles*, by whom peace was made, and in whom the eternal Word dwelt in a manner infinitely more august than in the cloud of glory.* Zechary prophesied that *their King*, by which they understood the Messias, was to be *meek and lowly*, and that he was to make his entrance in a very mean appearance, *riding on an ass:* but yet under that, he was to *bring salvation to them*, and they were to *rejoice greatly in him*. Malachi told them, that 'the Lord whom they sought, even the messenger of the covenant in whom they delighted, should suddenly come into his temple;' and that the day of his coming was to be dreadful; that he was to *refine and purify*, in particular, *the sons of Levi*; and a terrible destruction is denounced after that. One character

* ' It cannot be conceived how the glory of the second temple should be greater than the glory of the first, without the coming of the Messias to it. For the Jews themselves have observed that five signs of the divine glory were in the first temple, which were wanting in the second: as the Urim and Thummim, by which the highpriest was miraculously instructed of the will of God; the ark of the covenant, from whence God gave his answers by a clear and audible voice; the fire upon the altar, which came down from heaven, and immediately consumed the sacrifice; the divine presence or habitation with them, represented by a visible appearance, or given, as it were, to the king and high-priest by anointing with the oil of unction; and, lastly, the spirit of prophecy, with which those especially who were called to the prophetical office were endued. And there was no comparison between the beauty and glory of the structure and building of it, as appeared by the tears dropped from those eyes which had beheld the former, ("For many of the priests and Levites and chief of the fathers, who were ancient men, that had seen the first house, when the foundation of this house was laid before their eyes, wept with a loud voice;" Ezra iii. 12.) and by those words which God commanded Haggai to speak to the people for the introducing of this prophecy, "Who is left among you that saw this house in her first glory? And how do you see it now? Is it not in your eyes in comparison of it as nothing?" (Hag. ii. 3.) Being then the structure of the second temple was so far inferior to the first, being all those signs of the divine glory were wanting in it with which the former was adorned; the glory of it can no other way be imagined greater, than by the coming of Him into it, in whom all the signs of the divine glory were far more eminently contained; and this person alone is the *Messias*. For he was to be the glory of the people Israel, yea, even of the God of Israel; he the Urim and Thummim, by whom the will of God, as by a greater oracle, was revealed; he the true ark of the covenant, the only propitiatory by his blood; he which was to baptize with the Holy Ghost and with fire, the true fire which came down from heaven; he which was to take up his habitation in our flesh, and to dwell among us that we might behold his glory; he who received the Spirit without measure, and from whose fulness we do all receive. In him were all those signs of the Divine Glory united, which were thus divided in the first temple; in him they were all more eminently contained than in those; therefore his coming to the second temple was, as the sufficient, so the only means by which the glory of it could be greater than the glory of the first. If then the *Messias* was to come while the second temple stood, as appeared by God's prediction and promise; if that temple many ages since hath ceased to be, there being not one stone left upon a stone; if it certainly were before the destruction of it in greater glory than ever the former was; if no such glory could accrue unto it but by the coming of the *Messias*: then is that *Messias* already come.' *Pearson on the Creed*, pp. 127, 128. *Dobson's edition.*—[Ed.]

of his coming was, that *Elijah the prophet* was to come before that *great and dreadful day,* who should convert many, old and young. Now it is certain that no other person came, during the second temple, to whom these words can be applied: so that they were not accomplished, unless it was in the person of our Saviour, to whom all these characters do well agree.

ART. VII.

Mal. iv. 5, 6.

But to conclude with that prophecy which of all others is the most particular: when Daniel at the end of the seventy years' captivity was interceding for that nation, an angel was sent to him to tell him, that they were to have a new period of seventy weeks, that is, seven times seventy years, 490 years; and that after sixty-two weeks, *Messiah the Prince was to come, and to be cut off;* and that then the *people of a prince should destroy the city and the sanctuary;* and the *end of these was to be* as with *a flood* or inundation, and *desolations were determined to the end of the war.* They were to be destroyed by abominable armies, that is, by idolatrous armies; they were to be made desolate, till an utter end or consummation should be made of them. The pomp, with which this destruction is set forth, plainly shews, that the final ruin of the Jews by the Roman armies is meant by it. From which it is justly inferred, not only that, if that vision was really sent from God by an angel to Daniel, and in consequence to that was fulfilled, then the Messiah did come, and was cut off during the continuance of Jerusalem and the temple; but that it happened within a period of time designed in that vision. Time was then computed more certainly than it had been for many ages before. Two great measures were fixed; one at Babylon by Nabonasser, and another in Greece in the Olympiads. Here a prediction is given almost five hundred years before the accomplishment, with many very nice reckonings in it. I will not now enter upon the chronology of this matter, on which some great men have bestowed their labours very happily. Archbishop Usher has stated this matter so, that the interval of time is clearly four hundred eighty-six years. The covenant was to be confirmed with many for one week, in the midst of which God was to cause the sacrifice and oblation for sin to cease; which seems to be a mystical way of describing the death of Christ, that was to put an end to the virtue of the Judaical sacrifices; so sixty-nine weeks and a half make just four hundred eighty-six years and a half. But without going farther into this calculation, it is evident, that during the second temple, the Messias was to come, and to be cut off, and that soon after that a prince was to send an army to destroy both city and sanctuary. The Jews do not so much as pretend that during that temple the Messias thus set forth did come, or was cut off; so either the prediction failed in the event: or the Messias did come within that period.

Dan. ix. 24—27.

And thus, a thread of the prophecies of the Messias being

ART. VII. carried down through the whole Old Testament, it seems to be fully made out, that he was to be of the seed of Abraham, and of the posterity of David: that the tribe of Judah was to be a distinct policy, till he should come: that he should work many miracles: that he was to be meek and lowly: that his function was to consist in preaching to the afflicted, and in comforting them: that he was to call the Gentiles, and even the remote islands, to the knowledge of God: that he was to be born of a virgin, and at Bethlehem: that he was to be a new lawgiver, as Moses had been: that he was to settle his followers upon a new covenant, different from that made by Moses: that he was to come during the second temple: that he was to make a mean, but a joyful entrance to Jerusalem: that he was to be cut off: that the iniquities of us all were to be laid on him; and that his life was to be made an offering for sin; but that God was to give him a glorious reward for these his sufferings; and that his doctrine was to be internal, accompanied with a free offer of pardon, and of inward assistances; and that after his death the Jews were to fall under a terrible curse, and an utter extirpation. When this is all summed up together; when it appears, that there was never any other person to whom those characters did agree, but that they did all meet in our Saviour, we see what light the Old Testament has given us in this matter. Here a nation that hates us and our religion, who are scattered up and down the world, who have been for many ages without their temple, and without their sacrifices, without priests, and without their genealogies, who yet hold these books among them in a due veneration, which furnish us with so full a proof, that the Messiah whom they still look for, is the Lord Jesus whom we worship. We do now proceed to other matters.

The Jews pretend, that it is a great argument against the authority of the New Testament, because it acknowledges the Old to be from God, and yet repeals the far greater part of the laws enacted in it; though those laws are often said to be 'laws for ever,' and 'throughout all generations.' Now they seem to argue with some advantage, who say, that what God does declare to be a law that shall be perpetual by any one prophet, cannot be abrogated or reversed by another, since that other can have no more authority than the former prophet had: and if both are of God, it seems the one cannot make void that which was formerly declared by the other in the name of God. But it is to be considered, that by the phrases of 'a statute for ever,' or 'throughout all generations,' can only be meant, that such laws were not transient laws, such as were only to be observed whilst they marched through the wilderness, or upon particular occasions; whereas such laws, which were constantly and generally to be observed, were to them perpetual. But that does not import that the lawgiver himself had parted with all the authority, that naturally belongs to him, over his own laws. It only says, that the people had no power over such laws to repeal or change them: they were to bind them always; but that puts no limitation on the lawgiver himself, so that he might not alter his own constitutions. Positive precepts, which have no real value in themselves, are of their own nature alterable: and as in human laws the words of enacting a law for all future times do only make that to be a perpetual law for the subjects, but do not at all limit the legislative power, which is as much at liberty to abrogate or alter it, as if no such words had been in the law; there are also many hints in the Old Testament, which shew that the precepts of the Mosaical law were to be altered: many plain intimations are given of a time and state, in which the knowledge of God was to be spread over all the earth: and that God was every where to be worshipped. Now this was impossible to be done without a change in their law and rituals: it being impossible that all the world should go up thrice a year to worship at Jerusalem, or could be served by priests of the Aaronical family. Circumcision was a distinction of one particular race, which needed not to be continued after all were brought under one denomination, and within the same common privileges.

These things hitherto mentioned belong naturally to this part of the Article: yet, in the intention of those who framed it, these words relate to an extravagant sort of enthusiasts that lived in those days; who, abusing some ill-understood phrases concerning justification by Christ without the works of the law, came to set up very wild notions, which were bad in themselves, but much more pernicious in their consequences. They therefore fancied that a Christian was tied by no law, as a rule or yoke; all these being taken away by Christ: they said indeed, that a Christian by his renovation became a law to himself; he obeyed not any written rule or law, but a new inward nature: and thus as it is said that Sadocus mistook his master Antigonus, who taught his disciples to serve God, not for the hope of a reward, but without any expectations, as if he by that affectation of sublimity had denied that there was any reward; and from thence sprung the sect of the Sadducees: so these men, perhaps at first mistaking the meaning of the New Testament, went wrong only in their notions; and still meant to press the necessity of true holiness, though in another set of phrases, and upon other motives; yet from thence many wild and ungoverned notions arose then, and were not long ago revived among us: all which flowed from their not understanding the importance of the word *law* in the New Testament, in which it stands most commonly for the complex of the whole Jewish religion, in opposition to the Christian; as the word *law*, when it stands for a book, is meant of the five books of Moses.

The maintaining the whole frame of that dispensation, in

ART VII.
opposition to that liberty which the apostles granted to the Gentiles, as to the ritual parts of it, was the controversy then in debate between the apostles and the Judaizing Christians. The stating that matter aright is a key that will open all those difficulties, which with it will appear easy, and without it insuperable. In opposition to these, who thought then that the Old Testament, having brought the world on to the knowledge of the Messias, was now of no more use, this Article was framed.

The second part of the Article relates to a more intricate matter; and that is, whether in the Old Testament there were any promises made, other than transitory or temporal ones, and whether they might look for eternal salvation in that dispensation, and upon what account? Whether Christ was the Mediator in that dispensation, or if they were saved by virtue of their obedience to the laws that were then given them? Those who deny that Christ was truly God, think that in order to the raising him to those great characters in which he is proposed in the New Testament, it is necessary to assert that he gave the first assurances of eternal happiness, and of a free and full pardon of all sins in his gospel: and that in the Old Testament neither the one nor the other were certainly and distinctly understood.

It is true, that if we take the words of the covenant that Moses made between God and the people of Israel strictly and as they stand, they import only temporal blessings: that was a covenant with a body of men and with their posterity, as they were a people engaged to the obedience of that law. Now a national covenant could only be established in temporal promises of public and visible blessings, and of a long continuance of them upon their obedience, and in threatenings of as signal judgments upon the violation of them: but under those general promises of what was to happen to them collectively, as they made up one nation, every single person among them might, and the good men among them did, gather the hopes of a future state. It is clear that Moses did all along suppose the being of God, the creation of the world, and the promise of the Messias, as things fully known and carried down by tradition to his days: so it seems he did also suppose the knowledge of a future state, which was then generally believed by the Gentiles as well as the Jews; though they had only dark and confused notions about it. But when God was establishing a covenant with the Jewish nation, a main part of which was his giving them the land of Canaan for an inheritance, it was not necessary that eternal rewards or punishments should be then proposed to them; but from the tenor of the promises made to their forefathers, and from the general principles of natural religion, not yet quite extinguished among them, they might gather this, that under those carnal promises, blessings of a higher nature were to be understood. And so we see that David had the hope of arriving 'at the presence of God,' and 'at his right hand,' where he believed there was 'a fulness of joy, and pleasures for evermore:' and he puts himself in this opposition to the wicked, that whereas 'their portion was in this life, and they left their substance to their children;' he says, that as for him, he should 'behold God's face in righteousness,' and should 'be satisfied when he awaked with his likeness;' which seems plainly to relate to a state after this life, and to the resurrection. He carries this opposition farther in another Psalm, where after he had said, that 'men in honour did not continue, but were like the beasts that perished: that none of them could purchase immortality for his brother; that he should still live for ever, and not see corruption: they all died and left their wealth to others, and like sheep they were laid in the grave, where death should feed on them:' in opposition to which he says, that 'the upright should have dominion over them in the morning:' which is clearly a poetical expression for another day that comes after the night of death. As for himself in particular, he says, that 'God shall redeem my soul (that is, his life, or his body, for in those senses the word *soul* is used in the Old Testament) from the power of the grave:' that is, from continuing in that state of death; for 'he shall receive me.' This does very clearly set forth David's belief both of future happiness, and of the resurrection of his body. To which might be added some other passages in the Psalms, Ecclesiastes, Isaiah, and Daniel: in all which it appears, that the holy men in that dispensation did understand, that under those promises in the books of Moses that seemed literally to belong to the land of Canaan, and other temporal blessings, there was a spiritual meaning hid, which it seems was conveyed down by that succession of prophets, that was among them, as the mystical sense of them.

ART VII.

Ps. xvi. 11.
Ps. xvii. 14, 15.

Ps. xlix. 14, 15.

Ps. lxxxiv. 11.
lxxxvii. 6.
xc. 17.
xcvi. 13.
Eccl. xi. 9.
xii. 14.
Is. xxv. 8.
xxvi. 19
Dan. xii. 2.

It is to this that our Saviour seems to appeal, when the Sadducees came to puzzle him with that question of the seven brethren, who had all married one wife: he first tells them, 'they erred, not knowing the Scriptures;' which plainly imports, that the doctrine, which they denied, was contained in the scriptures: and then he goes to prove it, not from those more express passages that are in the prophets and holy writers, which as some think the Sadducees rejected; but from the law, which being the source of their religion, it might seem a just prejudice against any doctrine, especially if it was of great consequence, that it was not contained in the law. Therefore he cites these words that are so often repeated, and that were so much considered by the Jews, as containing in them the foundation of God's love to them; that God said upon many occasions, particularly at his first appearance to Moses, 'I am the God of Abraham, the God of Isaac, and the God of Jacob.' Which words imported not only that

Matt. xxii. 29.

Ver. 31, 32.
Exod. iii. 6.

ART. VII. God had been their God, but still was their God: now when God is said to be a God to any, by that is meant, that he is their benefactor, or *exceeding rich reward*, as was promised to Abraham. And that therefore Abraham, Isaac, and Jacob *lived unto God*, that is, were not dead; but were then in a happy state of life, in which God did reward them, and so was their God. Whether this argument rests here, our Saviour designing only to prove, against the main error of the Sadducees, that we have souls distinct from our bodies, that shall outlive their separation from them; or if it goes further to prove the rising of the body itself, I shall not determine. On the one hand our Saviour seems to apply himself particularly to prove the resurrection of the body; so we must see how to find here an argument for that, to answer the scope of the whole discourse: yet on the other hand it may be said, that he having proved the main point of the soul's subsisting after death, which is the foundation of all religion; the other point which was chiefly denied, because that was thought false, would be more easily both acknowledged and believed.

As for the resurrection of the body, all that can be brought from hence as an argument to prove it is, that since God was the God of Abraham, Isaac, and Jacob, and by consequence their benefactor and rewarder, and yet they were pilgrims on this earth, and suffered many tossings and troubles, that therefore they must be rewarded in another state: or because God promised that to them he would give the land of Canaan, as well as to their seed after them, and since they never had any portion of it in their own possession, that therefore they shall rise again, and with the other saints reign on earth, and have that promise fulfilled in themselves.

From all this the assertion of the Article is as to one main point made good, that the old fathers looked for more than transitory promises: it is also clear, that they looked for a further pardon of sin, than that which their law held forth to them in the expiation made by sacrifices. Sins of ignorance, Heb. x. 28. or sins of a lower sort, were those only for which *sin* or *trespass-offerings were appointed*. The sins of a higher order were punished by death, by the hand of Heaven, or by cutting off; so that such as sinned in that kind were to die without mercy: yet when David had fallen into the most Psal. li. 1, heinous of those sins, he prays to God for a pardon, accord-2, 16, 17. ing to God's loving-kindness, and the multitude of his tender mercies: for he knew that they were beyond the expiation by sacrifice. The prophets do often call the Jews to repent of their idolatry and other crying sins, such as oppression, injustice, and murder; with the promise of the pardon of Isa. i. 18. them; even though they were of the deepest dye, as crimson and scarlet. Since then for lesser sins an expiation was appointed by sacrifice, besides their confessing and repenting of it; and since it seems, by St. Paul's way of arguing, that they held it for a maxim, that 'without shedding of blood there was no remission of sins;' this might naturally lead them to think that there was some other consideration that was interposed in order to the pardoning of those more heinous sins: for a greater degree of guilt seems by a natural proportion to demand a higher degree of sacrifice and expiation. But after all, whatsoever Isaiah, Daniel, or any other prophet, might have understood or meant by those sacrificatory phrases that they use in speaking of the Messiah, yet it cannot be said from the Old Testament, that in that dispensation it was clearly revealed that the Messias was to die, and to become a sacrifice for sin: the Messias was indeed promised under general terms; but there was not then a full and explicit revelation of his being to die for the redemption of mankind; yet since the most heinous sins were then pardoned, though not by virtue of the sacrifices of that covenant, nor by the other means prescribed in it, we have good reason to affirm, that, according to this Article, life was offered to mankind in the old dispensation by Christ, who was, with relation to obtaining the favour of God, and everlasting life, the Mediator of that as well as of the new dispensation. In the New Testament he is set in opposition to the old Adam, 'that as in the one all died, so in the other all were made alive:' nor is it any way incongruous to say, that the merit of his death should by an anticipation have saved those who died before he was born: for that being in the view of God as certain before, as after it was done, it might be in the divine intention the sacrifice for the old, as well as it is expressly declared to be the sacrifice for the new dispensation. And this being so, God might have pardoned sins in consideration of it, even to those who had no distinct apprehensions concerning it. For as God applies the death of Christ, by the secret methods of his grace, to many persons whose circumstances do render them incapable of the express acts of laying hold on it, the want of those (for instance, in infants and idiots) being supplied by the goodness of God: so though the revelation that was made of the Messias to the fathers under the old dispensation, was only in general and prophetical terms, of which they could not have a clear and distinct knowledge; yet his death might be applied to them, and their sins pardoned through him, upon their performing such acts as were proportioned to that dispensation, and to the revelation that was then made; and so they were reconciled to God even after sins, for which no sacrifices were appointed by their dispensation, upon their repentance and obedience to the fœderal acts and conditions then required, which supplied the want of more express acts with relation to the death of Christ, not then distinctly revealed to them. But though the old fathers had a conveyance of the hope of

ART. VII.

Heb. ix. 22.

Isa. liii.
Dan. ix.

1 Cor. xv. 22.

ART. VII.

2 Pet. i. 19.

Rom. iii. 24, 25.

eternal life made to them, with a resurrection of their bodies, and a confidence in the mercy of God, for pardoning the most heinous sins; yet it cannot be denied, but that it was as 'a light that shined in a dark place, till the day-star did arise,' and that Christ 'brought life and immortality to light by his gospel;' giving us fuller and clearer discoveries of it, both with relation to our souls and bodies; and that by him also God 'has declared his righteousness for the remission of sins, through the forbearance of God, through the redemption that is in Christ Jesus, and through faith in his blood.'

The third branch of this Article will not need much explanation, as it will bear no dispute, except with Jews, who do not acknowledge the New Testament. The ceremonial parts of the Mosaical law, which comprehends all both the negative and the positive precepts, were enjoined the Jews either with relation to the worship of God and service at the temple, or to their persons and course of life.

That which is not moral of its own nature, or that had no relation to civil society, was commanded them, to separate them not only from the idolatrous and magical practices of other nations, but to distinguish them so entirely as to all their customs, even in the rules of eating and of cleanness, that they might have no familiar commerce with other nations, but live within and among themselves; since that was very likely to corrupt them, of which they had very large experience. Some of those rituals were perhaps given them as punishments for their frequent revolts, and were as a yoke upon them, who were so prone to idolatry. They were as rudiments and remembrances to them: they were as it were subdued by a great variety of precepts, which were matter both of much charge and great trouble to them: by these they were also amused; for it seems they did naturally love a pompous exterior in religion; they were also, by all that train of performances which were laid on them, kept in mind both of the great blessings of God to them, and of the obligations that lay on them towards God; and many of those, particularly their sacrifices and washings, were typical. All this was proper and necessary to restrain and govern them, while they were the only people in the world that renounced idolatry, and worshipped the true God: and therefore so soon as that of which they had an emblem in the structure of their temple (of a court of the Gentiles separated with a middle wall of partition, from the place in which the Israelites worshipped) was to be removed, and that the house of God was to become 'a house of prayer to all nations,' then all those distinctions were to be laid aside, and all that service was to determine and come to an end. The apostles did declare, that the Gentiles were not to be brought under that heavy yoke, which

Acts xv. their fathers were not able to bear; yet the apostles themselves, as born Jews, and while they lived among the Jews, did continue in the observance of their rites, as long as God seemed to be waiting for the remnant of that nation that was to be saved, before his wrath came upon the rest to the uttermost. They went to the temple, they purified themselves; and, in a word, 'to the Jews they became Jews;' and in this compliance, the first converts of the Jewish nation continued till the destruction of Jerusalem; after which, it became impossible to observe the greatest part of their most important rituals, even all those that were tied to the temple. But that nation losing its genealogies, and all the other characters that they formerly had of a nation under the favour and protection of God, could no more know after a few ages, whether they were the seed of Abraham or not, or whether there were any left among them of the tribe of Levi, or of the family of Aaron. So that now all those ceremonies are at an end; many of them are become impossible, and the rest useless; as the whole was abrogated by the authority of the apostles, who being sent of God, and proving their mission by miracles, as well as Moses had done his, they might well have *loosed* and dissolved those precepts upon earth, upon which, according to our Saviour's words, they are to be esteemed as *loosed in heaven*.

ART. VII.

Heb. x.

The judiciary parts of the law were those that related to them as they were a society of men, to whom God by a special command gave authority to drive out and destroy a wicked race of people, and to possess their land; which God appointed to be divided equally among them, and that every portion should be as a perpetuity to a family; so that though it might be mortgaged out for a number of years, yet it was afterwards to revert to the family. Upon this bottom they were at first set; and they were still to be preserved upon it; so that many laws were given them as they were a civil society, which cannot belong to any other society: and therefore their whole judiciary law, except when any parts of it are founded on moral equity, was a complicated thing, and can belong to no other nation, that is not in its first and essential constitution made and framed as they were. For instance; the prohibition of taking use for money, being a mean to preserve that equality which was among them, and to keep any of them from becoming excessively rich, or others from becoming miserably poor, this is by no means to be applied to other constitutions, where men are left to their industry, and neither have their inheritance by a grant from heaven, nor are put by any special appointment of God all upon a level. So that it is certain, and can bear no debate, that the Mosaical dispensation, as to all the parts of it that are not of their own nature moral, is determined and abrogated by the gospel. The decisions which the apostles made in this matter are so clear, and for the proof of them, the whole tenor of the Epistles to the Galatians and the Hebrews is so full, that no doubt can rest concerning this with any man who reads them.

130   AN EXPOSITION OF

ART. VII.   The last branch of this Article that remains to be considered, is concerning the moral law, by which the Ten Commandments are meant, together with all such precepts as do belong to them, or are corollaries arising out of them. By *moral law* is to be understood, in opposition to *positive*, a law which has an antecedent foundation in the nature of things, that arises from eternal reason, is suitable to the frame and powers of our souls, and is necessary for maintaining human society. All such laws are commanded, because they are in themselves good, and suitable to the state in which God has put us here. The two sources, out of which all the notions of morality flow, are, first, the consideration of ourselves as we are single individuals, and that with relation both to soul and body; and next, the consideration of human society, what is necessary for the peace and order, the safety and happiness, of mankind. There are two orders of moral precepts; some relate to things that of their own nature are inflexibly good or evil, such as truth and falsehood; whereas other things by a variety of circumstances may so change their nature, that they may be either morally good or evil: a merciful or generous temper is always a good moral quality, and yet it may run to excesses: there may be many things that are not unalterably moral in themselves, which yet may be fit subjects of perpetual laws about them. For instance; in the degrees of kindred with relation to marriage, there are no degrees but direct ascendants or descendants, that is, parents and children, that by an eternal reason can never marry; for where there is a natural subordination, there can never be such an equality as that state of life requires: but collateral degrees, even the nearest, brothers and sisters, are not by any natural law barred marriage, and therefore in a case of necessity they might marry: yet since their intermarrying must be attended with vast inconveniences, and would tend to the defilement of all families, and hinder the conjunction of mankind by the intermixture of different families; it becomes therefore a fit subject for a perpetual law, to strike a horror at the thought of such commixtures, and so to keep the world pure; which, considering the freedoms in which those of the same family do live, could not be preserved without such a law. It is also the interest of mankind, and necessary for the careful education of the rising generation, that marriages should be for life; for if it were free for married persons to separate at pleasure, the issue of marriages so broken would be certainly much neglected: and since a power to break a marriage would naturally inflame such little quarrellings as may happen among all persons that live together, which will on the contrary be certainly repressed, when they know that the marriage cannot be dissolved, and when, by such a dissolution of marriages, the one half of the human species, I mean womankind, is exposed to great mise‧ries, and subject to much tyranny, it is a fit subject for a perpetual law; so that it is moral in a secondary order. It were easy to give instances of this in many more particulars, and to shew, that a precept may be said to be moral, when there is a natural suitableness in it to advance that which is moral in the first order, and that it cannot be well preserved without such a support. It will appear what occasion there is for this distinction, when we consider the Ten Commandments; which are so many heads of morality, that are instanced in the highest act of a kind; and to which are to be reduced all such acts as by the just proportions of morality belong to that order and series of actions.

The foundation of morality is religion. The sense of God, that he is, and that he is both a rewarder and a punisher, is the foundation of religion. Now this must be supposed as antecedent to his laws, for we regard and obey them from the persuasion that is formed in us concerning the being and the justice of God: the two first commandments are against the two different sorts of idolatry; which are, the worshipping of false gods, or the worshipping the true God in a corporeal figure: the one is the giving the honour of the true God to an idol, and the other is the depressing the true God to the resemblance of an idol. These were the two great branches of idolatry, by which the true ideas of God were corrupted. Religion was by them corrupted in its source. Nobody can question but that it is immoral to worship a false god; it is a transferring the honour, which belongs immediately and singly to the great God, to a creature, or to some imaginary thing which never had a real existence. This is the robbing God of what is due to him, and the exalting another thing to a degree and rank that cannot belong to it. Nor is it less immoral to propose the great and true God to be worshipped under appearances that are derogatory to his nature, that tend to give us low thoughts of him, and that make us think him like, if not below, ourselves. This way of worshipping him is both unsuitable to his nature, and unbecoming ours; while we pay our adorations to that which is the work of an artificer. This is confirmed by those many express prohibitions in scripture, to which reasons are added, which shew that the thing is immoral in its own nature: it being often repeated, that no similitude of God was ever seen: and 'to whom will ye liken me?' All things in heaven and earth are often called the 'work of his hands:' which are plain indications of a moral precept, when arguments are framed from the nature of things to enforce obedience to it. The reason given in the very command itself, is taken from the nature of God, who is jealous; that is, so tender of his glory, that he will not suffer a diminution of it to go unpunished; and if this precept is clearly founded upon natural justice, and the proportion that ought to be kept between all human acts and their objects, then it must be perpetual; and that

ART.
VII.

the rather, because we do plainly see that the gospel is a refining upon the law of Moses, and does exalt it to a higher pitch of sublimity and purity; and by consequence the ideas of God, which are the first seeds and principles of religion, are to be kept yet more pure and undefiled in it, than they were in a lower dispensation.

Ex. iii, 1.
Lev. xix. 12.
Matt. v. 33.

The third precept is against false swearing: for the word *vain* is often used in the scripture in that sense: and since in all the other commandments, the sin which is named is not one of the lowest, but of the chief sins that relate to that head; there is no reason therefore to think, that *vain* or idle swearing, which is a sin of a lower order, should be here meant, and not rather false swearing, which is the highest sin of the kind. The morality of this command is very apparent; for since God is the God of truth, and every oath is an appeal to him, therefore it must be a gross wickedness to appeal to God, or to call him to vouch for our lies.

The fourth commandment cannot be called moral in the first and highest sense; for from the nature of things no reason can be assigned, why the seventh day, rather than the sixth, or the eighth, or any other day, should be separated from the common business of life, and applied to the service of God. But it is moral that a man should pay homage to his Maker, and acknowledge him in all his works and ways: and since our senses and sensible objects are apt to wear better things out of our thoughts, it is necessary that some solemn times should be set apart for full and copious meditations on these subjects; this should be universal, lest, if the time were not the same every where, the business of some men might interfere with the devotions of others. It ought to have such an eminent character on it, like a cessation from business: which may both awaken a curiosity to inquire into the reason of that stop, and also may give opportunity for meditations and discourses on those subjects. It is also clear, that such days of rest must not return so oft, that the necessary affairs of life should be stopped by them, nor so seldom, that the impressions of religion should wear out, if they were too seldom awakened: but what is the proper proportion of time, that can best agree both with men's bodies and minds, is only known to the great Author of nature. Howsoever, from what has been said, it appears that this is a very fit matter to be fixed by some sacred and perpetual law, and that from the first creation; because there being then no other method for conveying down knowledge, besides oral tradition, it seems as highly congruous to that state of mankind, as it is agreeable to the words in Genesis, to believe that God should then have appointed one day in seven for commemorating the creation, and for acknowledging the great Creator of all things. But though it seems very clear, that here a perpetual law was given the world for the separating the seventh day; yet it was a mere circumstance, and does not at all belong to the standing use of the law, in what end of the week this day was to be reckoned, whether the first or the last: so that even a less authority than the apostles, and a less occasion than the resurrection of Christ, might have served to have transferred the day. There being in this no breach made on the good and moral design of this law, which is all in it that we ought to reckon sacred and unalterable: the degree of the rest might be also more severely urged under the Mosaical law, than either before it or after it. Our Saviour having given plain intimations of an abatement of that rigour, by this general rule, that 'the sabbath was made for man, and not man for the sabbath.' We, who are called to a state of freedom, are not under such a strictness as the Jews were. Still the law stands for separating a seventh day from the common business of life, and applying it to a religious rest, for acknowledging at first the Creator, and now, by a higher relation, the Redeemer, of the world.

These four commandments make the first table, and were generally reckoned as four distinct commandments, till the Roman church having a mind to make the second disappear, threw it in as an appendix to the first, and then left it quite out in her catechisms: though it is plain that these commandments relate to two very different matters, the one being in no sort included in the other. Certainly they are much more different than the coveting the neighbour's wife is from the coveting any of his other concerns; which are plainly two different acts of the same species; and the *house* being set before the *wife* in Exodus (though it comes after it in Deuteronomy, which, being a repetition, is to be governed by Exodus, and not Exodus by it) stands for the whole substance, which is afterwards branched out in the particulars; and so it is clear that there is no colour for dividing this in two; but the first two commandments relating to things of such a different sort, as is the worshipping of more gods than one, and the worshipping the true God in an image, ought still to be reckoned as different: and though the reason given from the jealousy and justice of God may relate equally to both, yet that does not make them otherwise one, than as both might be reduced to one common head of idolatry, so that both were to be equally punished.

In the second table this order is to be observed. There are four branches of a man's property, to which every thing that he can call his own may be reduced: his person, his wife and children, his goods, and his reputation: so there is a negative precept given to secure him in every one of these, against killing, committing adultery, stealing, and bearing false witness: to which, as the chief acts of their kind, are to be reduced all those acts that may belong to those heads: such as injuries to a man in his person, though not carried on nor designed to kill him; every temptation to uncleanness, and all those ex-

ART. VII.

Mark ii. 27.

Ex. xx. 17.
Deut. v. 21.

cesses that lead to it; every act of injustice, and every lie or defamation. To these four are added two fences; the one exterior, the other interior. The exterior is the settling the obedience and order that ought to be observed in families, according to the law of nature: and, by a parity of reason, if families are under a constitution, where the government is made as a common parent, the establishing the obedience to the civil powers, or to such orders of men who may be made as parents, with relation to matters of religion: this is the foundation of peace and justice, of the security and happiness of mankind. And therefore it was very proper to begin the second table, and those laws that relate to human society, with this; without which the world would be like a forest, and mankind, like so many savages, running wildly through it.

The last commandment is an inward fence to the law: it checks desires, and restrains the thoughts. If free scope should be given to these, as they would very often carry men to unlawful actions, for a man is very apt to do that which he desires, so they must give great disturbance to those that are haunted or overcome by them. And therefore as a mean both to secure the quiet of men's minds, and to preserve the world from the ill effects which such desires might naturally have, this special law is given; 'Thou shalt not covet.' It will not be easy to prove it *moral* in the strictest sense, yet in a secondary order it may be well called *moral:* the matter of it being such both with relation to ourselves and others, that it is a very proper subject for a perpetual law to be made about it. And yet, as St. Paul says, he had not known it to be a sin, if it had not been for the law that forbids it; for, after all that can be said, it will not be easy to prove it to be of its own nature moral. Thus, by the help of that distinction of what is moral in a primary and in a secondary order, the morality of the Ten Commandments is demonstrated.

That this law obliges Christians as well as Jews, is evident from the whole scope of the New Testament. Instead of derogating from the obligation of any part of that law, our Saviour after he had affirmed, that 'he came not to dissolve the law, but to fulfil it,' and 'that heaven and earth might pass away, but that one tittle of the law should not pass away;' he went through a great many of those laws, and shewed how far he extended the commentary he put upon them, and the obligations that he laid upon his disciples, beyond what was done by the Jewish rabbies: all the rest of his gospel, and the writings of his apostles, agree with this, in which there is not a tittle that looks like a slackening of it, but a great deal to the contrary: a strictness that reaches to idle words, to passionate thoughts, and to all impure desires, being enjoined as indispensably necessary; for 'without holiness no man can see the Lord.'

And thus every thing relating to this Article is considered, and I hope both explained and proved.

ARTICLE VIII.

Of the Three Creeds.

𝕿𝖍𝖊 𝕿𝖍𝖗𝖊𝖊 𝕮𝖗𝖊𝖊𝖉𝖘, Nice 𝕮𝖗𝖊𝖊𝖉, Athanasius 𝕮𝖗𝖊𝖊𝖉, 𝖆𝖓𝖉 𝖙𝖍𝖆𝖙 𝖜𝖍𝖎𝖈𝖍 𝖎𝖘 𝖈𝖔𝖒𝖒𝖔𝖓𝖑𝖞 𝖈𝖆𝖑𝖑𝖊𝖉 𝖙𝖍𝖊 Apostles' 𝕮𝖗𝖊𝖊𝖉, 𝖔𝖚𝖌𝖍𝖙 𝖙𝖍𝖗𝖔𝖚𝖌𝖍𝖑𝖞 𝖙𝖔 𝖇𝖊 𝖗𝖊𝖈𝖊𝖎𝖛𝖊𝖉 𝖆𝖓𝖉 𝖇𝖊𝖑𝖎𝖊𝖛𝖊𝖉; 𝖋𝖔𝖗 𝖙𝖍𝖊𝖞 𝖒𝖆𝖞 𝖇𝖊 𝖕𝖗𝖔𝖛𝖊𝖉 𝖇𝖞 𝖒𝖔𝖘𝖙 𝖈𝖊𝖗𝖙𝖆𝖎𝖓 𝖂𝖆𝖗𝖗𝖆𝖓𝖙𝖘 𝖔𝖋 𝕳𝖔𝖑𝖞 𝕾𝖈𝖗𝖎𝖕𝖙𝖚𝖗𝖊.

ALTHOUGH no doubt seems to be here made of the names or designations given to those creeds, except of that which is ascribed to the apostles, yet none of them are named with any exactness: since the article of the procession of the Holy Ghost, and all that follows it, is not in the Nicene creed, but was used in the church as a part of it; for so it is in Epiphanius, before the second general council at Constantinople; and it was confirmed and established in that council: only the article of the Holy Ghost's *proceeding from the Son*, was afterwards added first in Spain, anno 447, which spread itself over all the west: so that the creed here called the Nice creed is indeed the Constantinopolitan creed, together with the addition of *filioque* made by the western church. That which is called Athanasius's creed is not his neither; for as it is not among his works, so that great article of the Christian religion having been settled at Nice, and he and all the rest of the orthodox referring themselves always to the creed made by that council, there is no reason to imagine that he would have made a creed of his own; besides, that not only the Macedonian,* but both the Nesto-

In Ancho-reto.

---

* The Macedonian heresy, so called from Macedonius, its founder. Upon the death of Eusebius, bishop of Constantinople, Paulus, who had been before displaced by the Emperor, was again chosen to that see. The Arians at the same time chose Macedonius. When the Emperor Constantius became acquainted with this matter, he sent instructions to the president, to remove Paulus, and to establish Macedonius in that see. The installation of Macedonius was accompanied with an awful event—the slaughter of (according to Socrates) about 3150 persons. Such, says that historian, were the means that Macedonius and the Arians used to climb by slaughter and murder to be magistrates in the church. Afterwards, Macedonius gave place to Paulus, who, however, was not long after banished through the influence of the Arians, and in his exile murdered. Macedonius again took possession of the see of Constantinople, and grievously persecuted the orthodox, who adhered to the article of 'one substance,' or the essential deity of Christ; not only cutting them off from the churches, but banishing them from the city. He continued for a time to make war with and wear out those who held the truth as in Jesus, but was at length deposed. He was first an Arian, and then fell into another heresy. His opinion was, that although the Son of God was like unto the Father, as well in substance as in all other things, yet the Holy Ghost had not these titles of honour, but 'was only the servant or drudge of the Father and the Son.' His followers were called Macedonians, or Pneumatomachians. His heresy was condemned at the second general council at Constantinople, A.D. 381, at which 150 bishops were present, and 'the finishing touch' was there given to the decrees of Nice respecting the three persons in the Godhead.—[ED.]

rian* and the Eutychian† heresies are expressly condemned by this creed; and yet those authorities never being urged in those disputes, it is clear from thence, that no such creed was then known in the world; as indeed it was never heard of before the eighth century; and then it was given out as the creed of Athanasius, or as a representation of his doctrine, and so it grew to be received by the western church; perhaps the more early, because it went under so great a name, in ages that were not critical enough to judge of what was genuine and what was spurious.

There is one great difficulty that arises out of several expressions in this creed, in which it is said, that *whosoever will be saved, must believe it;* that the belief of it is *necessary to salvation;* and that such as do not *hold it pure and undefiled* shall without doubt *perish everlastingly:* where many explanations of a mystery hard to be understood are made indispensably necessary to salvation; and it is affirmed, that all such as do not so believe must perish everlastingly. To this two answers are made: 1. That it is only the Christian faith in general that is hereby meant, and not every period and article of this creed; so that all those severe expressions are thought to import only the necessity of believing the Christian religion: but this seems forced; for the words that follow, *and the catholic faith is,* do so plainly determine the signification of that word to the explanation that comes after, that the word *catholic faith,* in the first verse, can be no other than the same word, as it is defined in the third and following verses; so that this answer seems not natural. 2. The common answer in which the most eminent men of this church, as far as the memory of all such as I have known could go up, have agreed, is this, that these condemnatory expressions are only to be understood to relate to those who, having the means of instruction offered to them, have rejected them,

---

* For an account of Nestorius, see page 63.

† The Eutychian heresy, so called from Eutyches, its founder. Eutyches was abbot of a convent of monks at Constantinople. His opposition to the doctrines of Nestorius (see pp. 63, 64) led him into an error of the opposite extreme, equally prejudicial to the interests of the Christian church. The 'poisonous heresy' of Eutyches caused a provincial council to be summoned, which was accordingly held at Constantinople. At that council Eutyches thus delivered his doctrine: 'I confess that our Lord consisted of two natures before the divinity was coupled with the humanity, but after the uniting of them I affirm that he had but one nature.' He said, moreover, ' that the body of the Lord was not of the same substance with ours.' Wherefore he was degraded. Upon his application to the Emperor Theodosius, another council was called, which met at Ephesus. At this council Flavianius, bishop of Constantinople, who procured the condemnation of Eutyches, was, owing to the influence of Dioscorus, bishop of Alexandria, who was the declared enemy of the Bishop of Constantinople, condemned to be publicly scourged, and afterwards banished. He died of his wounds in Epipas, a city of Lydia, the place of his banishment. This council was called *conventus latronum.* Another, known as the fourth general council, was however summoned, and held at Chalcedon in the year 451, where Eutyches, who had been already sent into banishment, was condemned, and the following decreed—' That in Christ two distinct natures were united in one person, and that without any change, mixture, or confusion.' *Evagrius Scholasticus and Mosheim.*—[Ed.]

and have stifled their own convictions, holding the truth in unrighteousness, and choosing darkness rather than light: upon such as do thus reject this great article of the Christian doctrine, concerning one God and three Persons, Father, Son, and Holy Ghost, and that other concerning the incarnation of Christ, by which God and man were so united as to make one person, together with the other doctrines that follow these, are those anathemas denounced: not so as if it were hereby meant, that every man who does not believe this in every tittle must certainly perish, unless he has been furnished with sufficient means of conviction, and that he has rejected them, and hardened himself against them. The wrath of God 'is revealed against all sin,' and 'the wages of sin is death:' so that every sinner has the wrath of God abiding on him, and is in a state of damnation: yet a sincere repentance delivers him out of it, even though he lives and dies in some sins of ignorance; which though they may make him liable to damnation, so that nothing but true repentance can deliver him from it; yet a general repentance, when it is also special for all known sins, does certainly deliver a man from the guilt of unknown sins, and from the wrath of God due to them. God only knows our hearts, the degrees of our knowledge, and the measure of our obstinacy, and how far our ignorance is affected or invincible; and therefore he will deal with every man according to what he has received. So that we may believe that some doctrines are necessary to salvation, as well as that there are some commandments necessary for practice; and we may also believe that some errors as well as some sins are exclusive of salvation; all which imports no more than that we believe such things are sufficiently revealed, and that they are necessary conditions of salvation; but by this we do not limit the mercies of God towards those who are under such darkness as not to be able to see through it, and to discern and acknowledge these truths. It were indeed to be wished, that some express declaration to this purpose were made by those who have authority to do it: but in the mean while, this being the sense in which the words of this creed are universally taken, and it agreeing with the phraseology of the scripture upon the like occasions, this is that which may be rested upon. And allowing this large explanation of these severe words, the rest of this creed imports no more than the belief of the doctrine of the Trinity, which has been already proved, in treating of the former Articles.

As for the creed called the Apostles' creed, there is good reason for speaking so doubtfully of it as the Article does, since it does not appear that any determinate creed was made by them: none of the first writers agree in delivering their faith in a certain form of words; every one of them gives an abstract of his faith, in words that differ both from one

ART. VIII.

another, and from this form. From thence it is clear that there was no common form delivered to all the churches; and if there had been any tradition, after the times of the council of Nice, of such a creed composed by the apostles, the Arians had certainly put the chief strength of their cause on this, that they adhered to the Apostles' creed, in opposition to the innovations of the Nicene fathers; there is therefore no reason to believe that this creed was prepared by the apostles, or that it was of any great antiquity, since Ruffin* was the first that published it: it is true, he published it as the creed of the church of Aquileia; but that was so late, that neither this nor the other creeds have any authority upon their own account. Great respect is indeed due to things of such antiquity, and that have been so long in the church; but, after all, we receive those creeds, not for their own sakes, nor for the sake of those who prepared them, but for the sake of the doctrine that is contained in them; because we believe that the doctrine which they declare is contained in the scriptures, and chiefly that which is the main intent of them, which is to assert and profess the Trinity, therefore we do receive them; though we must acknowledge that the creed ascribed to Athanasius, as it was none of his, so it was never established by any general council.

* For an account of Ruffin, see page 69.

ARTICLE IX.

Of the Original or Birth-Sin.

Original Sin standeth not in the following of Adam (as the * Pelagians do vainly talk), but it is the fault or corruption of the nature of every man, that naturally is engendered of the Offspring of Adam, whereby man is very far gone from Original Righteousness, and is of his own nature inclined to evil, so that the Flesh lusteth always contrary to the Spirit, and therefore in every Person born into the World it deserveth God's Wrath and Damnation: And this Infection of Nature doth remain, yea in them that are regenerated, whereby the Lust of the Flesh, called in Greek φρόνημα σαρκὸς, which some do expound the Wisdom, some Sensuality, some the Affection, some the Desire of the Flesh, is not subject to the Law of God. And though there is no Condemnation for them that believe and are baptized, yet the Apostle doth confess, That Concupiscence and Lust hath of itself the nature of Sin.

AFTER the first principles of the Christian religion are stated, and the rule of faith and life was settled, the next thing that was to be done, was to declare the special doctrines of this religion; and that first with relation to all Christians, as they

---

* 'A new controversy arose in the church during the fifth century, and its pestilential effects extended themselves through the following ages. The authors of it were Pelagius and Cælestius, both monks; the former a Briton, the latter a native of Ireland: they lived at Rome in the greatest reputation, and were universally esteemed on account of their extraordinary piety and virtue. These monks looked upon the doctrines which were commonly received, 'concerning the original corruption of human nature, and the necessity of divine grace to enlighten the understanding, and purify the heart, as prejudicial to the progress of holiness and virtue, and tending to lull mankind in a presumptuous and fatal security. They maintained that these doctrines were as false as they were pernicious; that the sins of our first parents were imputed to them alone, and not to their posterity; that we derive no corruption from their fall, but are born as pure and unspotted as Adam came out of the forming hand of his Creator: that mankind, therefore, are capable of repentance and amendment, and of arriving to the highest degrees of piety and virtue by the use of their natural faculties and powers; that, indeed, external grace is necessary to excite their endeavours, but that they have no need of the internal succours of the Divine Spirit.' These notions, and some others intimately connected with them, were propagated at Rome, though in a private manner, by the two monks already mentioned, who, retiring from that city, A. D. 410, upon the approach of the Goths, went first into Sicily, and afterwards into Africa, where they published their doctrine with more freedom. From Africa, Pelagius passed into Palestine, while Cælestius remained at Carthage, with a view to preferment, desiring to be admitted among the presbyters of that city. But the discovery of his opinions having blasted his hopes, and his errors being condemned in a council held at Carthage, A. D. 412, he departed from that city, and went into the east.' *Mosheim.* In the east Pelagius met a friend and supporter in John, bishop of Jerusalem, whose attachment to the sentiments of Origen led him to favour those of Pelagius.

are single individuals, for the directing every one of them in order to the working out his own salvation; which is done from this to the nineteenth Article: and then with relation to them as they compose a society called the church; which is carried on from the nineteenth to the end.

In all that has been hitherto explained, the whole church of England has been all along of one mind. In this and in some that follow there has been a greater diversity of opinion; but both sides have studied to prove their tenets to be at least not contrary to the Articles of the Church. These different parties have disputed concerning the decrees of God, and those assistances which, pursuant to his decrees, are afforded to us. But because the foundation of those decrees, and the necessity of those assistances, are laid in the sin of Adam, and in the effects it had on mankind, therefore these controversies begin on this head. The Pelagians and the Socinians agree in saying, that Adam's sin was personal: that by it, as being the first sin, it is said that sin *entered into the world:* but that as Adam was made mortal, and had died whether he had sinned or not; so they think the liberty of human nature is still entire; and that every man is punished for his own sins, and not for the sin of another; to do otherwise, they say, seems contrary to justice, not to say, goodness.

Ver. 15. In opposition to this, *judgment* is said to have *come upon many to condemnation through one* (either man or sin). *Death* is said *to have reigned by one*, and *by one man's offence;* and *many* are said to be *dead through the offence of one.* All these passages do intimate that death is the consequence of Adam's sin; and that in him, as well as in all others, *death* was the wages of *sin*, so also that we die upon the account of his sin.

Under the patronage of John, Pelagius assumed more boldness in the propagation of his heresy. Augustin sent into Palestine a Spanish presbyter named Orosius, who accused Pelagius before a council of bishops at Jerusalem. He was, however, dismissed without the least censure; and was shortly afterwards acquitted of all errors by the council of Diospolis (a city of Palestine known in scripture as Lydda), at which Eulogius of Cæsarea, metropolitan of Palestine, presided. The African bishops, nothing dismayed by the apostacy of the eastern church, assembled at Carthage, A. D. 416, while the Numidian bishops met at Milevum, and condemned anew the antiscriptural doctrines of Pelagius and his companion. Upon this Pelagius and Cælestius appealed to Zosimus, bishop of Rome, whom, by a confession of faith drawn up in a sufficiently artful manner to impose on the *infallibility!* of the papal see, they induced to pronounce in their favour, and declare them sound in the faith and unjustly persecuted by their adversaries. The African bishops, however, with Augustin at their head, continued their war against this heresy, until at last Zosimus changed his mind, and condemned Pelagius and Cælestius, the very persons whom a little before he had pronounced orthodox, and to whom he had extended his protecting influence. Sometime afterwards this heresy was condemned by the third general council at Ephesus, and by the Gauls, Britons, and Africans, in their councils. Thus was this heresy crushed; and to the great Head of the church thanks are due, for having, at that time, raised up such a bold and uncompromising champion of the faith in Augustin, bishop of Hippo; by whose unwearied exertions it was that this sect was suppressed in its very birth.—[Ed.]

We are said to bear the *image of the first Adam*, as true **ART.** Christians bear the *image of the second:* now we are sure that **IX.** there is both a derivation of righteousness, and a communi- 1 Cor. xv. cation of inward holiness, transferred to us through Christ: so 49. it seems to follow from thence, that there is somewhat both transferred to us, and conveyed down through mankind, by the first Adam; and particularly that by it we are all made subject to death; from which we should have been freed, if Adam had continued in his first state, and that by virtue of the *tree of life*: in which some think there was a natural vir- Gen.iii.22. tue to cure all diseases, and relieve against all accidents, while others do ascribe it to a divine blessing, of which that tree was only the symbol or *sacrament;* though the words said after Adam's sin, as the reason of driving him out of paradise, lest he put forth his hand, and 'take of the tree of life, and eat, and live for ever,' seem to import that there was a physical virtue in the tree, that could so fortify and restore life, as to give immortality. These do also think that the threatening made to Adam, that upon his eating the forbidden fruit he should surely die, is to be taken literally, and is to be carried no further than to a natural death. This subjection to death, and to the fear of it, brings men under a slavish bondage, many terrors, and other passions and miseries that arise out of it, which they think is a great punishment; and that it is a condemnation and sentence of death passed upon the whole race; and by this they are *made sinners*, that is, treated as guilty persons, and severely punished.

This they think is easily enough reconciled with the notions of justice and goodness in God, since this is only a temporary punishment relating to men's persons: and we see in the common methods of Providence, that children are in this sort often punished for the sins of their fathers; most men that come under a very ill habit of body, transmit the seeds of diseases and pains to their children. They do also think that the communication of this liableness to death is easily accounted for; and they imagine, that as the tree of life might be a plant that furnished men with an universal medicine, so the forbidden fruit might derive a slow poison into Adam's body, that might have exalted and inflamed his blood very much, and might, though by a slower operation, certainly have brought on death at the last. Our being thus adjudged to death, and to all the miseries that accompany mortality, they think may be well called the *wrath of God, and damnation:* so temporary judgments are often expressed in scripture. And to this they add, that Christ has entirely redeemed us from this, by the promise he has given us of raising us up at the last day: and that therefore when St. Paul is so copiously discoursing of the resurrection, he brings this in, that as we have borne the 'image of the first Adam, who was earthly,' so we shall also 'bear the image of the heavenly:' and 'since

142   AN EXPOSITION OF

ART. IX.

1 Cor. xv. 21, 22.
In Ep. ad Rom. passim.

by man came death, by man came also the resurrection from the dead;' and that 'as in Adam all die, so in Christ shall all be made alive;' and that this is the universal redemption and reparation that all mankind shall have in Christ Jesus. All this these divines apprehend is conceivable, and no more; therefore they put original sin in this only, for which they pretend they have all the fathers with them before St. Austin, and particularly St. Chrysostom and Theodoret, from whom all the later Greeks have done little more than copied out their words. This they do also pretend comes up to the words of the Article; for as this general adjudging of all men to die may be called, according to the style of the scriptures, *God's wrath and damnation*; so the fear of death, which arises out of it, corrupts men's natures, and inclines them to evil.

Others do so far approve of all this, as to think that it is a part of original sin, yet they believe it goes much further: and that there is a corruption spread through the whole race of mankind, which is born with every man. This the experience of all ages teaches us but too evidently; every man feels it in himself, and sees it in others. The philosophers, who were sensible of it, thought to avoid the difficulty that arises from it, when it might be urged, that a good God could not make men to be originally depraved and wicked; they therefore fancied that all our souls pre-existed in a former and a purer state, from which they fell, by descending too much into corporeal pleasure, and so both by a lapse and for a punishment they sunk into grosser bodies, and fell differently according to the different degrees of the sins they had committed in that state: and they thought that a virtuous life did raise them up to their former pitch, as a vicious one would sink them lower into more depraved and more miserable bodies. All this may seem plausible: but the best that can be said for it is, that it is an hypothesis that saves some difficulties; but there is no sort of proofs to make it appear to be true. We neither perceive in ourselves any remembrances of such a state, nor have we any warning given us either of our fall, or of the means of recovering out of it: so since there is no reason to affirm this to be true, we must seek for some other source of the corruption of human nature. The Manichees imputed it to the evil god, and thought it was his work, which some say might have set on St. Austin the more earnestly to look for another hypothesis to reconcile all.

Gen. vi. 5. viii. 21.
1 Kings viii. 46.
Prov. xxiv. 16.
Jer. xvii.9.
2 Cor.v.17.
Eccl. vii. 29.

But before we go to that, it is certain, that in scripture this general corruption of our nature is often mentioned. 'The imaginations of man's thoughts are only evil continually: What man is he that liveth and sinneth not? The just man falleth seven times a day: The heart of man is deceitful above all things, and desperately wicked; who can know it? All that are in Christ must become new creatures: old things must be done away, and every thing must become new. God made man upright, but he sought out to himself many inventions. The flesh is weak; The flesh lusteth against the spirit; The carnal mind is enmity to the law of God, and is not subject to the law of God, neither indeed can be:' and 'they that are in the flesh cannot please God:' where by *flesh* is to be meant the natural state of mankind, according to those words, 'That which is born of the flesh is flesh, and that which is born of the Spirit is spirit.' These, with many other places of scripture to the same purpose, when they are joined to the universal experience of all mankind concerning the corruption of our whole race, lead us to settle this point, that in fact it has overrun our whole kind, the contagion is spread over all. Now this being settled, we are next to inquire, how this could happen: we cannot think that God made men so: for it is expressly said, that 'God made man after his own image.'

ART. IX.

Gal. v. 17.
Rom. viii. 7, 8.

John iii. 6.

Gen. i. 27.

The surest way to find out what this *image* was at first, is to consider, what the New Testament says of it, when we come to be restored to it. 'We must put on the new man, after the image of him that created him;' or as elsewhere, the 'new man in righteousness and true holiness.' This then was the *image of God*, in which man was at first made. Nor ought the image of God to be considered only as an expression that imports only our representing him here on earth, and having dominion over the creatures: for in Genesis the creation of man in the image of God is expressed as a thing different from his dominion over the creatures, which seems to be given to him as a consequent of it. The image of God seems to be this, that the soul of man was a being of another sort and order than all those material beings till then made, which were neither capable of thought nor liberty, in which respect the soul was made after the *image of God*. But Adam's soul being put in his body, his brain was a *tabula rasa*, as white paper, had no impressions in it, but such as either God put in it, or such as came to him by his senses. A man born deaf and blind, newly come to hear and see, is not a more ignorant and amazed-like creature than Adam must have been, if God had not conveyed some great impressions into him; such as first the acknowledging and obeying him as his Maker, and then the managing his body so as to make it an instrument, by which he could make use of and observe the creation. There is no reason to think that his body was at first inclined to appetite, and that his mind was apt to serve his body, but that both were restrained by supernatural assistances. It is much more natural and more agreeable to the words of the *wise man*, to think that *God made man upright*, that his body craved modestly, and that his mind was both judge and master of those cravings; and if a natural hypothesis may be offered but only as an hypothesis, it may be supposed, that a man's blood was naturally low and cool, but that it was capable of a vast inflammation and elevation, by which a man's powers

Eph. iv. 22, 24.

Gen. i. 27, 28.

ART.
IX.
might be exalted to much higher degrees of knowledge and capacity: the animal spirits receiving their quality from that of the blood, a new and a strong fermentation in the blood might raise them, and by consequence exalt a man to a much greater sublimity of thought: but with that it might dispose him to be easily inflamed by appetites and passions; it might put him under the power of his body, and make his body much more apt to be fired at outward objects, which might sink all spiritual and pure ideas in him, and raise gross ones with much fury and rapidity. Hereby his whole frame might be much corrupted, and that might go so deep in him, that all those who descended from him might be defiled by it, as we see madness and some chronical diseases pass from parents to their children.

All this might have been natural, and as much the physical effect of eating the forbidden fruit, as it seems immortality would have been that of eating the fruit of the tree of life: this might have been in its nature a slow poison, which must end in death at last. It may be very easy to make all this appear probable from physical causes. A very small accident may so alter the whole mass of the blood, that in a very few minutes it may be totally changed: so the eating the forbidden fruit might have, by a natural change of things, produced all this. But this is only an hypothesis, and so is left as such. All the assistance that revealed religion can receive from philosophy, is to shew, that a reasonable hypothesis can be offered upon physical principles, to shew the possibility, or rather probability, of any particulars that are contained in the scriptures. This is enough to stop the mouths of Deists, which is all the use that can be made of such schemes.

To return to the main point of the fall of Adam: he himself was made liable to death: but not barely to cease to live; for death and life are terms opposite to one another in scripture. In treating upon these heads, it is said, that 'the wages of sin is death, but the gift of God is eternal life.' And though the addition of the word *eternal* makes the signification of the one more express, yet where it is mentioned without that addition, no doubt is to be made, but that it is to be so meant: as where it is said, that 'to be carnally minded is death, but to be spiritually minded is life and peace:' and 'believing, we have life through his name: Ye will not come unto me, that ye may have life.' So, by the rule of opposites, *death* ought to be understood as a word of a general signification, which we, who have the comment of the New Testament to guide us in understanding the Old, are not to restrain to a natural death; and therefore when we are said to be 'the servants of sin unto death,' we understand much more by it than a natural death: so God's threatening Adam with *death*, ought not to be restrained to a *natural death*. Adam being thus defiled, all emanations from him must partake of that vitiated state to which he had brought himself. But then the

Rom. vi. 23.

Rom. viii. 6.
John xx. 31.
John v. 40.

question remains, how came the souls of his posterity to be defiled; for if they were created pure, it seems to be an unjust cruelty to them, to condemn them to such an union to a defiled body, as should certainly corrupt them? All that can be said in answer to this is,

ART. IX.

That God has settled it as a law in the creation, that a soul should inform a body according to the texture of it, and either conquer it, or be mastered by it, as it should be differently made: and that as such a degree of purity in the texture of it might make it both pure and happy; so a contrary degree of texture might have very contrary effects. And if, with this, God made another general law, that when all things were duly prepared for the propagation of the species of mankind, a soul should be always ready to go into and animate those first threads and beginnings of life; those laws being laid down, Adam, by corrupting his own frame, corrupted the frame of his whole posterity, by the general course of things, and the great law of the creation. So that the suffering this to run through all the race, is no more (only different in degrees and extent) than the suffering the folly or madness of a man to infect his posterity. In these things God acts as the Creator of the world by general rules, and these must not be altered because of the sins and disorders of men: but they are rather to have their course, that so sin may be its own punishment. The defilement of the race being thus stated, a question remains, whether this can be properly called a sin, and such as deserves *God's wrath and damnation?* On the one hand an opposition of nature to the Divine nature must certainly be hateful to God, as it is the root of much malignity and sin. Such a nature cannot be the object of his love, and of itself it cannot be accepted of God: now since there is no mean in God, between *love* and *wrath*, *acceptation* and *damnation*, if such persons are not in the first order, they must be in the second.

Yet it seems very hard, on the other hand, to apprehend, how persons who have never actually sinned, but are only unhappily descended, should be, in consequence to that, under so great a misery. To this several answers are made: some have thought that those who die before they commit any actual sin, have indeed no share in the favour of God, but yet that they pass unto a state in the other world, in which they suffer little or nothing. The stating this more clearly, will belong to another opinion, which shall be afterwards explained.

There is a further question made, whether this vicious inclination is a sin, or not? Those of the church of Rome, as they believe that original sin is quite taken away by baptism, so finding that this corrupt disposition still remains in us, they do from thence conclude, that it is no part of original sin; but that this is the natural state in which Adam was made at first, only it is in us without the restraint or bridle of supernatural assistances, which was given to him, but lost by sin, and re-

L

stored to us in baptism. But, as was said formerly, Adam in his first state was made after the image of God, so that his bodily powers were perfectly under the command of his mind; this revolt, that we feel our bodies and senses are always in, cannot be supposed to be God's original workmanship. There are great disputings raised concerning the meaning of a long discourse of St. Paul's in the seventh of the Romans concerning a constant struggle that he felt within himself; which some, arguing from the scope of the whole Epistle, and the beginning of that chapter, understand only of the state that St. Paul represents himself to have been in while yet a Jew, and before his conversion: whereas others understand it of him in his converted and regenerated state. Very plausible things have been said on both sides, but without arguing any thing from words, the sense of which is under debate, there are other places which do manifestly express the struggle that is in a good man: 'The flesh is weak, though the spirit is willing: the flesh lusteth against the spirit, as the spirit lusteth against the flesh:' we ought to be still 'mortifying the deeds of the body;' and we feel many sins 'that do so easily beset us,' that from these things we have reason to conclude, that there is a corruption in our nature, which gives us a bias and propensity to sin. Now there is no reason to think that baptism takes away all the branches and effects of original sin: it is enough if we are by it delivered from the wrath of God, and brought into a state of favour and acceptation: we are freed from the curse of death, by our being entitled to a blessed resurrection: and if we are so far freed from the corruption of our nature, as to have a fœderal right to such assistances as will enable us to resist and repress it, though it is not quite extinct in us, so long as we live in these frail and mortal bodies, here are very great effects of our admission to Christianity by baptism; though this should not go so far as to root all inclinations to evil out of our nature. The great disposition that is in us to appetite and passion, and that great heat with which they inflame us; the aversion that we naturally have to all the exercises of religion, and the pains that must be used to work us up to a tolerable degree of knowledge, and an ordinary measure of virtue, shews that these are not natural to us: whereas sloth and vice do grow on us without any care taken about them: so that it appears, that they are the natural, and the other the forced, growth of our souls. These ill dispositions are so universally spread through all mankind, and appear so early, and in so great a diversity of ill inclinations, that from hence it seems reasonable and just to infer, that this corruption is spread through our whole nature and species, by the sin and disobedience of Adam. And beyond this a great many among ourselves think that they cannot go, in asserting of original sin.

But there is a further step made by all the disciples of St.

Austin, who believe that a covenant was made with all mankind in Adam, as their first parent: that he was a person constituted by God to represent them all; and that the covenant was made with him, so that if he had obeyed, all his posterity should have been happy, through his obedience; but by his disobedience they were all to be esteemed to have sinned in him, his act being imputed and transferred to them all. St. Austin considered all mankind as lost in Adam, and in that he made the decree of election to begin: there being no other reprobation asserted by him, than the leaving men to continue in that state of damnation, in which they were by reason of Adam's sin; so that though by baptism all men were born again and recovered out of that lost state, yet unless they were within the decree of election, they could not be saved, but would certainly fall from that state, and perish in a state of sin; but such as were not baptized were shut out from all hope. Those word's of Christ's, 'Except ye be born again of water and of the Spirit, ye cannot enter into the kingdom of God,' being expounded so as to import the indispensable necessity of baptism to eternal salvation; all who were not baptized were reckoned by him among the damned: yet this damnation, as to those who had no actual sin, was so mitigated, that it seemed to be little more than an exclusion out of heaven, without any suffering or misery, like a state of sleep and inactivity. This was afterwards dressed up as a division or partition in hell, called the *Limbo of Infants;* so by bringing it thus low, they took away much of the horror that this doctrine might otherwise have given the world.

ART. IX.

John iii. 3, 5.

It was not easy to explain the way how this was propagated: they wished well to the notion of a soul's propagating a soul, but that seemed to come too near creation: so it was not received as certain. It was therefore thought, that the body being propagated defiled, the soul was created and infused at the time of conception: and that though God did not create it impure, yet no time was interposed between its creation and infusion: so that it could never be said to have been once pure, and then to have become impure. All this, as it afforded an easy foundation to establish the doctrine of absolute decrees upon it, no care being taken to shew how this sin came into the world, whether from an absolute decree or not, so it seemed to have a great foundation in that large discourse of St. Paul's: where, in the fifth of the Romans, he compares the blessings that we receive by the death of Christ, with the guilt and misery that was brought upon us by the sin of Adam. Now it is confessed, that by Christ we have both an imputation or communication of the merits of his death, and likewise a purity and holiness of nature conveyed to us by his doctrine and spirit. In opposition then to this, if the comparison is to be closely pursued, there must be

ART. IX. an imputation of sin, as well as a corruption of nature, transfused to us from Adam. This is the more considerable as to the point of imputation, because the chief design of St. Paul's discourse seems to be levelled at that, since it is begun upon the head of reconciliation and atonement: upon which it follows, that 'as by one man sin entered into the world, and death by sin, and death passed upon all men, for that (or, as others render it, *in whom*) all have sinned.' Now they think it is all one to their point, whether it be rendered *for that,* or *in whom:* for though the latter words seem to deliver their opinion more precisely, yet it being affirmed, that, according to the other rendering, all who die have sinned; and it being certain, that many infants die who have never actually sinned, these must have *sinned in Adam,* they could sin no other way. It is afterwards said by St. Paul, that 'by the offence of one many were dead: that the judgment was by one to condemnation: that by one man's offence death reigned by one. That by the offence of one, judgment came upon all men to condemnation: and that by one man's disobedience many were made sinners.' As these words are positive, and of great importance in themselves, so all this is much the stronger, by the opposition in which every one of them is put to the effects and benefits of Christ's death; particularly to our justification through him, in which there is an imputation of the merits and effects of his death, that are thereby transferred to us; so that the whole effect of this discourse is taken away, if the imputation of Adam's sin is denied. And this explication does certainly quadrate more entirely to the words of the Article, as it is known that this was the tenet of those who prepared the Articles, it having been the generally-received opinion from St. Austin's days downward.

Rom.v.12, to the end.

But to many other divines this seems a harsh and unconceivable opinion; it seems repugnant to the justice and goodness of God, to reckon men guilty of a sin which they never committed, and to punish them in their souls eternally for that which is no act of theirs: and though we easily enough conceive how God, in the riches of his grace, may transfer merit and blessing from one person to many, this being only an economy of mercy, where all is free, and such a method is taken as may best declare the goodness of God: but in the imputation of sin and guilt, which are matters of strict justice, it is quite otherwise. Upon that head God is pleased often to appeal to men for the justice of all his ways: and therefore no such doctrine ought to be admitted, that carries in it an idea of cruelty, beyond what the blackest tyrants have ever invented. Besides that in the scripture such a method as the punishing children for their fathers' sins, is often disclaimed, and it is positively affirmed, that every man that sins is punished Now though, in articles relating to the nature of God,

Jer. xxxi. 29, 30.
Ezek. xviii. 20.

they acknowledge it is highly reasonable to believe, that there ART.
may be mysteries which exceed our capacity; yet in moral IX.
matters, in God's fœderal dealings with us, it seems unreasonable, and contrary to the nature of God, to believe that there may be a mystery contrary to the clearest notions of justice and goodness; such as the condemning mankind for the sin of one man, in which the rest had no share; and as contrary to our ideas of God, and upon that to set up another mystery that shall take away the truth and fidelity of the promises of God; justice and goodness being as inseparable from his nature, as truth and fidelity can be supposed to be. This seems to expose the Christian religion to the scoffs of its enemies, and to objections that are much sooner made than answered: and since the foundation of this is a supposed covenant with Adam as the representative head of mankind, it is strange that a thing of that great consequence should not have been more plainly reported in the history of the creation; but that men should be put to fetch out the knowledge of so great and so extraordinary a thing, only by some remote consequences. It is no small prejudice against this opinion, that it was so long before it first appeared in the Latin church; that it was never received in the Greek; and that even the western church, though perhaps for some ignorant ages it received it, as it did every thing else, very implicitly, yet has been very much divided both about this, and many other opinions related to it, or arising out of it.

As for those words of St. Paul's, that are its chief, if not its only foundation, they say many things upon them. First, it is a single proof. Now when we have not a variety of places proving any point, in which one gives light, and leads us to a sure exposition of another, we cannot be so sure of the meaning of any one place, as to raise a theory, or found a doctrine, upon it. They say further, that St. Paul seems to argue, from that opinion of our having sinned in Adam, to prove that we are justified by Christ. Now it is a piece of natural logic not to prove a thing by another, unless that other is more clear of itself, or at least more clear by its being already received and believed. This cannot be said to be more clear of itself, for it is certainly less credible or conceivable, than the reconciliation by Christ. Nor was this clear from any special revelation made of it in the Old Testament: therefore there is good reason to believe, that it was then a doctrine received among the Jews, as there are odd things of this kind to be found among the Cabbalists, as if all the souls of all mankind had been in Adam's body. Now when an argument is brought in scripture to prove another thing by, though we are bound to acknowledge the conclusion, yet we are not always sure of the premises; for they are often founded upon received opinions. So that it is not certain that St. Paul meant to offer this doctrine to our belief as true, but only

ART. IX.

that he intended by it to prove our being reconciled to God through the death of Christ; and the medium by which he proved it might be, for aught that appears from the words themselves, only an opinion held true among those to whom he writes. For he only supposes it, but says nothing to prove it: which it might be expected he would have done, if the Jews had made any doubt of it. But further they say, that when comparisons or oppositions, such as this, are made in scripture, we are not always to carry them on to an exact equality: we are required not only 'to be holy as God is holy, but to be perfect as he is perfect:' where by the *as* is not to be meant a true equality, but some sort of resemblance and conformity. Therefore those who believe that there is nothing imputed to Adam's posterity on the account of his sin, but this temporary punishment of their being made liable to death, and to all those miseries that the fear of it, with our other concerns about it, bring us under, say that this is enough to justify the comparison that is there stated: and that those, who will carry it on to be an exact parallel, make a stretch beyond the phraseology of the scripture, and the use of parables, and of the many comparisons that go only to one or more points, but ought not to be stretched to every thing.

1 Pet. i.15, 16.
Matt.v.48.

These are the things that other great divines among us have opposed to this opinion. As to its consonancy to the Article, those who oppose it do not deny, but that it comes up fully to the highest sense that the words of the Article can import: nor do they doubt, but that those who prepared the Articles, being of that opinion themselves, might perhaps have had that sense of the words in their thoughts. But they add, that we are only bound to sign the Articles in a literal and grammatical sense: since therefore the words, *God's wrath and damnation*, which are the highest in the Article, are capable of a lower sense, temporary judgments being often so expressed in the scriptures, therefore they believe the loss of the favour of God, the sentence of death, the troubles of life, and the corruption of our faculties, may be well called *God's wrath and damnation*. Besides, they observe, that the main point of the imputation of Adam's sin to his posterity, and its being considered by God as their own act, not being expressly taught in the Article, here was that moderation observed, which the compilers of the Articles have shewed on many other occasions. It is plain from hence, that they did not intend to lay a burden on men's consciences, or oblige them to profess a doctrine that seems to be hard of digestion to a great many. The last prejudice that they offer against that opinion is, that the softening the terms of *God's wrath and damnation*, that was brought in by the followers of St. Austin's doctrine, to such a moderate and harmless notion, as to be only a loss of heaven, with a sort of unactive sleep, was an effect of their apprehending that the world could very ill bear

Ex. xxxii. 10. and through the whole Old Testament.
Mat. iii. 7.
1 Thess. ii. 16.
Luke xxiii. 40.
1 Cor. xi. 29.
1Pet.iv.17.
Rom. xiii. 2.
2 Cor. vii. 3.
John viii. 10, 11.
Rom. xiv. 23.

an opinion of so strange a sound, as that all mankind were to be damned for the sin of one man: and that therefore, to make this pass the better, they mitigated *damnation* far below the representation that the scriptures generally give of it, which propose it as the being adjudged to a place of torment, and a state of horror and misery.

Thus I have set down the different opinions in this point, with that true indifference that I intend to observe on such other occasions, and which becomes one who undertakes to explain the doctrines of the church, and not his own; and who is obliged to propose other men's opinions with all sincerity, and to shew what are the senses that the learned men, of different persuasions in these matters, have put on the words of the Article. In which one great and constant rule to be observed is, to represent men's opinions candidly, and to judge as favourably both of them and their opinions as may be: to bear with one another, and not to disturb the peace and union of the church, by insisting too much and too peremptorily upon matters of such doubtful disputation; but willingly to leave them to all that liberty, to which the church has left them, and which she still allows them.

ARTICLE X.

Of Free-Will.

The Condition of Man after the fall of Adam is such that he cannot turn and prepare himself by his own natural strength and good works to faith and calling upon God. Wherefore we have no power to do good works pleasant and acceptable to God, without the Grace of God by Christ preventing us, that we may have a good will, and working with us when we have that good will.

WE shall find the same moderation observed in this Article, that was taken notice of in the former; where all disputes concerning the degree of that feebleness and corruption, under which we are fallen by the sin of Adam, are avoided, and only the necessity of a preventing and a co-operating grace is asserted against the Semipelagians* and the Pelagians. But before we enter upon that, it is fitting first to state the true notion of free-will, in so far as it is necessary to all rational

---

* 'A new and different modification was given to the doctrine of Augustin by the monk Cassian, who came from the east into France, and erected a monastery near Marseilles. Nor was he the only one who attempted to fix upon a certain temperature between the errors of Pelagius and the opinions of the African oracle; several persons embarked in this undertaking about the year 430, and hence arose a new sect, which were called by their adversaries, Semipelagians.

'The opinions of this sect have been misrepresented, by its enemies, upon several occasions; such is generally the fate of all parties in religious controversies. Their doctrine, as it has been generally explained by the learned, amounted to this: "That inward preventing grace was not necessary to form in the soul the first beginnings of true repentance and amendment; that every one was capable of producing these by the mere power of their natural faculties, as also of exercising faith in Christ, and forming the purposes of a holy and sincere obedience." But they acknowledged, at the same time, "That none could persevere or advance in that holy and virtuous course which they had the power of beginning, without the perpetual support and the powerful assistance of the divine grace."†

'The disciples of Augustin, in Gaul, attacked the Semipelagians, with the utmost vehemence, without being able to extirpate or overcome them. The doctrine of this sect was so suited to the capacities of the generality of men, so conformable to the way of thinking that prevailed among the monastic orders, so well received among the gravest and most learned Grecian doctors, that neither the zeal nor industry of its adversaries could stop its rapid and extensive progress. Add to its other advantages, that neither Augustin, nor his followers, had ventured to condemn it in all its parts, nor to brand it as an impious and pernicious heresy.' *Mosheim*.—[ED.]

---

† 'The leading principles of the Semipelagians were the five following :—
1. That God did not dispense his grace to one more than another, in consequence of predestination, i. e. an eternal and absolute decree; but was willing to save all men, if they complied with the terms of his gospel. 2. That Christ died for all men. 3. That the grace purchased by Christ, and necessary to salvation, was offered to all men. 4. That man, before he received grace, was capable of faith and holy desires. 5. That man, born free, was consequently capable of resisting the influences of grace, or complying with its suggestions.' *Maclaine.*

agents to make their actions morally good or bad; since it is ART. a principle that seems to rise out of the light of nature, that X. no man is accountable, rewardable, or punishable, but for that in which he acts freely, without force or compulsion; and so far all are agreed.

Some imagine, that liberty must suppose a freedom to do, or not to do, and to act contrariwise at pleasure. To others it seems not necessary that such a liberty should be carried to denominate actions morally good or bad: God certainly acts in the perfectest liberty, yet he cannot sin. Christ had the most exalted liberty in his human nature, of which a creature was capable, and his merit was the highest, yet he could not sin. Angels and glorified saints, though no more capable of rewards, are perfect moral agents, and yet they cannot sin: and the devils, with the damned, though not capable of further punishment, yet are still moral agents, and cannot but sin: so this indifferency to do, or not to do, cannot be the true notion of liberty. A truer one seems to them to be this, that a rational nature is not determined as mere matter, by the impulse and motion of other bodies upon it, but is capable of thought, and, upon considering the objects set before it, makes reflection, and so chooses. Liberty therefore seems to consist in this inward capacity of thinking, and of acting and choosing upon thought. The clearer the thought is, and the more constantly that our choice is determined by it, the more does a man rise up to the highest acts, and sublimest exercises of liberty.

A question arises out of this, whether the will is not always determined by the understanding, so that a man does always choose and determine himself upon the account of some idea or other? If this is granted, then no liberty will be left to our faculties. We must apprehend things as they are proposed to our understanding; for if a thing appears true to us, we must assent to it; and if the will is as blind to the understanding, as the understanding is determined by the light in which the object appears to it, then we seem to be concluded under a fate, or necessity. It is, after all, a vain attempt to argue against every man's experience: we perceive in ourselves a liberty of turning our minds to some ideas, or from others; we can think longer or shorter of these, more exactly and steadily, or more slightly and superficially, as we please; and in this radical freedom of directing or diverting our thoughts, a main part of our freedom does consist: often objects as they appear to our thoughts do so affect or heat them, that they do seem to conquer us, and carry us after them; some thoughts seeming as it were to intoxicate and charm us. Appetites and passions, when much fired by objects apt to work upon them, do agitate us strongly; and, on the other hand, the impressions of religion come often into our minds with such a secret force, so much of terror and such secret joy mixing with them, that they seem to master us; yet in all this a man acts freely, because he thinks and chooses for himself; and though perhaps he does not feel himself so entirely balanced, that he is indifferent to both sides, yet he has still such a remote liberty, that he can turn himself to other objects and thoughts, so that he can divert, if not all of a sudden resist, the present impressions that seem to master him. We do also feel that in many trifles we do act with an entire liberty, and do many things upon no other account, and for no other reason, but because we will do them: and yet more important things depend on these.

Our thoughts are much governed by those impressions that are made upon our brain: when an object proportioned to us appears to us with such advantages as to affect us much, it makes such an impression on our brain, that our animal spirits move much towards it; and those thoughts that answer it arise oft and strongly upon us, till either that impression is worn out and flatted, or new and livelier ones are made on us by other objects. In this depressed state in which we now are, the ideas of what is useful or pleasant to our bodies are strong; they are ever fresh, being daily renewed; and, according to the different construction of men's blood and their brains, there arises a great variety of inclinations in them. Our animal spirits, that are the immediate organs of thought, being the subtiler parts of our blood, are differently made and shaped, as our blood happens to be acid, salt, sweet, or phlegmatic: and this gives such a bias to all our inclinations, that nothing can work us off from it, but some great strength of thought that bears it down: so learning, chiefly in mathematical sciences, can so swallow up and fix one's thought, as to possess it entirely for some time; but when that amusement is over, nature will return and be where it was, being rather diverted than overcome by such speculations.

The revelation of religion is the proposing and proving many truths of great importance to our understandings, by which they are enlightened, and our wills are guided; but these truths are feeble things, languid and unable to stem a tide of nature, especially when it is much excited and heated: so that in fact we feel, that, when nature is low, these thoughts may have some force to give an inward melancholy, and to awaken in us purposes and resolutions of another kind; but when nature recovers itself, and takes fire again, these grow less powerful. The giving those truths of religion such a force that they may be able to subdue nature, and to govern us, is the design of both natural and revealed religion. So the question comes now according to the Article to be, whether a man by the powers of nature and of reason, without other inward assistances, can so far turn and dispose his own mind, as to believe and 'to do works pleasant and acceptable to God.' Pelagius thought that man was so entire in his liberty, that there was no need of any other grace but that of *pardon*, and of proposing the truths of religion to men's knowledge, but that the use of these was in every man's power. Those who were called Semipelagians thought that an assisting inward grace was necessary to enable a man to go through all the harder steps of religion; but with that they thought that the first turn or conversion of the will to God, was the effect of a man's own free choice.

ART. X.

In opposition to both which, this Article asserts both an assisting and a preventing grace. That there are inward assistances given to our powers, besides those outward blessings of Providence, is first to be proved. In the Old Testament, it is true, there were not express promises made by Moses of such assistances; yet it seems both David and Solomon had a full persuasion about it. David's prayers do every where relate to somewhat that is internal: he prays God 'to open and turn his eyes; to unite and incline his heart; to quicken him; to make him to go; to guide and lead him; to create in him a clean heart, and renew a right spirit within him.' Solomon says, that 'God gives wisdom; that he directs men's paths, and giveth grace to the lowly.' In the promise that Jeremy gives of a new covenant, this is the character that is given of it; 'I will put my law in their inward parts, and write it in their hearts: They shall all know me, from the least of them unto the greatest.' Like to that is what Ezekiel promises; 'A new heart also will I give you, and a new spirit will I put within you; and I will take away the stony heart out of your flesh, and I will give you an heart of flesh; and I will put my spirit within you, and cause you to walk in my statutes, and ye shall keep my judgments and do them.' That these prophecies relate to the new dispensation cannot be questioned, since Jeremy's words, to which the other are equivalent, are cited and applied to it in the Epistle to the Hebrews. Now the opposition of the one dispensation to the other, as it is here stated, consists in this, that whereas the old dispensation was made up of laws and statutes that were given on tables of stone, and in writing, the new dispensation was to have somewhat in it beside that external revelation, which was to be internal, and which should dispose and enable men to observe it.

Ps. cxix. 18, 27, 32, 35.
Ps. li. 10, 11.
Prov. ii. 6. iii. 6, 34.

Jer. xxxi. 33, 34.

Ezek. xxxvi. 26, 27.

A great deal of our Saviour's discourse concerning the Spirit, which he was to pour on his disciples, did certainly belong to that extraordinary effusion at Pentecost, and to those wonderful effects that were to follow upon it; yet as he had formerly given this as an encouragement to all men to pray, that 'his heavenly Father would give the Holy Spirit to every one that asked him,' so there are many parts of that his last discourse that seem to belong to the constant necessities of all Christians. It is as unreasonable to limit all to that time, as the first words of it, 'I go to prepare a place for

Luke xi. 13.

John xiv. 2.

ART. X.

you;' and 'because I live, ye shall live also.' The prayer which comes after that discourse, being extended beyond them to all that should 'believe in his name through their word,' we have no reason to limit these words, 'I will manifest myself to him; My Father and I will make our abode with him; In me ye shall have peace;' to the apostles only; so that the guidance, the conviction, the comforts, of that Spirit, seem to be promises which in a lower order belong to all Christians. St. Paul speaks of 'the love of God shed abroad in their hearts by the Holy Ghost:' when he was under temptation, and prayed thrice, he had this answer, ' My grace is sufficient for thee; my strength is made perfect in weakness.' He prays often for the churches in his Epistles to them, that 'God would stablish, comfort, and perfect them, enlighten and strengthen them;' and this in all that variety of words and phrases that import inward assistances. This is also meant by 'Christ's living and dwelling in us,' and by our being 'rooted and grounded in him;' our being 'the temples of God, a holy habitation to him, through his Spirit;' our being 'sealed by the Spirit of God to the day of redemption;' by all those directions to pray for 'grace to help in time of need,' and 'to ask wisdom of God that gives liberally to all men;' as also by the phrases of 'being born of God,' and 'the having his seed abiding in us.' These and many more places, which return often through the New Testament, seem to put it beyond all doubt, that there are inward communications from God, to the powers of our souls; by which we are made both to apprehend the truths of religion, to remember and reflect on them, and to consider and follow them more effectually.

Rom. v. 5.

2 Cor. xii. 9.

Eph. iii. 17.
2 Cor. vi. 16.
Eph. ii. 22.
i. 13, 14.
Heb. iv. 16.
Jam. i. 5.
1 John iii. 9.

How these are applied to us is a great difficulty indeed, but it is to little purpose to amuse ourselves about it. God may convey them immediately to our souls, if he will; but it is more intelligible to us to imagine that the truths of religion are by a divine direction imprinted deep upon our brain; so that naturally they must affect us much, and be oft in our thoughts: and this may be an hypothesis to explain regeneration or habitual grace by. When a deep impression is once made, there may be a direction from God, in the same way that his providence runs through the whole material world, given to the animal spirits to move towards and strike upon that impression, and so to excite such thoughts as by the law of the union of the soul and body to correspond to it: this may serve for an hypothesis to explain the conveyance of actual grace to us: but these are only proposed as hypotheses, that is, as methods, or possible ways, how such things may be done, and which may help us to apprehend more distinctly the manner of them. Now as this hypothesis has nothing in it but what is truly philosophical, so it is highly congruous to the nature and attributes of God, that if our faculties are fallen under a decay and corruption, so that bare instruction is not like to prevail over us, he should by some secret methods rectify this in us. Our experience tells us but too often what a feeble thing knowledge and speculation is, when it engages with nature strongly assaulted; how our best thoughts fly from us and forsake us: whereas at other times the sense of these things lies with a due weight on our minds, and has another effect upon us. The way of conveying this is invisible; our Saviour compared it to the 'wind that bloweth where it listeth; no man knows whence it comes, and whither it goes.' No man can give an account of the sudden changes of the wind, and of that force with which the air is driven by it, which is otherwise the most yielding of all bodies; to which he adds, 'so is every one that is born of the Spirit.' This he brings to illustrate the meaning of what he had said, that 'except a man was born again of water and of the Spirit, he could not enter into the kingdom of God:' and to shew how real and internal this was, he adds, 'that which is born of the flesh is flesh;' that is, a man has the nature of those parents from whom he is descended, by *flesh* being understood the fabric of the human body, animated by the soul: in opposition to which he subjoins, 'that which is born of the Spirit is spirit;' that is to say, a man thus regenerated by the operation of the Spirit of God, comes to be of a spiritual nature.

With this I conclude all that seemed necessary to be proved, that there are inward assistances given to us in the new dispensation. I do not dispute whether these are fitly called *grace*, for perhaps that word will scarce be found in that sense in the scriptures; it signifying more largely the love and favour of God, without restraining it to this act or effect of it. The next thing to be proved is, that there is a *preventing grace*, by which the will is first moved and disposed to turn to God. It is certain that the first promulgation of the gospel to the churches that were gathered by the apostles, is ascribed wholly to the riches and freedom of the grace of God. This is fully done in the Epistle to the Ephesians, in which their former ignorance and corruption is set forth under the figures of *blindness*, of 'being without hope, and without God in the world, and dead in trespasses and sins, they following the course of this world, and the prince of the power of the air, and being by nature children of wrath;' that is, under wrath. I dispute not here concerning the meaning of the word *by nature*, whether it relates to the corruption of our nature in Adam, or to that general corruption that had overspread heathenism, and was become as it were another nature to them. In this single instance we plainly see that there was no previous disposition to the first preaching of the gospel at Ephesus: many expressions of this kind, though perhaps not of this force, are in the other Epistles. St. Paul, in his Epistle to the Romans, puts God's choosing of Abraham upon

ART. X.

Rom. iv. 2.

Rom. xi. 20.

1 Cor. i. 26, 27, 29.

1 Cor. iv. 7.

Isa. lxv. 1.

Acts xvi. 14.

John xv. 5, 16. vi. 44. i. 13
Phil. ii. 13.

this, that it was 'of grace, not of debt, otherwise Abraham might have had whereof to glory.' And when he speaks of God's casting off the Jews, and grafting the Gentiles upon that stock from which they were cut off, he ascribes it wholly to the goodness of God towards them, and charges them 'not to be highminded, but to fear.' In his Epistle to the Corinthians he says, that 'not many wise, mighty, nor noble, were chosen, but God had chosen the foolish, the weak, and the base things of this world, so that no flesh should glory in his presence:' and he urges this further, in words that seem to be as applicable to particular persons, as to communities or churches: 'Who maketh thee to differ from another? and what has thou, that thou didst not receive? Now if thou didst receive it, why dost thou glory as if thou hadst not received it?' From these and many more passages of the like nature it is plain, that in the promulgation of the gospel, 'God was found of them that sought not to him, and heard of them that called not upon him;' that is, he prevented them by his favour, while there were no previous dispositions in them to invite it, much less to merit it. From this it may be inferred, that the like method should be used with relation to particular persons.

We do find very express instances in the New Testament of the conversion of some by a preventing grace: it is said, that 'God opened the heart of Lydia, so that she attended to the things that were spoken of Paul.' The conversion of St. Paul himself was so clearly from a preventing grace, that if it had not been miraculous in so many of its circumstances, it would have been a strong argument in behalf of it. These words of Christ seem also to assert it; 'Without me ye can do nothing; ye have not chosen me, but I you; and no man can come to me, except the Father which has sent me draw him.' Those who received Christ were 'born not of blood, nor of the will of the flesh, nor of the will of man, but of the will of God.' God is said 'to work in us both to will and to do of his own good pleasure:' the one seems to import the first beginnings, and the other the progress, of a Christian course of life. So far all among us, that I know of, are agreed, though perhaps not as to the force that is in all those places to prove this point.

There do yet remain two points in which they do not agree; the one is the efficacy of this preventing grace; some think that it is of its own nature so efficacious, that it never fails of converting those to whom it is given: others think that it only awakens and disposes, as well as it enables them to turn to God, but that they may resist it, and that the greater part of mankind do actually resist it. The examining of this point, and the stating the arguments on both sides, will belong more properly to the seventeenth Article. The other head, in which many do differ, is concerning the extent of this preventing grace; for whereas such as do hold it to be efficacious of itself, restrain it to the number of those who are elected and converted by it; others do believe, that as Christ died for all men, so there is an universal grace which is given in Christ to all men, in some degree or other, and that it is given to all baptized Christians in a more eminent degree; and that as all are corrupted by Adam, there is also a general grace given to all men in Christ. This depends so much on the former point, that the discussing the one is indeed the discussing of both; and therefore it shall not be further entered upon in this place.

ARTICLE XI.

Of the Justification of Man.

We are accounted Righteous before God only for the Merit of our Lord and Saviour Jesus Christ, by Faith, and not for our own Works or Deservings. Wherefore that we are justified by Faith only, is a most wholesome Doctrine, and very full of Comfort, as more largely is expressed in the Homily of Justification.

In order to the right understanding this Article, we mu.t first consider the true meaning of the terms of which it is made up: which are *justification, faith, faith only,* and *good works;* and then, when these are rightly stated, we will see what judgments are to be passed upon the questions that do arise out of this Article. *Just,* or *justified,* are words capable of two senses; the one is, a man who is in the favour of God by a mere act of his grace, or upon some consideration not founded on the holiness or the merit of the person himself. The other is, a man who is truly holy, and as such is beloved of God. The use of this word in the New Testament was probably taken from the term *chasidim* among the Jews, a designation of such as observed the external parts of the law strictly, and were believed to be upon that account much in the favour of God; an opinion being generally spread among them, that a strict observance of the external parts of the law of Moses did certainly put a man in the favour of God. In opposition to which, the design of a great part of the New Testament is to shew that these things did not put men in the favour of God. Our Saviour used the word *saved* in opposition to *condemned;* and spoke of men who were *condemned already,* as well as of others who were *saved.* St. Paul enlarges more fully into many discourses; in which our being *justified* and the *righteousness of God,* or his *grace towards us,* are all terms equivalent to one another. His design in the Epistle to the Romans was to prove that the observance of the Mosaical law could not *justify,* that is, could not put a man under the *grace* or *favour* of God, or the *righteousness* of God, that is, into a state of *acceptation* with him, as that is opposite to a state of *wrath* or *condemnation:* he upon that shews that Abraham was in the favour of God before he was circumcised, upon the account of his trusting to the promises of God, and obeying his commands; and that God reckoned upon these acts of his, as much as if they had been an entire course of obedience; for that is the meaning of these words, 'And it was imputed to him for righteousness.' These promises were freely made to him by God, when by no previous works of

John iii. 18.

Gen. xv. 6. Rom. iv. 3, 22.

his he had made them to be due to him of debt; therefore that covenant which was founded on those promises, was the 'justifying of Abraham freely by grace.' Upon which St. Paul, in a variety of inferences and expressions, assumes that we are in like manner 'justified freely by grace through the redemption in Christ Jesus.' That God has of his own free goodness offered a new covenant, and new and better promises to mankind in Christ Jesus, which whosoever believe as Abraham did, they are justified as he was. So that whosoever will observe the scope of St. Paul's Epistles to the Romans and Galatians, will see that he always uses *justification* in a sense that imports our being put in the favour of God. The Epistle to the Galatians was indeed writ upon the occasion of another controversy, which was, whether, supposing Christ to be the Messias, Christians were bound to observe the Mosaical law or not: whereas the scope of the first part of the Epistle to the Romans is to shew that we are not justified nor saved by the law of Moses, as a mean of its own nature capable to recommend us to the favour of God, but that even that law was a dispensation of *grace*, in which it was a true faith like Abraham's that put men in the favour of God; yet in both these Epistles, in which *justification* is fully treated of, it stands always for the receiving one into the favour of God.

ART. XI.

Rom. iii. 24.

In this, the consideration upon which it is done, and the condition upon which it is offered, are two very different things. The one is a dispensation of God's mercy, in which he has regard to his own attributes, to the honour of his laws, and his government of the world: the other is the method in which he applies that to us, in such a manner, that it may have such ends as are both perfective of human nature, and suitable to an infinitely holy Being to pursue. We are never to mix these two together, or to imagine that the condition, upon which justification is offered to us, is the consideration that moves God; as if our holiness, faith, or obedience, were the moving cause of our justification;* or that God *justifies*

---

* ' Faith is the only hand which putteth on Christ unto justification; and Christ the only garment, which, being so put on, covereth the shame of our defiled natures, hideth the imperfection of our works, preserveth us blameless in the sight of God, before whom, otherwise, the weakness of our faith were cause sufficient to make us culpable, yea, to shut us from the kingdom of heaven, where nothing that is not absolute can enter.'—*Hooker*.

' Justification is the office of God only, and is not a thing which we render unto him, but which we receive of him: not which we give to him, but which we take of him, by his free mercy, and by the only merits of his most dearly beloved Son, our only Redeemer, Saviour, and Justifier, Jesus Christ: so that the true understanding of this doctrine, we be justified freely by faith without works, or that we be justified by faith in Christ only, is not, that this our own act to believe in Christ, or this our faith in Christ, which is within us, doth justify us, and deserve our justification unto us (for that were to count ourselves to be justified by some act or virtue that is within ourselves); but the true understanding and meaning thereof is, that although we hear God's word and believe it, although we have faith, hope, charity, repentance, dread, and fear of God within us, and do never so many works thereunto: yet we must renounce the merit of all our said virtues, of faith,

M

us, because he sees that we are truly *just:* for though it is not to be denied, but that in some places of the New Testament, *justification* may stand in that sense, because the word in its true signification will bear it; yet in these two Epistles, in which it is largely treated of, nothing is plainer than that the design is to shew us what it is that brings us to the favour of God, and to a state of pardon and acceptation: so that *justification* in those places stands in opposition to accusation and *condemnation.*

The next term to be explained is *faith;* which in the New Testament stands generally for the complex of Christianity, in opposition to the law, which stands as generally for the complex of the whole Mosaical dispensation. So that the *faith of Christ* is equivalent to this, the gospel of Christ; because Christianity is a fœderal religion, founded on God's part, on the promises that he has made to us, and on the rules he has set us; and on our part, on our believing that revelation, our trusting to those promises, and our setting ourselves to follow those rules: the believing this revelation, and that great article of it, of Christ's being the Son of God, and the true Messias, that came to reveal his Father's will, and to offer himself up to be the sacrifice of this new covenant, is often represented as the great and only condition of the covenant on our part; but still this *faith* must receive the whole gospel, the precepts as well as the promises of it, and receive Christ as a Prophet to teach, and a King to rule, as well as a Priest to save us.

By *faith only,* is not to be meant faith as it is separated from the other evangelical graces and virtues; but faith, as it is opposite to the rites of the Mosaical law: for that was the great question that gave occasion to St. Paul's writing so fully upon this head; since many Judaizing Christians, as they acknowledged Christ to be the true Messias, so they thought that the law of Moses was still to retain its force: in opposition to whom St. Paul says, that 'we are justified by

---

Rom. iii. 28.
Gal. ii. 16.

hope, charity, and all other virtues and good deeds, which we either have done, shall do, or can do, as things that be far too weak, and insufficient, and imperfect, to deserve remission of our sins, and our justification; and therefore we must trust only in God's mercy, and that sacrifice which our High-priest and Saviour Christ Jesus, the Son of God, once offered for us upon the cross, to obtain thereby God's grace and remission, as well of our original sin in baptism, as of all actual sin committed by us after our baptism, if we truly repent and turn unfeignedly to him again. So that as St. John Baptist, although he were never so virtuous and godly a man, yet in this matter of forgiving of sin, he did put the people from him, and appointed them unto Christ, saying thus unto them, Behold, yonder is the Lamb of God, which taketh away the sins of the world: even so, as great and as godly a virtue as the lively faith is, yet it putteth us from itself, and remitteth or appointeth us into Christ, for to have only by him remission of our sins, or justification. So that our faith in Christ (as it were) saith unto us thus, It is not I that take away your sins, but it is Christ only, and to him only I send you for that purpose, forsaking therein all your good virtues, words, thoughts, and works, and only putting your trust in Christ.' *Homily of the Salvation of Mankind: Second Part.*—[Ed.]

faith, without the works of the law.' It is plain that he means the Mosaical dispensation, for he had divided all mankind into those 'who were in the law,' and those 'who were without the law,' that is, into Jews and Gentiles. Nor had St. Paul any occasion to treat of any other matter in those Epistles, or to enter into nice abstractions, which became not one that was to instruct the world in order to their salvation: those metaphysical notions are not easily apprehended by plain men, not accustomed to such subtilties, and are of very little value, when they are more critically distinguished: yet when it seems some of those expressions were wrested to an ill sense and use, St. James treats of the same matter, but with this great difference, that though he says expressly that 'a man is justified by his works, and not by faith only;' yet he does not say, *by the works of the law;* so that he does not at all contradict St. Paul; the works that he mentions not being the circumcision or ritual observances of Abraham, but his offering up his son Isaac, which St. Paul had reckoned a part of the *faith of Abraham:* this shews that he did not intend to contradict the doctrine delivered by St. Paul, but only to give a true notion of the *faith* that *justifies;* that it is not a bare believing, such as devils are capable of, but such a believing as exerted itself in good works. So that the *faith* mentioned by St. Paul is the complex of all Christianity; whereas that mentioned by St. James is a bare believing, without a life suitable to it. And as it is certainly true that we are taken into the favour of God, upon our receiving the whole gospel, without observing the Mosaical precepts; so it is as certainly true, that a bare professing or giving credit to the truth of the gospel, without our living suitably to it, does not give us a right to the favour of God. And thus it appears that these two pieces of the New Testament, when rightly understood, do in no wise contradict, but agree well with one another.

ART. XI.

Rom. ii. 12.

James ii. 24.

In the last place, we must consider the signification of *good works:* by them are not to be meant some voluntary and assumed pieces of severity, which are no where enjoined in the gospel, that arise out of superstition, and that feed pride and hypocrisy: these are so far from deserving the name of *good works,* that they have been in all ages the methods of imposture, and of impostors, and the arts by which they have gained credit and authority. By *good works* therefore are meant acts of true holiness, and of sincere obedience to the laws of the gospel.

The terms being thus explained, I shall next distinguish between the questions arising out of this matter, that are only about words, and those that are more material and important. If any man fancy that the remission of sins is to be considered as something previous to *justification,* and distinct from it, and acknowledge that to be freely given in Christ Jesus; and that

ART. XI.

in consequence of this there is such a grace infused, that thereupon the person becomes truly *just*, and is considered as such by God: this, which must be confessed to be the doctrine of a great many in the church of Rome, and which seems to be that established at Trent, is indeed very visibly different from the style and design of those places of the New Testament, in which this matter is most fully opened: but yet after all it is but a question about words; for if that which they call *remission* of sins, be the same with that which we call *justification*; and if that which they call *justification* be the same with that which we call *sanctification*, then here is only a strife of words; yet even in this we have the scriptures clearly of our side; so that we hold the *form of sound words*, from which they have departed. The scripture speaks of *sanctification* as a thing different from, and subsequent to, *justification*. 'Now ye are washed, ye are sanctified, ye are justified.' And since justification, and the being in the love and favour of God, are in the New Testament one and the same thing, the remission of sins must be an act of God's favour: for we cannot imagine a middle state of being neither accepted of him, nor yet under his *wrath*, as if the remission of sins were merely an extinction of the guilt of sin without any special favour. If therefore this remission of sins is acknowledged to be given freely to us through Jesus Christ, this is that which we affirm to be *justification*, though under another name: we do also acknowledge that our natures must be sanctified and renewed, that so God may take pleasure in us, when his image is again visible upon us; and this we call *sanctification*; which we acknowledge to be the constant and inseparable effect of *justification:* so that as to this, we agree in the same doctrine, only we differ in the use of the terms; in which we have the phrase of the New Testament clearly with us.

1 Cor. vi. 11.

But there are two more material differences between us: it is a tenet in the church of Rome, that the use of the sacraments, if men do not put a bar to them, and if they have only imperfect acts of sorrow accompanying them, does so far complete those weak acts, as to *justify* us.* This we do utterly deny, as a doctrine that tends to enervate all religion; and to make the sacraments, that were appointed to be the solemn acts of religion, for quickening and exciting our piety, and for conveying grace to us, upon our coming devoutly to them, become means to flatten and deaden us; as if they were of the nature of charms, which, if they could be come at, though

---

* ' Si quis dixerit, sacramenta novæ legis non continere gratiam, quam significant, aut gratiam ipsam non ponentibus obicem non conferre, quasi signa tantum externa sint, acceptæ per fidem gratiæ, vel justitiæ, et notæ quidam Christianæ professionis, quibus apud homines discernuntur fideles ab infidelibus: Anathema sit.'
' Si quis dixerit, per ipsa novæ legis sacramenta ex opere operato non confern gratiam, sed solam fidem divinæ promissionis ad gratiam consequendam sufficere Anathema sit.' *Conc. Trident. canon. et decret. Sessio* viii. *Can.* vi. *et* viii.—[ED.

with ever so slight a preparation, would make up all defects. The doctrine of sacramental justification is justly to be reckoned among the most mischievous of all those practical errors that are in the church of Rome.* Since, therefore, this is no where mentioned in all these large discourses that are in the New Testament concerning justification, we have just reason to reject it: since also the natural consequence of this doctrine is to make men rest contented in low imperfect acts, when they can be so easily made up by a sacrament, we have just reason to detest it, as one of the depths of Satan; the tendency of it being to make those ordinances of the gospel, which were given us as means to raise and heighten our faith

* It is of vital importance that the doctrine of the church of Rome respecting the justification of a sinner should be well understood; for this is, after all, the grand distinguishing difference between us and the papacy. Unacquaintance with this article has led many to charge upon the papal church what she does not receive, while it has deprived them of the opportunity and power of attacking her system where it is most vulnerable; thereby giving to the adversary an easy triumph, and to true religion a severe blow. It will not, therefore, be deemed out of place to here point out, in the words of the great Hooker, how far we agree, and wherein we differ from, and protest against the church of Rome, in this momentous question: 'There is a glorifying righteousness of men in the world to come: as there is a justifying and sanctifying righteousness here. The righteousness wherewith we shall be clothed in the world to come, is both perfect and inherent. That whereby here we are justified is perfect; but not inherent. That whereby we are sanctified is inherent, but not perfect. This openeth a way to the understanding of that grand question, which hangeth yet in controversy between us and the church of Rome, about the matter of justifying righteousness. First, although they imagine, that the mother of our Lord and Saviour Jesus Christ were, for his honour, and by his special protection, preserved clean from all sin: yet touching the rest, they teach as we do, that infants that never did actually offend, have their natures defiled, destitute of justice, averted from God; that in making man righteous, none do efficiently work with God, but God. They teach as we do, that unto justice no man ever attained, but by the merits of Jesus Christ. They teach as we do, that although Christ, as God, be the efficient; as man, the meritorious cause of our justice: yet in us also there is something required. God is the cause of our natural life, in him we live: but he quickeneth not the body without the soul in the body. Christ hath merited to make us just: but, as a medicine, which is made for health, doth not heal by being made, but by being applied, so, by the merits of Christ there can be no justification, without the application of his merit. Thus far we join hands with the church of Rome.

' Wherein then do we disagree? We disagree about the nature and essence of the medicine, whereby Christ cureth our disease; about the manner of applying it; about the number and the power of means, which God requireth in us for the effectual applying thereof to our souls' comfort. When they are required to shew what the righteousness is whereby a Christian man is justified: they answer, that it is a divine spiritual quality; which quality, received into the soul, doth first make it to be one of them, who are born of God: and secondly, endue it with power to bring forth such works, as they do that are born of him; even as the soul of man being joined to his body doth first make him to be of the number of reasonable creatures; and secondly, enable him to perform the natural functions which are proper to his kind; that it maketh the soul amiable and gracious in the sight of God, in regard whereof it is termed grace; that it purgeth, purifieth, and washeth out all the stains and pollutions of sins; that by it, through the merit of Christ, we are delivered as from sin, so from eternal death and condemnation, the reward of sin. This grace they will have to be applied by infusion; to the end, that as the body is warm by the heat which is in the body, so the soul might be righteous by inherent grace: which grace they make capable of increase; as the body may be more and more warm, so the soul more and more justified, according as grace should be augmented; the augmentation whereof is merited by good works, as good works are made meritorious by it. Wherefore the first receipt of grace in their divinity is, the first justification; the increase thereof,

166   AN EXPOSITION OF

ART. XI. and repentance, become engines to encourage sloth and impenitence.

There is another doctrine that is held by many, and is still taught in the church of Rome, not only with approbation, but favour; that the inherent holiness of good men is a thing of its own nature so perfect, that, upon the account of it, God is so bound to esteem them just, and to *justify* them, that he were unjust if he did it not. They think there is such a real *condignity* in it, that it makes men God's adopted children. Whereas we, on the other hand, teach, that God is indeed pleased with the inward reformation that he sees in good men, in whom his grace dwells; that he approves and accepts of

---

the second justification. As grace may be increased by the merit of good works: so it may be diminished by the demerit of sins venial—it may be lost by mortal sin. In as much, therefore, as it is needful in the one case to repair, in the other to recover, the loss which is made: the infusion of grace hath her sundry after-meals; for the which cause, they make many ways to apply the infusion of grace. It is applied to infants, through baptism, without either faith or works, and in them really it taketh away original sin, and the punishment due unto it; it is applied to infidels and wicked men in the first justification, through baptism without works, yet not without faith; and it taketh away both sins actual and original together, with all whatsoever punishment, eternal or temporal, thereby deserved. Unto such as have attained the first justification, that is to say the first receipt of grace, it is applied farther by good works to the increase of former grace, which is the second justification. If they work more and more, grace doth more increase, and they are more and more justified. To such as diminished it by venial sins, it is applied by holy water, Ave Mary's, crossings, papal salutations, and such like, which serve for reparations of grace decayed. To such as have lost it through mortal sin, it is applied by the sacrament (as they term it) of penance: which sacrament hath force to confer grace anew, yet in such sort, that being so conferred, it hath not altogether so much power, as at the first; for it only cleanseth out the stain or guilt of sin committed, and changeth the punishment eternal into a temporary satisfactory punishment here, if time do serve; if not, hereafter to be endured, except it be lightened by masses, works of charity, pilgrimages, fasts, and such like; or else shortened by pardon for term, or by plenary pardon quite removed and taken away. This is the mystery of the man of sin. This maze the church of Rome doth cause her followers to tread when they ask her the way to justification.

'Whether they speak of the first or second justification, they make it the essence of a divine quality inherent, they make it righteousness which is in us. If it be in us then it is ours, as our souls are ours though we have them from God, and can hold them no longer than pleaseth Him; for if he withdraw the breath of our nostrils, we fall to dust: but the righteousness wherein we must be found, if we will be justified, is not our own; therefore we cannot be justified by any inherent quality. Christ hath merited righteousness for as many as are found in him. In him God findeth us if we be faithful, for by faith we are incorporated into Christ. Then although in ourselves we be altogether sinful and unrighteous, yet even the man which is impious in himself, full of iniquity, full of sin; him being found in Christ through faith, and having his sin remitted through repentance; him God upholdeth with a gracious eye, putteth away his sin by not imputing it, taketh quite away the punishment due thereunto, by pardoning it, and accepteth him in Jesus Christ, as perfectly righteous, as if he had fulfilled all that was commanded him in the law: shall I say more perfectly righteous than if himself had fulfilled the whole law? I must take heed what I say: but the apostle saith, "God made him to be sin for us, who knew no sin: that we might be made the righteousness of God in him." Such we are in the sight of God the Father, as is the very Son of God himself. Let it be counted folly, or frenzy, or fury, whatsoever; it is our comfort, and our wisdom; we care for no knowledge in the world but this, that man hath sinned, and God has suffered; that God hath made himself the Son of Man, and that men are made the righteousness of God. You see therefore that the church of Rome, in teaching justification by inherent grace, doth pervert the truth of Christ, and that, by the hands of the Apostles, we have received otherwise than she teacheth.'—[ED.]

their sincerity; but that with this there is still such a mix- ART.
ture, and in this there is still so much imperfection, that even XI.
upon this account, if God did straitly mark iniquity, none
could stand before him: so that even his acceptance of this is
an act of mercy and grace. This doctrine was commonly
taught in the church of Rome at the time of the Reformation,
and, together with it, they reckoned that the chief of those
works that did justify, were either great or rich endowments,
or excessive devotions towards images, saints, and relics; by
all which, Christ was either forgot quite, or remembered only
for form sake, esteemed perhaps as the chief of saints: not to
mention the impious comparisons that were made between him
and some saints, and the preferences that were given to them
beyond him. In opposition to all this, the reformers began,
as they ought to have done, at the laying down this as the
foundation of all Christianity, and of all our hopes, that we
were reconciled to God merely through his mercy, by the
redemption purchased by Jesus Christ; and that a firm believing the gospel, and a claiming to the death of Christ, as
the great propitiation for our sins, according to the terms on
which it is offered us in the gospel, was that which united us
to Christ; that gave us an interest in his death, and thereby
justified us. If, in the management of this controversy, there
was not so critical a judgment made of the scope of several
passages of St. Paul's Epistles; and if the dispute became
afterwards too abstracted and metaphysical, that was the effect
of the infelicity of that time, and was the natural consequence
of much disputing: therefore though we do not now stand to
all the arguments, and to all the citations and illustrations,
used by them; and though we do not deny but that many of
the writers of the church of Rome came insensibly off from
the most practical errors, that had been formerly much taught,
and more practised, among them; and that this matter was so
stated by many of them, that, as to the main of it, we have no
just exceptions to it: yet, after all, this beginning of the Reformation was a great blessing to the world, and has proved
to, even to the church of Rome; by bringing her to a juster
sense of the atonement made for sins by the blood of Christ;
and by taking men off from external actions, and turning them
to consider the inward acts of the mind, faith and repentance,
as the conditions of our justification. And therefore the approbation given here to the homily, is only an approbation
of the doctrine asserted and proved in it; which ought not to
be carried to every particular of the proofs or explanations that
are in it. To be *justified*, and to be accounted righteous, stand
for one and the same thing in the Article: and both import
our being delivered from the guilt of sin, and entitled to the
savour of God. These differ from God's intending from all
eternity to save us, as much as a decree differs from the execution of it.

A R T. XI.

A man is then only *justified*, when he is freed from wrath, and is at peace with God: and though this is freely offered to us in the gospel through Jesus Christ, yet it is applied to none but to such as come within those qualifications and conditions set before us in the gospel. That God pardons sin, and receives us into favour only through the death of Christ, is so fully expressed in the gospel, as was already made out upon the second Article, that it is not possible to doubt of it, if one does firmly believe, and attentively read, the New Testament. Nor is it less evident, that it is not offered to us absolutely, and without conditions and limitations. These conditions are, *repentance*, with which *remission of sins* is often joined; and *faith*, but a 'faith that worketh by love, that purifies the heart, and that keeps the commandments of God;' such a faith as shews itself to be alive by good works, by acts of charity, and every act of obedience; by which we demonstrate, that we truly and firmly believe the divine authority of our Saviour and his doctrine. Such a faith as this *justifies*, but not as it is a work or meritorious action, that of its own nature puts us in the favour of God, and makes us truly just; but as it is the condition upon which the mercy of God is offered to us by Christ Jesus; for then we correspond to his design of coming into the world, that 'he might redeem us from all iniquity,' that is, justify us: and 'purify unto himself a peculiar people, zealous of good works;' that is, sanctify us. Upon our bringing ourselves therefore under these qualifications and conditions, we are actually in the favour of God; our sins are pardoned, and we are entitled to eternal life.

Gal. v. 6.
Luke xxiv. 47.
Acts ii. 38.

Tit. ii. 14.

Our faith and repentance are not the valuable considerations for which God pardons and justifies; that is done merely for the death of Christ; which God having out of the riches of his grace provided for us, and offered to us, justification is upon those accounts said to be *free;* there being nothing on our part which either did or could have procured it. But still our faith, which includes our hope, our love, our repentance, and our obedience, is the condition that makes us capable of receiving the benefits of this redemption and free grace. And thus it is clear, in what sense we believe, that *we* are *justified* both *freely*, and yet through Christ; and also through *faith*, as the condition indispensably necessary on our part.

In strictness of words, we are not *justified* till the final sentence is pronounced; till upon our death we are solemnly acquitted of our sins, and admitted into the presence of God; this being that which is opposite to *condemnation:* yet as a man, who is in that state that must end in *condemnation*, is said to be *condemned already*, and *the wrath of God* is said *to abide upon him;* though he be not yet adjudged to it: so, on the contrary, a man in that state which must end in the full enjoyment of God, is said now to be *justified*, and to be at peace with God; because he not only has the promises of

John iii. 18.

that state now belonging to him, when he does perform the conditions required in them; but is likewise receiving daily marks of God's favour, the protection of his providence, the ministry of angels, and the inward assistances of his grace and Spirit.

This is a doctrine full of comfort; for if we did believe that our justification was founded upon our inherent justice, or sanctification, as the consideration on which we receive it, we should have just cause of fear and dejection; since we could not reasonably promise ourselves so great a blessing, upon so poor a consideration: but when we know that this is only the condition of it, then when we feel it is sincerely received and believed, and carefully observed by us, we may conclude that we are *justified:* but we are by no means to think, that our certain persuasion of Christ's having died for us in particular, or the certainty of our salvation through him, is an act of *saving faith*, much less that we are justified by it. Many things have been too crudely said upon this subject, which have given the enemies of the Reformation great advantages, and have furnished them with much matter of reproach. We ought to believe firmly, that Christ died for all penitent and converted sinners; and when we feel these characters in ourselves, we may from thence justly infer, that he died for us, and that we are of the number of those who shall be saved through him: but yet if we may fall from this state, in which we do now feel ourselves, we may and must likewise forfeit those hopes; and therefore we must 'work out our salvation with fear and trembling.' Our believing that we shall be saved by Christ, is no act of divine faith; since every act of faith must be founded on some divine revelation: it is only a collection and inference that we may make from this general proposition, that Christ is the propitiation for the sins of those who do truly repent and believe his gospel; and from those reflections and observations that we make on ourselves, by which we conclude that we do truly both repent and believe.

ARTICLE XII.

Of Good Works.

Albeit that Good Works, which are the fruits of Faith, and follow after Justification, cannot put away our Sins, and endure the severity of God's Judgment: yet are they pleasing and acceptable to God and Christ, and do spring out necessarily of a true and lively Faith, insomuch that by them a lively Faith may be as evidently known, as a Tree discerned by the fruit.

THAT good works are indispensably necessary to salvation; that 'without holiness no man shall see the Lord;' is so fully and frequently expressed in the gospel, that no doubt can be made of it by any who reads it: and indeed a greater disparagement to the Christian religion cannot be imagined, than to propose the hopes of God's mercy and pardon barely upon believing without a life suitable to the rules it gives us. This began early to corrupt the theories of religion, as it still has but too great an influence upon the practice of it. What St. James writ upon this subject must put an end to all doubting about it; and whatever subtilties some may have set up, to separate the consideration of faith from a holy life, in the point of *justification;* yet none among us have denied that it was absolutely necessary to salvation: and so it be owned as necessary, it is a nice curiosity to examine whether it is of itself a condition of justification, or if it is the certain distinction and constant effect of that faith which justifies. These are speculations of very little consequence, as long as the main point is still maintained; that Christ came to *bring us to God,* to change our natures, to mortify the old man in us, and to raise up and restore that *image of* God, from which we had fallen by sin. And therefore even where the thread of men's speculations of these matters may be thought too fine, and in some points of them wrong drawn; yet so long as this foundation is preserved, 'that every one who nameth the name of Christ does depart from iniquity,' so long the doctrine of Christ is preserved pure in this capital and fundamental point.

2 Tim. ii. 19.

There do arise out of this Article only two points, about which some debates have been made. 1st. Whether the good works of holy men are in themselves so perfect, that they can endure the severity of God's judgment, so that there is no mixture of imperfection or evil in them, or not? The council of Trent has decreed, that men by their good works have so fully satisfied the law of God, according to the state of this life, that nothing is wanting to them.* The second point is, whether these good works are of their own nature meritorious of eternal life, or not? The council of Trent has decreed that they are: yet a long softening is added to the decree, importing, *That none ought to glory in himself, but in the Lord; whose goodness is such, that he makes his own gifts to us, to be merits in us:* and it adds, *That because in many things we offend all, every one ought to consider the justice and severity, as well as the mercy and goodness, of God; and not to judge himself, even though he should know nothing by himself.* So then that in which all are agreed about this matter, is, 1. That our works cannot be good or acceptable to God but as we are assisted by his grace and Spirit to do them: so that the real goodness that is in them flows from those assistances which enable us to do them. 2. That God does certainly reward good works: he has promised it, and 'he is faithful, and cannot lie; nor is he unrighteous to forget our labour of love.' So the favour of God and eternal happiness is the reward of good works. Mention is also made of 'a full reward, of the reward of a righteous man, and of a prophet's reward.' 3. That this reward is promised in the gospel, and could not be claimed without that, by any antecedent merit founded upon equality: 'Since our light affliction, which is but for a moment, worketh for us a far more exceeding and eternal weight of glory.'

ART. XII.

Matt. x. 41, 42.

2 Cor. iv. 17.

The points in which we differ are, 1. Whether the good works of holy men are so perfect, that there is no defect in

* 'Nihil ipsis justificatis amplius deesse credendum est, quominus plene illis quidem operibus, quæ in Deo sunt facta, divinæ legi pro hujus vitæ statu satisfecisse, et vitam æternam suo etiam tempore, si tamen in gratia decesserint consequendam, vere promeruisse censeantur.'—*Sessio* vi. cap. xvi.

'Si quis dixerit justitiam acceptam non conservari, atque etiam augeri coram Deo per bona opera; sed opera ipsa fructus solummodo et signa esse justificationis adeptæ, non autem ipsius augendæ causam: anathema sit.—*Can.* xxiv. *Sess.* vi.

'Si quis dixerit, hominis justificati bona opera ita esse dona Dei, ut non sint etiam bona ipsius justificati merita, aut, ipsum justificatum bonis operibus, quæ ab eo per Dei gratiam, et Jesu Christi meritum, cujus vivum membrum est, fiunt, non vere mereri augmentum gratiæ, vitam æternam, et ipsius vitæ æternæ, si tamen in gratia decesserit, consecutionem, atque etiam gloriæ augmentum: anathema sit.'—*Can.* xxxii. *Sess.* vi.

'Turn thee yet again, and thou shalt see greater abominations than they do.' The following, from the same *infallible* source of truth, will shew that good works not only deserve increase of grace and eternal life, but that by them we can make satisfaction to God the Father; and, wonderful to relate, not only satisfaction for oneself, but actually for another!!

'Docet præterea, tantam esse divinæ munificentiæ largitatem, ut non solum pœnis sponte a nobis pro vindicando peccato susceptis, aut sacerdotis arbitrio pro mensura delicti impositis, sed etiam, quod maximum amoris argumentum est, temporalibus flagellis a Deo inflictis, et a nobis patienter toleratis, apud Deum Patrem per Christum Jesum satisfacere voleamus.'—*Sessio* xiv. cap. ix.

'In eo vero summa Dei bonitas, et clementia maximis laudibus, et gratiarum actionibus prædicanda est, qui humanæ imbecillitati hoc condonavit, ut unus posset pro altero satisfacere, quod quidem hujus partis Pœnitentiæ maxime proprie est: ut enim, quod ad contritionem, et confessionem attinet, nemo pro altero dolere, aut confiteri potest; ita, qui divina gratia præditi sunt, alterius nomine possunt, quod Deo debetur, persolvere; quare fit, ut quodam pacto alter alterius onera portare videatur.' *Catechis. ex decreto Concil. Trident. ad Paroch. De Pœnitentia.—Quæ ad veram satisfactionem requirantur.*—[Ed.]

them; or whether there is still some such defect mixed with them, that there is occasion for mercy, to pardon somewhat even in good men? Those of the church of Rome think that a work cannot be called *good*, if it is not entirely *good;* and that nothing can please God in which there is a mixture of sin. Whereas we, according to the Article, believe that human nature is so weak and so degenerated, that as far as our natural powers concur in any action, there is still some allay in it: and that a *good work* is considered by God according to the main, both of the action and of the intention of him that does it; and as a father *pities* his childsen, so God passes over the defects of those who serve him sincerely, though not perfectly. 'The imaginations of the heart of man are only evil continually: In many things we offend all,' says St. James: and St. Paul reckons that 'he had not yet apprehended, but was forgetting the things behind, and reaching to those before, and still pressing forward.'

We see, in fact, that the best men in all ages have been complaining and humbling themselves even for the sins of their holy things, for their vanity and desire of glory, for the distraction of their thoughts in devotion, and for the affection which they bore to earthly things. It were a doctrine of great cruelty, which might drive men to despair, if they thought that no action could please God, in which they were conscious to themselves of some imperfection or sin. The midwives of Egypt *feared God*, yet they excused themselves by a lie: but God accepted of what was good, and passed over what was amiss in them, and 'built them houses.' St. Austin urges this frequently, that our Saviour, in teaching us to pray, has made this a standing petition, 'Forgive us our trespasses,' as well as that, 'Give us this day our daily bread;' for we sin daily, and do always need a pardon. Upon these reasons we conclude, that somewhat of the man enters into all that men do: we are made up of infirmities, and we need the intercession of Christ to make our best actions to be accepted of by God: for 'if he should straitly mark iniquity, who can stand before him? but mercy is with him, and forgiveness.' So that with Hezekiah we ought to pray, that 'though we are not purified according to the purification of the sanctuary, yet the good Lord would pardon every one that prepareth his heart to seek God.'

The second question arises out of this, concerning *the merit of good works*; for upon the supposition of their being completely good, that merit is founded; which will be acknowledged to be none at all, if it is believed that there are such defects in them, that they need a pardon; since where there is guilt, there can be no pretension to merit. The word *merit* has also a sound that is so daring, so little suitable to the humility of a creature, to be used towards a Being of infinite majesty, and with relation to endless rewards, that though we do not deny but that a sense is given to it by many of the church of Rome, to which no just exception can be made, yet there ART. seems to be somewhat too bold in it, especially when *condig-* XII. *nity* is added to it: and since this may naturally give us an idea of a buying and selling with God, and that there has been a great deal of this put in practice, it is certain that on many respects this *word* ought not to be made use of. There is somewhat in the nature of man apt to swell and to raise itself out of measure, and to that no indulgence ought to be given, in words that may flatter it; for we ought to subdue this temper by all means possible, both in ourselves and others. On the other hand, though we confess that there is a disorder and weakness that hangs heavy upon us, and that sticks close to us, yet this ought not to make us indulge ourselves in our sins, as if they were the effects of an infirmity that is inseparable from us. To consent to any sin, if it were ever so small in itself, is a very great sin: we ought to go on, still 'cleansing ourselves' more and more, 'from all filthiness both of 2 Cor. vii. the flesh and of the spirit, and perfecting holiness in the fear 1. of God.' Our readiness to sin should awaken both our diligence to watch against it, and our humility under it. For though we grow not up to a pitch of being above all sin, and of absolute perfection, yet there are many degrees both of purity and perfection, to which we may arrive, and to which we must constantly aspire. So that we must keep a just temper in this matter, neither to ascribe so much to our own works as to be lifted up by reason of them, or to forget our daily need of a Saviour both for pardon and intercession; nor on the other hand so far to neglect them, as to take no care about them. The due temper is 'to make our calling and Phil. ii. 12. election sure, and to work out our own salvation with fear and trembling;' but to do 'all in the name of the Lord Jesus,' Col. iii. 17. ever trusting to him, and 'giving thanks to God by him.'

ARTICLE XIII.

Of Works before Justification.

Works done before the Grace of Christ, and the Inspiration of his Spirit, are not pleasant to God; forasmuch as they spring not of Faith in Jesus Christ, neither do they make men meet to receive Grace, or (as the School-Authors say) deserve Grace of Congruity: Yea rather, for that they are not done as God hath commanded and willed them to be done, we doubt not but that they have the nature of Sin.

THERE is but one point to be considered in this Article, which is, whether men can, without any inward assistances from God, do any action that shall be in all its circumstances so good, that it is not only acceptable to God, but meritorious in his sight, though in a lower degree of merit. If what was formerly laid down concerning a corruption that was spread over the whole race of mankind, and that had very much vitiated their faculties, be true, then it will follow from thence, that unassisted nature can do nothing that is so good in itself, that it can be pleasant or meritorious in the sight of God. A great difference is here to be made between an external action as it is considered in itself, and the same action as it was done by such a man. An action is called good, from the morality and nature of the action itself; so actions of justice and charity are in themselves good, whatsoever the doer of them may be: but actions are considered by God with relation to him that does them, in another light; his principles, ends, and motives, with all the other circumstances of the action, come into this account; for unless all these be good, let the action in its own abstracted nature be ever so good, it cannot render the doer acceptable or meritorious in the sight of God.

Another distinction is also to be made between the methods of the goodness and mercy of God, and the strictness of justice: for if God had such regard to the feigned humiliation of Ahab, as to grant him and his family a reprieve for some time from those judgments that had been denounced against them and him; and if Jehu's executing the commands of God upon Ahab's family, and upon the worshippers of Baal, procured him the blessing of a long continuance of the kingdom in his family, though he acted in it with a bad design, and retained still the old idolatry of the calves set up by Jeroboam; then we have all reason to conclude, according to the infinite mercy and goodness of God, that no man is rejected by him, or denied inward assistances, that is making the most of his fa-

1 Kings xxi. 29.
2 Kings x. 30, 31.

culties, and doing the best that he can; but that he who is ART.
faithful in his little, shall be made ruler over more. XIII.

The question is only, whether such actions can be so pure, as to be free from all sin, and to merit at God's hand, as being works naturally perfect? For that is the formal notion of the *merit of congruity*, as the notion of the *merit of condignity* is, that the work is perfect in the supernatural order.

To establish the truth of this Article, beside what was said upon the head of original sin, we ought to consider what St. Paul's words in the 7th of the Romans do import: nothing was urged from them on the former Articles, because there is just ground of doubting whether St. Paul is there speaking of himself in the state he was in when he writ it, or whether he is personating a Jew, and speaking of himself as he was while yet a Jew. But if the words are taken in that lowest sense, they prove this, that an unregenerate man has in himself such a principle of corruption, that even a good and a holy *law* revealed to him, cannot reform it; but that, on the contrary, it will 'take occasion from that very law to deceive him, and Rom. vii. to slay him.' So that all the benefit that he receives even 11, 12, 13. from that revelation is, that 'sin in him becomes exceeding sinful;' as being done against such a degree of light, by which it appears that he is 'carnal, and sold under sin;' and that Ver. 14, though his understanding may be enlightened by the revelation of the law of God made to him, so that he has some inclinations to obey it, yet he does not that which he would, but that which he would not: and though his *mind* is so far convinced, that he 'consents to the law that it is good,' yet 16. 'he still does that which he would not;' which was the effect of 'sin that dwelt in him;' and from hence he knew, 'that 17, in him, that is, in his flesh,' in his carnal part, or carnal state, 18, 'there dwelt no good thing; for 'though to will,' that is, to resolve on obeying the law, 'was present, yet he found not a way how to perform that which was good;' the good that he wished to do, that he did not; but he did the evil that he wished not to do; which he imputed to the 'sin that dwelt in him.' He found then a *law*, a bent and bias within him, that when he wished, resolved, and endeavoured, to do good, 'evil was present with him,' it sprung up naturally within 21, him; for though in his rational powers he might so far approve the law of God as to *delight* in it; yet he found 'an- 23, other law' arising upon his mind from his body, 'which warred against the law of his mind, and brought him into captivity to the law of sin which was in his members:' all this made him conclude, that 'he was carnal, and sold under sin;' and cry out, 'O wretched man that I am, who shall deliver me from 24, the body of this death?' For this 'he thanks God through 25. our Lord Jesus Christ:' and he sums all up in these words; 'So then, with the mind I myself serve the law of God, but with the flesh the law of sin.'

ART.
XIII.
If all this discourse is made by St. Paul of himself, when he had the light which a divinely inspired law gave him, he being educated in the exactest way of that religion, both zealous for the law, and blameless in his own observance of it; we may from thence conclude how little reason there is to believe that a heathen, or indeed an unregenerated man, can be better than he was, and do actions that are both good in themselves, which it is not denied but that he may do; and do them in such a manner that there shall be no mixture or imperfection in them, but that they shall be perfect in a natural order, and be by consequence meritorious in a secondary order.

By all this we do not pretend to say, that a man in that state can do nothing; or that he has no use of his faculties: he can certainly restrain himself on many occasions; he can do many good works, and avoid many bad ones; he can raise his understanding to know and consider things according to the light that he has; he can put himself in good methods and good circumstances; he can pray, and do many acts of devotion, which though they are all very imperfect, yet none of them will be lost in the sight of God, who certainly will never be wanting to those who are doing what in them lies, to make themselves the proper objects of his mercy, and fit subjects for his grace to work upon. Therefore this Article is not to be made use of to discourage men's endeavours, but only to increase their humility; to teach them not to think of themselves above measure, but soberly; to depend always on the mercy of God, and ever to fly to it.

ARTICLE XIV.

Of Works of Supererogation.

Voluntary Works, besides, over and above God's Commandments, which they call works of Supererogation, cannot be taught without Arrogancy and Impiety. For by them men do declare, That they do not only render unto God as much as they are bound to do: but that they do more for his sake, than of bounden Duty is required. Whereas Christ saith plainly, when ye have done all that are commanded to you, say, We are unprofitable Servants.

THERE are two points that arise out of this Article to be considered, 1st. Whether there are in the New Testament counsels of perfection given; that is to say, such rules which do not oblige all men to follow them, under the pain of sin; but yet are useful to carry them on to a sublimer degree of perfection, than is necessary in order to their salvation. 2d. Whether men by following these do not more than they are bound to do, and, by consequence, whether they have not thereby a stock of merit to communicate to others. The first of these leads to the second; for if there are no such counsels, then the foundation of supererogation fails. [Luke xvii. 10.]

We deny both upon this ground, that the great obligations of 'loving God with all our heart, soul, strength, and mind, and our neighbour as ourselves,' which are reckoned by our Saviour the 'two great commandments, on which hang all the Law and the Prophets,' are of that extent, that it seems not possible to imagine, how any thing can be acceptable to God, that does not fall within them. Since if it is acceptable to God, then that obligation to love God so entirely must bind us to it; for if it is a sin not to love God up to this pitch, then it is a sin not to do every thing that we imagine will please him: and, by consequence, if there is a degree of pleasing God, whether precept or counsel, that we do not study to attain to, we do not *love* him in a manner suitable to that. It seems a great many in the church of Rome are aware of this consequence, and therefore they have taken much pains to convince the world that we are not bound to love God at all, or, as others more cautiously word it, that we are only bound to value him above all things, but not to have a *love* of such a vast intention for him. This is a proposition that, after all their softening it, gives so much horror to every Christian, that I need not be at any pains to confute it. [Matt. xxii. 36—40.]

We are further required in the New Testament, 'to cleanse [2 Cor. vii. 1.]

ART. XIV.

1 Cor. vi. 20.

ourselves from all filthiness both of the flesh and spirit, perfecting holiness in the fear of God;' and to reckon ourselves 'his, and not our own,' and that 'we are bought with a price;' and that therefore 'we ought to glorify him both in our bodies, and in our spirits, which are his.' These and many more like expressions are plainly precepts of general obligation, for nothing can be set forth in more positive words than these are: and it is not easy to imagine, how any thing can go beyond them; for if we are Christ's property, purchased by him, then we ought to apply ourselves to every thing in which his honour, or the honour of his religion, can be concerned, or which will be pleasing to him.

Isai. xxix. 13. Matt. xv. 7—9. Coloss. ii. 18.

Our Saviour having charged the Pharisees so often, for adding so many of their ordinances to the laws of God, 'teaching his fear by the precepts of men,' and the apostles condemning 'a show of will-worship and voluntary humility,' seem to belong to this matter, and to be designed on purpose to repress the pride and singularities of affected hypocrites.

Matt. xix. 16, 17.

Our Saviour said to him that asked, 'What he should do that he might have eternal life?—Keep the commandments.' These words I do the rather cite, because they are followed with a passage, that, of all others in the New Testament, seems to look the likest a counsel of perfection; for when he, who made the question, replied upon our Saviour's answer,

Ver. 20, 21. that 'he had kept all these from his youth up,' and added, 'what lack I yet?' to that our Saviour answered, 'If thou wilt be perfect, go sell all that thou hast, and give to the poor, and thou shalt have treasure in heaven; and come and follow me:' and by the words that follow, of the difficulty of a 'rich man's entering into the kingdom of heaven,' this is more fully explained. The meaning of all that whole passage is this; Christ called that person to abandon all, and come and follow him, in such a manner as he had called his apostles. So that here is no counsel, but a positive command given to that particular person upon this occasion. By *perfect* is only to be meant complete, in order to that to which he pretended, which was *eternal life*. And that also explains the word in that period, *treasures in heaven*, another expression for *eternal life*, to compensate the loss which he would have made by the sale of his possessions. So that here is no counsel, but a special command given to this person, in order to his own attaining *eternal life*.

Nor is it to be inferred from hence, that this is proposed to others in the way of a counsel; for as in cases either of a famine or persecution, it may come to be to some a command, *to sell all* in order to the relief of others, as it was in the first beginnings of Christianity; so in ordinary cases to do it, might be rather a tempting of Providence than a trusting to it, for then a man should part with the means of his subsistence, which God has provided for him, without a necessary and pressing occasion. Therefore our Saviour's words, 'Sell that ye have, and give alms,' as they are delivered in the strain and peremptoriness of a command, so they must be understood to bind as positive commands do: not so constantly as a negative command does, since in every minute of our life that binds: but there is a rule and order in our obeying positive commands. We must not rest on the *sabbath-day*, if a work of necessity or charity calls us to put to our hands: we must not obey our parents in disobeying a public law: so if we have families, or the necessities of a feeble body, and a weak constitution, for which God hath supplied us with that which will afford us 'food convenient for us,' we must not throw up those provisions, and cast ourselves upon others. Therefore that precept must be moderated and expounded, so as to agree with the other rules and orders that God has set us.

ART. XIV. Luke xii. 33. Prov. xxx. 8.

A distinction is therefore to be made between those things that do universally and equally bind all mankind, and those things that do more specially bind some sorts of men, and that only at some times. There are greater degrees of charity, gravity, and all other virtues, to which the clergy for instance are more bound than other men; but these are to them precepts, and not counsels. And in the first beginnings of Christianity there were greater obligations laid upon all Christians, as well as greater gifts were bestowed on them. It is true, in the point of marriage St. Paul does plainly allow, that such as 'marry do well, but that such as marry not do better.' But the meaning of that is not as if an unmarried life were a state of perfection, beyond that which a man is obliged to: but only this; that as to the course of this life, and the *present distress;* and as to the judgment that is to be made of men by their actions, no man is to be thought to do amiss who *marries;* but yet he who marries not, is to be judged to do *better.* But yet inwardly and before God this matter may be far otherwise: for he who *marries not* and burns, certainly does worse than he who *marries and lives chastely.* But he who finding that he can limit himself without endangering his purity; though no law restrains him from marrying, yet seeing that he is like to be tempted to be too careful about the concerns of this life if he *marries,* is certainly under obligations to follow that course of life in which there are fewer temptations, and greater opportunities to attend on the service of God.

1 Cor. vii. 38.

With relation to outward actions, and to the judgments that from visible appearances are to be made of them, some actions may be said to be better than others, which yet are truly good: but as to the particular obligations that every man is under, with relation to his own state and circumstances, and for which he must answer at the last day, these being secret, and so not subject to the judgments of men, certainly every man is strictly bound to do the best he can; to choose that course of life in which he thinks he may do the best services to God and man: nor are these free to him to choose or not: he is under obligations, and he sins if he sees a more excellent thing that he might have done, and contents himself with a lower or less valuable thing. St. Paul had wherein to *glory;* for whereas it was lawful for him as an apostle to suffer the Corinthians to supply him in temporals, when he was serving them in spiritual things; yet he chose rather for the honour of the gospel, and to take away all occasion of censure from those who sought for it, 'to work with his own hands, and not to be burdensome to them.' But in that state of things, though there was no law or outward obligation upon him to *spare them;* he was under an inward law of doing all things to the glory of God: and by this law he was as much bound, as if there had been an outward compulsory law lying upon him.

Acts xx. 34.
1 Cor. ix. 18.
2 Cor. xii. 13.

This distinction is to be remembered, between such an obligation as arises out of a man's particular circumstances, and such other motives as can be only known to a man himself, and such an obligation as may be fastened on him by stated and general rules: he may be absolutely free from the latter of these, and yet be secretly bound by those inward and stronger constraints of the love of God, and zeal for his glory. Enough seems to be said to prove that there are no counsels of perfection in the gospel; that all the rules set to us in it are in the style and form of precepts; and that though there may be some actions of more heroical virtue, and more sublime piety, than others, to which all men are not obliged by equal or general rules; yet such men, to whose circumstances and station they do belong, are strictly obliged by them, so that they should sin, if they did not put them in practice.

This being thus made out, the foundation of works of supererogation is destroyed. But if it should be acknowledged that there were such counsels of perfection in the scripture, there are still two other clear proofs, to shew that there can be no such thing as supererogating with God. First, every man not only has sinned, but has still so much corruption about him, as to feel the truth of that of St. James, 'in many things we offend all.' Now unless it can be supposed that, by obeying those counsels, a man can compensate with Almighty God for his sins, there is no ground to think that he can supererogate. He must first clear his own score, before he can imagine that any thing upon his account can be forgiven or imputed to another: and if the guilt of sin is eternal, and the pretended merit of obeying counsels is only temporary, no temporary merit can take off an eternal guilt. So that it must first be supposed, that a man both is and has been perfect as to the precepts of obligation, before it can be thought that he should have an overplus of merit.

James iii.2.

The other clear argument from scripture against works of supererogation is, that there is nothing in the whole New

Testament that does in any sort favour them; we are always taught to trust to the mercies of God, and to the death and intercession of Christ, and 'to work out our own salvation with fear and trembling:' but we are never once directed to look for any help from saints, or to think that we can do any thing for another man's soul, in this way. The Psalm has it, 'No man can by any means give a ransom for his brother's soul:' the words of Christ cited in the Article are full and express against it.

ART. XIV.
Phil. ii. 12.
Ps. xlix. 7.

The words in the parable of the five foolish virgins and the five wise, may seem to favour it, but they really contradict it; for it was the foolish virgins that desired the wise to give them of their *oil;* which if any will apply to a supposed communication of merit, they ought to consider that the proposition is made by the *foolish,* and the answer of the wise virgins is full against it: 'Not so, lest there be not enough for us and you.' What follows, of bidding them 'go to them that sell, and buy for themselves,' is only a piece of the fiction of the parable, which cannot enter into any part of the application of it. What St. Paul says of his 'filling up that which was behind of the afflictions of Christ in his flesh, for his body's sake, which is the church,' is, as appears by the words that follow, 'whereof I am made a minister,' only applicable to the edification that the church received from the sufferings of the apostles; it being a great confirmation to them of the truth of the gospel, when those who preached it suffered so constantly and so patiently for it; by which they both confirmed what they had preached, and set an example to others, of adhering firmly to it. And since Christ is related to his church, as a head to the members, it is in some sort his suffering himself, when his members suffer: and that conformity which they ought to express to him as their head was necessary to make up the due proportion, that ought to be between the head and the members. So St. Paul rejoiced in his being made *conformable to him:* and this, as it is a sense that the words will well bear, so it is certain they are capable of no other sense; for if the sufferings of the apostles were meritorious in behalf of the other Christians, some plain account must have been given of this in the New Testament, at least to do honour to the memory of such apostles as had then died for the faith. If it is suggested, that the living apostles were too modest to claim it to themselves, that will not satisfy; all runs quite in a contrary style: the mercies of God and the blood of Christ being always repeated, whereas these are never once named. Now to imagine that there can be any thing of such great use to us, in which the scripture should be not only silent, but should run in a strain totally different from it, is not conceivable: for if in any thing, the gospel ought to be full and explicit in all that which

Matt. xxv. 9.
Col. i. 24

ART. XIV.

Mark xi. 17.

concerns our peace and reconciliation with God, and the means of our escaping his wrath, and obtaining his favour.

There is another doctrine that does also belong to this head, which is purgatory, that is not to be entered on here, but is referred to its proper place. Thus it appears, how ill this doctrine of works of supererogation is founded; and upon how many accounts it is evidently false; and yet upon it has been built not only a theory of a communication of those merits, and a treasure in the church, but a practice of so foul a nature; that in it the words of our Saviour spoken to the Jews, 'My house is a house of prayer, but ye have made it a den of thieves,' are accomplished in a high and most scandalous manner. It has been pretended that this was of the nature of a bank, of which the pope was the keeper; and that he could grant such bills and assignments upon it as he pleased:* this was done in so base and so crying a manner, that all who had any sense of probity in their own church were ashamed of it.

In the primitive church there were very severe rules made, obliging all that had sinned publicly (and they were afterwards applied to such as had sinned secretly) to continue for many years in a state of separation from the sacrament, and of penance and discipline. But because all such general rules admit of a great variety of circumstances, taken from men's sins, their persons, and their repentance, there was a power given to all bishops by the council of Nice, to shorten the time, and to relax the severity, of those canons; and such favour as they saw cause to grant was called *indulgence*. This was just and necessary, and was a provision without which no constitution or society can be well governed. But after the tenth century, as the popes came to take this power in the whole extent of it into their own hands, so they found it too feeble to carry on the great designs that they grafted upon it.

They gave it high names, and called it a plenary remission, and the pardon of all sins: which the world was taught to look on as a thing of a much higher nature, than the bare excusing of men from discipline and penance. Purgatory†

---

* 'Upon the whole then it is evident, that the doctrine of purgatory is of heathen original; that the fire of it is, like the thunder of the Vatican, a harmless thing, which no wise man would be afraid of, were it not too often attended with church thunderbolts, persecutions, and massacres; and that it only serves to cheat the simple and ignorant out of their money, by giving them bills of exchange upon the other world for cash paid in *this*, without any danger of the bills returning protested.' *Meagher's Popish Mass.* A just exposure of this iniquitous traffic.—[ED.]

† 'The doctrine of purgatory is the mother of indulgences, and the fear of that hath introduced these: for the world happened to be abused like the countryman in the fable, who, being told he was likely to fall into a *delirium* in his feet, was advised for remedy to take the juice of cotton. He feared a disease that was not, and looked for a cure as ridiculous.' *Bishop Taylor.*—[ED.]

was then got to be firmly believed, and all men were strangely possessed with the terror of it: so a deliverance from purgatory, and by consequence an immediate admission into heaven, was believed to be the certain effect of it. And to support all this, the doctrine of *counsels of perfection*, of works of *supererogation*, and of the *communication* of those merits, was set up; and to that this was added, that a treasure made up of these, was at the pope's disposal, and in his keeping. The use that this was put to, was as bad as the forgery itself. Multitudes were by these means engaged to go to the Holy Land to recover it out of the hands of the Saracens: afterwards they armed vast numbers against the heretics to extirpate them: they fought also all those quarrels which their ambitious pretensions engaged them in with emperors and other princes, by the same pay; and at last they set it to sale with the same impudence, and almost with the same methods, that mountebanks use in the venting of their secrets.

This was so gross even in an ignorant age, and among the ruder sort, that it gave the first rise to the Reformation: and as the progress of it was a very signal work of God, so it was in a great measure owing to the scandals that this shameless practice had given the world. And upon this single reason it is that this matter has been more fully examined than was necessary; for the thing is so plain, that it has no sort of difficulty in it.

ARTICLE XV.

Of Christ alone without Sin.

Christ in the truth of our nature was made like unto us in all things (sin only except) from which he was clearly void both in his flesh and in spirit. He came to be a Lamb without spot, who, by sacrifice of himself once made, should take away the sins of the World: and sin, as St. John saith, was not in him. But all we the rest (although baptized and born again in Christ) yet offend in many things; and if we say we have no sin, we deceive ourselves, and the truth is not in us.

THIS Article relates to the former, and is put here as another foundation against all works of supererogation: for that doctrine, with the consequences of it, having given the first occasion to the Reformation, it was thought necessary to overthrow it entirely; and because the perfection of the saints must be supposed, before their supererogation can be thought on, that was therefore here opposed.

Heb. vii. 26.
1 Pet. ii. 22.
Acts x. 38.
1 Pet. i. 19.

That Christ was 'holy, without spot and blemish, harmless, undefiled, and separate from sinners;' that there was 'no guile in his mouth;' that he never did amiss, but 'went about always doing good,' and was as a 'lamb without spot,' is so oft affirmed in the New Testament, that it can admit of no debate. This was not only true in his rational powers, the superior part called the *spirit*, in opposition to the lower part, but also in those appetites and affections that arise from our bodies, and from the union of our souls to them, called the *flesh*. For though in these Christ, having the human nature truly in him, had the appetites of hunger in him, yet the Devil could not tempt him by that to distrust God, or to desire a miraculous supply sooner than was fitting: he overcame even that necessary appetite, whensoever there was

John iv. 34.

an occasion given him 'to do the will of his heavenly Father:' he had also in him the aversions to pain and suffering, and the horror at a violent and ignominious death, which are planted in our natures; and in this it was natural to him to wish and to pray that the cup might pass from him. But in this his purity appeared the most eminently, that though he felt the weight of his nature to a vast degree, he did, notwithstanding that, limit and conquer it so entirely, that he

Matt. xxvi. 37—39.

resigned himself absolutely to his Father's will: 'Not my will, but thy will be done.'

Besides all that has been already said upon the former Articles, to prove that some taint and degree of the original corruption remains in all men; the peculiar character of Christ's holiness so oft repeated, looks plainly to be a distinction proper to him, and to him only. We are called upon to follow him, to learn of him, and to imitate him, without restriction; whereas we are required to 'follow the apostles, only as they were the followers of Christ:' and though we are commanded 'to be holy as he was holy in all manner of conversation;' that does no more prove that any man can arrive at that pitch, than our being commanded 'to be perfect as our heavenly Father is perfect,' will prove that we may become as perfect as God is: the importance of these words being only this, that we ought in all things to make God and Christ our patterns; and that we ought to endeavour to imitate and resemble them all we can. {ART. XV. 1 Cor. xi.1. 1 Pet.i.15. Matt. v.48.}

There seems to be a particular design in the contexture and writing of the scriptures, to represent to us some of the failings of the best men: for though Zacharias and Elizabeth are said to have been *blameless*, that must only be meant of the exterior and visible part of their conversation, that it was free from blame, and of their being accepted of God; but that is not to be carried to import a sinless purity before God: for we find the same Zachary guilty of misbelieving the message of the angel to him, to such a degree, that he was punished for it with a dumbness of above nine months' continuance. Perhaps the Virgin's question to the angel had nothing blameworthy in it: but our Saviour's answers to her, both when she came to him in the temple, when he was twelve years old, and more particularly when she moved him, at the marriage in Cana, to furnish them with wine, look like a reprimand. The contentions among the apostles about the pre-eminence, and in particular the ambition of James and John, cannot be excused. St. Peter's dissimulation at Antioch in the Judaizing controversy, and the sharp contention that happened between Paul and Barnabas, are recorded in scripture, and they are both characters of the sincerity of those who penned them, and likewise marks of the frailties of human nature, even in its greatest elevation, and with its highest advantages. So that all the high characters that are given of the best men, are to be understood either comparatively to others whom they exceeded, or with relation to their outward actions, and the visible parts of their life: or they are to be meant of their zeal and sincerity, which is valued and accepted of God: and, as it was to Abraham, is imputed to them for righteousness. {Luke i. 6. Ver. 20. Luke ii.49. John ii. 4. Matt. xx. 20, 24. Gal. ii. 11, 12, 13, 14. Acts xv. 39.}

Yet this is not to be abused by any to be an encouragement to live in sin; for we may carry this purity and perfection certainly very far, by the grace of God. In every sin that we commit we do plainly perceive, that we do it with so much freedom, that we might not have done it; here is still

ART. XV.

just matter for humiliation and repentance. By this doctrine our church intends only to repress the pride of vain-glorious and hypocritical men, and to strike at the root of that filthy merchandise that has been brought into the house of God, under the pretence of the perfection, and even the overdoing or supererogating, of the saints.

ARTICLE XVI.

Of Sin after Baptism.

Not every deadly sin willingly committed after Baptism is the sin against the Holy Ghost, and unpardonable. Wherefore the grant of repentance is not to be denied to such as fall into sin after Baptism. After we have received the Holy Ghost, we may depart from grace given, and fall into sin, and by the grace of God we may arise again and amend our Lives. And therefore they are to be condemned, which say they can no more sin as long as they live here, or deny the place of forgiveness to such as truly repent.

THIS Article, as it relates to the sect of the Novatians of old, so it is probable it was made a part of our doctrine, upon the account of some of the enthusiasts, who, at that time, as well as some do in our days, might boast their perfection, and join with that part of the character of a Pharisee, this other of an unreasonable rigour of censure and punishment against offenders. By *deadly sin* in the Article, we are not to understand such sins as in the church of Rome are called *mortal*, in opposition to others that are *venial:* as if some sins, though offences against God, and violations of his law, could be of their own nature such slight things, that they deserved only temporal punishment, and were to be expiated by some piece of penance or devotion, or the communication of the merits of others. The scripture no where teaches us to think so slightly of the majesty of God, or of his law. There is a *curse* upon every one 'that continueth not in all things which are written in the book of the law to do them;' and the same curse must have been on us all, if Christ had not redeemed us from it: 'The wages of sin is death.' And St. James asserts, that there is such a complication of all the precepts of the law of God, both with one another, and with the authority of the lawgiver, that 'he who offends in one point is guilty of all.' So, since God has in his word given us such dreadful apprehensions of his *wrath* and of the *guilt of sin*, we dare not soften these to a degree below the majesty of the eternal God, and the dignity of his most holy laws. But, after all, we are far from the conceit of the Stoics, who made all sins alike. We acknowledge that some sins of ignorance and infirmity may consist with a state of grace; which is either quite destroyed, or at least much eclipsed and clouded by other sins, that are more heinous in their nature, and more deliberately gone about. It is in this sense that the word *deadly sin* is to be understood in the Article: for though in

Gal. iii. 10.

Rom. vi. 23.

Jam. ii. 10, 11.

ART. XVI.

Matt. xii. 24, 31.

the strictness of justice every sin is *deadly*, yet in the dispensation of the gospel, those sins are only *deadly*, that do deeply wound the conscience, and that drive away grace.

Another term in the Article needs also to be a little explained; *the sin against the Holy Ghost*; concerning which, since there is so severe a sentence pronounced by Christ, it is necessary that it be rightly understood; and that can only be done by considering the occasion of those words, as well as the words themselves. Christ wrought such miracles in the sight of his enemies, that when there was no room left for any other cavil, they betook themselves to that, that 'he did not cast out devils but by Beelzebub, the prince of devils.' And this was the occasion that led our Saviour to speak of the sin or *blasphemy against the Holy Ghost*. It was their rejecting the clearest evidence that God could give to prove any thing by: the power by which those miracles were wrought, and which was afterwards communicated to the apostles, is called through the whole New Testament, the *Holy Ghost*. By which is not to be meant here the third person of the Trinity, but the wonderful effusion of those extraordinary gifts and powers that were then communicated, the economy and dispensation of which is said to be derived from that *one Spirit*. This was the utmost proof that could be given of truth: and when men set themselves to blaspheme this, and to ascribe the works of Christ to a collusion with the Devil, they did thereby so wilfully oppose God, and reproach his power, they did so stifle their own conviction, and set themselves against the conviction of others, that nothing could be done further for their conviction; this being the highest degree of evidence and proof: and this was so high an indignity to God, when he descended so far to satisfy their scruples, that it was not to be pardoned; as their impenitence and incredulity was so obstinate as not to be overcome.

Upon this occasion given, our Saviour makes a difference between their blaspheming him, and, instead of owning him to be the Messias, calling him a *deceiver*, a *glutton*, and a *wine-bibber*; of which, upon hearing his doctrine, and seeing his life, they were still guilty. This was indeed a great sin, but yet there were means left of convincing them of the truth of his being the great prophet sent of God; and by these they might be so far prevailed on as to repent and believe, and so to obtain pardon: but when they had those means set before them; when they saw plain and uncontested miracles done before them; and when, instead of yielding to them, they set up such an opposition to them, which might have been as reasonably said of every miracle that could have been wrought, then it was not possible to convince them. This is an impious rejecting of the highest method that God himself uses for proving a thing to us. The scorn put upon it, as it flows from a nature so depraved, that it cannot be wrought on, so it is a sin not to be pardoned. All things of extreme severity in a doctrine that is so full of grace and mercy as the gospel is, ought to be restrained as much as may be. From thence we infer, that those dreadful words of our Saviour's ought to be restrained to the subject to which they are applied, and ought not to be carried further. Since miracles have ceased, no man is any more capable of this sin.

ART. XVI.

These terms being thus explained, the question in the Article is now to be explained. There are words in St. John's Epistle, and elsewhere, that seem to import, that *men born of God*, that is to say, baptized or regenerated Christians, *sin not:* 'Whosoever abideth in him, sinneth not: Whosoever sinneth hath not seen him, neither known him: Whosoever is born of God doth not commit sin, for his seed remaineth in him; and he cannot sin, for he is born of God.' This is again repeated in the end of that Epistle, together with these words, 'He that is begotten of God keepeth himself, and that wicked one toucheth him not.' As these words seem to import that a true Christian sins not, so in the Epistle to the Hebrews it is said to be 'impossible to renew again, by repentance, those who fall away, after they had been once enlightened, and had tasted of the heavenly gift, had been made partakers of the Holy Ghost, and had tasted the good word of God, and the powers of the world to come.' Upon these expressions, and some others, though not quite of their force, it was, that in the primitive church, some that fell after baptism were cast out of the communion of the church; and though they were not cut off from all hopes of the mercy of God, yet they were never restored to the peace of the church; this was done in Tertullian's time, if what he says on this subject is not to be reckoned as a piece of his *Montanism*.

1 John iii. 6, 9. v. 18.

Heb. vi. 4, 5, 6.

But soon after there were great contests upon this head, while the Novatians withdrew from the communion of the church, and believed it was defiled by the receiving of apostates into it: though that was not done so easily as some proposed, but after a long separation and a severe course of penance. Upon this followed all those penitentiary canons concerning the several measures and degrees of penance, and that not only for acts of apostacy from the Christian religion, but for all other crying sins. According to what has been already said upon the former Articles, it has appeared, that the sanctification of regenerated men is not so perfected in this life, but that there is still a mixture of defects and imperfections left in them: and the state of the new covenant is a continuance of repentance and remission of sins; for as oft as one sins, if he repents truly of it, and forsakes his sins, there is a standing offer of the pardon of all sins; and therefore Christ has taught us to pray daily, 'Forgive us our sins.' If there were but one general pardon offered in baptism, this would signify little to those who feel their infirmities, and the sins that do so easily

ART.
XVI.

beset them, so apt to return upon them. It was no wonder if the entertaining this conceit brought in a superstitious error in practice among the ancient Christians, of delaying baptism till death; as hoping that all sins were then certainly pardoned; a much more dangerous error than even the fatal one of trusting to a death-bed repentance. For baptism might have been more easily compassed; and there was more offered in the way of argument for building upon it, than has been offered at for a death-bed repentance.

St. Peter's denial, his repentance, and his being restored to his apostolical dignity, seem to be recorded, partly on this account, to encourage us, even after the most heinous offences, to return to God, and never to reckon our condition desperate, were our sins ever so many, but as we find our hearts hardened in them into an obstinate impenitency. Our Saviour has made our pardoning the offences that others commit against us, the measure upon which we may expect pardon from God; and he being asked what limits he set to the number of the faults that we were bound to pardon, by the day, if seven was not enough, he carried it up to *seventy times seven*, a vast number, far beyond the number of offences that any man will in all probability commit against another in a day. But if they should grow up to all that vast number of four hundred and ninety, yet if our brother still 'turns again and repents,' we are still bound to forgive. Now since this is joined with what he declared, that if we pardoned our brother his offences, 'our heavenly Father would also forgive us,' then we may depend upon this, that according to the sincerity of our repentance, our sins are always forgiven us. And if this is the nature of the new covenant, then the church, which is a society formed upon it, must proportion the rules both of her communion and censure to those set in the gospel: a heinous sin must give us a deeper sorrow, and higher degrees of repentance; scandals must also be taken off and forgiven, when the offending persons have repaired the offence that was given by them, with suitable degrees of sorrow. St. Paul, in the beginnings of Christianity, in which it, being yet tender and not well known to the world, was more apt to be both blemished and corrupted, did yet order the Corinthians to receive back into their communion the incestuous person, whom by his own directions they had 'delivered to Satan;' they had excommunicated him, and, by way of reverse to the gifts of the Holy Ghost poured out upon all Christians, he was possessed or haunted with an evil spirit: and yet, as St. Paul declares that he forgave him, so he orders them to forgive him likewise; and he gives a reason for this conduct, from the common principles of pity and humanity, 'lest he should be swallowed up by overmuch sorrow.' What is in that place mentioned only in a particular instance, is extended to a general rule in the Epistle to the Galatians: 'If any one is overtaken in a fault, ye which are

1 Cor. v. 5.

2 Cor. ii. 7.

spiritual restore such a one in the spirit of meekness, considering thyself, lest thou also be tempted.' Where both the supposition that is made, and the reason that is given, do plainly insinuate that all men are subject to their several infirmities; so that every man may be overtaken in faults. The charge given to Timothy and Titus to 'rebuke and exhort,' does suppose that Christians, and even bishops and deacons, were subject to faults that might deserve correction.

A R T. XVI.

Gal. vi. 1.

2 Tim.iv.2. Tit. i. 13.

In that passage, cited out of St. John's Epistle, as mention is made of a 'sin unto death,' for which they were not to pray, so mention is made both there and in St. James's Epistle of 'sins for which they were to pray,' and which upon their prayers were to be forgiven. All which places do not only express this to be the tenor of the new covenant, that the sins of regenerated persons were to be pardoned in it, but they are also clear precedents and rules for the churches to follow them in their discipline. And therefore those words in St. John, that 'a man born of God doth not and cannot sin, must be understood in a larger sense, of their not living in the practice of known sins; of their not allowing themselves in that course of life, nor going on deliberately with it.

1 John v. 16.

Jam. v. 15, 16.

By the 'sin unto death,' is meant the same thing with that apostasy mentioned in the 6th of the Hebrews. Among the Jews some sins were punished by a total excision or cutting off, and this probably gave the rise to that designation of a 'sin unto death.' The words in the Epistle to the Hebrews do plainly import those who, being not only baptized, but having also received a share of the extraordinary effusion of the Holy Ghost, had totally renounced the Christian religion, and apostatized from the faith, which 'was a crucifying of Christ anew.' Such apostates to Judaism were thereby involved in the crime and guilt of the crucifying of Christ, and 'the putting him to open shame.' Now persons so apostatizing could not be renewed again by repentance, it not being possible to do any thing toward their conviction that had not been already done; and they, hardening themselves against all that was offered for their conviction, were arrived at such a degree in wickedness, that it was impossible to work upon them; there was nothing left to be tried that had not been already tried, and proved to be ineffectual. Yet it is to be observed, that it was an unjustifiable piece of rigour, to apply these words to all such as had fallen in a time of trial and persecution; for as they had not those miraculous means of conviction, which must be acknowledged to be the strongest, the sensiblest, and the most easily apprehended, of all arguments; so they could not sin so heinously as those had done, who, after what they had seen and felt, revolted from the faith.

Heb. vi. 6.

Great difference is also to be made between a deliberate sin, that a man goes into upon choice, and in which he continues; and a sin, that the fears of death and the infirmities of human nature betray him into, and out of which he quickly recovers himself, and for which he mourns bitterly. There was no reason to apply what is said in the New Testament against the wicked apostates of that time, to those who were overcome in the persecution. The latter sinned grievously; yet it was not in the same kind, nor are they in any sort to be compared to the former. All affectations of excessive severity look like pharisaical hypocrisy; whereas the Spirit of Christ, which is made up of humility and charity, will make us look so severely to ourselves, that on that very account we will be gentle even to the failings of others.

Yet, on the other hand, the church ought to endeavour to conform herself so far to her Head, and to his doctrine, as to 'note those who obey not the gospel, and to have no company with them, that they may be ashamed; yet not so as to hate such a one, or count him as an enemy, but to admonish him as a brother.' Into what neglect or prostitution soever any church may have fallen in this great point of separating offenders, of making them ashamed, and of keeping others from being corrupted with their ill example and bad influence, that must be confessed to be a very great defect and blemish. The church of Rome had slackened all the ancient rules of discipline, and had perverted this matter in a most scandalous manner; and the world is now sunk into so much corruption, and to such a contempt of holy things, that it is much more easy here to find matter for lamentation, than to see how to remedy or correct it.

ARTICLE XVII.

Of Predestination and Election.

Predestination to life is the everlasting purpose of God, whereby (before the foundations of the World were laid) he hath constantly decreed by his Counsel, secret to us, to deliver from curse and damnation, those whom he hath chosen in Christ out of mankind, and to bring them by Christ unto everlasting Salvation as vessels made to honour. Wherefore they which be endued with so excellent a benefit of God, be called according to God's purpose, by his Spirit working in due season. They through grace obey the calling, they be justified freely, they be made Sons of God by Adoption, they be made like the Image of his only begotten Son Jesus Christ: They walk religiously in good works, and at length by God's mercy they attain to everlasting felicity.

As the godly consideration of Predestination and our Election in Christ is full of sweet, pleasant, and unspeakable comfort to godly persons, and such as feel in themselves the working of the Spirit of Christ, mortifying the works of the Flesh, and their earthly members, and drawing up their mind to high and heavenly things, as well because it doth greatly establish and confirm their Faith of eternal Salvation to be enjoyed through Christ, as because it doth fervently kindle their love towards God: So for curious and carnal persons, lacking the Spirit of Christ, to have continually before their Eyes the sentence of God's Predestination, is a most dangerous downfall, whereby the Devil doth thrust them either into desperation, or into wretchlessness of most unclean living, no less perilous than desperation.

Furthermore, We must receive God's promises in such wise, as they be generally set forth to us in holy Scripture: And in our doings, that Will of God is to be followed, which we have expressly declared unto us in the Word of God.

THERE are many things in several of the other Articles which depend upon this; and therefore I will explain it more fully: for as this has given occasion to one of the longest, the subtilest, and indeed the most intricate, of all the questions in divinity; so it will be necessary to open and examine it as fully as the importance and difficulties of it do require. In treating of it, I shall,

First, State the question, together with the consequences, that arise out of it.

ART.
XVII.

Secondly, Give an account of the differences that have arisen upon it.

Thirdly, I shall set out the strength of the opinions of the contending parties, with all possible impartiality and exactness.

Fourthly, I shall shew how far they agree, and how far they differ; and shall shew what reason there is for bearing with one another's opinions in these matters; and in the

Fifth and last place, I shall consider how far we of this church are determined by this Article, and how far we are at liberty to follow any of those different opinions.

The whole controversy may be reduced to this single point as its head and source: Upon what views did God form his purposes and decrees concerning mankind? Whether he did it merely upon a design of advancing his own glory, and for manifesting his own attributes, in order to which he settled the great and universal scheme of his whole creation and providence? Or whether he considered all the free motions of those rational agents that he did intend to create, and according to what he foresaw they would choose and do, in all the various circumstances in which he might put them, formed his decrees? Here the controversy begins: and when this is settled, the three main questions that arise out of it will be soon determined.

The first is, whether both God and Christ intended that Christ should only die for that particular number whom God intended to save? Or whether it was intended that he should die for all, so that every man that would, might have the benefit of his death, and that no man was excluded from it, but because he willingly rejected it?

The second is, Whether those assistances, that God gives to men to enable them to obey him, are of their own nature so efficacious and irresistible, that they never fail of producing the effect for which they are given? Or whether they are only sufficient to enable a man to obey God; so that their efficacy comes from the freedom of the will, that either may co-operate with them, or may not, as it pleases?

The third is, Whether such persons do, and must certainly persevere to whom such grace is given? Or, whether they may not fall away both entirely and finally from that state?

There are also other questions concerning the true notion of liberty, concerning the feebleness of our powers in this lapsed state, with several lesser ones; all which do necessarily take their determination from the decision of the first and main question; about which there are four opinions.

The first is of those commonly called Supralapsarians, who think that God does only consider his own glory in all that he does: and that whatever is done arises, as from its first cause, from the decree of God: that in this decree God, considering only the manifestation of his own glory, intended to make the world, to put a race of men in it, to constitute them under Adam as their fountain and head: that he decreed Adam's sin, the lapse of his posterity, and Christ's death, together with the salvation or damnation of such men as should be most for his own glory: that to those who were to be saved he decreed to give such efficacious assistances, as should certainly put them in the way of salvation; and to those whom he rejected he decreed to give such assistances and means only as should render them inexcusable: that all men do continue in a state of grace, or of sin, and shall be saved or damned, according to that first decree: so that God views himself only, and in that view he designs all things singly for his own glory, and for the manifesting of his own attributes.

The second opinion is of those called the Sublapsarians, who say, that Adam having sinned freely, and his sin being imputed to all his posterity, God did consider mankind, thus lost, with an eye of pity; and, having designed to rescue a great number out of this lost state, he decreed to send his Son to die for them, to accept of his death on their account, and to give them such assistances as should be effectual both to convert them to him, and to make them persevere to the end: but for the rest, he framed no positive act about them, only he left them in that lapsed state, without intending that they should have the benefit of Christ's death, or of efficacious and persevering assistances.

The third opinion is of those who are called Remonstrants, Arminians,* or Universalists, who think that God intended to create all men free, and to deal with them according to the use that they should make of their liberty: that therefore he, foreseeing how every one would use it, did, upon that, decree all things that concerned them in this life, together with their salvation and damnation in the next: that Christ died for all men; that sufficient assistances are given to every man, but that all men may choose whether they will use them, and persevere in them, or not.

The fourth opinion is of the Socinians,† who deny the certain prescience of future contingencies; and therefore they think the decrees of God from all eternity were only general; that such as believe and obey the gospel shall be saved, and that such as live and die in sin shall be damned: but that there were no special decrees made concerning particular persons, these being only made in time, according to the state in which they are: they do also think that man is by nature so free and so entire, that he needs no inward grace; so they deny a special predestination from all eternity, and do also deny inward assistances.

This is a controversy that arises out of natural religion: for if it is believed that God governs the world, and that the wills

* See note, p. 202.
† For an account of the heresy of Socinus, see note, p. 60.

ART. XVII.

of men are free; then it is natural to inquire which of these is subject to the other, or how they can be both maintained? whether God determines the will? or if his Providence follows the motions of the will? Therefore all those that believed a Providence have been aware of this difficulty. The Stoics put all things under a fate; even the gods themselves: if this fate was a necessary series of things, a chain of matter and motion that was fixed and unalterable, then it was plain and downright atheism. The Epicureans set all things at liberty, and either thought that there was no God, or at least that there was no Providence. The philosophers knew not how to avoid this difficulty, by which we see Tully and others were so differently moved, that it is plain they despaired of getting out of it. The Jews had the same question among them; for they could not believe their law, without acknowledging a Providence: and yet the Sadducees among them asserted liberty in so entire a manner, that they set it free from all restraints: on the other hand, the Essens put all things under an absolute fate: and the Pharisees took a middle way; they asserted the freedom of the will, but thought that all things were governed by a Providence. There are also subtle disputes concerning this matter among the Mahometans, one sect asserting liberty, and another fate, which generally prevails among them.

Joseph. Ant. Jud. lib. xviii. c. 1—de Bell. Jud. lib. ii. c. 7.

In the first ages of Christianity, the Gnostics fancied that the souls of men were of different ranks, and that they sprang from different principles, or gods, who made them. Some were carnal, that were devoted to perdition; others were spiritual, and were certainly to be saved; others were animal of a middle order, capable either of happiness or misery. It seems that the Marcionites and Manichees thought that some souls were made by the bad god, as others were made by the good. In opposition to all these, Origen asserted, that all souls were by nature equally capable of being either good or bad; and that the difference among men arose merely from the freedom of the will, and the various use of that freedom: that God left men to this liberty, and rewarded and punished them according to the use of it; yet he asserted a Providence: but as he brought in the Platonical doctrine of pre-existence into the government of the world; and as he explained God's loving Jacob, and his hating of Esau, before they were born, and had done either good or evil, by this of a regard to what they had done formerly; so he asserted the fall of man in Adam, and his being recovered by grace; but he still maintained an unrestrained liberty in the will. His doctrine, though much hated in Egypt, was generally followed over all the east, particularly in Palestine and at Antioch. St. Gregory Nazianzen and St. Basil drew a system of divinity out of his works, in which that which relates to the liberty of the will is very fully set forth: that book was much studied in the east. Chrysostom, Isidore of Damiete, and Theodoret, with all their followers,

Iren. adv. Her. lib. i. c. 1. sect. 11.
Epiph. Her. 31.
Clem. Al. Pæd. lib. i. c. 6.
Orig. Periarchon.
l iii. Philocal c. 21.
Explan. Ep. ad. Rom. l. vi. c. 3.

Orig. Philocal.

taught it so copiously, that it became the received doctrine of the eastern church. Jerome was so much in love with Origen, that he translated some parts of him, and set Ruffin on translating the rest. But as he had a sharp quarrel with the bishops of Palestine, so that perhaps disposed him to change his thoughts of Origen: for ever after that, he set himself much to disgrace his doctrine; and he was very severe on Ruffin for translating him: though Ruffin confesses, that, in translating his works, he took great liberties in altering several passages that he disliked. One of Origen's disciples was Pelagius, a Scottish monk, in great esteem at Rome, both for his learning and the great strictness of his life. He carried these doctrines further than the Greek church had done; so that he was reckoned to have fallen into great errors both by Chrysostom and Isidore (as it is represented by Jansenius, though that is denied by others, who think they meant another of the same name). He denied that we had suffered any harm by the fall of Adam, or that there was any need of inward assistances; and he asserted an entire liberty in the will. St. Austin, though in his disputes with the Manichees he had said many things on the side of liberty, yet he hated Pelagius's doctrine, which he thought asserted a sacrilegious liberty, and he set himself to beat down his tenets, which had been but feebly attacked by Jerome. Cassian, a disciple of St. Chrysostom's, came to Marseilles about this time, having left Constantinople perhaps when his master was banished out of it. He taught a middle doctrine, asserting an inward grace, but subject to the freedom of the will; and that all things were both decreed and done, according to the prescience of God, in which all future contingents were foreseen: he also taught, that the first conversion of the soul to God was merely an effect of its free choice; so that all preventing grace was denied by him; which came to be the peculiar distinction of those who were afterwards called the Semipelagians. Prosper and Hilary gave an account of this system to St. Austin, upon which he writ against it, and his opinions were defended by Prosper, Fulgentius, Orosius, and others, as Cassian's were defended by Faustus, Vincentius, and Gennadius. In conclusion, St. Austin's opinions did generally prevail in the west; only Pelagius, it seems, retiring to his own country, he had many followers among the Britains: but German and Lupus, being sent over once and again from France, are said to have conquered them so entirely, that they were all freed from those errors: whatever they did by their arguments, the writers of their legends took care to adorn their mission with many very wonderful miracles, of which the gathering all the pieces of a calf, some of which had been dressed, and the putting them together in its skin, and restoring it again to life, is none of the least. The ruin of the Roman empire, and the disorders that the western provinces fell under by their new and barbarous masters, occa-

ART. XVII.

Ruffin. Peror. in Vers.Com. Orig. in Ep. ad. Rom. Chrys. Ep. 4. ad Olymp. Isid.Pelus. lib. Ep. 514.

sioned in those ages a great decay of learning: so that few writers of fame coming after that time, St. Austin's great labours and piety, and the many vast volumes that he had left behind him, gave him so great a name, that few durst contest what had been so zealously and so copiously defended by him: and though it is highly probable, that Celestine was not satisfied with his doctrine; yet both he and the other bishops of Rome, together with many provincial synods, have so often declared his doctrine in those points to be the doctrine of the church, that this is very hardly got over by those of that communion.

The chief, and indeed the only material, difference that is between St. Austin's doctrine and that of the Sublapsarians is, that he, holding that with the sacrament of baptism there was joined an inward regeneration, made a difference between the *regenerate* and the *predestinate*, which these do not: he thought persons thus regenerate might have all grace, besides that of *perseverance*; but he thought that they, not being predestinated, were certainly to fall from that state, and from the grace of regeneration. The other differences are but forced strains to represent him and the Calvinists as of different principles: he thought, that overcoming delectation, in which he put the efficacy of grace, was as irresistible, though he used not so strong a word for it as the Calvinists do; and he thought that the decree was as absolute, and made without any regard to what the free-will would choose, as any of these do. So in the main points, the absoluteness of the decree, the extent of Christ's death, the efficacy of grace, and the certainty of perseverance, their opinions are the same, though their ways of expressing themselves do often differ. But if St. Austin's name and the credit of his books went far, yet no book was more read in the following ages than Cassian's Collations. There was in them a clear thread of good sense, and a very high strain of piety that run through them; and they were thought the best institutions for a monk to form his mind, by reading them attentively: so they still carried down, among those who read them, deep impressions of the doctrine of the Greek church.

This broke out in the ninth century, in which Godescalcus, a monk, was severely used by Hincmar, and by the church of Rhemes, for asserting some of St. Austin's doctrines; against which Scotus Erigena wrote; as Bertram, or Ratramne, wrote for them. Remigius, bishop of Lyons, with his church, did zealously assert St. Austin's doctrine, not without great sharpness against Scotus. After this, the matter slept, till the school-divinity came to be in great credit: and Thomas Aquinas being accounted the chief glory of the Dominican order, he not only asserted all St. Austin's doctrine, but added this to it; that whereas formerly it was in general held, that the providence of God did extend itself to all things whatsoever, he thought this was done by God's concurring immediately to the production of every thought, action, motion, or mode; so that God was the first and immediate cause of every thing that was done: and in order to the explaining the joint production of every thing by God as the first, and by the creature as the second cause, he thought, at least as his followers have understood him, that by a physical influence the will was predetermined by God to all things, whether good or bad; so that the will could not be said to be free in that particular instance *in sensu composito*, though it was in general still free in all its actions *in sensu diviso:* a distinction so sacred, and so much used among them, that I choose to give it in their own terms, rather than translate them. To avoid the consequence of making God the author of sin, a distinction was made between the positive act of sin, which was said not to be evil, and the want of its conformity to the law of God, which being a negation was no positive being, so that it was not produced. And thus, though the action was produced jointly by God as the first cause, and by the creature as the second, yet God was not guilty of the sin, but only the creature. This doctrine passed down among the Dominicans, and continues to do so to this day. Scotus, who was a Franciscan, denied this predetermination, and asserted the freedom of the will. Durandus denied this immediate concourse; in which he has not had many followers, except Adola, and some few more.

When Luther began to form his opinions into a body, he clearly saw, that nothing did so plainly destroy the doctrine of merit and justification by works, as St. Austin's opinions: 'he found also in his works very express authorities against most of the corruptions of the Roman church: and being of an order that carried his name, and by consequence was accustomed to read and reverence his works, it was no wonder if he, without a strict examining of the matter, espoused all his opinions. Most of those of the church of Rome who wrote against him, being of the other persuasions, any one reading the books of that age would have thought that St. Austin's doctrine was abandoned by the church of Rome: so that when Michael Baius, and some others at Louvain, began to revive it, that became a matter of scandal, and they were condemned at Rome: yet at the council of Trent the Dominicans had so much credit, that great care was taken, in the penning their decrees, to avoid all reflections upon that doctrine. It was at first received by the whole Jesuit order, so that Bellarmine formed himself upon it, and still adhered to it: but soon after, that order changed their mind, and left their whole body to a full liberty in those points, and went all quickly over to the other hypothesis, that differed from the Semipelagians only in this, that they allowed a preventing-grace, but such as was subject to the freedom of the will.

200 AN EXPOSITION OF

ART. XVII. Molina and Fonseca invented a new way of explaining God's foreseeing future contingents, which they called a *middle*, or *mean science;* by which they taught, that as God sees all things as possible in his knowledge of *simple apprehension*, and all things that are certainly future, as present in his knowledge of *vision;* so by this knowledge he also sees the chain of all conditionate futurities, and all the connections of them, that is, whatsoever would follow upon such or such conditions. Great jealousies arising upon the progress that the order of the Jesuits was making, these opinions were laid hold on to mortify them; so they were complained of at Rome for departing from St. Austin's doctrine, which in these points was generally received as the doctrine of the Latin church: and many conferences were held before pope Clement the Eighth, and the cardinals; where the point in debate was chiefly, What was the doctrine and tradition of the church? The advantages that St. Austin's followers had were such, that before fair judges they must have triumphed over the other: pope Clement had so resolved; but he dying, though pope Paul the Fifth had the same intentions, yet he happening then to be engaged in a quarrel with the Venetians about the ecclesiastical immunities, and having put that republic under an *interdict*, the Jesuits who were there chose to be banished, rather than to break the *interdict:* and their adhering so firmly to the papal authority, when most of the other orders forsook it, was thought so meritorious at Rome, that it saved them the censure: so, instead of a decision, all sides were commanded to be silent, and to quarrel no more upon those heads.

About forty years after that, Jansenius,* a doctor of Lou-

* Cornelius Jansenius, bishop of Ypres, a man of much learning and piety, flourished in the early part of the seventeenth century. He was the author of a celebrated work, entitled 'Augustinus,' the publication of which, after his death, revived the controversy respecting the nature and extent of grace, and disturbed the temporary calm into which the fierce contests between the Jesuits and Dominicans had, owing to the skilful management of Paul V., subsided. 'This celebrated work,' writes Mosheim, 'which gave such a wound to the Romish church, as neither the power nor wisdom of the pontiffs will ever be able to heal, is divided into three parts. The first is historical, and contains a relation of the Pelagian controversy, which arose in the fifth century. In the second, we find an accurate account and illustration of the doctrine of Augustin, relating to the constitution and powers of the human nature, in its original, fallen, and renewed state. The third contains the doctrine of the same great man, relating to the aids of sanctifying grace, procured by Christ, and to the eternal predestination of men and angels.'

The publication of this work was so detrimental to the cause of the Jesuits, by placing them in direct opposition to Augustin, that they left no means untried to procure the condemnation of it by the papal see. In this they succeeded by, in the first place, having the perusal of it prohibited by the Roman inquisitors, and in the next place by inducing Urban VIII. to issue a bull against it as a work infected with errors. This condemnation was, however, very far from reaching the end proposed—the overthrow of the system of Divine truth propounded in Jansenius's work; and many distinguished men (amongst them the doctors of Louvain) set at nought the papal bull by openly espousing the cause of Jansenius. Each party continued to defend their peculiar tenets with much zeal and no small degree of sophistry, by means of which the followers of Jansenius contrived to evade the fury

vain, being a zealous disciple of St. Austin's, and seeing the ART.
progress that the contrary doctrines were making, did, with XVII.
great industry, and an equal fidelity, publish a voluminous
system of St. Austin's doctrine in all the several branches of
the controversy: and he set forth the Pelagians and the
Semipelagians in that work under very black characters; and,
not content with that, he compared the doctrines of the modern innovators with theirs. This book was received by the
whole party with great applause, as a work that had decided
the controversy. But the author having writ with an extraordinary force against the French pretensions on Flanders,
which recommended him so much to the Spanish court, that
he was made a bishop upon it: all those in France who followed St. Austin's doctrine, and applauded this book, were
represented by their enemies as being in the same interests
with him, and by consequence as enemies to the French greatness; so that the court of France prosecuted the whole party.
This book was at first only prohibited at Rome, as a violation
of that silence that the pope had enjoined; afterwards articles
were picked out of it, and condemned, and all the clergy of
France were required to sign the condemnation of them.

---

of the Jesuits, who were the more powerful party, and who scrupled not to have recourse to their familiar weapons, 'even the secular arm, and a competent number of dragoons.' The Jansenists endeavoured to establish the truth of their system by an appeal to miracles; and must have triumphed over their opponents, were it not that at that time the papacy was deeply interested in keeping itself apart from the truth laid down by Augustin, and which had been wielded with such force against it by Luther, and his followers. Accordingly, on the 31st of May, 1653, Innocent X., turning a deaf ear to the numerous entreaties of a large body of the clergy to suspend his decision, condemned by a bull these five propositions, extracted by his opponents from the book of Jansenius:—'1st. That there are divine precepts which good men, notwithstanding their desire to observe them, are, nevertheless, absolutely unable to obey; nor has God given them that measure of grace that is essentially necessary to render them capable of such obedience.—2d. That no person, in his corrupt state of nature, can resist the influence of divine grace, when it operates upon the mind.—3d. That in order to render human actions meritorious, it is not requisite that they be exempt from necessity, but only that they be free from constraint.—4th. That the Semipelagians err grievously in maintaining that the human will is endowed with the power of either receiving or resisting the aids and influences of preventing grace.—5th. That whosoever affirms that Jesus Christ made expiations, by his sufferings and death, for the sins of all mankind, is a Semipelagian.' The four first of these propositions were declared heretical, the fifth rash, impious, and injurious to the Supreme Being. An ingenious device was then set up, by means of which the Jansenists contrived, notwithstanding the pope's bull, to maintain their opinions, and yet remain within the pale of the papal church. This was by subscribing to the correctness of the pope's decision respecting these propositions; which was the *questio de jure*. The other, by denying that these propositions were in the book of Jansenius, on the ground that the pope had not declared himself in this point; this was the *questio de facto*. Alexander VII. put an end to this distinction by, in the year 1656, issuing a bull, in which it was positively declared, that the five propositions were the tenets of Jansenius, and were to be found in his book.

After this the Jesuits set upon their opponents with such fury and persecution, that those who refused to comply with the papal decree were cast into prison, or banished; others escaped by flight, and many took refuge under the wing of the Dutch government, and were thus enabled to smile at the storm, and defy the persecuting fury of the papal see.—[ED.]

These articles were certainly in his book, and were manifest consequences of St. Austin's doctrine, which was chiefly driven at; though it was still declared at Rome, that nothing was intended to be done in prejudice of St. Austin's doctrine. Upon this pretence his party have said, that those articles being capable of two senses, the one of which was strained, and was heretical, the other of which was clear, and according to St. Austin's doctrine, it must be presumed it was not in that second, but in the other sense, that they were condemned at Rome, and so they signed the condemnation of them: but then they said, that they were not in Jansenius's book in the sense in which they condemned them.

Upon that followed a most extravagant question concerning the pope's infallibility in matters of fact: it being said on the one side, that the pope having condemned them as Jansenius's opinions, the belief of his infallibility obliged them to conclude that they must be in his book: whereas the others with great truth affirmed, that it had never been thought that in matters of fact either popes or councils were infallible. At last a new cessation of hostilities upon these points was resolved on; yet the hatred continues and the war goes on, though more covertly and more indirectly than before.

Nor are the reformed more of a piece than the church of Rome upon these points. Luther went on long, as he at first set out, with so little disguise, that whereas all parties had always pretended that they asserted the *freedom* of the will, he plainly spoke out, and said the will was not *free*, but *enslaved*: yet before he died, he is reported to have changed his mind; for though he never owned that, yet Melancthon, who had been of the same opinion, did freely retract it; for which he was never blamed by Luther. Since that time all the Lutherans have gone into the Semipelagian opinions so entirely and so eagerly, that they will neither tolerate nor hold communion with any of the other persuasion. Calvin not only taught St. Austin's doctrine, but seemed to go on to the Supralapsarian way; which was more openly taught by Beza, and was generally followed by the reformed; only the difference between the Supralapsarians and the Sublapsarians was never brought to a decision; divines being in all the Calvinists' churches left to their freedom as to that point.

In England the first reformers were generally in the Sublapsarian hypothesis: but Perkins and others having asserted the Supralapsarian way, Arminius,* a professor in Leyden,

---

* James Arminius, professor of divinity in the university of Leyden, was 'a man who joined to unquestionable piety and meekness of spirit, a clear and acute judgment; and who had obtained no slight eminence by the talent with which he had extricated the doctrines of Christianity from the dry and technical mode in which they had hitherto been stated and discussed. His celebrity placed him in a situation ill suited to his habits and temper. As a pupil of Beza, he had embraced the extreme views to which that divine had carried the tenets advocated by the powerful pen of Calvin. It happened that one Coornhert had advanced some opinions,

THE XXXIX ARTICLES. 203

writ against him: upon this Gomarus and he had many disputes; and these opinions bred a great distraction over all the United Provinces. At the same time another political matter occasioning a division of opinion, whether the war should be carried on with Spain, or if propositions for a peace or truce should be entertained? it happened that Arminius's followers were all for a peace, and the others were generally for carrying on the war; which being promoted by the prince of Orange, he joined to them: and the Arminians were represented as men, whose opinions and affections leaned to popery: so that this, from being a doctrinal point, became the distinction of a party, and by that means the differences were inflamed. A

ART. XVII.

---

which, if not loose in themselves, were, at least, expressed in a very unguarded way. The ministers of Delft published a reply: in which the moderate and generally received Sublapsarian hypothesis was sustained; which gave little less offence to the high Calvinists than did the heterodox language of Coornhert. Arminius, therefore, as the most talented divine of the day, was applied to, in order to take up the pen, on both sides. On the one hand, his friend Martin Lydius, solicited him to vindicate the Supralapsarian views of his former tutor, Beza, against the reply of the ministers; and, on the other, he was invited by the synod of Amsterdam, to defend this same reply against Coornhert. Placed in this remarkable situation, Arminius felt compelled to enter into an examination of the whole question, and was induced to change his sentiments, and to adopt that view of the Divine dispensations which now bears his name.'—*Allport.*

The sentiments of the Arminians, or Remonstrants, concerning the questions of predestination and grace, were comprehended in five articles, generally denominated the five points, and which have been the subject of much discussion in our own church. They are—1st. 'That God, from all eternity, determined to bestow salvation on those whom he foresaw would persevere unto the end in their faith in Christ Jesus; and to inflict everlasting punishment on those who should continue in their unbelief, and resist unto the end his Divine succours.

' 2d. That Jesus Christ, by his death and sufferings, made an atonement for the sins of all mankind in general, and of every individual in particular;—that, however, none but those who believe in him can be partakers of this divine benefit.

' 3d. That true faith cannot proceed from the exercise of our natural faculties and powers, nor from the force and operation of free-will; since man, in consequence of his natural corruption, is incapable either of thinking or of doing any good thing; and that therefore it is necessary, to his conversion and salvation, that he be regenerated and renewed by the operation of the Holy Ghost, which is the gift of God through Jesus Christ.

' 4th. That this Divine grace, or energy of the Holy Ghost, which heals the disorder of a corrupt nature, begins, advances, and brings to perfection, every thing that can be called good in man; and that, consequently, all good works, without exception, are to be attributed to God alone, and to the operation of his grace: that, nevertheless, this grace does not force the man to act against his inclination, but may be resisted and rendered ineffectual by the perverse will of the impenitent sinner.

' 5th. That they who are united to Christ by faith are thereby furnished with abundant strength, and with succours sufficient to enable them to triumph over the seductions of Satan, and the allurements of sin and temptation; but that the question, ' Whether such may fall from their faith, and perfect finally this state of grace?' has not been yet resolved with sufficient perspicuity; and must, therefore, be yet more carefully examined by an attentive study of what the Holy Scriptures have declared in relation to this important point. " It is to be observed, that this last article was afterwards changed by the Arminians, who, in process of time, declared their sentiments with less caution, and positively affirmed that the saints might fall from a state of grace."'—*Mosheim.*

The opinions of Arminius were condemned at the famous synod of Dort. Of the life of Arminius, and the proceedings of the synod of Dort, the reader will find a concise and interesting account in Allport's translation of Davenant on the Colossians.—[ED.]

ART. XVII. great synod met at Dort; to which the divines were sent from hence, as well as from other churches. The Arminian tenets were condemned; but the difference between the Supralapsarians and Sublapsarians was not meddled with. The divines of this church, though very moderate in the way of proposing their opinions, yet upon the main adhered to St. Austin's doctrine. So the breach was formed in Holland: but when the point of state was no more mixed with it, these questions were handled with less heat.

Those disputes quickly crossed the seas, and divided us: the abbots adhered to St. Austin's doctrine; while bishop Overal, but chiefly archbishop Laud, espoused the Arminian tenets. All divines were by proclamation required not to preach upon those heads: but those that favoured the new opinions were encouraged, and the others were depressed. And unhappy disputes falling in at that time concerning the extent of the royal prerogative beyond law, the Arminians having declared themselves highly for that, they were as much favoured at court, as they were censured in the parliament: which brought that doctrine under a very hard character over all the nation.

Twisse carried it high to the Supralapsarian hypothesis, which grew to be generally followed by those of that side: but that sounded harshly; and Hobbes grafting afterwards a fate and absolute necessity upon it, the other opinions were again revived; and no political interests falling in with them, as all prejudices against them went off, so they were more calmly debated, and became more generally acceptable than they were before. Men are now left to their liberty in them, and all anger upon those heads is now so happily extinguished, that diversity of opinions about them begets no alienation nor animosity.

So far have I prosecuted a short view of the history of this controversy. I come now to open the chief grounds of the different parties: and first, for the Supralapsarians.

They lay this down for a foundation, that God is essentially perfect and independent in all his acts: so that he can consider nothing but himself and his own glory: that therefore he designed every thing in and for himself: that to make him stay his decrees till he sees what free creatures will do, is to make him decree dependently upon them; which seems to fall short of infinite perfection: that he himself can be the only end of his counsels; and that therefore he could only consider the manifestation of his own attributes and perfection; that infinite wisdom must begin its designs at that which is to come last in the execution of them; and since the conclusion of all things at the last day will be the manifestation of the wisdom, goodness, and justice of God, we ought to suppose, that God, in the order of things designed that first, though in the order of time there is no first nor second in God, this being supposed to be from all eternity. After this great design was laid, all the means in order to the end were next to be designed. Creatures in the sight of God are as nothing, and, by a strong figure, are said to be less than nothing, and vanity. Now if we in our designs do not consider ants or insects, not to say straws, or grains of sand and dust, then what lofty thoughts soever our pride may suggest to us, we must be confessed to be very poor and inconsiderable creatures before God; therefore he himself and his own glory can only be his own end in all that he designs or does.

This is the chief basis of their doctrine, and so ought to be well considered. They add to this, that there can be no certain prescience of future contingents. They say it involves a contradiction, that things which are not certainly to be, should be certainly foreseen; for if they are certainly foreseen, they must certainly be: so while they are supposed to be contingent, they are yet affirmed to be certain, by saying that they are certainly foreseen. When God decrees that any thing shall be, it has from that a certain futurition, and as such it is certainly foreseen by him: an uncertain foresight is an act of its nature imperfect, because it may be a mistake, and so is inconsistent with the divine perfection. And it seems to imply a contradiction to say that a thing happens freely, that is, may be, or may not be, and yet that it is certainly foreseen by God. God cannot foresee things, but as he decrees them, and so gives them a futurition, and, therefore, this prescience antecedent to his decree must be rejected as a thing impossible.

They say further, that conditionate decrees are imperfect in their nature, and that they subject the will and acts of God to a creature: that a conditionate decree is an act in suspense, whether it shall be or not; which is inconsistent with infinite perfection. A general will, or rather a willing that all men should be saved, has also plain characters of imperfection in it: as if God wished somewhat that he could not accomplish, so that his goodness should seem to be more extended than his power. Infinite perfection can wish nothing but what it can execute; and if it is fit to wish it, it is fit also to execute it. Therefore all that style, that ascribes passions or affections to God, must be understood in a figure; so that when his providence exerts itself in such acts as among us men would be the effects of those passions, then the passions themselves are in the phrase of the scripture ascribed to God. They say we ought not to measure the punishments of sin by our notions of justice: God afflicts many good men very severely, and for many years in this life, and this only for the manifestation of his own glory, for making their faith and patience to shine; and yet none think that this is unjust. It is a method in which God will be glorified in them: some sins are punished with other sins, and likewise with a course of severe miseries: if we transfer this from time to eternity, the whole will be then more conceivable; for if God may do for a little time that which is inconsistent with our notions, and with our rules of justice, he may do it for a longer duration; since it is as impossible that he can be unjust for a day, as for all eternity.

As God does every thing for himself and his own glory, so the scriptures teach us every where to offer up all praise and glory to God; to acknowledge that all is of him, and to humble ourselves as being nothing before him. Now if we were elected not by a free act of his, but by what he foresaw that we would be, so that his grace is not efficacious by its own force, but by the good use that we make of it, then the glory and praise of all the good we do, and of God's purposes to us, were due to ourselves: he designs, according to the other doctrine, equally well to all men; and all the difference among them will arise neither from God's intentions to them, nor from his assistances, but from the good use that he foresaw they would make of these favours that he was to give in common to all mankind: man should have whereof to glory, and he might say, that he himself made himself to differ from others. The whole strain of the scriptures in ascribing all good things to God, and in charging us to offer up the honour of all to him, seems very expressly to favour this doctrine; since if all our good is from God, and is particularly owing to his grace, then good men have somewhat from God that bad men have not; for which they ought to praise him. The style of all the prayers that are used or directed to be used in the scripture, is for a grace that opens our eyes, that turns our hearts, that makes us to go, that leads us not into temptation, but delivers us from evil. All these phrases do plainly import that we desire more than a power or capacity to act, such as is given to all men, and such as, after we have received it, may be still ineffectual to us. For to pray for such assistances as are always given to all men, and are such that the whole good of them shall wholly depend upon ourselves, would sound very oddly; whereas we pray for somewhat that is special, and that we hope shall be effectual. We do not and cannot pray earnestly for that, which we know all men as well as we ourselves have at all times.

Humility and earnestness in prayer seem to be among the chief means of working in us the image of Christ, and of deriving to us all the blessings of heaven. That doctrine which blasts both, which swells us up with an opinion that all comes from ourselves, and that we receive nothing from God but what is given in common with us to all the world, is certainly contrary both to the spirit and to the design of the gospel.

To this they add observations from Providence. The world was for many ages delivered up to idolatry; and since the Christian religion has appeared, we see vast tracts of coun-

tries which have continued ever since in idolatry: others are
fallen under Mahometanism; and the state of Christendom
is in the eastern parts of it under so much ignorance, and the
greatest part of the west is under so much corruption, that
we must confess the far greatest part of mankind has been in
all ages left destitute of the means of grace, so that the pro-
mulgating the gospel to some nations, and the denying it to
others, must be ascribed to the unsearchable ways of God,
that are past finding out. If he thus leaves whole nations
in such darkness and corruption, and freely chooses others
to communicate the knowledge of himself to them, then we
need not wonder if he should hold the same method with individuals, that he does with whole bodies: for the rejecting of
whole nations by the lump for so many ages, is much more
unaccountable than the selecting of a few, and the leaving
others in that state of ignorance and brutality. And whatever may be said of his extending mercy to some few of those
who have made a good use of that dim light which they had;
yet it cannot be denied but their condition is much more deplorable, and the condition of the others is much more hopeful; so that great numbers of men are born in such circumstances, that it is morally impossible that they should not
perish in them; whereas others are more happily situated and
enlightened.

This argument taken from common observation becomes
much stronger, when we consider what the apostle says, particularly in the Epistles to the Romans and the Ephesians, Rom. ix.
even according to the exposition of those of the other side: Eph. i. 3—
for if God *loved* Jacob, so as to choose his posterity to be his 6, 9—11.
people, and rejected or *hated* Esau and his posterity, and if ii. 1—9.
that was according to the *purpose* and design of his election;
if by the same purpose the Gentiles were to be grafted upon
that stock, from which the Jews were then to be cut off; and
if the counsel or purpose of God had appeared in particular to
those of Ephesus, though the most corrupted both in magic,
idolatry, and immorality, of any in the east; then it is plain,
that the applying the means of grace, arises merely from a
great design that was long hid in God, which did then break
out. It is reasonable to believe, that there is a proportion
between the application of the means, and the decree itself
concerning the end. The one is resolved into the unsearchable riches of God's grace, and declared to be free and absolute. God's choosing the nation of the Jews in such a distinction beyond all other nations, is by Moses and the pro- Deut. vii.
phets frequently said not to be on their own account, or on 7, 8.
the account of any thing that God saw in them, but merely x. 15, 16.
from the goodness of God to them. From all this it seems,
say they, as reasonable to believe that the other is likewise
free, according to those words of our Saviour's, 'I thank thee, Matt. xi.
O Father, Lord of heaven and earth, because thou hast hid 25, 26.

these things from the wise and prudent, and hast revealed them unto babes:' the reason of which is given in the following words, 'Even so, Father, for it seemed good in thy sight.' What goes before, of Tyre and Sidon, and the land of Sodom, that would have made a better use of his preaching, than the towns of Galilee had done, among whom he lived, confirms this, that the means of grace are not bestowed on those of whom it was foreseen that they would have made a good use of them; or denied to those who, as was foreseen, would have made an ill use of them; the contrary of this being plainly asserted in those words of our Saviour's. It is further observable, that he seems not to be speaking here of different nations, but of the different sorts of men of the same nation: the more learned of the Jews, the wise and prudent, rejected him, while the simpler, but better sort, *the babes*, received him: so that the difference between individual persons seems here to be resolved into the *good pleasure of God*.

It is further urged, that since those of the other side confess, that God by his prescience foresaw what circumstances might be happy, and what assistances might prove efficacious, to bad men; then his not putting them in those circumstances, but giving them such assistances only, which, how effectual soever they might be to others, he saw would have no efficacy on them, and his putting them in circumstances, and giving them assistances, which he foresaw they would abuse, if it may seem to clear the justice of God, yet it cannot clear his infinite holiness and goodness; which must ever carry him, according to our notions of these perfections, to do all that may be done, and that in the most effectual way, to rescue others from misery, to make them truly good, and to put them in a way to be happy. Since therefore this is not always done, according to the other opinion, it is plain that there is an unsearchable depth in the ways of God, which we are not able to fathom. Therefore it must be concluded, that since all are not actually good, and so put in a way to be saved, that God did not intend that it should be so; for 'who hath resisted his will? The counsel of the Lord standeth fast, and the thoughts of his heart to all generations.' It is true, his laws are his will in one respect: he requires all to obey them: he approves them, and he obliges all men to keep them. All the expressions of his desires that all men should be saved, are to be explained of the will of revelation, commonly called *the sign of his will*. When it is said, *What more could have been done?* that is to be understood of outward means and blessings: but still God has a secret will of his *good pleasure*, in which he designs all things; and this can never be frustrated.

From this they do also conclude, that though Christ's death was to be offered to all Christians, yet that intentionally and actually he only died for those whom the Father had chosen and given to him to be saved by him. They cannot think that Christ could have *died in vain,* which St. Paul speaks of as a vast absurdity. Now since, if he had died for all, he should have *died in vain,* with relation to the far greater part of mankind, who are not to be saved by him; they from thence conclude, that all those for whom he died are certainly saved by him. Perhaps with relation to some subaltern blessings, which are through him communicated, if not to all mankind, yet to all Christians, he may be said to have died for all: but as to eternal salvation, they believe his design went no further than the secret purpose and election of God, and this they think is implied in these words, 'all that are given me of my Father: thine they were, and thou gavest them me.' He also limits his intercession to those only; 'I pray not for the world, but for those that thou hast given me; for they are thine: and all thine are mine, and mine are thine.' They believe that he also limited to them the extent of his death, and of that sacrifice which he offered in it.

ART. XVII.
Gal. ii. 21.

John xvii. 6, 9, 10.

It is true, the Christian religion being to be distinguished from the Jewish in this main point, that whereas the Jewish was restrained to Abraham's posterity, and confined within one race and nation, the Christian was to be preached to *every creature;* universal words are used concerning the death of Christ: but as the words, 'preaching to every creature,' and to 'all the world,' are not to be understood in the utmost extent, for then they have never been verified; since the gospel has never yet, for aught that appears to us, been preached to every nation under heaven; but are only to be explained generally of a commission not limited to one or more nations; none being excluded from it: the apostles were to execute it in going from city to city, as they should be inwardly moved to it by the Holy Ghost: so they think that those large words, that are applied to the death of Christ, are to be understood in the same qualified manner; that no nation or sort of men are excluded from it, and that some of all kinds and sorts shall be saved by him. And this is to be carried no further, without an imputation on the justice of God: for if he has received a sufficient oblation and satisfaction for the sins of the whole world, it is not reconcileable to justice, that all should not be saved by it, or should not at least have the offer and promulgation of it made them; that so a trial may be made whether they will accept of it or not.

Mark xvi. 15.

The *grace of God* is set forth in scripture by such figures and expressions as do plainly intimate its efficacy; and that it does not depend upon us to use it, or not to use it, at pleasure. It is said to be a creation; 'we are created unto good works, and we become new creatures:' it is called a regeneration, or a *new birth;* it is called a quickening and a resurrection; as our former state is compared to a feebleness, a blindness, and a death. God is said 'to work in us both to will

Eph. ii. 10.
2 Cor. v. 17.
Phil. ii. 13.
Ps. cx. 3
Jer. xxxi. 33, 34.

P

ART. XVII.

Ezek. xxxvi. 26, 27.
Rom. ix. 21.

and to do: His people shall be willing in the day of his power: He will write his laws in their hearts, and make them to walk in them.' Mankind is compared to a mass of clay in the hand of the *potter*, who of the same lump makes at his pleasure 'vessels of honour or of dishonour.' These passages, this last in particular, do insinuate an absolute and a conquering power in grace; and that the love of God constrains us, as St. Paul speaks expressly.

All outward coaction is contrary to the nature of liberty, and all those inward impressions that drove on the prophets, so that they had not the free use of their faculties, but felt themselves carried they knew not how, are inconsistent with it; yet when a man feels that his faculties go in their method, and that he assents or chooses from a thread of inward conviction and ratiocination, he still acts freely, that is, by an internal principle of reason and thought. A man acts as much according to his faculties, when he assents to a truth, as when he chooses what he is to do: and if his mind were so enlightened, that he saw as clearly the good of moral things, as he perceives speculative truths, so that he felt himself as little able to resist the one as the other, he would be no less a free and a rational creature, than if he were left to a more unlimited range: nay the more evidently that he saw the true good of things, and the more that he were determined by it, he should then act more suitably to his faculties, and to the excellence of his nature. For though the saints in heaven being made perfect in glory are no more capable of further rewards, yet it cannot be denied but they act with a more accomplished liberty, because they see all things in a true light, according

Ps. xxxvi.

to that, 'in thy light we shall see light:' and therefore they conclude that such an overcoming degree of grace, by which a man is made willing through the illumination of his understanding, and not by any blind or violent impulse, is no way contrary to the true notion of liberty.

After all, they think, that if a debate falls to be between the sovereignty of God, his acts and his purposes, and the freedom of man's will, it is modest and decent rather to make the abatement on man's part, than on God's; but they think there is no need of this. They infer, that besides the outward enlightening of a man by knowledge, there is an inward enlightening of the mind, and a secret forcible conviction stamped on it; otherwise what can be meant by the prayer of St. Paul for the Ephesians, who had already heard the gospel

Eph. i. 17, 18, 19.

preached, and were instructed in it; 'that the eyes of their understanding being enlightened, they might know what was the hope of his calling, and what the riches of the glory of his inheritance in the saints, and what was the exceeding greatness of his power towards them that believed.' This seems to be somewhat that is both internal and efficacious. Christ compares the union and influence that he communicates to believers, to that union of a head with the members, and of a root with the branches, which imports an internal, a vital, and an efficacious influence. And though the outward means that are offered may be, and always are, rejected, when not accompanied with this overcoming grace, yet this never returns empty; these outward means coming from God, the resisting of them is said to be the 'resisting God, the grieving or quenching his Spirit;' and so in that sense we resist the grace or favour of God; but we can never withstand him when he intends to overcome us.

ART. XVII.

Acts vii. 51.
Eph. iv. 30.

As for perseverance, it is a necessary consequence of absolute decrees, and of efficacious grace; for since all depends upon God, and that as 'of his own will he begat us,' so with him 'there is neither variableness nor shadow of turning: whom he loves he loves to the end;' and he has promised, that 'he will never leave nor forsake those to whom he becomes a God:' we must from thence conclude, that 'the purpose and calling of God is without repentance.' And therefore though good men may fall into grievous sins, to keep them from which there are dreadful things said in scripture, against their falling away, or apostasy; yet God does so uphold them, that, though he suffers them often to feel the weight of their natures, yet of all that are given by the Father to the Son to be saved by him, none are lost.

Jam. i. 17, 18.
Joh. xiii. 1.
Heb. xiii. 5.
Rom. xi. 29.

John xvii. 11, 12.
xviii. 8, 9.

Upon the whole matter, they believe that God did in himself and for his own glory *foreknow* such a determinate number, whom he pitched upon, to be the persons in whom he would be both sanctified and glorified: that, having thus foreknown them, he *predestinated* them to be holy, conformable to the image of his Son: that these were to be *called* not by a general calling in the sense of these words, 'many are called, but few are chosen;' but to be 'called according to his purpose:' and those he *justified* upon their obeying that calling; and he will in conclusion *glorify* them. Nor are these words only to be limited to the sufferings of good men; they are to be extended to all the effects of the love of God, according to that which follows, that 'nothing can separate us from the love of God in Christ.' The whole reasoning in the 9th of the Romans does so plainly resolve all the acts of God's mercy and justice, his *hardening* as well as his pardoning, into an absolute freedom, and an unsearchable depth, that more express words to that effect can hardly be imagined.

Matt. xx. 16.
Rom. viii. 29, 30.

Rom. ix. 18.

It is in general said, that 'the children being yet unborn, neither having done good or evil; that the purpose of God according to election might stand, not of works, but of him that calleth; Jacob was loved and Esau hated;' that God 'raised up Pharaoh, that he might shew his power in him;' and when an objection is suggested against all this, instead of answering it, it is silenced with this, 'Who art thou, O man, that repliest against God?' And all is illustrated with the

Ver. 11—13.

Ver. 17.

Ver. 20.

ART. figure of the potter; and concluded with this solemn question,
XVII. 'What if God, willing to shew his wrath, and to make his
Ver. 22. power known, endured with much long-suffering the vessels
of wrath fitted to destruction?' This carries the reader to
consider what is so often repeated in the book of Exodus, con-
Exod. iv. cerning God's 'hardening the heart of Pharaoh, so that he
21. x. 20. would not let his people go.' It is said, that God 'has made
xi. 10. the wicked man for the day of evil:' as it is written on the
xiv. 8. other hand, that 'as many believed the gospel, as were ap-
Prov. xvi. pointed to eternal life.' Some are said to be 'written in the
4. book of life, of the Lamb slain before the foundation of the
Acts xiii. world, or according to God's purpose before the world began.'
48. Ungodly men are said to be 'of old ordained to condemnation,
Rev. xiii. and to be given up by God unto vile affections, and to be
8. iii. 5. given over by him to a reprobate mind.' Therefore they think
xx. 12. that reprobation is an absolute and free act of God, as well as
xxi. 27. election, to manifest his holiness and justice in them who are
2 Tim. i. 9. under it, as well as his love and mercy is manifested in the
Jude 4. elect. Nor can they think with the Sublapsarians, that re-
Rom. i. 26, probation is only God's passing by those whom he does not
21. elect; this is an act unworthy of God, as if he forgot them,
which does clearly imply imperfection. And as for that which
is said concerning their being fallen in Adam, they argue, that
either Adam's sin, and the connection of all mankind to him
as their head and representative, was absolutely decreed, or it
was not: if it was, then all is absolute; Adam's sin and the
fall of mankind were decreed, and by consequence all from the
beginning to the end are under a continued chain of absolute
decrees; and then the Supralapsarian and the Sublapsarian
hypothesis will be one and the same, only variously expressed.
But if Adam's sin was only foreseen and permitted, then a
conditionate decree founded upon prescience is once admitted,
so that all that follows turns upon it; and then all the arguments either against the perfection of such acts, or the certainty of such a prescience, turn against this; for if they are
admitted in any one instance, then they may be admitted in
others as well as in that.

The Sublapsarians do always avoid to answer this; and it
seems they do rather incline to think that Adam was under
an absolute decree; and if so, then though their doctrine may
seem to those, who do not examine things nicely, to look
more plausible; yet really it amounts to the same thing with
the other. For it is all one to say, that God decreed that
Adam should sin, and that all mankind should fall in him, and
that then God should choose out of mankind, thus fallen by
his decree, such as he would save, and leave the rest in that
lapsed state to perish in it; as it is to say, that God intending
to save some, and to damn others, did, in order to the carrying this on in a method of justice, decree Adam's fall, and the
fall of mankind in him, in order to the saving of his elect, and

the damning of the rest. All that the Sublapsarians say in this particular for themselves is, that the scripture has not declared any thing concerning the fall of Adam, in such formal terms, that they can affirm any thing concerning it. A liberty of another kind seems to have been then in man, when he was made after the image of God, and before he was corrupted by sin. And therefore though it is not easy to clear all difficulties in so intricate a matter, yet it seems reasonable to think, that man in a state of innocency was a purer and a freer creature to good, than now he is. But after all, this seems to be only a fleeing from the difficulty, to a less offensive way of talking of it; for if the prescience of future contingents cannot be certain, unless they are decreed, then God could not certainly foreknow Adam's sin, without he had made an absolute decree about it; and that, as was just now said, is the same thing with the Supralapsarian hypothesis; of which I shall say no more, having now laid together in a small compass the full strength of this argument. I go next to set out with the same fidelity and exactness the Remonstrants' arguments.

ART. XVII.

They begin with this, that God is just, holy, and merciful: that, in speaking of himself in the scripture with relation to those attributes, he is pleased to make appeals to men, to call them to reason with him: thus his prophets did often bespeak the Jewish nation; the meaning of which is, that God acts so, that men, according to the notions that they have of those attributes, may examine them, and will be forced to justify and approve them. Nay, in these God proposes himself to us, as our pattern; we ought to imitate him in them, and by consequence we may frame just notions of them. We are required to be holy and merciful as he is merciful. What then can we think of a justice that shall condemn us for a fact that we never committed, and that was done many years before we were born? as also that designs first of all to be glorified by our being eternally miserable, and that decrees that we shall commit sins, to justify the previous decree of our reprobation? If those decrees are thus originally designed by God, and are certainly effectuated, then it is inconceivable how there should be a justice in punishing that which God himself appointed by an antecedent and irreversible decree should be done: so this seems to lie hard upon justice. It is no less hard upon infinite holiness, to imagine that a Being of 'purer eyes than that it can behold iniquity,' should by an antecedent decree fix our committing so many sins, in such a manner that it is not possible for us to avoid them: this is to make us to be born indeed under a necessity of sin; and yet this necessity is said to flow from the act and decrees of God: God represents himself always in the scriptures as 'gracious, merciful, slow to anger, and abundant in goodness and truth.' It is often said, that 'he desires that no man should perish, but that all should come to the knowledge of the truth:' and this

Hab. i. 13.

Ex. xxxiv. 6.

2 Pet. iii. 9.

ART. XVII.
Ezek. xviii. 32.
xxxiii. 11.

is said sometimes with the solemnity of an oath; 'As I live, saith the Lord, I take no pleasure in the death of sinners.' They ask, what sense can such words bear, if we can believe that God did by an absolute decree reprobate so many of them? If all things that happen do arise out of the decree of God as its first cause, then we must believe that God takes pleasure both in his own decrees and in the execution of them; and, by consequence, that he takes pleasure in the death of sinners, and that in contradiction to the most express and most solemn words of scripture. Besides, what can we think of the truth of God, and of the sincerity of those offers of grace and mercy, with the obtestations, the exhortations, and expostulations upon them, that occur so often in scripture, if we can think that by antecedent acts of God he determined that all these should be ineffectual; so that they are only so many solemn words that do indeed signify nothing, if God intended that all things should fall out as they do, and if they do so fall out only because he intended it? The chief foundation of this opinion lies in this argument as its basis, that nothing can be believed that contradicts the justice, holiness, the truth, and purity, of God; that these attributes are in God according to our notions concerning them, only they are in him infinitely more perfect; since we are required to imitate them. Whereas the doctrine of absolute decrees does manifestly contradict the clearest ideas that we can form of justice, holiness, truth, and goodness.

From the nature of God they go to the nature of man; and they think that such an inward freedom by which a man is the master of his own actions, and can do or not do what he pleases, is so necessary to the morality of our actions, that without it our actions are neither good nor evil, neither capable of rewards or punishment. Mad men, or men asleep, are not to be charged with the good or evil of what they do; therefore at least some degrees of liberty must be left with us, otherwise why are we praised or blamed for any thing that we do? If a man thinks that he is under an inevitable decree, as he will have little remorse for all the evil he does, while he imputes it to that inevitable force that constrains him, so he will naturally conclude that it is to no purpose for him to struggle with impossibilities: and men being inclined both to throw all blame off from themselves, and to indulge themselves in laziness and sloth, these practices are too natural to mankind to be encouraged by opinions that favour them. All virtue and religion, all discipline and industry, must arise from this as their first principle; that there is a power in us to govern our own thoughts and actions, and to raise and improve our faculties. If this is denied, all endeavours, all education, all pains either on ourselves or others, are vain and fruitless things. Nor is it possible to make a man believe other than this; for he does so plainly perceive that he is a free agent; he feels himself balance matters in his thoughts, and deliberate about them so evidently, that he certainly knows he is a free being.

This is the image of God that is stamped upon his nature; and though he feels himself often hurried on so impetuously, that he may seem to have lost his freedom in some turns, and upon some occasions: yet he feels that he might have restrained that heat in its first beginnings; he feels he can divert his thoughts, and master himself in most things, when he sets himself to it: he finds that knowledge and reflection, that good company and good exercises, do tame and soften him, and that bad ones make him wild, loose, and irregular. From all this they conclude that man is free, and not under inevitable fate, or irresistible motions either to good or evil. All this they confirm from the whole current of the scripture, that is full of persuasions, exhortations, reproofs, expostulations, encouragements, and terrors; which are all vain and theatrical things, if there are no free powers in us to which they are addressed: to what purpose is it to speak to dead men, to persuade the blind to see, or the lame to run? If we are under an impotence till the irresistible grace comes, and if, when it comes, nothing can withstand it, then what occasion is there for all those solemn discourses, if they can have no effect on us? They cannot render us inexcusable, unless it were in our power to be bettered by them; and to imagine that God gives light and blessings to those whom he before intended to damn, only to make them inexcusable, when they could do them no good, and they will serve only to aggravate their condemnation, gives so strange an idea of that infinite goodness, that it is not fit to express it by those terms which do naturally arise upon it.

It is as hard to suppose two contrary wills in God, the one commanding us our duty, and requiring us with the most solemn obtestations to do it, and the other putting a certain bar in our way, by decreeing that we shall do the contrary. This makes God look as if he had a *will* and a *will;* though a heart and a heart import no good quality, when applied to men: the one *will* requires us to do our duty, and the other makes it impossible for us not to sin: the *will* for the good is ineffectual, while the will that makes us sin is infallible. These things seem very hard to be apprehended; and whereas the root of true religion is the having right and high ideas of God and of his attributes, here such ideas arise as naturally give us strange thoughts of God; and if they are received by us as originals, upon which we are to form our own natures, such notions may make us grow to be spiteful, imperious, and without bowels, but do not seem proper to inspire us with love, mercy, and compassion; though God is always proposed to us in that view. All preaching and instruction does also suppose this: for to what purpose are men called upon, taught,

ART. XVII. and endeavoured to be persuaded, if they are not free agents, and have not a power over their own thoughts, and if they are not to be convinced and turned by reason? The offers of peace and pardon that are made to all men are delusory things, if they are by an antecedent act of God restrained only to a few, and all others are barred from them.

It is further to be considered, say they, that God having made men free creatures, his governing them accordingly, and making his own administration of the world suitable to it, is no diminution of his own authority: it is only the carrying on of his own creation according to the several natures that he has put in that variety of beings of which this world is composed, and with which it is diversified: therefore if some of the acts of God, with relation to man, are not so free as his other acts are, and as we may suppose necessary to the ultimate perfection of an independent Being, this arises not from any defect in the acts of God, but because the nature of the creature that he intended to make free is inconsistent with such acts.

The Divine Omnipotence is not lessened when we observe some of his works to be more beautiful and useful than others are; and the irregular productions of nature do not derogate from the order in which all things appear lovely to the Divine Mind. So if that liberty, with which he intended to endue thinking beings, is incompatible with such positive acts, and so positive a providence as governs natural things and this material world, then this is no way derogatory to the sovereignty of his mind. This does also give such an account of the evil that is in the world, as does no way accuse or lessen the purity and holiness of God; since he only suffers his creatures to go on in the free use of those powers that he has given them; about which he exercises a special providence, making some men's sins to be the immediate punishments of their own or of other men's sins, and restraining them often in a great deal of that evil that they do design, and bringing out of it a great deal of good that they did not design; but all is done in a way suitable to their natures, without any violence to them.

It is true, it is not easy to shew how those future contingencies, which depend upon the free choice of the will, should be certain and infallible. But we are on other accounts certain that it is so; for we see through the whole scriptures a thread of very positive prophecies, the accomplishment of which depended on the free will of man; and these predictions, as they were made very precisely, so they were no less punctually accomplished. Not to mention any other prophecies, all those that related to the death and sufferings of Christ were fulfilled by the free acts of the priests and people of the Jews: they sinned in doing it, which proves that they acted in it with their natural liberty. By these and all the

other prophecies that are in both Testaments, it must be ART.
confessed, that these things were certainly foreknown; but XVII.
where to found that certainty, cannot be easily resolved; the
infinite perfection of the Divine Mind ought here to silence
all objections. A clear idea, by which we apprehend a thing
to be plainly contrary to the attributes of God, is indeed a
just ground of rejecting it; and therefore they think that they
are in the right to deny all such to be in God, as they plainly
apprehend to be contrary to justice, truth, and goodness: but
if the objection against any thing supposed to be in God lies
only against the manner and the unconceivableness of it, there
the infinite perfection of God answers all.

It is further to be considered, that this prescience does not
make the effects certain, because they are foreseen; but they
are foreseen because they are to be; so that the certainty of
the prescience is not antecedent or causal, but subsequent
and eventual. Whatsoever happens, was future before it
happened; and since it happened, it was certainly future from
all eternity; not by a certainty of fate, but by a certainty
that arises out of its being once, from which this truth, that it
was future, was eternally certain: therefore the Divine Prescience being only the knowing all things that were to come,
that does not infer a necessity or causality.

The scripture plainly shews on some occasions a conditionate prescience: God answered David, that Saul was come to 1 Sam.
Keilah, and that the men of Keilah were to deliver him up; xxiii. 11,
and yet both the one and the other was upon the condition of 12.
his staying there; and he going from thence, neither the one
nor the other ever happened: here was a conditionate prescience. Such was Christ's saying, that those of Tyre and Matt. xi.
Sidon, Sodom and Gomorrah, would have turned to him, if 21. x. 15.
they had seen the miracles that he wrought in some of the
towns of Galilee. Since then this prescience may be so certain, that it can never be mistaken, nor misguide the designs
or providence of God; and since by this both the attributes
of God are vindicated, and the due freedom of the will of man
is asserted, all difficulties seem to be easily cleared this way.

As for the giving to some nations and persons the means of
salvation, and the denying these to others, the scriptures do
indeed ascribe that wholly to the riches and freedom of God's
grace; but still they think, that he gives to all men that which
is necessary to the state in which they are, to answer the
obligations they are under in it; and that this light and
common grace is sufficient to carry them so far, that God will
either accept of it, or give them further degrees of illumination: from which it must be inferred, that all men are inexcusable in his sight; and that 'God is always just and clear Psal. li. 4.
when he judges;' since every man had that which was sufficient, if not to save him, yet at least to bring him to a state
of salvation. But besides what is thus simply necessary, and

ART.
XVII.
is of itself sufficient, there are innumerable favours, like largesses of God's grace and goodness; these God gives freely as he pleases.

And thus the great designs of Providence go on according to the goodness and mercy of God. None can complain, though some have more cause to rejoice and glory in God than others. What happens to nations in a body may also happen to individuals; some may have higher privileges, be put in happier circumstances, and have such assistances given them as God foresees will become *effectual*, and not only those, which though they be in their nature *sufficient*, yet in the event will be *ineffectual:* every man ought to complain of himself for not using that which was sufficient, as he might have done; and all good men will have matter of rejoicing in God, for giving them what he foresaw would prove effectual. After all, they acknowledge there is a depth in this, of God's not giving all nations an equal measure of light, nor putting all men into equally happy circumstances, which they cannot unriddle: but still justice, goodness, and truth, are saved; though we may imagine a goodness that may do to all men what is absolutely the best for them: and there they confess there is a difficulty, but not equal to those of the other side.

From hence it is that they expound all those passages in the New Testament, concerning the *purpose*, the *election*, the *foreknowledge*, and the *predestination*, of God, so often mentioned. All those, they say, relate to God's design of calling the Gentile world to the knowledge of the Messias: this was kept secret, though hints of it are given in several of the Prophets; so it was a mystery; but it was then revealed, when, according to Christ's commission to his apostles, to 'go and teach all nations,' they went preaching the gospel to the Gentiles. This was a stumbling-block to the Jews, and it was the chief subject of controversy betwixt them and the apostles at the time when the Epistles were writ: so it was necessary for them to clear this very fully, and to come often over it. But there was no need of amusing people in the beginnings of Christianity, and in that first infancy of it, with high and unsearchable speculations concerning the decrees of God: therefore they observe, that the apostles shew how that Abraham at first, Isaac and Jacob afterwards, were chosen by a discriminating favour, that they and their posterity should be in covenant with God: and upon that occasion the apostle goes on to shew, that God had always designed to call in the Gentiles, though that was not executed but by their ministry.

With this key one will find a plain coherent sense in all St. Paul's discourses on this subject, without asserting antecedent and special decrees as to particular persons. Things that happen under a permissive and directing Providence, may be also in a largeness of expression ascribed to the will and counsel of God; for a permissive and directing will is really a will, though it be not antecedent nor causal. The *hardening Pharaoh's heart* may be ascribed to God, though it is said that his *heart hardened itself;* because he took occasion, from the stops God put in those plagues that he sent upon him and his people, to encourage himself, when he saw there was a new respite granted him: and he who was a cruel and bloody prince, deeply engaged in idolatry and magic, had deserved such judgments for his other sins; so that he may be well considered as actually under his final condemnation, only under a reprieve, not swallowed up in the first plagues, but preserved in them, and raised up out of them, to be a lasting monument of the justice of God against such hardened impenitency. 'Whom he will he hardeneth,' must be still restrained to such persons as that tyrant was.

ART. XVII.

Exod. vii. 22.
Exod. viii. 15, 19, 32.

Rom. ix. 18.

It is endless to enter into the discussion of all the passages cited from the scripture to this purpose; this key serving, as they think it does, to open most of them. It is plain these words of our Saviour concerning those 'whom the Father had given him,' are only to be meant of a dispensation of Providence, and not of a decree; since he adds, 'And I have lost none of them, except the son of perdition:' for it cannot be said, that he was in the decree, and yet was lost. And in the same period in which God is said 'to work in us both to will and to do,' we are required to 'work out our own salvation with fear and trembling.' The word rendered, 'ordained to eternal life,' does also signify, fitted or predisposed to eternal life. That question, 'Who made thee to differ?' seems to refer to those gifts which in different degrees and measures were poured out on the first Christians; in which men were only passive, and discriminated from one another by the freedom of those gifts, without any thing previous in them to dispose them to them.

John xvii. 12.

Phil. ii. 12, 13.

Acts xiii. 48.

1 Cor. iv. 7.

Christ is said to be the 'propitiation for the sins of the whole world;' and the wicked are said to 'deny the Lord that bought them;' and his death, as to its extent to all men, is set in opposition to the sin of Adam: so that 'as by the offence of one, judgment came upon all men to condemnation; so by the righteousness of one, the free gift came upon all men to justification of life.' The *all* of the one side must be of the same extent with the *all* of the other: so since *all* are concerned in Adam's sin, *all* must be likewise concerned in the death of Christ. This they urge further, with this argument, that all men are obliged to believe in the death of Christ, but no man can be obliged to believe a lie; therefore it follows that he must have died for *all*. Nor can it be thought that grace is so efficacious of itself, as to determine us; otherwise why are we required 'not to grieve God's Spirit?' Why is it said, 'Ye do always resist the Holy Ghost: as your fathers did, so do ye. How often would I have gathered you under

1 John ii. 2.
2 Pet. ii. 1.

Rom. v. 18.

Acts vii. 51.
Matt. xxiii. 37.

my wings, but ye would not? What more could I have done in my vineyard, that has not been done in it?' These seem to be plain intimations of a power in us, by which we not only can, but often do, resist the motions of grace.

If the determining efficacy of grace is not acknowledged, it will be yet much harder to believe that we are efficaciously determined to *sin*. This seems to be not only contrary to the purity and holiness of God, but is so manifestly contrary to the whole strain of the scriptures, that charges sin upon men, that in so copious a subject it is not necessary to bring proofs. 'O Israel, thou hast destroyed thyself; but in me is thy help:' and, 'Ye will not come unto me, that ye may have life: why will you die, O house of Israel?' And as for that nicety of saying, that the evil of sin consists in a negation, which is not a positive being, so that though God should determine men to the action that is sinful, yet he is not concerned in the sin of it: they think it is too metaphysical to put the honour of God and his attributes upon such a subtilty: for in sins against moral laws, there seems to be an antecedent immorality in the action itself, which is inseparable from it. But suppose that sin consisted in a negative, yet that privation does immediately and necessarily result out of the action, without any other thing whatsoever intervening; so that if God does infallibly determine a sinner to commit the action to which that guilt belongs, though that should be a sin only by reason of a privation that is dependent upon it, then it does not appear but that he is really the author of sin; since if he is the author of the sinful action, on which the sin depends as a shadow upon its substance, he must be esteemed, say they, the author of sin.

And though it may be said, that sin being a violation of God's law, he himself, who is not bound by his law, cannot be guilty of sin; yet an action that is immoral is so essentially opposite to infinite perfection, that God cannot be capable of it, as being a contradiction to his own nature. Nor is it to be supposed that he can damn men for that, which is the necessary result of an action to which he himself determined them.

As for perseverance, the many promises made in the scriptures to them that *overcome*, that continue *stedfast* and *faithful to the death*, seem to insinuate, that a man may fall from a good state. Those famous words in the 6th of the Hebrews do plainly intimate, that such men may 'so fall away, that it may be impossible to renew them again by repentance.' And in that Epistle where it is said, 'The just shall live by faith;' it is added, 'but if he draw back (*any man* is not in the original), my soul shall have no pleasure in him.' And it is positively said by the prophet, 'When the righteous turneth away from his righteousness, and committeth iniquity, all his righteousness that he hath done shall not be mentioned; in his sin that he hath sinned shall he die.' These suppositions, with a great many more of the same strain that may be brought out of other places, do give us all possible reason to believe that a good man may fall from a good state, as well as that a wicked man may turn from a bad one. In conclusion, the end of all things, the final judgment at the last day, which shall be pronounced according to what men have done, whether good or evil, and their being to be rewarded and punished according to it, seems so effectually to assert a freedom in our wills, that they think this alone might serve to prove the whole cause.

ART. XVII.

So far I have set forth the force of the argument on the side of the Remonstrants. As for the Socinians, they make their plea out of what is said by the one and by the other side. They agree with the Remonstrants in all that they say against absolute decrees, and in urging all those consequences that do arise out of them: and they do also agree with the Calvinists in all that they urge against the possibility of a certain prescience of future contingents: so that it will not be necessary to set forth their plea more specially, nor needs more be said in opposition to it, than what was already said as part of the Remonstrants' plea. Therefore, without dwelling any longer on that, I come now to make some reflections upon the whole matter.

It is at first view apparent, that there is a great deal of weight in what has been said of both sides: so much, that it is no wonder if education, the constant attending more to the difficulties of the one side than of the other, and a temper some way proportioned to it, does fix men very steadily to either the one or the other persuasion. Both sides have their difficulties, so it will be natural to choose that side where the difficulties are least felt: but it is plain there is no reason for either of them to despise the other, since the arguments of both are far from being contemptible.

It is further to be observed, that both sides seem to be chiefly concerned to assert the honour of God, and of his attributes. Both agree in this, that whatever is fixed as the primary idea of God, all other things must be explained so as to be consistent with that. Contradictions are never to be admitted; but things may be justly believed, against which objections may be formed that cannot be easily answered.

The one side think, that we must begin with the idea of infinite perfection, of independency, and absolute sovereignty: and if in the sequel difficulties occur which cannot be cleared, that ought not to shake us from this primary idea of God.

Others think, that we cannot frame such clear notions of independency, sovereignty, and infinite perfection, as we can do of justice, truth, holiness, goodness, and mercy: and since the scripture proposes God to us most frequently under

ART. XVII. those ideas, they think that we ought to fix on these as the primary ideas of God, and then reduce all other things to them.

Thus both sides seem zealous for God and his glory; both lay down general maxims that can hardly be disputed; and both argue justly from their first principles. These are great grounds for mutual charity and forbearance in these matters.

It is certain, that one who has long interwoven his thoughts of infinite perfection with the notions of absolute and unchangeable decrees, of carrying on every thing by a positive will, of doing every thing for his own glory, cannot apprehend decrees depending on a foreseen free will, a grace subject to it, a merit of Christ's death that is lost, and a man's being at one time loved, and yet finally hated, of God, without horror. These things seem to carry in them an appearance of feebleness, of dependence, and of changeableness.

On the other hand, a man that has accustomed himself to think often on the infinite goodness and mercy, the long-suffering, patience, and slowness to anger, that appears in God; he cannot let the thought of absolute reprobation, or of determining men to sin, or of not giving them the grace necessary to keep them from sin and damnation, enter into his mind, without the same horror that another feels in the reverse of all this.

So that the source of both opinions being the different ideas that they have of God, and both these ideas being true; men only mistaking in the extent of them, and in the consequences drawn from them; here are the clearest grounds imaginable for a mutual forbearance, for not judging men imperiously, nor censuring them severely upon either side. And those who have at different times of their lives been of both opinions, and who upon the evidence of reason, as it has appeared to them, have changed their persuasions, can speak more affirmatively here; for they know, that in great sincerity of heart they have thought both ways.

Each opinion has some practical advantages of its side. A Calvinist is taught, by his opinions, to think meanly of himself, and to ascribe the honour of all to God; which lays in him a deep foundation for humility: he is also much inclined to secret prayer, and to a fixed dependence on God; which naturally both brings his mind to a good state, and fixes it in it: and so though perhaps he cannot give a coherent account of the grounds of his watchfulness and care of himself; yet that temper arises out of his humility, and his earnestness in prayer. A Remonstrant, on the other hand, is engaged to awaken and improve his faculties, to fill his mind with good notions, to raise them in himself by frequent reflection, and by a constant attention to his own actions: he sees cause to reproach himself for his sins, and to set about his duty to purpose: being assured that it is through his own fault if he miscarries: he has no dreadful terrors upon his mind; nor is he tempted to an undue security, or to swell up in (perhaps) an imaginary conceit of his being unalterably in the favour of God.

Both sides have their peculiar temptations as well as their advantages: the Calvinist is tempted to a false security, and sloth: and the Arminian may be tempted to trust too much to himself, and too little to God: so equally may a man of a calm temper, and of moderate thoughts, balance this matter between both the sides, and so unreasonable it is to give way to a positive and dictating temper in this point. If the Arminian is zealous to assert liberty, it is because he cannot see how there can be good or evil in the world without it: he thinks it is the work of God, that he has made for great ends; and therefore he can allow of nothing that he thinks destroys it. If on the other hand a Calvinist seems to break in upon liberty, it is because he cannot reconcile it with the sovereignty of God, and the freedom of his grace: and he grows to think that it is an act of devotion to offer up the one to save the other.

The common fault of both sides is to charge one another with the consequences of their opinions, as if they were truly their tenets. Whereas they are apprehensive enough of these consequences, they have no mind to them, and they fancy that by a few distinctions they can avoid them. But each side thinks the consequences of the other are both worse, and more certainly fastened to that doctrine, than the consequences that are urged against himself are. And so they think they must choose that opinion that is the least perplexed and difficult: not but that ingenuous and learned men of all sides confess, that they feel themselves very often pinched in these matters.

Another very indecent way of managing these points is, that both sides do too often speak very boldly of God. Some petulant wits, in order to the representing the contrary opinion as absurd and ridiculous, have brought in God, representing him, with indecent expressions, as acting or decreeing, according to their hypothesis, in a manner that is not only unbecoming, but that borders upon blasphemy. From which, though they think to escape by saying that they are only shewing what must follow if the other opinion were believed; yet there is a solemnity and gravity of style, that ought to be most religiously observed, when we poor mortals take upon us to speak of the glory or attributes, the decrees or operations, of the great God of heaven and earth: and every thing relating to this, that is put in a burlesque air, is intolerable. It is a sign of a very daring presumption, to pretend to assign the order of all the acts of God, the ends proposed in them, and the methods by which they are executed. We, who do not know how our thoughts carry our bodies to obey and second our minds, should not imagine that we can conceive how God

ART.
XVII.
may move or bend our wills. The hard thing to digest in this whole matter, is reprobation: they who think it necessary to assert the freedom of election, would fain avoid it: they seek soft words for it, such as the passing by or leaving men to perish: they study to put that on Adam's sin, and they take all the methods they can to soften an opinion that seems harsh, and that sounds ill. But howsoever they will bear all the consequences of it, rather than let the point of absolute election go.

On the other side, those who do once persuade themselves that the doctrine of reprobation is false, do not see how they can deny it, and yet ascribe a free election to God. They are once persuaded that there can be no reprobation but what is conditionate, and founded on what is foreseen concerning men's sins: and from this they are forced to say the same thing of election. And both sides study to begin the controversy with that which they think they can the most easily prove; the one at the establishing of election, and the other at the overthrowing of reprobation. Some have studied to seek out middle ways: for they observing that the scriptures are writ in a great diversity of style, in treating of the good or evil that happens to us, ascribing the one to God, and imputing the other to ourselves, teaching us to ascribe the honour of all that is good to God, and to cast the blame of all that is evil upon ourselves, have from thence concluded, that God must have a different influence and causality in the one, from what he has in the other: but when they go to make this out, they meet with great difficulties; yet they choose to bear these rather than to involve themselves in those equally great, if not greater difficulties, that are in either of the other opinions. They wrap up all in two general assertions, that are great practical truths, *Let us arrogate no good to ourselves, and impute no evil to God*, and so let the whole matter rest. This may be thought by some the lazier, as well as the safer way: which avoids difficulties, rather than answers them; whereas they say of both the contending sides, that they are better at the starting of difficulties than at the resolving of them.

Thus far I have gone upon the general, in making such reflections as will appear but too well grounded to those who have with any attention read the chief disputants of both sides. In these great points all agree: that mercy is freely offered to the world in Christ Jesus: that God did freely offer his Son to be our propitiation, and has freely accepted the sacrifice of his death in our stead, whereas he might have condemned every man to have perished for his own sins: that God does, in the dispensation of his gospel, and the promulgation of it to the several nations, act according to the freedom of his grace, upon reasons that are to us mysterious and past finding out: that every man is inexcusable in the sight of God: that all men are so far free as to be praiseworthy or blameworthy for the good or evil that they do: that every man ought to employ his faculties all he can, and to pray and depend earnestly upon God for his protection and assistance: that no man in practice ought to think that there is a fate or decree hanging over him, and so become slothful in his duty, but that every man ought to do the best he can, as if there were no such decree, since, whether there is or is not, it is not possible for him to know what it is: that every man ought to be deeply humbled for his sins in the sight of God, without excusing himself by pretending a decree was upon him, or a want of power in him: that all men are bound to obey the rules set them in the gospel, and are to expect neither mercy nor favour from God, but as they set themselves diligently about that: and finally, that at the last day all men shall be judged, not according to secret decrees, but according to their own works. In these great truths, of which the greater part are practical, all men agree. If they would agree as honestly in the practice of them, as they do in confessing them to be true, they would do that which is much more important and necessary, than to speculate and dispute about niceties; by which the world would quickly put on a new face, and then those few, that might delight in curious searches and arguments, would manage them with more modesty and less heat, and be both less positive and less supercilious.

 I have hitherto insisted on such general reflections as seemed proper to these questions. I come now in the last place to examine how far our church hath determined the matter, either in this Article or elsewhere: how far she hath restrained her sons, and how far she hath left them at liberty. For those different opinions being so intricate in themselves, and so apt to raise hot disputes, and to kindle lasting quarrels, it will not be suitable to that moderation which our church hath observed in all other things, to stretch her words on these heads beyond their strict sense. The natural equity or reason of things ought rather to carry us, on the other hand, to as great a comprehensiveness of all sides, as may well consist with the words in which our church hath expressed herself on those heads.

 It is not to be denied, but that the Article seems to be framed according to St. Austin's doctrine: it supposes men to be under a *curse and damnation*, antecedently to *predestination*, from which they are delivered by it; so it is directly against the Supralapsarian doctrine: nor does the Article make any mention of reprobation, no, not in a hint; no definition is made concerning it. The Article does also seem to assert the efficacy of grace: that in which the knot of the whole difficulty lies, is not defined; that is, whether God's eternal purpose or decree was made according to what he foresaw his creatures would do, or purely upon an absolute will, in order to his own glory. It is very probable, that those who penned it meant that the decree was absolute; but yet since they have not said it, those who subscribe the Articles do not seem to be bound to any thing that is not expressed in them: and therefore since the Remonstrants do not deny but that God having foreseen what all mankind would, according to all the different circumstances in which they should be put, do or not do, he upon that did, by a firm and eternal decree, lay that whole design in all its branches, which he executes in time; they may subscribe this Article without renouncing their opinion as to this matter. On the other hand, the Calvinists have less occasion for scruple; since the Article does seem more plainly to favour them. The three cautions, that are added to it, do likewise intimate that St. Austin's doctrine was designed to be settled by the Article: for *the danger of men's having the sentence of God's predestination always before their eyes, which may occasion either desperation on the one hand, or the wretchlessness of most unclean living on the other*, belongs only to that side; since these mischiefs do not arise out of the other hypothesis. The other two, of taking *the promises of God in the sense in which they are set forth to us in holy scriptures*, and *of following that will of God that is expressly declared to us in the word of God*, relate very visibly to the same opinion: though others do infer from these cautions, that the doctrine laid down in the Article must be so understood as to agree with these cautions; and therefore they argue, that since absolute predestination cannot consist with them, that therefore the Article is to be otherwise explained. They say the natural consequence of an absolute decree is either presumption or despair: since a man upon that bottom reckons, that which way soever the decree is made, it must certainly be accomplished. They also argue, that because we must receive the promises of God as conditional, we must also believe the decree to be conditional; for absolute decrees exclude conditional promises. An offer cannot be supposed to be made in earnest by him that has excluded the greatest number of men from it by an antecedent act of his own. And if we must only follow the revealed will of God, we ought not to suppose that there is an antecedent and positive will of God, that has decreed our doing the contrary to what he has commanded.

Thus the one side argues, that the Article as it lies, in the plain meaning of those who conceived it, does very expressly establish their doctrine: and the other argues, from those cautions that are added to it, that it ought to be understood so as that it may agree with these cautions: and both sides find in the Article itself such grounds, that they reckon they do not renounce their opinions by subscribing it. The Remonstrant side have this further to add, that the universal extent of the death of Christ seems to be very plainly affirmed in the most solemn part of all the offices of the church: for in the office of Communion, and in the Prayer of Consecration, we own that Christ, *by the one oblation of himself once offered, made there a full, perfect, and sufficient sacrifice, oblation, and satisfaction, for the sins of the whole world.* Though the others say, that by *full, perfect, and sufficient,* is not to be understood that Christ's death was intended to be a complete sacrifice and satisfaction for *the whole world,* but that in its own value it was capable of being such. This is thought too great a stretch put upon the words. And there are yet more express words in our Church Catechism to this purpose; which is to be considered as the most solemn declaration of the sense of the church, since that is the doctrine in which she instructs all her children: and in that part of it which seems to be most important, as being the short summary of the Apostles' Creed, it is said, *God the Son, who hath redeemed me and all mankind:* where *all* must stand in the same extent of universality, as in the precedent and in the following words; *The Father who made me and all the world; the Holy Ghost who sanctifieth me and all the elect people of God;* which being to be understood severely, and without exception, this must also be taken in the same strictness. There is another argument brought from the office of Baptism, to prove that men may fall from a state of grace and regeneration; for in the whole office, more particularly in the Thanksgiving after the Baptism, it is affirmed, that the person baptized is *regenerated by God's holy Spirit,* and is *received for his own child by adoption:* now since it is certain that many who are baptized fall from that state of grace, this seems to import, that some of the regenerate may fall away: which though it agrees well with St. Austin's doctrine, yet it does not agree with the Calvinists' opinions.

ART. XVII.

Thus I have examined this matter in as short a compass as was possible; and yet I do not know that I have forgot any important part of the whole controversy, though it is large, and has many branches. I have kept, as far as I can perceive, that indifference which I proposed to myself in the prosecuting of this matter; and have not on this occasion declared my own opinion, though I have not avoided the doing it upon other occasions. Since the church has not been peremptory, but that a latitude has been left to different opinions, I thought it became me to make this explanation of the Article such: and therefore I have not endeavoured to possess the reader with that which is my own sense in this matter, but have laid the force of the arguments, as well as the weight of the difficulties, of both sides, before him, with all the advantages that I had found in the books either of the one or of the other persuasion. And I leave the choice as free to my reader as the church has done.

ARTICLE XVIII.

Of obtaining Eternal Salvation only by the Name of Christ.

They also are to be accursed, that presume to say, That every man shall be saved by the Law or Sect which he professeth; so that he be diligent to frame his Life according to that Law, and the Light of Nature. For Holy Scripture doth set out unto us only the Name of Jesus Christ, whereby men must be saved.

THE impiety, that is condemned in this Article, was first taught by some of the heathen orators and philosophers in the fourth century, who, in their addresses to the Christian emperors for the tolerance of *paganism*, started this thought, that how lively soever it may seem, when well set off in a piece of eloquence, will not bear a severe argument: that God is more honoured by the varieties and different methods of worshipping and serving him, than if all should fall into the same way: that this diversity has a beauty in it, and a suitableness to the infinite perfections of God; and it does not look so like a mutual agreement or concert, as when all men worship him one way. But this is rather a flash of wit than true reasoning.

The *Alcoran* has carried this matter further, to the asserting, that all men in all religions are equally acceptable to God, if they serve him faithfully in them. The infusing this into the world, that has a show of mercy in it, made men more easy to receive their law; and they took care by their extreme severity to fix them in it, when they were once engaged: for though they use no force to make men Musselmans, yet they punish with all extremity every thing that looks like apostacy from it, if it is once received. The doctrine of Leviathan, that makes *law* to be *religion* and *religion* to be *law*, that is, that obliges subjects to believe that religion to be true, or at least to follow that which is enacted by the laws of their country, must be built either on this foundation, that there is no such thing as revealed religion, but that it is only a political contrivance: or that all religions are equally acceptable to God.

Others having observed that it was a very small part of mankind that had the advantages of the Christian religion, have thought it too cruel to damn in their thoughts all those who have not heard of it, and yet have lived morally and virtuously, according to their light and education. And some, to make themselves and others easy, in accommodating their religion to their secular interests, to excuse their changing, and to quiet their consciences, have set up this notion, that seems to have a largeness both of good nature and charity in it; looks plausible, and is calculated to take in the greatest numbers: they therefore suppose that God in his infinite goodness will accept equally the services that all his creatures offer to him, according to the best of their skill and strength.

In opposition to all which, they are here condemned, who think that every man shall be saved by the *law* or *sect* which he professeth: where a great difference is to be observed between the words *saved by the law*, and *saved in the law*; the one is condemned, but not the other. To *be saved by a law* or *sect*, signifies, that by the virtue of that *law* or *sect* such men who follow it may be *saved:* whereas to be *saved in a law* or *sect* imports only, that God may extend his compassions to men that are engaged in false religions. The former is only condemned by this article, which affirms nothing concerning the other. In sum; if we have fully proved that the Christian religion was delivered to the world in the name of God, and was attested by miracles, so that we believe its truth, we must believe every part and tittle of it, and by consequence those passages which denounce the wrath and judgments of God against impenitent sinners, and that promise mercy and salvation only upon the account of Christ and his death: 'We must believe with our hearts, and confess it with our mouths: we must not be ashamed of Christ, or of his words, lest he should be ashamed of us, when he comes in the glory of his Father, with his holy angels.' This, I say, being a part of the gospel, must be as true as the gospel itself is; and these rules must bind all those to whom they are proposed, whether they are enacted by *law* or not; for if we are assured that they are a part of the *law of the King of kings*, we are bound to believe and obey them, whether human laws do favour them or not; it being an evident thing, that no subordinate authority can derogate from that which is superior to it: so if the laws of God are clearly revealed, and certainly conveyed down to us, we are bound by them, and no human law can dissolve this obligation. If God has declared his will to us, it can never be supposed to be free to us to choose whether we will obey it or not, and serve him under that or under another form of religion, at our pleasure and choice. We are limited by what God has declared to us, and we must not fancy ourselves to be at liberty after he has revealed his will to us.

As to such to whom the Christian religion is revealed, there no question can be made, for it is certain they are under an indispensable obligation to obey and follow that which is so graciously revealed to them: they are bound to follow it according to what they are in their consciences persuaded is its true sense and meaning. And if for any secular interest they choose to comply with that which they are convinced is an important error, and is condemned in the scripture, they do

ART. XVIII. plainly shew that they prefer lands, houses, and life, to the authority of God, in whose will, when revealed to them, they are bound to acquiesce.

The only difficulty remaining is concerning those who never heard of this religion; whether, or how, can they be saved? St. Paul having divided the world into Jews and Gentiles, called by him those who were in the law, and who were with- Rom. ii. 12, 14, 15. out law; he says, those 'who sinned without law,' that is, out of the Mosaical dispensation, 'shall be judged without law,' that is, upon another foot. For he adds, when 'the Gentiles, which have not the law, do by nature the things contained in the law (that is, the moral parts of it), these, having not the law, are a law unto themselves (that is, their consciences are to them instead of a written law); which shew the work of the law written in their hearts, their conscience also bearing witness, and their thoughts the meanwhile accusing or else excusing one another.' This implies that there are either seeds of knowledge and virtue laid in the nature of man, or that such notions pass among them, as are carried down by tradi- Rom. x. 14. tion. The same St. Paul says, 'How can they call on him in whom they have not believed? and how can they believe in him of whom they have not heard? and how can they hear without a preacher?' which seems plainly to intimate, that men cannot be bound to believe, and by consequence cannot be punished for not believing, unless the gospel is preached Acts x. 34, 35. to them. St. Peter said to Cornelius, 'Of a truth I perceive that God is no respecter of persons; but in every nation he that feareth God, and worketh righteousness, is accepted of him.' Those places seem to import, that those who make the best use they can of that small measure of light that is given them, shall be judged according to it; and that God will not require more of them than he has given them. This also agrees so well with the ideas which we have both of justice and goodness, that this opinion wants not special colours to make it look well. But, on the other hand, the pardon of sin, and the favour of God, are so positively limited to the believing in Christ Jesus, and it is so expressly said, that Acts iv. 12. 'there is no salvation in any other;' and that 'there is none other name (or authority) under heaven given among men, whereby we must be saved;' that the distinction which can only be made in this matter is this, that it is only on the account, and in the consideration of the death of Christ, that sin is pardoned, and men are saved.

This is the only sacrifice in the sight of God; so that whosoever are received into mercy have it through Christ as the channel and conveyance of it. But it is not so plainly said, that, no man can be saved unless he has an explicit knowledge of this, together with a belief in it. Few in the old dispensation could have that: infants and innocents, or idiots, have it not; and yet it were a bold thing to say, that they may not be saved by it. So it does not appear to be clearly revealed, ART. that none should be saved by the death of Christ, unless they XVIII. do explicitly both know it, and believe in it: since it is certain, that God may pardon sin only upon that score, without obliging all men to believe in it, especially when it is not revealed to them. And here another distinction is to be made, which will clear this whole matter, and all the difficulties that arise out of it.

A great difference is to be made between a fœderal certainty of salvation, secured by the promises of God, and of this new covenant in Christ Jesus, and the extent to which the goodness and mercy of God may go. None are in the fœderal state of salvation but Christians: to them is given the covenant of grace, and to them the promises of God are made and offered; so that they have a certainty of it upon their performing those conditions that are put in the promises. All others are out of this promise, to whom the tidings of it were never brought; but yet a great difference is to be made between them, and those who have been invited to this covenant, and admitted to the outward profession, and the common privileges of it, and that yet have in effect rejected it: these are under such positive denunciations of wrath and judgment, that there is no room left for any charitable thoughts or hopes concerning them: so that if any part of the gospel is true, that must be also true, that they are under condemnation, for 'having loved darkness more than light,' when the light shone John iii. upon them, and visited them. But as for them whom God 19. has left in darkness, they are certainly out of the covenant, out of those promises and declarations that are made in it. So that they have no fœderal right to be saved, neither can we affirm that they shall be saved: but, on the other hand, they are not under those positive denunciations, because they were never made to them: therefore since God has not declared that they shall be damned, no more ought we to take upon us to damn them.

Instead of stretching the severity of justice by an inference, we may rather venture to stretch the mercy of God, since that is the attribute which of all others is the most magnificently spoken of in the scriptures: so that we ought to think of it in the largest and most comprehensive manner. But indeed the most proper way is, for us to stop where the revelation of God stops; and not to be wise beyond what is written; but to leave the secrets of God as mysteries too far above us to examine, or to sound their depth. We do certainly know on what terms we ourselves shall be saved or damned: and we ought to be contented with that, and rather study to 'work out our own salvation with fear and trembling,' than to let our minds run out into uncertain speculations concerning the measures and the conditions of God's uncovenanted mercies: we ought to take all possible care that we ourselves come not into

ART. XVIII. condemnation, rather than to define positively of others, who must, or who must not, be condemned.

It is therefore enough to fix this according to the design of the Article, that it is not free to men to choose at pleasure what religion they will, as if that were left to them, or that all religions were alike; which strikes at the foundation, and undermines the truth, of all revealed religion. None are within the covenant of grace but true Christians; and all are excluded out of it, to whom it is offered, who do not receive and believe it, and live according to it. So, in a word, all that are saved, are saved through Christ; but whether all these shall be called to the explicit knowledge of him, is more than we have any good ground to affirm. Nor are we to go into that other question; whether any that are only in a state of nature, live fully up to its light? This is that about which we can have no certainty, no more than whether there may be a common grace given to them all, proportioned to their state, and to the obligations of it. This in general may be safely believed, that God will never be wanting to such as do their utmost endeavours in order to the saving of their souls: but that, as in the case of Cornelius, an angel will be sent, and a miracle be wrought, rather than such a person shall be left to perish. But whether any of them do ever arrive at that state, is more than we can determine; and it is a vain attempt for us to endeavour to find it out.

ARTICLE XIX.

Of the Church.

The Visible Church* of Christ is a Congregation of faithful Men, in the which the pure Word of God is preached, and the Sacraments be duly administered according to Christ's Ordinance, in all those things that of necessity are requisite to the same.

As the Church of Jerusalem, Alexandria, and Antioch, have erred, so also the Church of Rome hath erred, not only in their living and manner of Ceremonies, but also in matters of Faith.

THIS Article, together with some that follow it, relates to the fundamental difference between us and the church of Rome: they teaching that we are to judge of doctrines by the authority and the decisions of the church; whereas we affirm, that we are first to examine the doctrine, and according to that to judge of the purity of a church. Somewhat was already said on the sixth Article relating to this matter: what remains is now to be considered.

The whole question is to be reduced to this point, whether we ought to examine and judge of matters of religion, according to the light and faculty of judging that we have; or if we

---

* ' The word church is ambiguous, having, both in holy scripture and common use, divers senses, somewhat different: for

' 1st. Sometimes any assembly or company of Christians is called a church; as when mention is made of *the church in* such *a house* (whence *Tertullian* saith, *where there are three, even laics, there is a church*).

' 2d. Sometimes a particular society of Christians, living in spiritual communion, and under discipline; as when, *the church* at such *a town; the churches of* such *a province;* the churches, all the churches, are mentioned: according to which notion St. *Cyprian* saith, that there is a church, where there is *a people united to a priest, and a flock adhering to their shepherd:* and so *Ignatius* saith, that *without the orders of the clergy a church is not called.*

' 3d. A larger collection of divers particular societies combined together in order, under direction and influence of a common government, or of persons acting in the public behalf, is termed a church: as the church of *Antioch,* of *Corinth,* of *Jerusalem,* &c., each of which, at first, probably might consist of divers congregations, having dependencies of less towns annexed to them; all being united under the care of the bishops and presbytery of those places; but however soon after the apostles' times, it is certain that such collections were, and were named churches.

' 4th. The society of those who at present, or in course of time, profess the faith and gospel of Christ, and undertake the evangelical covenant, in distinction to all other religions; particularly to that of the Jews; which is called the synagogue.

' 5th. The whole body of God's people that is, ever hath been, or ever shall be, from the beginning of the world to the consummation thereof, who, having (formally or virtually) believed in Christ, and sincerely obeyed God's laws, shall finally, by the meritorious performances and sufferings of Christ, be saved, is called the church.'—*Barrow on the Unity of the Church.* The reader ought also to consult ' Pearson on the Creed,' Art. IX.; and Bishop Taylor's discourse ' Of the Church,' &c.—[ED.]

AN EXPOSITION OF

ART. XIX.

are bound to submit in all things to the decision of the church? Here the matter must be determined against private judgment, by very express and clear authorities, otherwise the other side proves itself. For we having naturally a faculty of judging for ourselves, and using it in all other things, this freedom being the greatest of all our other rights, must be still asserted, unless it can be made appear that God has in some things put a bar upon it by his supreme authority.

That authority must be very express, if we are required to submit to it in a point of such vast importance to us. We do also see that men are apt to be mistaken, and are apt likewise willingly to mistake, and to mislead others; and that particularly in matters of religion the world has been so much imposed upon and abused, that we cannot be bound to submit to any sort of persons implicitly, without very good and clear grounds that do assure us of their infallibility: otherwise we have just reason to suspect that in matters of religion, chiefly in points in which human interests are concerned, men may either through ignorance, and weakness, or corruption, and on design, abuse and mislead us. So that the authorities or proofs of this infallibility must be very express; since we are sure no man nor body of men can have it among them, but by a privilege from God; and a privilege of so extraordinary a nature must be given, if at all, in very plain, and with very evident characters; since without these human nature cannot and ought not to be so tame as to receive it. We must not draw it from an inference, because we think we need it, and cannot be safe without it, that therefore it must be so, because, if it were not so, great disorders would arise from the want of it. This is certainly a wrong way of arguing. If God has clearly revealed it, we must acquiesce in it, because we are sure, if he has lodged infallibility any where, he will certainly maintain his own work, and not require us to believe any one implicitly, and not at the same time preserve us from the danger of being deceived by him. But we must not presume, from our notions of things, to give rules to God. It were, as we may think, very necessary that miracles should be publicly done from time to time, for convincing every age and succession of men; and that good men should be so assisted as generally to live without sin: these and several other things may seem to us extremely convenient, and even necessary; but things are not so ordered for all that.* It is also certain, that if God has lodged such

---

* This is one of the chief arguments in favour of infallibility on which the Romanist erects his building. He first concludes that there must be a living, speaking, infallible judge in the church; and then wisely, and not less modestly, concludes in favour of his pope, or pope and councils. In his reply to Cressy, Whitby thus answers this assumption:

'He, through the whole chapter, slily supposes, and sometimes asserts, a necessity of an infallible judge, as if without such a one the way to salvation were uncertain, and controversies endless.

'1. But he should first prove, that God hath appointed an infallible judge, and therefore it is necessary there should be one, and not conclude that he hath ap-an infallibility on earth, it ought not to be in such hands as do naturally heighten our prejudices against it. It will go against the grain to believe it, though all outward appearances looked ever so fair for it: but it will be an inconceivable method of Providence, if God should lodge so wonderful an authority in hands that look so very unlike it, that of all others we should the least expect to find it with them.

If they have been guilty of notorious impostures, to support their own authority, if they have committed great violences to extend it, and have been for some ages together engaged in as many false, unjust, and cruel practices, as are perhaps to be met with in any history; these are such prejudices, that at least they must be overcome by very clear and unquestionable proofs: and finally, if God has settled such a power in his

---

pointed one, because he conceives a necessity of it. I could name a hundred privileges, that Mr. C. could conceive to be highly beneficial to the church, which yet God never granted to it; and if we may deduce infallibility from the necessity or convenience of it to secure us in our way to heaven, and decide our controversies, then why may we not conclude, that somebody else beside your pope and council is infallible? Is it not more conducive to these ends, that every bishop should be infallible? more still, that every preacher? and more yet, that every individual Christian? Would not these infallibly secure them from all danger of erring? Might not God send some infallible interpreter from heaven to expound all obscure and doubtful places of scripture? Might not the apostles have left us such a commentary? Might not God (if he had pleased) have spoken so perspicuously in scripture, that there should be no need of an infallible interpreter to make it plainer? But if from the advantage and use of these dispensations we should infer their actual existence, the conclusion would confute the premises.

'2. The plea for an infallible guide, to secure us from wandering out of the way to heaven, is invalidated by the plainness and easiness of the way, which we cannot miss unless we will; so that he who will keep his eyes open, is in no more danger of losing his way than in the walks of his own garden; for we know the conditions which God hath made necessary to salvation are clear and easy, unless God should bind us upon pain of damnation fully to know and believe articles obscure and ambiguous, and so damn men for not believing that, the truth whereof they could not discover, which is highly repugnant both to his revealed goodness and justice. We, therefore, distinguish between points fundamental and points not fundamental, those being clearly revealed, and so of a necessary belief; to determine their sense, there is no more need of a judge, than for any other perspicuous truth. What need of a judge to decide whether scripture affirms that there is but one God? that this God cannot lie? that Jesus was crucified and rose again? that without faith and obedience we cannot come to heaven? These, and such like, are the truths we entitle fundamental, and if the sense of these need an infallible judge, then let us bring Euclid's elements to the bar, and call for a judge to decide whether twice two make four. Then for points not fundamental, their belief being not absolutely necessary to salvation, we may err about them, and not err damnably, and so this plea for an infallible judge is wholly evacuated. And with no more difficulty may we baffle the other, taken from its necessity to determine controversies; for if any man oppose fundamental doctrines, or any other evident truths, our church can censure him, without pretending to be infallible. What need of an infallible judge to convict him of heresy, that shall deny the resurrection of the dead? (which yet some of your own popes have not believed, if some of your own historians may be believed.) Therefore, doctrines not fundamental, being not clearly revealed, our church doth not take upon her to determine these, but if any disputes arise about such points, it is her work to silence and suppress them; and when she gives her judgment of that side she thinks most probable, though she doth not expect that all her children should be so wise as to be of her opinion, yet she expects they should be so modest, as not to contradict her, which is as effectually available to end controversies as is your pretended infallibility.'
—[ED.]

ART.
XIX.
church, we must be distinctly directed to those in whose hands it is put, so that we may fall into no mistake in so important a matter. This will be the more necessary, if there are different pretenders to it: we cannot be supposed to be bound to believe an infallibility in general, unless we have an equal evidence directing us to those with whom it rests, and who have the dispensing of it. These general considerations are of great weight in deciding this question, and will carry us far into some preliminaries, which will appear to be indeed great steps towards the conclusion of the matter.

There are three ways by which it may be pretended that infallibility can be proved: the one is the way of Moses and the prophets, of Christ and his apostles, who, by clear and unquestionable miracles publicly done, and well attested, or by express and circumstantiated prophecies of things to come, that came afterwards to be verified, did evidently demonstrate that they were sent of God: wheresoever we see such characters, and that a miracle is wrought by men who say they are sent of God, which cannot be denied nor avoided; and if what such persons deliver to us is neither contrary to our ideas of God, and of morality, nor to any thing already revealed by God; there we must conclude that God has lodged an infallible authority with them, as long and as far as that character is stamped upon it.

That is not pretended here: for though they study to persuade the world that miracles are still among them, yet they do not so much as say that the miracles are wrought by those with whom this infallibility is lodged, and that they are done to prove them to be infallible. For though God should bestow the gift of miracles upon some particular persons among them, that is no more an argument that their church is infallible, than the miracles that Elijah or Elisha wrought were arguments to prove that the Jewish church was infallible. Indeed the public miracles that belonged to the whole body, such as the cloud of glory, the answers by the Urim and Thummim, the trial of jealousy, and the constant plenty of the sixth year, as preparatory to the sabbatical year, seem more reasonably to infer an infallibility; because these were given to that whole church and nation.* But yet the Jewish

* This line of argument, here alluded to by our author, is the most easy and satisfactory answer to the absurd pretence of the papal church to infallibility. They cannot urge any one scripture from the New Testament containing promises to the Christian church (which too they unwarrantably limit to themselves), to which the Jew cannot reply by the production of similar, and, in some instances, much more enlarged promises made to his church. If, for instance, the man who refuses to hear the church is to be accounted a heathen and publican, (Matt. xviii. 17.) the man that did presumptuously, and would not hearken to the Jewish priest, was commanded to be put to death. (Deut. xvii. 12.) The same argument will hold good in all the other scriptures advanced by the papal church in her behalf. Now, although they have no right to appeal to scripture until the authority and infallibility of their church be first proved, since, according to their doctrine, it is the peculiar province of the Roman church to, in the first place, decide what is

church was far from being infallible all that while; for we see they fell all in a body into idolatry upon several occasions:

scripture, and in the second, what is the meaning or sense of any particular verse or passage—yet, giving them full permission to make use of that book which they are so prone to insult by calling it obscure, insufficient, and a dead letter—what do they prove? The infallibility of the Jewish church! 'For if,' writes Dr. Whitby, ' Roman Catholics conclude from these ambiguous and obscure places for the infallibility of councils, or the major part of the church-guides concurring with the pope in any sentence or decree, although these places do not speak one syllable of any pope or major part of the church-guides, and much less of the Romish prelates, and less of their *infallible* assistance; what ovations and triumphs would they have made, had it been said expressly of their cardinals and councils, as it is said of Jewish priests, that they were *set for judgment and for controversy?* had God fixed his glorious presence at Rome, as he did at Jerusalem, and settled there a *seat of judgment*, and a continual court of highest judicature, as was that Sanhedrin, which in Jerusalem was settled? had he dwelt in St. Peter's, as he dwelt in the temple? had he left with them, as he did with the Jewish priests, a standing oracle, a *Urim* and a *Thummim*, to consult with upon all occasions? So that this plea being much stronger for the infallibility of the superiors of the Jewish church, than for the infallibility of the whole western church, or any of its councils, the Roman doctors must acknowledge, either that they fallaciously urge it against Protestants, or must confess that it stands also good against the Christian, and is a confirmation of all those traditions which were condemned by our Saviour, and a sufficient plea for all those errors and corruptions, which, as the prophets do complain, were generally taught and practised by the church-guides in the declining ages of the Jewish church: for if these arguments be good now, they were so then; and if they were good then, for aught that I can see, the high-priest, and the major part of the church rulers of the Jews, were always in the right; and Christ, and his apostles, with the holy prophets, must be in the wrong.'†

To avoid the force of this argument, which so completely turns the weapons of the papacy against itself, some of that party have devised this reply—more ingenious than solid or satisfactory: That the Jewish church was infallible, but that its infallibility disappeared and centred in the Lord Jesus Christ, the greater authority, when he appeared on earth. To this argument, if it can be called one, of which the Editor has known, indeed heard, priests of the Roman church avail themselves, the answer is easy, and more than ever shews the difficulties in which they, who use it, are placed. 1st. The Jewish church did sin in matters fundamental before the coming of Christ—' They err in vision, they stumble in judgment,' ' and the prophets prophesy falsely, and the priests bear rule by their means,' was the testimony of God concerning the church-guides. Apostacy from the truth and idolatry were sins of the Jewish church. But, 2d., if they were infallible until the appearing of the Saviour on earth, which the Bible proves that they were not, how were the people assured of the departure of this high privilege from their own church-guides (whom they were to obey under pain of death), and of its lodgment in the Lord Jesus? This is the point. How did the Saviour convince them? By his doctrine and by miracles. The former was an appeal to their private judgment—the latter to their senses; and if these be allowed, the papal system against the right of private judgment, and in favour of transubstantiation, is demolished. Thus they cannot evade the force of this argument against infallibility without destroying their own building. We cannot but conclude this article in the words of Whitby:—' If this be truly the result of the most specious pretences of the Roman party to draw our souls into their deadly snares, if all their fairest pleas do make for Judaism, more naturally than they do for popery; if what they urge, to prove the Protestant divines to be deceivers of the people, doth more strongly prove our blessed Jesus a deceiver, which is the highest blasphemy; I hope that no true lover of this Jesus will be much tempted by such pleas to entertain a good opinion of the Romish faith: it being certainly that faith, which cannot be established but on the ruins of Christianity, nor embraced by any Protestant, but with the greatest hazard, if not the ruin, of his soul.'—[ED.]

---

† Whitby: Sermon on John vii. 47—49, which every student ought not merely to read, but well digest. It is to be found in his Commentary, at the end of the gospel of St. John.

ART. XIX.

those public miracles proved nothing but that for which they were given, which was, that Moses was sent of God, and that his law was from God, which they saw was still attested in a continuance of extraordinary characters. If infallibility had been promised by that law, then the continuance of the miracles might have been urged to prove the continuance of the infallibility; but that not being promised, the miracles were only a standing proof of the authority of their law, and of God's being still among them. And thus though we should not dispute the truth of the many legends that some are daily bringing forth, which yet we may well do, since they are believed to be true by few among themselves, they being considered among the greater part of the knowing men of that church, as arts to entertain the credulity and devotion of the people, and to work upon their fears and hopes, but chiefly upon their purses: all these, I say, when confessed, will not serve to prove that there is an infallibility among them, unless they can prove that these miracles are wrought to prove this infallibility.

The second sort of proofs that they may bring, is from some passages in scripture, that seem to import that it was given by Christ to the church. But though in this dispute all these passages ought to be well considered and answered, yet they ought not to be urged to prove this infallibility, till several other things are first proved; such as, that the scriptures are the word of God; that the book of the scriptures is brought down pure and uncorrupted to our hands; and that we are able to understand the meaning of it: for before we can argue from the parts of any book, as being of divine authority, all these things must be previously certain, and be well made out to us: so that we must be well assured of all those particulars, before we may go about to prove any thing by any passages drawn out of the scriptures. Further, these passages suppose that those to whom this infallibility belongs are a church: we must then know what a church is, and what makes a body of men to be a church, before we can be sure that they are that society to whom this infallibility is given: and since there may be, as we know that in fact there are, great differences among several of those bodies of men called churches, and that they condemn one another as guilty of error, schism, and heresy; we are sure that all these cannot be infallible: for contradictions cannot be true. So then we must know which of them is that society where this infallibility is to be found. And if in any one society there should be different opinions about the seat of this infallibility, those cannot be all true, though it is very possible that they may be all false: we must be then well assured in whom this great privilege is vested, before we can be bound to acknowledge it, or to submit to it. So here a great many things must be known, before we can either argue from, or apply, those passages of scripture in which it is pretended that infallibility is promised to the church: and if private judgment is to be trusted in the inquiries that arise about all these particulars, they being the most important and most difficult matters that we can search into, then it will be thought reasonable to trust it yet much further.

It is evident, by their proceeding this way, that both the authority and the sense of the scriptures must be known antecedently to our acknowledging the authority or the infallibility of any church. For it is an eternal principle and rule of reason, never to prove one thing by another, till that other is first well proved: nor can any thing be proved afterwards by that which was proved by it. This is as impossible, as if a father should beget a son, and should be afterwards begotten by that son. Therefore the scriptures cannot prove the infallibility of the church, and be afterwards proved by the testimony of the church. So the one or the other of these must be first settled and proved, before any use can be made of it to prove the other by it.

The last way they take to find out this church by, is from some notes* that they pretend are peculiar to her, such as the name *catholic; antiquity; extent; duration; succession of bishops; union among themselves, and with their head; conformity of doctrine with former times; miracles; prophecy; sanctity of doctrine; holiness of life; temporal felicity; curses upon their enemies; and a constant progress or efficacy of doctrine; together with the confession of their adversaries*: and they fancy, that wheresoever we find these, we must believe that body of men to be infallible. But upon all this, endless questions will arise, so far will it be from ending controversies, and settling us upon infallibility. If all these must be believed to be the marks of the infallible church, upon the account of which we ought to believe it, and submit to it, then two inquiries upon every one of these notes must be discussed, before we can be obliged to acquiesce in the infallibility: First, whether that is a true mark of infallibility, or not? And next, whether it belongs to the church which they call infallible, or not? And then another very intricate question will arise upon the whole, whether they must be all found together? or, how many, or which, of them together, will give us the entire characters of the infallible church?

In discussing the questions, whether every one of these is

---

* In order to the full understanding of this point, the reader must refer to Gibson's *Preservative against Popery*, vol. 1, in which 'the notes of the church as laid down by Cardinal Bellarmine are examined and confuted.' This examination of the notes, &c., may also be found in a small quarto, published in 1687, entitled 'A brief Discourse concerning the Notes of the Church, with some Reflections on Cardinal Bellarmine's Notes.' The quarto edition contains also two papers not found in Gibson's collection: 'A vindication of the discourse concerning the Notes;' and 'A defence of the confuter of Bellarmine's second note of the church, Antiquity, against the cavils of the adviser.'—[ED.]

a true mark, or not, no use must be made of the scriptures; for if the scriptures have their authority from the testimony, or rather the decisions, of the infallible church, no use can be made of them till that is first fixed. Some of these notes are such as did not at all agree to the church in the best and purest times; for then she had but a little extent, a short-lived duration, and no temporal felicity: and she was generally reproached by her adversaries. But out of which of these topics can one hope to fetch an assurance of the infallibility of such a body? Can no body of men continue long in a constant series, and with much prosperity, but must they be concluded to be infallible? Can it be thought that the assuming a name can be a mark? Why is not the name *Christian* as solemn as *catholic?* Might not the philosophers have concluded from hence against the first Christians, that they were, by the confession of all men, the *true lovers of wisdom;* since they were called philosophers much more unanimously than the church of Rome is called catholic?

If a conformity of doctrine with former times, and a sanctity of doctrine, are notes of the church, these will lead men into inquiries of such a nature, that if they are once allowed to go so far with their private judgment, they may well be suffered to go much further. Some standard must be fixed on, by which the sanctity of doctrine may be examined; they must also be allowed to examine what was the doctrine of former times: and here it will be natural to begin at the first times, the age of the apostles. It must therefore be first known what was the doctrine of that age, before we can examine the conformity of the present age with it. A succession of bishops is confessed, to be still kept up among corrupted churches. An union of the church with its head cannot be supposed to be a note, unless it is first made out by some other topics, that this church must have a head; and that he is infallible: for unless it is proved by some other argument that she ought to have a head, she cannot be bound to adhere to him, or to own him; and unless it is also proved that he is infallible, she cannot be bound absolutely, and without restrictions, to adhere to him. Holiness of life cannot be a mark, unless it is pretended that those in whom the infallibility is are all holy. A few holy men here and there are indeed an honour to any body; but it will seem a strange inference, that because some few in a society are eminently holy, that therefore others of that body who are not so, but are perhaps as eminently vicious, should be infallible. Somewhat has been already said concerning miracles: the pretence to prophecy falls within the same consideration; the one being as wonderful a communication of omniscience, as the other is of omnipotence. For the confession of adversaries, or some curses on them; these cannot signify much, unless they were universal. Fair enemies will acknowledge what is good among

their adversaries: but as that church is the least apt, of any ART.
society we know, to speak good of those who differ from her, XIX.
so she has not very much to boast as to others saying much
good of her. And if signal providences have now and then
happened, these are such things, and they are carried on with
such a depth, that we must acquiesce in the observation of the
wisest men of all ages, that 'the race is not to the swift, nor Eccl. ix.
the battle to the strong: but that time and chance happeneth 11.
to all things.'

And thus it appears, that these pretended notes, instead of giving us a clear thread to lead us up to infallibility and to end all controversies, do start a great variety of questions, that engage us into a labyrinth, out of which it cannot be easy for any to extricate themselves. But if we could see an end of this, then a new set of questions will come on, when we go to examine all churches by them: Whether the church of Rome has them all? And if she alone has them so, that no other church has them equally with her or beyond her?

If all these must be discussed before we can settle this question, which is the true infallible church? a man must stay long ere he can come to a point in it.

Therefore there can be no other way taken here, but to examine first, what makes a particular church: and then since the catholic church is an united body of all particular churches, when the true notion of a particular church is fixed, it will be easy from that to form a notion of the catholic church.

It would seem reasonable by the method of all creeds, in particular of that called the Apostles' Creed, that we ought first to settle our faith as to the great points of the Christian religion, and from thence go to settle the notion of a true church: and that we ought not to begin with the notion of a church, and from thence go to the doctrine.

The doctrine of Christianity must be first stated, and from this we are to take our measures of all churches; and that chiefly with respect to that doctrine, which every Christian is bound to believe: here a distinction is to be made between those capital and fundamental articles, without which a man cannot be esteemed a true Christian, nor a church a true church; and other truths, which, being delivered in scripture, all men are indeed obliged to believe them, yet they are not of that nature that the ignorance of them, or an error in them, can exclude from salvation.

To make this sensible: it is a proposition of another sort, that Christ died for sinners, than this, that he died at the third or at the sixth hour. And yet if the second proposition is expressly revealed in scripture, we are bound to believe it, since God has said it, though it is not of the same nature with the other.

Here a controversy does naturally arise that wise people are

R

ART. XIX.

unwilling to meddle with, what articles are fundamental, and what are not?

The defining of fundamental articles seems, on the one hand, to deny salvation to such as do not receive them all, which men are not willing to do.

And, on the other hand, it may seem a leaving men at liberty, as to all other particulars that are not reckoned up among the fundamentals.

But after all, the covenant of grace, the terms of salvation, and the grounds on which we expect it, seem to be things of another nature than all other truths, which, though revealed, are not of themselves the means or conditions of salvation. Wheresoever true baptism is, there it seems the essentials of this covenant are preserved: for, if we look on baptism as a fœderal admission into Christianity, there can be no baptism where the essence of Christianity is not preserved. As far then as we believe that any society has preserved that, so far we are bound to receive her baptism, and no further. For unless we consider baptism as a sort of a charm, that such words joined with a washing with water make one a Christian; which seems to be expressly contrary to what St. Peter says of it, that 'it is not the washing away the filth of the flesh, but the answer of a good conscience towards God, that saves us;' we must conclude, that baptism is a fœderal thing, in which, after that the sponsions are made, the seal of regeneration is added.

1 Pet. iii. 21.

From hence it will follow, that all who have a true baptism, that makes men believers and Christians, must also have the true faith as to the essentials of Christianity; the fundamentals of Christianity seem to be all that is necessary to make baptism true and valid. And upon this a distinction is to be made, that will discover and destroy a sophism that is often used on this occasion. A true church* is, in one sense, a society that

* It is of vital importance that the controversialist should study this question, 'What constitutes any church a true church?' Many Protestants have, in their zeal without knowledge, denied the title of true church to the church of Rome, thereby entangling themselves in difficulties. If the papacy be not a true church, how, as Calvin asked, can Antichrist sit in the temple of God? Or how, we might add, can she be charged with being the mother of harlots, if she have not some claim to be the bride? Her sin is not that she directly denies or overturns the truth of Christ, but that she makes void his truth by adopting a new creed, thus indirectly and far more effectually overturning the foundation of faith. When Bishop Hall published his 'Old Religion,' he was assailed by many as favouring popery, because he called the Roman a true church, they not knowing, or not considering, the exact meaning of the word true; nor what an advantage is given to the enemy by denying the Roman to be a church. Hall submitted the matter to his friend Bishop Davenant, who returned the following answer, in which the question is handled in a concise and masterly manner, and for which the Editor is indebted to the Rev. J. Allport's valuable life of Davenant, prefixed to his translation of that bishop's exposition of the Epistle to the Colossians.

'To the Right Rev. Father in God, Joseph, Lord Bishop of Exon, these.

'MY LORD,

'You desire my opinion concerning an assertion of yours, whereat some have taken offence.

'The proposition was this, "That the Roman church remains yet a true visible church."

preserves the essentials and fundamentals of Christianity: in another sense it stands for a society, all whose doctrines are true, that has corrupted no part of this religion, nor mixed any errors with it. A true man is one who has a soul and a body, that are the essential constituents of a man: whereas, in another sense, a man of sincerity and candour is called a true man. Truth in the one sense imports the essential constitution, and in the other it imports only a quality that is accidental to it. So when we acknowledge that any society is a true church, we ought to be supposed to mean no other, than

ART. XIX.

'The occasion, which makes this an ill-sounding proposition in the ears of Protestants, especially such as are not thoroughly acquainted with school distinctions, is the usual acceptation of the word "true" in our English tongue; for, though men skilled in metaphysics hold it for a maxim, *Ens, Verum, Bonum convertuntur;* yet, with us, he, which shall affirm such a one is a true Christian, a true gentleman, a true scholar, or the like, he is conceived not only to ascribe trueness of being unto all these, but those due qualities or requisite actions whereby they are made commendable or praiseworthy in their several kinds. In this sense the Roman church is no more a true church in respect of Christ, or those due qualities and proper actions which Christ requires, than an arrant whore is a true and loyal wife unto her husband.

'I durst, upon mine oath, be one of your compurgators, that you never intended to adorn that strumpet with the title of a true church in this meaning. But your own writings have so fully cleared you herein, that suspicion itself cannot reasonably suspect you on this point.

'I therefore can say no more respecting your mistaken proposition, than this: If, in that treatise wherein it was delivered, the antecedents or consequents were such as served fitly to lead the reader into that sense, which under the word true comprehended only truth of Being or Existence, and not the due qualities of the thing or subject, you have been causelessly traduced. But, on the other side, if that proposition comes *ex abrupto*, or stands solitary in your discourse, you cannot marvel though, by taking the word true according to the more ordinary acceptation, your true meaning was mistaken.

'In brief, your proposition admits a true sense; and, in that sense, is, by the learned in our reformed church, not disallowed: for, the being of a church does principally stand upon the gracious action of God, calling men out of darkness and death unto the participation of light and life in Christ Jesus. So long as God continues this calling unto any people, though they as much as in them lies, darken this light, and corrupt the means which should bring them to light and salvation in Christ; yet, when God calls men unto the participation of life in Christ by the word and by the sacrament, there is the true being of a Christian church, let men be never so false in their exposition of God's word, or never so untrusty in mingling their own traditions with God's ordinances.

'Thus, the church of the Jews lost not her being of a church when she became an idolatrous church.

'And thus, under the government of the Scribes and Pharisees, who voided the commandments of God by their own traditions, there was yet standing a true church, in which Zacharias, Elizabeth, the Virgin Mary, and our Saviour himself was born, who were members of that church, and yet participated not in the corruptions thereof.

'Thus, to grant that the Roman was, and is, a true visible Christian church, though in doctrine a false, and in practice an idolatrous church, is a true assertion; and of greater use and necessity in our controversy with papists about the perpetuity of the Christian church, than is understood by those who gainsay it.

'This, in your Reconciler, is so well explicated, as, if any shall continue in traducing you in regard of that proposition so explained, I think it will be only those, who are better acquainted with wrangling than reasoning, and deeper in love with strife than truth. And, therefore, be no more troubled with other men's groundless suspicions, than you would be in like case with their idle dreams. Thus I have enlarged myself beyond my first intent. But my love to yourself, and the assurance of your constant love unto the truth, enforced me thereunto. I rest always, your loving brother,

'*Jan.* 30, 1628.   JOHN SARUM.'—[ED.]

ART.
XIX.

that the covenant of grace in its essential constituent parts is preserved entire in that body; and not that it is true in all its doctrines and decisions.

The second thing to be considered in a church is, their association together in the use of the sacraments. For these are given by Christ to the society, as the rites and badges of that body. That which makes particular men believers, is their receiving the fundamentals of Christianity: so that which constitutes the body of the church, is the profession of that faith, and the use of those sacraments, which are the rites and distinctions of those who profess it.

In this likewise a distinction is to be made between what is essential to a sacrament, and what is the exact observance of it according to the institution. Additions to the sacraments do not annul them, though they corrupt them with that adulterate mixture. Therefore where the sponsions are made, and a washing with water is used with the words of Christ, there we own that there is a true baptism: though there may be a large addition of other rites, which we reject as superstitious, though we do not pretend that they null the baptism. But if any part of the institution is cut off, there we do not own the sacrament to be true: because it being an institution of Christ, it can no more be esteemed a true sacrament, than as it retains all that, which by the institution appears to be the main and essential part of the action.

Upon this account it is, that since Christ appointed bread and wine for his other sacrament, and that he not only blessed both, but distributed both, with words appropriated to each kind, we do not esteem that to be a true sacrament, in which either the one or the other of these kinds is withdrawn.

But in the next place, there may be many things necessary, in the way of precept and order, both with relation to the sacraments, and to the other public acts of worship, in which though additions or defects are erroneous and faulty, yet they do not annul the sacraments.

We think none ought to baptize but men dedicated to the service of God, and ordained according to that constitution that was settled in the church by the apostles; and yet baptism by laics, or by women, such as is most commonly practised in the Roman church, is not esteemed null by us, nor is it repeated: because we make a difference between what is essential to a sacrament, and what is requisite in the regular way of using it.

None can deny this among us, but those who will question the whole Christianity of the Roman church, where the midwives do generally baptize: but if this invalidates the baptism, then we must question all that is done among them: persons so baptized, if their baptism is void, are neither truly ordained, nor capable of any other act of church-communion. Therefore men's being in orders, or their being duly ordained, is not necessary to the essence of the sacrament of baptism, but only to the regularity of administering it: and so the want of it does not void it, but does only prove such men to be under some defects and disorder in their constitution.

ART. XIX.

Thus I have laid down those distinctions that will guide us in the right understanding of this Article. If we believe that any society retains the fundamentals of Christianity, we do from that conclude it to be a true church, to have a true baptism, and the members of it to be capable of salvation. But we are not upon that bound to associate ourselves to their communion: for if they have the addition of false doctrines, or any unlawful parts of worship among them, we are not bound to join in that which we are persuaded is error, idolatry, or superstition.

If the sacraments that Christ has appointed are observed and ministered by any church as to the main of them, according to his institution, we are to own those for valid actions: but we are not for that bound to join in communion with them, if they have adulterated these with many mixtures and additions.

Thus a plain difference is made between our owning that a church may retain the fundamentals of Christianity, a true baptism, and true orders, which are a consequent upon the former, and our joining with that church in such acts as we think are so far vitiated, that they become unlawful to us to do them. Pursuant to this, we do neither repeat the baptism, nor the ordinations, of the church of Rome: we acknowledge that our forefathers were both baptized and ordained in that communion: and we derive our present Christianity or baptism, and our orders, from thence: yet we think that there were so many unlawful actions, even in those rituals, besides the other corruptions of their worship, that we cannot join in such any more.

The being baptized in a church does not tie a man to every thing in that church; it only ties him to the covenant of grace. The stipulations which are made in baptism, as well as in ordination, do only bind a man to the Christian faith, or to the faithful dispensing of that gospel, and of those sacraments, of which he is made a minister: so he who, being convinced of the errors and corruptions of a church, departs from them, and goes on in the purity of the Christian religion, does pursue the true effect both of his baptism, and of his ordination vows. For these are to be considered as ties upon him only to God and Christ, and not to adhere to the other dictates of that body in which he had his birth, baptism, and ordination.

The great objection against all this is, that it sets up a private judgment, it gives particular persons a right of judging churches: whereas the natural order is, that private persons ought to be subject and obedient to the church.

This must needs feed pride and curiosity, it must break al

ART. XIX.

order, and cast all things loose, if every single man, according to his reading and presumption, will judge of churches and communions.

On this head it is very easy to employ a great deal of popular eloquence, to decry private men's examining of scriptures, and forming their judgments of things out of them, and not submitting all to the judgment of the church. But how absurd soever this may seem, all parties do acknowledge that it must be done.

Those of the church of Rome do teach, that a man born in the Greek church, or among us, is bound to lay down his error, and his communion too, and to come over to them; and yet they allow our baptism, as well as they do the ordinations of the Greek church.

Thus they allow private men to judge, and that in so great a point, as what church and what communion ought to be chosen or forsaken. And it is certain, that to judge of churches and communions is a thing of that intricacy, that if private judgment is allowed here, there is no reason to deny it its full scope as to all other matters.

God has given us rational faculties to guide and direct us; and we must make the most of these that we can: we must judge with our own reasons, as well as see with our own eyes: neither can we, or ought we to resign up our understandings to any others, unless we are convinced that God has imposed this upon us, by his making them infallible, so that we are secured from error if we follow them.

All this we must examine, and be well assured of it, otherwise it will be a very rash, unmanly, and base thing in us, to muffle up our own understandings, and to deliver our reason and faith over to others blindfold. Reason is God's image in us; and as the use and application of our reason, as well as of the freedom of our wills, are the highest excellencies of the rational nature; so they must be always claimed, and ought never to be parted with by us, but upon clear and certain authorities in the name of God, putting us implicitly under the dictates of others.

We may abuse the use of our reason, as well as the liberty of our will; and may be damned for the one as well as the other. But when we set ourselves to make the best use we can of the freedom of our wills, we may and do upon that expect secret assistances. We have both the like promises, direction to the like prayers, and reason to expect the same illumination, to make us *see*, know, and comprehend the truths of religion, that we have to expect that our powers shall be inwardly strengthened to love and obey them. David prays

Ps. cxix. 18, 35.
Is. liv. 13.
Jer. xxxi. 33, 34.

that God may 'open his eyes,' as well as that he may 'make him to go in his ways.' The promises in the prophets concerning the gospel dispensation carry in them the being taught of God, as well as the being made to walk in his ways; and 'the enlightening the mind, and the eyes of the mind' to know, is prayed for by St. Paul, as well as that 'Christ may dwell in their hearts.'

ART. XIX.
Eph. i. 18.
iii. 17.

Since then there is an assistance of the Divine grace given to fortify the understanding, as well as to enable the will, it follows that our understanding is to be employed by us in order to the finding out of the truth, as well as our will in order to the obeying of it. And though this may have very ill consequences, it does not follow from thence, that it is not true. No consequences can be worse than the corruption that is in the world, and the damnation that follows upon sin; and yet God permits it, because he has made us free creatures. Nor can any reason be given why we should be less free in the use of our understanding, than we are in the use of our will; or why God should make it to be less possible for us to fall into errors, than it is to commit sins. The wrath of God is as much denounced against men that 'hold the truth in unrighteousness,' as against other sins: and it is reckoned among the heaviest of curses, to be given up to 'strong delusions, to believe a lie.' Upon all these reasons therefore it seems clear, that our understandings are left free to us as well as our wills; and if we observe the style and method of the scriptures, we shall find in them all over a constant appeal to a man's reason, and to his intellectual faculties.

Rom. i. 18. 24, 26.
2 Thess. ii. 11.

If the mere dictates of the church, or of infallible men, had been the resolution or foundation of faith, there had been no need of such a long thread of reasoning and discourse, as both our Saviour used while on earth, and as the apostles used in their writings. We see the way of authority is not taken, but explanations are offered, proofs and illustrations are brought to convince the mind; which shews that God, in the clearest manifestation of his will, would deal with us as with reasonable creatures, who are not to believe but upon persuasion; and are to use our reasons in order to the attaining that persuasion. And therefore upon the whole matter we ought not to believe doctrines to be true, because the church teaches them; but we ought to 'search the scriptures,' and then, according as we find the doctrine of any church to be true in the fundamentals, we ought to believe her to be a true church; and if, besides this, the whole extent of the doctrine and worship, together not only with the essential parts of the sacraments, but the whole administration of them and the other rituals of any church, are pure and true; then we ought to account such a church true in the largest extent of the word *true;* and by consequence we ought to hold communion with it.

Another question may arise out of the first words of this Article, concerning the visibility of this church; Whether it must be always visible? According to the distinction hitherto made use of, the resolution of this will be soon made. There seem to be promises in the scriptures, of a perpetual duration

ART. XIX.
Matth. xxviii. 20.
Matt. xvi. 18.

of the Christian church: 'I will be with you always, even to the end of the world:' and, 'The gates of hell shall not prevail against the church.' The Jewish religion had a period prefixed, in which it was to come to an end: but the prophecies that are among the prophets, concerning the new dispensation, seem to import not only its continuance, but its being continued still visible in the world. But as the Jewish dispensation was long continued, after they had fallen generally into some very gross errors; so the Christian church may be visible still, though not infallible. God may preserve the succession of a true church, as to the essentials and fundamentals of faith, in the world, even though this society should fall into error. So a visible society of Christians in a true church, as to the essentials of our faith, is not controverted by us. We do only deny the infallibility of this true church, and therefore we are not afraid of that question, *Where was your church before Henry the Eighth?** We answer, It was

---

* To confound the two questions (the falling of a church from its *being* and its *visibility*), is as absurd as to maintain that 'the stars fail every day, and the sun every night.' Some churches may fall from their purity, but yet not from their being or visibility. Some may so fail as to fulfil the threat, 'I will remove thy candlestick out of its place,' and there be left not so much as the name of a Christian church. With us in these kingdoms the church for a time fell from its purity, but not from its being or visibility, for even in the most corrupt ages there were many true Christians, who too frequently were called to seal their testimony with their blood. In order then to entangle us in any difficulty by the question, 'Where was your religion before Henry the Eighth?' Romanists ought to prove that England was obliged, not merely by the bonds of love which ought to bind all pure churches together, but, *jure divino*, to communicate with the papal see; and to receive, with brutish submission, all its degrading additions to Christianity, as the 'true catholic faith out of which no man can be saved.'

Henry VIII. resisted and overturned the pope's usurped authority over these dominions. The church then, being delivered from her oppressor, ceased to teach the papal additions and novelties, and returned to the primitive truth, by continuing to teach what popery herself is compelled to acknowledge as the catholic faith.

This is simply and powerfully stated by Sir H. Lynde, in his 'Via Tuta,' in reply to the question, 'Where was your religion before Luther?'

'He then that shall question us, where our church was before Luther? let him look back into the primitive church; nay, let him look into the bosom of the present Roman church, and there he shall find and confess, that, if ever antiquity and universality were marks of the true church, of right and necessity they must belong to ours. Look into the four creeds, which the church of Rome professes, (the Apostles', the Nicene, the Athanasian, and the creed of pope Pius IV.) and you shall find that three of those creeds are taught and believed by our church; and these, by our adversaries' confession, were instituted by the apostles, and the fathers of the primitive church, *not created by Luther*. Look into the seven sacraments, which the church of Rome holds, and you shall acknowledge that two of these sacraments are professed by us; and these, by our adversaries' confession, were instituted by Christ, *not broached by Luther*. Look into the canon of our Bible, and you shall observe, that the books of canonical scripture which our church allows, were universally received in all ages, and are approved at this day by the church of Rome for canonical scripture, *not devised by Luther*. Look into our book of Common Prayer, and compare it with the ancient liturgies, and it will appear that the same forms of prayer (for substance) were read, and published in a known tongue, in the ancient churches, *not broached by Luther*. Look into the ordination, and calling of pastors, and it will appear, that the same essential form of ordination, which at this day is practised in our church, was used by the apostles and their successors, and *not devised by Luther*. If therefore the three creeds, the two principal sacraments of the church, the books of canonical scripture, the ancient liturgies, the ordination of pastors: if, I say, all these were an-where it is now, here in England, and in the other kingdoms of the world: only it was then corrupted, and it is now pure. There is therefore no sort of inconvenience in owning the constant visibility of a constant succession and church of *true* Christians: *true* as to the essentials of the covenant of grace, though not *true* in all their doctrines. This seems to be a part of the glory of the Messias, and of his kingdom, that he shall be still visibly worshipped in the world by a body of men called by his name. But when visibility is thus separated from infallibility, and it is made out that a church may be a true church, though she has a large allay of errors and corruptions mixed in her constitution and decisions; there will be no manner of inconvenience in owning a constant visibility, even at the same time that we charge the most eminent part of this visible body with many errors and with much corruption.

ART. XIX.

So far has the first part of this article been treated of: from it we pass to the second, which affirms, that as the other patriarchal and apostolical churches, such as Jerusalem, Alexandria, and Antioch, have erred, so the church of Rome has likewise erred, and that not only in their living, and manner of ceremoines, but also in matters of *faith*.

It is not questioned but that the other patriarchal churches

---

ciently taught, and universally, in all ages, in the bosom of the Roman church, even by the testimonies of our adversaries themselves, is it not a silly and senseless question to demand of us, where our church was before Luther? The positive doctrine which we teach, is contained in a few principal points, and those also have antiquity, and universality, with the consent of the Roman church. The points in controversy, which are *sub judice* and in question, are, for the most part, if not all, *additions obtruded upon the church*, and certainly, from those *additions* and *new articles of faith*, the question, truly and properly, results upon themselves: where was *your* church (that is, where was your *Trent doctrine*, and articles of the *Roman creed*, received *de fide*) before Luther? If, therefore, our doctrine lay involved in the bosom of the Roman church (which no Romanist can deny), if I say, it became hidden, as good corn covered with chaff, or as fine gold overlaid with a greater quantity of dross, was it therefore new and unknown, because popery sought, by a prevailing faction, to obscure it? Was there no *good corn* in the granary of the church, for many years' space, until Luther's days, because *it was not severed* from the *chaff?* No *pure gold*, because our adversaries *would not refine it by the fire of God's word?* If the chaff and dross be ours, or if our church savour of nothing but novelty and heresy (as some of these men pretend), *let them remove from the bosom of their own church*, that *new* and *heretical doctrine*, which they say was never heard of before Luther; and tell me if their church will not prove *a poor and senseless carcass, and a dead body without a soul*. Take away the three creeds, which we profess, our two sacraments, the books of canonical scripture, and tell me, if such light chaff and new heresies (as they now style them) were removed, whether *their twelve new articles, their five* (improperly called) *sacraments*, their *Apocryphal* scriptures, their *unwritten* verities and *traditions, will be able to make a true visible church?* Nay, more; the church of Rome does not only acknowledge those things which we hold, but the most ingenuous members of it *are ashamed also of those* ADDITIONS of theirs, which we deny. As for instance, we charge them with the worship of images (contrary to Exod. xx. 4, 5): they deny it, or at least excuse their manner of adoration; but they condemn not us for not worshipping. We accuse them for praying in an unknown tongue (contrary to 1st Cor. xiv.); they excuse it, that God knows the meaning of the heart; but they do not condemn us for praying with the spirit, and with the understanding. We condemn them for adoring the elements of bread and wine in the sacrament, because it contradicts God's word, and depends upon the intention of the priest: they excuse it, that they adore upon condition, if the consecrated bread be Christ; but they do not condemn

ART. XIX.

have erred; both that where our Saviour himself first taught, and which was governed by two of the apostles successively, and those which were founded by St. Peter in person, or by proxy, as church-history represents Alexandria and Antioch to have been. Those of the church of Rome, by whom they are at this day condemned both of heresy and schism, do not dispute this. Nor do they dispute that many of their popes have led bad and flagitious lives: they deny not that the canons, ceremonies, and government of the church, are very much changed by the influence and authority of their popes: but the whole question turns upon this, Whether the see of Rome has erred in matters of faith or not? In this those of that communion are divided: some, by the church or see of Rome, mean the popes personally; so they maintain, that they never have, and never can fall into error: whereas others, by the see of Rome, mean that whole *body* that holds communion with Rome, which they say cannot be tainted with error; and these separate this from the personal infallibility of *popes:* for if a pope should err, they think that a general council has authority to proceed against him, and to deprive him: and thus, though he should err, the *see* might be kept free from error. I shall upon this Article only consider the first opinion, reserving the consideration of the second to the Article concerning general councils.

---

us for adoring Christ's real body in heaven. We accuse them for taking away the cup from the lay people: they excuse it, but they do not condemn us for following Christ's example, and receiving in both kinds. And what is *remarkable* and *comfortable* to all believing Protestants, we charge them with flat idolatry in the adoration of the sacrament, of relics, of saints, of images. And, howsoever they excuse themselves in distinguishing their manner of adoration, yet, I say, *to our endless comfort* be it spoken, *they cannot charge us, in the doctrine of our church, no, not with the least suspicion of idolatry.*'

Others would trace the church in the footsteps of the various churches and individuals that have been persecuted by the papal see.

This course is adopted and well handled by Mournay, count de Plessis, in his address to 'the Friends and Followers of the Church of Rome,' at the beginning of his 'Mystery of Iniquity, the History of the Papacy,' in which he points out where our church was all the time preceding the Reformation, and ably retorts, calling on them to shew where their church was in 'those six hundred years next after Christ.'

The former part he winds up in the following beautiful sentence, which, although this note is unavoidably long, the Editor cannot deny himself and the reader the pleasure of quoting and perusing:

' And now thou knowest where our church was in all this time. Thou, rude and simple as thou art, thinkest, perhaps, when thou seest the sun to set in the west, that it is swallowed up in the ocean, and quite extinguished, wherein indeed, when it sets to thee, it riseth to others, and returns again to thee in his due time, and misseth not a minute; the river Rosny, when it entereth into the Lake of Lozanna, thou thinkest it is quite devoured, but that lively and running water cutteth and divideth that dead and standing pool, making way through her swallowing depths: our church in like manner hath made her way through many ages, hath run into the lake, yet not overwhelmed, but hath past through the bottomless gulfs thereof with glory and triumph; and many rivers meeting her, she passeth through many countries, and at the last falls into her ocean, the church of Christ into God, the bottomless sea of all goodness, and there is drowned, losing herself to find herself in Him.'

The reader should also, on this point, read Stillingfleet's Rational Account of the Grounds of the Protestant Religion; art. 'the Reformation of the Church of England justified.'—[ED.]

THE XXXIX ARTICLES. 251

As to the popes their being subject to error, that must be confessed, unless it can be proved, that, by a clear and express privilege granted them by God, they are excepted out of the common condition of human nature. It is further highly probable that there is no such privilege, since the church continued for many ages before it was so much as pretended to; and that in a time when that see was not only claiming all the rights that belonged to it, but challenging a great many that were flatly denied and rejected: such as the right of receiving appeals from the African churches; in which reiterated instances, and a bold claim upon a spurious canon, pretended to be of the council of Nice, were long pursued: but those churches asserted their authority of ending all matters within themselves. In all this contest infallibility was never claimed; no more than it had been by Victor, when he excommunicated the Asian churches for observing Easter on the fourteenth day of the moon, and not on the Lord's-day after, according to the custom of the Roman as well as of other churches. ART. XIX.

When pope Stephen quarrelled with St. Cyprian about the rebaptizing of heretics, Cyprian and Firmilian were so far from submitting to his authority, that they speak of him with a freedom used by equals, and with a severity that shewed they were far from thinking him infallible. When the whole east was distracted with the disputes occasioned by the Arian controversy, there was so much partiality in all their councils, that it was decreed, that appeals should be made to pope Julius, and afterwards to his successors; though here was an occasion given to assert his infallibility, if it had been thought on, yet none ever spoke of it. Great reverence was paid to that church, both because they believed it was founded by St. Peter and St. Paul, and chiefly because it was the imperial city; for we see that all other sees had that degree of dignity given them, which by the constitution of the Roman empire was lodged in their cities: and so when Byzance was made the imperial city, and called New Rome, though more commonly Constantinople, it had a patriarchal dignity bestowed on it; and was in all things declared equal to Old Rome, only the point of rank and order excepted. This was decreed in two general councils, the second and the fourth, in so express a manner, that it alone before equitable judges would fully shew the sense of the church in the fourth and fifth century upon this head. When pope Liberius condemned Athanasius, and subscribed to semi-Arianism, this was never considered as a new decision in that matter, so that it altered the state of it. No use was made of it, nor was any argument drawn from it. Liberius was universally condemned for what he had done; and when he repented of it, and retracted it, he was again owned by the church. Euseb. His. Eccl. l.v.c. 23—25. Cypr. Ep. 74 et 75. Firmil. Oxon. Con. Sard. c. 3, et 7.

Con. Const. Cap. 3. Con. Chalced. c. 28.

We have in the sixth century a most undeniable instance of the sense of the whole church in this matter. Pope

ART. XIX.

Conc. Sinuess. An. 303.
—tom. 1. Conc.

Honorius was by the sixth general council condemned as a Monothelite; and this in the presence of the pope's legates, and he was anathematized by several of the succeeding popes. It is to no purpose here to examine whether he was justly or unjustly condemned; it is enough that the sense both of the eastern and western church appeared evidently in that age upon these two points; that a pope might be a heretic; and that, being such, he might be held accursed for it: and in that time there was not any one that suggested, that either he could not fall into heresy, since our Saviour had prayed that St. Peter's *faith might not fail;* or that, if he had fallen into it, he must be left to the judgment of God; but that the holy see (according to the fable of P. Marcellin) could be judged by no body. The confusions that followed for some ages in the western parts of Europe, more particularly in Italy, gave occasion to the bishops of Rome to extend their authority.

The emperors at Constantinople, and their exarchs at Ravenna, studied to make them sure to their interests, yet still asserting their authority over them. The new conquerors studied also to gain them to their side; and they managed their matters so dexterously, that they went on still increasing and extending their authority; till being much straitened by the kings of the Lombards, they were protected by a new conquering family, that arose in France in the eighth century; who, to give credit both to their usurpation of that crown, and to the extending their dominions into Italy, and the assuming the empire of the west, did both protect and enrich them, and enlarged their authority; the greatness of which they reckoned could do them no hurt, as long as they kept the confirmation of their election to themselves. That family became quickly too feeble to hold that power long, and then an imposture was published, of a volume of the *Decretal Epistles* of the popes of the first ages, in which they were represented as acting according to those high claims to which they were then beginning to pretend. Those ages were too blind and too ignorant to be capable of searching critically into the truth of this collection; it quickly passed for current; and though some in the beginning disputed it, yet that was soon borne down, and the credit of that work was established. It furnished them with precedents that they were careful enough not only to follow, but to outdo. Thus a work, which is now as universally rejected by the learned men of their own body as spurious, as it was then implicitly taken for genuine, gave the chief foundation during many ages to their unbounded authority: and this furnishes us with a very just prejudice against it, that it was managed with so much fraud and imposture; to which they added afterwards much *cruelty* and *violence;* the two worst characters possible, and the least likely to be found joined with infallibility: for it is reasonable enough to apprehend, that, if God had lodged such a privilege any where, he would have so influenced those who were the depositaries of it, that they should have appeared somewhat like that authority to which they laid claim; and that he would not have forsaken them so, that for above eight hundred years the papacy, as it is represented by their own writers, is perhaps the worst succession of men that is to be found in history.*

But now to come more close, to prove what is here asserted in this part of the Article. If all those doctrines which were established at Trent, and that have been confirmed by popes, and most of them brought into a new creed, and made parts of it, are found to be gross errors; or if but any one of them should be found to be an error, then there is no doubt to be made but that the church of Rome hath erred; so the proof brought against every one of these is likewise a proof against their infallibility. But I shall here give one instance of an error, which will not be denied by the greater part of the church of Rome. They have now for above six hundred years asserted, that they had an authority over princes, not only to convict and condemn them of heresy, and to proceed against them with church-censures; but that they had a power to depose them, to absolve their subjects from their oaths of allegiance, and to transfer their dominions to such persons as should undertake to execute their sentences. This they have often put in execution, and have constantly kept up their claim to it to this day. It will not serve them to get clear here, to say, that these were the violent practices of some popes: what they did in many particular instances may be so turned off, and left as a blemish on the memories of some of them.

---

* 'The ancient canons are more reverently regarded in the church of England, than in the church of Rome; for how well you have observed them in former ages, let your own Baronius testify. "How foul (saith he) was then the face of the holy Roman church, when most potent, and withal most filthy, harlots did bear all the sway at Rome? at whose lust sees were changed, bishops appointed, and (which is horrible to be heard, and not to be uttered) whose lovers, the false popes, were thrust into the seat of Peter, which were not to be written in the catalogue of the Roman bishops, but only for the noting of the times: for who may say they were lawful popes which were thus, without right, thrust in by such strumpets? No where we find any mention of clergy choosing, or giving consent afterward; all canons were put to silence; the pontifical decrees were choked, ancient traditions proscribed, and the old customs, sacred rites, and former use in choosing the high bishop, utterly extinguished." And for later times, your own learned friends also complain as followeth. Budeus: "The holy canons and rules of church discipline, made in better times to guide the life of clergymen, are now become leaden rules, such as Aristotle saith the rules of Lesbian buildings were. For as leaden and soft rules do not direct the building with an equal tenor, but are bowed to the building at the lust of the builders; so are the popes' canons made flexible as lead or wax, that now this great while the world cannot endure them. Neither is it only to the offence of the little ones, but of the great ones also. No man seeketh a dispensation but he obtaineth it: yea, at Rome there are which give attendance to see if any be willing to crave dispensation of all things established by law; all that crave it have it."' *Mason: On the Orders of the Church of England.*—[Ed.]

But the point at present in question is, whether they have not laid claim to this, as a right belonging to their see, as a part of St. Peter's authority descended to them? whether they have not founded it on his being *Christ's vicar*, who was the 'King of kings, and Lord of lords; to whom all power in heaven and in earth was given?' Whether they have not founded it on Jeremy's 'being set over nations and kingdoms, to root out, pluck down, and to destroy?' and on other places of scripture; not forgetting, that the first words of the Bible are, 'In the beginning,' and not 'In the beginnings;' from which they inferred, that there is but one principle, from whence all power is derived: and that God made 'two great lights, the sun to rule by day;' which they applied to themselves.

This, I say, is the question: Whether they did not assume this authority as a power given them by God? As for the applying it to particular instances, to those kings and emperors whom they deposed, that is, indeed, a personal thing, whether they were guilty of heresy, or of being favourers of it, or not? And whether the popes proceeded against them with too much violence or not?

The point now in question is, Whether they declared this to be a doctrine, that there was an authority lodged with their see for doing such things, and whether they alleged scripture and tradition for it?*

Now this will appear evident to those who will read their bulls: in the preambles of which those quotations will be found, as some of them are in the body of the canon law; and it is decreed in it, that the belief of this is *absolutely necessary to salvation*.

This was pursued in a course of many ages. General councils, as they are esteemed among men, have concurred with the popes both in general decrees asserting this power to be in them, and in special sentences against princes: this became the universally received doctrine of those ages: *No university nor nation declaring against it; not so much as one divine, civilian, canonist, or casuist, writ against it*, as Card. Perron truly said. It was so certainly believed, that those writers, whom the deposed princes got to undertake their defence, do not in any of their books pretend to call the doctrine in general in question.

Two things were disputed: one was, Whether popes had a direct power in temporals over princes; so that they were as much subject to them as feudatory princes were to their superior lords? This, to which Boniface the Eighth laid claim, was indeed contradicted. The other point was, Whether those particulars for which princes had been deposed, such as the giving the investiture to bishoprics, were heresies or not? This was much contested: but the power, in the case

---

* The reader will find this question very fully and ably discussed in the Introduction to Barrow's 'Treatise of the Pope's Supremacy.'—[ED.]

of manifest heresy, or of favouring it, to depose princes, and transfer their crowns to others, was never called in question. This was certainly a definition made in the chair, *ex cathedra:* for it was addressed to all their community, both laity and clergy: plenary pardons were bestowed with it on those who executed it: the clergy did generally preach the croisades upon it. Princes, that were not concerned in him that was deposed, gave way to the publication of those bulls, and gave leave to their subjects to take the cross, in order to the executing of them: and the people did in vast multitudes gather about the standards that were set up for leading on armies to execute them; while many learned men writ in defence of this power, and not one man durst write against it.

ART. XIX.

This argument lies not only against the infallibility of popes, but against that of general councils likewise; and also against the authority of oral tradition: for here, in a succession of many ages, the tradition was wholly changed from the doctrine of former times, which had been, that the clergy were subject to princes, and had no authority over them or their crowns. Nor can it be said, that that was a point of discipline; for it was founded on an article of doctrine, whether there was such a power in the popes or not? The prudence of executing or not executing it, is a point of discipline and of the government of the church: but it is a point of doctrine, whether Christ has given such an authority to St. Peter and his followers. And those points of speculation, upon which a great deal turns as to practice, are certainly so important, that in them, if in any thing, we ought to expect an infallibility: for in this case a man is distracted between two contrary propositions: the one is, that he must obey the civil powers, as set over him by an ordinance of God; so that if he resist them, he shall receive in himself damnation: the other is, that the pope being Christ's vicar, is to be obeyed when he absolves him from his former oath and allegiance; and that the new prince set up by him, is to be obeyed under the pain of damnation likewise.

Here a man is brought into a great strait, and therefore he must be guided by infallibility, if in any thing.

So the whole argument comes to this head; that we must either believe that the *deposing power* is lodged by Christ in the see of Rome; or we must conclude, with the Article, that they have erred; and by consequence, that they are not infallible: for the erring in any one point, and at any one time, does quite destroy the claim of *infallibility*.

Before this matter can be concluded, we must consider what is brought to prove it: what was laid down at first must be here remembered, that the proofs brought for a thing of this nature must be very express and clear. A privilege of such a sort, against which the appearances and prejudices are so strong, must be very fully made out, before we can be

ART XIX. bound to believe it: nor can it be reasonable to urge the authority of any passages from scripture, till the grounds are shewn for which the scriptures themselves ought to be believed.

Those who think that it is in general well proved, that there must be an infallibility in the church, conclude from thence, that it must be in the pope: for if there must be a living speaking judge always ready to guide the church, and to decide controversies, they say this cannot be in the diffusive body of Christians; for these cannot meet to judge. Nor can it be in a general council, the meeting of which depends upon so many accidents, and on the consent of so many princes, that the infallibility will lie dormant for some ages, if the general council is the seat of it. Therefore they conclude, that since it is certainly in the church, and can be nowhere else but in the pope, therefore it is lodged in the see of Rome. Whereas we, on the other hand, think this is a strong argument against the infallibility in general, that it does not appear in whom it is vested: and we think that every side does so effectually confute the other, that we believe them all as to that; and think they argue much stronger when they prove where it cannot be, than when they pretend to prove where it must be.*

* So far from the church of Rome, which, if we believe its own testimony, is most united, being agreed in this matter, the very seat of infallibility, the only means according to them of preserving unity, is itself the great cause of strife and division. When they are urged to point out where this infallibility may be found and consulted, they are at their wits' end. One says that it is lodged in the pope when he speaks *ex cathedra*. No, says another, who is entangled in this inextricable difficulty—that popes have contradicted popes, and that too while professing to speak in the full plenitude of their authority. Another will have it to be in general councils; but the same difficulty meets us here. Another asserts that it is vested in councils when confirmed by popes; but we are not more fortunate here, for councils confirmed by popes have taught and decreed contrary to councils confirmed by popes. No wonder then that Chillingworth should exclaim—' I, for my part, after a long and (as I verily believe and hope) impartial search of the true way to eternal happiness, do profess plainly that I cannot find any rest for the sole of my foot but upon this rock only (the Bible). I see plainly and with mine own eyes, that there are popes against popes, councils against councils, some fathers against others, the same fathers against themselves, a consent of fathers of one age against a consent of fathers of another age, the church of one age against the church of another age,' and, he might have added, the church of the council of Trent diametrically opposite to the word of God.† If therefore Romanists themselves cannot agree as to the seat of this infallibility, it is too much to ask Protestants to submit to such an uncertain authority.

But indeed it is quite evident that Romanists themselves have not been able to find out this infallible tribunal, for notwithstanding all their boasting, what advantage do they possess over the members of any other church? They have not preserved themselves from internal divisions; for no communion was ever more distracted. If they say, 'our divisions are about non-essential points,' we may reply, according to Chillingworth, that those who differ from us, do so in points fundamental, or they do not. If in points fundamental, they cannot possibly belong to our church. If they differ from us in points not fundamental, why may not we have our differences as well as you? But how can that communion be undivided when, as we have said, the centre or seat of unity is itself the cause of strife?

Again, the church of Rome has not furnished its members with an infallible exposition of the word of God, which, to any reasonable mind, would appear to be the

† The reader should furnish himself from history with some facts proving each of the positions above mentioned.

This, in the point now in hand, concerning the pope, seems as evident as any thing can possibly be: it not appearing, that, after the words of Christ to St. Peter, the other apostles thought the point was thereby decided, who among them should be the greatest. For that debate was still on foot, and was canvassed among them in the very night in which our Saviour was betrayed. Nor does it appear, that after the effusion of the Holy Ghost, which certainly inspired them with the full understanding of Christ's words, they thought there was any thing peculiarly given to St. Peter beyond the rest. He was questioned upon his baptizing Cornelius: he was not singly appealed to in the great question of subjecting the Gentiles to the yoke of the Mosaical law; he delivered his opinion as one of the apostles: after which St. James summed up the matter, and settled the decision of it. He was charged by St. Paul as guilty of dissimulation in that matter, for which St. Paul withstood him to his face: and he justifies that in an Epistle that is confessed to be writ by divine inspiration. St. Paul does also in the same Epistle plainly assert the equality of his own authority with his; and that he received no authority from him, and owed him no dependence: nor was he ever appealed to in any of the points that appear to have been disputed in the times that the Epistles were written. So that we see no cha-

ART. XIX.

Acts xi. 2 —18.

Acts xv. 19. Gal. ii. 11 —14. & i. 1, 12, 17.

---

great end for which such a privilege as that of infallibility would have been bestowed upon any church. In this important matter, that church which claims to be the interpreter of holy writ has grossly neglected the edification of its members.

Well is this vain pretence thus exposed by Chillingworth: 'Besides, what an impudence it is to pretend, that *your church is infallibly directed concerning the true meaning of the scripture*, whereas there are thousands of places in scripture, which you do not pretend certainly to understand, and about the interpretation whereof your own doctors differ among themselves; if your church be infallibly directed concerning the true meaning of scripture, why do not your doctors follow her infallible direction? And if they do, how comes such difference among them in their interpretations?

' Again, Why does your church thus put her candle under a bushel, and keep her talent of interpreting scripture infallibly, thus long wrapt up in napkins? Why sets she not forth infallible commentaries or expositions upon all the Bible? Is it, because this would not be profitable for Christians, that scripture should be interpreted? It is blasphemous to say so. The scripture itself tells us, *All scripture is profitable*. And the scripture is not so much the words as the sense. And if it be not profitable, why does she employ particular doctors to interpret scriptures fallibly? unless we must think, that fallible interpretations of scripture are profitable, and infallible interpretations would not be so!'

But again; this infallible tribunal has not furnished even an authorized version of the Bible! There were so many disagreeing editions of the Vulgate, which the council of Trent decreed should be held as authentic, that, in order to remedy this confusion, Sixtus V., in the year 1590, published an edition which he declared to be the authentic Vulgate, which had been the object of search by the council of Trent; and pronounced an anathema against any who should presume to alter it, *etiam minima aliqua particula*. Notwithstanding this, his successor Clement VIII., in less than three years, caused it to be suppressed, and published another authentic edition, which differs from that of Sixtus V.† in only two thousand places! Upon these infallibility-destroying changes and contradictions, Dr. James thus writes:—

' There is a great controversy between us and the papists concerning the version

---

† The reader may see this question of the variations of the Vulgate and the several editions, &c. &c., treated in the Editor's letters to a Romish priest.—See Page's 'Three Letters to a Romish Priest,' pp. 43—49.

s

racters of any special infallibility that was in him, besides that which was the effect of the inspiration, that was in the other apostles as well as in him: nor is there a tittle in the scripture, not so much as by a remote intimation, that he was to derive that authority, whatsoever it was, to any successor, or to lodge it in any particular city or see.

The silence of the scripture in this point seems to be a full proof that no such thing was intended by God: otherwise we have all reason to believe that it would have been clearly expressed. St. Peter himself ought to have declared this: and since both Alexandria and Antioch, as well as Rome, pretend to derive from him, and that the succession to those sees began in him, this makes a decision in this point so much the more necessary.

When St. Peter writ his second Epistle, in which he mentions a revelation that he had from Christ, of his *approaching dissolution*, though that was a very proper occasion for declaring such an important matter, he says nothing that relates to it, but gives only a new attestation of the truth of Christ's divine mission, and of what he himself had been a witness to in the mount, when he saw 'the excellent glory, and heard the voice out of it.' He leaves a provision in writing for the following ages, but says nothing of any succession or see: so

---

of Jerome. That Jerome was learned, and that he put forth a version, is received by Protestants and papists; but what this is, and where it is, is disputed. But let us grant that the edition papists now use, called the Vulgate, is the same which Jerome handed down, yet when we have so many of our adversaries acknowledging *various editions* of the Vulgate, improved and corrected by Stephanus, Hentenius, the doctors of Louvain (" *Louvaniensibus*"), Sixtus V., and Clement VIII., may we not ask, what copy they wish to be received, *amidst so many disagreeing editions*, for the *true, legitimate, authentic*, and *undoubted?* If they praise the industry of Stephanus, they condemn the labours of Hentenius; if they approve Hentenius, the labours of the Louvain doctors are useless; if the Louvain were diligent (and they certainly were), what need of the double labour of Sixtus V.? Some may say, all the other editions must lie by, and Sixtus V.'s be received, because he is pope, and as such, in a matter of faith, he neither can deceive, nor be deceived. But *Sixtus* and *Clement* are *opposed*. Sixtus says, Clement denies; Clement says, Sixtus denies. (*O Concordia discors!!*) Sixtus put forth his edition to last for ever! edit. anno 1590. In 1592, Clement VIII. published a new edition so *contrary to Sixtus*', that *you would not know it to be the same*. Which must be received —which believed?'§

Thus, it is evident that, in all things, the Romanist, although deceived by this ignis fatuus of infallibility, is cast upon a sea of uncertainty, and can find no rest but in the adoption of the principles of our church. For whether we consider the notes of the church—these he must examine and judge of by his private reason: or the seat of his church's infallibility—this likewise he must search for by his private judgment, amongst the many and distracting controversies to which it has given rise: or does he search for an infallible commentary? he has no such thing—no way of ascertaining the meaning of scripture but that which is common to us: or for even an authorized version of the word of God? his church has here likewise forsaken him, and by decreeing the Vulgate to be the authentic, without authorizing any edition of the same, has consigned him to either ignorance or despair.

We may then indeed conclude with Burnet, that Romanists 'argue much stronger, when they prove where it (infallibility) cannot be, than when they pretend to prove where it must be,' or what it has done for its deceived votaries.— [ED.]

§ Bellum Papale.

that here the greatest of all privileges is pretended to be lodged in a succession of bishops, without any one passage in scripture importing it.

ART. XIX.

Another set of difficulties arise, concerning the persons who have a right to choose these popes in whom this right is vested, and what number is necessary for a canonical election: how far simony voids it, and who is the competent judge of that; or who shall judge in the case of two different elections, which has often happened. We must also have a certain rule to know when the popes judge as private persons, and when they judge infallibly: with whom they must consult, and what solemnities are necessary to make them speak *ex cathedra*, or *infallibly*. For if this infallibility comes as a privilege from a grant made by Christ, we ought to expect, that all those necessary circumstances to direct us, in order to the receiving and submitting to it, should be fixed by the same authority that made the grant. Here then are very great difficulties: let us now see what is offered to make out this great and important claim.

The chief proof is brought from these words of our Saviour, when upon St. Peter's confessing, that 'he was the Christ, the Son of the living God;' he said to him, 'Thou art Peter, and upon this Rock* I will build my church, and the gates of hell shall not prevail against it. I will give unto thee the keys of the kingdom of heaven; and whatsoever thou

Matt. xvi. 16, 18, 19.

* 'But, for as much as they seem to make greatest account of these words of Christ, "Thou art Peter, and upon this rock I will build my church," therefore, for answer hereunto, understand thou good Christian reader, that the old Catholic fathers, have written and pronounced, not any mortal man as Peter was, but Christ himself, the Son of God, to be this rock. Gregorius Nyssenus saith, " Tu es Petrus," &c. &c. "Thou art Peter, and upon this rock I will build my church." He meaneth the confession of Christ: for he had said before, " Thou art Christ, the Son of the living God." So saith St. Hilary, " Hæc est una felix fidei Petra, quam Petrus ore suo confessus est."—" This is that only blessed rock of faith that Peter confessed with his mouth." Again he saith, " Upon this rock of Peter's confession is the building of the church." So Cyrillus, " Petra nihil aliud est, quam firma et inconcussa discipuli fides."—" The rock is nothing else, but the strong and assured faith of the disciple." So likewise Chrysostome, " Super hanc petram, id est, in hac fide, et confessione ædificabo ecclesiam meam."—" Upon this rock, that is to say, upon this faith and this confession I will build my church." Likewise St. Augustine, " Petra erat Christus super quod fundamentum etiam ædificatus est Petrus."—" Christ was the rock, upon whose foundation Peter himself was also built." And addeth further besides, " Non me ædificabo super te, sed te ædificabo super me."—" Christ saith unto Peter, I will not build myself upon thee: but I will build thee upon me." All these fathers be plain, but none so plain as Origen; his words be these: " Petra est, quicunque est discipulus Christi: et super talem petram construitur omnis ecclesiastica doctrina. Quod in super unum illum Petrum tantum existimas ædificare totam ecclesiam, quid dicturus es de Johanne filio Tonitrui, et apostolorum unoquoque? Num audebis dicere quod adversus Petrum unum non prevaliturae sint portae inferorum? Au soli Petro dantur a Christo claves regni coelorum?"—" He is the rock, whosoever is the disciple of Christ: and upon such a rock all ecclesiastical learning is built. If thou think that the whole church is built only upon Peter, what then wilt thou say of John, the son of the thunder, and of every of the apostles? shall we dare to say, that the gates of hell shall not prevail only against Peter? or are the keys of the kingdom of heaven given *only unto Peter?*" By these few it may appear, what right the pope hath to claim his authority by God's word, and, as Mr. Harding saith, *De jure divino.*' *Jewell's reply to Harding.*—[ED.]

shalt bind on earth shall be bound in heaven, and whatsoever thou shalt loose on earth shall be loosed in heaven.' This begins with an allusion to his name; and discourses built upon such allusions are not to be understood strictly or grammatically. By the *Rock* upon which Christ promises to *build his church*, many of the fathers have understood the *person of Christ*, others have understood the *confession of him*, or *faith in him*, which indeed is but a different way of expressing the same thing. And it is certain that, strictly speaking, the *church* can only be said to be founded upon Christ, and upon his doctrine. But in a secondary sense it may be said to be founded upon the apostles, and upon St. Peter as the first in order; which is not to be disputed.

Now though this is a sense which was not put on these words for many ages; yet when it should be allowed to be their true sense, it will not prove any thing to have been granted to St. Peter but what was common to the other apostles; who are all called the 'foundations upon which the church is built.' That which follows, of the *gates of hell* not being able *to prevail against the church*, may be either understood of death, which is often called *the gate to the grave;* which is the sense of the word that is rendered *hell:* and then the meaning of these words will be, that the church, which Christ was to raise, should never be extinguished, nor die, or come to a period, as the Jewish religion then did: or, according to the custom of the Jews, of holding their courts and councils about their gates, by the gates of hell may be understood, the designs and contrivances of the powers of darkness, which should never prevail over the *church* to root it out, and destroy it; for the word rendered *prevail* does signify an entire victory: this only imports, that the church should be still preserved against all the attempts of hell, but does not intimate that no error was ever to get into it.

By the words *kingdom of heaven*, generally through the whole gospel, the dispensation of the Messias is understood. This appears evidently from the words with which both St. John Baptist and our Saviour began their preaching, 'Repent, for the kingdom of heaven is at hand:' and the many parables and comparisons that Christ gave of the kingdom of heaven, can only be understood of the preaching of the gospel. This being then agreed to, the most natural and the least forced exposition of those words must be, that St. Peter was to open the dispensation of the gospel.* The proper use of a

* 'And in relation to this promise of our Lord, as well as the completion of it by the conversion of the Gentiles, it seems to be that this apostle doth, in the synod met at Jerusalem, speak thus, " Men and brethren, ye know how that a good while ago, ἀφ' ἡμερῶν ἀρχαίων, God chose me out among you, that by my mouth the Gentiles should hear the word." (Acts xv. 7.) He therefore was assuredly the person who first preached the gospel to the Gentiles, and by doing so opened the kingdom of heaven to them: he was the person chosen by Christ to perform this work. . . . . Nor is this exposition any new fancy of my own; it is as ancient

key is to open a door: and as this agrees with these words, 'he that hath the key of the house of David, that openeth and no man shutteth, and shutteth and no man openeth;' and with the phrase of the 'key of knowledge,' by which the lawyers are described; for they had a key with writing tables given them, as the badges of their profession: so it agrees with the accomplishment of this promise in St. Peter, who first opened the gospel to the Jews, after the wonderful effusion of the Holy Ghost: and more eminently when he first opened the door to the Gentiles, preaching to Cornelius, and baptizing him and his household, to which the phrase of the *kingdom of heaven* seems to have a more particular relation. This dispensation was committed to St. Peter, and seems to be claimed by him as his peculiar privilege in the council at Jerusalem. This is a clear and plain sense of these words. For those who would carry them further, and understand by the kingdom of heaven our eternal happiness, must use many distinctions; otherwise, if they expound them literally, they will ascribe to St. Peter that which certainly could only belong to our Saviour himself. Though at the same time it is not to be denied, but that under the figure of keys, the power of discipline, and the conduct and management of Christians, may be understood. But as to this, all the pastors of the church have their share in it; nor can it be appropriated to any one person. As for that of *binding* and *loosing*, and the confirming in *heaven* what he should do in *earth*, whatever it may signify, it is no special grant to St. Peter: for the same words are spoken by our Saviour elsewhere to all the apostles: so this is given equally to them all. The words *binding* and *loosing* are used by the Jewish writers, in the sense of affirming or denying the obligation of any precept of the law that might be in dispute. So according to this common form of speech, and the sense formerly given to the words *kingdom of heaven*, the meaning of these words must be, that Christ committed to the apostles the dispensing his gospel to the world, by which he authorized them to dissolve the obligation of the Mosaical laws; and to give other laws to the Christian church, which they should do under such visible characters of a divine authority, empowering and conducting them in it, that it should be very

ART. XIX.
Rev. iii 7.
Luke xi. 52.

---

as Tertullian, who saith (*De Pudicitia*) that Christ did personally confer this honour on St. Peter, saying, " Upon thee will I build my church." " Sic enim exitus docuit, in ipso ecclesia exstructa est, i.e. per ipsum, ipse clavem imbuit."—" So the event doth teach, the church was built on him, that is, by him, he hanselled the first key :" he preached that sermon by which three thousand Jews were brought into the faith ; he laid the first foundation of a church among the Gentiles; he first, by baptism, gave them entrance into the kingdom of heaven. . . . .
. . . . This being so, it is evident that in this matter St. Peter neither hath nor can have a successor; and that it is absurd to claim a title of succession to this prerogative of St. Peter; this being in effect to say, that the foundations of the church of Christ are not yet laid, and to pretend to a commission to perform at present what was fully done above a thousand six hundred years ago.' *Whitby*.— [ED.]

ART.
XIX.

evident, that what they did on earth was also ratified in heaven. These words, thus understood, carry in them a clear sense, which agrees with the whole design of the gospel. But whatsoever their sense may be, it is plain that there was nothing given peculiarly to St. Peter by them, which was not likewise given to the rest of the apostles. Nor do these words of our Saviour to St. Peter import any thing of a successive infallibility that was to be derived from him with any distinction beyond the other apostles: unless it were a priority of order and dignity; and whatever that was, there is not so much as a hint given, that it was to descend from him to any see or succession of bishops.

Luke xxii. 32.
John xxi. 15, 16, 17.

As for our Saviour's praying that St. Peter's 'faith might not fail,' and his restoring him to his apostolical function, by a thrice repeated charge, 'Feed my sheep, Feed my lambs,' that has such a visible relation to his fall, and to his denying him, that it does not seem necessary to enlarge further on the making it out, or on shewing that these words are capable of no other signification, and cannot be carried further.

The importance of this argument, rather than the difficulty of it, has made it necessary to dwell fully upon it: so much depends upon it, and the missionaries of the church of Rome are so well instructed in it, that it ought to be well considered; for how little strength soever there may be in the arguments brought to prove this infallibility, yet the colours are specious, and they are commonly managed both with much art and great confidence.

ARTICLE XX.

Of the Authority of the Church.

The Church hath power to decree Rites or Ceremonies, and Authority in Matters of Faith. And yet it is not lawful for the Church to ordain any thing that is contrary to God's Word written; neither may it so expound one place of Scripture, that it be repugnant to another. Wherefore although the Church be a Witness and keeper of Holy Writ, yet as it ought not to decree any thing against the same, so besides the same ought it not to enforce any thing to be believed for necessity of Salvation.

This Article consists of two parts; the first asserts a power in the church both to decree rites and ceremonies, and to judge in matters of faith: the second limits this power over matters of faith to the scriptures: so that it must neither contradict them, nor add any articles as necessary to salvation to those contained in them.* This is suitable to some words that were once in

---

* The question between us and the papal church in this point is, not whether the church has power to decree rites or ceremonies, and authority in matters of faith—this cannot be denied; every church has this power within itself—but whether the church has authority to enlarge the catholic and apostolic faith by decreeing as necessary to salvation certain articles, which by her own confession have not any other foundation except only her decree. This is the question at issue between the Reformed and the Church of Rome. Our articles are articles of church communion or church discipline, drawn up for the better furtherance of the faith of Christ, and rendered necessary for the reasons given by our author in his Introduction, p. 5. But it must ever be borne in mind, that so far from adding any thing to the faith of Christ, two of those articles, the 6th and 20th, declare the Bible to be the sole standard of faith; and that, as it is not lawful to decree any thing contrary to it, so it is not in the power of the church to add any thing, even though it be not contrary, to that revelation given in the inspired word of God. This which we reject is the power usurped by the church of Rome; in which matter she has not only daringly set at nought the solemn injunctions in the word of God, but also the decrees of councils which she professes to so highly reverence: —which conduct is well reproved by Bishop Taylor, in the following extract:

'First, we allege that this very power of making new articles is a novelty, and expressly against the doctrine of the primitive church ; and we prove it, first, by the words of the apostle, (Gal. i. 8.) saying, "If we, or an angel from heaven, shall preach unto you any other gospel (viz. in whole, or in part, for there is the same reason of them both) than that which we have preached, let him be anathema ;" and, secondly, by the sentence of the Fathers in the third general council, that at Ephesus,† "That it shall not be lawful for any man to publish or compose another faith or creed than that which was defined by the Nicene Council: and that whosoever shall dare to compose or offer any such to any persons willing to be converted from paganism, Judaism, or heresy, if they were bishops, or clerks, they should be deposed; if laymen, they should be accursed!" And yet, in the church of Rome, faith and Christianity increase like the moon; Bromyard complained of it long since, and the mischief increases daily.'—ED.

---

† This is the decree of the council of Ephesus, to which Burnet refers in his Introduction: (see pp. 1, 3.)

the fifth Article, but were afterwards left out; instead of which the first words of this Article were put in this place, according to the printed editions; though they are not in the original of the Articles signed by both houses of convocation, that are yet extant.

As to the first part of the Article, concerning the power of the church, either with relation to ceremonies or points of faith, the dispute lies only with those who deny all church power, and think that churches ought to be in all things limited by the rules set in scripture; and that where the scriptures are silent, there ought to be no rules made, but that all men should be left to their liberty; and, in particular, that the appointing new ceremonies looks like a reproaching of the apostles, as if their constitutions had been so defective, that those defects must be supplied by the inventions of men: which they oppose so much the more, because they think that all the corruptions of popery began at some rites which seemed at first not only innocent, but pious; but were afterwards abused to superstition and idolatry, and swelled up to that bulk as to oppress and stifle true religion with their number and weight.

A great part of this is in some respect true; yet that we may examine the matter methodically, we shall first consider, what power the church has in those matters; and then, what rules she ought to govern herself by in the use of that power. It is very visible, that in the Gospels and Epistles there are but few rules laid down as to ritual matters: in the Epistles there are some general rules given, that must take in a great many cases: such as, 'Let all things be done to edification, to order, and to peace:' and in the Epistles to Timothy and Titus, many rules are given in such general words, as, 'Lay hands suddenly on no man,' that in order to the guiding of particular cases by them, many distinctions and specialities were to be interposed to the making them practicable and useful. In matters that are merely ritual, the state of mankind in different climates and ages is apt to vary; and the same thing that in one scene of human nature may look grave, and seem fit for any society, may in another age look light, and dissipate men's thoughts. It is also evident that there is not a system of rules given in the New Testament about all these; and yet a due method in them is necessary to maintain the order and decency that become divine things. This seems to be a part of the gospel *liberty*, that it is not 'a law of ordinances;' these things being left to be varied according to the diversities of mankind.

The Jewish religion was delivered to one nation, and the main parts of it were to be performed in one place; they were also to be limited in rituals, lest they might have taken some practices from their neighbours round about them, and so by the use of their rites have rendered idolatrous practices more familiar and acceptable to them: and yet they had many rites among them in our Saviour's time, which are not mentioned in any part of the Old Testament; such was the whole constitution of their synagogues, with all the service and officers that belonged to them: they had a baptism among them, besides several rites added to the paschal service. Our Saviour reproved them for none of these; he hallowed some of them to be the fœderal rites of his new dispensation; he went to their synagogues; and though he reproved them for overvaluing their rites, for preferring them to the laws of God, and making these void by their traditions, yet he does not condemn them for the use of them. And while of the greater precepts he says, 'These things ye ought to have done;' he adds concerning their rites and lesser matters, 'and not to have left the other undone.' Matt. xxiii. 23.

If then such a liberty was allowed in so limited a religion, it seems highly suitable to the sublimer state of the Christian liberty, that there should be room left for such appointments or alterations as the different state of times and places should require. In hotter countries, for instance, there is no danger in dipping; but if it is otherwise in colder climates, then since 'mercy is better than even sacrifice,' a more sparing use may be made of water; aspersion may answer the true end of baptism. A stricter or gentler discipline of offenders must be also proportioned to what the times will bear, and what men can be brought to submit to. The dividing of Christians into such districts, that they may have the best conveniences to assemble themselves together for worship, and for keeping up of order; the appointing the times as well as the places of worship, are certainly to be fixed with the best regard to present circumstances that may be. The bringing Christian assemblies into order and method, is necessary for their solemnity, and for preventing that dissipation of thought that a diversity of behaviour might occasion. And though a *kiss of peace*, and an order of deaconesses, were the practices of the apostolical time; yet when the one gave occasion to raillery, and the other to scandal, all the world was, and still is, satisfied with the reasons of letting both fall. Hos. vi. 6. Matt. xii. 7.

Now if churches may lay aside apostolical practices in matters that are ritual, it is certainly much easier to justify their making new rules for such things; since it is a higher attempt to alter what was settled by the apostles themselves, than to set up new rules in matters which they left untouched. Habits and postures are the necessary circumstances of all public meetings: the times of fasting and of prayer, the days of thanksgiving and communions, are all of the same nature. The public confession of sins by scandalous persons; the time and manner of doing it; the previous steps that some churches have made for the trial of those who were to be received into holy orders, that so by a longer inspection into their behaviour, while in lower orders, they might discover how fit they were to be admitted into the sacred ones; and chiefly the prescribing stated forms for the several acts of religious worship, and not leaving that to the capacities or humours, to the inventions, and often to the extravagancies, of those who are to officiate: all these things, I say, fall within those general rules given by the apostles to the churches in their time: where we find that the *apostles* had their *customs*, as well as *the churches of God;* which were then opposed to the innovating and the contentious humours of some factious men. And such a pattern have the apostles set us of complying with those things that are regularly settled, wheresoever we are, that we find 'they became all things to all men: to the Jews they became Jews;' though that was a religion then extinguished in its obligation, by the promulgation of the gospel; and was then fallen under great corruption: yet, in order to the gaining of some of them, such was the spirit of charity and edification with which the apostles were acted, that while they were among them they complied in the practice of those abrogated rites; though they asserted both the liberty of the Gentiles, and even their own, in that matter: it was only a compliance, and not a submission, to their opinions, that made them *observe days*, and distinguish *meats*, while among them. If then such rites, and the rites of such a church, were still complied with by inspired men, this is an infallible pattern to us; and let us see, upon how much stronger reasons we, who are under those obligations to unity and charity with all Christians, ought to maintain the *unity of the body*, and the decency and order that is necessary for *peace and mutual edification.*

Therefore, since there is not any one thing that Christ has enjoined more solemnly and more frequently than love and charity, union and agreement, amongst his disciples; since we are also required to assemble ourselves together, to constitute ourselves in a body, both for worshipping God jointly, and for maintaining of order and love among the society of Christians, we ought to acquiesce in such rules as have been agreed on by common consent, and which are recommended to us by long practice, and that are established by those who have the lawful authority over us. Nor can we assign any other bounds to our submission in this case, than those that the gospel has limited. We must 'obey God, rather than man;' and we must in the first place 'render to God the things that are God's,' and then 'give to Cæsar the things that are Cæsar's.' So that if either church or state have power to make rules and laws in such matters, they must have this extent given them, that till they break in upon the laws of God and the gospel, we must be bound to obey them. A mean cannot be put here; either they have no power at all, or they have a power that must go to every thing that is not forbid by any law of

God. This is the only measure that can be given in this matter.

But a great difference is here to be made between those rules that both church and state ought to set to themselves in their enacting of such matters, and the measures of the obedience of subjects: the only question in the point of obedience must be, lawful or unlawful. For expedient or inexpedient ought never to be brought into question, as to the point of obedience; since no inexpediency whatsoever can balance the breaking of order, and the dissolving the constitution and society. This is a consideration that arises out of a man's apprehensions of the fitness or usefulness of things; in which though he might be in the right as to the antecedent fitness of them, and yet even there he may be in the wrong, and in common modesty every man ought to think that it is more likely that he should be in the wrong, than the governors and rulers of the society; yet, I say, allowing all this, it is certain that order and obedience are, both in their own nature, and in their consequences, to be preferred to all the particular considerations of expediency or inexpediency. Yet still those in whose hands the making of those rules is put, ought to carry their thoughts much further: they ought to consider well the genius of the Christian religion, and therefore they are to avoid every thing that may lead to idolatry, or feed superstition; every thing that is apt to be abused to give false ideas of God, or to make the world think that such instituted practices may balance the violation of the laws of God. They ought not to overcharge the worship of God with too great a number of them: the rites ought to be grave, simple, and naturally expressive of that which is intended by them. Vain pomp and indecent levity ought to be guarded against; and next to the honour of God and religion, the peace and edification of the society ought to be chiefly considered. Due regard ought to be had to what men can bear, and what may be most suitable to the present state of the whole; and finally, a great respect is due to ancient and established practices. Antiquity does generally beget veneration; and the very changing of what has been long in use does naturally startle many, and discompose a great part of the body. So all changes, unless the expediency of making them is upon other accounts very visible, labour under a great prejudice with the more staid sort of men; for this very reason, because they are changes. But in this matter, no certain or mathematical rules can be given: every one of these that has been named is capable of that variety, by the diversity of times and other circumstances; that since prudence and discretion must rule the use that is to be made of them, that must be left to the conscience and prudence of every person who may be concerned in the management of this authority. He must act as he will answer it to God and to the church; for he must be at liberty in

ART. XX.
applying those general rules to particular times and cases. And a temper must be observed: we must avoid a sullen adhering to things because they were once settled, as if points of honour were to be maintained here; and that it looked like a reproaching a constitution, or the wisdom of a former age, to alter what they did; since it is certain that what was wisely ordered in one time, may be as wisely changed in another: as, on the other hand, all men ought to avoid the imputation of a desultory levity; as if they loved changes for changes' sake. This might give occasion to our adversaries to triumph over us, and might also fill the minds of the weaker among ourselves with apprehensions and scruples.

The next particular asserted in this Article is, *That the church hath authority in matters of faith.* Here a distinction is to be made between an authority that is absolute, and founded on infallibility, and an authority of order. The former is very formally disclaimed by our church; but the second may be well maintained, though we assert no unerring authority. Every single man has a right to search the scriptures, and to take his faith from them; yet it is certain that he may be mistaken in it. It is therefore a much surer way for numbers of men to meet together, and to examine such differences as happen to arise; to consider the arguments of all hands, with the importance of such passages of scripture as are brought into the controversy; and thus to inquire into the whole matter: in which as it is very natural to think that a great company of men should see further than a less number; so there is all reason to expect a good issue of such deliberations, if men proceed in them with due sincerity and diligence; if pride, faction, and interest, do not sway their councils, and if they seek for truth more than for victory.

But what abuses soever may have crept since into the public consultations of the clergy, the apostles at first met and
Act xv. 6. consulted together upon that controversy which was then moved concerning the imposing the Mosaical law upon the Gentiles: they ordered the pastors of the church to be able
Titus i. 9. to convince gainsayers, and not to reject a man as a heretic,
—iii. 10. till after a first and a second admonition. The most likely method both to find out the truth, and to bring such as are in error over to it, is to consult of these matters in common; and that openly and fairly. For if every good man, that prays earnestly to God for the assistance and direction of his Spirit, has reason to look for it; much more may a body of pastors, brought together to seek out the truth, in any point under debate, look for it, if they bring with them sincere and unprejudiced minds, and do pray earnestly to God. In that case, they may expect to be directed and assisted of him. But this depends upon the purity of their hearts, and the earnestness of their endeavours and prayers.

When any synod of the clergy has so far examined a point,

as to settle their opinions about it, they may certainly decree that such is their doctrine: and as they judge it to be more or less important, they may either restrain any other opinion, or may require positive declarations about it, either of all in their communion, or at least of all whom they admit to minister in holy things.

This is only an authority of order for the maintaining of union and edification: and in this a body does no more as it is a body, than what every single individual has a right to do for himself. He examines a doctrine that is laid before him, he forms his own opinion upon it, and pursuant to that he must judge with whom he can hold communion, and from whom he must separate.

When such definitions are made by the body of the pastors of any church, all persons within that church do owe great respect to their decision. Modesty must be observed in descanting upon it, and in disputing about it. Every man that finds his own thoughts differ from it, ought to examine the matter over again, with much attention and care, freeing himself all he can from prejudice and obstinacy; with a just distrust of his own understanding, and an humble respect to the judgment of his superiors.

This is due to the considerations of peace and union, and to that authority which the church has to maintain it. But if, after all possible methods of inquiry, a man cannot master his thoughts, or make them agree with the public decisions, his conscience is not under bonds; since this authority is not absolute, nor grounded upon a promise of infallibility.

This is a tenet that, with relation to national churches and their decisions, is held by the church of Rome, as well as by us: for they place infallibility either in the pope, or in the universal church: but no man ever dreamt of infallibility in a particular or national church: and the point in this Article is only concerning particular churches; for the head of general councils comes in upon the next. *That no church can add any thing as necessary to salvation*, has been already considered upon the sixth Article.

It is certain, that as we owe our hopes of salvation only to Christ, and to what he has done for us; so also it can belong only to him, who procured it to us, to fix the terms upon which we may look for it: nor can any power on earth clog the offers that he makes us in the gospel, with new or other terms than those which we find made there to us. There can be no dispute about this: for unless we believe that there is an infallible authority lodged in the church, to explain the scripture, and to declare tradition; and unless we believe that the scriptures are both obscure and defective, and that the one must be helped by an infallible commentary, and the other supplied by an authentical declarer of tradition; we cannot ascribe an authority to the church, either to contradict the scripture, or to add necessary conditions of salvation to it.

We own, after all, that the church is the depository of the whole scriptures, as the Jews were of the Old Testament: but in that instance of the Jews, we may see that a body of men may be faithful in the copying of a book exactly, and in the handing it down without corrupting it, and yet they may be mistaken in the true meaning of that which they preserve so faithfully. They are expressly called 'the keepers of the oracles of God;' and are nowhere reproved for having attempted upon this *depositum:* and yet for all that fidelity they fell into great errors about some of the most important parts of their religion: which exposed them to the rejecting the Messias, and to their utter ruin.

The church's being called the witness of holy writ, is not to be resolved into any judgment that they pass upon it as a body of men that have authority to judge and give sentence, so that the canonicalness or the uncanonicalness of any book shall depend upon their testimony: but is resolved into this, that such successions and numbers of men, whether of the laity or clergy, have in a course of many ages had these books preserved and read among them; so that it was not possible to corrupt that upon which so many men had their eyes in all the corners and ages of Christendom.

And thus we believe the scriptures to be a book written by inspired men, and delivered by them to the church, upon the testimony of the church that at first received it; knowing that those great matters of fact, contained and appealed to in it, were true: and also upon the like testimony of the succeeding ages, who preserved, read, copied, and translated that book, as they had received it from the first.

The church of Rome is guilty of a manifest circle in this matter: for they say they believe the scriptures upon the authority of the church, and they do again believe the authority of the church, because of the testimony of the scripture concerning it.

This is as false reasoning as can be imagined: for nothing can be proved by another authority till that authority is first fixed and proved: and therefore if the testimony of the church is believed to be sacred, by virtue of a divine grant to it, and that from thence the scriptures have their credit and authority, then the credit due to the church's testimony is antecedent to the credit of the scripture; and so must not be proved by any passages brought from it; otherwise that is a manifest circle. But no circle is committed in our way, who do not prove the scriptures from any supposed authority in the church, that has handed them down to us; but only as they are vast companies of men, who cannot be presumed to have been guilty of any fraud in this matter; it appearing further to be morally impossible for any that should have attempted a fraud in it, to have executed it. When therefore the scripture itself is proved by moral arguments of this kind, we may, according to the strictest rules of reasoning, examine what authority the scripture gives to the pastors of the church met in lesser or greater councils.

ARTICLE XXI.

Of the Authority of General Councils.

General Councils may not be gathered together without the Commandment and will of Princes. And when they be gathered together (forasmuch as they be an Assembly of Men whereof all be not governed with the Spirit and Word of God) they may err, and sometimes have erred even in things pertaining unto God. Wherefore things ordained by them as necessary to Salvation, have neither Strength nor Authority, unless it may be declared that they are taken out of Holy Scriptures.

THERE are two particulars settled in this Article: the one is, the power of calling of councils, at least, an assertion that they cannot be called without the will of princes: the other is, the authority of general councils, that they are not infallible, and that some have erred: and therefore the inference is justly made, that whatever authority they may have in the rule and government of the church, their decisions in matters necessary to salvation ought to be examined by the word of God, and are not to be submitted to, unless it appears that they are conform to the scripture.

The first of these is thus proved: clergymen are subject to their princes, according to these words, 'Let every soul be subject to the higher powers:' if they are then subject to them, they cannot be obliged to go out of their dominions upon the summons of any other; their persons being under the laws and authority of that country to which they belong. This is plain, and seems to need no other proof. It is very visible how much the peace of kingdoms and states is concerned in this point: for if a foreign power should call their clergy away at pleasure, they might be not only left in a great destitution as to religious performances, but their clergy might be practised upon, and sent back to them with such notions, and upon such designs, that, chiefly supposing the immunity of their persons, they might become, as they often were in dark and ignorant ages, the incendiaries of the world, and the disturbers and betrayers of their countries. This is confirmed by the practice of the first ages, after the church had the protection of Christian magistrates: in these the Roman emperors called the first general councils, which is expressly mentioned not only in the histories of the councils, but in their acts; where we find both the writs that summoned them, and their letters, sometimes to the emperors, and sometimes to the churches, which do all set forth their being summoned by the sacred authority of their emperors, without

Rom. xiii. 1.

THE XXXIX ARTICLES.

mentioning any other. In calling some of these councils, it does not appear that the popes were much consulted; and in others we find popes indeed supplicating the emperors to call a council, but nothing that has so much as a shadow of their pretending to an authority to summon it themselves.

This is a thing so plain, and may be so soon seen into by any person who will be at the pains to turn to the editions of the first four general councils made by themselves, not to mention those that followed in the Greek church, that the confidence with which it has been asserted, that they were summoned by the popes, is an instance to shew us that there is nothing at which men, who are once engaged, will stick when their cause requires it. But even since the popes have got this matter into their own hands, though they summon the council, yet they do not pretend to it, nor expect that the world would receive a council as general, or submit to it, unless the princes of Christendom should allow of it, and consent to the publication of the bull. So that, by reason of this, councils are now become almost unpracticable things.

When all Christendom was included within the Roman empire, then the calling of a council lay in the breast and power of one man; and, during the ages of ignorance and superstition, the world was so subjected to the pope's authority, that princes durst seldom oppose their summons, or deny their bishops leave to go when they were so called. But after the scandalous schism in the popedom,* in which there were

---

* 'After the death of Gregory XI. (which happened in the year 1378) the cardinals assembled to consult about choosing a successor, when the people of Rome, fearing lest the vacant dignity should be conferred on a Frenchman, came in a tumultuous manner to the conclave, and with great clamours, accompanied with many outrageous threatenings, insisted that an Italian should be advanced to the popedom. The cardinals, terrified by this uproar, immediately proclaimed Bartholomew de Pergnano, who was a Neapolitan, and archbishop of Bari, and assumed the name of Urban VI. This new pontiff, by his unpolite behaviour, injudicious severity, and intolerable arrogance, had made himself many enemies among people of all ranks, and especially among the leading cardinals. These latter, therefore, tired of his insolence, withdrew from Rome to Agnœni, and from thence to Fondi, a city in the kingdom of Naples, where they elected to the pontificate, Robert, count of Geneva, who took the name of Clement VII., and declared, at the same time, that the election of Urban was nothing more than a mere ceremony, which they had found themselves obliged to perform, in order to calm the turbulent rage of the populace. Which of these two is to be considered as the true and lawful pope, is, to this day, matter of doubt; nor will the records or writings, alleged by the contending parties, enable us to adjust that point with any certainty. Urban remained at Rome: Clement went to Avignon in France. His cause was espoused by France and Spain, Scotland, Sicily, and Cyprus, while all the rest of Europe acknowledged Urban to be the true Vicar of Christ.

'Thus the union of the Latin church under one head was destroyed at the death of Gregory XI., and was succeeded by that deplorable dissension commonly known by the name of the Great Western Schism. This dissension was fomented with such dreadful success, and arose to such a shameful height, that, for the space of fifty years, the church had two or three different heads at the same time; each of the contending popes forming plots, and thundering out anathemas against their competitors.' . . . .

'The great purpose that was aimed at in the convocation of this grand assembly (the council of Constance, A. D. 1414) was the healing of the schism that had so long rent the papacy; and this purpose was happily accomplished. It was solemnly

T

ART. XXI.

for a great while two popes, and at last three at a time, councils began to pretend that the power of governing the church, and of censuring, depriving, and making of popes, was radically in them, as *representing the universal church:* so they fell upon methods to have frequent councils, and that whether both popes and princes should oppose it or not; for they declared both the one and the other to be fallen from their dignity, that should attempt to hinder it. Yet they carried the claim of the freedom of elections, and of the other ecclesiastical immunities, so high, that all that followed upon this was, that the popes being terrified with the attempts begun at Constance, and prosecuted at Basil and Pisa, took pains to have princes on their side, and then made bargains and *concordates* with them, by which they divided all the rights of the church, at least the pretensions to them, between themselves and the princes. Matters of gain and advantage were reserved to the see of Rome; but the points of power and jurisdiction were generally given up to the princes. The temporal authority has by that means prevailed over the spiritual, as much as the spiritual authority had prevailed over the temporal for several ages before. Yet the pretence of a general council is still so specious, that all those in the Roman communion that do not acknowledge the infallibility of their popes, do still support this pretension, that the infallibility is given by Christ to his church; and that in the interval of councils it is in the community of the bishops and pastors of the church; and that when a council meets, then the infallibility is lodged with it; according to that, 'It seemed good to the Holy Ghost, and to us.'

Acts xv. 28.

The first thing to be settled in every question is the mean-

---

declared, in the fourth and fifth sessions of this council, by two decrees, that the Roman pontiff was inferior and subject to a general assembly of the universal church; and the authority of councils was vindicated and maintained by the same decrees in the most effectual manner. This vigorous proceeding prepared the way for the degradation of John XXIII., who, during the twelfth session, was unanimously deposed from the pontificate on account of several flagitious crimes that were laid to his charge, and more especially on account of the scandalous violation of a solemn engagement he had taken, about the beginning of the council, to resign the papal chair if that should appear necessary to the peace of the church; which engagement he broke some weeks after, by a clandestine flight. In the same year (1415) Gregory XII. sent to the council Charles de Malatesta, to make in his name, and as his proxy, a solemn and voluntary resignation of the pontificate. About two years after this, Benedict XIII. was deposed by a solemn resolution of the council, and Otto de Colonna raised, by the unanimous suffrages of the cardinals, to the high dignity of head of the church, which he ruled under the title of Martin V. Benedict, who resided still at Perpignan, was far from being disposed to submit either to the decree of the council which deposed him, or to the determination of the cardinals, with respect to his successor. On the contrary, he persisted until the day of his death, which happened in the year 1423, in assuming the title, the prerogatives, and the authority, of the papacy. And when this obstinate man was dead, a certain Spaniard, named Giles Munios, was chosen pope in his place, by two cardinals, under the auspicious patronage of Alphonsus king of Sicily, and adopted the title of Clement VIII.; but this sorry pontiff, in the year 1429, was persuaded to resign his pretensions to the papacy, and to leave the government of the church to Martin V.' *Mosheim.*—[Ed.]

ing of the terms: so we must begin and examine what makes ART.
a general council; whether all the bishops must be present in XXI.
person, or by proxy? And what share the laity, or the princes
that are thought to represent their people, ought to have in a
council? It is next to be considered, whether a general citation
is enough to make a council general, were the appearance of
the bishops ever so small at their first opening? It is next to
be considered, whether any come thither and sit there as representing others; and if votes ought to be reckoned according to the numbers of the bishops, or of the others who depute and send them? And whether nations ought to vote in a
body as integral parts of the church; or every single bishop
by himself? And finally, whether the decisions of councils
must be unanimous, before they can be esteemed infallible?
or whether the major vote, though exceeding only by one, or
if some greater inequality is necessary; such as two-thirds, or
any other proportion? That there may be just cause of raising
scruples upon every one of these, is apparent at first view. It
is certain, a bare name cannot qualify a number of bishops
sitting together, to be this general council. The number of
bishops does it not neither. A hundred and fifty was a small
number at Constantinople: even the famous three hundred
and eighteen at Nice were far exceeded by those at Arimini.
All the first general councils were made up for the most part
of eastern bishops; there being a very inconsiderable number
of the western among any of them; scarce any at all being to
be found in some. If this had been the body to whom Christ
had left this infallibility, it cannot be imagined but that some
definition or description of the constitution of it would have
been given us in the scripture: and the profound silence that
is about it gives just occasion to think, that how wise and how
good soever such a constitution may be, if well pursued, yet it
is not of a divine institution; otherwise somewhat concerning
so important a head as this is must have been mentioned in
the scripture.

The natural idea of a general council, is a meeting of all the
bishops of Christendom, or at least of proxies instructed by
them and their clergy. Now if any will stand to this description, then we are very sure that there was never yet a true
general council; which will appear to every one that reads the
subscriptions of the councils. Therefore we must conclude,
that general councils are not constituted by a divine authority;
since we have no direction given us from God, by which we
may know what they are, and what is necessary to their constitution. And we cannot suppose that God has granted any
privileges, much less infallibility, which is the greatest of all,
to a body of men, of whom, or of whose constitution, he has
said nothing to us. For suppose we should yield that there
were an infallibility lodged in general in the church diffusive,
so that the church in some part or other shall be always pre-

ART.
XXI.
served from error; yet the restraining this to the greater number of such bishops as shall happen to come to a council, they living perhaps near it, or being more capable and more forward to undertake a journey, being healthier, richer, or more active, than others; or, which is as probable, because it has often fallen out, they being picked out by parties or princes to carry on cabals, and manage such intrigues as may be on foot at the council; the restraining the infallibility, I say, to the greater number of such persons, unless there is a divine authority for doing it, is the transferring the infallibility from the whole body to a select number of persons, who of themselves are the least likely to consent to the engrossing this privilege to the majority of their body, it being their interest to maintain their right to it, free from intrigue or management.

We need not wonder if such things have happened in the latter ages, when Nazianzen laments the corruptions, the ambition, and the contentions, that reigned in those assemblies in his own time; so that he never desired to see any more of them. He was not only present at one of the general councils, but he himself felt the effects of jealousy and violence in it.

Further, it will appear a thing incredible, that there is an infallibility in councils because they are called general, and are assembled out of a great many kingdoms and provinces; when we see them go backward and forward, according to the influences of courts, and of interests directed from thence. We know how differently councils decreed in the Arian controversies; and what a variety of them Constantius set up against that at Nice. So it was in the Eutychian heresy, approved in the second council at Ephesus, but soon after condemned at Chalcedon. So it was in the business of images, condemned at Constantinople in the east; but soon after upon another change at court maintained in the second at Nice; and not long after condemned in a very numerous council at Francfort. And in the point in hand, as to the authority of councils, it was asserted at Constance and Basil, but condemned in the Lateran; and was upon the matter laid aside at Trent. Here were great numbers of all hands; both sides took the name of general councils.

It will be a further prejudice against this, if we see great violence and disorders entering into the management of some councils; and craft and artifice into the conduct of others. Numbers of factious and furious monks came to some councils, and drove on matters by their clamours; so it was at Ephesus. We see gross fraud in the second at Nice, both in the persons set up to represent the absent patriarchs, and in the books and authorities that were vouched for the worship of images. The intrigues at Trent, as they are set out even by cardinal Pallavicini, were more subtile, but not less apparent, nor less scandalous. Nothing was trusted to a session, till it was first canvassed in congregations; which were what a committee of the whole house is in our parliaments; and then every man's vote was known; so that there was hereby great occasion given for practice. This alone, if there had been no more, shewed plainly that they themselves knew they were not guided by the Spirit of God, or by infallibility; since a session was not thought safe to be ventured on, but after a long previous canvassing.

Another question remains yet to be cleared, concerning their manner of proceeding; whether the infallibility is affixed to their vote, whatsoever their proceedings may be? or whether they are bound to discuss matters fully? The first cannot be said, unless it is pretended that they vote by a special inspiration. If the second is allowed, then we must examine both what makes a full discussion; and whether they have made it?

If we find opinions falsely represented; if books that are spurious have been relied on; if passages of scripture, or of the fathers, on which it appears the stress of the decision has turned, have been manifestly misunderstood and wrested, so that in a more enlightened age no person pretends to justify the authority that determined them, can we imagine that there should be more truth in their conclusions, than we do plainly see was in the premises out of which they were drawn? So it must either be said, that they vote by an immediate inspiration, or all persons cannot be bound to submit to their judgment till they have examined their methods of proceeding, and the grounds on which they went: and when all is done, the question comes, concerning the authority of such decrees after they are made; whether it follows immediately upon their being made, or must stay for the confirmatory bulls? If it must stay for the bull, then the infallibility is not in the council: and that is only a more solemn way of preparing matters in order to the laying them before the pope. If they are infallible before the confirmation, then the infallibility is wholly in the council; and the subsequent bull does, instead of confirming their decrees, derogate much from them: for to pretend to confirm them, imports that they wanted that addition of authority, which destroys the supposition of their infallibility, since what is infallible cannot be made stronger; and the pretending to add strength to it, implies that it is not infallible. Human constitutions may be indeed so modelled, that there must be a joint concurrence before a law can be made: and though it is the last consent that settles the law, yet the previous consents were necessary steps to the giving it the authority of a law.

And thus it is not to be denied, but that, as to the matters of government, the church may cast herself into such a model, that as by a decree of the council of Nice the bishops of a province might conclude nothing without the consent of the

ART.
XXI.
metropolitan; so another decree might even limit a general council to stay for the consent of one or more patriarchs. But this must only take place in matters of order and government, which are left to the disposal of the church, but not in decisions about matters of faith. For if there is an infallibility in the church, it must be derived from a special grant made by Christ to his church: and it must go according to the nature of that grant, unless it can be pretended that there is a clause in that grant, empowering the church to dispose of it, and model it at pleasure. For if there is no such power, as it is plain there is not, then Christ's grant is either to a single person, or to the whole community: if to a single person, then the infallibility is wholly in him, and he is to manage it as he thinks best: for if he calls a council, it is only an act of his humility and condescension, to hear the opinions of many in different corners of the church, that so he may know all that comes from all quarters: it may also seem a prudent way to make his authority to be the more easily borne and submitted to, since what is gently managed is best obeyed: but after all, these are only prudential and discreet methods. The infallibility must be only in him, if Christ has by the grant tied him to such a succession. Whereas on the other hand, if the infallibility is granted to the whole community, or to their representatives, then all the applications that they may make to any one *see* must only be in order to the execution of their decrees, like the addresses that they make to princes for the civil sanction. But still the infallibility is where Christ put it. It rests wholly in their decision, and belongs only to that: and any other confirmation that they desire, unless it be restrained singly to the execution of their decrees, is a wound given by themselves to their own infallibility, if not a direct disclaiming of it.

When the confirmation of the council is over, a new difficulty arises concerning the receiving the decrees: and here it may be said, that if Christ's grant is to the whole community, so that a council is only the authentical declarer of the tradition, the whole body of the church that is possessed of the tradition, and conveys it down, must have a right to examine the decision that the council has made, and so is not bound to receive it, but as it finds it to be conformable to tradition.

Here it is to be supposed, that every bishop, or at the least all the bishops of any national church, know best the tradition of their own church and nation: and so they will have a right to re-examine things after they have been adjudged in a general council.

This will entirely destroy the whole pretension to infallibility: and yet either this ought to have been done after the councils at Arimini, or the second of Ephesus, or else the world must have received semi-Arianism, or Eutychianism, implicitly from them. It is also no small prejudice against this opinion, that the church was constituted, the scriptures were received, many heresies were rejected, and the persecutions were gone through, in a course of three centuries; in all which time there was nothing that could pretend to be called a general council. And when the ages came, in which councils met often, neither the councils themselves, who must be supposed to understand their own authority best, nor those who wrote in defence of their decrees, who must be supposed to be inclined enough to magnify their authority, being of the same side; neither of these, I say, ever pretended to argue for their opinions, from the infallibility of those councils that decreed them.

They do indeed speak of them with great respect, as of bodies of men that were guided by the Spirit of God: and so do we of our reformers, and of those who prepared our Liturgy: but we do not ascribe infallibility to them, and no more did they. Nor did they lay the stress of their arguments upon the authority of such decisions; they knew that the objection might have been made as strong against them, as they could put the argument for them; and therefore they offered to wave the point, and to appeal to the scripture, setting aside the definitions that had been made in councils both ways.

To conclude this argument.

If the infallibility is supposed to be in councils, then the church may justly apprehend that she has lost it: for as there has been no council that has pretended to that title, now during one hundred and thirty years, so there is no great probability of our ever seeing another. The charge and noise, the expectations and disappointments, of that at Trent, has taught the world to expect nothing from one: they plainly see that the management from Rome must carry every thing in a council: neither princes nor people, no nor the bishops themselves, desire or expect to see one.

The claim set up at Rome for infallibility makes the demand of one seem not only needless there, but to imply a doubting of their authority, when other methods are looked after, which will certainly be always unacceptable to those who are in possession, and act as if they were infallible: nor can it be apprehended, that they will desire a council to reform those abuses in discipline, which are all occasioned by that absolute and universal authority of which they are now possessed.

So by all the judgments that can be made from the state of things, from the interests of men, and the last management at Trent, one may without a spirit of prophecy conclude, that, unless Christendom puts on a new face, there will be no more general councils. And so here infallibility

ART. XXI.

Matt. xviii. 17.

is at an end, and has left the church at least for a very long interval.

It remains that those passages should be considered that are brought to support this authority. Christ says, 'Tell the church; and if he neglects to hear the church, let him be unto thee as a heathen man, and a publican.'

These words in themselves, and separated from all that went before, seem to speak this matter very fully: but when the occasion of them, and the matter that is treated of in them, are considered, nothing can be plainer than that our Saviour is speaking of such private differences as may arise among men, and of the practice of forgiving injuries, and composing their differences. 'If thy brother sin against thee;' first, private endeavours were to be used; then the interposition of friends was to be tried; and finally, the matter was to be referred to the body, or assembly, to which they belonged: and those who could not be gained by such methods, were no more to be esteemed brethren, but were to be looked on as very bad men, like heathens. They might upon such refractoriness be excommunicated, and prosecuted afterwards in temporal courts, since they had by their perverseness forfeited all sort of right to that tenderness and charity that is due to true Christians.

This exposition does so fully agree to the occasion and scope of these words, that there is no colour of reason to carry them further.*

1 Tim. iii. 15.

The character given to the church of Ephesus, in St. Paul's Epistle to Timothy, that it was 'the pillar and ground of truth,' is a figurative expression: and it is never safe to build upon metaphors, much less to lay much weight upon them.

The Jews described their synagogues by such honourable characters, in which it is known how profuse all the eastern nations are. These are by St. Paul applied to the church of Ephesus: for he there speaks of the church where Timothy was then, in which he instructs him to behave himself well. It has visibly a relation to those inscriptions that were made on pillars which rested upon firm pedestals: but whatsoever the strict importance of the metaphor may be, it is a metaphor, and therefore it can be no argument. Christ's promise

John xvi. 13.

of the Spirit to his apostles, that should 'lead them into all

---

* 'But the command to tell the offence of our private brother is not a command to tell it to the church catholic met in council; for then this precept could not have been obeyed for the first three centuries, no such council ever meeting till the time of Constantine. Then, secondly, the church must always be assembled in such a council, because doubtless there are, and will be always, persons thus offending against their Christian brethren. And thirdly, then every private person must be obliged, at what distance soever he be from it, and how unable soever he may be to do so, to travel to this council, and lay his private grievance before them: all which are palpable absurdities.' *Whitby.*—[ED.]

truth,' relates visibly to that extraordinary inspiration by which they were to be acted, and that was, 'to shew them things to come;' so that a succession of prophecy may be inferred from these words, as well as of infallibility. ART. XXI

Those words of our Saviour, with which St. Matthew concludes his Gospel, 'Lo, I am with you always, even to the end of the world,' infer no infallibility, but only a promise of assistance and protection: which was a necessary encouragement to the apostles, when they were sent upon so laborious a commission, that was to involve them in so much danger. God's 'being with any,' his 'walking with them,' his 'being in the midst of them,' his 'never leaving nor forsaking them,' are expressions often used in the scripture, which signify no more but God's watchful providence, guiding, supporting, and protecting his people: all this is far from infallibility. Mat.xxviii. 20.

2 Cor. vi. 16.
Heb. xiii. 5.

The last objection to be proposed is that which seems to relate most to the point in hand, taken from the decree made by a council at Jerusalem, which begins, 'It seemed good to the Holy Ghost, and to us:' from which they infer, that the Holy Ghost is present with councils, and that what seems good to them is also approved by the Holy Ghost. But it will not be easy to prove that this was such a council, as to be a pattern to succeeding ones to copy after it. We find *brethren* are here joined with the apostles themselves: now since these were no other than the laity, here an inference will be made, that will not easily go down. If they sat and voted with the apostles, it will seem strange to deny them the same privilege among bishops. By *elders* here it seems *presbyters* are meant, and this will give them an entrance into a general council, out of which they cannot be well excluded, if the laity are admitted. But here was no citation, no time given to all churches to send their bishops or proxies: it was an occasional meeting of such of the apostles as happened to be then at Jerusalem, who called to them the *elders* or *presbyters*, and other Christians at Jerusalem: for the Holy Ghost was then poured out so plentifully on so many, that no wonder if there were then about that truly *mother church* a great many of both sorts, who were of such eminence, that the apostles might desire them to meet and to join with them. Acts xv. 28.

The apostles were divinely assisted in the delivering that commission which our Saviour gave them in charge, 'To preach to every creature;' and so were infallibly assisted in the executing of it: yet when other matters fell in, which were no parts of that commission, they, no doubt, did as St. Paul, who sometimes *writ by permission*, as well as at other times *by commandment*: of which he gives notice, by saying, 'It is I, and not the Lord:' he suggested advices, which to him, according to his prudence and experience, seemed to be well Mark xvi. 15.
1 Cor. vii. 6, 12.

ART. XXI.
Ver. 40.
Ver. 25.

founded; and he offered them with great sincerity; for though he had some reason to think that what he proposed, flowed from the 'Spirit of the Lord,' from that inspiration that was acting him; yet because that did not appear distinctly to him, he speaks with reserves, and says, he 'gives his judgment as one that had obtained mercy of the Lord to be faithful.' So the apostles here, receiving no inspiration to direct them in this case, but observing well what St. Peter put them in mind of, concerning God's sending him by a special vision to preach to the Gentiles, and that God had poured out the Holy Ghost on them, even as he had done upon the apostles, who were

Acts xv. 9. Jews by nature, and that 'he did put no difference in that between Jews and Gentiles, purifying the hearts of the Gentiles by faith:' they upon this did by their judgment conclude from thence, that what God had done in the particular instance of Cornelius, was now to be extended to all the Gentiles. So by this we see that those words, 'seemed good to the Holy Ghost,' relate to the case of Cornelius; and those words, 'seemed good to us,' import that they resolved to extend that to be a general rule to all the Gentiles.

This gives the words a clear and distinct sense, which agrees with all that had gone before; whereas it will otherwise look very strange to see them add their authority to that of the Holy Ghost; which is too absurd to suppose: nor will it be easy to give any other consisting sense to these words.

Here is no precedent of a council, much less of a general one: but a decision is made by men that were in other things divinely inspired, which can have no relation to the judgments of other councils. And thus it appears that none of those places, which are brought to prove the infallibility of councils, come up to the point: for so great and so important a matter as this is, must be supposed to be either expressly declared in the scriptures, or not at all.

The Article affirming, that *some general councils have erred*, must be understood of councils that pass for such; and that may be called general councils, much better than many others that go by that name: for that at Arimini was both very numerous, and was drawn out of many different provinces. As to the strict notion of a general council, there is great reason to believe that there was never any assembly to which it will be found to agree. And for the four general councils, which this church declares she receives, they are received only because we are persuaded from the scriptures that their decisions were made according to them: that the Son is truly God, of the same substance with the Father. That the Holy Ghost is also truly God. That the divine nature was truly united to the human in Christ; and that in one person. That both natures remained distinct; and that the human nature was not swallowed up of the divine. These truths we find in the scriptures, and therefore we believe them. We reverence those councils for the sake of their doctrine; but do not believe the doctrine for the authority of the councils. There appeared too much of human frailty in some of their other proceedings, to give us such an implicit submission to them, as to believe things only because they so decided them.

ARTICLE XXII.

Of Purgatory.

The Romish Doctrine concerning Purgatory, Pardons, Worshipping and Adoration, as well of Images as of Relicks, and also Invocation of Saints, is a fond thing, vainly invented and grounded upon no Warrant of Scripture, but rather repugnant to the Word of God.

THERE are two small variations in this Article, from that published in king Edward's reign. What is here called the *Romish doctrine*, is there called the *doctrine of schoolmen*. The plain reason of this is, that these errors were not so fully espoused by the body of the Roman church, when those Articles were first published, so that some writers that softened matters threw them upon the schoolmen; and therefore the Article was cautiously worded, in laying them there: but before these that we have now were published, the *decree* and *canons* concerning the *mass* had passed at Trent, in which most of the heads of this Article are either affirmed or supposed; though the formal decree concerning them was made some months after these Articles were published.* This will serve

---

* This point deserves serious attention. Many of those articles against which we protest are so far from being Catholic doctrines, that they were not defined, and therefore not universally received even in the papal church until after the Reformation. This fact the champions of popery cannot deny. This subject is discussed by Stillingfleet with great ability in his ' Reformation of the Church of England justified,' in which he thus notices the assertion that we have rejected catholic truth:—' According to your principles that which differenceth a catholic doctrine from a particular opinion, is the church's definition; before then the church had passed a definition in these points, they could not be held as catholic doctrines. To make this somewhat clearer, because it is necessary for undeceiving those who are told, as you tell us here, that at the Reformation we rejected such things which were universally owned for catholic doctrines, which is so far from being true, that it is impossible they should be owned for such by the church of Rome upon your own principles. For, I pray, tell us, are there not several sorts of opinions among you at this day, none of which are pretended to be catholic doctrines? and this you constantly tell us, when we object to you your dissensions about them. As for instance, the pope's personal infallibility, the superiority of popes over general councils, the immaculate conception of the blessed Virgin, the disputes about predestination, &c. When we tell you of your differences in these points, you answer, that these hinder not the unity of the church, because these are only in matters of opinion; and that it is not *de fide* that men should hold either way. When we demand the reason of this difference concerning these things, your answer is, that the church hath defined some things to be believed, and not others; that what the church hath defined, is to be looked on as catholic doctrine, and the deniers of it are guilty of heresy; but where the church hath not defined, those are not catholic doctrines, but only at best but pious opinions, and men may be good catholics and yet differ about them. I pray, tell me, is this your doctrine or is it not? If not, there may be heretics within your church, as well as without. If it be your doctrine, apply it to the matters in hand. Were these things defined by the church at the beginning of the Reformation? If they were, produce those definitions for all those things which

to justify that diversity. The second difference is only the leaving out of a severe word. *Perniciously repugnant to the word of God*, was put at first; but *perniciously* being considered to be only a hard word, they judged very right in the second edition of them, that it was enough to say *repugnant to the word of God.*

There are in this Article five particulars, that are all ingredients in the doctrine and worship of the church of Rome; purgatory, pardons, the worship of images, and of relics, and the invocation of saints; that are rejected not only as illgrounded, brought in and maintained without good warrants from the scripture, but as contrary to it.

The first of these is purgatory; concerning which, the doctrine of the church of Rome is, that every man is liable both to temporal and to eternal punishment for his sins; that God, upon the account of the death and intercession of Christ, does indeed pardon sin as to its eternal punishment; but the sinner is still liable to temporal punishment, which he must expiate by acts of penance and sorrow in this world, together with such other sufferings as God shall think fit to lay upon him: but if he does not expiate these in this life, there is a state of suffering and misery in the next world, where the soul is to bear the temporal punishment of its sins; which may continue longer or shorter, till the day of judgment. And in order to the shortening this, the prayers and supererogations of men here on earth, or the intercession of the saints in heaven, but above all things, the sacrifice of the mass, are of great efficacy. This is the doctrine of the church of Rome, asserted in the councils of Florence and Trent.* What has been taught among

---

you say were owned as catholic doctrines then ; that we may see, that at least in the judgment of your church they were accounted so. Tell us, when and where those doctrines were defined before the Council of Trent? and, I hope you will not say, that was before the beginning of the Reformation. If then there were no such definitions concerning them, they could not by your church be accounted as catholic doctrines ; at the most, they could be but only pious opinions, as that of the pope's infallibillity among you is, and consequently men might be catholics still, though they disputed or denied them. And how then come the Protestants to be accounted heretics in their reformation, if, upon your own principles, those things which they denied were then no catholic doctrines ?'—[ED.]

* The council of Florence decreed, 'That if true penitents depart in the love of God, before they have satisfied for their sins of omission, or commission, by fruits of repentance, their souls go to purgatory to be purged.' The council of Trent has thus decreed concerning this doctrine :—

'*Decretum de purgatorio.*

'Cum catholica ecclesia, spiritu sancto edocta, ex sacris litteris, et antiqua patrum traditione, in sacris conciliis, et novissime in hac œcumenica synodo docuerit, purgatorium esse ; animasque ibi detentas, fidelium suffragiis, potissimum vero acceptabili altaris sacrificio juvari ; præcipit sancta synodus episcopis, ut sanam de purgatorio doctrinam, a sanctis patribus et sacris conciliis traditam, a Christi fidelibus credi, teneri, doceri, et ubique prædicari diligenter studeant. Apud rudem vero plebem difficiliores ac subtiliores quæstiones, quæque ad ædificationem non faciunt, et ex quibus plerumque nulla fit pietatis accessio, a popularibus concionibus secludantur. Incerta item, vel quæ specie falsi laborant, evulgari ac tractari non permittant. Ea vero quæ ad curiositatem quamdam aut superstitionem spectant, vel turpe lucrum sapiunt, tanquam scandala et fidelium offendicula prohibeant. Curent autem episcopi ut fidelium vivorum suffragia, missarum scilicet

ART. them concerning the nature and the degrees of those torments,
XXII. though supported by many pretended apparitions and revelations, is not to be imputed to the whole body; and is indeed only the doctrine of schoolmen, though it is generally preached and infused into the consciences of the people. Therefore I shall only examine that which is the established doctrine of the whole Roman church. And first as to the foundation of it, that sins are only pardoned, as to their eternal punishment,
Rom. v. 1. to those 'who being justified by faith have peace with God through our Lord Jesus Christ:' there is not a colour for it in the scriptures. Remission of sins is in general that with which the preaching of the gospel ought always to begin; and this is so often repeated, without any such reserve, that it is a high assuming upon God, and his attributes of goodness and mercy, to limit these when he has not limited them; but has expressly said, that this is a main part of the new covenant, that
Jer. xxxi. 'he will remember our sins and iniquities no more.' Now it
34.
Heb. viii. seems to be a maxim, not only of the law of nations, but of
12. nature, that all offers of pardon are to be understood in the full extent of the words, without any secret reserves or limitations; unless they are plainly expressed. An indemnity being offered by a prince to persuade his subjects to return to their obedience, in the fullest words possible, without any reserves made in it, it would be looked on as a very perfidious thing, if when the subjects come in upon it, trusting to it, they should be told that they were to be secured by it against capital punishments; but that, as to all inferior punishments, they were still at mercy. We do not dispute whether God, if he had thought fit so to do, might not have made this distinction; nor do we deny that the grace of the gospel had been infinitely valuable, if it had offered us only the pardon of sin with relation to its eternal punishment, and had left the temporal punishment on us, to be expiated by ourselves. But then we say, this ought to have been expressed: the distinction ought to have been made between temporal and eternal: and we ought not to have been drawn into a covenant with God, by words that do plainly import an entire pardon and oblivion, upon which there lay a limited sense that was not to be told the

---

sacrificia, orationes, eleemosynæ, aliaque pietatis opera, quæ a fidelibus pro aliis fidelibus defunctis fieri consuverunt, secundum ecclesiæ instituta pie et devote fiant; et quæ pro illis ex testatorum fundationibus, vel alia ratione debentur, non perfunctorie, sed a sacerdotibus, et ecclesiæ ministris, et aliis, qui hoc præstare tenentur, diligenter et accurate persolvantur.'—*Sessio* xxv.

We see from the above how careful the council was not to entangle itself in the dispute respecting the nature of purgatory; the decree simply stating that there is such a place. Equally vague is the article in the creed of pope Pius IV. on this subject. The catechism of the council of Trent made, however, a bolder step, and has informed us that purgatory is a fire in which the souls of the faithful are tormented.

'Præterea est purgatorius ignis, quo piorum animæ ad definitum tempus cruciatæ, expiantur ut eis in æternam patriam ingressus patere possit, in quam nihil coinquinatum ingreditur.' *Cat. ad Par. De Symbolo, Art. descendit ad inferos.*
—[ED.]

world till it was once well engaged in the Christian religion. Upon these reasons it is that we conclude, that this doctrine not being contained in the scriptures, is not only without any warrant in them, but that it is contrary to those full offers of mercy, peace, and oblivion, that are made in the gospel; it is contrary to the truth and veracity, and to the justice and goodness of God, to affirm that there are reserves to be understood for punishments, when the offers and promises are made to us in such large and unlimited expressions.

ART. XVII.

Thus we lay our foundation in this matter, which does very fully overthrow theirs. We do not deny but that God does in this world punish good men for those sins, which yet are forgiven them through Christ, according to those words in the Psalm, 'Thou wast a God that forgavest them, though thou tookest vengeance of their inventions:' but this is a consideration quite of another nature. God, in the government of this world, thinks fit, by his Providence, sometimes to interpose in visible blessings, as well as judgments, to shew how he protects and favours the good, and punishes the bad; and that the bad actions of good men are odious to him, even though he has received their persons into his favour. He has also in the gospel plainly excepted the government of this world, and the secret methods of his Providence, out of the mercy that he has promised, by the warnings that are given to all Christians to prepare for crosses and afflictions in this life. He has made faith and patience in adversities a main condition of this new covenant; he has declared, that these are not the punishments of an angry God, but the chastisements of a kind and merciful Father, who designs by them both to shew to the world the impartiality of his justice in punishing some crying sins in a very signal manner, and to give good men deep impressions of their odiousness, to oblige them to a severer repentance for them, and to a greater watchfulness against them; as also to give the world such examples of resignation and patience under them, that they may edify others by that, as much as by their sins they may have offended them. So that, upon all these accounts, it seems abundantly clear, that no argument can be drawn from the temporal punishments of good men for their sins in this world, to a reserve of others in another state. The one are clearly mentioned and reserved in the offers of mercy that are made in the gospel, whereas the others are not. This being the most plausible thing that they say for this distinction of those twofold punishments, it is plain that there is no foundation for it.

Ps. xcix. 8.

As for those words of Christ's, 'ye shall not come out till ye have paid the uttermost farthing;' from which they would infer, that there is a state in which, after we shall be cast into prison, we are paying off our debts: this, if an argument at all, will prove too much; that in hell the damned are clearing

Mat. v. 26.

scores; and that they shall be delivered when all is paid off. For by *prison* there, that only can be meant, as appears by the whole contexture of the discourse, and by other parables of the like nature. It is a figure taken from a man imprisoned for a great debt; and the continuance of it, till the last farthing is paid, does imply their perpetual continuance in that state, since the debt is too great to be ever paid off. From a phrase in a parable, no consequence is to be drawn, beyond that which is the true scope of the parable, which in this particular is only intended by our Saviour, to shew the severe punishment of those who hate implacably, which is a sin that does certainly deserve hell, and not purgatory.

Our Saviour's words concerning the *sin* against 'the Holy Ghost,' that 'it is neither forgiven in this life, nor in that which is to come,' is also urged to prove, that some sins are pardoned in the next life, which are not pardoned in this. But still this will seem a stronger argument against the eternity of hell-torments, than for purgatory; and will rather import, that the damned may at last be pardoned their sins, since these are the only persons whose sins are not pardoned in this world; for of those who are justified, it cannot be said that their sins are not forgiven them, and such only go to purgatory: therefore, either this is only a general way of speaking, to exclude all hopes of pardon, and to imply that God's judgments will pursue such blasphemers, both in this life, and in the next; or, if we will understand them more critically, by *this life*, or *this age*, and the *next*, according to a common opinion and phrase of the Jews, which is founded on the prophecies, are to be understood the *dispensation of the Law*, and the *dispensation of the Messias*; the *age to come* being a common phrase for the times of the Messias; according to those words in the Epistle to the Hebrews, 'He hath not put in subjection to angels the world to come.' By the Mosaical law, sacrifices were only received, and by consequence pardon was offered for sins of a less heinous nature; but those that were more heinous were to be punished by death, or by *cutting off* without mercy; whereas a full promise of the pardon of all sins is offered in the gospel: so that the meaning of these words of Christ's is, that such a blasphemy was a sin not only beyond the pardon offered in the Law of Moses, which was the *age* that then was; but that it was a sin beyond that pardon which was to be offered by the Messias in the *age to come*, that is, in the kingdom of heaven, that was then at hand. But these words can by no means be urged to prove this distinction of temporal and eternal punishment; therefore we must conclude, that since 'repentance and remission of sins' are joined together in the first commission to preach the gospel; and since life, peace, and salvation, are promised to such as believe, that all this is to be understood simply and plainly, without any other limitation or exception than that

which is expressed, which is only of such chastisements as ART. XXII.
God thinks fit to exercise good men with in this life.

In the next place, we shall consider what reason we have to reject the doctrine of purgatory; as we have already seen how weak the foundation is upon which it is built. The scripture speaks to us of two states after this life, of happiness, and misery; and as it divides all mankind into good and bad, into those that do good and those that do evil, into believers and unbelievers, righteous and sinners; so it proposes always the end of the one to be everlasting happiness and the end of the other to be everlasting punishment, without the least hint of any middle state after death. So that it is very plain there is nothing said in scripture of men too good to be damned, but not so good as to be immediately saved. Now, if there had been yet a great deal to be suffered after death, and that there were many very effectual ways to prevent and avoid, or at least to shorten those sufferings; and if the apostles knew this, and yet said not a word of it, neither in their first sermons nor in their Epistles; here was a great treachery in the discharge of their function, and that to the souls of men, not to warn them of their danger, nor to direct them to the proper methods of avoiding it; but, on the contrary, to speak and write to them, just as we can suppose impostors would have done, to terrify those who would not receive their gospel, with eternal damnation, but not to say a word to those who received it, of their danger, in case they lived not up to that exactness that their religion required, and yet upon the main adhered to it and followed it. This is a method that does not agree with common honesty, not to say inspiration. A fair way of proceeding, is to make men sensible of dangers of all sorts, and to shew them how to avoid them; the apostles told their converts, that 'through much tribulation we must enter into the kingdom of heaven;' they assured them, that 'their present sufferings were not worthy to be compared to the glory that was to be revealed;' and that 'those light afflictions, which are for a moment, wrought for them a more exceeding and eternal weight of glory.' Here, if they knew any thing of purgatory, a powerful consideration was passed over in silence, that by these afflictions they should be delivered from those torments. Acts xiv. 22. Rom. viii. 18. 2 Cor. iv. 17.

This argument goes further than mere silence; though that is very strong. The scriptures speak always as if the one did immediately follow the other; and that the saints, or true Christians, pass from the miseries of this state to the glories of the next. So does our Saviour represent the matter in the parable of Lazarus and the rich glutton; whose souls were presently carried to their different abodes; the one to be comforted, as the other was tormented. He promised also to the repenting thief, 'To-day thou shalt be with me in paradise.' St. Paul comforts himself, in the apprehension of his dissolu- Luke xvi. 25. Luke xxiii. 43.

U

ART XXII.
2 Tim. iv. 8.
Phil. i. 23.
2 Cor. v. 6, 8.
v. 1, 2.

Heb. xi. 10.

Rev. xiv. 13.

2 Ep. John, ver. 8.
1 Cor. xv. 41.

tion that was approaching, with the prospect of the 'crown of righteousness that should be given him' after death; and so he states these two as certain consequents one of another, 'to be dissolved and to be with Christ, to be absent from the body, and present with the Lord:' and he makes it appear that it was no peculiar privilege that he promised to himself, but that which all Christians had a right to expect; for he says in general, this 'we know that if our earthly house of this tabernacle be dissolved, we have a building of God, a house not made with hands, eternal in the heavens.' In the Epistle to the Hebrews the patriarchs under the old dispensation are represented as 'looking for that city whose builder and founder is God:' though in that state the manifestations of another life were more imperfect than in this; in which 'life and immortality are brought to light;' they being veiled and darkened in that state. And finally, St. John heard a voice commanding him to write, 'Blessed are the dead who die in the Lord (that is, being true Christians) from henceforth (or immediately): Yea, saith the Spirit, that they may rest from their labours; and their works do follow them.' From the solemnity with which these words are delivered, they carry in them an evidence sufficient to determine the whole matter. So that we must have very hard thoughts of the sincerity of the writers of the New Testament, and very much disparage their credit, not to say their inspiration, if we can imagine that there are scenes of suffering, and those very dismal ones, to be gone through, of which they gave the world no sort of notice; but spoke in the same style that we do, who believe no such dismal interval between the death of good men and their final blessedness. The scriptures do indeed speak of a *full reward* and of different degrees of glory, 'as one star exceeds another.' They do also represent the day of judgment upon the resurrection of the body, as that which gives the full and entire possession of blessedness; so that from hence some have thought, upon very probable grounds, that the blessed, though admitted to happiness immediately upon their death, yet were not so completely happy as they shall be after the resurrection: and in this there arose a diversity of opinions, which is very natural to all who will go and form systems out of some general hints. Some thought that the souls of good men were at rest, and in a good measure happy, but that they did not see God before the resurrection. Others thought that Christ was to come down and reign visibly upon earth a thousand years before the end of the world; and that the saints were to rise and to reign with him, some sooner and some later. Some thought that the last conflagration was so to affect all, that every one was to pass through it, and that it was to give the last and highest purification to those bodies that were then to be glorified; but that the better Christians that any had been, they should feel the less of the pain of that

last fire. These opinions were very early entertained in the ART.
church: an itch of intruding too far into things which men did XXII.
not thoroughly understand, concerning angels, began to disturb the church even in the days of the apostles: which made
St. Paul charge the Colossians to beware of vain philosophy. Col. ii 8,
Plato thought there was a middle sort of men, who though 18.
they had sinned, yet had repented of it, and were in a curable
condition, and that they went down for some time into hell,
to be purged and absolved by grievous torments. The Jews
had also a conceit, that the souls of some men continued for
a year, going up and down in a state of purgation. From
these opinions somewhat of a curiosity in describing the
degrees of the next state began pretty early to enter into the
church.

As for that opinion of the Platonists, and the fictions of
Homer and Virgil, setting forth the complaints of souls departed, for their not being relieved by prayers and sacrifices,
though these perhaps are the true sources of the doctrine of
purgatory, and of redeeming souls out of it, yet we are not so
much concerned in them, as in what is represented to us by
the author of the second book of the Maccabees, concerning
the sacrifice that was offered by Judas Maccabeus, for those,
about whom, after they were killed, they found such things
as shewed that they had defiled themselves with the idolatry
of the heathens. All this is of less authority with us, who do
not acknowledge that book to be canonical: according to
what was set out in its proper place. And although we set a
due value upon some of the apocryphal books, yet others are
of a lower character. The first book of Maccabees is a very
grave history, writ with much exactness and a true judgment;
but the second is the work of a mean writer: he was an
abridger of a larger work; and as he has the modesty to ask
his readers pardon for his defects, so it is very plain to every
one that reads him, that he needs often many grains of allowance. So that this book is one of the least valuable pieces of
the Apocrypha; and there are very probable reasons to question the truth of that relation, concerning those who were
thus prayed for. But because that would occasion too long a
digression, we are to make a difference between the story that
he relates, and the author's own reflections upon it; for as we
ought not to make any great account of his reflections, these
being only his private thoughts, who might probably have imbibed some of the principles of the Greek philosophy, as some
of the Jews had done, or he might have believed that notion
which is now very generally received by the Jews, that every
Jew shall have a share in the world to come, but that such as
have lived ill must be purged before they arrive at it. It is
of much more importance to consider what Judas Maccabeus 2 Maccab.
did; which even by that relation seems to be no more than xii. 40
this, that he finding some things consecrated to the idols of

the Jamnites, about the bodies of those who were killed, concluded that to have been the cause of their death: and upon this he and all his men betook themselves to prayer, and besought God that the sin might be wholly put out of remembrance: he exhorted his people to keep themselves, by that example, from the like sin; and he made a collection of a sum of money, and sent it to Jerusalem to offer a sin-offering before the Lord. So far the matter agrees well enough with the Jewish dispensation. It had appeared in the days of Joshua, how much guilt the sin of Achan, though but one person, had brought upon the whole congregation; and their law had upon another occasion prescribed a sin-offering for the whole congregation to expiate blood that was shed, when the murderer could not be discovered: that so the judgments of God might not come upon them, by reason of the cry of that blood. And by a parity of reason, Judas might have offered such an offering to free himself and his men from the guilt which the idolatry of a few might have brought upon greater numbers; such a sacrifice as this might, according to the nature of that law, have been offered: but to offer a *sin-offering* for the dead, was a new thing without ground, or any intimation of any thing like it in their law. So there is no reason to doubt, but that, if the story is true, Judas offered this sin-offering for the living, and not for the dead. If they had been alive then, by their law no sin-offering could have been made for them: for idolatry was to be punished by *cutting off*, and not to be expiated by sacrifice: what then could not have been done for them if alive, could much less be done for them after their death. So we have reason to conclude that Judas offered this sacrifice only for the living: and we are not much concerned in the opinion which so slight a writer, as the author of that book, had concerning it. But whatever might be his opinion, it was far from that of the Roman church. By this instance of the Maccabees, men who died in a state of mortal sin, and that of the highest nature, had sacrifices offered for them: whereas, according to the doctrine of the church of Rome, hell, and not purgatory, is to be the portion of all such: so this will prove too much, if any thing at all, that sacrifices are to be offered for the damned. The design of Judas's sending to make an offering for them, as that writer states it, was, that their sins might be forgiven, and that they might have a happy resurrection. Here is nothing of redeeming them out of misery, or of shortening or alleviating their torments: so that the author of that book seems to have been possessed with that opinion, received commonly among the Jews, that no Jew could finally perish; as we find St. Jerome expressing himself with the like partiality for all Christians. But whatever the author's opinion was, as that book is of no authority, it is highly probable that Judas's design in that oblation was misunderstood by the historian; and we are sure that eve his sense of it differs totally from that of the church of Rome. A passage in the New Testament is brought as a full proof of the fire of purgatory. When St. Paul in his Epistle to the Corinthians is reflecting on the divisions that were among them, and on that diversity of teachers that formed men into different principles and parties, he compares them to different builders. Some raised upon a rock an edifice like the temple at Jerusalem, of *gold* and *silver*, and noble *stones*, called *precious stones;* whereas others upon the same rock raised a mean hovel of *wood, hay, and stubble;* of both he says, 'every man's work shall be made manifest. For the day shall reveal it; because it shall be revealed by fire; for the fire shall try every man's work of what sort it is.' And he adds, 'If any man's work abide which he hath built thereupon, he shall receive a reward; and if any man's work shall be burnt, he shall suffer loss; but he himself shall be saved, yet so as by fire.' From the first view of these words it will not be thought strange if some of the ancients, who were too apt to expound places of scripture according to their first appearance, might fancy, that at the last day all were to pass through a great fire; and to suffer more or less in it: but it is visible that that opinion is far enough from the doctrine of purgatory. These words relate to a fire that was soon to appear, and that was to try every man's work. It was to be revealed, and in it every man's work was to be made manifest. So this can have no relation to a secret purgatory fire.* The meaning of it can be no other, but that whereas some with the apostles were building up the church, not only upon the foundation of Jesus Christ, and the belief of his doctrine, but were teaching men doctrines and rules that were virtuous, good, and great; others at the same time were daubing with a profane mixture, both of Judaism and Gentilism, joining these with some of the precepts of Christianity; a *day* would soon appear, which probably is meant of the destruction of Jerusalem, and of the Jewish nation; or it may be applied to the persecution that was soon to break out; in that day, those who had true notions, generous principles, and suitable practices, would weather that storm: whereas others, that were entangled with weak and superstitious conceits, would then run a great risk, though their firm believing that Jesus was the Messias would preserve them: yet the weakness and folly of

ART. XXII.
1 Cor. iii. 10—15.

* 'But whether we understand these words of that day (of the destruction of Jerusalem) or any other day of judgment, this is certain, that the apostle cannot be here supposed to speak of the *Roman purgatory fire*; (1) because the fire the apostle speaks of, as Origen hath noted, is not τῦε ὑλικὸς καὶ αἰσθητὸς, ἀλλὰ τροπολογικὸς, *fire properly, but metaphorically, so called,* as appears from those words, *he shall escape as by fire.* (2) Because this fire is to try *every man's work, Paul and Apollos's, as well as theirs* who built on the foundation hay and stubble; and sure they will not say Paul and Apollos went to purgatory. (3) This fire shall try every man's work, *of what sort it is:* now purgatory fire doth not try every man's works, but punishes them for them.' *Whitby.*—[ED.]

ART. those teachers would appear, their opinions would involve
XXII. them in such danger, that their escaping would be difficult; like
one that gets out of a house that is all on fire round about him.
So that these words cannot possibly belong to purgatory; but
must be meant of some signal discrimination that was to be
made, in some very dreadful appearances which would distinguish between the true and the false apostles; and that could
be no other but either in the destruction of Jerusalem, or in
the persecution that was to come on the church; though the
first is the more probable.

It were easy to pursue this argument further, and to shew,
that the doctrine of purgatory, as it is now in the Roman
church, was not known in the church of God for the first six
hundred years; that then it began to be doubtfully received.
But in an ignorant age, visions, legends, and bold stories prevailed much; yet the Greek church never received it. Some
of the fathers speak indeed of the last probatory fire; but
though they did not think the saints were in a state of con-
summate blessedness, enjoying the vision of God, yet they
thought they were in a state of ease and quiet, and that in
Aug. de heaven. St. Austin speaks in this whole matter very doubt-
Civit. Dei, fully; he varies often from himself; he seems sometimes very
l. 21. c.
18. ad 22. positive only for two states; at other times, as he asserts the
Enchir. c. last probatory fire, so he seems to think that good souls might
67, 68, 69.
Ad Dul- suffer some grief in that sequestered state before the last day,
cid. upon the account of some of their past sins, and that by de-
quæst.
prima. grees they might arise up to their consummation. All these
contests were proposed very doubtfully before Gregory the
Great's days; and even then some doubts seem to have been
made: but the legends were so copiously played upon all those
doubts, that this remnant of paganism got at last into the
western church. It was no wonder, that the opinions formerly mentioned, which began to appear in the second age,
had produced in the third the practice of praying for the
Tertul. de dead; of which we find such full evidence in Tertullian and
Cor. Mil.
c.3. de Ex- St. Cyprian's writings, that the matter of fact is not to be de-
hor. c. 13. nied. This appears also in all the ancient liturgies: and
Cypr. Epiphanius charges Aerius with this of rejecting all prayers
Ep. 34, 37.
Epiph. for the dead, asking, why were they prayed for? The opinions
Hær. 75. that they fell into concerning the state of departed souls, in
l. 3. n. 3. the interval between their death and the day of judgment,
gave occasion enough for prayer; they thought they were capable of making a progress, and of having an early resurrection. They also had this notion among them; that it was the
peculiar privilege of Jesus Christ to be above all our prayers;
but that no men, not excepting the apostles, nor the blessed
Virgin, were above the prayers of the church. They thought
this was an act of church-communion, that we were to hold
Dion. de even with the saints in heaven, to pray for them. Thus in the
Eccl. Hier.
cap. 7. Apostolical Constitutions, in the books of the Ecclesiastical

Hierarchy, and in the Liturgies that are ascribed to St. Basil and St. Chrysostom, they offer unto God these prayers, which they thought their reasonable service, for those who were at rest in the faith, their forefathers, fathers, patriarchs, prophets, and apostles; preachers, evangelists, martyrs, confessors, religious persons, and for every spirit perfected in the faith; especially for our most holy, immaculate, most blessed Lady, the mother of God, the ever Virgin Mary. Particular instances might also be given of this out of St. Cyprian, St. Ambrose, Nazianzen, and St. Austin; who in that famous and much cited passage concerning his mother, Monica, as he speaks nothing of any temporal pains that she suffered, so he plainly intimates his belief that God had done all that he desired. Thus it will appear to those who have examined all the passages which are brought out of the fathers, concerning their prayers for the dead, that they believed they were then in heaven, and at rest; and by consequence, though these prayers for the dead did very probably give the chief rise to the doctrine of purgatory; yet, as they then made them, they were utterly inconsistent with that opinion. Tertullian, who is the first that is cited for them, says, we make oblations for the dead, and we do it for that second nativity of theirs *(natalitia)* once a year. The signification of the word *natalitia*, as they used it, was the saint's day of death, in which they reckoned he was born again to heaven: so, though they judged them there, yet they offered up prayers for them: and when Epiphanius brings in Aerius asking, why those prayers were made for the dead? though it had been very natural, and indeed unavoidable, if he had believed purgatory, to have answered, that it was to deliver them from thence: yet he makes no such answer, but only asserts, that it had been the practice of the church so to do. The Greek church retains that custom, though she has never admitted of purgatory. Here then an objection may be made to our constitution, that in this of praying for the dead we have departed from the practice of the ancients: we do not deny it, both the church of Rome and we in another practice, of equal antiquity, of giving the eucharist to infants, have made changes, and let that custom fall. The curiosities in the second century seem to have given rise to those prayers in the third; and they gave the rise to many other disorders in the following centuries. Since, therefore, God has commanded us, while we are on earth, to pray for one another, and has made that a main act of our charity and church-communion, but has nowhere directed us to pray for those that have finished their course; and since the only pretence that is brought from scripture, of St. Paul's praying, that 'Onesiphorus might find mercy in the day of the Lord,' cannot be wrought up into an argument, for it cannot be proved that he was then dead; and since the fathers reckon this of praying for the dead only as one of their customs, for

ART. XXII.

Aug.conf. l. 9. c. 13.

De Cor. Mil.

2 Tim. i. 18.

ART. XXII. which they vouch no other warrant but practice; since, also, this has been grossly abused, and has been applied to support a doctrine totally different from theirs; we think that we have as good a plea for not following them in this, as we have for not giving infants the sacrament, and therefore we think it no imputation on our church, that we do not in this follow a groundless and a much abused precedent, though set us in ages which we highly reverence.

The greatest corruption of this whole matter comes in the last place to be considered; which is, the methods proposed for redeeming souls out of purgatory. If this doctrine had rested in a speculation, we must still have considered it as derogatory to the death of Christ, and the truth of the gospel: but it raises our zeal a little more, when we consider the use that was made of it; and that fears and terrors being by this means infused into men's minds, new methods were proposed to free them from these. The chief of which was the saying of *masses* for departed souls. It was pretended, that this being the highest act of the communion of Christians, and the most sublime piece of worship, therefore God was so well pleased with the frequent repetition of it, with the prayers that accompanied it, and with those that made provisions for men who should be constantly employed in it, that this was a most acceptable sacrifice to God. Upon this followed all those vast endowments for saying *masses* for departed souls; though in the institution of that sacrament, and in all that is spoken of it in the scripture, there is not an hint given of this. Sacraments are positive precepts, which are to be measured only by the institution, in which there is not room left for us to carry them further. We are 'to take, eat and drink, and thereby shew forth the Lord's death till his second coming:' all which has no relation to the applying this to others who are gone off the stage; therefore if we can have any just notions either of superstition, or of will-worship, they are applicable here. Men will fancy that there is a virtue in an action, which we are sure it has not of itself, and we cannot find that God has put in it; and yet they, without any authority from God, do set up a new piece of worship, and imagine that God will be pleased with them in every thing they do or ask, only because they are perverting this piece of worship, clearly contrary to the institution, to be a solitary mass. In the primitive church, where all the service of the whole assembly ended in a communion, there was a roll read, in which the names of the more eminent saints of the catholic church, and of the holy bishops, martyrs, or confessors of every particular church, were registered. This was an honourable remembrance that was kept up of such as had died in the Lord. When the soundness of any person's faith was brought in suspicion, his name was not read till that point was cleared, and then either his name continued to be read, or it was quite dashed out. This was thought an honour due to the memory of those who had died in the faith: and in St. Cyprian's time, in the infancy of this practice, we see he counted the leaving a man's name out as a thing that only left a blot upon him, but not as a thing of any consequence to his soul; for when a priest had died, who had by his last will named another priest the tutor (or guardian) of his children, this seemed to him a thing of such ill example, to put those secular cares upon the minds of the clergy, that he appointed that his name should be no more read in the daily sacrifice: which plainly shews, unless we will tax St. Cyprian with a very unreasonable cruelty, that he considered that only as a small censure laid on his memory, but not as a prejudice to his soul. This gives us a very plain view of the sense that he had of this matter. After this roll was read, then the general prayer followed, as was formerly acknowledged, for all their souls; and so they went on in the communion service. This has no relation to a mass said by a single priest to deliver a soul out of purgatory. ART. XXII. Cypr. Epist. 1. ad pleb. Furnit. Oxon.

Here, without going far in tragical expressions, we cannot hold saying what our Saviour said upon another occasion, 'My house is a house of prayer, but ye have made it a den of thieves.' A trade was set up on this foundation. The world was made to believe, that by virtue of so many masses, which were to be purchased by great endowments, souls were redeemed out of purgatory; and scenes of visions and apparitions, sometimes of the tormented, and sometimes of the delivered souls, were published in all places: which had so wonderful an effect, that in two or three centuries endowments increased to so vast a degree, that if the scandals of the clergy on the one hand, and the statutes of *mortmain* on the other, had not restrained the profuseness that the world was wrought up to upon this account, it is not easy to imagine how far this might have gone; perhaps to an entire subjecting of the temporalty to the spiritualty. The practices by which this was managed, and the effects that followed on it, we can call by no other name than downright impostures; worse than the making or vending false coin: when the world was drawn in by such arts to plain bargains, to redeem their own souls, and the souls of their ancestors and posterity, so many masses were to be said, and forfeitures were to follow upon their not being said: thus the masses were really the price of the lands. An endowment to a religious use, though mixed with error or superstition in the rules of it, ought to be held sacred, according to the decision given concerning the censers of those that were in the rebellion of Corah: so that we do not excuse the violation of such from sacrilege; yet we cannot think so of endowments, where the only consideration was a false opinion first of purgatory, and then of redemption out of it by masses; this being expressed in the very deeds themselves. By the same reasons, by which private persons Mark xi. 17. Numb. xvi. 38.

ART. XXII.

are obliged to restore what they have drawn from others by base practices, by false deeds, or counterfeit coin; bodies are also bound to restore what they have got into their hands by such fraudulent practices; so that the states and princes of Christendom were at full liberty upon the discovery of these impostures, to void all the endowments that had followed upon them; and either to apply them to better uses, or to restore them to the families from which they had been drawn, if that had been practicable, or to convert them to any other use. This was a crying abuse, which those who have observed the progress that this matter made from the eighth century to the twelfth, cannot reflect on without both amazement and indignation. We are sensible enough that there are many political reasons and arguments for keeping up the doctrine of purgatory. *But we have not so learned Christ.* We ought not to lie even for God, much less for ourselves, or for any other pretended ends of keeping the world in awe and order: therefore all the advantages that are said to arise out of this, and all the mischief that may be thought to follow on the rejecting of it, ought not to make us presume to carry on the ends of religion by unlawful methods. This were to call in the assistance of the Devil to do the work of God; if the just apprehensions of the wrath of God, and the guilt of sin, together with the fear of everlasting burnings, will not reform the world, nor restrain sinners, we must leave this matter to the wise and unsearchable judgments of God.

The next particular in this Article is the condemning the Romish doctrine concerning *pardons:* that is founded on the distinction between the temporal and eternal punishment of sin; and the pardon is of the temporal punishment, which is believed to be done by a power lodged singly in the pope, derived from those words, 'Feed my sheep,' and 'To thee will I give the keys of the kingdom of heaven.' This may be by him derived, as they teach, not only to bishops and priests, but to the inferior orders, to be dispensed by them; and it excuses from penance, unless he who purchases it thinks fit to use his penance in a medicinal way, as a preservative against sin. So the virtue of indulgences* is the applying

---

* The system of indulgences had its foundation in the early ages of Christianity, when many of those who had apostatized under the persecution of Decius were anxious to be re-admitted to the communion of the church, 'without submitting to that painful course of penitential discipline, which the ecclesiastical laws indispensably required. The bishops were divided upon this matter: some were for shewing the desired indulgence, while others opposed it with all their might. In Egypt and Africa, many, in order to obtain more speedily the pardon of their apostacy, interested the martyrs in their behalf, and received from them letters of reconciliation and peace, i. e. a formal act, by which they (the martyrs) declared in their last moments, that they looked upon them as worthy of their communion, and desired, of consequence, that they should be restored to their place among the brethren.'—*Mosheim.*

The subsequent scandalous abuse of this practice, and the iniquitous traffic in indulgences which called forth the zeal of Martin Luther, are too well known to require any further remarks.—[ED.]

the treasure of the church upon such terms as popes shall think fit to prescribe, in order to the redeeming souls from purgatory, and from all other temporal punishments, and that for such a number of years as shall be specified in the bulls; some of which have gone to thousands of years; one I have seen to ten hundred thousand: and as these indulgences are sometimes granted by special tickets, like tallies struck on that treasure; so sometimes they are affixed to particular churches and altars, to particular times, or days, chiefly to the year of jubilee; they are also affixed to such things as may be carried about, to *Agnus Dei's*, to medals, to rosaries and scapularies; they are also affixed to some prayers, the devout saying of them being a mean to procure great indulgences. The granting these is left to the pope's discretion, who ought to distribute them as he thinks may tend most to the honour of God, and the good of the church; and he ought not to be too profuse, much less to be too scanty, in dispensing them.

This has been the received doctrine and practice of the church of Rome since the twelfth century; and the council of Trent* in a hurry, in its last session, did in very general words approve of the practice of the church in this matter, and decreed that indulgences should be continued; only they restrained some abuses, in particular that of selling them; yet even those restraints were wholly referred to the popes themselves: so that this crying abuse, the scandal of which had occasioned the first beginnings and progress of the Reformation, was upon the matter established; and the correcting the excesses in it was trusted to those who had been the authors of them, and the chief gainers by them. This point of their doctrine is more fully opened than might perhaps seem necessary, if it were not that a great part of the confutation of some doctrines is the exposing of them. For though in ages and places of ignorance these things have been, and still are,

---

* '*Decretum de Indulgentiis.*

'Cum potestas conferendi indulgentias a Christo ecclesiæ concessa sit; atque hujusmodi potestate, divinitus sibi tradita, antiquissimis etiam temporibus illa usa fuerit: sacrosancta synodus indulgentiarum usum, Christiano populo maxime salutarem, et sacrorum conciliorum auctoritate probatum, in ecclesia retinendum esse docet et præcipit; eosque anathemate damnat, qui aut inutiles esse asserunt, vel eas concedendi in ecclesia potestatem esse negant: in his tamen concedendis moderationem, juxta veterem et probatam in ecclesia consuetudinem, adhiberi cupit; ne nimia facilitate ecclesiastica disciplina enervetur. Abusus vero, qui in his irrepserunt, et quorum occasione insigne hoc indulgentiarum nomen ab hæreticis blasphematur, emendatos et correctos cupiens, præsenti decreto generaliter statuit pravos quæstus omnes pro his consequendis, unde plurima in Christiano populo abusuum causa fluxit, omnino abolendos esse. Cæteros vero, qui ex superstitione, ignorantia, irreverentia, aut aliunde quomodocumque provenerunt, cum ob multiplices locorum et provinciarum, apud quas hi committuntur, corruptelas commode nequeant specialiter prohiberi; mandat omnibus episcopis, ut diligenter quisque hujusmodi abusus ecclesiæ suæ colligat, eosque in prima synodo provinciali referat: ut aliorum quoque episcoporum sententia cogniti, statim ad summum romanum pontificem deferantur: cujus auctoritate et prudentia, quod universali ecclesiæ expediet, statuatur; ut ita sanctarum indulgentiarum munus, pie, sancte, et incorrupte omnibus fidelibus dispensitur.' *Sessio* xxv.—[Ed.]

practised with great assurance, and to very extravagant excesses; yet in countries and ages of more light, when they come to be questioned, they are disowned with an assurance equal to that with which they are practised elsewhere. Among us some will perhaps say, that these are only exemptions from penance; which cannot be denied to be within the power of the church; and they argue, that though it is very fit to make severe laws, yet the execution of these must be softened in practice. This is all that they pretend to justify, and they give up any further indulgences as an abuse of corrupt times. Whereas at the same time a very different doctrine is taught among them, where there is no danger, but much profit, in owning it. All this is only a pretence; for the episcopal power, in the inflicting, abating, or commuting of penance, is stated among them as a thing wholly different from the power of indulgences. They are derived from different originals; and designed for ends totally different from one another. The one is for the outward discipline of the church, and the other is for the inward quiet of consciences, and in order to their future state. The one is in every bishop, and the other is asserted to be peculiar to the pope. Nor will they escape by laying this matter upon the ignorance and abuses of former times. It was published in bulls, and received by the whole church: so that if either the pope, or the diffusive body of the church are infallible, there must be such a power in the pope; and the decree of the council of Trent confirming and approving the practice of the church in that point, must bind them all. For if this doctrine is false, then their infallibility must go with it; for in every hypothesis in which infallibility is said to be lodged, whether in the pope or in councils, this doctrine has that seal to it.

As for the doctrine itself, all that has been already said against the distinction of temporal and eternal punishment, and against purgatory, overthrows it; since the one is the foundation on which it is built, and the other is that which it pretends to secure men from: and therefore this falls with those. All that was said upon the head of the sufficiency of the scriptures comes also in here; for if the scriptures ought to be our rule in any thing, it must be chiefly in those matters which relate to the pardon of sin, to the quiet of our consciences, and to a future state. Therefore a doctrine and practice that have not so much as colours from scripture in a matter of such consequence, ought to be rejected by us upon this single account. If from the scripture we go to the practice and tradition of the church, we are sure that this was not thought on for above ten centuries; all the indulgences that were then known being only the abatements of the severity of the penitentiary canons; but in the ages in which aspiring and insolent popes imposed on ignorant and superstitious multitudes, a jumble was made of indulgences formerly granted, of purgatory, and of the papal authority, that was then very implicitly submitted to; and so out of all that mixture this arose; which was as ill managed as it was ill grounded. The natural tendency of it is not only to relax all public discipline, but also all secret penance, when shorter methods to peace and pardon may be more easily purchased. The vast application to the executing the many trifling performances to which indulgences are granted, has brought in among them such a prostitution of holy things, that either it must be said that those are public cheats, and that they were so from the beginning, or that their virtue is now exhausted, though the bulls that grant them are perpetual; or else a man may on very easy terms preserve himself and redeem his friends out of purgatory. If the saying a prayer before a privileged altar, or the visiting some churches in the time of jubilee, with those slight devotions that are then enjoined, have such efficacy in them, it is scarce possible for any man to be in danger of purgatory.

ART. XXII.

The *third* head rejected in this Article is the worshipping of images. Here those of the church of Rome complain much of the charge of idolatry, that our church has laid upon them, so fully and so severely in the Homilies. Some among ourselves have also thought that we must either renounce that charge, or that we must deny the possibility of salvation in that church, and in consequence to that conclude, that neither the baptism nor the orders of that church are valid: for since idolaters are excluded from the kingdom of heaven, they argue, that if there can be no salvation where idolatry is committed by the whole body of a church, then that can be no church, and in it there is no salvation. But here we are to consider, before we enter upon the specialities of this matter, that idolatry is a general word, which comprehends many several sorts and ranks of sins under it. As lying is capable of many degrees, from an officious lie to the swearing falsely against the life of an innocent man in judgment: the one is the lowest, and the other is the highest act of that kind; but all are lying: and yet it would appear an unreasonable thing to urge every thing that is said of any act in general, and which belongs to the highest acts of it, as if all the inferior degrees did necessarily involve the guilt of the highest. There is another distinction to be made between actions, as they signify either of themselves, or by the public constructions that are put on them, by those who authorize them, and those same actions as they may be privately intended by particular persons. We, in our weighing of things, are only to consider what actions signify of their own nature, or by public authority, and according to that we must form our judgments about them, and in particular in the point of idolatry: but as for the secret thoughts or intentions of men, we must leave these to the 'udgment of God, who only knows them, and who being infinitely gracious, slow to anger, and ready to forgive, will, we do not doubt, make all the abatements in the weighing men's actions that there is reason for. But we ought not to enter into that matter; we ought neither to aggravate nor to mollify things too much: we are to judge of things as they are in themselves, and to leave the case of men's intentions and secret notions to that God who is to judge them. As for the business of images, we know that the heathens had them of several sorts. Some they believed were real resemblances of those deities that they worshipped: those divinities had been men, and the statues made for them resembled them. Other images they believed had a divine virtue affixed to them, perhaps from the stars, which were believed to be gods; and it was thought that the influences of their aspects and positions were by secret charms called down, and fastened to some figures. Other images were considered as emblems and representations of their deities: so that they only gave them occasion to represent them to their thoughts. These images, thus of different sorts, were all worshipped; some more, some less: they kneeled before them; they prayed to them, and made many oblations to them; they set lights before them, and burnt incense to them; they set them in their temples, market-places, and highways; and they had them in their houses: they set them off with much pomp, and had many processions to their honour. But in all this, though it is like the vulgar among them might have gross thoughts of those images, yet the philosophers, not only after the Christian religion had obliged them to consider well of that matter, and to express themselves cautiously about it; but even while they were in the peaceable possession of the world, did believe that the deity was not in the image, but was only represented by it; that the deity was worshipped in the image, so that the honour done the image did belong to the deity itself. Here then were two false opinions: the one was concerning those deities themselves; the other was concerning this way of worshipping them; and both were blamed; not only the worshipping a false god, but the worshipping that god by an image. If idolatry had only consisted in the acknowledging a false god, and if the worshipping the true God in an image had not been idolatry, then all the fault of the heathenish idolaters should have consisted in this, that they worshipped a false god; but their worshipping images should not of itself have been an additional fault. But in opposition to this, what can we think of those full and copious words, in which God did not only forbid the having of false gods, but the making of 'a graven image, or the likeness of any thing in heaven, in earth, or under the earth?' The 'bowing down to it, and the worshipping it,' are also forbid. Where, besides the copiousness of these words, we are to consider, that Moses, in the rehearsal of that law in Deuteronomy, does over and over again add and insist on this, that 'they saw no manner of similitude,' when God spoke to them, 'lest they should corrupt themselves, and make to them a graven image;' an enumeration is made of many different likenesses; and after that comes another species of idolatry, 'the worshipping the host of heaven;' and therefore Moses charges them in that chapter again and again 'to take heed, to take good heed to themselves, lest they should forget the covenant of the Lord their God, and make them a graven image:' and he lays the same charge a third time upon them in the same chapter. A special law is also given against the most innocent of all the images that could be made: they were required not only not to have idols, nor graven images, but 'not to rear up a standing image or pillar; nor to set up any image of stone, or any carved stone;' such were the *Baitulia*; the least tempting or ensnaring of all idols: 'they were not to bow down before it;' and the reason given is, 'For I am the Lord your God.' The importance of those laws will appear clearer, if they are compared with the practice of those times, and particularly in those symbolical images, which were sacred emblems and hieroglyphics, that were not meant to be a true representation of the Divine Being, but were a combination of many symbols, intended to represent at once to the thoughts of the worshipper many of the perfections of God: these were most particularly practised in Egypt, and to them the copiousness of the Second Commandment seems to have a particular respect, such having been the images which they had lately seen, and which seem the most excusable of all others: when, I say, all this is laid together, with the commandment itself, and with those other laws that accompany and explain it, nothing seems more evident, than that God intended to forbid all outward representations, that should be set up as the objects of worship. It is also very plain, that the prophets expostulated with the people of Israel for their carved and molten images, as well as for their false gods: and among the reasons given against images, one is often repeated, 'To whom will ye liken me?' which seems to import, that by these images they represented the living God. And Isaiah often, as also both Jeremiah and Habakkuk, when they set forth the folly of making an image, of praying to it, and trusting in it, bring in the greatness and glory of the living God, in opposition to these images. Now though it is possible enough to apprehend, how that the Jews might make images in imitation of the heathen, to represent that God whom they served; yet it is no way credible that they could have fallen into such a degree of stupidity, as to fancy that a piece of wood, which they had carved into such a figure, was a real deity. They might think it a god by representation, as the heathens thought their idols were; but more than this cannot be easily apprehended. So that it is most reasonable to think, that they knew the God they had thus

ART. XXII.
Deut. iv. 13, 15, 17, 23.
Deut. xii. 30.
Levit. xxvi. 1.
Deut. xv. 22.

Isaiah xl. 18—27.
xliv. 9—21.
Jer. x. 1—17.
Hab. ii. 18, 19, 20.

ART.
XXII.

made, and prayed to, was only a piece of wood; but they might well fall into that corruption of many of the heathen, of thinking that they honoured God by serving him in such an image. If the sin of the Jews was only their having other gods; and if the worshipping an image was only evil, because a false deity was honoured by it, why is image-worship condemned, with reasons that will hold full as strong against the images of the true God, as of false gods, if it had not been intended to condemn simply all image-worship? Certainly, if the prophets had intended to have done it, they could not have expressed themselves more clearly and more fully than they did.

To this it is to be added, that it seems very clear from the history of the golden calf, that the Israelites did not intend,

Ex. xxxii. 1, 4, 5.

by setting it up, to cast off the true Jehovah, that 'had brought them out of Egypt.' They plainly said the contrary, and appointed a feast to Jehovah. It is probable they thought Moses was either burnt or starved on Mount Sinai, so they desired some visible representation of the Deity to go before them; they intended still to serve him; but since they thought they had lost their prophet and guide, they hoped that this should have been perhaps as a *teraphim* to them; yet for all

Acts vii.41. Psal. cvi. 19, 20.

this, the calf is called an *idol*: and they are said 'to have changed their glory into the similitude of an ox that eateth grass.' So that here an emblem of the Deity is called an idol. They could take the *calf* for no other, but as a visible sign or

1 Kings xii. 27— 33.

symbol in which they intended to worship their God or Elohim, and the Lord or Jehovah. Such very probably were also the calves of Dan and Bethel, set up by Jeroboam, who seemed to have no design to change the object of their worship, or the nature of their religion; but only to divert them from going up to Jerusalem, and to furnish them with conveniences to worship the living God nearer home. His design was only to establish the kingdom to himself; and in order to that, we must think, that he would venture on no more than was necessary for his purpose. Besides, we do clearly

1 Kings xvi. 31. 2 Kings x. 28, 29.

see an opposition made between the calves set up by Jeroboam, and the worship of Baal brought from Tyrus by Ahab. Those who hated that idolatry, such as Jehu and his family, yet continued in the sin of Jeroboam; and they are represented as 'zealous for Jehovah,' though they worshipped the

Hos.viii.4, 5.

calves of Dan and Bethel. These are called *idols* by Hosea. From all which it seems to be very evident that the ten tribes still feared and worshipped the true Jehovah. This appears yet more clear from the sequel of their history, when they were carried away by the kings of Assyria; and new inhabitants were sent to people the country, who brought their idols along with them, and did not acknowledge 'Jehovah the true God;' but upon their being plagued with lions, to prevent this, the king of Assyria sent one of the priests, that had been carried out of the country, who taught them how they should 'fear the Lord:' out of which that mixture arose, that they 'feared the Lord, and served their own images.' This proves, beyond all contradiction, that the ten tribes did still worship Jehovah in those calves that they had at Dan and Bethel: and thus it appears very clear, that, through the whole Old Testament the use of all images in worship was expressly forbid; and that the worshipping them, even when the true God was worshipped by them, was called idolatry. The words in which this matter is expressed are copious and full, and the reasons given for the precept are taken from the nature of God; who could be likened to nothing, and who had shewed no similitude of himself when he appeared to their fathers, and delivered their law to them. [ART. XXII. 2 Kings xvii. 28, 32, 41.]

The new dispensation does in all respects carry the ideas of God and of true religion much higher, and raises them much above those compliances that were in the old, to men's senses, and to sensitive natures; and it would seem to contradict the whole design of it, if we could imagine that such things were allowed in it, which were so expressly forbid in the old. Upon this occasion it is remarkable, that the two fullest passages in the New Testament concerning images, are written upon the occasion of the most refined idolatry that was then in the world, which was at Athens. When St. Paul was there, his spirit was moved within him, when he saw that city 'full of idols:' he upon that charges them for thinking that the 'Godhead was like unto gold or silver, or stone graven by art or man's device?' he argues from the majesty of God, who made the world and all things therein, and was the Lord of heaven and earth, and therefore was not to be 'shipped by men's hands (that is, images made by them), who needed nothing, since he gives us life, breath (or the continuance of life), and all things.' He therefore condemns that way of worship as an effect of *ignorance*, and tells them, 'of a day in which God will judge the world.' It is certain that the Athenians at that time did not think their images were the proper resemblances of the Divinity. Tully, who knew their theology well, gives us a very different account of the notion that they had of their images. Some images were of no figure at all, but were only stones and pillars that had no particular shape; others were hieroglyphics made up of many several emblems, of which some signified one perfection of the Deity, and some another; and others were indeed the figures of men and women; but even in these the wiser among them said, they worshipped one Eternal Mind, and under him some inferior beings, demons, and men; who they believed were subordinate to God, and governed this world. So it could not be said of such worshippers, that they thought that the Godhead was like unto their images; since the best writers among them tell us plainly that they thought no such thing. [Acts xvii. 16, 24—29. Cic. de Nat. Deor. l. i. cap. 27.]

x

ART.
XXII.

St. Paul therefore only argues in this against image-worship in itself, which does naturally lead men to these low thoughts of God; and which is a very unreasonable thing in all those who do not think so of him. It is contrary to the nature and perfections of God: few men can think God is like to those images, therefore that is a very good argument against all worshipping of them. And we may upon very sure grounds say that the Athenians had such elevated notions both of God and of their images, that whatsoever was a good argument against image-worship among them, will hold good against all image-worship whatsoever.

But as St. Paul stayed long enough at Athens to understand their opinions well, and that no doubt he learned their doctrine very particularly from his convert Dionysius, so at his coming to Corinth from thence, when he had learned from Aquila and Priscilla the state of the church in Rome, and no doubt had learned among other things that the Romans admired the Greeks, and made them their patterns; he in the beginning of his Epistle to them, having still deep impressions upon his spirit of what he had seen and known at Athens, arraigns the whole Greek philosophy; and especially

Rom. i. 20 —32.

those among them 'who professed themselves wise, but became fools; who though they knew God, yet glorified him not as God, nor were thankful; but became vain in their imaginations, so that their foolish heart was darkened.' They had high speculations of the unity and simplicity of the Divine Essence; but they set themselves to find such excuses for the idolatry of the vulgar, that they not only continued to comply with them in the grossest of all their practices, but they studied more laboured defences for them, than the ruder multitudes could ever have fallen upon. They knew the true God; for God had shewed to them 'that which might be known of him: but they held the truth in unrighteousness, and changed the glory of the incorruptible God into an image made like to corruptible man, and to birds and four-footed beasts, and to creeping things:' which seems to be a description of hieroglyphic figures, the most excusable of all those images by which they represented the Deity. This St. Paul makes to be the original of all the corruption and immorality that was spread over the Gentile world, which came in, partly as the natural consequence of idolatry, of its debasing the ideas of God, and wounding true religion and virtue in its source and first seeds, and partly as an effect of the just judgments of God upon those who thus dishonoured him, that was to a very monstrous degree spread over both Greece and Rome. Of these St. Paul gives us some very enormous instances, with a catalogue of the vices that sprang from those vitiated principles. These two passages, the one of St. Paul's preaching, and the other of his writing, being both applied to those who had the finest speculations among the heathen, do evidently demonstrate how contrary the Christian doctrine is to the worshipping of images of all sorts, how speciously soever that may be disguised.

ART. XXII.

If these things wanted an explanation, we find it given us very fully in all the writings of the fathers during their disputes with the heathens. They do not only charge them with the false notions that they had of God, the many deities they worshipped, the absurd legends that they had concerning them; but in particular they dwell long upon this of the worshipping God in or by an image, with arguments taken both from the pure and spiritual nature of God, and from the plain revelation he made of his will in this matter. Upon this argument many long citations might be gathered from Justin Martyr, from Clemens* of Alexandria, Origen, Tertullian, Cyprian, Arnobius, Minutius Felix, Lactantius, Eusebius, Ambrose, and St. Austin. Their reasonings are so clear and so full, that nothing can be more evident than that they condemned all the use of images in the worship of God: and yet both Celsus, Porphyry, Maximus Tyrius, and Julian, told them very plainly, that they did not believe that the Godhead was like their images, or was shut up within them; they only used them as helps to their imagination and apprehension, that from thence they might form suitable thoughts of the Deity. This did not satisfy the fathers, who insisted on it to the last, that all such images as were made the objects of worship were idols; so that if in any one thing we have a very full account of the sense of the whole church for the first four centuries, it is in this matter. They do not speak of it now and then only by the way, as in a digression; in which the heat of argument, or of rhetoric, may be apt to carry men too far: they set themselves to treat of this argument very nicely; and they were engaged in it with philosophers, who were as good at subtleties and distinctions as other men. This was one of the main parts of the controversy: so, if in any head whatsoever, they writ exactly upon those subjects. They attacked the established religion of the Roman empire; and this was not to be done with clamour, nor could they offer at it in a plain contradiction to such principles as are consistent with the Christian religion, if the doctrine of the Roman church is true. Here then we have not only the scripture but tradition fully of our side.

Some pretended Christians, it is true, did very early worship images; but those were the Gnostics, held in detestation by all the orthodox. Irenæus, Epiphanius, and St. Austin tell us, that they worshipped the images of Christ, together

Iren. l. i.
c. 24.
Epiph.
Hæres. 27.
August. de
Hæres.
cap. 7.

* Just. Mart. Apol. l. i. c. 5. Clem. Alex. Strom. l. i. c. 15. Protr. Orig. cont. Cels. l. i. sect. 2, 3, 5, 7. Tertull. Apol. c. 12. Cypr. de Idol. Vanitate. Arnob. lib. v. Minut. Felix. Oct. c. 18. Euseb. Præp. Evang. l. iii. Lactan. l. ii, c. 2. Ambros. ad. Valent. Imperat. relat. Sym. respond. Epist. 31. August. de Civitate Dei, l. vii. c. 5.
Orig. con. Cels. l. vii. c. 44. Euseb. Præp. Ev. l. iii. c. 4. Max. Tyr. diss. 38. Jul. Frag. Ep. Euseb. Præp. Evang. l. iv. c. 1.

with Pythagoras, Plato, and Aristotle: nor are they only blamed for worshipping the images of Christ, together with these of the philosophers; but they are particularly blamed for having several sorts of images, and worshipping these as the heathens did; and that among these there was an image of Christ, which they pretended to have had from Pilate. Besides these corrupters of Christianity, there were no others among the Christians of the first ages that worshipped images. This was so well known to the heathens, that they bring this, among other things, as a reproach against the Christians, that they had no images: which the first apologists are so far from denying, that they answered them, that it was impossible for him who knew God, to worship images. But as human nature is inclined to visible objects of worship, so it seems some began to paint the walls of their churches with pictures, or at least moved for it. In the beginning of the fourth century this was condemned by the council of Eliberis, Can. 36. *It pleases us to have no pictures in churches, lest that which is worshipped should be painted upon the walls.* Towards the end of that century, we have an account given us by Epiphanius, of his indignation occasioned by a picture that he saw upon a veil at Anablatha. He did not much consider whose picture it was, whether a picture of Christ or of some saint; he positively affirms it was against the authority of the scriptures, and the Christian religion, and therefore he tore it, but supplied that church with another veil. It seems, private persons had statues of Christ and the apostles; which Eusebius censures, where he reports it as a *remnant of heathenism.** It is plain enough from some passages in St. Austin, that he knew of no images in churches in the beginning of the fifth century. It is true, they began to be brought before that time into some of the churches of Pontus and Cappadocia, which was done very probably to

---

* The following is the passage from Eusebius referred to by our author:
'In so much as we have made mention of this city, Paneas, I think I shall offend if I pass over with silence a certain history worthy to be related to the posterity. The report goeth, that the woman whose bloody flux we learn to have been cured by our Saviour in the gospel, was of the aforesaid city, and that her house is there to be seen, and a worthy monument yet there to continue of the benefit conferred by our Saviour upon her. That there standeth over an high stone, right over against the door of her house, an image of brass resembling the form of a woman kneeling upon her knees, holding her hands before her, after the manner of supplication. Again, that there standeth over against this another image of a man molten of the same metal, comely arrayed in a short vesture, stretching forth his hand unto the woman, at whose feet in the same pillar there groweth up from the ground a certain unknown kind of herb in the height unto the hem of the brazen image's vesture, curing all kinds of maladies. This picture of the man, they report to be the image of Jesus. It hath continued unto our time, and is to be seen of travellers that frequent the same city. Neither is it any marvel at all, that they which of the Gentiles were cured by our Saviour, made and set up such things, for that we have seen the pictures of his apostles, to wit, of Paul, of Peter, and of Christ himself, being graven in their colours, to have been kept and reverenced. *For the men of old of a heathenish custom, were wont to honour after this manner such as they counted saviours.*'—[ED.]

draw the heathens, by this piece of conformity to them, to ART.
like the Christian worship the better. For that humour XXII.
began to work, and appeared in many instances of other
kinds as well as in this.
It was not possible that people could see pictures in their
churches long, without paying some marks of respect to
them, which grew in a little time to the downright worship
of them. A famous instance we have of this in the sixth
century: Serenus, bishop of Marseilles, finding that he could
not restrain his people from the worship of images, broke
them in pieces; upon which pope Gregory writ to him, Greg.
blaming him indeed for breaking the images, but commending Epist. l. ix.
him for not allowing them to be worshipped: this he pro- Ep. 9.
secutes in a variety of very plain expressions; *It is one thing
to worship an image, and another thing to learn by it what is to
be worshipped:* he says they were set up, not to be worshipped, but to instruct the ignorant, and cites our Saviour's
words, 'Thou shalt worship the Lord thy God, and him only
shalt thou serve,' to prove that it was not lawful to worship
the work of men's hands. We see by a fragment cited in the
second Nicene council, that both Jews and Gentiles took
advantages from the worship of images, to reproach the
Christians soon after that time. The Jews were scandalized
at their worshipping images, as being expressly against the
command of God. The Gentiles had also by it great advantages of turning back upon the Christians all that had
been written against their images in the former ages.

At last, in the beginning of the eighth century, the famous
controversy about the having or breaking of images grew hot.
The churches of Italy were so set on the worshipping of them,
that pope Gregory the Second* gives this for the reason of
their rebelling against the emperor, because of his opposition
to images. And here in little more than an hundred years
the see of Rome changed its doctrine, pope Gregory the
Second being as positive for the worshipping them, as the
first of that name had been against it. Violent contentions
arose upon this head. The breakers of images were charged
with Judaism, Samaritanism, and Manicheism; and the worshippers of them were charged with Gentilism and idolatry.
One general council at Constantinople, consisting of about
three hundred and thirty-eight bishops, condemned the worshipping them as idolatrous: but another at Nice, of three
hundred and fifty bishops, though others say they were only
three hundred, asserted the worship of them. Yet as soon
as this was known in the west, how active soever the see
of Rome was for establishing their worship, a council of about
three hundred bishops met at Francfurt, under Charles the

* This is owned by all the historians of that age, Anastasius, Zonaras, Cedrenus, Glycas, Theophanes, Sigebert, Otho, Fris. Urspergensis, Sigonius, Rubens, and Ciaconius.

Great, which condemned the Nicene council, together with the worship of images. The Gallican church insisted long upon this matter; books were published in the name of Charles the Great against them. A council held at Paris under his son did also condemn image-worship as contrary to the honour that is due to God only, and to the commands that he has given us in scripture. The Nicene council was rejected here in England, as our historians tell us, because it asserted the adoration of images, *which the church of God abhors.* Agobard, bishop of Lyons, and Claud of Turin, writ against it; the former writ with great vehemence: the learned men of that communion do now acknowledge, that what he writ was according to the sense of the Gallican church in that age: and even Jonas of Orleans, who studied to moderate the matter, and to reconcile the Gallican bishops to the see of Rome, yet does himself declare against the worship of images.

We are not concerned to examine how it came that all this vigorous opposition to image-worship went off so soon. It is enough to us, that it was once made so resolutely; let those who think it so incredible a thing, that churches should depart from their received traditions, answer this as they can. As for the methods then used, and the arguments that were then brought to infuse this doctrine into the world, he who will read the history and acts of the Nicene council, will find enough to incline him to a very bad opinion, both of the men and of their doctrine; though he were ever so much inclined to think well of them. After all, though that council laid the foundation of image-worship, yet the church of Rome has made great improvements in it since. Those of Nice expressed a detestation of an image made to represent the Deity; they go no higher than the images of Christ and the saints; whereas since that time the Deity and the Trinity have been represented by images and pictures: and that not only by connivance, but by authority in the church of Rome. Bellarmine,* Suarez, and others, prove the lawfulness of such images from the general practice of the church. Others go further, and from the caution given in the decree of the council of Trent, concerning the images of God, do infer, that they are allowed by that council, provided they be decently made. Directions are also given concerning the use of the image of the Trinity in public offices among them. In a word, all their late doctors agree, that they are lawful, and reckon the calling that in question to be not only rashness, but an error; and such as have held it unlawful to make such images were especially condemned at Rome, December 17, 1690. The varieties of those images, and the boldness of them, are things apt to give horror to modest minds, not accustomed to

---

* Bellarm. l. ii. c. 8. De Relig. et imagin. Sanct. Suarez, M. 3. Ysambert de Mist. Incarn. ad quæst. 25. dis. 3. Vasquez in 3 Aquin. disp. 113. c. 3. et d'sp. cxlv. cc. 3. 4. Cajetan. in 3 Aquin. quæst. 25. A. 3.

THE XXXIX ARTICLES. 311

such attempts. It must be acknowledged, that the old emblematical images of the Egyptians, and the grosser ones now used by the Chinese, are much more instructing, and much less scandalous figures.

ART. XXII.

As the Roman church has gone beyond the Nicene council in the images that they allow of, so they have also gone beyond them in the degrees of the worship that they offer to them. At Nice the worship of images was very positively decreed, with anathemas against those who did it not:* a bare honour they reckoned was not enough. They thought it was a very valuable argument, that was brought from those words of Christ to the Devil, 'Thou shalt worship the Lord thy God, and him only shalt thou serve;' that here service is only appropriated to God, but not worship. Among the acts of worship they reckon the oblation of incense and lights; and the reason given by them for all this is, because the *honour of the image, or type, passes to the original, or prototype;* so that plain and direct worship was to terminate on the image itself: and Durandus passed for little less than a heretic, because he thought that images were worshipped only improperly and abusively, because at their presence we call to mind the object represented by them, which we worship before the image, as if the object itself were before us.

Con. Nic. 2. Act. 7. Act. 6.

Con. Nic. Act. 5.

Duran. in Senten. l. 3. dist. 9. q. 2. n. 15.

The council of Nice did plainly assert the direct worship of images, but they did as positively declare,† that they meant

* *Nice, 2, Act. 1. Labbæi et Cossartii,* vol. vii. p. 60. *Paris,* 1671. *Adrian I. Pope, anno* 787.

' Sanctæ et universali synodo Theodosius exiguus Christianus. Confiteor, et polliceor, et recipio amplector atque adoro principaliter intemeratam iconam domini Nostri Jesu Christi veri Dei Nostri, et iconam Dei genetricis, quæ illum sine semine peperit; et auxilium et protectionem ejus, et intercessiones illius unaquaque die ac nocte invoco ut peccator in adjutorium meum, tanquam eam, quæ habeat confidentiam apud Christum Dominum Nostrum, qui ex ea natus est. Pari modo sanctorum et laudabilissimorum Apostolorum, prophetarum, et martyrum, et patrum atque cultorum eremi iconas recipio et adoro, non tanquam deos (absit) sed affectum et amorem animæ meæ, quem habebam prius in eos, etiam nunc ostendens, rogo cunctos illos ex tota anima ut intercedant pro me ad Deum, quatenus det mihi per intercessiones eorum invenire misericordiam penes se in die judicii. Similiter et lipsana sanctorum adoro et honoro, et amplector, tanquam eorum qui decertaverint pro Christo, et acceperint gratiam ab ipso ad sanitatis efficiendas, et languores curandos, et dæmones ejiciendos, quemadmodum ecclesia Christianorum suscepit a sanctis Apostolis et patribus, et usque ad nos. Pingi autem consentio in ecclesiis sanctorum principaliter iconam domini Nostri Jesu Christi et sanctæ Dei genetricis, ex varia materia auri et argenti, et omni colore: ut carnea dispensatio ipsius omnibus innotescat.—His qui non adorant, anathema. His qui audent detrahere, &c. vel vocare illas idola, anathema. His qui non docent diligenter cunctum Christi amatorem populum adorare venerabiles iconas, &c. &c. anathema.'—[ED.]

† *Act* 7. Vol. vii. p. 556.

' Definimus in omni certitudine ac diligentia, sicut figuram preciosæ ac vivificæ crucis, ita venerabiles ac sanctas imagines proponendas, tam quæ de coloribus et tessellis, quam quæ ex alia materia congruentur in sanctis Dei ecclesiis, et sacris vasis, et vestibus, et in parietibus ac tabulis, domibus et viis: tam videlicet imaginem domini Dei et salvatoris nostri Jesu Christi quam intemeratæ dominæ nostræ sanctæ Dei genetricis, honorabilumq. angelorum, et omnium sanctorum simul et almorum virorum. Quanto enim frequentius per imaginalem formationem videntur, tanto qui has contemplantur, alacrius eriguntur ad primitivorum earum memoriam et desi-

ART. XXII.

only that it should be an honorary adoration, and not the true *latria*, which was only due to God. And whatever some modern representers and expositors of the Roman doctrine may say, to soften the harshness of the worship of images, it is very copiously proved, both from the words of the council of Nice, and from all the eminent writers in that communion, even from the time of Aquinas,* and of the modern schoolmen, and writers of controversy, that direct worship ought to be offered to the image itself: this reserve of the *latria* to God, being an evident proof, that all inferior acts of worship were allowed them. But this reserve does no way please the later writers; for Aquinas, and many from him do teach, that the same acts and degrees of worship which are due to the original, are also due to the image; they think an image has such a relation to the original, that both ought to be worshipped by the same act, and that to worship the image with any other sort of acts, is to worship it on its own account, which they think is idolatry. Whereas others adhering to the Nicene doctrine, think that the image is to be worshipped with an inferior degree, that otherwise idolatry must follow. So here the danger of idolatry is threatened of both sides; and since one of them must be chosen, thus it will follow, that let a man do what he can, he must commit idolatry, according to the opinion of some very subtile and learned men among them.

Con. Nic. Act. 2.

Con. Trid. Sess. 25.

The council of Trent did indeed decline to give a clear decision in this matter, and only decreed, that *due worship* should be given to images;† but did not determine what that *due*

---

derium, et ad osculum, et ad honorariam his adorationem tribuendam. Non tamen ad veram latriam, quæ secundum fidem est, quæq. solam divinam naturam decet, impartiendam: ita ut istis, sicuti figuræ preciosæ ac vivificæ crucis et sanctis evangeliis et reliquis sacris monumentis, incensorum et luminum oblatio ad harum honorem efficiendum exhibeatur, quemadmodum et antiquis piæ consuetudinis erat. Imaginis enim honor ad primitivum transit: et qui adorat imaginem, adorat in ea depicti subsistentiam.'

And in the same council we have the following adoration of the cross—see Act VII. p. 583. 'Crucem tuam adoramus domine, et adoramus lauceam quæ aperuit vivificum latus tuæ bonitatis.'—[ED.]

* Aquin. 2. p. q. 25. art. 3. See to the same purpose, Alex. Hales, Bonaventure, Ricardus de Media villa palud. Almans. Biel Summa Angelica, and many more cited by bishop Stillingfleet's Defence of the Charge of Idolatry, part II. chap. 2.

† The following is the decree of the council of Trent concerning the worship of relics and images:

'Sanctorum quoque martyrum, et aliorum cum Christo viventium sancta corpora, quæ viva membra fuerunt Christi, et templum Spiritus sancti, ab ipso ad æternam vitam suscitanda et glorificanda, a fidelibus venerande esse: per quæ multa beneficia a Deo hominibus præstantur: ita ut affirmantes, sanctorum reliquiis venerationem atque honorem non deberi; vel eas aliaque sacra monumenta a fidelibus inutiliter honorari; atque eorum opis impetrandæ causa sanctorum memorias frustra frequentari; omnino damnandos esse, prout jampridem eos damnavit, et nunc etiam damnat ecclesia. Imagines proro Christi, deiparæ Virginis, et aliorum sanctorum, in templis præsertim habendas et retinendas, iisque debitum honorem et venerationem impertiendam; non quod credatur inesse aliqua in iis divinitas, vel virtus, propter quam sint colendæ; vel quod ab eis sit aliquid petendum; vel quod fiducia in imaginibus sit figenda, veluti olim fiebat a gentilibus, quæ in idolis spem

worship was. And though it appears by the decree, that there were abuses committed among them in that matter, yet they only appoint some regulations, concerning such images as were to be suffered, and that others were to be removed; but they left the divines to fight out the matter concerning the *due worship* that ought to be given to images. They were then in haste, and intended to offend no party; and as they would not justify all that had been said or done concerning the worship of images, so they would condemn no part of it: yet they confirmed the Nicene council, and in particular made use of that maxim of theirs, that the *honour of the type goes to the prototype;* and thus they left it as they found it. So that the dispute goes on still as hot as ever. The practice of the Roman church is express for the *latria* to be given to images: and therefore all that write for it do frequently cite that hymn, *Crux Ave spes unica, auge piis justitiam, reisque dona veniam.* It is expressly said in the Pontifical, *Cruci debetur latria,* and the prayers used in the consecration of a cross; it is prayed,* that the *blessing of that cross, on which Christ hung, may be in it, that it may be a healthful remedy to mankind, a strengthener of faith, an increaser of good works, the redemption of souls, and a comfort, protection, and defence, against the cruelty of our enemies.* These with all the other acts of adoration used among them, seem to favour those who are for a *latria* to be given to all those images, to the originals of which it is due; and in the like proportion for *dulia* and *hyperdulia* to other images. It is needless to prosecute this matter further.

It seemed necessary to say so much, to justify our church, which has in her Homilies laid this charge of idolatry very severely on the church of Rome; and this is so high an imputation, that those who think it false, as they cannot, with a good conscience, subscribe, or require others to subscribe the Article concerning the Homilies, so they ought to retract their own subscriptions, and to make solemn reparations in justice and honour, for laying so heavy an imputation unjustly upon that whole communion.

There is nothing that can be brought from scripture, that

---

suam collocabant; sed quoniam honos, qui eis exhibetur, refertur ad prototypa, quæ illæ repræsentant: ita ut per imagines, quas osculamur, et coram quibus caput aperimus et procumbimus, Christum adoremus, et sanctos, quorum illæ similitudinem gerunt veneremur; id quod conciliorum, præsertim vero secundæ Nicænæ synodi, decretis contra imaginum oppugnatores est sancitum.' *Sessio* xxv. In this Sessio the council of Trent, it will be observed, appeals to the authority of the second Nicene council on the subject of image-worship.—[ED.]

* In benedictione novæ Crucis.

Rogamus te Domine, sancte Pater, omnipotens sempiterne Deus, ut digneris benedicere hoc lignum Crucis tuæ, ut sit remedium salutare generi humano, sit soliditas fidei, profectus bonorum operum, redemptio animarum, sit solamen et protectio ac tutela contra sæva jacula inimicorum. Per Dom.

Sanctificetur lignum istud in nomine Patris et Filii et Spiritus Sancti, et benedictio illius ligni in quo membra sancta Salvatoris suspensa sunt sit in isto ligno, ut orantes inclinantesque se propter Deum ante istam crucem inveniant corporis et animæ sanitatem per eundem.

ART. XXII.

Heb. ix. 3, 5, 7.

has a show of an argument for supporting image-worship, unless it be that of the cherubims that were in the 'holiest of all;' and they, as is supposed, were worshipped, at least by the high-priest when he went thither, once a year, if not by the whole people. But first there is a great difference to be made between a form of worship immediately prescribed by God, and another form that not only has no warrant for it, but seems to be very expressly forbidden. It is plain, the cherubims were not seen by the people, and so they could be no visible object of worship to them. They were scarce seen by the high-priest himself, for the holiest of all was quite dark; no light coming into it, but what came through the veil from the holy place; and even that had very little light. Nor is there a word concerning the high-priest's worshipping either the ark or the cherubim. It is true, there is a place in the Psalms that seems to favour this; as it is rendered by the Vulgar, 'worship his footstool, for it is holy;' but both the Hebrew and the Septuagint have it, as it is in our translation, 'worship at his footstool, for he is holy;' and all the Greek fathers cite these words so. Many of the Latin fathers do also cite them according to the Greek; and the last words of the Psalm, in which the same words are repeated, make the sense of it evident: for there it is thus varied, 'Exalt ye the Lord our God, and worship at his holy hill, for the Lord our God is holy.' These words coming so soon after the former, are a paraphrase to them, and determine their sense. No doubt the high-priest worshipped God, who dwelt between the cherubims, in that cloud of glory in which he shewed himself visibly present in his temple; but there is no sort of reason to think, that in so majestic a presence, adoration could be offered to any thing else; or that after the high-priest had adored the divine essence so manifested, he would have fallen to worship the ark and the cherubims. This agrees ill with the figure that is so much used in this matter of a king and his chair of state; for in the presence of the king, all respects terminate in his person, whatsoever may be done in his absence.

Psal. xcix. 5, 9.

And thus, this being not so much as a precedent, much less an argument, for the use of images; and there being nothing else brought from scripture, that with any sort of wresting can be urged for it, and the sense and practice of the whole church being so express against it, the progress of it having been so long and so much disputed, the tendency of it to superstition and abuse being by their own confession so visible; the scandal that it gives to Jews and Mahometans being so apparent, and it carrying in its outward appearances such a conformity (to say at present no more) to heathenish idolatry, we think we have all possible advantages in this argument. We adhere to that purity of worship which is in both Testaments so much insisted on; we avoid all scandal, and make no approaches to heathenism, and follow the pattern set us by the primitive church. And as our simplicity of worship needs not be defended, since it proves itself; so no proofs are brought for the other side, but only a pretended usefulness in outward figures, to raise the mind by the senses to just apprehensions of spiritual objects; which, allowing it true, will only conclude for the historical use of images, but not for the directing our worship towards them. But the effect is quite contrary to the pretence; for, instead of raising the mind by the senses, the mind is rather sunk by them into gross ideas.

ART. XXII.

The bias of human nature lies to sense, and to form gross imaginations of incorporeal objects; and therefore, instead of gratifying these, we ought to wean our minds from them, and to raise them above them all we can. Even men of speculation and abstraction feel nature in this grows too hard for them; but the vulgar is apt to fall so headlong into these conceits, that it looks like the laying of snares for them, to furnish them with such methods and helps for their having gross thoughts of spiritual objects. The fondness that the people have for images, their readiness to believe the most incredible stories concerning them, the expense they are at to enrich and adorn them, their prostrations before them, their confidence in them, their humble and tender embracing and kissing of them, their pompous and heathenish processions to do them honour, the fraternities erected for particular images, not to mention the more universal and established practices of directing their prayers to them, of setting lights before them, and of incensing them; these, I say, are things too well known, to such as have seen the way of that religion, that they should need to be much enlarged on; and yet they are not only allowed of, but encouraged. Those among them who have too much good sense that they should sink into those foolish apprehensions themselves, yet must not only bear with them, but often comply with them to avoid the giving of scandal, as they call it; not considering the much greater scandal that they give, when they encourage others by their practice to go on in these follies. The enlarging into all the corruptions occasioned by this way of worship would carry me far; but it seems not necessary, the thing is so plain in itself.

The next head in this Article is a full instance of it, which is, the worship of relics. It is no wonder that great care was taken in the beginnings of Christianity, to shew all possible respect and tenderness even to the bodies of the martyrs. There is something of this planted so deep in human nature, that though the philosophy of it cannot be so well made out, yet it seems to be somewhat more than an universal custom; humanity is of its side, and is apt to carry men to the profusions of pomp and cost: all religions do agree in this, so that we need not wonder if Christians, in the first fervour of their religion, believing the resurrection so firmly as they did, and having a high sense of the honour done to Christ and his religion by the sufferings of the martyrs; if, I say, they studied to gather their bones and ashes together, and bury them decently. They thought it a sign of their being joined with them in one body, to hold their assemblies at the places where they were buried: this might be also considered as a motive to encourage others to follow the example that they had given them, even to martyrdom: and therefore all the marks of honour were put even upon their bodies that could be thought on, except worship. After the ages of persecution were over, a fondness of having and keeping their relics began to spread itself in many places. Monks fed that humour by carrying them about. We find in St. Austin's works, that superstition was making a great progress in Afric upon these heads, of which he complains frequently. Vigilantius had done it to more purpose in Spain; and did not only complain of the excesses, but of the thing in itself. St. Jerome fell unmercifully upon him for it, and sets a high value upon relics, yet he does not speak one word of worshipping them; he denies and disclaims it, and seems only to allow of a great fondness for them; and, with most of that age, he was very apt to believe, that miracles were oft wrought by them. When superstition is once suffered to mix with religion, it will be still gaining ground, and it admits of no bounds: so this matter went on, and new legends were invented; but when the controversy of image-worship began, it followed that as an accessary. The enshrining of relics occasioned the most excellent sort of images; and they were thought the best preservatives possible both for soul and body; no presents grew to be more valued than relics; and it was an easy thing for the popes to furnish the world plentifully that way, but chiefly since the discovery of the catacombs, which has furnished them with stores not to be exhausted. The council of Trent did in this, as in the point of images ; it appointed *relics* to be *venerated*, but did not determine the degree;* so it left the world in possession of a most excessive dotage upon them They are used every where by them as sacred charms, kissed. and worshipped, they are served with lights and incense.

In opposition to all this, we think, that all decent honours are indeed due to the bodies of the saints, which were once the 'temples of the Holy Ghost;' but since it is said, that God took that care of the *body of Moses*, so as to bury it in such a manner that no man knew of his sepulchre, there seems to have been in this a peculiar caution guarding against that superstition, which the Jews might very probably have fallen into with relation to his body. And this seems so clear an indication of the will of God in this matter, that we reckon we

---

* For the decree concerning relic-worship, see note, p. 313.—[ED.]

are very safe when we do no further honour to the body of a saint, than to bury it. And though that saint had been ever so eminent, not only for his holiness, but even for miracles wrought by him, by his shadow, or even by looking upon him; yet the history of the *brazen serpent* shews us, that a fondness even on the instruments, that God made use of to work miracles by, degenerates easily to the superstition of burning incense to them; but when that appears, it is to be checked, even by breaking that which was so abused. Hezekiah is commended for breaking in pieces that noble remain of Moses's time till then preserved; neither its antiquity, nor the signal miracles once wrought by it, could balance the ill use that was then made of it: that good king broke it, for which he might have had a worse name than an *iconoclast*, if he had lived in some ages. It is true, miracles were of old wrought by Aaron's rod, by Elisha's bones after his death, and the one was preserved, but not worshipped; nor was there any superstition that followed on the other. Not a word of this fondness appears in the beginnings of Christianity; though it had been an easy thing at that time to have furnished the world with pieces of our Saviour's garments, hair, or nails; and great store might have been had of the Virgin's and the apostles' relics: St. Stephen's and St. James's bones might have been then parcelled about: and if that spirit had then reigned in the church, which has been in the Roman church now above a thousand years, we should have heard of the relics that were sent about from Jerusalem to all the churches. But when such things might have been had in great abundance, and have been known not to be counterfeits, we hear not a word of them. If a fondness for relics had been in the church upon Christ's ascension, what care would have been taken to have made great collections of them!

Then we see no other care about the body of St. Stephen but to bury it; and not long after that time upon St. Polycarp's martyrdom, when the Jews, who had set on the prosecution against him, suggested, that, if the Christians could gain his body, they would perhaps forsake Christ and worship him; they rejected the accusation with horror; for in the epistle which the church of Smyrna writ upon his martyrdom, after they mention this insinuation, they have those remarkable words, which belong both to this head, and to that which follows it of the invocation and worship of saints. *These men know not that we can neither forsake Christ, who suffered for the salvation of all that are saved, the innocent for the guilty, nor worship any other; Him truly being the Son of God we adore: but the martyrs, and disciples, and followers of the Lord, we justly love, for that extraordinary good mind, which they have expressed toward their King and Master, of whose happiness God grant that we may partake, and that we may learn by their examples.* The Jews had so persuaded the

ART. XXII.

2 Kings xviii. 4.

2 Kings xiii. 21.

Ep. Euseb. l. iv. c. 15.

318   AN EXPOSITION OF

ART XXII.

Gentiles of Smyrna of this matter, that they burnt St. Polycarp's body; but the Christians gathered up his bones with much respect, so that it appeared how they honoured them, though they could not worship them; and they buried them in a convenient place,* which they intended to make the place where they *should hold, by the blessing of God, the yearly commemoration of that birth-day of his martyrdom, with much joy and gladness, both to honour the memory of those who had overcome in that glorious engagement, and to instruct and confirm all others by their example.* This is one of the most valuable pieces of true and genuine antiquity; and it shews us very fully the sense of that age both concerning the relics, and the worship of the saints. In the following ages, we find no characters of any other regard to the bones or bodies of the saints, but that they buried them very decently, and did annually commemorate their death, calling it their *birth-day.* And it may incline men strongly to suspect the many miracles that were published in the fourth century, as wrought at the tombs, or memories of the martyrs, or by their relics, that we hear of none of those in the former three centuries; for it seems there was more occasion for them during the persecution, than after it was over; it being much more necessary then to furnish Christians with so strong a motive as this must have been, to 'resist even to blood,' when God was pleased to glorify himself so signally in his saints. This, I say, forces us to fear, that credulity and imagination, or somewhat worse than both these, might have had a large share in those extraordinary things that are related to us by great men in the fourth century. He must have a great disposition to believe wonderful things, that can digest the extraordinary relations that are even in St. Basil, St. Ambrose, and St. Austin; and most signally in St. Jerome: for instance, that after one had stolen Hilarion's body out of Cyprus, and brought it to Palestine, upon which Constantia, that went constantly to his tomb, was ready to have broke her heart; God took such pity on her, that as the true body wrought

Basil.
Hom. xix.
in Sanct.
quadragint.
Martyr. in
Hom. xxiii.
in Sanct.
Mart.
Maman.
Paul. in
vita
Ambros.
Aug. de
Civit. Dei,
lib. xxii.
c. 8.

* In reference to this subject, Dr. Milner, in his 'End of Religious Controversy,' thus writes:—

'The whole history of the martyrs, from St. Ignatius and St. Polycarp, the disciples of the apostles, whose relics, after their execution, were carried away by the Christians, as "more valuable than gold and precious stones," down to the latest martyr, incontestibly proves the veneration which the church has ever entertained for these sacred objects.' We might fairly conclude from these words that the early Christians held the popish doctrine of the worship of relics; and indeed Dr. Milner refers with such confidence to Eusebius, that one not acquainted with the sophistry and dishonesty of the advocates of popery would unhesitatingly conclude that the historian of the early church had clearly established this position. But what is the fact? Let Eusebius himself speak: 'So we gathered his (Polycarp's) bones, more precious than pearls, and better tried than gold, and *buried them in the place that was fit for that purpose,'* &c. This is the passage to which Dr. M. refers; and those marked are the words which immediately follow the Doctor's quotation from Eusebius, but which, in his defence of relic-worship, have been so carefully suppressed.—[ED.]

great miracles in Palestine, so likewise very great miracles continued still to be wrought at the tomb, where it was at first laid. One, in respect to those great men, is tempted to suspect that many things might have been foisted into their writings in the following ages. A great many practices of this kind have been made manifest beyond contradiction.* Whole books have been made to pass for the writings of fathers, that do evidently bear the marks of a much later date, where the fraud was carried too far not to be discovered. At other times parcels have been laid in among their genuine productions, which cannot be so easily distinguished; they not being liable to so many critical inquiries, as may be made on a larger work. It is a little unaccountable how so many marvellous things should be published in that age; and yet that St. Chrysostom, who spent his whole life between two of the publickest scenes of the world, Antioch and Constantinople, and was an active and inquisitive man, should not so much as have heard of any such wonderful stories; but should have taken pains to remove a prejudice out of the minds of his hearers, that might arise from this, that whereas they heard of many miracles that were wrought in the times of the apostles, none were wrought at that time; upon which, he gives very good reason why it was so. His saying so positively, *That none were wrought at that time*, without so much as a *salvo* for what he might have heard from other parts, shews plainly, that he had not heard of any at all. For he was orator enough to have made even looser reports look probable. This does very much shake the credit of those amazing relations that we find in St. Jerome, St. Ambrose, and St. Austin. It is true, there seems to have been an opinion very generally received both in the east and the west, at that time, which must have very much heightened the growing superstition for relics. It was a remnant both of Judaism and Gentilism, that the souls of the martyrs hovered about their tombs, called their memories; and that therefore they might be called upon, and spoke to there. This appears even in the council of Elliberis, where the superstition of lighting candles about their tombs in daylight is forbidden: the reason given is, because the *spirits were not to be disquieted*. St. Basil, and the other fathers, that do so often mention the going to their memories, do very plainly insinuate their being present at them, and hearing themselves called upon. This may be the reason why, among all the saints that are so much magnified in that age, we never find the blessed Virgin so much as once mentioned. They knew not where her body was laid, they had no tomb for her, no nor any of her relics

ART. XXII.

Chrysost. Hom. 6. in 1 ad Cor. ii.

Basil. Hom. xix. in Sanct. quadragint. Martyr.

* The reader will find valuable information on this subject in Dr. James's 'Treatise of the Corruptions of Scripture, Councils, and Fathers, by the Prelates, Pastors, and Pillars of the church of Rome, for maintenance of Popery,' in which the bastardy of the false Fathers and the corruption of the true Fathers are demonstrated beyond the possibility of contradiction.—[ED.]

ART. XXII.

margin: ART. XXII.

or utensils. But upon the occasion of Nestorius's denying her to be the *mother of God,* and by carrying the opposition to that too far, a superstition for her was set on foot; it made a progress sufficient to balance the slowness of its beginning; the whole world was then filled with very extravagant devotions for her.

The great noise we find concerning relics in the end of the fourth century, has all the characters of novelty possible in it; for those who speak of it, do not derive it from former times. One circumstance in this is very remarkable, that neither Trypho, Celsus, Lucian, nor Cecilius, do object to the Christians of their time their fondness for dead bodies, or praying about their tombs, which they might well have alleged in opposition to what the Christians charged them with, if there had been any occasion for it. Whereas this custom was no sooner begun, than both Julian and Eunapius reproach the Christians for it. Julian, it is true, speaks only of their calling on God over sepulchres: Eunapius writ after him; and it seems, in his time, that which Julian sets forth as a calling upon God, was advanced to an invocation of them. He says, they *heaped together the bones and skulls of men that had been punished for many crimes* (it was natural enough for a spiteful heathen to give this representation of their martyrdom), *holding them for gods:* and after some scurrilous invectives against them, he adds, *they are called martyrs, and made the ministers and messengers of prayer to the gods.* This seems to be a very evident proof of the novelty of this matter. As for the adoring them, when Vigilantius asked, *Why dost thou kiss and adore a little dust put up in fine linen?* St. Jerome, though excessively fond of them, denies this very positively, and that in very injurious terms, being offended at the injustice of the reproach. Yet as long as the bodies of the martyrs were let lie quietly in their memories, the fond opinion of their being present, and hearing what was said to them, made the invocating them look like one man's desiring the assistance of another good man's prayers; so that this step seemed to have a fair colour. But when their bodies were pulled asunder, and carried up and down, so that it was believed miracles abounded every where about them; and when their bones and relics grew to increase and multiply, so that they had more bones and limbs than God and nature had given them; then new hypotheses were to be found out to justify the calling upon them every where, as their relics were spread. St. Jerome, in his careless way, says, *they followed the Lamb whithersoever he went,* and seems to make no doubt of their being, if not every where, yet in several places at once. But St. Austin, who could follow a consequence much further in his thoughts, though he doubted not but that men were much the better for the prayers of the martyrs, yet he confesses that it passed the strength of his understanding to

margin: Ap. Cyr. lib. 10. con. Julian. Eunap. in vita Ædess.

margin: Hieron. adv. Vigilant. Aug. cura pro mortuis, c. 16.

determine, whether they heard those who called upon them at their memories, or wheresoever else they were believed to have appeared, or not. But the devotions that are spoken of by all of that age, are related as having been offered at their memories; so that this seems to have been the general opinion, as well as it was the common practice of that age, though it is no wonder if this conceit once giving some colour and credit to the invocating them, that did quickly increase itself to a general invocation of them every where. And thus a fondness for their relics, joined with the opinion of their relation and nearness to them, did in a short time grow up to a direct worshipping of them; and, by the fruitfulness that always follows superstition, did spread itself further, to their clothes, utensils, and every thing else that had any relation to them.

_{ART. XXII.}

There was cause given in St. Austin's time to suspect that many of the bones which were carried about by monks, were none of their bones, but impostures, which very much shakes the credit of the miracles wrought by them, since we have no reason to think that God would support such impostures with miracles; as, on the other hand, there is no reason to think that false relics would have passed upon the world, if miracles had been believed to accompany true ones, unless they had their miracles likewise to attest their value: so let this matter be turned which way it may, the credit both of relics, and of the miracles wrought by them, is not a little shaken by it. But in the following ages we have more than presumptions, that there was much of this false coin that went abroad in the world. It was not possible to distinguish the false from the true. The freshness of colour and smell, so often boasted, might have been easily managed by art; the varieties of those relics, the different methods of discovering them, the shinings that were said to be about their tombs, with the smells that broke out of them, the many apparitions that accompanied them, and the signal cures that were wrought by them, as they grew to fill the world with many volumes of legends, many more lying yet in the manuscripts in many churches, than have been published: all these, I say, carry in them such characters of fraud and imposture on the one hand, and of cruelty and superstition on the other; so much craft, and so much folly, that they had their full effect upon the world, even in contradiction to the clearest evidence possible; the same saints having more bodies and heads than one, in different places, and yet all equally celebrated with miracles. A great profusion of wealth and pomp was laid out in honouring them, new devotions were still invented for them: and though these things are too palpably false to be put upon us now, in ages of more light, where every thing will not go down because it is confidently affirmed; yet as we know how great a part of the devotion of the Latin church this continued to be for many ages before the Reformation, so the same trade is still

Aug. de opere monach. c. 28.

Y

ART. XXII. carried on, where the same ignorance, and the same superstition, does still continue.

I come now to consider the last head of this Article, which is the invocation of saints,* of which much has been already said by an anticipation: for there is that connection between the worship of relics and the invocation of saints, that the treating of the one does very naturally carry one to say somewhat of the other. It is very evident that saints were not invocated in the Old Testament. God being called so oft the God of Abraham, Isaac, and Jacob, seems to give a much better warrant for it, than any thing that can be alleged from the New Testament. Moses was their lawgiver, and their mediator and intercessor with God; and his intercession, as it had been very effectual for them, so it had shewed itself in a very extraordinary instance of his desiring that his name might be 'blotted out of the book which he had written,' rather than the people should perish; when God had offered to him, that he would raise up a new nation to himself, out of his posterity God had also made promises to that nation by him: so that it might be natural enough, considering the genius of superstition, for the Jews to have called to him in their miseries, to obtain the performance of those promises made by him to them. We may upon this refer the matter to every man's judgment, whether Abraham and Moses might not have been much more reasonably invocated by the Jews according to what we find in the Old Testament, than any saint can be under the New: yet we are sure they were not prayed to. Elijah's going up to heaven in so miraculous a manner, might also have been thought a good reason for any to have prayed to him: but nothing of that kind was then practised. They understood prayer to be a part of that worship which they owed to God only: so that the praying to any other, had been to a certain degree the having another God *before*, or besides the *true Jehovah*. They never prayed to any other, they called upon him, and made mention of no other: the rule was without exception, 'Call upon me in the time of trouble; I will hear thee, and thou shalt glorify me.' Upon this point there is no dispute.

Exod. xxxii. 32.

Psal. l. 15.

* The council of Trent thus decreed in the matter of saint-worship:—' Mandat sancta synodus omnibus episcopis, et cæteris docendi munus curamque sustinentibus, ut, juxta catholicæ et apostolicæ ecclesiæ usum, a primævis Christianæ religionis temporibus receptum, sanctorumque patrum consensionem, et sacrorum conciliorum decreta, in primis de sanctorum intercessione, invocatione, reliquiarum honore, et legitimo imaginum usu, fideles diligenter instruant, docentes eos, sanctos, una cum Christo regnantes, orationes suas pro hominibus Deo offerre, bonum atque utile esse suppliciter eos invocare; et ob beneficia impetranda a Deo per Filium ejus Jesum Christum, Dominum nostrum qui solus noster redemptor et salvator est, ad eorum orationes, opem, auxilium confugere: illos vero qui negant sanctos æterna felicitate in cœlo fruentes, invocandos esse; aut qui asserunt, vel illos pro hominibus non orare, vel eorum, ut pro nobis etiam singulis orent, invocationem esse idololatriam; vel pugnare cum verbo Dei, adversarique honori unius mediatoris Dei et hominum Jesu Christi; vel stultum esse, in cœlo regnantibus voce vel mente supplicare; impie sentire.' *Sessio* xxv.—[ED.]

In the New Testament we see the same method followed, with this only exception, that Jesus Christ is proposed as our Mediator; and that not only in the point of redemption, which is not denied by those of the church of Rome, but even in the point of intercession; for when St. Paul is treating concerning the prayers and supplications that are to be offered 'for all men,' he concludes that direction in these words: 'For there is one God and one Mediator between God and man, the man Christ Jesus.' We think the silence of the New Testament might be a sufficient argument for this: but these words go further, and imply a prohibition to address our prayers to God by any other mediator. All the directions that are given us of trusting in God, and praying to him, are upon the matter prohibitions of trusting to any other, or of calling on any other. Invocation and faith are joined together: 'How shall they call on him in whom they have not believed?' So that we ought only to pray to God, and to Christ, according to those words, 'Ye believe in God, believe also in me.' We do also know that it was a part of heathenish idolatry to invocate either demons or departed men, whom they considered as good beings subordinate to the Divine Essence, and employed by God in the government of the world; and they had almost the same speculations about them, that have been since introduced into the church, concerning angels and saints. In the condemning all idolatry, no reserve is made in scripture for this, as being faulty, only because it was applied wrong; or that it might be set right when directed better. On the contrary, when some men, under the pretence of 'humility and of will-worship,' did, according to the Platonic notions, offer to bring in the 'worship of angels' into the church of Colosse, pretending, as is probable, that those spirits who were employed by God in the ministry of the gospel, ought, in gratitude for that service, and out of respect to their dignity, to be worshipped: St. Paul condemns all this, without any reserves made for lower degrees of worship; he charges the Christians to 'beware of that vain philosophy,' and not to be deceived by those shows of *humility*, or the speculations of men, who pretended to explain that which they did not know, as 'intruding into things which they had not seen, vainly puffed up by their fleshly mind.' If any degrees of invocating saints or angels had been consistent with the Christian religion, this was the proper place of declaring them: but the condemning that matter so absolutely, looks as a very express prohibition of all sort of worship to angels. And when St. John fell down to worship the angel, that had made him such glorious discoveries upon two several occasions, the answer he had was, 'See thou do it not: worship God: I am thy fellow-servant.' It is probable enough that St. John might imagine, that the angel, who had made such discoveries to him, was *Jesus*

ART. XXII.

1 Tim. ii. 5.

Rom. x. 14.

John xiv. 1.

Col. ii. 18.

Ver. 8, 9, 10.

Rev. xix. 10. Rev. xxii. 9.

ART. XXII. Christ: but the answer plainly shews, that no sort of worship ought to be offered to angels, nor to any but God. The reason given excludes all sorts of *worship*, for that cannot be among fellow-servants.

As angels are thus forbid to be worshipped, so no mention is made of worshipping or invocating any saints that had died for the faith, such as St. Stephen and St. James. In the Epistle to the Hebrews, they are required to 'remember them which had the rule over them, and to follow their faith;' but not a word of praying to them. So that if either the silence of the scriptures on this head, or if plain declarations to the contrary, could decide this matter, the controversy would soon be at an end. Christ is always proposed to us as the only person by whom we come unto God: and when St. Paul speaks against the worshipping of angels, he sets Christ out in his glory in opposition to it. 'For in him dwelleth all the fulness of the Godhead bodily; and ye are complete in him, which is the head of all principality and power;' pursuing that reason in a great many particulars.

From the scriptures, if we go to the first ages of Christianity, we find nothing that favours this, but a great deal to the contrary. Irenæus disclaims the invocation of angels. The memorable passage of the church of Smyrna, formerly cited, is a full proof of their sense in this matter. Clemens Alexandrinus and Tertullian do often mention the worship that was given to God only by prayer: and so far were they at that time from praying to saints, that they prayed for them, as was formerly explained: they thought they were not yet in the presence of God, so they could not pray to them as long as that opinion continued. That form of praying for them is in the Apostolical Constitutions. In all that collection, which seems to be a work of the fourth or fifth century, there is not a word that intimates their praying to saints. In the council of Laodicea,* there is an express condemnation of those who invocated angels;† this is called *a secret idolatry, and a forsaking of our Lord Jesus Christ.* The first apologists for Christianity do arraign the worship of demons, and of such as had once lived on earth, in a style that shewed they did not apprehend that the argument could be turned against them, for their worshipping either angels or departed saints. When the Arian controversy arose, the invocation of Christ is urged by Athanasius, Basil, Cyril, and other fathers, as an evident

---

* Con. Laod. c. 35. Just. Mart. Apol. 2. Iren. l. 2. c. 35. Orig. con. Cels. l. 8. Tert. de Orat. c. 1. Athanas. ad adelph. frat. et confess. cont. Arian. epist. Greg. Nazianz. in sanct. Lumin. Orat. orat. 30. Greg. Niss. in Basil. cont. Eunap. Basil. Hom. in sanct. Christ. generat. cont. Eunom. l. 4. Epiph. Hæres. 64, 69, 78, 79. Theod. de Hær. Fabul. l. 5. c. 3. Chrysost. de Trinit.

† Council of Laodicea, c. 25. s. 24. decreed, 'That we ought not to forsake the church of God, and depart aside, and invocate angels (Αγγιλους ονομαζειν), and make meetings, which are things forbidden: if any man therefore be found to give himself to this privy idolatry, let him be accursed, because he hath forsaken our Lord Jesus Christ the Son of God, and betaken himself to idolatry.'—[ED.]

argument that he was neither made nor created; since they did not pray to angels, or any other creatures; from whence they concluded that Christ was God. These are convincing proofs of the doctrine of the three first, and of a good part of the fourth century.

ART. XXII.

It is true, as was confessed upon the former head, they began with martyrs in the end of the fourth century. They fancied they heard those that called to them; and upon that it was no wonder if they invocated them, and so private prayers to them began. But, as appears both by the Constitutions, and several of the writers of that time, the public offices were yet preserved pure. St. Austin says plainly, *The Gentiles built temples, raised altars, ordained priests, and offered sacrifices to their gods: but we do not erect temples to our martyrs, as if they were gods; but memories as to dead men, whose spirits live with God; nor do we erect altars, upon which we sacrifice to martyrs; but to one God only do we offer, to the God of martyrs, and our God; at which sacrifice they are named in their place and order, as men of God, who in confessing him have overcome the world; but they are not invocated by the priest that sacrifices.* It seems the form of praying for the saints mentioned in the Constitutions, was not used in the churches of Afric in St. Austin's time: he says very positively, that they did not pray for them, but did praise God for them: and he says in express words, *Let not the worship of dead men be any part of our religion; they ought so to be honoured, that we may imitate them, but not worshipped.* God was indeed prayed to, in the fifth century, to hear the intercession of the saints and martyrs; but there is a great difference between praying to God to favour us on their account, and praying immediately to them to hear us.

Aug. con. Serm. Ar. c. 29. con. Max. 1.13. c. 4. Aug. de Civ. Dei, 1.22. c. 10. l. 8. c. 27.

Aug. de vera Rel. c. 55.

The praying to them imports either their being every where, or their knowing all things; and as it is a blasphemous piece of idolatry to ascribe that to them without a divine communication; so it is a great presumption in any man to fancy that they may be prayed to, and to build so many parts of worship upon it, barely upon some probabilities and inferences, without an express revelation about it. For the saints may be perfectly happy in the enjoyment of God without seeing all things in him; nor have we any reason to carry that further than the scripture has done. But as the invocating of martyrs grew from a calling to them at their memories, to a general calling to them in all places; so from the invocating martyrs, they went on to pray to other saints; yet that was at first ventured on doubtfully, and only in funeral orations; where an address to the dead person to pray for those that were then honouring his memory, might, perhaps, come in as a figure of pompous eloquence; in which Nazianzen, one of the first that uses it, did often give himself a very great compass; yet he and others

ART. soften such figures with this, *If there is any sense or know-*
XXII. *ledge of what we do below.*

From prayers to God to receive the intercessions of martyrs and saints, it came in later ages to be usual to have litanies to them, and to pray immediately to them; but at first this was only a desire to them to pray for those who did thus invocate them, *Ora pro nobis.* But so impossible is it to restrain superstition, when it has once got head, and has prevailed, that in conclusion all things that were asked either of God or Christ, came to be asked from the saints in the same humility both of gesture and expression; in which if there was any difference made, it seemed to be rather on the side of the blessed Virgin and the saints, as appears by the ten *Ave's* for one *Pater*, and that humble prostration in which all fall down every day to worship her: the prayer used constantly to her, *Maria, Mater gratiæ, Mater misericordiæ, tu nos ab hoste protege, et hora mortis suscipe,* is an immediate acknowledgment of her as the giver of these things; such are, *Solve vincla reis, profer lumen cæcis;* with many others of that nature. The collection of these swells to a huge bulk, *Jure Matris impera Redemptori,* is an allowed address to her; not to mention an infinity of most scandalous ones, that are not only tolerated, but encouraged, in that church.* Altars are consecrated to her honour, and to the honour of other saints; but which is more, the sacrifice of the mass is offered up to her honour, and to the honour of the saints: and in the form of absolution, the pardon of sins, the increase of grace, and eternal life, are prayed for to the penitent by the virtue of the passion of Christ, and the merits of the blessed Virgin, and of all the saints. The pardon of sins and eternal life are also prayed for from angels, *Angelorum concio sacra, archangelorum turma inclyta, nostra diluant jam peccata, præstando supernam*

---

* We pass over the many proofs of this idolatry to be found in the writings of papal divines; and extract two from works in which we are sure to find the most moderate statement of their views on this subject. The first, from the catechism of the council of Trent, is as follows:—

'Jure autem sancta Dei ecclesia huic gratiarum actioni preces etiam et implorationem sanctissimæ Dei Matris adjunxit, qua pie atque suppliciter ad eam confugeremus, ut nobis peccatoribus sua intercessione conciliaret Deum, bonaque tum ad hanc, tum ad æternam vitam necessaria impetraret. Ergo nos exules, filii Evæ, qui hanc lacrymarum vallem incolimus, assidue misericordiæ matrem, ac fidelis populi advocatam invocare debemus, ut oret pro nobis peccatoribus, ab eaque hac prece opem et auxilium implorare, cujus et præstantissima merita apud Deum esse, et summam voluntatem juvandi humanum genus, nemo, nisi impie et nefarie, dubitare potest.' *Cat. ad Paroch. De oratione, Pro quibus orandum sit.* The other is given according to the translation in the Laity's Directory (a popish publication) for the year 1833. 'We select for the date of our letter this most joyful day on which we celebrate the solemn festival of the most blessed Virgin's triumphant assumption into heaven, that she who has been through every great calamity our patroness and protectress, may watch over us writing to you, and lead our mind by her heavenly influence to those counsels which may prove most salutary to Christ's flock. . . . . But that all may have a successful and happy issue, let us raise our eyes to the most blessed Virgin Mary, who alone destroys heresies, who is our greatest hope, yea, the entire ground of our hope.' *Encyclical Letter of pope Gregory XVI. (the present pontiff.)*—[ED.]

cœli gloriam. Many strains of this kind are to be found in the hymns and other public offices of that church: and though in the late corrections of their offices, some of the more scandalous are left out, yet those here cited, with a great many more to the same purpose, are still preserved. And the council of Trent did plainly intend to connive at all these things, for they did not restrain the invocation of saints, only to be an address to them to pray for us, which is the common disguise with which they study to cover this matter: but by the decree of the council, the flying to *their help and assistance*, as well as to their *intercession*, is encouraged; which shews that the council would not limit this part of their devotion to a bare *Ora pro nobis;* that might have seemed flat and low, and so it might have discouraged it; therefore they made use of words that will go as far as superstition can carry them. So that if the invocating them, if the making vows to them, the dedicating themselves to them; if the flying to them in all distresses, in the same acts, and in the same words, that the scriptures teach us to fly to God with; and if all the studied honours of processions and other pompous rites towards their images, that are invented to do them honour; if, I say, all this does amount to idolatry, then we are sure they are guilty of it; since they *honour the creature* not only *besides*, but (in the full extent of that phrase) *more than the Creator.*

ART. XXII.

Rom. i. 25.

And now let us see what is the foundation of all these devotions, against which we bring arguments, that, to speak modestly of them, are certainly such that there should be matters of great weight in the other scale to balance them. Nothing is pretended from scripture, nor from any thing that is genuine, for above three hundred and fifty years after Christ. In a word, the practice of the church, since the end of the fourth century, and the authority of tradition, of popes and councils, must bear this burden. These are consequences that do not much affect us; for though we pay great respect to many great men that flourished in the fourth and fifth centuries, yet we cannot compare that age with the three that went before it. Those great men give us a sad account of the corruptions of that time, not only among the laity, but the clergy; and their being so flexible in matters of faith, as they appeared to be in the whole course of the Arian controversy, gives us very just reason to suspect the practices of that age, in which the protection and encouragements that the church received from the first Christian emperors, were not improved to the best advantage.

The justest abatement that we can offer for this corruption, which is too manifest to be either denied or justified, is this, they were then engaged with the heathens, and were much set on bringing them over to the Christian religion. In order to that it was very natural for them to think of all methods possible to accommodate Christianity to their taste. It was, perhaps, observed how far the apostles complied with the Jews, that they might gain them. St. Paul had said, that to 'the Jews he became a Jew;' and 'to them that were without law,' that is, the Gentiles, 'as one without law; that by all means he might gain some.' They might think that if the Jews, who had abused the light of a revealed religion, who had rejected and crucified the Messias, and persecuted his followers, and had in all respects corrupted both their doctrine and their morals, were waited on and complied with, in the observance of that very law which was abrogated by the death of Christ, but was still insisted on by them as of perpetual obligation; and yet that after the apostles had made a solemn decision in the matter, they continued to conform themselves to that law; all this might be applied with some advantages to this matter. The Gentiles had nothing but the light of nature to govern them; they might seem willing to become Christians, but they still despised the nakedness and simplicity of that religion. And it is reasonable enough to think that the emperors and other great men might in a political view, considering the vast strength of *heathenism*, press the bishops of those times to use all imaginable ways to adorn Christianity with such an exterior form of worship, as might be most acceptable to them, and might most probably bring them over to it.

The Christians had long felt the weight of persecution from them, and were, no doubt, much frightened with the danger of a relapse in Julian's time. It is natural to all men to desire to be safe, and to weaken the numbers of their implacable enemies. In that state of things we do plainly see they began to comply in lesser matters: for whereas in the first ages the Christians were often reproached with this, that they had no temples, altars, sacrifices, nor priests, they changed their dialect in all those points: so we have reason to believe that this was carried further. The vulgar are more easily wrought upon in greater points of speculation, than in some small ritual matters; because they do not understand the one, and so are not much concerned about it: but the other is more sensible, and lies within their compass. We find some in Palestine kept images in their houses, as Eusebius tells us; others began in Spain to light candles by daylight, and to paint the walls of their churches: and though these things were condemned by the council of Elliberis; yet we see by what St. Jerome has cited out of Vigilantius, that the spirit of superstition did work strongly among them: we hear of none that writ against those abuses besides Vigilantius; yet Jerome tells us, that many bishops were of the same mind with him, with whom he is so angry as to doubt, whether they deserved to be called bishops. Most of these abuses had also specious beginnings, and went on insensibly: where they made greater steps, we find an opposition to them. Epiphanius is very severe upon the Collyridians, for their worshipping the blessed Virgin. And though they did it by offering up a cake to her, yet if any will read all that he says against that superstition, they will clearly see, that no prayers were then offered up to her by the orthodox; and that he rejects the thought of it with indignation. But the respect paid the martyrs, and the opinion that they were still hovering about their tombs, might make the calling to them for their prayers, seem to be like one man's desiring the prayers of other good men; and when a thing of this kind is once begun, it naturally goes on. Of all this we see a particular account in a discourse writ on purpose on this argument, of curing the affections and inclinations of the Greeks, by Theodoret, who may be justly reckoned among the greatest men of antiquity, and in it he insists upon this particular of proposing to them the saints and martyrs, instead of their gods. And there is no doubt to be made, but that they found the effects of this compliance; many heathens were every day coming over to the Christian religion. And it might then perhaps be intended to lay those aside, when the heathens were once brought over.

ART. XXII.

Theod. de cur. Gr. affect. l. 8. de Martyr.

To all which this must be added, that the good men of that time had not the spirit of prophecy, and could not foresee what progress this might make, and to what an excess it might grow; they had nothing of that kind in their view: so that between charity and policy, between a desire to bring over multitudes to their faith, and an inclination to secure themselves, it is not at all to be wondered at, by any who considers all the circumstances of those ages, that these corruptions should have got into the church, and much less, having once got in, they should have gone on so fast, and be carried so far.

Thus I have offered all the considerations that arise from the state of things at that time, to shew how far we do still preserve the respect due to the fathers of those ages, even when we confess that they were men, and that something of human nature appeared in this piece of their conduct. This can be made no argument for later ages, who having no heathens among them, are under no temptations to comply with any of the parts of heathenism, to gain them. And now that the abuse of these matters is become so scandalous, and has spread itself so far, how much soever we may excuse those ages, in which we discern the first beginnings, and as it were the small heads, of that which has since overflowed Christendom; yet we can by no means bear even with those beginnings, which have had such dismal effects; and therefore we have reduced the worship of God to the simplicity of the scripture times, and of the first three centuries: and for the fourth, we reverence it so much on other accounts, that for the sake of these we are unwilling to reflect too much on this.

ART.
XXII.

Another consideration urged for the invocation of saints is, that, they seeing God, we have reason to believe that they see in him, if not all things, yet at least all the concerns of the church, of which they are still parts; and they being in a most perfect state of charity, they must certainly love the souls of their brethren here below: so that if saints on earth, whose charity is not yet perfect, do pray for one another here on earth, they in that state of perfection do certainly pray most fervently for them. And as we here on earth do desire the prayers of others, it may be as reasonable and much more useful to have recourse to their prayers, who are both in a higher state of favour with God, and have a more exalted charity: by which their intercessions will be both more earnest, and more prevalent. They think also that this honour paid the saints, is an honour done to God, who is glorified in them: and since he is the acknowledged fountain of all, they think that all the worship offered to them ends and terminates in God. They think, as princes are come at by the means of those that are in favour with them; so we ought to come to God by the intercession of the saints: that all our prayers to them are to be understood to amount to no more than a desire to them, to intercede for us; and finally, that the offering of sacrifice is an act of worship, that can indeed be made only to God, but that all other acts of devotion and respect may be given to the saints: and the sublimest degrees of them may be offered to the blessed Virgin, as the mother of Christ, in a peculiar rank by herself. For they range the order of worship into *latria*, that is due only to God; *hyperdulia*, that belongs to the blessed Virgin; and *dulia*, that belongs to the other saints.

It were easy to retort all this, by putting it into the mouth of a heathen; and shewing how well it would fit all those parts of worship, that they offered to demons or intelligent spirits, and to deified men among them. This is obvious enough, to such as have read what the first apologists for Christianity have writ upon those heads. But to take this to pieces; we have no reason to believe that the saints see all the concerns of the church. God can make them perfectly happy without this; and if we think the seeing them is a necessary ingredient of perfect happiness, we must from thence conclude, that they do also see the whole chain of Providence: otherwise they may seem to be in some suspense, which, according to our notions, is not consistent with perfect happiness. For if they see the persecutions of the church, and the miseries of Christians, without seeing on to the end, in what all that will issue, this seems to be a stop to their entire joy. And if they see the final issue, and know what God is to do, then we cannot imagine that they can intercede against it, or indeed for it. To us, who know not the hidden counsels of God, prayer is necessary and commanded: but it seems inconsistent with a state in which all these events are known. This which they lay for the foundation of prayers to saints, is a thing concerning which God has revealed nothing to us, and in which we can have no certainty. God has commanded us to pray for one another, to join our prayers together, and we have clear warrants for desiring the intercession of others. It is a high act of charity, and a great instance of the mutual love that ought to be among Christians: it is a part of the communion of the saints: and as they do certainly know, that those, whose assistance they desire, understand their wants when they signify them to them; so they are sure that God has commanded this mutual praying one for another. It is a strange thing therefore to argue from what God has commanded, and which may have many good effects, and can have no bad one, to that which he has not commanded; on the contrary, against which there are many plain intimations in scripture, and which may have many bad effects, and we are not sure that it can have any one that is good. Beside, that the solemnity of devotion and prayer is a thing very different from our desiring the prayers of such as are alive; the one is as visibly an act of religious worship, as the other is not. God has called himself 'a jealous God, that will not give his glory to another.' And through the whole scripture, prayer is represented as a main part of the service due to him; and as that in which he takes the most pleasure. It is a sacrifice, and is so called: and every other sacrifice can only be accepted of God, as it is accompanied with the internal acts of prayers and praises; which are the spiritual sacrifices with which God is well pleased. The only thing, which the church of Rome reserves to God, proves to be the *sacrifice of the mass*: which, as shall appear upon another Article, is a sacrifice that they have invented, but which is no where commanded by God; so that if this is well made out, there will be nothing reserved to God to be the act of their *latria*: though it is not to be forgotten, that even the Virgin and the saints have a share in that sacrifice.

ART. XXII.

Isa. xlii. 8.

Ps. cxli. 2.
Hos. xiv. 2.
Ps. lxv. 2.

The excusing this, from the addresses made to princes by those that are in favour with them, is as bad as the thing itself; it gives us a low idea of God, and of Christ, and of that goodness and mercy, that is so often declared to be infinite, as if he were to be addressed to by those about him, and might not be come to without an interposition: whereas the scriptures speak always of God, as *a hearer of prayer*, and as ready to accept of and answer the prayers of his people: to seek to other assistances, looks as if the mercies of God were not infinite, or the intercessions of Christ were not of infinite efficacy. This is a corrupting of the main design of the gospel, which is to draw our affections wholly to God, to free us from all low notions of him, and from every thing that may incline us to idolatry and superstition.

ART.
XXII.
Thus I have gone through all the heads contained in this Article. It seemed necessary to explain these with a due copiousness; they being not only points of speculation, in which errors are not always so dangerous, but practical things, which enter into the worship of God, and that run through it. And certainly it is the will of God, that we should preserve it pure, from being corrupted with heathenish or idolatrous practices. It seems to be the chief end of revealed religion to deliver the world from idolatry; a great part of the Mosaical law did consist of rites of which we can give no other account, that is so like to be true, as, that they were fences and hedges, that were intended to keep that nation in the greatest opposition, and at the utmost distance possible from idolatry: we cannot therefore think that in the Christian religion, in which we are carried to higher notions of God, and to a more spiritual way of worshipping him, there should be such an approach to some of the worst pieces of Gentilism, that it seems to be outdone by Christians in some of its most scandalous parts; such as the worship of subordinate gods, and of images. These are the chief grounds upon which we separate from the Roman communion; since we cannot have fellowship with them, unless we will join in those acts, which we look on as direct violations of the First and Second Commandments. God is a jealous God, and therefore we must rather venture on their wrath, how *burning* soever it may be, than on his, who is a *consuming fire*.

ARTICLE XXIII.

Of Ministering in the Congregation.

It is not lawful for any Man to take upon him the Office of public Preaching or Ministering the Sacraments in the Congregation, before he be lawfully called and sent to execute the same. And those we ought to judge lawfully called and sent, which be chosen and called to this Work by Men, who have public Authority given unto them, in the Congregation, to call and send Ministers into the Lord's Vineyard.*

WE have two particulars fixed in this Article: the *first* is against any that shall assume to themselves, without a lawful vocation, the authority of dispensing the things of God: the *second* is, the defining, in very general words, what it is that makes a lawful call. As to the first, it will bear no great difficulty: we see in the old dispensation, that the family, the age, and the qualifications, of those that might serve in the priesthood, are very particularly set forth. In the New Testament our Lord called the twelve apostles, and sent them out: he also sent out upon another occasion seventy disciples: and before he left his apostles, he told them, that 'as his Father had sent him, so he sent them:' which seems to import, that as he was sent into the world with this, among other powers, that he might send others in his name; so he likewise empowered them to do the same: and when they went planting churches, as they took some to be companions of labour with themselves, so they appointed others over the particular churches in which they fixed them: such were Epaphras, or Epaphroditus at Colosse, Timothy at Ephesus, and Titus in Crete. To them the apostles gave authority: otherwise it was a needless thing to write so many directions to them, in order to their conduct. They had the *depositum* of the faith, with which they were chiefly intrusted: concerning the succession in which that was to be continued, we have these words of St. Paul: 'The things which thou hast heard of me, among many witnesses, the same commit thou to faithful men, who shall be able to teach others also.' To them directions are given, concerning all the different parts of their worship; 'supplications, prayers, intercessions, and giving of thanks:' and also the keep- John xx. 21.

2 Tim. i. 13.

2 Tim. ii. 2.

1 Tim. ii. 1, 2, 3. ii. 12.

---

* On the question of Holy Orders, the reader should examine Mason's celebrated work in Defence of the Orders of the Church of England. He will also find this point ably discussed in a work undertaken by the command of archbishop Sancroft, and entitled, 'A Legacy to the Church of England, vindicating her orders from the objections of Papists and Dissenters,' by the Rev. Luke Milbourn. This subject is also handled by bishop Taylor in his 'Episcopacy Asserted.'—[ED.]

ing up the decency of the worship, and the not suffering of women to teach; like the women priests among the heathens, who were believed to be filled with a Bacchic fury. To them are directed all the qualifications of such as might be made either *bishops* or *deacons:* they were to examine them according to these, and either to receive or reject them. All this was directed to Timothy, that he might know how he ought to 'behave himself in the house of God.' He had authority given him to *rebuke* and *intreat*, to *honour* and to *censure*. He was to order what widows might be received into the *number*, and who should be refused. He was *to receive accusations against elders*, or presbyters, according to directed methods, and was either to censure some, or to lay hands on others, as should agree with the rules that were set him; and in conclusion, he is very solemnly charged, to 'keep that which was committed to his trust.' He is required rightly to 'divide the word of truth,' to 'preach the word,' to 'be instant in season and out of season,' to 'reprove, rebuke, and exhort, and to do the work of an evangelist, and to make full proof of his ministry.' Some of the same things are charged upon Titus, whom St. Paul had left in Crete, to 'set in order the things that were wanting, and to ordain elders in every city:' several of the characters by which he was to try them are also set down: he is charged to *rebuke the people sharply*, and to *speak the things that became sound doctrine:* he is instructed concerning the doctrines which he was to *teach*, and those which he was to *avoid;* and also how to censure an heretic: he was to *admonish him twice;* and if that did not prevail, he was to *reject him*, by some public censure.

These rules given to Timothy and Titus do plainly import, that there was to be an authority in the church, and that no man was to assume this authority to himself; according to that maxim, that seems to be founded on the light of nature, as well as it is set down in scripture, as a standing rule agreed to in all times and places: 'no man taketh this honour to himself, but he that is called of God, as was Aaron.'

St. Paul, in his Epistles to the Romans and Corinthians, did reckon up the several orders and functions that God had set in his church, and in his Epistle to the Ephesians he shews, that these were not transient but lasting constitutions; for there, as he reckons the *apostles, prophets, evangelists, pastors*, and *teachers*, as the *gifts* which Christ at his ascension had given to men; so he tells the ends for which they were given; 'for the perfecting the saints,' (by perfecting seems to be meant the initiating them by holy mysteries, rather than the compacting or putting them in joint; for as that is the proper signification of the word, so it being set first, the other things that come after it make that the strict sense of *perfecting;* that is, *completing* does not so well agree with the period,) 'for the work of the ministry,' (the whole ecclesiastical or sacred services,) 'for the edifying the body of Christ,' (to which instructing, exhorting, comforting, and all the other parts of preaching may well be reduced;) and then the duration of these gifts is defined, 'Till we all come in the unity of the faith, and of the knowledge of the Son of God, unto a perfect man.' This seems to import the whole state of this life.

We cannot think that all this belonged only to the infancy of the church, and that it was to be laid aside by her when she was further advanced; for when we consider that in the beginnings of Christianity there was so liberal an effusion of the Holy Spirit poured out upon such great numbers, who had very extraordinary credentials, miracles, and the gift of tongues, to prove their mission; it does not seem so necessary in such a time, or rather for the sake of such a time only, to have settled those functions in the church, and that the apostles should have 'ordained elders in every church.' Those extraordinary gifts that were then, without any authoritative settlement, might have served in that time to have procured to men so qualified all due regards. We have therefore much better reason to conclude, that this was settled at that time, chiefly with respect to the following ages, which as they were to fall off from that zeal and purity that did then reign among them, so they would need rule and government to maintain the unity of the church, and the order of sacred things. And for that reason chiefly we may conclude, that the apostles settled order and government in the church, not so much for the age in which they themselves lived, as once to establish and give credit to constitutions, that they foresaw would be yet more necessary to the succeeding ages.

This is confirmed by that which is in the Epistle to the Hebrews, both concerning those 'who had ruled over them,' and those who were then their guides. St. Peter gives directions to the elders of the churches to whom he writ, how they ought both to 'feed and govern the flock;' and his charging them not to do it out of covetousness, or with ambition, insinuates that either some were beginning to do so, or that, in a spirit of prophecy, he foresaw that some might fall under such corruptions. This is hint enough to teach us, that, though such things should happen, they could furnish no argument against the function. Abuses ought to be corrected, but upon that pretence the function ought not to be taken away.

If from the scriptures we go to the first writings of Christians, we find that the main subject of St. Clemens' and St. Ignatius' Epistles is to keep the churches in order and union, in subjection to their pastors, and in the due subordination of all the members of the body one to another. After the first age the thing grows too clear to need any further proof. The argument for this from the standing rules of order, of decency, of the authority in which the holy things ought to be maintained, and the care that must be taken to repress v

ART. XXIII. and insolence, and all the extravagancies of light and ungoverned fancies, is very clear. For if every man may assume authority to preach and perform holy functions, it is certain religion must fall into disorder, and under contempt. Hotheaded men of warm fancies and voluble tongues, with very little knowledge and discretion, would be apt to thrust themselves on to the teaching and governing others, if they themselves were under no government. This would soon make the public service of God to be loathed, and break and dissolve the whole body.

A few men of livelier thoughts, that begin to set on foot such ways, might for some time maintain a little credit; yet so many others would follow in at that breach which they had once made on public order, that it could not be possible to keep the society of Christians under any method, if this were once allowed. And therefore those who in their heart hate the Christian religion, and desire to see it fall under a more general contempt, know well what they do, when they encourage all those enthusiasts that destroy order; hoping, by the credit which their outward appearances may give them, to compass that which the others know themselves to be too obnoxious to hope that they can ever have credit enough to persuade the world to. Whereas those poor deluded men do not see what properties the others make of them. The morals of infidels shew that they hate all religions equally, or with this difference, that the stricter any are, they must hate them the more; the root of their quarrel being at all religion and virtue. And it is certain, as it is that which those who drive it on see well, and therefore they drive it on, that if once the public order and national constitution of a church is dissolved, the strength and power, as well as the order and beauty, of all religion will soon go after it: for, humanly speaking, it cannot subsist without it.

I come in the next place to consider the second part of this Article, which is the definition here given of those that are lawfully called and sent: this is put in very general words, far from that magisterial stiffness in which some have taken upon them to dictate in this matter. The Article does not resolve this into any particular constitution, but leaves the matter open and at large for such accidents as had happened, and such as might still happen. They who drew it had the state of the several churches before their eyes, that had been differently reformed; and although their own had been less forced to go out of the beaten path than any other, yet they knew that all things among themselves had not gone according to those rules that ought to be sacred in regular times: necessity has no law, and is a law to itself.

This is the difference between those things that are the means of salvation, and the precepts that are only necessary, because they are commanded. Those things which are the means, such as faith, repentance, and new obedience, are indispensable; they oblige all men, and at all times alike; because they have a natural influence on us, to make us fit and capable subjects of the mercy of God: but such things as are necessary only by virtue of a command of God, and not by virtue of any real efficiency which they have to reform our natures, do indeed oblige us to seek for them, and to use all our endeavours to have them. But as they of themselves are not necessary in the same order with the first, so much less are all those methods necessary in which we may come at the regular use of them. This distinction shall be more fully enlarged on when the sacraments are treated of. But to the matter in hand. That which is simply necessary as a mean to preserve the order and union of the body of Christians, and to maintain the reverence due to holy things, is, that no man enter upon any part of the holy ministry, without he be chosen and called to it by such as have an authority so to do; that, I say, is fixed by the Article: but men are left more at liberty as to their thoughts concerning the subject of this lawful authority.

ART. XXIII.

That which we believe to be *lawful authority*, is that rule which the body of the pastors, or bishops and clergy of a church, shall settle, being met in a body under the due respect to the powers that God shall set over them: rules thus made, being in nothing contrary to the word of God, and duly executed by the particular persons to whom that care belongs, are certainly the *lawful authority*. Those are the pastors of the church, to whom the care and watching over the souls of the people is committed; and the prince, or supreme power, comprehends virtually the whole body of the people in him: since, according to the constitution of the civil government, the wills of the people are understood to be concluded by the supreme, and such as are the subject of the legislative authority. When a church is in a state of persecution under those who have the civil authority over her, then the *people*, who receive the faith, and give both protection and encouragement to those that labour over them, are to be considered as the body that is governed by them. The natural effect of such a state of things, is to satisfy the people in all that is done, to carry along their consent with it, and to consult much with them in it. This does not only arise out of a necessary regard to their present circumstances, but from the rules given in the gospel, of not ruling as the kings of the several nations did; nor *lording* it, or carrying it with a high authority over *God's heritage* (which may be also rendered over their several *lots* or *portions*). But when the church is under the protection of a Christian magistrate, then he comes to be in the stead of the whole people; for they are concluded in and by him; he gives the protection and encouragement, and therefore great regard is due to him, in the exercise of his lawful authority, in which he has a great share, as shall be explained in its

ART.
XXIII.

proper place. Here, then, we think this authority is rightly lodged, and set on its proper basis.

And in this we are confirmed, because, by the decrees of the first general councils, the concerns of every province were to be settled in the province itself; and it so continued till the usurpations of the papacy broke in every where, and disordered this constitution. Through the whole Roman communion the chief jurisdiction is now in the pope; only princes have laid checks upon the extent of it; and by *appeals* the secular court takes cognizance of all that is done either by the pope or the clergy. This we are sure is the effect of usurpation and tyranny: yet since this authority is in fact so settled, we do not pretend to annul the acts of that power, nor the missions or orders given in that church; because there is among them an order *in fact*, though not as it ought to be, *in right*. On the other hand, when the body of the clergy comes to be so corrupted that nothing can be trusted to the regular decisions of any synod or meeting, called according to their constitution, then if the prince shall select a peculiar number, and commit to their care the examining and reforming both of doctrine and worship, and shall give the legal sanction to what they shall offer to him; we must confess that such a method as this runs contrary to the established rules, and that therefore it ought to be very seldom put in practice; and never, except when the greatness of the occasion will balance this irregularity that is in it. But still here is an authority both in *fact* and *right;* for if the magistrate has a power to make laws in sacred matters, he may order those to be prepared, by whom, and as he pleases.

Finally, if a company of Christians find the public worship where they live to be so defiled that they cannot with a good conscience join in it, and if they do not know of any place to which they can conveniently go, where they may worship God purely, and in a regular way; if, I say, such a body finding some that have been ordained, though to the lower functions, should submit itself entirely to their conduct, or finding none of those, should by a common consent desire some of their own number to minister to them in holy things, and should upon that beginning grow up to a regulated constitution, though we are very sure that this is quite out of all rule, and could not be done without a very great sin, unless the necessity were great and apparent; yet if the necessity is real and not feigned, this is not condemned or annulled by the Article; for when this grows to a constitution, and when it was begun by the consent of a body, who are supposed to have an authority in such an extraordinary case, whatever some hotter spirits have thought of this since that time; yet we are very sure, that not only those who penned the Articles, but the body of this church for above half an age after, did, notwithstanding those irregularities, acknowledge the foreign churches so constituted, to be true churches as to all the essentials of a church, though they had been at first irregularly formed, and continued still to be in an imperfect state. And therefore the general words in which this part of the Article is framed, seem to have been designed on purpose not to exclude them.

ART. XXIII.

Here it is to be considered, that the high-priest among the Jews was the chief person in that dispensation; not only the chief in rule, but he that was by the divine appointment to officiate in the chief act of their religion, the yearly expiation for the sins of the whole nation; which was a solemn renewing their covenant with God, and by which atonement was made for the sins of that people. Here it may be very reasonably suggested, that since none besides the high-priest might make this atonement, then no atonement was made, if any other besides the high-priest should so officiate. To this it is to be added, that God had by an express law fixed the high-priesthood in the eldest of Aaron's family; and that therefore, though that being a theocracy, any prophets empowered of God might have transferred this office from one person or branch of that family to another; yet without such an authority no other person might make any such change. But after all this, not to mention the Maccabees, and all their successors of the Asmonean family, as Herod had begun to change the high-priesthood at pleasure; so the Romans not only continued to do this, but in a most mercenary manner they set this sacred function to sale. Here were as great nullities in the high-priests that were in our Saviour's time, as can be well imagined to be; for, the Jews keeping their genealogies so exactly as they did, it could not but be well known in whom the right of this office rested; and they all knew that he who had it, purchased it, yet these were in fact high-priests: and since the people could have no other, the atonement was still performed by their ministry. Our Saviour owned Caiaphas, the sacrilegious and usurping high-priest, and as such he *prophesied*. This shews that where the necessity was real and unavoidable, the Jews were bound to think that God did, in consideration of that, dispense with his own precept. This may be a just inducement for us to believe, that whensoever God by his providence brings Christians under a visible necessity of being either without all order and joint worship, or of joining in an unlawful and defiled worship, or finally, of breaking through rules and methods in order to the being united in worship and government; that of these three, of which one must be chosen, the last is the least evil, and has the fewest inconveniences hanging upon it, and that therefore it may be chosen.

John xi. 51. xviii. 22, 23.

Our reformers had also in view two famous instances in church-history of laymen that had preached and converted nations to the faith. It is true, they came, as they ought to

ART.
XXIII.
have done, to be regularly ordained, and were sent to such as had authority so to do. So Frumentius preached to the Indians, and was afterwards made a priest and a bishop by Athanasius. The king of the Iberians, before he was baptized himself, did convert his subjects; and, as says the historian, he became the apostle of his country before he himself was *initiated*. It is indeed added, that he sent an embassy to Constantine the emperor, desiring him that he would send priests for the further establishment of the faith there.

These were regular practices; but if it should happen that princes or states should take up such a jealousy of their own authority, and should apprehend that the suffering their subjects to go elsewhere for regular ordinations, might bring them under some dependance on those that had ordained them, and give them such influence over them, that the prince of such a neighbouring and regular church should by such ordinations have so many creatures spies, or instruments in their own dominions; and if upon other political reasons they had just cause of being jealous of that, and should thereupon hinder any such thing in that case, neither our reformers, nor their successors for near eighty years after those Articles were published, did ever question the constitution of such churches.

We have reason to believe that none ought to baptize but persons lawfully ordained; yet since there has been a practice so universally spread over the Christian church, of allowing the baptism, not only of laics, but of women, to be lawful, though we think that this is directly contrary to the rules given by the apostles; yet since this has been in fact so generally received and practised, we do not annul such baptisms, nor rebaptize persons so baptized; though we know that the original of this bad practice was from an opinion of the indispensable necessity of baptism to salvation. Yet since it has been so generally received, we have that regard to such a common practice, as not to annul it, though we condemn it. And thus what thought soever private men, as they are divines, may have of those irregular steps, the Article of the church is conceived in such large and general words, that no man, by subscribing it, is bound up from freer and more comprehensive thoughts.

ARTICLE XXIV.

Of speaking in the Congregation in such a Tongue as the People understandeth.

It is a thing plainly repugnant to the Word of God, and the Custom of the Primitive Church, to have Public Prayer in the Church, or to minister the Sacraments, in a Tongue not understanded of the People.

This Article, though upon the matter very near the same, yet was worded much less positively in those at first set forth by king Edward.

It is most fit, and most agreeable to the Word of God, that nothing be read or rehearsed in the Congregation in a Tongue not known unto the People; which St. Paul hath forbidden to be done, unless some be present to interpret.

In king Edward's Articles they took in *preaching* with *prayer*, but in the present Article this is restrained to *prayer*. The former only affirms the use of a known tongue to be most fit and agreeable to the word of God; the latter denies the worship in an unknown tongue to be lawful, and affirms it to be repugnant to the *word of God;* to which it adds, *and the custom of the primitive church.*

THIS Article seems to be founded on the law of nature. The worship of God is a chain of acts by which we acknowledge God's attributes, rejoice in his goodness, and lay claim to his mercies. In all which the more we raise our thoughts, the more seriousness, earnestness, and affection that animates our mind, so much the more acceptably do we serve God, who is a *spirit*, and will be worshipped in 'spirit and in truth.' John iv. All the words used in devotion are intended to raise in us 23, 24. the thoughts that naturally belong to such words. And the various acts, which are as it were the breaks in the service, are intended as rests to our minds, to keep us the longer without weariness and wandering in those exercises. One great end of continuance in worship is, that, by the frequent repeating and often going over of the same things, they may come to be deeply rooted in our thoughts. The chief effect that the worship of God has by its own efficiency, is the infixing those things, about which the branches of it are employed, the deeper on our minds; upon which God gives his blessing as we grow to be prepared for it, or capable of it. Now all this is lost, if the worship of God is a thread of such sounds, as makes the person who officiates a barbarian to the rest. They have nothing but noise and show to amuse them, which how much soever they may strike upon and entertain the senses, yet they cannot affect the heart, nor excite the mind: so that the natural effect of such a way of worship is to make religion a pageantry, and the public service of God an opera.

If from plain sense, and the natural consequences of things, we carry on this argument to the scriptures, we find the whole practice of the Old Testament was to worship God, not only in a tongue that was understood, for it may be said there was no occasion then to use any other; but that the expressions used in the prayers and psalms that we find in the Old Testament, shew they were intended to affect those who were to use them; and if that is acknowledged, then it will clearly follow that all ought to understand them; for who can be affected with that which he does not understand? So this shews that the end of public devotion is the exciting and inflaming those who bear a share in it. When Ezra and Nehemiah were instructing the people out of the law, they took care to have it read 'distinctly, one giving the sense of it.' After they were long in captivity, though it had not worn out quite the knowledge of the Hebrew, yet the Chaldee was more familiar to them, so a paraphrase was made of the Hebrew into that language, though it was rather a different dialect than another language; and by the forms of their prayers, we see that one cried with a loud voice, 'Stand up, and bless the Lord your God for ever and ever;' which shews that all did understand the service. When the Syriac tongue became more familiar to them, the Jews had their prayers in Syriac; and they did read the law in their synagogues in Greek, when that language was more familiar to them; when they read the law in Greek, we have reason to believe that they prayed likewise in it. In the New Testament, we see the gift of tongues was granted to enable the apostles, and others, to go every where preaching the gospel, and performing holy functions in such a language as might be understood: the world was amazed when every man heard them speak in his own language.

One of the general rules given by St. Paul, with relation to the worship of God, is, 'Let every thing be done to edification.' Since then the speaking either to God in the name of the people, or to the people in the name of God, in an unknown tongue, can edify no person; then by this rule it is to be understood to be forbidden. When some who had the gift of tongues did indiscreetly shew it in the church of Corinth, St. Paul was so offended at that, and thought it would appear to the world so undecent, as well as unfruitful, that he bestows a whole chapter upon it; and though a great part of the discourse is against the pretending to teach the

people in an unknown tongue, which yet is not near so bad ART. XXIV.
as the reading the word of God to them in a tongue not understood by them, it being much more important that the people should understand the words of the living God than the expositions of men; yet there are many passages in that chapter that belong to prayer: the reason of the thing is common to both, since, unless the words were understood, they who uttered them spoke only to the air; and how should it be known what was spoken? For if the meaning of the voice was not known, they would be barbarians to one another. As to prayer, he says, 'If I pray in an unknown tongue, my 1 Cor. xiv. spirit (that is, the inspiration or gift that is in me) prayeth; 14. but my understanding (that is, my rational powers) is unfruitful;' and therefore he concludes that he will both *pray* Ver. 15. and *give thanks* with the *spirit*, and with the *understanding also;* he will do it in such a manner, that the inspiration with which he was acted and his rational powers should join together. The reason given for this seems evident enough to determine the whole matter: 'Else when thou shalt bless Ver. 16, with the spirit, how shall he that occupieth the room of the 17. unlearned say *Amen* at thy giving of thanks, seeing he understandeth not what thou sayest? For thou verily givest thanks well, but the other is not edified.' In which words it is plain that the people, even the most unlearned among them, were to join in the prayers and praises, and to testify that by saying *Amen* at the conclusion of them; and in order to their doing this as became reasonable creatures, it was necessary that they should understand what that was which they were to confirm by their *Amen*. It is also evident that St. Paul judged, that the people ought to be edified by all that was said in the church; and so he says a little after this, 'Let all Ver. 26. things be done to edifying.' After such plain authorities from scripture, supporting that which seems to be founded on the light of nature, we need go no further to prove that which is mainly designed by this Article.

The custom of the primitive church is no less clear in this point. As the Christian religion was spread to different nations, so they all worshipped God in their own tongue. The Syriac, the Greek, and the Latin, were indeed of that extent, that we have no particular history of any churches that lay beyond the compass of those languages; but there was the same reason for putting the worship of God in other languages, that there was for these: that which is drawn from the three languages, in which the title on our Saviour's cross was written, is too trifling a thing to deserve an answer; as if a humour of Pilate's were to be considered as a prophetical warrant, what he did being only designed to make that title to be understood by all who were then at Jerusalem. There are very Cont. Cellarge passages both in Origen and St. Basil, which mention sum, l. 8. every tongue's *praising of God;* and that the gospel being p. 402. Cantab. Basil. in

ART. XXIV.
epist. ad clericos Neocesarien.
Johan. 8. Ep. 247. Concil. tom. 9.

spread to many nations, he was in every nation praised in the language of that nation. This continued so long to be the practice even of the Latin church,* that in the ninth century, when the Slavons were converted, it was considered at Rome by pope John VIII. in what language they should be allowed to worship God. And, as it is pretended, a voice was heard, *Let every tongue confess to God;* upon which that pope wrote both to the prince and to the bishop of the Slavons, allowing them to have their public service in their own tongue. But in the other parts of the western church, the Latin tongue continued to be so universally understood by almost all sorts of people, till the tenth or eleventh century, that there was no occasion for changing it; and by that time the clergy were affecting to keep the people in ignorance, and in a blind dependance upon themselves; and so were willing to make them think that the whole business of reconciling the people to God lay upon them, and that they were to do it for them. A great part of the service of the mass was said so low, that even they who understood some Latin could not be the better for it, in an age in which there was no printing, and so few copies were to be had of the public offices. The scriptures were likewise kept from the people, and the service of God was filled with many rites, in all which the clergy seemed to design to make the people believe that these were sacred charms, of which they only had the secret. So that all the edification which was to be had in the public worship was turned to pomp and show, for the diversion and entertainment of the spectators.

Con. Trid. Cap. 8. Sess. 22.

In defence of this worship in an unknown tongue, the main argument that is brought is the authority and infallibility of the church, which has appointed it; and since she ought to be supposed not to have erred, therefore this must be believed to be lawful. We are not much moved with this, especially with the authority of the later ages; so the other arguments must be considered, which indeed can scarce be called arguments. The modern tongues change so fast, that they say, if the worship were in them, it must either be often changed, or

---

* That such was the practice of the Latin church even in the thirteenth century appears from the following decree of the fourth Lateran council, held under pope Innocent III., A.D. 1215.

'*4th Lateran, Innocent III.,* 1215. Can. ix. p. 161, *Labb.* vol. XI.

' Quoniam in plerisque partibus intra eandem civitatem atque diœcesim permixti sunt populi diversarum linguarum, habentes sub una fide varios ritus et mores: districte præcipimus, ut pontifices hujusmodi civitatum sive diœcesim provideant viros idoneos, qui secundum diversitates rituum et linguarum Divina officia illis celebrent, et ecclesiastica sacramenta ministrent, instruendo eis verbo pariter et exemplo.'—*De diversis ritibus in eadem fide.*

With this the following canon of the council of Trent affords a curious contrast: ' Si quis dixerit ecclesiæ Romanæ ritum, quo summisa voce pars canonis, et verba consecrationis proferuntur, damnandum esse; aut lingua tantum vulgari missam celebrari debere: aut aquam non miscendam esse vino in calice offerendo, eo quod sit contra Christi institutionem : anathema sit.'—[ED.]

the phrases would grow old, and sound harshly. A few alterations once in an age will set this matter right; besides, that the use of such forms does fix a language, at least as to those phrases that are used in it, which grow to be so familiar to our ears by constant use, that they do not so easily wear out. It is above eighty years since the present translation of the Bible was made, and above one hundred and forty since our Liturgy was compiled, and yet we perceive no uncouthness in the phrases. The simplicity, in which such forms must be drawn, makes them not so subject to alteration as other composures, of rhetoric or poetry; but can it be thought any inconveniency now and then to alter a little the words or phrases of our service? Much less can that be thought of weight enough to balance the vaster prejudice of keeping whole nations in ignorance, and of extinguishing devotion by entertaining it with a form of worship that is not understood.

Nor can this be avoided by saying, that the people are furnished with forms in their own language, into which the greatest part of the public offices are translated: for as this is not done but since the Reformation began, and in those nations only where the scandal that is given by an unknown language might have, as they apprehend, ill effects; so it is only an artifice to keep those still in their communion, whom such a gross practice, if not thus disguised, might otherwise drive from them. But still the public worship has no edification in it; nor can those who do not understand it say *Amen*, according to St. Paul. Finally, they urge the *communion of saints*, in order to which they think it is necessary that priests, wheresoever they go, may be able to officiate, which they cannot do if every nation worships God in its own language. And this was indeed very necessary in those ages in which the see of Rome did by provisions, and the other inventions of the canonists, dispose of the best benefices to their own creatures and servants. That trade would have been spoiled, if strangers might not have been admitted till they had learned the language of the country; and thus, instead of taking care of the people that ought to be edified by the public worship, provision was made at their cost for such vagrant priests as have been in all ages the scandals of the church, and the reproaches of religion.

ARTICLE XXV.

Of the Sacraments.

Sacraments ordained of Christ be not only Badges or Tokens of Christian Men's Profession, but rather they be certain sure Witnesses, and effectual Signs of Grace, and God's Will towards us, by the which he doth work invisibly in us, and doth not only quicken, but also strengthen and confirm, our Faith in him.

There are Two Sacraments ordained of Christ our Lord in the Gospel: that is to say, Baptism, and the Supper of the Lord.

Those five commonly called Sacraments, that is to say, Confirmation, Penance, Orders, Matrimony, and extreme Unction, are not to be counted for Sacraments of the Gospel; being such as have grown partly of the corrupt following of the Apostles, partly are States of Life allowed in the Scriptures, but yet have not like Nature of Sacraments with Baptism, and the Lord's Supper; for that they have not any visible Sign or Ceremony ordained of God.

The Sacraments were not ordained of Christ to be gazed upon, or to be carried about, but that we should duly use them. And in such only as worthily receive the same they have a wholesome Effect or Operation; but they that receive them unworthily, purchase to themselves Damnation, as St. Paul saith.

THERE is a great diversity between the form of this Article, as it is now settled, and that published by king Edward, which begun in these words: *Our Lord Jesus Christ gathered his people into a society by sacraments, very few in number, most easily to be kept, and of most excellent signification; that is to say, Baptism, and the Supper of the Lord.* There is nothing in that edition instead of the paragraph concerning the other five pretended sacraments. Next comes the paragraph which is here the last, only with the addition of these words after operation: *Not as some say,* ex opere operato, *which terms, as they are strange and utterly unknown to the holy scripture, so do they yield a sense which savoureth of little piety, but of much superstition:* and, in conclusion, the paragraph comes, with which the Article does now begin; so that in all this diversity there is no real difference: for the virtue of the sacraments being put in the worthy receiving, excludes the doctrine of *opus operatum*,* as formally as if it had expressly been condemned; and the naming the two sacraments

---

* For the canons of the Council of Trent respecting the sacraments, and doctrine of *opus operatum*, see note, page 164.—[ED.]

instituted by Christ, is upon the matter the rejecting of all the rest.

ART. XXV.

It was most natural to begin this article with a description of sacraments in general. This difference is to be put between sacraments and other ritual actions; that whereas other rites are badges and distinctions by which the Christians are known, a sacrament is more than a bare matter of form; and as, in the Old Testament, circumcision and propitiatory sacrifices were things of a different nature and order from all the other ritual precepts concerning the cleansings, the distinctions of days, places, and meats. These were indeed precepts given them of God, but they were not federal acts of renewing the covenant, or reconciling themselves to God. By circumcision they received the seal of the covenant, and were brought under the obligation of the whole law: they were by it made debtors to it; and when by their sins they had provoked God's wrath, they were reconciled to him by their sacrifices, with which atonement was made, and so their sins were forgiven them. The nature and end of those was to be federal acts, in the offering of which the Jews kept to their part of the covenant, and in the accepting of which God maintained it on his part; so we see a plain difference between these and a mere rite, which, though commanded, yet must pass only for the badge of a profession, as the doing of it is an act of obedience to a divine law. Now, in the new dispensation, though our Saviour has eased us of that *law of ordinances*, that *grievous yoke*, and those *beggarly elements* which were laid upon the Jews; yet, since we are still in the body, subject to our senses, and to sensible things, he has appointed some federal actions, to be both the visible stipulations and professions of our Christianity, and the conveyances to us of the blessings of the gospel.

There are two extremes to be avoided in this matter. The one is of the church of Rome, that teaches, that as some sacraments imprint a character upon the soul, which they define to be a physical quality, that is, supernatural and spiritual, so they do all carry along with them such a divine virtue, that by the very receiving them (the *opus operatum*) it is conveyed to the souls of those to whom they are applied, unless they themselves put a bar in the way of it by some mortal sin. In consequence of this, they reckon, that by the sacraments given to a man in his agonies, though he is very near past all sense, and so cannot join any lively acts of his mind with the sacraments, yet he is justified; not to mention the common practice of giving extreme unction in the last agony, when no appearance of any sense is left. This we reckon a doctrine that is not only without all foundation in scripture, but that tends to destroy all religion, and to make men live on securely in sin, trusting to this, that the sacraments may be given them when they die. The conditions of

ART.
XXV.
the new covenant are, repentance, faith, and obedience; and we look on this as the corrupting the vitals of this religion, when any such means are proposed, by which the main design of the gospel is quite overthrown. The business of a character is an unintelligible notion. We acknowledge baptism is not to be repeated; but that is not by virtue of a character imprinted in it, but because it being a dedication of the person to God in the Christian religion, what is once so done is to be understood to continue still in that state, till such a person falls into an open apostacy. In case of the repentance of such a person, we finding that the primitive church did reconcile, but not rebaptize apostates, do imitate that their practice; but not because of this late and unexplicable notion of a character. We look on all sacramental actions as acceptable to God only with regard to the temper, and the inward acts of the person to whom they are applied, and cannot consider them as medicines or charms, which work by a virtue of their own, whether the person to whom they are applied co-operates with them, or not. Baptism is said by St. Peter 'to save us,' not as it is an action that washes us; 'not the putting away the filth of the flesh, but the answer of a good conscience towards God.' And therefore baptism without this profession is no baptism, but seems to be used as a charm; unless it is said, that this answer or profession is implied, whensoever baptism is desired. When a person of age desires baptism, he must make those answers and sponsions, otherwise he is not truly baptized; and though his outward making of them being all that can fall under human cognizance, he who does that must be held to be truly baptized, and all the outward privileges of a baptized person must belong to him; yet as to the effect of baptism on the soul of him that is baptized, without doubt that depends upon the sincerity of the professions and vows made by him. The wills of infants are by the law of nature and nations in their parents, and are transferred by them to their sureties; the sponsions that are made on their behalf are considered as made by themselves; but there the outward act is sufficient; for the inward acts of one person cannot be supposed necessary to give the sacrament its virtue in another.

1 Pet. iii. 21.

1Cor.x.16.
In the eucharist, by our 'shewing forth our Lord's death till he comes,' we are admitted to the 'communion of his body and blood;' to a share in partnership with other Christians in the effects and merits of his death. But the unworthy receiver is guilty of his body and blood, and brings thereby down judgments upon himself; so that to fancy a virtue in sacraments that works on the person to whom they are applied, without any inward acts accompanying it, and upon his being only passive, is a doctrine of which we find nothing in the scriptures; which teach us that every thing we do is only accepted of God, with regard to the disposition of mind that

he knows us to be in when we go about it. Our prayers and sacrifices are so far from being accepted of God, that they are *abomination* to him, if they come from wicked and defiled hearts. The making men believe that sacraments may be effectual to them when they are next to a state of passivity, not capable of any sensible thoughts of their own, is a sure way to raise the credit of the clergy, and of the sacrament; but at the same time it will most certainly dispose men to live in sin, hoping that a few rites, which may be easily procured at their death, will clear all at last. And thus we reject, not without great zeal against the fatal effects of this error, all that is said of the *opus operatum*; the very doing of the sacrament: we think it looks more like the incantations of heathenism, than the purity and simplicity of the Christian religion.

But the other extreme, that we likewise avoid, is that of sinking the sacraments so low, as to be mere rites and ceremonies. St. Peter says, 'Baptism saves us.' St. Paul calls it, the 'laver of regeneration;' to which he joins 'the renewing of the Holy Ghost.' Our Saviour saith, 'He that believeth, and is baptized, shall be saved;' and, 'Except ye are born again of water and of the Spirit, ye cannot enter into the kingdom of God.' These words have a sense and signification that rises far above a mere ceremony done to keep up order, and to maintain a settled form. The phrase 'communion of the body and blood of Christ,' is above the nature of an anniversary, or memorial feast. This opinion we think is very unsuitable to those high expressions; and we do not doubt but that Christ, who instituted those sacraments, does still accompany them with a particular presence in them, and a blessing upon them; so that we coming to them with minds well prepared, with pure affections and holy resolutions, do certainly receive in and with them particular largesses of the favour and bounty of God. They are not bare and naked remembrances and tokens; but are actuated and animated by a divine blessing that attends upon them. This is what we believe on this head, and these are the grounds upon which we found it.

A sacrament is an institution of Christ, in which some material thing is sanctified by the use of some form or words, in and by which federal acts of this religion do pass on both sides; on ours, by stipulations, professions, or vows; and on God's by his secret assistances: by these we are also united to the body of Christ, which is the church. It must be instituted by Christ: for though ritual matters, that are only the expressions of our duty, may be appointed by the church; yet federal acts, to which a conveyance of divine grace is tied, can only be instituted by him who is the Author and Mediator of this new covenant, and who lays down the rules or conditions of it, and derives the blessings of it by what methods and in what channels he thinks fit. Whatsoever his apostles settled, was by authority and commission from him; therefore it is

ART XXV.

Tit. iii. 5.
Mark xvi. 16.
John iii. 3, 5.

ART.
XXV.

not to be denied, but that if they had appointed any sacramental action, that must be reckoned to be of the same authority, and is to be esteemed Christ's institution, as much as if he himself, when on earth, had appointed it.

Matter is of the essence of a sacrament; for words without some material thing, to which they belong, may be of the nature of prayers or vows, but they cannot be sacraments: receiving a sacrament is on our part our faith plighted to God in the use of some material substance or other; for in this consists the difference between sacraments and other acts of worship. The latter are only acts of the mind declared by words or gesture, whereas sacraments are the application of a material sign, joined with acts of the mind, words, and gestures. With the *matter* there must be a *form*, that is, such words joined with it as do appropriate the matter to such an use, and separate it from all other uses, at least in the act of the sacrament. For in any piece of *matter* alone, there cannot be a proper suitableness to such an end, as seems to be designed by sacraments, and therefore a *form* must determine and apply it; and it is highly suitable to the nature of things, to believe that our Saviour, who has instituted the sacrament, has also either instituted the form of it, or given us such hints as to lead us very near it. The end of sacraments is double; the one is by a solemn federal action both to unite us to Christ, and also to derive a secret blessing from him to us: and the other is to join and unite us by this public profession, and the joint partaking of it, with his body, which is the church. This is, in general, an account of a sacrament. This, it is true, is none of those words that are made use of in scripture, so that it has no determined signification given to it in the word of God; yet it was very early applied by Pliny to those vows by which the Christians tied themselves to their religion, taken from the oaths by which the soldiery among the Romans were sworn to their colours or officers; and from that time this term has been used in a sense consecrated to the federal rites of religion. Yet if any will dispute about words, we know how much St. Paul condemns all those curious and vain questions, which have in them the subtilties and ' oppositions of science falsely so called.' If any will call every rite used in holy things, a sacrament, we enter into no such contentions.

The rites, therefore, that we understand when we speak of sacraments, are the constant federal rites of Christians, which are accompanied by a divine grace and benediction, being instituted by Christ to unite us to him, and to his church; and of such we own that there are two, *Baptism*, and the *Supper of the Lord*. In Baptism, there is *matter*, *water*; there is a *form*, the person *dipped* or *washed*, with words, ' I baptize thee in the name of the Father, and of the Son, and of the Holy Ghost:' there is an institution, ' Go preach and

lib. x.
Ep. 97.

1 Tim. vi. 20.

Matt.
xxviii. 19.

baptize;' there is a federal sponsion, 'The answer of a good ART.
conscience;' there is a blessing conveyed with it, 'Baptism   XXV.
saves us;' there is 'one baptism, as there is one body and 1 Pet. iii.
one spirit; we are all baptized into one body.' So that here 21.
all the constituent and necessary parts of a sacrament are
found in baptism. In the Lord's Supper, there is *bread* and Matt. xxvi.
wine for the *matter*. The giving it to be eat and drunk, with 26, 27.
the words that our Saviour used in the first supper, are the
form: 'Do this in remembrance of me,' is the institution. 1 Cor. xi.
'Ye shew forth the Lord's death till he come again,' is the 23—27.
declaration of the federal act of our part: it is also the 'com- 1 Cor. x.
munion of the body and of the blood of Christ,' that is, the 16, 17.
conveyance of the blessings of our partnership in the effects
of the death of Christ. 'And we being many, are one bread
and one body, for we are all partakers of that one bread;' this
shews the union of the church in this sacrament. Here then
we have in these two sacraments, both matter, form, institution, federal acts, blessings conveyed, and the union of the
body in them. All the characters which belong to a sacrament agree fully to them.

In the next place we must, by these characters, examine
the other pretended sacraments. It is no wonder if, the word
sacrament being of a large extent, there should be some passages in ancient writers, that call other actions so besides
Baptism and the *Lord's Supper;* for in a larger sense every
holy rite may be so called. But it is no small prejudice
against the number of seven sacraments, that Peter Lombard,
a writer in the twelfth century, is the first that reckons *seven*
of them: from that mystical expression of the seven spirits of
God, there came a conceit of the sevenfold operation of the
Spirit; and it looked like a good illustration of that, to assert
seven sacraments. This pope Eugenius put in his instruction Lib. 3.
to the Armenians, which is published with the Council of dist. 2.
Florence; and all was finally settled at Trent.* Now there
might have been so many fine allusions made on the number
seven, and some of the ancients were so much set on such
allusions, that since we hear nothing of that kind from any
of them, we may well conclude, that this is more than an
ordinary negative argument against their having believed that
there were seven sacraments. To go on in order with them:

The first that we reject, which is reckoned by them the
second, is *confirmation.* But to explain this, we must con-

---

* The following is the canon of the council of Trent, in which she adds her five new sacraments to those appointed by our Lord:—' Si quis dixerit, sacramenta novæ legis non fuisse omnia a Jesu Christo, Domino nostro, instituta; aut esse plura vel pauciora quam septem, videlicet, baptismum, confirmationem, eucharistiam, pœnitentiam, extremam unctionem, ordinem, et matrimonium; aut etiam aliquod horum septem non esse vere et proprie sacramentum: anathema sit.' S*s,io* vii. can. 1.
The reader will find the same doctrine embodied in the creed of pope Pius IV. See Appendix.—[ED.]

sider in what respect our church receives *confirmation*, and upon what reasons it is that she does not acknowledge it to be a sacrament. We find that after Philip, the deacon and evangelist, had converted and baptized some in Samaria, Peter and John were sent thither by the apostles, who 'laid their hands' on such as were baptized, and 'prayed that they might receive the Holy Ghost;' upon which it is said, that 'they received the Holy Ghost.' Now though ordinary functions, when performed by the apostles, such as their laying on of hands on those whom they ordained or confirmed, had extraordinary effects accompanying them; but when the extraordinary effects ceased, the end for which these were at first given being accomplished, the gospel having been fully attested to the world, yet the functions were still continued of confirmation as well as ordination: and as the 'laying on of hands,' that is reckoned among the principles of the Christian doctrine, after *repentance* and *faith*, and subsequent to *baptism*, seems very probably to belong to this; so from these warrants we find in the earliest writings of Christianity mention of a *confirmation* after *baptism*, which for the greater solemnity and awe of the action, and from the precedent of St. Peter and St. John, was reserved to the bishop, to be done only by him.

Upon these reasons we think it is in the power of the church to require all such as have been baptized, to come before the bishop and renew their baptismal vow, and pray for God's holy Spirit to enable them to keep their vow; and, upon their doing this, the bishop may solemnly pray over them, with that ancient and almost natural ceremony of laying his hands upon them, which is only a designation of the persons so prayed over, and blessed, that God may seal and defend them with his holy Spirit; in which, according to the nature of the new covenant, we are sure that such as do thus vow and pray, do also receive the Holy Spirit, according to the promise that our Saviour has made us. In this action there is nothing but what is in the power of the church to do, even without any other warrant or precedent. The doing all things to *order*, and to *edifying*, will authorize a church to all this; especially, since the now universal practice of *infant baptism* makes this more necessary than it was in the first times, when chiefly the *adult* were baptized. It is highly reasonable that they, who gave no actual consent of their own, should come, and by their own express act make the stipulations of baptism. It may give greater impressions of awe and respect, when this is restrained to the highest order in the church. Upon the sincere vows and earnest prayers of persons thus confirmed, we have reason to believe that a proportioned degree of God's grace and Spirit will be poured out upon them. And in all this we are much confirmed, when we see such warrants for it in scripture. A thing so good in

THE XXXIX ARTICLES. 353

itself, that has at least a probable authority for it, and was ART.
certainly a practice of the first ages, is upon very just grounds XXV.
continued in our church. Would to God it were as seriously
gone about, as it is lawfully established!

But, after all this, here is no sacrament, no express institution, neither by Christ nor his apostles; no rule given to practise it, and, which is the most essential, there is no matter here; for the laying on of hands is only a gesture in prayer; nor are there any federal rites declared to belong to it; it being indeed rather a ratifying and confirming the baptism, than any new stipulation. To supply all this, the church of Rome has appointed *matter* for it. The *chrism*, which is a mixture of *oil*-olive and *balm* (*opobalsamum*), the *oil* signifying the clearness of a good conscience, and the *balm* the savour of a good reputation. This must be peculiarly blessed by the bishop, who is the only minister of that function. The *form* of this sacrament is the applying the *chrism* to the forehead, with these words, *Signo te signo crucis, et confirmo te chrismate salutis, in nomine Patris, Filii, et Spiritus Sancti:* ' I sign thee with the sign of the cross, and confirm thee with the chrism of salvation, in the name of the Father, the Son, and the Holy Ghost.' They pretend Christ did institute this; but they say the Holy Ghost which he breathed on his disciples, being a thing that transcended all sacraments, he settled no determined *matter* nor *form* to it; and that the succeeding ages appropriated this *matter* to it.

We do not deny, but that the Christians began very early to use oil in holy functions; the climates they lived in making it necessary to use oil much, for stopping the perspiration, that might dispose them the more to use oil in their sacred rites. It is not to be denied, but that both Theophilus and Tertullian, in the end of the second, and the beginning of the third century, do mention it. The frequent mention of *oil*, and of *anointing*, in the scripture, might incline them to this: it was prophesied of Christ, that he was to be 'anointed with the oil of joy and gladness above his fellows:' and the names of *Messias* and *Christ* do also import this; but yet we hold all *that* to be mystical, and that it is to be meant of that fulness of the Spirit which he received *without measure*. Upon the same account we do understand those words of St. Paul in the same mystical sense: ' He that establisheth us with you in Christ, and hath anointed us, is God; who hath also sealed us, and given the earnest of the Spirit in our hearts:' as also those words of St. John: ' But ye have an unction from the Holy One, and ye know all things. The anointing which ye have received of him abideth in you; and ye need not that any man teach you, but as the same anointing teacheth you all things.' These words do clearly relate to somewhat that the Christians received immediately from God; and so must be understood figuratively: for we do not see the least hint

Theophil. l. i. ad Autolyc. Tert. de Bapt. c. 7, 8. de Re-sur. Car. c. 8. Cypr. Ep. 70.

2 Cor. i. 21, 22.

1 John ii. 20, 27.

2 A

of the apostles using of oil, except to the sick; of which afterwards. So that if this use of oil is considered only as a ceremony of a natural signification, that was brought into the rituals of the church, it is a thing of another nature: but if a sacrament is made of it, and a divine virtue is joined to that, we can admit of no such thing, without an express institution and declaration in scripture.

The invention that was afterwards found out, by which the bishop was held to be the only minister of *confirmation*, even though presbyters were suffered to *confirm*, was a piece of superstition without any colour from scripture. It was settled, that the bishop only might consecrate the *chrism*; and though he was the ordinary minister of confirmation, yet presbyters were also suffered to do it, the chrism being consecrated by the bishop: presbyters thus confirming was thought like the deacons giving the sacrament, though priests only might consecrate the eucharist. In the Latin church Jerome tells us, that in his time the bishop only confirmed; and though he makes the reason of this to be rather for doing an honour to them, than from any necessity of the law, yet he positively says, the bishops went round praying for the Holy Ghost on those whom they confirmed. It is said by Hilary, that in Egypt *the presbyters did confirm in the bishop's absence:* so that custom, joined with the distinction between the consecration, and the applying of the chrism, grew to be the universal practice of the Greek church. The greatness of dioceses, with the increasing numbers of the Christians, made that both in France, in the councils of Orange; and in Spain, in the council of Toledo, the same rule was laid down that the Greeks had begun. In Spain some priests did consecrate the chrism, but that was severely forbid in one of the councils of Toledo: yet at Rome the ancient custom was observed of appropriating the whole business of confirmation to the bishop, even in Gregory the Great's time: therefore he reproved the clergy of Sardinia, because among them the priest did confirm, and he appointed it to be reserved to the bishop. But, when he understood that some of them were offended at this, he writ to the bishop of Carali, that though his former order was made according to the ancient practice of the church of Rome, yet he consented that for the future the priest might *confirm* in the bishop's absence. But pope Nicholas in the ninth century pressed this with more rigour: for the Bulgarians being then converted to the Christian religion, and their priests having both baptized and confirmed the new converts, pope Nicholas sent bishops among them, with orders to confirm even those who had already been confirmed by priests: upon which, the contest being then on foot between Rome and Constantinople, Photius got it to be decreed in a synod at Constantinople, that the chrism being hallowed by a bishop, it might be administered by presbyters: and Photius affirmed, that a presbyter might do this, as well as baptize or offer at the altar. But pope Nicholas, with the confidence that was often assumed by that see upon as bad grounds, did affirm, that this had never been allowed of. And upon this many of the Latins did, in the progress of their disputes with the Greeks, say, that they had no confirmation. This has been more enlarged on, than was necessary by the designed shortness of this work, because all those of the Roman communion among us have now no confirmation, unless a bishop happens to come amongst them. And therefore it is now a common doctrine among them, that though confirmation is a sacrament, yet it is not necessary.

ART. XXV. In Decr. Con. Florent.

About this there were fierce disputes among them about sixty years ago, whether it was necessary for them to have a bishop here to confirm, according to the ancient custom, or not. The Jesuits, who had no mind to be under any authority but their own, opposed it; for the bishop being by pope Eugenius declared to be the ordinary minister of it, from thence it was inferred, that a bishop was not simply necessary. This was much censured by some of the Gallican church. If confirmation were considered only as an ecclesiastical rite, we could not dispute the power of the church about it; but we cannot allow that a sacrament should be thus within the power of the church; or that a new function of consecrating oil, without applying it, distinct from confirmation, and yet necessary to the very essence of it, could have been set up by the power of the church; for if sacraments are federal conveyances of grace, they must be continued according to their first institution, the grace of God being only tied to the actions with which it is promised.

We go next to the second of the sacraments here rejected, which is *Penance*, that is reckoned the fourth in order among them. *Penance*, or *penitence*, is formed from the Latin translation of a Greek word that signifies a *change* or *renovation of mind;* which Christ has made a necessary condition of the new covenant. It consists in several acts; by all which, when joined together, and producing this real change, we become true penitents, and have a right to the *remission of sins*, which is in the New Testament often joined with *repentance*, and is its certain consequent. The first act of this repentance is, confession to God, before whom we must humble ourselves, and confess our sins to him; upon which we believe that 'he is faithful,' and true to his promises, and 'just to forgive us our sins;' and if we have wronged others, or have given public offence to the body, or church to which we belong, we ought to *confess our faults* to them likewise; and as a mean to quiet men's consciences, to direct them to complete their repentance, and to make them more humble and ashamed of their sins, we advise them to use secret confession to *their priest*,

1 John i. 9.

James v. 16.

ART. XXV. or to any other minister of God's word; leaving this matter wholly to their discretion.*

When these acts of sorrow have had their due effect, in reforming the natures and lives of sinners, then their sins are forgiven them: in order to which, we do teach them to pray much, to give alms according to their capacity, and to fast as often as their health and circumstances will admit of; and most indispensably to restore or repair, as they find they have sinned against others. And as we teach them thus to look back on what is past, with a deep and hearty sorrow, and a profound shame, so we charge them to look chiefly forward, not thinking that any acts with relation to what is past can, as it were, by an account or compensation, free us from the guilt of our former sins, unless we amend our lives and change our tempers for the future; the great design of repentance being to make us like God, pure and holy as he is. Upon such a repentance sincerely begun and honestly pursued, we do in general, as the heralds of God's mercy, and the ministers of his gospel, pronounce to our people daily, the offers that are made us of mercy and pardon by Christ Jesus. This we do in our daily service, and in a more peculiar manner before we

* 'The church of England *commands* confession to be made *only to God.* She *allows* or *recommends* to the sick a confession of those things that afflict their minds, to their ministers, *in order to obtain advice or consolation.*—Is this the doctrine you are sworn to teach? Far from it. Must I then, besides exposing your sophistry, correct your ignorance of your own doctrines, by stating them from your (pretended) infallible councils?

'The TRENT DOCTRINE is, that by the bare receiving of the sacraments grace is conferred. (See council of Trent, sessio vii. canon viii.) Confession you make part of one of your *new* sacraments, viz. of the sacrament of penance, as you call it, perverting the scripture where the word is *repentance,* and *not* penance, although you also translate the word repentance as we do, when it suits your purpose. (See Acts v. 31, Rhemish Testament.) 'You make confession, which only consists of words, the *matter* of your new sacrament!—" *Sunt autem quasi materia hujus sacramenti ipsius pœnitentis actus, nempe contritio, confessio et satisfactio."* (Council of Trent, sessio xiv. cap. 3.) Confession, according to TRENT, is part of the sacrament of penance, by which grace is conferred *" ex opere operato."*

'You have then not only recommended confession to the minister or priest, but *commanded, under pain of being accursed,* secret or auricular confession to be made at stated times—not to GOD, as we say, but unto the priest—not in order to obtain *advice,* as we say, but in order to obtain *grace and absolution!!* The question then is, *not* whether it be *adviseable* to make confession to the minister of those things that afflict our minds, *in order to obtain advice, but* whether to confess all our greater sins, and all that upon strict inquiry we remember, not to GOD, as we admit, but to a priest, be *necessary* to salvation. You assert that it is necessary to salvation; this the church of England denies; and protests against your unscriptural domination over the consciences and souls of men. The council of Trent (sessio xiv. can. 6, 7, 8.) decrees, " that to confess all and every mortal sin, which after diligent inquiry we remember, and every evil thought or desire, and the circumstances that change the nature of the sin," is necessary to salvation, and of divine institution, and whosoever denies this, is to be accursed! And that all is to be done according to the constitution of the great council of Lateran. The order of which council was, that all persons of years of discretion should confess their sins once at least every year to their own priest, or with his leave to another priest; otherwise, when living, they were to be driven from entrance into the church, and when dead, they were to have no Christian burial. Now how do you support this unscriptural tyranny over the consciences and souls of men? When, and where, was such a system as this of Trent and Lateran instituted by CHRIST, or commanded, or practised, by the Apostles?' *Page's Letters to a Romish Priest.*—[ED.]

go to the holy communion. We do also, as we are a body that may be offended with the sins of others, forgive the scandals committed against the church; and that such as we think die in a state of repentance, may die in the full peace of the church, we join both absolutions in one; in the last office likewise praying to our Saviour that he would forgive them, and then we, as the officers of the church, authorized for that end, do forgive all the offences and scandals committed by them against the whole body. This is our doctrine concerning repentance; in all which we find no characters of a sacrament, no more than there is in prayer or devotion. Here is no matter, no application of that matter by a peculiar form, no institution, and no peculiar federal acts. The scene here is the mind, the acts are internal, the effect is such also; and therefore we do not reckon it a sacrament, not finding in it any of the characters of a sacrament.

ART. XXV.

The matter that is assigned in the church of Rome, are the acts of the penitent; his confession by his mouth to the priest, the contrition of his heart, and the satisfaction of his work, in doing the enjoined penance. The aggregate of all these is the *matter*; and the *form*, are the words, *Ego te absolvo*. Now besides what we have to say from every one of these particulars, the matter of a sacrament must be some visible sign applied to him that receives it. It is therefore a very absurd thing to imagine that a man's own thoughts, words, or actions, can be the *matter* of a sacrament: how can this be sanctified or applied to him? It will be a thing no less absurd to make the *form* of a sacrament to be a practice not much elder than four hundred years; since no ritual can be produced, nor author cited, for this form, for above a thousand years after Christ; all the ancient forms of receiving penitents having been by a blessing in the form of a prayer, or a declaration; but none of them in these positive words, *I absolve thee.* We think this want of *matter*, and this new invented *form*, being without any institution in scripture, and different from so long a practice of the whole church, are such reasons, that we are fully justified in denying penance to be a sacrament. But because the doctrine of repentance is a point of the highest importance, there arise several things here that ought to be very carefully examined.

Innoc.3. in 4 Later. Can. 21, 22. Con. Trid. Sess. 14. c. 5.

As to *confession*, we find in the scriptures, that such as desired St. John's baptism came 'confessing their sins;' but that was previous to baptism. We find also that scandalous persons were to be 'openly rebuked before all,' and so to be put to shame; in which, no doubt, there was a confession, and a publication of the sin; but that was a matter of the discipline and order of the church: which made it necessary to 'note such persons as walked disorderly, and to have no fellowship with them,' sometimes not so much as to eat with them, who being Christians, and such as were called *brothers*,

Matt. iii. 6.

1 Tim. v. 20.

2 Thess. iii. 14. 1 Cor. v. 11.

ART. were a reproach to their profession. But besides the power
XXV. given to the apostles of *binding and loosing*, which, as was said
on another head, belonged to other matters; we find that
when our Saviour breathed on his apostles, and gave them
John xx. the Holy Ghost, he with that told them, that 'whose soever
23. sins they remitted, they were remitted; and whose soever sins
they retained, they were retained.' Since a power of remitting or retaining sin was thus given to them, they infer, that
it seems reasonable, that, in order to their dispensing it with
a due caution, the knowledge of all sins ought to be laid open
to them.

Some have thought that this was a personal thing given to
the apostles with that miraculous effusion of the Holy Ghost;
with which such a discerning of spirits was communicated to
them, that they could discern the sincerity or hypocrisy of
Acts v. those that came before them. By this St. Peter discovered
3, 9. the sin of Ananias and Sapphira; and he also saw that Simon
Acts viii.
23. of Samaria was 'in the gall of bitterness, and in the bond
of iniquity:' so they conclude that this was a part of that extraordinary and miraculous authority which was given to the
apostles, and to them only. But others, who distinguish
between the full extent of this power, and the ministerial
authority that is still to be continued in the church, do believe
that these words may in a lower and more limited sense belong to the successors of the apostles; but they argue very
strongly, that if these words are to be understood in their
full extent as they lie, a priest has by them an absolute and
unlimited power in this matter, not restrained to conditions
or rules; so that if he does pardon or retain sins, whether in
that he does right or wrong, the sins must be pardoned or
retained accordingly: he may indeed sin in using it wrong,
for which he must answer to God; but he seems, by the
literal meaning of these words, to be clothed with such a plenipotentiary authority, that his act must be valid, though he
may be punished for employing it amiss.*

* The Trent doctrine of absolution is—' Si quis dixerit, absolutionem sacramentalem sacerdotis non esse *actum judicialem, vd nudum ministerium pronuntiandi et declarandi remissa esse peccata* confitenti, modo tantum credat se esse absolutum ; *aut sacerdos non serio, sed joco absolvat* ; aut dixerit non requiri confessionem pœnitentis, ut sacerdos eum absolvere possit; anathema sit !!!' *Sessio* xiv. canon ix.

' The absolution of the church of England is simply declaratory. The words, as you will find them in the daily form of prayer, are, " Almighty GOD the Father of our LORD JESUS CHRIST, who desireth not the death of a sinner, but rather that he may turn from his wickedness and live ; and hath given power and commandment to his ministers, *to declare and pronounce to his people, being penitent,* the absolution and remission of their sins. HE pardoneth and absolveth all them that truly repent, and unfeignedly believe his holy gospel." But because the minister pronounces it thus in the visitation of the sick—" Our LORD JESUS CHRIST, who hath left power to his church to absolve all sinners who truly repent and believe in him, of his great mercy forgive thee thine offences : And by his authority committed to me, I absolve thee from all thy sins, in the name of the FATHER, and of the SON, and of the HOLY GHOST"—you would, I suppose, *wisely* conclude, that when the reformers reached this part of the prayer book, they forgot what they had said in the commencement, and here claim a power which there is vested *only in God*. Or that

An ambassador that has full powers, though limited by ART. secret instructions, does bind him that so empowered him by XXV. every act that he does pursuant to his powers, how much soever it may go beyond his instructions; for how obnoxious soever that may render him to his master, it does not at all lessen the authority of what he has done, nor the obligation that arises out of it. So these words of Christ's, if applied to all priests, must belong to them in their full extent; and if so, the salvation or the damnation of mankind is put absolutely in the priest's power. Nor can it be answered, that the conditions of the pardon of sin that are expressed in the other parts of the gospel, are here to be understood, though they are not expressed; as we are said to be saved if we believe, which does not imply that a single act of believing the gospel without any thing else, puts us in a state of salvation. In opposition to this, we answer, that the gospel having so described *faith* to us, as the root of all other graces and virtues, as that which produces them, and which is known by them,

---

by saying "by his authority committed unto me, I absolve" &c. &c.; it necessarily follows that they contradict what they had said before, "that power and commandment is given unto the minister, *to declare and pronounce* to his people, being penitent," &c. &c. But a few words will explain this, and may discover to you, that in the language of scripture a thing is said to *be done by a person*, when his doing it *only consists in his declaring and pronouncing it*—See Jeremiah i. 9, 10.— "And the LORD said unto me, Behold I have put my words in thy mouth. See I have this day set thee over the nations and over the kingdoms, to root out, and to pull down, and to destroy, and to throw down, to build and to plant." Now we must all grant that Jeremiah had power over the kingdoms, to root out and to pull down, &c. &c.; for GOD gave it to him. We must likewise grant that Jeremiah exercised this power, and did throw down and destroy kingdoms: otherwise GOD's purpose in raising him up would have failed. The point then is, how, and in what way, did Jeremiah exercise this power, and throw down and destroy the kingdoms? There are but two ways. 1st—By being actively engaged in the battle in the day of the falling of these kingdoms, and by his own act and deed destroying them; or, 2dly—By his declaring and pronouncing their downfall by the authority committed to him, and by proclaiming the word of destruction. That he pulled down and destroyed the kingdoms in the first way, you must maintain: or contradict the council of Trent. That he did it in the second way we maintain, and say, just so hath CHRIST given power to his ministers to remit sin ; but this power is *only* to be exercised *by their declaring* and *pronouncing* the absolution and remission of their sins to " all that truly repent, and unfeignedly believe his holy gospel." And the minister, pronouncing and declaring this absolution, may be said to absolve, in the same way that Jeremiah, declaring and pronouncing the downfall of nations and kingdoms, may be said, and is said, to have pulled down, rooted out, and destroyed them. . . . . .
' Another portion of scripture, to which I refer, is that which concerns the cleansing of the leper; which is exactly parallel, as the leper typified the sinner defiled with sin. In Leviticus xiii. 3, 6, &c. " And the priest shall look upon him, and shall PRONOUNCE him *unclean* ;" and again, " And the priest shall PRONOUNCE him *clean*." Here then we see, that the priest had *only* the power of declaring and pronouncing, and not the power of killing or curing, of making clean or unclean: and yet in the 14th chap. 11th verse, the thing is said to be done by the priest :— " And the priest that MAKETH him clean," &c. &c. This is plain, and proves, that in the language of scripture a thing is said to be done by a person, when his doing it *only* consists in his *declaring* and *pronouncing* it. Apply this now, and you shall discover that we may use the words " I absolve," and yet maintain that the absolution is *only declaratory*, without agreeing with the impious doctrine of the council of Trent, or "*annihilating the book of Common Prayer.*" *Page's Letters to a Romish Priest.*—[ED.]

ART. XXV. all that is promised upon our *faith* must be understood of a faith so qualified as the gospel represents it; and therefore that cannot be applied to this case, where an unlimited authority is so particularly expressed, that no condition seems to be implied in it. If any conditions are elsewhere laid upon us, in order to our salvation, then, according to their doctrine, we may say that of them which they say of contrition upon this occasion, that they are necessary when we cannot procure the priest's pardon; but that by it the want of them all may be supplied, and that the obligation to them all is superseded by it:* and if any conditions are to be understood as limits upon this power, why are not all the conditions of the gospel, faith, hope, and charity, contrition and new obedience, made necessary, in order to the lawful dispensing of it, as well as confession, attrition, and the doing the penance enjoined? Therefore since no condition is here named as a restraint upon this general power, that is pretended to be given to priests by those words of our Saviour, they must either be understood as simple and unconditional, or they must be limited to all the conditions that are expressed in the gospel; for there is not the colour of a reason to restrain them to some of them, and to leave out the rest: and thus we think we are fully justified by saying, that by these words our Saviour did indeed fully empower the apos-

---

* 'The absolution of the priest is, according to Trent, of such importance and value, that it can, by some strange process, make attrition contrition, and save a man who has only imperfect repentance, in which there is no love of God. The Lord Jesus Christ says, "Except ye repent, ye shall all likewise perish:" Trent says, If ye have even attrition, (i. e. imperfect repentance, arising from base motives, such as fear of hell, &c.) ye shall surely be saved, if only ye can get the priest's absolution. You say, that contrition (perfect repentance) is indispensably necessary to give efficacy to the absolution. How can you assert this, when Trent lays down such soul-destroying doctrine as this, that attrition is sufficient, if the person can get the priest's absolution !!! This is such awful doctrine, that I shall give your own authorities, lest any should conclude that I misrepresent your system. The council of Trent speaks thus :—" Illam vero contritionem imperfectam, quæ attritio dicitur, quoniam vel ex turpitudinis peccati consideratione, vel ex gebennæ et pœnarum metu communiter concipitur, si voluntatem peccandi excludat, cum spe veniæ; declarat non solum non facere hominem hypocritam, et magis peccatorem, verum, etiam donum Dei esse, et Spiritus sancti impulsum, non adhuc quidem inhabitantis, sed tantum moventis, quo penitens adjutus, viam sibi ad justitiam parat. Et quamvis sine sacramento pœnitentiæ per se ad justificationem perducere peccatorem nequeat; tamen eum ad Dei gratiam in sacramento pœnitentiæ impetrandum disponit." *Sessio* xiv. cap. 4. You must now have another statement of this doctrine, from the " Abridgment of Christian Doctrine" revised by Dr. Doyle. (See the article on penance.) " Q. What is attrition? *A*. It is imperfect contrition, arising from the consideration of the turpitude of sin, or fear of punishment; and if it contain a detestation of sin with the hope of pardon, it is so far from being itself wicked, that though alone it justify not, yet it prepares th· way to justification, and disposes us, at least remotely, towards obtaining God's grace in the sacrament. Q. What, if a dying man be in mortal sin, and cannot have a priest? *A. Then* nothing but perfect contrition will suffice, it being impossible to be saved without the love of God." So that, according to this impious doctrine, the absolution of the priest supplies the place of the love of God, which is lacking in attrition!! Need I say, that the church of England has too much respect for the character of God, and his truth, not to protest loudly against such a system as this?' *Page's Letters to a Romish Priest*.—[ED.]

tles to publish his gospel to the world, and to declare the terms of salvation, and of obtaining the pardon of sin, in which they were to be infallibly assisted, so that they could not err in discharging their commission; and the terms of the covenant of grace being thus settled by them, all who were to succeed them were also empowered to go on with the publication of this pardon and of those glad tidings to the world: so that whatsoever they declared in the name of God, conform to the tenor of that which the apostles were to settle, should be always made good. We do also acknowledge, that the pastors of the church have, in the way of censure and government, a ministerial authority to remit or to retain sins, as they are matters of scandal or offence; though that indeed does not seem to be the meaning of those words of our Saviour; and therefore we think that the power of pardoning and retaining is only declaratory, so that all the exercises of it are then only effectual, when the declarations of the pardon are made conform to the conditions of the gospel. This doctrine of ours, how much soever decried of late in the Roman church, as striking at the root of the priestly authority, yet has been maintained by some of their best authors, and some of the greatest of their schoolmen.

Thus we have seen upon what reason it is that we do not conclude from hence, that auricular confession is necessary; in which we think that we are fully confirmed by the practice of many of the ages of the Christian church, which did not understand these words as containing an obligation to secret confession. It is certain, that the practice and tradition of the church must be relied on here, if in any thing, since there was nothing that both clergy and laity were more concerned both to know and to deliver down faithfully, than this, on which the authority of the one, and the salvation of the other, depended so much. Such a point as this could never have been forgot or mistaken; many and clear rules must have been given about it. It is a thing to which human nature has so much repugnancy, that it must, in the first forming of churches, have been infused into them as absolutely necessary in order to pardon and salvation.

A church could not now be formed, according to the doctrine and practice of the church of Rome, without very full and particular instructions, both to priests and people, concerning confession and absolution. It is the most intricate part of their divinity, and that which the clergy must be the most ready at. In opposition to all this, let it be considered, that though there is a great deal said in the New Testament concerning sorrow for sin, repentance, and remission of sins, yet there is not a word said, nor a rule given, concerning confession to be made to a priest, and absolution to be given by him. There is indeed a passage in St. James's Epistle relating to confession; but it is 'to one another;' not restrained

James v. 16.

ART. XXV. to the priest; as the word rendered *faults* seems to signify those offences by which others are wronged; in which case confession is a degree of reparation, and so is sometimes necessary: but whatever may be in this, it is certain, that the confession, which is there appointed to be made, is a thing that was to be mutual among Christians; and it is not commanded in order to absolution, but in order to the procuring the intercessions of other good men; and therefore it is added, and 'pray for one another.' By the words that follow, 'that ye may be healed,' joined with those that went before concerning the *sick*, it seems the direction given by St. James belongs principally to sick persons; and the conclusion of the whole period shews, that it relates only to the private prayers of good men for one another; 'the effectual fervent prayer of a righteous man availeth much :' so that this place does not at all belong to auricular confession or absolution.

Nor do there any prints appear, before the apostacies that happened in the persecution of Decius, of the practice even of confessing such heinous sins as had been publicly committed. Then arose the famous contests with the Novatians, concerning the receiving the lapsed into the communion of the church again. It was concluded not to exclude them from the hopes of mercy, or of reconciliation; yet it was resolved not to do that till they had been kept at a distance for some time from the holy communion; at last they were admitted to make their confession, and so they were received to the communion of the church. This time was shortened, and many things were passed over, to such as shewed a deep and sincere repentance; and one of the characters of a true repentance, upon which they were always treated with a great distinction of favour, was, if they came and first accused themselves. This shewed that they were deeply affected with the sense of their sins, when they could not bear the load of them, but became their own accusers, and discovered their sins. There are several canons that make a difference in the degrees and time of the penance, between those who had accused themselves, and those against whom their sins were proved. A great deal of this strain occurs often in the writings of the fathers, which plainly shews that they did not look on the necessity of an enumeration of all their sins as commanded by God; otherwise it would have been enforced with considerations of another nature, than that of shortening their penance.

The first occasion that was given to the church to exercise this discipline, was from the frequent apostacies, into which many had lapsed during the persecutions; and when these went off, another sort of disorders began to break in upon the church, and to defile it. Great numbers followed the example of their princes, and became Christians; but a mixed multitude came among them, so that there were many scandals amongst that body, which had been formerly remarkable for the purity of their morals, and the strictness of their lives. It was the chief business of all those councils that met in the fourth and fifth centuries, to settle many rules concerning the degrees and time of penance, the censures both of the clergy and laity, the orders of the penitents and the methods of receiving them to the communion of the church. In some of those councils they denied reconciliation after some sins, even to the last, though the general practice was to receive all at their death; but while they were in a good state of health, they kept them long in penance, in a public separation from the common privileges of Christians, and chiefly from the holy sacrament, and under severe rules, and that for several years, more or fewer, according to the nature of their sins, and the characters of their repentance; of which a free and unextorted confession being one of the chief, this made many prevent that, and come in of their own accord to confess their sins, which was much encouraged and magnified. *ART. XXV. Dallæus de Confessione. Morinus de Pœnitentia.*

Confession was at first made publicly; but the inconveniencies of that appearing, and particularly many of those sins being capital, instead of a public, there was a private confession practised. The bishops either attended upon these themselves, or they appointed a penitentiary priest to receive them: all was in order to the executing the canons, and for keeping up the discipline of the church. Bishops were warranted by the council of Nice to excuse the severity of the canons, as the occasion should require. The penitents went through the penance imposed, which was done publicly; the separation and penance being visible, even when the sin was kept secret; and when the time of the penance was finished, they received the penitents by prayer and imposition of hands, into the communion of the church, and so they were received. This was all the absolution that was known during the first six centuries.

Penitents were enjoined to publish such of their secret sins, as the penitentiary priest did prescribe. This happened to give great scandal at Constantinople, when Nectarius was bishop there; for a woman being in a course of penance, confessed publicly that she had been guilty of adultery, committed with a deacon in the church. It seems, by the relation that the historian gives of this matter, that she went beyond the injunction given her; but whether the fault was in her, or in the penitentiary priest, this gave such offence, that Nectarius broke that custom. And Chrysostom, who came soon after him to that see, speaks very fully against secret confession, and advises Christians to confess only to God; yet the practice of secret confession was kept up elsewhere. But it appears by a vast number of citations from the fathers, both in different ages, and in the different corners of the church, that though they pressed confession much, and magnified the *Socr. Hist. l. v. c. 19. Thirteen passages out of him cited and explained by Daillé de Conf. l. iv. c. 25.*

ART.
XXV.

value of it highly, yet they never urged it as necessary to the pardon of sin, or as a sacrament; they only pressed it as a mean to complete the repentance, and to give the sinner an interest in the prayers of the church. This may be positively affirmed concerning all the quotations that are brought in this matter, to prove that auricular confession is necessary in order to the priest's pardon, and that it is founded on those words of Christ, ' Whose sins ye remit,' &c. that they prove quite the contrary; that the fathers had not that sense of it, but considered it, either as a mean to help the completing of repentance, or as a mean to maintain the purity of the Christian church, and the rigour of discipline.

In the fifth century a practice begun, which was no small step to the ruin of the order of the church. Penitents were suffered, instead of the public penance that had been formerly enjoined, to do it secretly in some monastery, or in any other private place, in the presence of a few good men, and that at the discretion of the bishop, or the confessor; at the end of which, absolution was given in secret. This was done to draw what professions of repentance they could from such persons who would not submit to settled rules: this temper was found neither to lose them quite, nor to let their sins pass without any censure. But in the seventh century, all public penance for secret sins was taken quite away. Theodore, archbishop of Canterbury, is reckoned the first of all the bishops of the western church that did quite take away all public penance for secret sins.

Another piece of the ancient severity was also slackened, for they had never allowed penance to men that had relapsed into any sin; though they did not cut them off from all hope of the mercy of God, yet they never gave a second absolution to the relapse. This the church of Rome has still kept up in one point, which is heresy; a relapse being delivered to the secular arm, without admitting him to penance. The ancients did indeed admit such to penance, but they never reconciled them. Yet in the decay of discipline, absolution came to be granted to the relapse, as well as to him that had sinned but once.

About the end of the eighth century, the commutation of penance began; and, instead of the ancient severities, vocal prayers came to be all that was enjoined; so many *Paters* stood for so many days of fasting, and the rich were admitted to buy off their penance under the decenter name of giving alms. The getting many masses to be said, was thought a devotion by which God was so much honoured, that the commuting penance for masses was much practised. Pilgrimages and wars came on afterwards; and in the twelfth century, the trade was set up of selling indulgences. By this it appears, that confession came by several steps into the church; that in the first ages it was not heard of; that the apostacies in time of persecution gave the first rise to it: all which demonstrates that the primitive church did not consider it as a thing appointed by Christ to be the matter of a sacrament.

It may be in the power of the church to propose confession, as a mean to direct men in their repentance, to humble them deeper for their sins, and to oblige them to a greater strictness. But to enjoin it as necessary to obtain the pardon of sin, and to make it an indispensable condition, and indeed the most indispensable of all the parts of repentance, is beyond the power of the church; for since Christ is the Mediator of this new covenant, he alone must fix the necessary conditions of it. In this, more than in any thing else, we must conclude that the gospel is express and clear; and therefore so hard a condition as this is cannot be imposed by any other authority. The obligation to auricular confession is a thing to which mankind is naturally so little disposed to submit, and it may have such consequences on the peace and order of the world, that we have reason to believe, that if Christ had intended to have made it a necessary part of repentance, he would have declared it in express words, and not have left it so much in the dark, that those who assert it, must draw it by inferences from those words, 'Whose sins ye remit,' &c. Some things are of such a nature, that we may justly conclude, that either they are not at all required, or that they are commanded in plain terms.

As for the good or evil effects that may follow on the obliging men to a strictness in confession, that does not belong to this matter: if it is acknowledged to be only a law of the church, other considerations are to be examined about it; but if it is pretended to be a law of God, and a part of a sacrament, we must have a divine institution for it; otherwise all the advantages that can possibly be imagined in it, without that, are only so many arguments to persuade us, that there is somewhat that is highly necessary to the purity of Christians, of which Christ has not said a word, and concerning which his apostles have given us no directions. We do not deny but it may be a mean to strike terror in people, to keep them under awe and obedience; it may, when the management of it is in good hands, be made a mean to keep the world in order, and to guide those of weaker judgments more steadily and safely, than could be well done any other way. In the use of confession, when proposed as our church does, as matter of advice, and not of obligation, we are very sensible many good ends may be attained; but while we consider those, we must likewise reflect on the mischief that may arise out of it; especially supposing the greater part both of the clergy and laity to be what they ever were, and ever will be, depraved and corrupted. The people will grow to think that the priest is in *God's stead* to them; that their telling their sins to him, is as if they confessed them to God; they will expect to be

ART.
XXV.

easily discharged for a gentle penance, with a speedy absolution; and this will make them as secure, as if their consciences were clear, and their sins pardoned; so the remedy being easy and always at hand, they will be encouraged to venture the more boldly on sin. It is no difficult matter to gain a priest, especially if he himself is a bad man, to use them tenderly upon those occasions. On the other hand, corrupt priests will find their account in the dispensing this great power, so as to serve their own ends. They will know all people's tempers and secrets; and how strict soever they may make the seal of confession, to draw the world to trust to it; yet in bodies so knit together, as communities and orders are, it is not possible to know what use they make of this. Still they know all themselves, and see into the weakness, the passions, and appetites, of their people. This must often be a great snare to them, especially in the supposition that cannot be denied to hold generally true, of their being bad men themselves: great advantages are hereby given to infuse fears and scruples into people's minds, who, being then in their tenderest minutes, will be very much swayed and wrought on by them. A bad priest knows by this whom he may tempt to any sort of sin: and thus the good and the evil of confession, as it is a general law upon all men's consciences, being weighed one against the other; and it being certain that the far greater part of mankind is always bad, we must conclude that the evil does so far preponderate the good, that they bear no comparison or proportion to one another. The matter at present under debate is only whether it is one of the laws of God, or not? and it is enough for the present purpose to shew, that it is no law of God; upon which we do also see very good reason why it ought not to be made a law of the church; both because it is beyond her authority, which can only go to matters of order and discipline, as also because of the vast inconveniencies that are like to arise out of it.

The next part of repentance is *contrition*, which is a sorrow for sin upon the motives of the love of God, and the hatred of sin joined with a renovation of heart. This is that which we acknowledge to be necessary to complete our repentance; but this consisting in the temper of a man's mind, and his inward acts, it seems a very absurd thing to make this the matter of a sacrament, since it is of a spiritual and invisible nature. But this is not all that belongs to this head.

The casuists of the church of Rome have made a distinction between a perfect and an imperfect *contrition;* the imperfect they call *attrition;* which is any sorrow for sin, though upon an inferior motive, such as may be particular to one act of sin, as when it rises from the loss or shame it has brought with it, together with an act formed in detestation of it, without a resolution to sin no more. Such a sorrow as this is they teach does make the sacrament effectual, and puts a man in a state of justification, though they acknowledge that without the sacrament it is not sufficient to justify him.

ART. XXV.

This was settled by the council of Trent.* We think it strikes at the root of all religion and virtue, and is a reversing of the design for which sacraments were instituted, which was to raise our minds to a high pitch of piety, and to exalt and purify our acts. We think the sacraments are profaned when we do not raise our thoughts as high as we can in them. To teach men how low they may go, and how small a measure will serve turn, especially when the great and chief commandment, the consideration of the love of God, is left out, seems to be one of the greatest corruptions in practice of which any church can be guilty; a slackness in doctrine, especially in so great a point as this, in which human nature is under so fatal a bias, will always bring with it a much greater corruption in practice. This will indeed make many run to the sacrament, and raise its value; but it will rise upon the ruins of true piety and holiness. There are few men that can go long on in very great sins without feeling great remorses; these are to them rather a burden that they cannot shake off, than a virtue. Sorrow lying long upon their thoughts may be the beginning of a happy change, and so prove a great blessing to them: all which is destroyed by this doctrine: for if under such uneasy thoughts they go to confession, and are attrite, the sacrament is valid, and they are justified: then the uneasiness goes off, and is turned into joy, without their being any thing the better by it. They return to their sins with a new calm and security, because they are taught that their sins are pardoned, and that all scores are cleared. Therefore we conclude, that this doctrine wounds religion in its vitals; and we are confirmed in all this by what appears in practice, and what the best writers that have lived in that communion have said of the abuses that follow on the methods in which this sacrament is managed among them, which do arise mainly out of this part of their doctrine concerning *attrition*. All that they teach concerning those acts of *attrition*, or even *contrition*, is also liable to great abuse in practice: for, as a man may bring forth those acts in words, and not be the better for them; so he may force himself to think them, which is nothing but the framing an inward discourse within himself upon them; and yet these not arising genuinely from a new nature, or a change of temper, such acts can be of no value in the sight of God: yet the whole practice of their church runs upon these acts, as if a man's going through them, and making himself think them, could be of great value in the sight of God.

Trid. Sess. 14. c. 4.

The third branch of the matter of this sacrament is the

* For this decree, see note, p. 360.—[ED.]

ART. XXV. *satisfaction*, or the doing the penance; which, by the constant practice of the church for above twelve centuries, was to be performed before absolution could be given; except in extraordinary cases, such as death, or martyrdom; but in these latter ages, in which the necessity of confession is carried higher, the obligation to satisfaction or the doing of penance is let fall lower. A distinction is invented by which confession and contrition, attrition at least, are made essential parts of the sacrament, without which there is no sacrament; as soul and body are essential to the being of a man; and satisfaction is considered only as an integral part; such as an eye or a limb in a man, which is necessary to the order of it, but not to its being. If satisfaction is considered as that which destroys the habits of sin, and introduces the habits of virtue; if it is purgative and medicinal, and changes a man's principles and nature, then it ought to be reckoned the principal and least dispensable thing of all repentance. For our confessing past sins, and sorrowing for them, is only enjoined us as a mean to reform and purify our nature. If we imagine that our acts of repentance are a discounting with God, by so many pious thoughts whish are to be set against so many bad ones, this will introduce a sort of mechanical religion; which will both corrupt our ideas of God, and of the nature of good and evil.

The true and generous notion of religion is, that it is a system of many truths, which are of such efficacy, that if we receive them into our minds, and are governed by them, they will rectify our thoughts, and purify our natures; and by making us like God here, they will put us in a sure way to enjoy him eternally hereafter. Sorrow for past sins, and all reflections upon them, are enjoined us as means to make the sense of them go so deep in our minds, as to free us from all those bad habits that sin leaves in us, and from those ill inclinations that are in our nature. If we therefore set up a sorrowing for sin as a merchandise with God, by so many acts of one kind to take off the acts of another, here the true design of our sorrow is turned into a trafficking, by which how much soever priests may gain, or the value of sacraments may seem to rise, religion will certainly lose in its main design, which is the planting a new nature in us, and the making us become like God. Confession and contrition are previous acts, that lead to this reformation, which, as they teach, is wrought by the satisfaction; therefore we must needs condemn that doctrine which makes it less necessary and more dispensable than the other. In the case of death we confess all the rights of the church with relation to a man's scandals, and his obligations to make public penance, may and ought to be then forgiven him; but we think it one of the most fatal errors that can creep into any church, to encourage men to rely on a death-bed repentance. The nature of man leans so ART. much this way, that it is necessary to bend the point as XXV. strong as may be to the other hand.

The promises of the gospel run all upon the condition of repentance; which imports a renovation of the inner man, and a purity of life: so that no repentance can be esteemed true, but as we perceive that it has purified our hearts, and changed our course of life. What God may do with death-bed penitents, in the infinite extent and absoluteness of his mercy, becomes not us to define: but we are sure he has given no promises to such persons in his gospel. And since the function of clergymen is the dispensing of that, we cannot go beyond the limits set us in it: so there is no reason to make this part of repentance less necessary or obligatory than the other, but very much to the contrary. Another exception that we have to the allowed practice of that church, is the giving absolution before the satisfaction is made; upon its being enjoined and accepted by the penitent. This is so contrary to all ancient rules, that it were a needless labour to go to prove it; the thing being confessed by all: and yet the practice is so totally changed among them, that such as have blamed it, and have attempted to revive the ancient method, have been censured as guilty of an innovation, savouring of heresy: because they condemn so general a practice, that it would render the infallibility of the church very doubtful, if it should be pretended to have erred in so universal a practice.

Hasty absolutions, contrary both to the whole design of the gospel, and to the constant practice of the church, for at least twelve centuries, are now the avowed methods of that church; to which in a great measure all that corruption of morals that is among them owes its rise and continuance: for who can be supposed to set himself against those inclinations to sin, that are deeply rooted in his nature, and are powerfully recommended by the pleasure and gain that arises out of vicious practices, if the way to pardon is cast so wide open, that a man may sin as long and as securely as he will, and yet all at once, upon a few acts that he makes himself go through, he may get into a state of grace, and be pardoned and justified? The power that is left to the priest to appoint the penance, is a trust of a high nature, which yet is known to be universally ill applied; so that absolution is generally prostituted among them.

The true penance enjoined by the gospel is the forsaking of sin, and the doing acts of virtue. Fasting, prayers, and almsgiving, are acts that are very proper means to raise us to this temper. If fasting is joined with prayer, and if prayer arises out of an inward devotion of mind, and is serious and fervent, then we know that it has great efficacy; as being one of the

ART. XXV. chief acts of our religious service of God, to which the greatest promises are made, and upon which the best blessings do descend upon us. Alms-giving is also a main part of charity: which, when done from a right principle of loving God and our neighbour, is of great value in his sight. But if fasting is only an exercise of the body, and of abstaining so long, and from such things, this may perhaps trouble and pain the body; but bodily exercise profiteth nothing; so not to mention the mockery of fasting, when it is only a delay of eating, after which all liberties are taken, or an abstinence which is made up with other delicious and inflaming nutritives, these are of no value, being only inventions to deceive men, and to expose religion to mockery. But even severe and afflicting fasting, if done only as a punishment, which, when it is over, the penance is believed to be completed, gives such a low idea of God and religion, that from thence men are led to think very slightly of sin, when they know at what price they can carry it off. Such a continuance in fasting in order to prayer, as humbles and depresses nature, and raises the mind, is a great mean to reform the world; but fasting as a prescribed task to expiate our sins is a scorn put upon religion.

Prayer, when it arises from a serious heart that is earnest in it, and when it becomes habitual, is certainly a most effectual mean to reform the world, and to fetch down divine assistances. But to appoint so many vocal prayers to be gone through as a task; and then to tell the world that the running through these, with few or no inward acts accompanying them, is contrition or attrition, this is more like a design to root out all the impressions of religion, and all sense of that repentance which the gospel requires, than to promote it. This may be a task fit to accustom children to; but it is contrary to the true genius of religion, to teach men, instead of that *reasonable service* that we ought to offer up to God, to give him only the *labour of the lips*, which is the *sacrifice of fools*. Prayers gone through as a task can be of no value, and can find no acceptation in the sight of God. And as St. Paul said, that 'if he gave all his goods to the poor, and had not charity, he was nothing;' so the greatest profusion of alms-giving, when done in a mercenary way, to buy off and to purchase a pardon, is the turning of God's house from being a *house of prayer*, to be a *den of thieves*.

1 Cor. xiii. 1, 2, 3.

Upon all these reasons we except to the whole doctrine and practice of the church of Rome, as to the satisfaction made by doing penance. And in the last place we except to the form of absolution in these words, *I absolve thee*. We of this church, who use it only to such as are thought to be near death, cannot be meant to understand any thing by it, but the full peace and pardon of the church: for if we meant a pardon with relation to God, we ought to use it upon many other occasions. The pardon that we give in the name of God is only declaratory of his pardon, or supplicatory in a prayer to him for pardon. ART. XXV.

In this we have the whole practice of the church till the twelfth century universally of our side. All the fathers, all the ancient liturgies, all that have writ upon the offices, and the first schoolmen, are so express in this matter, that the thing in fact cannot be denied. Morinus has published so many of their old rituals, that he has put an end to all doubting about it. In the twelfth century some few began to use the words, *I absolve thee:* yet, to soften this expression, that seemed new and bold, some tempered it with these words, *in so far as it is granted to my frailty;* and others with these words, *as far as the accusation comes from thee, and as the pardon is in me.* Yet this form was but little practised: so that William, bishop of Paris, speaks of the form of absolution as given only in a prayer, and not as given in these words, *I absolve thee.* He lived in the beginning of the fourteenth century; so that this practice, though begun in other places before that time, yet was not known long after in so public a city as Paris. But some schoolmen began to defend it, as implying only a declaration of the pardon pronounced by the priest; and this having an air of more authority, and being once justified by learned men, did so universally prevail, that in little more than sixty years' time, it became the universal practice of the whole Latin church. So sure a thing is tradition, and so impossible to be changed, as they pretend, when within the compass of one age, the new form, *I absolve thee,* was not so much as generally known; and before the end of it the old form of doing it in a prayer, with imposition of hands, was quite worn out. The idea that arises naturally out of these words is, that the priest pardons sins; and since that is subject to such abuses, and has let in so much corruption upon that church, we think we have reason not only to deny that penance is a sacrament, but likewise to affirm, that they have corrupted this great and important doctrine of repentance, in all the parts and branches of it: nor is the matter mended with that prayer that follows the absolution; *The passion of our Lord Jesus Christ, the merits of the blessed Virgin and all the saints, and all the good that thou hast done, and the evil that thou hast suffered, be to thee for the remission of sins, the increase of grace, and the reward of eternal life.* Rituale Romanum de sacr. pœnitent.

The third sacrament rejected by this Article is *Orders;* which is reckoned the sixth by the church of Rome. We affirm, that Christ appointed a succession of pastors in different ranks, to be continued in his church, for the work of the gospel, and the care of souls: and that, as the apostles settled the churches, they appointed different orders of *bishops, priests,* and *deacons:* and we believe that all who are dedicated to serve in these ministries, after they are examined and judged worthy of them, ought to be separated to them by the

ART.
XXV.

marginal note: Haberti pontif. Græcum. Morinus de Ordinat. sacris.

imposition of hands, and by prayer. These were the only rites that we find practised by the apostles. For many ages the church of God used no other; therefore we acknowledge that *bishops, priests,* and *deacons,* ought to be blessed and dedicated to the holy ministry by imposition of hands and prayer; and that then they are received according to the order and practice settled by the apostles to serve in their respective degrees. Men thus separated have thereby authority to perfect the saints or Christians, that is, to perform the sacred functions among them, to minister to them, and to build them up in their most holy faith. And we think no other persons, without such a separation and consecration, can lawfully touch the holy things. In all which we separate the qualifications of the function from the inward qualities of the person; the one not at all depending on the other; the one relating only to the order and the good government of the society, and the other relating indeed to the salvation of him that officiates, but not at all to the validity of his office or service.

But in all this we see nothing like a sacrament: here is neither *matter, form,* nor *institution ;* here is only prayer: the laying on of hands is only a gesture in prayer, that imports the designation of the person so prayed over. In the Greek church there is indeed a different form; for though there are prayers in their office of Ordination, yet the words that do accompany the imposition of hands are only declaratory; *The grace of God, that perfects the feeble and heals the weak, promotes this man to be a deacon, a priest, or a bishop; let us therefore pray for him :* by which they pretend only to judge of a divine vocation: all the ancient rituals, and all those that treat of them for the first seven centuries, speak of nothing as essential to orders but *prayer* and *imposition of hands.* It is true, many rites came to be added, and many prayers were used that went far beyond the first simplicity. But in the tenth or eleventh century a new form was brought in, of delivering the *vessels* in ordaining priests; and words were joined with that, giving them power to *offer sacrifices to God, and to celebrate masses,* and then the orders were believed to be given by this rite. The delivering of the *vessels* looked like a *matter,* and these words were thought the *form* of the sacrament; and the prayer that was formerly used with the imposition of hands, was indeed still used, but only as a part of the office; no hands were laid on when it was used: and though the form of laying on of hands was still continued, the bishop with other priests laying their hands on those they ordained, yet it is now a dumb ceremony, not a word of a prayer being said while they lay on their hands. So that though both prayer and imposition of hands are used in the office, yet they are not joined together. In the conclusion of the office, a new benediction was added ever since the twelfth century. The bishop alone lays on his hands, saying, *Receive the Holy Ghost: whose sins ye remit, they are remitted; and whose sins ye retain, they are retained.* The number seven was thought to suit the sacraments best, so Orders were made one of them, and of these only priesthood; where the *vessels* were declared to be the *matter,* and the *form* was the delivering them with the words, *Take thou authority to offer up sacrifices to God, and to celebrate masses, both for the living and the dead; in the name of the Father, the Son, and the Holy Ghost.*

ART. XXV.

The schoolmen have taken a new way of explaining this whole matter, borrowed from the eucharist, that is made up of two parts, the consecration of the bread and of the wine; both so necessary, that without the one the other becomes void: so they teach that a priest has two powers, of *consecrating* and of *absolving;* and that he is ordained to the one by the delivery of the vessels, and to the other by the bishop's laying on of hands, with the words *Receive the Holy Ghost;* and they make the bishop and the priest's laying on of hands jointly, to be only their declaring as by a suffrage, that such a person ought to be ordained; so totally have they departed from the primitive forms.

If this is a sacrament, and if the sacrament consists in this matter and form by them assigned, then since all the rituals of the Latin church for the first ten centuries had no such form of ordaining priests, this cannot be the *matter* and *form* of a sacrament: otherwise the church had in a course of so many ages no true orders, nor any sacrament in them. Nor will it serve in answer to this to say, that Christ instituted no special *matter* nor *form* here, but has left the specifying those among the other powers that he has given to his church: for a sacrament being an institution of applying a *matter* designed by God, by a particular *form* likewise appointed; to say that Christ appointed here neither *matter* nor *form,* is plainly to confess that this is no sacrament. In the first nine or ten ages there was no matter at all used, nothing but an imposition of hands with prayer: so that by this doctrine the church of God was all that while without true orders, since there was nothing used that can be called the matter of a sacrament.

Therefore, though we continue this institution of Christ, as he and his apostles settled it in the church, yet we deny it to be a sacrament ; we also deny all the inferior orders to be sacred below that of deacon. The other orders we do not deny might be well, and on good reasons, appointed by the church as steps through which clerks might be made to pass, in order to a stricter examination and trial of them; like degrees in universities: but the making them, at least the subdiaconate, sacred, as it is reckoned by pope Eugenius, is, we think, beyond the power of the church; for here a degree

ART. XXV. of orders is made a sacrament, and yet that degree is not named in the scripture, nor in the first ages. It is true, it came to be soon used with the other inferior orders; but it cannot be pretended to be a sacrament, since no divine institution can be brought for it. And we cannot but observe, that in the definition that Eugenius has given of the sacraments, which is an authentical piece in the Roman church, where he reckons *priests, deacons,* and *subdeacons,* as belonging to the sacrament of orders, he does not name *bishops,* though their being of divine institution is not questioned in that church. Perhaps the spirit with which they acted at that time in Basil offended him so much, that he was more set on depressing than on raising them. In the council of Trent, in which so much zeal appeared for recovering the dignity of the episcopal order, at that time so much eclipsed by the papal usurpations, when the sacrament of *orders* was treated of, they reckon seven degrees of them, the highest of which is that of priest. So that though they decreed that a bishop was by the divine institution above a priest, yet they did not decree that the office was an order, or a sacrament. And the schoolmen do generally explain episcopate, as being a higher degree or extension of priesthood, rather than a new order, or a sacrament; the main thing in their thoughts being that which, if true, is the greatest of all miracles, the wonderful conversion made in transubstantiation, they seem to think that no order can be above that which qualifies a man for so great a performance.

I say nothing in this place concerning the power of offering sacrifices, pretended to be given in orders; for that belongs to another Article.

The fourth sacrament here rejected is *Marriage;* which is reckoned the last by the Roman account. In the point of argument there is less to say here than in any of the other; but there seems to be a very express warrant for calling it a *sacrament,* from the translation of a passage in St. Paul's Epistle to the Ephesians, in which he makes an allusion, while he treats of marriage, to the mutual relation that is between Christ and his church, from that state of life, and says, ' There is a great mystery here;' the Vulgar has translated the word *mystery* by *sacrament.* So though the words immediately following seem to turn the matter another way, ' but I speak concerning Christ and the church;' yet from the promiscuous use of those two words, and because *sacraments* were called the *mysteries* of the Christian religion, the translator, it seems, thought that all mysteries might be called *sacraments.* But it is so very hard here to find *matter, form,* a *minister,* and a *sacramental effect,* that though pope Eugenius, in that famous decree of his, is very punctual in assigning these, when he explains the other sacraments; yet he wisely

Ephes. v. 32.

passed them all over when he came to this, and only makes a true consent necessary to the making the sacrament.

ART XXV.

We do not deny marriage to be an ordinance of God; but we think that as it was at first made in the state of innocence, so it is still founded on the law of nature; and though the gospel gives rules concerning the duties belonging to this state of life, as it does concerning the duties of parents and children, which is another relation founded on the same law of nature, yet we cannot call it a sacrament; for we find neither *matter*, *form*, *institution*, nor *federal acts*, nor *effects* assigned to it in the gospel, to make us esteem it a sacrament.

The *matter* assigned by the Roman doctors is the inward consent, by which both parties do mutually give themselves to one another: the *form* they make to be the words or signs, by which this is expressed. Now* it seems a strange thing to make the secret thoughts of men the *matter*, and their words the *form* of a sacrament; all mutual compacts being as much sacraments as this, there being no visible material things applied to the parties who receive them; which is necessary to the being of a sacrament. It is also a very absurd opinion, which may have very fatal consequences, and raise very afflicting scruples, if any should imagine that the *inward consent* is the *matter* of this sacrament; here is a foundation laid down for voiding every marriage. The parties may and often do marry against their wills; and though they profess an outward consent, they do inwardly repine against what they are doing. If after this they grow to like their marriage, scruples must arise, since they know they have not the sacrament; because it is a doctrine in that church, that as intention is necessary in every sacrament, so here that goes further, the intention being the only *matter* of this sacrament; so that without it there is no marriage, and yet since they cannot be married again to complete, or rather to make the marriage, such persons do live only in a state of concubinage.

On the other hand, here is a foundation laid down for breaking marriages as often as the parties, or either of them, will solemnly swear that they gave no inward consent, which is often practised at Rome. All contracts are sacred things; but of them all, marriage is the most sacred, since so much depends upon it. Men's words, confirmed by oaths and other solemn acts, must either be binding according to the plain and acknowledged sense of them, or all the security and confidence of mankind is destroyed. No man can be safe if

* Upon the whole doctrine of the church of Rome, concerning the sacraments, as it is explained by the schoolmen, I have followed the account given by Honoratus Fabri, in his Summa Theologica, who is dead within these ten years. I knew him at Rome, anno 1685. He was a true philosopher, beyond the liberties allowed by his order, and studied to reduce their school-divinity to as clear ideas as it was capable of. So that in following him I have given the best, and not the worst, face of their doctrine. His book was printed at Lyons, anno 1669.

ART. XXV. this principle is once admitted; that a man is not bound by his promises and oaths, unless his inward consent went along with them: and if such a fraudulent thing may be applied to marriages, in which so many persons are concerned, and upon which the order of the world does so much depend, it may be very justly applied to all other contracts whatsoever, so that they may be voided at pleasure. A man's words and oaths bind him by the eternal laws of fidelity and truth; and it is a just prejudice against any religion whatsoever, if it should teach a doctrine in which, by the secret reserves of not giving an inward consent, the faith which is solemnly given may be broken. Here such a door is open to perfidy and treachery, that the world can be no longer safe while it is allowed; hereby lewd and vicious persons may entangle others, and in the mean while order their own thoughts so, that they shall be all the while free.

Next to *matter* and *form*, we must see for the institution of this sacrament. The church of Rome think that is strong here, though they feel it to be hardly defensible in the other points that relate to it. They think that though marriage, as it is a mutual contract, subsists upon the law of nature, yet a divine virtue is put in it by the gospel, expressed in these words, 'This is a great mystery, or sacrament;' so the explaining these words determines this controversy. The chief point in dispute at that time was, whether the Gentiles were to be received to equal privileges with the Jews, in the dispensation of the Messias. The Jews do not to this day deny, but that the Gentiles may be admitted to it; but still they think that they are to be considered as a distinct body, and in a lower order, the chief dignity being to be reserved to the seed of Abraham. Now St. Paul had in that Epistle, as well as in his other Epistles, asserted, that all were equal in Christ; that he had taken away the 'middle wall of partition;' that he had abolished the ground of the enmity, which was Eph. ii. 15, the Mosaical law, called 'the law of commandments contained 16, 20, 21. in ordinances; that he might make both Jew and Gentile one new man;' one entire body of a church; 'he being the chief corner-stone, in whom the whole building was fitly framed together: and so became a holy habitation to God.' Thus he made use of the figure of a body, and of a temple, to illustrate this matter; and to shew how all Christians were to make up but one body, and one church. So when he came to speak of the rules belonging to the several states of human life, he takes occasion to explain the duties of the married state, by comparing that to the relation that the church has to Christ: and when he had said that the married couple make but one body and one flesh; which declares that, according to the first institution, every man was to have but one wife; he adds upon that, 'this is a great mystery:' that is, from hence another mystical argument might be brought, to shew that

Jew and Gentile must make one body; for since the church was the spouse of Christ, he must, according to that figure, have but one wife; and by consequence the church must be one: otherwise the figure will not be answered; unless we suppose Christ to be in a state answering a polygamy, rather than a single marriage. Thus a clear account of these words is given, which does fully agree to them, and to what follows, 'but I speak concerning Christ and the church.'

This, which is all the foundation of making marriage a sacrament, being thus cleared, there remains nothing to be said on this head, but to examine one consequence, that has been drawn from the making it a sacrament, which is, that the bond is indissoluble; and that even adultery does not void it. The law of nature or of nations seems very clear, that adultery, at least on the wife's part, should dissolve it: for the end of marriage being the ascertaining of the issue, and the contract itself being a mutual transferring the right to one another's person, in order to that end; the breaking this contract and destroying the end of marriage does very naturally infer the dissolution of the bond: and in this both the Attic and Roman laws were so severe, that a man was infamous who did not divorce upon adultery. Our Saviour, when he blamed the Jews for their frequent divorces, established this rule, 'that whosoever puts away his wife, except it be for fornication, and shall marry another, committeth adultery.' Which seems to be a plain and full determination, that in the case of fornication, he may put her away and marry another. It is true, St. Mark and St. Luke repeat these words, without mentioning this exception; so some have thought that we ought to bring St. Matthew to them, and not them to St. Matthew. But it is an universal rule of expounding scriptures, that when a place is fully set down by one inspired writer, and less fully by another, that the place which is less full is always to be expounded by that which is more full. So though St. Mark and St. Luke report our Saviour's words generally, without the exception, which is twice mentioned by St. Matthew, the other two are to be understood to suppose it; for a general proposition is true when it holds generally; and exceptions may be understood to belong to it, though they are not named. The Evangelist that does name them must be considered to have reported the matter more particularly, than the others that do it not. Since then our Saviour has made the exception, and since that exception is founded upon a natural equity, that the innocent party has against the guilty, there can be no reason why an exception so justly grounded, and so clearly made, should not take place.

Both Tertullian, Basil, Chrysostom, and Epiphanius, allow of a divorce in case of adultery; and in those days they had no other notion of a divorce, but that it was the dissolution of the bond; the late notion of a separation, the tie continuing, not being known till the canonists brought it in. Such a divorce was allowed by the council of Elliberis. The council of Arles did indeed recommend it to the husband, whose wife was guilty of adultery, not to marry; which did plainly acknowledge that he might do it. It was, and still is, the constant practice of the Greek church; and as both pope Gregory and pope Zachary allowed the innocent person to marry, so in a synod held at Rome in the tenth century, it was still allowed. When the Greeks were reconciled to the Latins in the council of Florence, this matter was passed over, and the care of it was only recommended by the pope to the emperor. It is true, Eugenius put it in his instruction to the Armenians; but though that passes generally for a part of the council of Florence, yet the council was over and up before that was given out.

This doctrine of the indissolubleness of marriage, even for adultery, was never settled in any council before that of Trent. The canonists and schoolmen had indeed generally gone into that opinion; but not only Erasmus, but both Cajetan and Catherinus declared themselves for the lawfulness of it: Cajetan indeed used a salvo, in case the church had otherwise defined, which did not then appear to him. So that this is a doctrine very lately settled in the church of Rome. Our reformers here had prepared a title in the new body of the canon law, which they had digested, allowing marriage to the innocent party; and upon a great occasion, then in debate, they declared it to be lawful by the law of God: and if the opinion, that marriage is a sacrament, falls, the conceit of the absolute indissolubleness of marriage will fall with it.

The last sacrament which is rejected by this Article, that is, the fifth, as they are reckoned up in the church of Rome, is *Extreme Unction.** In the commission that Christ gave his

---

* The council of Trent having made this sacrament, thus describes its virtue:

'*De effectu hujus sacramenti.*'

'Res porro, et effectus hujus sacramenti illis verbis explicatur: et oratio fidei salvabit infirmum; et alleviabit eum Dominus; et, si in peccatis sit, dimittentur ei: Res etenim hæc gratia est Spiritus Sancti: cujus unctio delicta, si quæ sint adhuc expianda, ac peccati reliquias abstergit; et ægroti animam alleviat, et confirmat, magnam in eo divinæ misericordiæ fiduciam excitando; qua infirmus sublevatus; et morbi incommoda ac labores levius fert; et tentationibus dæmonis calcaneo insidiantis facilius resistit; et sanitatem corporis interdum, ubi saluti animæ expedierit, consequitur.' *Sessio* xiv. cap. 2.

In the following chapter, ' De ministro hujus sacramenti, et tempore quo dari debeat,' the council states the reason of the name extreme unction: ' Declaratur etiam, esse hanc unctionem infirmis adhibendam, illis vero præsertim qui tam periculose decumbunt, ut in exitu vitæ constituti videantur: unde et sacramentum exeuntium nuncupatur.'

In another place of the same session the council thus enforces her new article:

Canon 1.—' Si quis dixerit, extremam unctionem non esse vere et proprie sacramentum a Christo Domino nostro institutum, et a beato Jacobo apostolo promulgatum; sed ritum tantum acceptum a patribus, aut figmentum humanum: anathema sit.'

apostles, among the other powers that were given them to confirm it, one was to *cure diseases* and *heal the sick;* pursuant to which St. Mark tells, that 'they anointed with oil many that were sick, and healed them.' The prophets used some symbolical actions when they wrought miracles; so Moses used his rod often; Elisha used Elijah's mantle; our Saviour put his finger into the deaf man's ear, and made clay for the blind man; and oil being upon almost all occasions used in the eastern parts, the apostles made use of it; but no hint is given that this was a sacramental action. It was plainly a miraculous virtue that healed the sick, in which oil was made use of as a symbol accompanying it. It was not prescribed by our Saviour, for any thing that appears, as it was not blamed by him neither. It was no wonder, if, upon such a precedent, those who had that extraordinary gift, did apply it with the use of *oil;* not as if *oil* was the sacramental conveyance; it was only used with it. The end of it was miraculous · it was in order to the *recovery of the sick,* and had no relation to their souls, though with the cure wrought on the body there might sometimes be joined an operation upon the soul; and this appears clearly from St. James's words, 'Is any sick among you? let him call for the elders of the church; and let them pray over him, anointing him with oil in the name of the Lord: and the prayer of faith shall save the sick, and the Lord shall raise him up.' All hitherto is one period, which is here closed. The following words contain new matter quite of a different kind; 'and if he have committed sins, they shall be forgiven him.' It appears clearly that this was intended for the recovery of the sick person, which is the thing that is positively promised; the other concerning the pardon of sins, comes in on the bye, and seems to be added only as an accessary to the other, which is the principal thing designed by this whole matter. Therefore, since anointing was in order to healing, either we must say that the gift of healing is still deposited with the *elders of the church,* which nobody affirms; or this *oil* was only to be used by those who had that special gift; and therefore if there are none now who pretend to have it, and if the church pretends not to have it lodged with her, then the anointing with oil cannot be used any more; and therefore those who use it not in order to the recovery of the person, delaying it till there is little or no hope left, use not that unction mentioned by St. James, but another of their own devising, which they call the *sacrament of the dying.* It is a vain thing to say, that because *saving* and *raising up* are sometimes used in a spiritual sense, that therefore the *saving the sick* here, and that of the *Lord's raising him up,* are to be so meant. For the forgiveness of sin, which is

ART. XXV.

Mark vi. 13.

James v. 14, 15.

---

sit.'—Canon 2. ' Si quis dixerit, sacram infirmorum unctionem non conferre gratiam, nec remittere peccata, nec alleviare infirmos; sed jam cessasse, quasi olim tantum fuerit gratia curationum: anathema sit.'—[Ed.]

ART.
XXV. the spiritual blessing, comes afterwards, upon supposition that the sick person had committed sins. The *saving* and *raising up* must stand in opposition to the sickness: so since all acknowledge that the one is literal, the other must be so too. The supposition of sin is added, because some persons, upon whom this miracle might have been wrought, might be eminently pious; and if at any time it was to be applied to ill men who had committed some notorious sins, perhaps such sins as had brought their sickness upon them, these were also to be forgiven.

In the use of miraculous powers, those to whom that gift was given, were not empowered to use it at pleasure; they were to feel an inward impulse exciting them to it, and they were obliged upon that firmly to believe, that God, who had given them the impulse, would not be wanting to them in the execution of it. This confidence in God was the *faith of miracles*, of which Christ said, 'If ye have faith as a grain of mustard-seed, ye shall say to this mountain, Remove hence to yonder place, and nothing shall be impossible unto you.' Of this also St. Paul meant, when he said, 'If I have all faith.' So from this we may gather the meaning of the *prayer of faith*, and *the anointing with oil*; that if the *elders of the church*, or such others with whom this power was lodged, felt an inward impulse moving them to call upon God, in order to a miraculous cure of a sick person, then they were to 'anoint him with oil in the name of the Lord:' that is, by the authority that they had from Christ to heal all manner of diseases: and they were to pray, believing firmly that God would make good that inward motion which he had given them to work this miracle; and in that case the effect was certain, the sick person would certainly recover, for that is absolutely promised. Every one that was sick was not to be anointed, unless an authority and motion from Christ had been secretly given for doing it; but every one that was anointed was certainly healed. Christ had promised that 'whatsoever they should ask in his name, he would do it.' *His name* must be restrained to his authority, or pursuant to such secret motions as they shall receive from him. This is the *prayer of faith* here mentioned by St. James: it being an earnest application to God to join his omnipotent power to perform a wonderful work, to which a person so divinely qualified felt himself inwardly moved by the spirit of Christ. The supposition of the sick person's *having committed sins*, which is added, shews that sometimes this virtue was applied to persons of that eminent piety, that though all men are guilty in the sight of God, yet they could not be said to have committed sins in the sense in which St. John uses the phrase; signifying by it, either that they had lived in the habits of sin, or that they had committed some notorious sin: but if some should happen to be sick, who had been eminent sinners, and those sins had

Matt. xxi. 21.

1 Cor. xiii. 2.

John xiv. 13.

drawn down the judgments of God upon them, which seems to ART.
be the natural meaning of these words, 'if ye have committed XXV.
sins;' then, with his bodily health, he was to receive a much
greater blessing, even the pardon of his sins. And thus the
anointing mentioned by St. James was in order to a miraculous cure, and the cure did constantly follow it: so that it
can be no precedent for an extreme unction, that is never
given till the recovery of the person is despaired of, and
by which it is not pretended that any cure is wrought.*

The matter of it is *oil-olive* blessed by the bishop; the form
is the applying it to the five senses, with these words, *Per* Rituale
hanc sacram unctionem, et suam piissimam misericordiam in- Rom. Con.
dulgeat tibi Deus quicquid peccasti, per visum, auditum, olfac- 14.
tum, gustum, et tactum. The proper word to every sense
being repeated as the organ of that sense is anointed. It is
administered by a priest, and gives the final pardon, with all
necessary assistances, in the last agony. Here is then an
institution, that, if warranted, is matter of great comfort; and
if not warranted, is matter of as great presumption. In the Con. Apos.
first ages we find mention is made frequently of persons that l. vii. c. 42,
were cured by an anointing with oil: oil was then much used 44.
in all their rituals, the catechumens being anointed with oil Tertul. de
before they were baptized, besides the chrism that was given Cypr. Ep.
after it. Oil grew also to be used in ordinations, and the 70. Clem.
dead were anointed in order to their burial: so that the Alex.
ordinary use of oil on other occasions brought it to be very l. ii. c. 8.
frequently used in their sacred rites; yet how customary Dionys.
soever the practice of anointing grew to be, we find no men- Areop. de
tion of any unction of the sick before the beginning of the Hier. 7, 8.
fifth century. This plainly shews that they understood St.
James's words as relating to a miraculous power, and not to a
function that was to continue in the church, and to be
esteemed a sacrament.

That earliest mention of it by pope Innocent the First, how Innocent.
much soever it is insisted on, is really an argument that Ep. 1. ad
proves against it, and not for it. For not to enlarge on the Decent.
many idle things that are in that Epistle, which have made

* 'This passage in St. James speaks of the sick person, anointed and prayed over, being RAISED UP. How then do you prove a sacrament of extreme unction from unction not extreme, not to be used, as Trent says, on those *past being raised up*, but on these that were to be raised up, "*and the* LORD *shall raise him up?*" Again, how can you promise remission of the sick man's sin, when you cannot promise the sign of it, viz. the recovery of the sick person? Two questions more. If extreme unction confers grace, wipes away and remits sin, and resists the assaults of the devil, as Trent says, why do you not give it to criminals about to die? Is it because they have no need of what this sacrament professes to give? Surely they have more need than other persons. Again, if extreme unction remits sin and wipes away the remainder of sin, why is the mass necessary, that those who receive this *sacrament*, should have masses said afterwards for the release of their souls from purgatory, where they are supposed to be detained, until all their sins be wiped away? If unction be effectual to do all that Trent says, why send those to purgatory who receive this unction? If it be not effectual to the wiping away the remainder of sin (as Trent says it is) in the dying person, of what use is it?' *Page's Letters to a Romish Priest.*
—[ED.]

ART. XXV. some think that it could not be genuine, and that do very much sink the credit both of the testimony and of the man; for it seems to be well proved to be his: the passage relating to this matter is in answer to a demand that was made to him by the bishop of Eugubium, whether the sick might be anointed with the oil of the chrism? and whether the bishop might anoint with it? To these he answers, that no doubt is to be made but that St. James's words are to be understood of the faithful that were sick, who may be anointed by the chrism; which may be used not only by the priests, but by all Christians, not only in their own necessities, but in the necessities of any of their friends: and he adds, that it was a needless doubt that was made, whether a bishop might do it; for presbyters are only mentioned, because the bishop could not go to all the sick; but certainly he who made the chrism itself, might anoint with it. A bishop asking these questions of another, and the answers which the other gives him, do plainly shew that this was no sacrament practised from the beginnings of Christianity; for no bishop could be ignorant of those. It was therefore some newly begun custom, in which the world was not yet sufficiently instructed. And so it was indeed, for the subject of these questions was not pure oil, such as now they make to be the matter of extreme unction; but the oil of *chrism*, which was made and kept for other occasions; and it seems very clear, that the miraculous power of healing having ceased, and none being any more anointed in order to that; some began to get a portion of the oil of chrism, which the laity, as well as the priests, applied both to themselves and to their friends, hoping that they might be cured by it. Nothing else can be meant by all this, but a superstitious using the *chrism*, which might have arisen out of the memory that remained of those who had been cured by oil, as the use of *bread* in the eucharist brought in the *holy bread*, that was sent from one church to another; and as from the use of *water* in *baptism* sprung the use of *holy water*. This then being the clear meaning of those words, it is plain that they prove quite the contrary of that for which they are brought; and though in that Epistle the pope calls *chrism* a kind of sacrament, that turns likewise against them; to shew that he did not think it was a sacrament, strictly speaking. Besides, that the ancients used that word very largely, both for every mysterious doctrine, and for every holy rite that they used. In this very Epistle, when he gives directions for the carrying about that *bread*, which they blessed, and sent about as an emblem of their communion with other churches; he orders them to be sent about only to the churches within the city, because he conceived the sacraments were not to be carried a great way off; so these loaves are called by him not only a *kind of sacrament*, but are simply reckoned to be *sacraments*.

We hear no more of anointing the sick with the chrism, ART. among all the ancients; which shews, that as that practice XXV. was newly begun, so it did not spread far, nor continue long. No mention is made of this neither in the first three ages, nor in the fourth age; though the writers, and particularly the councils of the fourth age, are very copious in rules concerning the sacraments. Nor in all their penitentiary canons, when they define what sins are to be forgiven, and what not, when men were in their last extremities, is there so much as a hint given concerning the last unction. The Constitutions, and the pretended Dionysius, say not a word of it, though they are very full upon all the rituals of that time in which those works were forged, in the fourth or fifth century. In none of the lives of the saints before the ninth century, is there any mention made of their having extreme unction, though their deaths are sometimes very particularly related, and their receiving the eucharist is oft mentioned. Nor was there any question made in all that time concerning the persons, the time, and the other circumstances relating to this unction; which could not have been omitted, especially when almost all that was thought on, or writ of, in the eighth and ninth century, relates to the sacraments, and the other rituals of the church.

It is true, from the seventh century on to the twelfth, they Lib. Sa-began to use an anointing of the sick, according to that men-cram. Gre-tioned by pope Innocent, and a peculiar office was made for gor. Menar-it; but the prayers that were used in it, shew plainly that it di Notæ. was all intended only in order to their recovery.

Of this anointing many passages are found in Bede, and Bede Hist in the other writers and councils of the eighth and ninth cen-Angl. l. iii tury. But all these do clearly express the use of it, not as a c. 15. sacrament for the good of the soul, but as a rite that carried sive Ritual. with it health to the body; and so it is still used in the Greek Græc. p. church. No doubt they supported the credit of this with 408. many reports, of which some might be true, of persons that had been recovered upon using it. But because that failed so often, that the credit of this rite might suffer much in the esteem of the world, they began in the tenth century to say, that it did good to the soul, even when the body was not healed by it; and they applied it to the several parts of the body. This begun from the custom of applying it at first to the diseased parts. This was carried on in the eleventh century. And then in the twelfth, those prayers that had been formerly made for the souls of the sick, though only as a part of the office, the pardon of sin being considered as prepara-Dec. Eug. tory to their recovery, came to be considered as the main and in Con. most essential part of it: then the schoolmen brought it into Flor. shape, and so it was decreed to be a sacrament by pope Eu-Sess. 14. genius, and finally established at Trent.

The argument that they draw from a parity in reason, that

ART.
XXV.
because there is a sacrament for such as come into the world, there should be also one for those that go out of it, is very trifling; for Christ has either instituted this to be a sacrament, or it is not one: if he has not instituted it, this pretended fitness is only an argument that he ought to have done somewhat that he has not done. The eucharist was considered by the ancients as the only *viaticum* of Christians, in their last passage: with them we give that, and no more.

Thus it appears upon what reason we reject those five sacraments, though we allow both of *confirmation* and *orders* as holy functions, derived to us down from the apostles; and because there is a visible action in these, though in strictness they cannot be called a sacrament, yet so the thing be rightly understood, we will not dispute about the extent of a word that is not used in scripture. Marriage is in no respect to be called a sacrament of the Christian religion; though it being a state of such importance to mankind, we hold it very proper, both for the solemnity of it, and for imploring the blessing of God upon it, that it be done with prayers and other acts of religious worship; but a great difference is to be made between a pious custom begun and continued by public authority, and a sacrament appointed by Christ. We acknowledge true repentance to be one of the great conditions of the new covenant; but we see nothing of the nature of a sacrament in it: and, for extreme unction, we do not pretend to have the gift of healing among us: and therefore we will not deceive the world, by an office that shall offer at that, which we acknowledge we cannot do: nor will we make a sacrament for the good of the soul, out of that which is mentioned in scripture, only as a rite that accompanied the curing the diseases of the body.

The last part of this Article, concerning the use of the sacraments, consists of two parts: the *first* is negative, that they are not ordained to be gazed on, or to be carried about, but to be used: and this is so express in the scripture, that little question can be made about it. The institution of baptism is, ' Go preach and baptize :' and the institution of the eucharist is, ' Take, eat, and drink ye all of it :' which words being set down before those in which the consecrating them is believed to be made, ' This is my body ;' and ' This is my blood ;' and the consecratory words being delivered as the reason of the command, ' Take, eat, and drink ;' nothing can be more clearly expressed than this, that the eucharist is consecrated only that it may be used, that it may be *eat* and *drunk*.

The *second* part of this period is, that the effect of the sacraments comes only upon the worthy receiving of them; of this so much was already said, upon the first paragraph of this Article, that it is not necessary to add any more here. The pretending that sacraments have their effect any other way, is the bringing in the doctrine and practice of charms ART. into the Christian religion: and it tends to dissolve all obli- XXV. gations to piety and devotion, to a holiness of life, or a purity of temper, when the being in a passive and perhaps insensible state, while the sacraments are applied, is thought a disposition sufficient to give them their virtue. Sacraments are federal acts, and those visible actions are intended to quicken us, so that in the use of them we may raise our inward acts to the highest degrees possible; but not to supply their defects and imperfections. Our opinion in this point represents them as means to raise our minds, and to kindle our devotion; whereas the doctrine of the church of Rome represents them as so many charms, which may heighten indeed the authority of him that administers them, but do extinguish and deaden all true piety, when such helps are offered, by which the worst of men, living and dying in a bad state, may by a few feint acts, and perhaps by none at all of their own, be well enough taken care of and secured. But as we have not so learned Christ, so neither dare we corrupt his doctrine in its most vital and essential parts.

ARTICLE XXVI.

Of the Unworthiness of the Ministers, which hinders not the Effect of the Sacraments.

Although, in the Visible Church, the Evil be ever mingled with the Good, and sometimes the Evil have chief Authority in the Ministration of the Word and Sacraments; yet for as much as they do not the same in their own Name, but in Christ's, and do minister by his Commission and Authority, we may use their Ministry both in hearing the Word of God, and in receiving the Sacraments. Neither is the Effect of Christ's Ordinance taken away by their Wickedness: Nor the Grace of God's Gifts diminished from such as by faith and rightly do receive the Sacraments ministered unto them, which be Effectual because of Christ's Institution and Promise, although they be ministered by Evil Men.

Nevertheless it appertaineth to the Discipline of the Church, that Enquiry be made of Evil Ministers; and that they be accused by those that have knowledge of their Offences, and finally being found guilty, by just Judgment be deposed.

THE occasion that was given to this Article, was the heat of some in the beginnings of the Reformation; who, being much offended at the public scandal which was given by the enormous vices that were without any disguise practised by the Roman clergy of all ranks, did from thence revive the conceit of the Donatists, who thought that not only heresy and schism did invalidate sacred functions, but that personal sins did also make them void.

It cannot be denied but that there are many passages in St. Cyprian that look this way; and which seem to make the sacraments depend as much on the good state that he was in who administered them, as the answer of their other prayers did.

In the progress of the controversy with the Donatists, they carried this matter very far; and considered the effect of the sacraments as the answer of prayers: so since the prayers of a wicked man are abomination to God, they thought the virtue of these actions depended wholly on him that officiated.

Against this St. Augustin set himself very zealously; he answered all that was brought from St. Cyprian in such a manner, that by it he has set us a pattern, how we ought to separate the just respect that we pay the fathers, from an implicit receiving of all their notions. If this conceit were allowed of, it must go to the secret thoughts and inward state in which he is who officiates; for if the sacraments are to be considered only as prayers offered up by him, then a man can never be sure that he receives them; since it is impossible to see into the hearts, or know the secrets, of men. Sacraments therefore are to be considered only as the public acts of the church; and though the effect of them, as to him that receives them, depends upon his temper, his preparation and application; yet it cannot be imagined that the virtue of those federal acts to which Christians are admitted in them, the validity of them, or the blessings that follow them, can depend on the secret state or temper of him that officiates. Even in the case of public scandals, though they may make the holy things to be loathed by the aversion that will naturally follow upon them; yet after all, though that aversion may go too far, we must still distinguish between the things that the ministers of the church do as they are public officers, and what they do as they are private Christians. Their prayers, and every thing else that they do, as they are private Christians, have their effect only according to the state and temper that they are in when they offer them up to God: but their public functions are the appointments of Christ, in which they officiate; they can neither make them the better nor the worse by any thing that they join to them. And if miraculous virtues may be in bad men, so that in the great day some of those to whom Christ shall say, 'I never knew you; depart from me ye that work iniquity,' may yet say to him, 'Lord, Lord, have we not prophesied in thy name? and in thy name have cast out devils? and in thy name done many wonderful works?' then certainly this may be concluded much more concerning those standing functions and appointments that are to continue in the church. Nor can any difference be made in this matter between public scandals and secret sins; for if the former make void the sacraments, the latter must do so too. The only reason that can be pretended for the one, will also fall upon the other: for if the virtue of the sacraments is thought to be derived upon them as an answer of prayer; then since the prayers of hypocrites are as little effectual as the prayers of those who are openly vicious, the inference is good, that if the sacraments administered by a scandalous man are without any effect, the sacraments administered by a man that is inwardly corrupted, though that can be only known to God, will be also of no effect; and therefore this opinion that was taken up, perhaps from an inconsiderate zeal against the sins and scandals of the clergy, is without all foundation, and must needs cast all men into endless scruples, which can never be cured.

The church of Rome, though they reject this opinion, yet have brought in another very like it, which must needs fill the minds of men with endless distractions and fears; chiefly considering of what necessity and efficacy they make the

ART. XXVI.

sacraments to be. They do teach that the intention of him that gives the sacrament is necessary to the essence of it, so that without it no sacrament can be administered. This was expressly affirmed by pope Eugenius in his decree, and an anathema passed at Trent against those that deny it.* They do indeed define it to be only an intention of doing that which the church intends to do; and though the surest way, they say, is to have an actual intention, yet it is commonly taught among them, that an habitual or virtual intention will serve. But they do all agree in this, that, if a priest has a secret intention not to make a sacrament, in that case no sacrament is made; and this is carried so far, that in one of the rubrics of the Missal† it is given as a rule, that if a priest who goes to consecrate twelve Hosties, should have a general intention to leave out one of them from being truly consecrated, and should not apply that to any one, but let it run loosely through them all, that in such case he should not consecrate any one of the twelve; that loose exception falling upon them all, because it is not restrained to any one particular. And among the Articles that were condemned by pope Alexander the Eighth, the 7th of December 1690, the 28th runs thus; *Valet baptismus collatus a ministro, qui omnem ritum externum formamque baptizandi observat, intus vero in corde suo apud se resolvit, non intendo quod facit ecclesia.* And thus they make the secret acts of a priest's mind enter so far into those divine appointments, that by his malice, irreligion, or atheism, he can make those sacraments, which he visibly blesses and administers, to be only the outward shows of sacraments, but no real ones. We do not pretend that the sacraments are of the nature of charms; so that if a man should in a way of open mockery and profanation go about them, that therefore, because matter and form are observed, they should be true sacraments. But though we make the serious appearances of a Christian action to be necessary to the making it a sacrament; yet we carry this no further, to the inward and secret acts of the priest, as if they were essential to the being of it. If this is true, no man can have quiet in his mind.

It is a profanation for an unbaptized person to receive the eucharist; so if baptism is not true when a priest sets his intention cross to it, then a man in orders must be in perpetual doubts, whether he is not living in a continual state of sacrilege in administering the other sacraments while he is not yet baptized; and if baptism be so necessary to salvation, that no man who is not baptized can hope to be saved, here a perpetual scruple must arise, which can never be removed.

<small>Miss. Rom. Rubr. de defectu Intent. art. vii.</small>

---

* The doctrine of intention is thus stated by the council of Trent:—
' Si quis dixerit, in ministris, dum sacramenta conficiunt, et conferunt, non requiri intentionem saltem faciendi quod facit ecclesia: anathema sit.' *Sessio* vii. can. xi. —[ED.]

† For this and the other Rubrics, see Appendix.—[ED.]

Nor can a man be sure but that, when he thinks he is worshipping the true body of Jesus Christ, he is committing idolatry, and worshipping only a piece of bread; for it is no more, according to them, if the priest had an intention against consecrating it. No orders are given if an intention lies against them; and then he who passes for a priest is no priest; and all his consecrations and absolutions are so many invalid things, and a continued course of sacrilege.

ART. XXVI.

Now what reason soever men may have in this case to hope for the pardon of those sins, since it is certain that the ignorance is invincible; yet here strange thoughts must arise concerning Christ and his gospel; if in those actions that are made necessary to salvation, it should be in the power of a false Christian, or an atheistical priest or bishop, to make them all void; so that by consequence it should be in his power to damn them: for since they are taught to expect grace and justification from the sacraments, if these are no true sacraments which they take for such, but only the shadows and the phantasms of them, then neither grace nor justification can follow upon them. This may be carried so far as even to evacuate the very being of a church; for a man not truly baptized can never be in orders; so that the whole ordinations of a church, and the succession of it, may be broke by the impiety of any one priest. This we look on as such a chain of absurdities, that if this doctrine of intention were true, it alone might serve to destroy the whole credit of the Christian religion, in which the sacraments are taught to be both so necessary and so efficacious; and yet all this is made to depend on that which can neither be known nor prevented.

The last paragraph of this Article is so clear, that it needs no explanation, and is so evident, that it wants no proof. Eli was severely threatened for suffering his sons to go on in their vices, when by their means the sacrifice of God was abhorred. God himself struck Nadab and Abihu dead, when they offered strange fire at his altar; and upon that these words were uttered, 'I will be sanctified in them that come nigh me, and before all the people will I be glorified.' Timothy was required to receive 'an accusation of an elder,' when regularly tendered to him; and to 'rebuke before all, those that sinned;' and he was charged to withdraw himself from those teachers who 'consented not to wholesome words,' and that made a gain *of godliness*. A main part of the discipline of the primitive church lay heaviest on the clergy: and such of them as either apostatized, or fell into scandalous sins, even upon their repentance, were indeed received into the peace of the church; but they were appointed to communicate among the laity, and were never after that admitted to the body of the clergy, or to have a share in their privileges. Certainly there is nothing more incumbent on the whole body

1 Sam. iii. 11.

Levit. x. 3.

1 Tim. v. 1, 19, 20. vi. 3, 4, 5.

ART.
XXVI.

of the church, than that all possible care be taken to discover the bad practices that may be among the clergy: which will ever raise strong prejudices not only against their persons, but even against their profession, and against that religion which they seem to advance with their mouths, while in their works, and by their lives, they detract from it, and seem to deny its authority. But after all, our zeal must go along with justice and discretion: fame may be a just ground to inquire upon; but a sentence cannot be founded on it. The laity must discover what they know, that so these who have autho-

Gal. v. 12. rity may be able to 'cut off those that trouble the church.' Discretion will require that things which cannot be proved, ought rather to be covered than exposed, when nothing but clamour can follow upon it. In sum, this is a part of the government of the church, for which God will reckon severely with those who, from partial regards, or other feeble or carnal considerations, are defective in that, which is so great a part of their duty, and in which the honour of God, and of religion, and the good of souls, as well as the order and unity of the church, are so highly concerned.

ARTICLE XXVII.

Of Baptism.

Baptism is not only a Sign of Profession and Mark of Difference, whereby Christian Men are discerned from others that be not Christened; but it is also a Sign of Regeneration or New Birth, whereby, as by an Instrument, they that receive Baptism rightly, are grafted into the Church. The Promises of the Forgiveness of Sin, of our Adoption to be the Sons of God by the Holy Ghost, are visibly Signed and Sealed, Faith is confirmed and Grace increased by virtue of Prayer to God. The Baptism of young Children is in any wise to be retained in the Church, as most agreeable with the Institution of Christ.

WHEN St. John Baptist began first to baptize, we do plainly see by the first chapter of St. John's Gospel, that the Jews were not surprised at the novelty of the rite; for they sent to ask *who he was?* And when he said he was not the Messias, nor Elias, nor that Prophet, they asked, 'Why bap‑ John i. 25. tizest thou then?' Which shews, not only that they had clear notions of baptism, but in particular that they thought that if he had been the Messias, or Elias, or that Prophet, he might then have baptized. St. Paul does also say, that the Jews 'were all baptized unto Moses in the cloud, and in the 1 Cor. x. 2. sea;' which seems to relate to some opinion the Jews had, that by that *cloud*, and their passing through the *sea*, they were purified from the Egyptian defilements, and made meet to become Moses's disciples. Yet in the Old Testament we find no clear warrant for a practice that had then got among the Jews, which is still taught by them, that they were to receive a proselyte, if a male, by *baptism, circumcision, and sacrifice;* and if a female, only by *baptism and sacrifice*. Thus they reckoned, that when any came over from heathenism to their religion, they were to use a washing; to denote their purifying themselves from the uncleanness of their former idolatry, and their entering into a holy religion.

And as they do still teach, that when the Messias comes, they are all bound to set themselves to repent of their former sins; so it seems they then thought, or at least it would have been no strange thing to them, if the Messias had received such as came to him by baptism. St. John, by baptizing those who came to him, took them obliged to enter upon a course of repentance, and he declared to them the near ap‑ proach of the Messias, and that 'the kingdom of God was Matt. iii. 2.

ART. XXVII. at hand;' and it is very probable, that those who were baptized by Christ, that is, by his apostles; for though it is expressly said that he baptized none, yet what he did by his disciples he might in a more general sense be said to have done himself; that these, I say, were baptized upon the same sponsions, and with the same declarations, and with no other; for the dispensation of the Messias was not yet opened, nor was it then fully declared that he was the Messias: howsoever this was a preparatory initiation of such as were fitted for the coming of the Messias; by it they owned their expectations of him, as then near at hand, and they professed their repentance of their sins, and their purposes of doing what should be enjoined them by him.

Water was a very proper emblem, to signify the passing from a course of defilement to a greater degree of purity, both in doctrine and practice.

Gal. iv. 4. Our Saviour in his state of humiliation, as he was subject to the Mosaical law, so he thought fit to fulfil all the obligations that lay upon the other Jews; which by a phrase used Mat.iii.15. among them he expresses thus, 'to fulfil all righteousness.' For though our Saviour had no sins to confess, yet that not being known, he might come to profess his belief of the dispensation of the Messias, that was then to appear. But how well soever the Jews might have been accustomed to this rite, and how proper a preparation soever it might be to the manifestation of the Messias; yet the institution of baptism, as it is a federal act of the Christian religion, must be taken from the commission that our Saviour gave to his disciples; Matt. xxviii. 19, 20. 'to go preach and make disciples to him in all nations, (for that is the strict signification of the word,) baptizing them in the name of the Father, and of the Son, and of the Holy Ghost; teaching them to observe all things whatsoever I have commanded you.'

By the first *teaching* or making of *disciples*, that must go before baptism, is to be meant the convincing the world, that Jesus is the Christ, the true Messias, anointed of God, with a fulness of grace and of the Spirit without measure, and sent to be the Saviour and Redeemer of the world. And when they were brought to acknowledge this, then they were to baptize them, to initiate them to this religion, by obliging them to renounce all idolatry and ungodliness, as well as all secular and carnal lusts, and then they led them into the water; and with no other garments but what might cover nature, they at first laid them down in the water, as a man is laid in the grave, and then they said those words, 'I baptize or wash thee in the name of the Father, Son, and Holy Ghost:' then they raised them up again, and clean garments Rom. vi.3, 4, 5. were put on them: from whence came the phrases of 'being Col. ii. 12. baptized into Christ's death;' of 'being buried with him by iii. 1. baptism into death;' of 'our being risen with Christ,' and of 'our putting on the Lord Jesus Christ;' of 'putting off the old man, and putting on the new.' After baptism was thus performed, the baptized person was to be further instructed in all the specialities of the Christian religion, and in all the rules of life that Christ had prescribed.

ART. XXVII.

Col. iii. 9, 10. Rom. xiii. 14.

This was plainly a different baptism from St. John's; a profession was made in it, not in general, of the belief of a Messias soon to appear, but in particular, that 'Jesus was the Messias.'

The stipulation in St. John's baptism was *repentance;* but here it is the belief of the whole Christian religion. In St. John's baptism they indeed promised repentance, and he received them into the earnests of the kingdom of the Messias; but it does not appear that St. John either did promise them *remission of sins,* or that he had commission so to do; for *repentance* and *remission of sins* were not joined together till after the resurrection of Christ; that he appointed that 'repentance and remission of sins should be preached in his name among all nations, beginning at Jerusalem.'

Luke xxiv. 47.

In the baptism of Christ, I mean that which he appointed after his resurrection, (for the baptism of his disciples before that time was, no doubt, the same with St. John's baptism,) there was to be an instruction given in that great mystery of the Christian religion concerning the Father, the Son, and the Holy Ghost; which those who had only received St. John's baptism knew not: 'they did not so much as know that there was a Holy Ghost;' that is, they knew nothing of the extraordinary effusion of the Holy Ghost. And it is expressly said, that those of St. John's baptism, when St. Paul explained to them the difference between the baptism of Christ, and that of St. John, that 'they were baptized in the name of the Lord Jesus.' For St. John in his baptism had only initiated them to the belief of a Messias; but had not said a word of Jesus, as being that Messias. So that this must be fixed, that these two baptisms were different; the one was a dawning or imperfect beginning to the other, as he that administered the one was like the *morning star* before the *Sun of righteousness.*

Acts xix. 2—5.

Our Saviour had this ordinance (that was then imperfect, and was to be afterwards completed, when he himself had finished all that he came into the world to do)—he had, I say, this visibly in his eye, when he spake to Nicodemus, and told him, that ' except a man were born again, he could not see (or discern) the kingdom of God:' by which he meant that entire change and renovation of a man's mind, and of all his powers, through which he must pass, before he could discern the true characters of the dispensation of the Messias; for that is the sense in which the kingdom of God does stand, almost universally through the whole gospel. When Nicodemus was amazed at this odd expression, and seemed to take

John iii. 3, 5, 6.

it literally, our Saviour answered more fully, 'Verily, verily, I say unto thee, Except a man be born of water and of the Spirit, he cannot enter into the kingdom of God.' The meaning of which seems to be this, that except a man came to be renewed, by an ablution like the baptism which the Jews used, that imported the outward profession of a change of doctrine and of heart; and with that, except he were inwardly changed by a secret power called the *Spirit*, that should transform his nature, he could not become one of his disciples, or a true Christian; which is meant by his entering into the *kingdom of God*, or the dispensation of the Messias.

Upon this institution and commission given by Christ, we see the apostles went up and down preaching and baptising. And so far were they from considering baptism only as a carnal rite, or a low element, above which a higher dispensation of the Spirit was to raise them, that when St. Peter saw the Holy Ghost visibly descend upon Cornelius and his friends, he upon that immediately baptized them; and said, 'Can any man forbid (or deny) water, that these should not be baptized, which have received the Holy Ghost as well as we?' Our Saviour has also made baptism one of the *precepts*, though not one of the *means*, necessary to salvation. A *mean* is that which does so certainly procure a thing, that it being had, the thing to which it is a certain and necessary *mean* is also had; and without it the thing cannot be had; there being a natural connection between it and the end. Whereas a *precept* is an institution, in which there is no such natural efficiency; but it is positively commanded; so that the neglecting it is a contempt of the authority that commanded it: and therefore in obeying the *precept*, the value or virtue of the action lies only in the obedience. This distinction appears very clearly in what our Saviour has said both of *faith* and *baptism*. 'He that believeth and is baptized shall be saved; and he that believeth not shall be damned.'

Where it appears that faith is the *mean* of salvation with which it is to be had, and not without it; since such a believing as makes a man receive the whole gospel as true, and so firmly to depend upon the promises that are made in it, as to observe all the laws and rules that are prescribed by it; such a *faith* as this gives us so sure a title to all the blessings of this new covenant, that it is impossible that we should continue in this state, and not partake of them; and it is no less impossible that we should partake of them, unless we do thus believe. It were not suitable to the truth and holiness of the divine nature to void a covenant so solemnly made, and that in favour of wicked men, who will not be reformed by it: so *faith* is the certain and necessary mean of our salvation, and is so put by Christ; since upon our having it we shall be *saved*, as well as *damned* upon our not having it.

On the other hand, the nature of a ritual action, even when

commanded, is such, that unless we could imagine that there is a charm in it, which is contrary to the spirit and genius of the gospel, which designs to save us by reforming our natures, we cannot think that there can be any thing in it that is of itself effectual as a mean; and therefore it must only be considered as a command that is given us, which we are bound to obey, if we acknowledge the anthority of the command. But this being an action that is not always in our power, but is to be done by another, it were to put our salvation or damnation in the power of another, to imagine that we cannot be saved without baptism; and therefore it is only a precept which obliges us in order to our salvation; and our Saviour, by leaving it out when he reversed the words, saying only, 'he that believeth not,' without adding, and is not baptized, shall be *damned*, does plainly insinuate that it is not a mean, but only a precept, in order to our salvation. {ART. XXVII.}

As for the ends and purposes of baptism, St. Paul gives us two: the one is, that 'we are all baptized into one body, we are made members one of another:' we are admitted to the society of Christians, and to all the rights and privileges of that body, which is the church. And in order to this, the outward action of baptism, when regularly gone about, is sufficient. We cannot see into the sincerity of men's hearts; outward professions and regular actions are all that fall under men's observation and judgment. But a second end of baptism is internal and spiritual. Of this St. Paul speaks in very high terms, when he says, that 'God has saved us according to his mercy, by the washing of regeneration, and the renewing of the Holy Ghost.' It were a strange perverting the design of these words, to say, that somewhat spiritual is to be understood by this *washing of regeneration*, and not baptism; when as to the word *save*, that is here ascribed to it, St. Peter gives that undeniably to baptism; and St. Paul elsewhere, in two different places, makes our baptism to represent 'our being dead to sin, and buried with Christ;' and our being 'risen and quickened with him, and made alive unto God;' which are words that do very plainly import regeneration. So that St. Paul must be understood to speak of baptism in these words. Here then is the inward effect of baptism; it is a death to sin, and a new life in Christ, in imitation of him, and in conformity to his gospel. So that here is very expressly delivered to us somewhat that rises far above the badge of a profession, or a mark of difference. {1 Cor. xii. 13.   Tit. iii. 5.   Rom. vi.   Col. ii. 12.}

That does indeed belong to baptism; it makes us the visible members of that one body, into which we are baptized, or admitted by baptism; but that which *saves us* in it, which both deadens and quickens us, must be a thing of another nature. If baptism were only the receiving us into the society of Christians, there were no need of saying, 'I baptize thee in the name of the Father, and of the Son, and of the Holy Ghost.' It were more proper to say, *I baptize thee in the name or by the authority of the church.* Therefore these august words, that were dictated by our Lord himself, shew us that there is somewhat in it that is internal, which comes from God; that it is an admitting men into somewhat that depends only on God, and for the giving of which the authority can only be derived by him. But after all, this is not to be believed to be of the nature of a charm, as if the very act of baptism carried always with it an inward regeneration. Here we must confess, that very early some doctrines arose upon baptism, that we cannot be determined by. The words of our Saviour to Nicodemus were expounded so as to import the absolute necessity of baptism in order to salvation; for it not being observed that the dispensation of the Messias was meant by the kingdom of God, but it being taken to signify eternal glory, that expression of our Saviour's was understood to import this, that no man could be saved unless he were baptized; so it was believed to be simply necessary to salvation. A natural consequence that followed upon that, was to allow all persons leave to baptize, clergy and laity, men and women, since it seemed necessary to suffer every person to do that without which salvation could not be had. Upon this, these hasty baptisms were used, without any special sponsion on the part of those who desired it; of which it may be reasonably doubted whether such a baptism be true, in which no sponsion is made; and this cannot be well answered, but by saying, that a general and an implied sponsion is to be considered to be made by their parents while they desire them to be baptized.

Another opinion that arose out of the former, was the mixing of the outward and the inward effects of baptism; it being believed that every person that was 'born of the water,' was also 'born of the Spirit;' and that the 'renewing of the Holy Ghost' did always accompany the 'washing of regeneration.' And this obliged St. Austin (as was formerly told) to make that difference between the *regenerate* and the *predestinated;* for he thought that all who were baptized were also *regenerated.* St. Peter has stated this so fully, that if his words are well considered, they will clear the whole matter. He, after he had set forth the miserable state in which mankind was, under the figure of the deluge, in which an ark was prepared for Noah and his family, says upon that, 'the like figure whereunto even baptism doth also now save us.' Upon which he makes a short digression to explain the nature of baptism, 'not the putting away the filth of the flesh, but the answer (or the demand and interrogation) of a good conscience towards God; by the resurrection of Jesus Christ, who is gone into heaven.' The meaning of all which is, that Christ having risen again, and having then had 'all power in heaven and in earth' given to him, he had put that

1 Pet. iii. 21.

virtue in baptism, that by it we are *saved*, as in an ark, from that miserable state in which the world lies, and in which it must perish. But then he explains the way how it saves us; that it is not as a physical action, as it washes away the filthiness of the flesh, or of the body, like the notion that the Gentiles might have of their *februations;* or, which is more natural, considering to whom he writes, like the opinions that the Jews had of their *cleansings* after their *legal impurities,* from which their washings and bathings did absolutely free them. The salvation that we Christians have by baptism, is effected by that federation into which we enter, when upon the demands that are made of our renouncing the *Devil,* the *world,* and the *flesh,* and of our believing in Christ, and our *repentance* towards God, we make such *answers* from a *good conscience,* as agree with the end and design of baptism; then by our thus coming into covenant with God, we are saved in baptism. So that the salvation by baptism is given by reason of the federal compact that is made in it. Now this being made outwardly, according to the rules that are prescribed, that must make the baptism good among men, as to all the outward and visible effects of it: but since it is the 'answer of a good conscience' only that *saves,* then an answer from a bad conscience, from a hypocritical person, who does not inwardly think, or purpose, according to what he professes outwardly, cannot save, but does on the contrary aggravate his damnation. Therefore our Article puts the efficacy of baptism, in order to the forgiveness of our sins, and to our adoption and salvation, upon the virtue of prayer to God; that is, upon those vows and other acts of devotion that accompany them: so that when the seriousness of the mind accompanies the regularity of the action, then both the outward and inward effects of baptism are attained by it; and we are not only 'baptized into one body,' but are also 'saved by baptism.' So that upon the whole matter, baptism is a federal admission into Christianity, in which, on God's part, all the blessings of the gospel are made over to the baptized; and, on the other hand, the person baptized takes on him, by a solemn profession and vow, to observe and adhere to the whole Christian religion. So it is a very natural distinction to say, that the outward effects of baptism follow it as outwardly performed; but that the inward effects of it follow upon the inward acts: but this difference is still to be observed between inward acts and outward actions, that when the outward action is rightly performed, the church must reckon the baptism good, and never renew it: but if one has been wanting in the inward acts, those may be afterwards renewed, and that want may be made up by repentance.

Thus all that the scriptures have told us concerning baptism seems to be sufficiently explained. There remains only one place that may seem somewhat strange. St. Paul says, that 'Christ 1 Cor. i. 17.

ART.
XXVII.

Acts viii.
26. to the
end.

Acts xvi.
31, 32, 33.

Galat. v.3.

sent him not to baptize, but to preach;' which some have carried so far as to infer from thence, that preaching is of more value than baptism. But it is to be considered, that the preaching of the Apostles was of the nature of a promulgation made by heralds; it was an act of a special authority, by which he in particular was to convert the world from idolatry and Judaism, to acknowledge 'Jesus to be the true Messias.' Now when men, by the preaching of the apostles, and by the miracles that accompanied it, were so wrought on as to believe that 'Jesus was the Christ;' then, according to the practice of Philip towards the eunuch of Ethiopia, and of St. Paul to his jailor at Philippi, they might immediately baptize them; yet most commonly there was a special instruction to be used, before persons were baptized who might in general have some conviction, and yet not be so fully satisfied, but that a great deal of more pains was to be taken to carry them on to that full assurance of faith which was necessary. This was a work of much time, and was to be managed by the pastors or teachers of the several churches; so that the meaning of what St. Paul says was this, that he was to publish the gospel from city to city, but could not descend to the particular labour of preparing and instructing of the persons to be baptized, and to the baptizing them when so prepared. If he had entered upon this work, he could not have made that progress, nor have founded those churches, that he did. All this is therefore misunderstood, when it is applied to such preaching as is still continued in the church; which does not succeed the apostolical preaching that was inspired and infallible, but comes in the room of that instruction and teaching which was then performed by the pastors of the church.

The last head in this Article relates to the baptism of infants, which is spoken of with that moderation, which appears very eminently through the whole Articles of our church. On this head, it is only said to be most agreeable with the institution of Christ, and that therefore it is to be in any ways retained in the church. Now to open this, it is to be considered, that though baptism and circumcision do not in every particular come to a parallel, yet they do agree in two things: the one is, that both were the rites of admission into their respective covenants, and to the rights and privileges that did arise out of them; and the other is, that in them both there was an obligation laid on the persons to the observance of that whole law to which they were so initiated. St. Paul, arguing against circumcision, lays this down as an uncontested maxim, that if a man was circumcised, 'he became thereby a debtor to the whole law.'

Parents had, by the Jewish constitution, an authority given them to conclude their children under that obligation; so that the soul and will of the child was so far put in the power of the parents, that they could bring them under federal **ART** obligations, and thereby procure to them a share in federal **XXVII.** blessings. And it is probable, that from hence it was, that when the Jews made proselytes, they considered them as having such authority over their children, that they baptized them first, and then circumcised them, though infants.

Now since Christ took baptism from them, and appointed it to be the federal admission to his religion, as circumcision had been in the Mosaical dispensation, it is reasonable to believe, that, except where he declared a change that he made in it, in all other respects it was to go on and to continue as before; especially when the apostles in their first preaching told the Jews, that the promises were made to them and Acts ii. 39. to their children; which the Jews must have understood according to what they were already in possession of, that they could initiate their children into their religion, bring them under the obligations of it, and procure to them a share in those blessings that belonged to it. The law of nature and nations puts children in the power of their parents; they are naturally their guardians; and if they are entitled to any thing, their parents have a right to transact about it, because of the weakness of the child; and what contracts soever they make, by which the child does not lose, but is a gainer, these do certainly bind the child. It is then suitable both to the constitution of mankind, and to the dispensation of the Mosaical covenant, that parents may dedicate their children to God, and bring them under the obligations of the gospel; and if they may do that, then they certainly procure to them with it, or in lieu of it, a share in the blessings and promises of the gospel. So that they may offer their children either themselves, or by such others of their friends, to whom for that occasion they transfer that right which they have, to transact for and to bind their children.

All this receives a great confirmation from the decision which St. Paul makes upon a case that must have happened commonly at that time; which was, when one of the parties in a married state, *husband* or *wife*, was converted, while the other continued still in the former state of idolatry, or infidelity: here then a scruple naturally arose, whether a believer or Christian might still live in a married state with an infidel. Besides the ill usage to which that diversity of religion might give occasion, another difficulty might be made, whether a person defiled by idolatry did not communicate that impurity to the Christian, and whether the children born in such a marriage were to be reckoned a *holy seed*, according to the Jewish phrase, or an *unholy*, unclean children, that is heathenish children; who were not to be dedicated to God, nor to be admitted into covenant with him: for *unclean* in the Old Testament, and *uncircumcised*, signify sometimes the same thing; and so St. Peter said that in the case of Cornelius God had

ART. XXVII.

Acts x. 28.
1 Cor. vii. 14.

shewed him, that he should call no man *common* or *unclean*; in allusion to all which St. Paul determines the case, not by an immediate revelation, but by the inferences that he drew from what had been revealed to him; he does appoint the Christian to live with the infidel, and says, that the Christian is so far from being defiled by the infidel, that there is a communication of a blessing that passes from the Christian to the infidel; the one being the better for the prayers of the other, and sharing in the blessings bestowed on the other: the better part was accepted of God, 'in whom mercy rejoices over judgment.' There was a communication of a blessing that the Christian derived to the infidel; which at least went so far, that their children were not *unclean;* that is, shut out from being dedicated to God, but were *holy*. Now it is to be considered that in the New Testament *Christians*, and *saints*, or *holy*, stand all promiscuously. The purity of the Christian doctrine, and the dedication by which Christians offer up themselves to God, makes them *holy*.

In scripture, *holiness* stands in a double sense; the one is a true and real purity, by which a man's faculties and actions become holy; the other is a dedicated holiness, when any thing is appropriated to God; in which sense it stands most commonly in the Old Testament. So times, places, and not only persons, but even utensils applied to the service of God, are called *holy*. In the New Testament, *Christian* and *saint* are the same thing; so the saying that children are *holy* when one of the parents is a Christian, must import this, that the child has also a right to be made *holy*, or to be made a Christian; and by consequence, that by the parents' dedication that child may be made *holy*, or a *Christian*.

Upon these reasons we conclude, that though there is no express precept or rule given in the New Testament for the baptism of infants, yet it is most agreeable to the institution of Christ, since he conformed his institutions to those of the Mosaical law, as far as could consist with his design; and therefore in a thing of this kind, in which the just tenderness of the human nature does dispose parents to secure to their children a title to the mercies and blessings of the gospel, there is no reason to think that this being so fully set forth and assured to the Jews in the Old Testament, that Christ should not have intended to give parents the same comforts and assurances by his gospel that they had under the law of Moses: since nothing is said against it, we may conclude from the nature of the two dispensations, and the proportion and gradation that is between them, that children under the new testament are a *holy seed*, as well as they were under the old; and by consequence, that they may be now baptized as well as they were then circumcised.

If this may be done, then it is very reasonable to say what is said in the Article concerning it, that *it ought in any wise to be retained in the church:* for the same humanity that obliges parents to feed their children, and to take care of them while they are in such a helpless state, must dictate, that it is much more incumbent on them, and is as much more necessary as the soul is more valuable than the body, for them to do all that in them lies for the souls of their children, for securing to them a share in the blessings and privileges of the gospel, and for dedicating them early to the Christian religion. The office for baptizing infants is in the same words with that for persons of riper age; because infants being then in the power of their parents, who are of age, are considered as in them, and as binding themselves by the vows that they make in their name. Therefore the office carries on the supposition of an internal regeneration; and in that helpless state the infant is offered up and dedicated to God; and provided, that when he comes to age he takes those vows on himself, and lives like a person so in covenant with God, then he shall find the full effects of baptism; and if he dies in that state of incapacity, he being dedicated to God, is certainly accepted of by him; and by being put in the second Adam, all the bad effects of his having descended from the first Adam are quite taken away. Christ, when on earth, encouraged those who brought *little children* to him; 'he took them in his arms, and laid his hands on them, and blessed them,' and said, 'Suffer little children to come unto me, and forbid them not; for of such is the kingdom of God.' Whatever these words may signify mystically, the literal meaning of them is, that little children may be admitted into the dispensation of the Messias, and by consequence that they may be baptized.

ART. XXVII.

Matt. xix. 13, 14.

ARTICLE XXVIII.

Of the Lord's Supper.

The Supper of the Lord is not only a Sign of the Love that Christians ought to have among themselves one to another; but rather it is a Sacrament of our Redemption by Christ's Death: Insomuch that to such as rightly, worthily, and with Faith, receive the same, the Bread which we break is a partaking of the Body of Christ, and likewise the Cup of Blessing is a partaking of the Blood of Christ. Transubstantiation (or the Change of the Substance of Bread and Wine) in the Supper of the Lord, cannot be proved by Holy Writ, but it is repugnant to the plain Words of Scripture, overthroweth the Nature of a Sacrament, and hath given occasion to many Superstitions. The Body of Christ is given, taken, and eaten in the Supper only after a Heavenly and Spiritual Manner; and the mean whereby the Body of Christ is received and eaten in the Supper, is Faith. The Sacrament of the Lord's Supper was not by Christ's Ordinance reserved, carried about, lifted up, and worshipped.

In the edition of these Articles in Edward VI.'s Reign, there was another long paragraph against Transubstantiation added in these words: Forasmuch as the Truth of Man's Nature requireth that the Body of one and the self-same Man cannot be at one Time in divers Places, but must needs be in one certain Place; therefore the Body of Christ cannot be present at one Time in many and divers Places: and because, as Holy Scripture doth teach, Christ was taken up into Heaven, and there shall continue unto the End of the World; a Faithful Man ought not either to believe, or openly confess, the Real and Bodily Presence, as they term it, of Christ's Flesh and Blood in the Sacrament of the Lord's Supper.

WHEN these Articles were at first prepared by the convocation in queen Elizabeth's reign, this paragraph was made a part of them; for the original subscription by both houses of convocation, yet extant, shews this. But the design of the government was at that time much turned to the drawing over the body of the nation to the Reformation, in whom the old leaven had gone deep; and no part of it deeper than the belief of the corporeal presence of Christ in the sacrament; therefore it was thought not expedient to offend them by so particular a definition in this matter; in which the very word *real presence* was rejected. It might, perhaps, be also suggested, that here a definition was made that went too much upon the principles of natural philosophy; which how true ART. soever, they might not be the proper subject of an article of XXVIII. religion. Therefore it was thought fit to suppress this paragraph; though it was a part of the Article that was subscribed, yet it was not published, but the paragraph that follows, *The body of Christ*, &c. was put in its stead, and was received and published by the next convocation; which upon the matter was a full explanation of the way of Christ's presence in this sacrament; that *he is present in a heavenly and spiritual manner, and that faith is the mean by which he is received.* This seemed to be more theological; and it does indeed amount to the same thing. But howsoever we see what was the sense of the first convocation in queen Elizabeth's reign; it differed in nothing from that in king Edward's time: and therefore though this paragraph is now no part of our Articles, yet we are certain that the clergy at that time did not at all doubt of the truth of it; we are sure it was their opinion; since they subscribed it, though they did not think fit to publish it at first; and though it was afterwards changed for another, that was the same in sense.

In the treating of this Article, I shall first lay down the doctrine of this church, with the grounds of it; and then I shall examine the doctrine of the church of Rome, which must be done copiously; for next to the doctrine of infallibility, this is the most valued of all their other tenets; this is the most important in itself, since it is the main part of their worship, and the chief subject of all their devotions. There is not any one thing in which both clergy and laity are more concerned; which is more generally studied, and for which they pretend they have more plausible colours, both from scripture and the fathers: and if sense and reason seem to press hard upon it, they reckon, that, as they understand the words of St. Paul, 'every thought must be captivated into 2 Cor. x. 5. the obedience of faith.'

In order to the expounding our doctrine, we must consider the occasion and the institution of this sacrament. The Jews were required once a year to meet at Jerusalem, in remembrance of the deliverance of their fathers out of Egypt. Moses appointed that every family should kill a lamb, whose Exod. xii. blood was to be sprinkled on their door-posts and lintels, and 3—14. whose flesh they were to eat; at the sight of which *blood* thus sprinkled, the destroying angel, that was to be sent out to kill the firstborn of every family in Egypt, was to *pass over* all the houses that were so marked: and from that *passing by* or *over* the Israelites, the lamb was called *the Lord's passover,* as being then the sacrifice, and afterwards the memorial of that *passover.* The people of Israel were required to keep up the memorial of that transaction, by slaying a lamb before the place where God should set his name; and by eating it up that night: they were also to eat with it a salad of bitter

ART. XXVIII. herbs and unleavened bread; and when they went to eat of the lamb, they repeated these words of Moses; 'that it was the Lord's passover.' Now though the first lamb that was killed in Egypt was indeed the sacrifice upon which God promised to *pass over* their houses; yet the lambs that were afterwards offered were only the memorials of it; though they still carried that name, which was given to the first, and were called the *Lord's passover*.

So that the Jews were in the *paschal supper* accustomed to call the memorial of a thing by the name of that of which it was the memorial: and as the deliverance out of Egypt was a type and representation of that greater deliverance that we were to have by the Messias, the first lamb being the sacrifice of that deliverance, and the succeeding lambs the memorials of it; so, in order to this new and greater deliverance, Christ 1 Cor. v. 7. himself was our 'passover, that was sacrificed for us:' he was John i. 29. the 'Lamb of God' that was both to 'take away the sins of the world,' and was to 'lead captivity captive;' to bring us out of the bondage of sin and Satan into the obedience of his gospel.

Compare Matt. xxvi. 26. Mark xiv. 22. Luke xxii. 19. 1 Cor. xi. 23.

He therefore chose the time of the passover, that he might be then offered up for us; and did institute this memorial of it while he was celebrating the Jewish *pascha* with his disciples, who were so much accustomed to the forms and phrases of that *supper*, in which every master of a family did officiate among his household, that it was very natural to them to understand all that our Saviour said or did according to those forms with which they were acquainted.

There were after supper, upon a new covering of the table, loaves of unleavened bread, and cups of wine set on it; in which, though the bread was very unacceptable, yet they drank liberally of the wine: Christ took a portion of that bread, and brake it, and gave it to his disciples, and said, 'This is my body which is broken for you: Do this in remembrance of me.' He did not say only, 'This is my body,' but 'This is my body broken;' so that his body must be understood to be there in its broken state, if the words are to be expounded literally. And no reason can be assigned why the word *broken* should be so separated from *body*; or that the *bread* should be literally his *body*, and not literally his *body broken*: the whole period must be either literally true, or must be understood mystically. And if any will say, that his body cannot be there, but in the same state in which it is now in heaven; and since it is not now *broken*, nor is the *blood shed* or separated from the body there, therefore the words must be understood thus; 'This is my body which is to be broken.' But from thence we argue, that since all is one period, it must be all understood in the same manner; and since it is impossible that *broken* and *shed* can be understood literally of the *body* and *blood*, that therefore the whole is to be mystically understood: and this appears more evident, since the disciples, who were naturally slow at understanding the easiest mysteries that he opened to them, must naturally have understood those words as they did the other words of the paschal supper, 'This is the Lord's passover;' that is, this is the memorial of it: and that the rather, since Christ added these words, 'Do this in remembrance of me.' If they had understood them in any other sense, that must have surprised them, and naturally have led them to ask him many questions: which we find them doing upon occasions that were much less surprising, as appears by the questions in the 14th of St. John, that discourse coming probably immediately after this institution: whereas no question was asked upon this: so it is reasonable to conclude that they could understand these words, 'This is my body,' no other way, but as they understood that of the lamb, 'This is the Lord's passover.' And by consequence, as their celebrating the *pascha* was a constant memorial of the deliverance out of Egypt, and was a symbolical action by which they had a title to the blessings of the covenant that Moses made with their fathers; it was natural for them to conclude, that after Christ had made himself to be truly that, which the first lamb was in a type, the true *sacrifice* of a greater and better *passover;* they were to commemorate it, and to communicate in the benefits and effects of it, by continuing that action of *taking, blessing, breaking,* and *distributing* of bread: which was to be the memorial and the communion of his death in all succeeding ages.

ART. XXVIII.

This will yet appear more evident from the second part of this institution: he took the cup and blessed it, and gave it to them, saying, 'This cup is the new testament,' or new covenant, ' in my blood: drink ye all of it.' Or, as the other gospels report it, ' This is my blood of the new testament, which is shed for many for the remission of sins.' As Moses had enjoined the sprinkling of the blood of the lamb, so he himself sprinkled both the book of the law and all the people with the blood of calves and of goats, saying, ' This is the blood of the testament (or covenant) which God hath enjoined you.' The blood of the paschal lamb was the token of that covenant which God made then with them.

Heb.ix.20.

The Jews were under a very strict prohibition of eating no blood at all: but it seems by the Psalms, that when they paid their vows unto God, they took in their hands ' a cup of salvation,' that is, of an acknowledgment of their salvation, and so were to rejoice before the Lord.

Psal. cxvi.

These being the laws and customs of the Jews, they could not without horror have heard Christ, when he gave them the cup, say, ' This is my blood:' the prohibition of blood was given in such severe terms; as that ' God would set his face against him that did eat blood, and cut him off from among

Levit. vii 26, 27. xvii. 14.

ART.
XXVIII.
his people.'* And this was so often repeated in the books of Moses, that besides the natural horror which humanity gives at the mention of drinking a man's blood, it was a special part of their religion to make no use of blood: yet after all this, the disciples were not startled at it; which shews that they must have understood it in such a way as was agreeable to the law and customs of their country: and since St. Luke and St. Paul report the words that our Saviour said when he gave it, differently from what is reported by St. Matthew and St. Mark, it is most probable that he spake both the one and the other; that he first said, 'This is my blood,' and then, as a clearer explanation of it, he said, 'This cup is the new testament in my blood:' the one being a more easy expression, and in a style to which the Jews had been more accustomed. They knew that the blood of the lamb was sprinkled; and by their so doing they entered into a covenant with God: and though the blood was never to be sprinkled after the first passover; yet it was to be poured out before the Lord, in remembrance of that sprinkling in Egypt: in remembrance of that deliverance, they drank of the cup of blessing and salvation, and rejoiced before the Lord. So that they could not understand our Saviour otherwise, than that the cup so blessed was to be to them the assurance of a *new testament* or *covenant*, which was to be established by the blood of Christ; and which was to be shed: in lieu of which they were to drink this ' cup of blessing' and praise.

According to their customs and phrases, the disciples could understand our Saviour's words in this sense, and in no other. So that if he had intended that they should have understood him otherwise, he must have expressed himself in another manner; and must have enlarged upon it, to have corrected those notions, into which it was otherwise most natural for Jews to have fallen. Here is also to be remembered that which was formerly observed upon the word *broken*, that if the words are to be expounded literally, then if the cup is literally ' the blood of Christ,' it must be his blood *shed*, poured out of his veins, and separated from his body. And if it is impossible to understand it so, we conclude that we are in the

* ' Transubstantiation is built on this error; that our LORD JESUS CHRIST did, on the night of his instituting this sacrament, eat his own flesh, and drink his own blood, and give both to his disciples. And this makes our LORD a transgressor of the law of GOD, which forbids any man to eat blood, Levit. xvii. 14, " For it is the life of all flesh; the blood of it is for the life thereof: therefore I said unto the children of Israel, YE SHALL EAT THE BLOOD OF NO MANNER OF FLESH: for the life of all flesh is the blood thereof: whosoever eateth it shall be cut off." Perhaps you will say, that our LORD was not bound by this law, or that he had power to set it aside. He was bound by it inasmuch as he was the man CHRIST JESUS; for it is written in Gal. iv. 4, that he was, " made *under* the law." And although he had power to set aside the law, yet he did not do so, for he himself says in Matt. v. 17, " Think not that I am come to destroy the law, or the prophets: *I am not come to destroy, but to fulfil.*" The decree of the Apostles, Acts xv. 29, also binds the Christians to abstain from blood.' *Page's Letters to a Romish Priest.*—[ED.]

right to understand the whole period in a mystical and figurative sense. And therefore since a man born and bred a Jew, and more particularly accustomed to the paschal ceremonies, could not have understood our Saviour's words, chiefly at the time of that festivity, otherwise than of a new *covenant* that he was to make, in which his ' body was to be broken,' and his ' blood shed' for the ' remission of sins ;' and that he was to substitute bread and wine, to be the lasting memorials of it ; in the repeating of which, his disciples were to renew their covenant with God, and to claim a share in the blessings of it ; this, I say, was the sense that must naturally have occurred to a Jew ; upon all this, we must conclude, that this is the true sense of these words ; or, that otherwise our Saviour must have enlarged more upon them, and expressed his meaning more particularly. Since therefore he said no more than what, according to the ideas and customs of the Jews, must have been understood as has been explained, we must conclude, that it, and it only, is the true sense of them. ART XXVIII

But we must next consider the importance of a long discourse of our Saviour's, set down by St. John, which seems such a preparation of his apostles to understand this institution literally, that the weight of this argument must turn upon the meaning of that discourse. The design of that was to shew, that the doctrine of Christ was more excellent than the law of Moses ; that though Moses gave the Israelites manna from heaven to nourish their bodies, yet notwithstanding that ' they died in the wilderness :' but Christ was to give his followers such food that it should give them *life ;* so that if they 'did eat of it, they should never die :' where it is apparent, that the bread and nourishment must be such as the *life* was ; and that being eternal and spiritual, the bread must be so understood : for it is clearly expressed how that food was to be received ; ' he that believeth on me hath everlasting life.' John vi. 32, 33.

ver. 40.

Since then he had formerly said, that the *bread* which he was to give, should make them 'live for ever ;' and since here it is said, that this life is given by faith ; then this bread must be his doctrine : for, this is that which faith receives. And when the Jews desired him to give them evermore of that bread, he answered, ' I am the bread of life : he that comes to me shall never hunger ; and he that believeth on me shall never thirst.' ver. 47, 48, 51.

In these words he tells them that they received that bread by coming to him, and by believing on him. Christ calls himself that *bread,* and says, that a 'man must eat thereof ;' which is plainly a figure : and if figures are confessed to be in some parts of their discourse, there is no reason to deny that they run quite through it. Christ says, that this ' bread was his flesh, which he was to give for the life of the world ;'

ART. XXVIII.

John vi. 53, 54, 55.

which can only be meant of his offering himself up upon the cross for the sins of the world. The Jews murmured at this, and said, 'How can this man give us his flesh to eat?' To which our Saviour answers, that 'except they did eat the flesh and drink the blood of the Son of man, they had no life in them.'

Now if these words are to be understood of a literal eating of his flesh in the sacrament, then no man can be saved that does not receive it: it was a natural consequence of the expounding these words of the sacrament to give it to children, since it is so expressly said, that life is not to be had without it. But the words that come next carry this matter further; 'Whoso eateth my flesh, and drinketh my blood, hath eternal life.' It is plain that Christ is here speaking of that, without which no man can have *life*, and by which all who received it have *life*: if therefore this is to be expounded of the sacrament, none can be damned that does receive it, and none can be saved that receives it not.

Therefore since *eternal life* does always follow the 'eating of Christ's flesh,' and the 'drinking his blood,' and cannot be had without it; then this must be meant of an internal and spiritual feeding on him: for, as none are saved without that, so all are saved that have it. This is yet clearer from the words that follow, 'my flesh is meat indeed, and my blood is drink indeed:' it may well be inferred, that Christ's flesh is eaten in the same sense, in which he says it is *meat*: now certainly it is not literally *meat*; for none do say that the body is nourished by it; and yet there is somewhat emphatical in this, since the word *indeed* is not added in vain, but to give weight to the expression.

ver. 56.

It is also said, 'he that eats my flesh, and drinks my blood, dwells in me, and I in him.' Here the description seems to be made of that eating and drinking of his flesh and blood; that it is such as the mutual indwelling of Christ and believers is. Now that is certainly only internal and spiritual, and not carnal or literal: and therefore such also must the *eating* and *drinking* be.

All this seems to be very fully confirmed from the conclusion of that discourse, which ought to be considered as the key to it all; for when the Jews were offended at the hardness of Christ's discourse, he said, 'It is the spirit that quickeneth; the flesh profiteth nothing: the words I speak unto you, they are spirit, and they are life:' which do plainly import, that his former discourse was to be understood in a spiritual sense, that it was a divine *Spirit* that *quickened* them, or gave them that *eternal* life, of which he had been speaking; and that the *flesh*, his natural body, was not the conveyer of it.

ver. 63.

All that is confirmed by the sense in which we find *eating* and *drinking* frequently used in the scriptures, according to what is observed by Jewish writers; they stand for wisdom,

learning, and all intellectual apprehensions, through which the ART.
soul of man is preserved, by the perfection that is in them, as XXVIII.
the body is preserved by food: So, 'Buy and eat: eat fat
things; drink of wine well refined.'
Maimonides also observes, that whensoever eating and More Ne-
drinking are mentioned in the Book of Proverbs, they are to vochim.
be understood of wisdom and the law: and after he has
brought several places of scripture to this purpose, he concludes, that because *this acceptation of eating occurs so often,
and is so manifest, as if it were the primary and most proper
sense of the word; therefore hunger and thirst stand for a privation of wisdom and understanding.* And the Chaldee para-
phrast turns these words, 'ye shall draw water out of the Isa. xii. 3
wells of salvation;' thus, 'ye shall receive a new doctrine with
joy from some select persons.'

Since then the figure of *eating* and *drinking* was used among
the Jews, for receiving and imbibing a doctrine; it was no
wonder if our Saviour pursued it in a discourse, in which
there are several hints given to shew us that it ought to be
so understood.

It is further observable, that our Saviour did frequently
follow that common way of instruction among the eastern
nations, by figures, that to us would seem strong and bold.
These were much used in those parts to excite the attention
of the hearers; and they are not always to be severely expounded according to the full extent that the words will bear.
The parable of the unjust judge, of the unjust steward, of the
ten virgins, of plucking out the right eye, and cutting off the
right hand or foot, and several others, might be instanced.
Our Saviour in these considered the genius of those to whom
he spoke: so that these figures must be restrained only to
that particular, for which he meant them; and must not be
stretched to every thing to which the words may be carried.
We find our Saviour compares himself to a great many things;
to a vine, a door, and a way: and therefore when the scope of
a discourse does plainly run in a figure, we are not to go and
descant on every word of it; much less may any pretend to
say, that some parts of it are to be understood literally,
and some parts figuratively.

For instance, if that chapter of St. John is to be understood
literally, then Christ's *flesh* and *blood* must be the nourishment
of our bodies, so as to be *meat indeed;* and that we shall
'never hunger any more, and never die after' we have eat of
it. If therefore all do confess that those expressions are
to be understood figuratively, then we have the same reason
to conclude that the whole is a figure: for it is as reasonable for us to make all of it a figure, as it is for them
to make those parts of it a figure which they cannot conveniently expound in a literal sense. From all which it is
abundantly clear that nothing can be drawn from that dis-

ART. XXVIII. course of our Saviour's, to make it reasonable to believe that the words of the institution of this sacrament ought to be literally understood: on the contrary, our Saviour himself calls the wine, after those words had been used by him, the 'fruit of the vine,' which is as strict a form of speech as can well be imagined, to make us understand that the nature of the wine was not altered: and when St. Paul treats of it in those two chapters, in which all that is left us besides the history of the institution concerning the sacrament is to be found, he calls it five times bread, and never once *the body of Christ.* In one place he calls it the 'communion of the body, as the cup is the communion of the blood of Christ.' Which is rather a saying, that it is in some sort, and after a manner, the body and the blood of Christ, than that it is so strictly speaking.

1 Cor. x. 16.

If this sacrament had been that mysterious and unconceivable thing which it has been since believed to be, we cannot imagine but that the books of the New Testament, the Acts of the Apostles, and their Epistles, should have contained fuller explanations of it, and larger instructions about it.

There is enough indeed said in them to support the plain and natural sense that we give to this institution; and because no more is said, and the design of it is plainly declared to be to remember Christ's death, and to 'shew it forth till he come,' we reckon that by this natural simplicity, in which this matter is delivered to us, we are very much confirmed in that plain and easy signification, which we put upon our Saviour's words. Plain things need not be insisted on: but if the most sublime and wonderful thing in the world seems to be delivered in words that yet are capable of a lower and plainer sense, then unless there is a concurrence of other circumstances, to force us to that higher meaning of them, we ought not to go into it; for simple things prove themselves: whereas the more extraordinary that any thing is, it requires a fulness and evidence in the proof, proportioned to the uneasiness of conceiving or believing it.

We do therefore understand our Saviour's institution thus, that as he was to give 'his body to be broken' and his 'blood to be shed for our sins,' so he intended that this his death and suffering should be still commemorated by all such as look for 'remission of sins' by it, not only in their thoughts and devotions, but in a visible representation: which he appointed should be done in symbols, that should be both very plain and simple, and yet very expressive of that which he intended should be remembered by them.

Bread is the plainest food that the body of man can receive, and *wine* was the common nourishing liquor of that country; so he made choice of these materials, and in them appointed a representation and remembrance to be made of his *body broken,* and of his *blood shed;* that is, of his death and sufferings till his *second coming:* and he obliged his followers to repeat this frequently. In the doing of it according to his institution, they profess the belief of his death, for the remission of their sins, and that they look for his second coming.

ART. XXVIII.

This does also import, that as bread and wine are the simplest of bodily nourishments, so his death is that which restores the souls of those that do believe in him: as bread and wine convey a vital nourishment to the body, so the sacrifice of his death conveys somewhat to the soul that is vital, that fortifies and exalts it. And as water in baptism is a natural emblem of the purity of the Christian religion, bread and wine in the eucharist are the emblems of somewhat that is derived to us, that raises our faculties, and fortifies all our powers.

St. Paul does very plainly tell us, that 'unworthy receivers,' that did neither examine nor discern themselves, nor yet discern the Lord's body, ' were guilty of the body and blood of the Lord, and did eat and drink their own damnation:' that is, such as do receive it without truly believing the Christian religion, without a grateful acknowledgment of Christ's death and sufferings, without feeling that they are walking suitably to this religion that they profess, and without that decency and charity, which becomes so holy an action; but that receive the bread and wine only as bare bodily nourishments, without considering that Christ has instituted them to be the memorials of his death; such persons are guilty of the body and blood of Christ: that is, they are guilty either of a profanation of the sacrament of his body and blood, or they do in a manner crucify him again, and put him to an open shame; when they are so faulty as the Corinthians were, in observing this holy institution with so little reverence, and with such scandalous disorders, as those were for which he reproached them.

1 Cor. xi. 27, 29.

Of such as did thus profane this institution, he says further, that they do eat and drink their own *damnation,* or *judgment;* that is, punishment: for the word rendered *damnation* signifies sometimes only temporary punishments.

So it is said, that 'judgment (the word is the same) must begin at the house of God:' God had sent such judgments upon the Corinthians for those disorderly practices of theirs, that some had fallen sick, and others had died, perhaps by reason of their drinking to excess in those feasts: but as God's judgments had come upon them; so the words that follow shew that these judgments were only chastisements, in order to the delivering them from the condemnation under which the world lies. It being said, that ' when we are judged, we are chastened of the Lord, that we should not be condemned with the world.' Therefore though God may very justly and even in great mercy punish men who profane this

1 Pet. iv. 17.

holy ordinance; yet it is an unreasonable terror, and contrary to the nature of the gospel covenant, to carry this so far, as to think that it is an unpardonable sin; which is punished with eternal damnation.

We have now seen the ill effects of unworthy receiving, and from hence according to that gradation, that is to be observed in the mercy of God in the gospel, that it not only holds a proportion with his justice, but 'rejoiceth over it,' we may well conclude that the good effects upon the worthy receiving of it are equal if not superior to the bad effects upon the unworthy receiving of it: and that the nourishment which the types, the *bread* and the *wine*, give the *body*, are answered in the effects, that the thing signified by them has upon the *soul*.

In explaining this there is some diversity: some teach that this memorial of the death of Christ, when seriously and devoutly gone about, when it animates our faith, increases our repentance, and inflames our love and zeal, and so unites us to God and to our brethren; that, I say, when these follow it, which it naturally excites in all holy and good minds, then they draw down the returns of prayer, and a further increase of grace in us; according to the nature and promises of the new covenant: and in this they put the virtue and efficacy of this sacrament.

But others think that all this belongs only to the inward acts of the mind, and is not sacramental: and therefore they think that the eucharist is a federal act, in which as on the one hand we renew our baptismal covenant with God, so on the other hand we receive in the sacrament a visible consignation, as in a tradition by a symbol or pledge, of the blessings of the new covenant, which they think is somewhat superadded to those returns of our prayers, or of other inward acts.

This they think answers the nourishment which the body receives from the symbols of *bread* and *wine;* and stands in opposition to that of the unworthy receivers being guilty of *the body and blood of the Lord;* and their *eating* and *drinking* that which will bring some judgment upon themselves. This they also found on these words of St. Paul, 'The cup of blessing that we bless, is it not the communion of the blood of Christ? the bread which we break, is it not the communion of the body of Christ?'

St. Paul considers the *bread* which was offered by the people as an emblem of their unity, that as there was one loaf, so they were *one body;* and that they were all *partakers* of that one loaf: from hence it is inferred, that since the word rendered *communion* signifies a *communication in fellowship*, or partnership, that therefore the meaning of it is, that in the sacrament there is a distribution made in that symbolical action of the death of Christ, and of the benefits and effects of it. 'The communion of the Holy Ghost' is a common sharing in the effusion of the Spirit; the same is meant by that, 'if there is any fellowship of the Spirit;' that is, if we do all partake of the same Spirit, we are said to have a 'fellowship in the sufferings of Christ,' in which every one must take his share. 'The communication,' or fellowship, 'of the mystery of the gospel,' was its being shared equally among both Jews and Gentiles; and the fellowship in which the first converts to Christianity lived, was their liberal distribution to one another, they holding all things in common. In these and some other places it is certain, that communion signifies somewhat that is more real and effectual, than merely men's owning themselves to be joined together in a society; which it is true it does also often signify: and therefore they conclude, that as in bargains or covenants, the ancient method of them before writings were invented was the mutual delivering of some pledges, which were the symbols of that faith, which was so plighted, instead of which the sealing and delivering of writings is now used among us; so our Saviour instituted this in compliance with our frailty, to give us an outward and sensible pledge of his entering into covenant with us, of which the *bread* and *wine* are constituted the symbols.

ART. XXVIII. 2 Cor. xiii. 14. Phil. ii. 1. Eph. iii, 9. Phil.iii.10.

Others think, that by the communion of the body and blood of Christ can only be meant the joint owning of Christ and of his death, in the receiving the sacrament; and that no *communication* nor partnership can be inferred from it: because St. Paul brings it in to shew the Corinthians how detestable a thing it was for a Christian to join in the idols' feasts; that it was to be a 'partaker with devils:' so they think that the *fellowship* or communion of Christians in the sacrament must be of the same nature with the 'fellowship of devils' in acts of idolatry: which consisted only in their associating themselves with those that worshipped idols; for that upon the matter was the worshipping of devils: and this seems to be confirmed by that which is said of the Jews, that they 'who did eat of the sacrifices were partakers of the altar;' which it seems can signify no more but that they professed that religion of which the altar was the chief instrument; the sacrifices being offered there.

1 Cor. x. 18, 20.

To all this it may be replied, that it is reasonable enough to believe, that according to the power which God suffered the Devil to exercise over the idolatrous world, there might be some enchantment in the sacrifices offered to idols, and that the Devil might have some power over those that did partake of them: and in order to this, St. Paul removed an objection that might have been made, that there could be no harm in their joining to the idol feasts; for 'an idol was nothing;' and so that which was offered to an idol could contract no defilement from the idol, it being *nothing*. Now if the meaning of their being 'partakers with devils' imports only

ART. XXVIII. their joining themselves in acts of fellowship with idolaters, then the sin of this would have easily appeared, without such a reinforcing of the matter; for though an idol was *nothing*, yet it was still a great sin to join in the acts that were meant to be the worship of this *nothing;* this was a dishonouring of God, and a debasing of man. But St. Paul seems to carry the argument further; that how true soever it was that the *idol* was *nothing*, that is, a dead and lifeless thing, that had no virtue nor operation, and that by consequence could derive nothing to the sacrifice that was offered to it; yet since those idols were the instruments by which the Devil kept the world in subjection to him, all such as did *partake* in their sacrifices might come under the effects of that magic, that might be exerted about their temples or sacrifices: by which the credit of idolatry was much kept up.

And though every Christian had a sure defence against the powers of darkness, as long as he continued true to his religion, yet if he went out of that protection into the empire of the Devil, and joined in the acts that were as a homage to him, he then fell within the reach of the Devil, and might justly fear his being brought into a *partnership* of those magical possessions or temptations that might be suffered to fall upon such Christians, as should associate themselves in so detestable a service.

1 Cor. x. 18. In the same sense it was also said, 'that all the Israelites who did eat of the sacrifices were partakers of the altar:' that is, that all of them who joined in the acts of that religion, such as the offering their peace-offerings, for of those of that kind they might only eat, all these were 'partakers of the altar;' that is, of all the blessings of their religion, of all the expiations, the burnt-offerings and sin-offerings, that were offered on the altar, for the sins of the whole congregation: for that as a great stock went in a common dividend among such as observed the precepts of that law, and joined in the acts of worship prescribed by it: thus it appears that such as joined in the acts of idolatry became *partakers* of all that influence that devils might have over those sacrifices; and all that continued in the observances of the Mosaical law, had thereby a *partnership* in the expiations of the altar: so likewise all Christians who receive this sacrament *worthily*, have by their so doing a share in that which is represented by it, the death of Christ, and the expiation and other benefits that follow it.

This seemed necessary to be fully explained: for this matter, how plain soever in itself, has been made very dark, by the ways in which some have pretended to open it. With this I conclude all that belongs to the first part of the Article, and that which was first to be explained of our doctrine concerning the sacrament: by which we assert a *real presence* of the *body* and *blood* of Christ: but not of his *body* as it is now glorified in heaven, but of his *body* as it was *broken* on the cross, when his 'blood was shed' and separated from it: that is, his ART. death, with the merit and effects of it, are in a visible and XXVIII. federal act offered in this sacrament to all worthy believers.

By *real* we understand *true*, in opposition both to fiction and imagination: and to those shadows that were in the Mosaical dispensation, in which the *manna*, the *rock*, the *brazen serpent*, but most eminently the *cloud of glory*, were the types and shadows of the Messias that was to come: with whom came 'grace and truth;' that is, a most wonderful manifestation of the mercy or grace of God, and a verifying of the promises made under the Law: in this sense we acknowledge a *real presence* of Christ in the sacrament: though we are convinced that our first reformers judged right concerning the use of the phrase *real presence*, that it were better to be let fall than to be continued, since the use of it, and that idea which does naturally arise from the common acceptation of it, may stick deeper, and feed superstition more, than all those larger explanations that are given to it can be able to cure.

But howsoever in this sense it is innocent of itself, and may be lawfully used; though perhaps it were more cautiously done not to use it, since advantages have been taken from it to urge it further than we intend it; and since it has been a snare to some.

I go in the next place to explain the doctrine of the church of Rome concerning this sacrament. Transubstantiation does express it in one word: but that a full idea may be given of this part of their doctrine, I shall open it in all its branches and consequences.

The matter of this sacrament is not *bread* and *wine*: for they are annihilated when the sacrament is made. They are only the remote matter, out of which it is made: but when the sacrament is made, they cease to be; and instead of them their outward appearances or *accidents* do only remain: which though they are no *substances*, yet are supposed to have a nature and essence of their own, separable from matter: and these appearances, with the body of Christ under them, are the *matter* of the sacrament.

Now though the natural and visible *body of Christ* could not be the sacrament of his *body*, yet they think his *real body*, being thus veiled under the appearances of bread and wine, may be the sacrament of his glorified body.

Yet, it seeming somewhat strange to make a *true body* the sacrament of itself, they would willingly put the sacrament in the appearances; but that would sound very harsh, to make accidents which are not *matter* to be the *matter* of the sacrament: therefore since these words, *This is my body*, must be literally understood, the matter must be the *true body of Christ*; so that *Christ's body* is the sacrament of his *body*.

Christ's body, though now in heaven, is, as they think,

ART.
XXVIII.

presented in every place where a true consecration is made. And though it is in heaven in an extended state, as all other bodies are, yet they think that extension may be separated from matter, as well as the other appearances or accidents are believed to be separated from it. And whereas our souls are believed to be so in our bodies, that though the whole soul is in the whole body, yet all the soul is believed to be in every part of it; but so, that if any part of the body is separated from the rest, the soul is not divided, being one single substance, but retires back into the rest of the body: they apprehend that Christ's body is present after the manner of a spirit, without extension, or the filling of space; so that the space which the appearances possess is still a vacuum, or only filled by the accidents: for a body without extension, as they suppose Christ's body to be, can never fill up an extension.

Christ's body in the sacrament is denominated one; yet still, as the species are broken and divided, so many new bodies are divided from one another; every crumb of bread and drop of wine that is separated from the whole, is a new body, and yet without a new miracle, all being done in consequence of the first great one that was all at once wrought.

The body of Christ continues in this state as long as the accidents remain in theirs; but how it should alter is not easy to apprehend: the corruption of all other accidents arises from a change in the common substance, out of which new accidents do arise, while the old ones vanish; but accidents without a subject may seem more fixed and stable: yet they are not so, but are as subject to corruption as other accidents are: howsoever, as long as the alteration is not total; though the bread should be both musty and mouldy, and the wine both dead and sour, yet as long as the bread and wine are still so far preserved, or rather that their appearances subsist, so long the body of Christ remains: but when they are so far altered that they seem to be no more bread and wine, and that they are corrupted either in part or in whole, Christ's body is withdrawn, either in part or in whole.

It is a great miracle to make the accidents of bread and wine subsist without a subject; yet the new accidents that arise upon these accidents, such as mouldiness or sourness, come on without a miracle, but they do not know how. When the main accidents are destroyed, then the presence of Christ ceases: and a new miracle must be supposed to produce new matter, for the filling up of that space which the substance of bread and wine did formerly fill; and which was all this while possessed by the accidents. So much of the matter of this sacrament.

The form of it is in the words of consecration, which though they sound declarative, as if the thing were already done; 'This is my body,' and 'This is my blood;' yet they believe them to be productive. But whereas the common notion of the form of a sacrament is, that it sanctifies and applies the matter; here the former matter is so far from being consecrated by it, that it is annihilated, and new matter is not sanctified, but brought thither or produced: and whereas whensoever we say of any thing, *this is*, we suppose that the thing is, as we say it is, before we say it; yet here all the while that this is a saying till the last syllable is pronounced, it is not that which it is said to be, but in the minute in which the last syllable is uttered, then the change is made: and of this they are so firmly persuaded, that they do presently pay all that adoration to it, that they would pay to the person of Jesus Christ if he were visibly present: though the whole virtue of the consecration depends on the intention of a priest: so that he with a cross intention hinders all this series of miracles, as he fetches it all on, by letting his intention go along with it.*

ART. XXVIII.

> * The adoration of the Eucharist is thus decreed by the council of Trent.
>
> '*De cultu et veneratione huic sanctissimo sacramento exhibenda.*
>
> ' Nullus itaque dubitandi locus relinquitur, quin omnes Christi fideles pro more in catholica ecclesia semper recepto latriæ cultum, qui vero Deo debetur, huic sanctissimo sacramento in veneratione exhibeant; neque enim ideo minus est adorandum, quod fuerit a Christo Domino, ut sumatur, institutum: nam illum eundem Deum præsentem in eo adesse credimus, quem Pater æternus introducens in orbem terrarum, dicit; Et adorent eum omnes angeli Dei.' *Sessio* xiii. cap. 5.
>
> ' Si quis dixerit, in sancto eucharistiæ sacramento Christum unigenitum Dei filium non esse cultu latriæ, etiam externo, adorandum, atque ideo nec festiva peculiari celebritate venerandum, neque in processionibus secundum laudabilem et universalem ecclesiæ sanctæ ritum et consuetudinem, solemniter circumgestandum, vel non publice, ut adoretur, populo proponendum, et ejus adoratores esse idololatras; anathema sit.' *Sessio* xiii. canon 6.
>
> The novelty and danger of this adoration is clearly and forcibly stated in the following:
>
> ' Now touching the adoration of the sacrament, Mr. Harding is not able to shew, neither any commandment of Christ, nor any word or example of the Apostles, or ancient Fathers concerning the same. It is a thing very lately devised by pope Honorius, about the year of our Lord 1226. Afterward increased by the new solemn feast of Corpus Christi day by pope Urbanus, anno 1264. And last of all confirmed for ever by multitudes of pardons in the council of Vienna by pope Clement V. anno 1310. The church of Asia and Græcia never received it until this day. The matter is great, and cannot be attempted without great danger. To give the honour of God to a creature, that is no God, it is manifest idolatry. And all idolaters, as St. John saith, shall have their portion in the lake burning with fire, and brimstone, which is the second death.'
>
> ' The greatest doctors of that side say, that, unless transubstantiation be concluded, the people cannot freely worship the sacrament, without occasion of idolatry. Now it is known that transubstantiation is a new fantasy, newly devised in the council of Lateran, (A.D. 1215) in Rome. And Doctor Tonstal saith, that before that time it was free and lawful for any man to hold the contrary. Wherefore it is likely, that before that time, there was no such adoration. Otherwise, it must needs have been with great danger of idolatry. But after that, as it is said before, pope Honorius took order and gave commandment, that the people should adore: pope Urbanus added thereto a new solemn feast of Corpus Christi day: and pope Clement confirmed the same with great store of pardons. This is the antiquity and petite degree of this kind of adoration. The great danger and horror of idolatry that hereof riseth, Mr. Harding thinketh may easily be solved by the example of Rachel, and Leah: and thus he bringeth in God's mystical providence for defence of open error: and thus instead of Rachel to take Leah, and to honour a creature instead of God.
>
> ' Wherein it shall be necessary briefly to touch, how many ways, even by their

ART.
XXVIII.

If it may be said of some doctrines, that the bare exposing them is a most effectual confutation of them; certainly that is more applicable to this, than to any other that can be imagined: for though I have in stating it considered some of the most important difficulties, which are seen and confessed by the schoolmen themselves, who have poised all these with much exactness and subtilty; yet I have passed over a great many more, with which those that deal in school-divinity will find enough to exercise both their thoughts and their patience. They run out in many subtilties, concerning the accidents both *primary* and *secondary;* concerning the ubication, the production and reproduction of bodies; concerning the penetrability of matter, and the organization of a penetrable body; concerning the way of the destruction of the species; concerning the words of consecration; concerning the water that is mixed with the wine, whether it is first changed by natural causes into wine; and since nothing but wine is transubstantiated, what becomes of such particles of water that are not turned into wine? What is the grace produced by the sacrament, what is the effect of the presence of Christ so long as he is in the body of the communicant; what is got by his presence, and what is lost by his absence? In a word, let a man read the shortest body of school-divinity that he can find, and he will see in it a vast number of other difficulties in this matter, of which their own authors are aware, which I have quite passed over. For when this doctrine fell into the hands

---

own doctrine, the poor simple people may be deceived, and yield the honour of God to that thing, that in their own judgment is no God. Thus therefore they say, if the priest chance to forget to put wine into the cup, and so pass over the consecration without wine: or, if the bread be made of any other than wheaten flour, which may possibly and easily happen: or, if there be so much water in quantity, that it overcome and alter the nature of the wine: or, if the wine be changed into vinegar, and therefore cannot serve to consecration: or, if there be thirteen cakes upon the table, and the priest for his consecration determine only upon twelve, in which case they say not one of them all is consecrated: or, if the priest dissemble, or leave out the words of consecration: or, if he forget it, or mind it not, or think not of it: In every one of these, and other like defects, there is nothing consecrate, and therefore the people in these cases, honouring the sacrament, by their own doctrine giveth the glory of God to a creature: which is undoubted idolatry. And that the folly thereof may the better appear, one of them writeth thus: " Quod si Sacerdos," &c. If the priest having before him sundry cakes at the time of consecration, do mind only and precisely to consecrate that only cake that he holdeth in his hand, some say, the rest be not consecrate: but say thou, as Duns saith, they be all consecrate: yea, further he saith, If the priest do precisely determine to consecrate only the one half part of the cake, and not likewise the other half, that then, the cake being whole, that one part only is consecrate, and not the other. Pope Gregory saith, If the priest be a known adulterer, or fornicator, and continue still in the same, that his blessing shall be turned into cursing: and that the people knowing his life, and nevertheless bearing his mass, commit idolatry.

'In this case standeth the simple people: so many ways and so easily they may be deceived. For notwithstanding they may, in some part, know the priest's life and open dealing, yet how can they be assured of his secret words, of his intention, of his mind, and of his will? or, if they cannot, how can they safely adore the sacrament, without doubt and danger of idolatry?' *Jewel.*—[ED.]

of nice and exact men, they were soon sensible of all the consequences that must needs follow upon it, and have pursued all these with a closeness far beyond any thing that is to be found among the writers of our side.

ART. XXVIII.

But that they might have a salvo for every difficulty, they framed a new model of philosophy; new theories were invented, of substances and accidents, of matter and of spirits, of extension, ubication, and impenetrability; and by the new definitions and maxims to which they accustomed men in the study of philosophy, they prepared them to swallow down all this more easily, when they should come to the study of divinity.

The infallibility of the church that had expressly defined it, was to bear a great part of the burden; if the church was infallible, and if they were that church, then it could be no longer doubted of. In dark ages miracles and visions came in abundantly to support it: in ages of more light, the infinite power of God, the words of the institution, it being the testament of our Saviour then dying, and soon after confirmed with his blood, were things of great pomp, and such as were apt to strike men that could not distinguish between the shows and the strength of arguments. But when all our senses, all our ideas of things, rise up so strongly against every part of this chain of wonders, we ought at least to expect proofs suitable to the difficulty of believing such a flat contradiction to our reasons, as well as to our senses.

We have no other notion of accidents, but that they are the different shapes or modes of matter; and that they have no being distinct from the body in which they appear: we have no other notion of a body but that it is an extended substance, made up of impenetrable parts, one without another; every one of which fills its proper space: we have no other notion of a body's being in a place but that it fills it, and is so in it as that it can be nowhere else at the same time: and though we can very easily apprehend that an infinite power can both create and annihilate beings at pleasure; yet we cannot apprehend that God does change the essences of things, and so make them to be contrary to that nature and sort of being of which he has made them.

Another argument against transubstantiation is this; God has made us capable to know and serve him: and, in order to that, he has put some senses in us, which are the conveyances of many subtile motions to our brains, that give us apprehensions of the objects which by those motions are represented to us.

When those motions are lively, and the object is in a due distance; when we feel that neither our organs nor our faculties are under any disorder, and when the impression is clear and strong, we are determined by it; we cannot help being

ART.
XXVIII.

so. When we see the sun risen, and all is bright about us, it is not possible for us to think that it is dark night; no authority can impose it on us; we are not so far the masters of our own thoughts, as to force ourselves to think it, though we would; for God has made us of such a nature, that we are determined by such an evidence, and cannot contradict it. When an object is at too great a distance, we may mistake; a weakness or an ill disposition in our sight may misrepresent it; and a false medium, water, a cloud, or a glass, may give it a tincture or cast, so that we may see cause to correct our first apprehensions, in some sensations: but when we have duly examined every thing, when we have corrected one sense by another, we grow at last to be so sure, by the constitution of that nature that God has given us, that we cannot doubt, much less believe, in contradiction to the express evidence of our senses.

It is by this evidence only that God convinces the world of the authority of those whom he sends to speak in his name; he gives them a power to work miracles, which is an appeal to the senses of mankind; and it is the highest appeal that can be made; for those who stood out against the conviction of Christ's miracles, had no cloak for their sins. It is the utmost conviction that God offers, or that man can pretend to: from all which we must infer this, that either our senses in their clearest apprehensions, or rather representations of things, must be infallible, or we must throw up all faith and certainty; since it is not possible for us to receive the evidence that is given us of any thing but by our senses; and since we do naturally acquiesce in that evidence, we must acknowledge that God has so made us, that this is his voice in us; because it is the voice of those faculties that he has put in us; and is the only way by which we can find out truth, and be led by it: and if our faculties fail us in any one thing, so that God should reveal to us any thing, that did plainly contradict our faculties, he should thereby give us a right to disbelieve them for ever.

If they can mistake when they bring any object to us with the fullest evidence that they can give, we can never depend upon them, nor be certain of any thing, because they shew it. Nay, we are not and cannot be bound to believe that, nor any other revelation that God may make to convince us. We can only receive a revelation by hearing or reading, by our ears or our eyes. So if any part of this revelation destroys the certainty of the evidence, that our senses, our eyes, or our ears, give us, it destroys itself: for we cannot be bound to believe it upon the evidence of our senses, if this is a part of it, that our senses are not to be trusted. Nor will this matter be healed, by saying, that certainly we must believe God more than our senses: and therefore, if he has revealed any thing to us, that is contrary to their evidence, we must as to that particular believe God before our senses; but that as to all other things where we have not an express revelation to the contrary, we must still believe our senses.

ART. XXVIII.

There is a difference to be made between that feeble evidence that our senses give us of remote objects, or those loose inferences that we may make from a slight view of things, and the full evidence that sense gives us; as when we see and smell to, we handle and taste the same object: this is the voice of God to us; he has made us so that we are determined by it: and as we should not believe a prophet that wrought ever so many miracles, if he should contradict any part of that which God had already revealed; so we cannot be bound to believe a revelation contrary to our sense; because that were to believe God in contradiction to himself; which is impossible to be true. For we should believe that revelation certainly upon an evidence, which itself tells us is not certain; and this is a contradiction. We believe our senses upon this foundation, because we reckon there is an intrinsic certainty in their evidence; we do not believe them as we believe another man, upon a moral presumption of his truth and sincerity; but we believe them, because such is the nature of the union of our souls and bodies, which is the work of God, that upon the full impressions that are made upon the senses, the soul does necessarily produce, or rather feel those thoughts and sensations arise with a full evidence, that correspond to the motions of sensible objects, upon the organs of sense. The soul has a sagacity to examine these sensations, to correct one sense by another; but when she has used all the means she can, and the evidence is still clear, she is persuaded, and cannot help being so; she naturally takes all this to be true, because of the necessary connection that she feels between such sensations, and her assent to them. Now, if she should find that she could be mistaken in this, even though she should know this, by a divine revelation, all the intrinsic certainty of the evidence of sense, and that connection between those sensations and her assent to them, should be hereby dissolved.

To all this another objection may be made from the mysteries of the Christian religion: which contradict our reason, and yet we are bound to believe them; although reason is a faculty much superior to sense. But all this is a mistake; we cannot be bound to believe any thing that contradicts our reason; for the evidence of reason as well as that of sense is the voice of God to us. But as great difference is to be made between a feeble evidence that sense gives us of an object that is at a distance from us, or that appears to us through a false medium; such as a concave or a convex glass; and the full evidence of an object that is before us, and that is clearly apprehended by us: so there is a great difference to be made between our reasonings upon difficulties that we can neither understand nor resolve, and our reasonings upon clear principles. The one may be false, and the other must be true: we are sure that a thing cannot be one and three in the same respect; our reason assures us of this, and we do and must believe it; but we know that in different respects the same thing may be one and three. And since we cannot know all the possibilities of those different respects, we must believe upon the authority of God revealing it, that the same thing is both *one* and *three;* though if a revelation should affirm that the same thing were *one* and *three* in the same respect, we should not, and indeed could not, believe it.

This argument deserves to be fully opened; for we are sure either it is true, or we cannot be sure that any thing else whatsoever is true. In confirmation of this we ought also to consider the nature and ends of miracles. They put nature out of its channel, and reverse its fixed laws and motions; and the end of God's giving men a power to work them, is, that by them the world may be convinced, that such persons are commissionated by him, to deliver his pleasure to them in some particulars. And as it could not become the infinite wisdom of the great Creator, to change the order of nature (which is his own workmanship) upon slight grounds; so we cannot suppose that he should work a chain of extraordinary miracles to no purpose. It is not to give credit to a revelation that he is making; for the senses do not perceive it; on the contrary, they do reject and contradict it: and the revelation, instead of getting credit from it, is loaded by it, as introducing that which destroys all credit and certainty.

In other miracles our senses are appealed to; but here they must be appealed from; nor is there any spiritual end served in working this miracle: for it is acknowledged, that the effects of this sacrament are given upon our due coming to it, independent upon the corporal presence: so that the grace of the sacrament does not always accompany it, since unworthy receivers, though, according to the Romish doctrine, they receive the true body of Christ, yet they do not receive grace with it: and the grace that is given in it to the worthy receivers, stays with them after that, by the destruction of the species of the bread and wine, the body of Christ is withdrawn. So that it is acknowledged, that the spiritual effect of the sacrament does not depend upon the corporal presence.

Here then it is supposed, that God is every day working a great many miracles, in a vast number of different places; and that of so extraordinary a nature, that it must be confessed, they are far beyond all the other wonders, even of omnipotence; and yet all this is to no end, that we can apprehend; neither to any sensible and visible end, nor to any internal and spiritual one. This must needs seem an amazing thing, that God should work such a miracle on our behalf, and yet should not acquaint us with any end for which he should work it.

ART. XXVIII.

To conclude this whole argument, we have one great advantage in this matter, that our doctrine concerning the sacrament, of a mystical presence of Christ in the symbols, and of the effects of it on the worthy and unworthy receivers, is all acknowledged by the church of Rome; but they have added to this the wonder of the corporal presence: so that we need bring no proofs to them at least, for that which we teach concerning it; since it is all confessed by them. But as to that which they have added, it is not necessary for us to give proofs against it; it is enough for us, if we shew that all the proofs that they bring for it are weak and unconcluding. They must be very demonstrative, if it is expected, that, upon the authority and evidence of them, we should be bound to believe a thing which they themselves confess to be contrary both to our sense and reason. We cannot by the laws of reasoning be bound to give arguments against it; it is enough if we can shew that neither the words of the institution, nor the discourse in the sixth of St. John, do necessarily infer it; and if we shew that those passages can well bear another sense, which is agreeable both to the words themselves, and to the style of the scriptures, and more particularly to the phraseology to which the Jews were accustomed, upon the occasion on which this was instituted; and if the words can well bear the sense that we give them, then the other advantages that are in it, of its being simple and natural, of its being suitable to the design of a sacrament, and of its having no hard consequences of any sort depending upon it; then, I say, by all the rules of expounding scripture, we do justly infer, that our sense of those words ought to be preferred.

This is according to a rule that St. Augustin gives to judge what expressions in scripture are figurative, and what not; 'If any place seems to command a crime or horrid action, it is figurative: and for an instance of this he cites those words, "Except ye eat the flesh and drink the blood of the Son of man, you have no life in you:" which seems to command a crime and a horrid action; and therefore it is a figure commanding us to communicate in the passion of our Lord, and to lay up in our memory with delight and profit, that his flesh was crucified and wounded for us.' As this was given for a rule by the great doctor of the Latin church, so the same maxim had been delivered almost two ages before him, by the great doctor of the Greek church, Origen, who says, 'that the understanding our Saviour's words of eating his flesh, and drinking his blood, according to the letter, is a letter that kills.' These passages I cite by an anticipation, before I enter upon the inquiry into the sense of the ancient church, concerning this matter; because they belong to the

Lib. iii. de Doct. Chris.c.16.

Hom. 7. in Levit.

ART. XXVIII. words of the institution, at least to the discourse in St. John: now if the sense that we give to these words is made good, we need be at no more pains to prove that they are capable of no other sense; since this must prove that to be the only true sense of them.

So that for all the arguments that have been brought by us against this doctrine, arising out of the fruitfulness of the matter, we were not bound to use them: for, our doctrine being confessed by them, it wants no proof; and we cannot be bound to prove a negative. Therefore though the copiousness of this matter has afforded us many arguments for the negative, yet that was not necessary: for as a negative always proves itself; so that holds more especially here, where that which is denied is accompanied with so many and so strange absurdities, as do follow from this doctrine.

The last topic in this matter is the sense that the ancient church had of it: for, as we certainly have both the scriptures and the evidence of our senses and reason of our side, so that will be much fortified, if it appears that no such doctrine was received in the first and best ages; and that it came in not all at once, but by degrees. I shall first urge this matter by some general presumptions; and then I shall go to plain proofs. But though the presumptions shall be put only as presumptions; yet if they appear to be violent, so that a man cannot hold giving his assent to the conclusion that follows from them, then though they are put in the form of presumptive arguments, yet that will not hinder them from being considered as concluding ones.

By the stating this doctrine it has appeared how many difficulties there are involved in it: these are difficulties that are obvious and soon seen: they are not found out by deep inquiry and much speculation: they are soon felt, and are very hardly avoided: and ever since the time that this doctrine has been received by the Roman church, these have been much insisted on; explanations have been offered to them all; and the whole principles of natural philosophy have been cast into a new mould, that they might ply to this doctrine: at least those, who have studied their philosophy in that system, have had such notions put in them, while their minds were yet tender and capable of any impressions, that they have been thereby prepared to this doctrine before they came to it, by a train of philosophical terms and distinctions, so that they were not much alarmed at it, when it came to be set before them.

They are accustomed to think that ubication, or the being in a place, is but an accident to a substance: so that the same body's being in more places, is only its having a few more of those accidents produced in it by God: they are accustomed to think that accidents are beings different from matter: like a sort of clothing to it, which do indeed require the having of a substance for their subject: but yet since ART. they are believed to have a being of their own, God may XXVIII. make them subsist: as the skin of a man may stand out in its proper shape and colour, though there were nothing but air or vacuity within it.

They are accustomed to think, that as an accident may be without its proper substance, so substance may be without its proper accidents; and they do reckon extension and impenetrability, that is, a body's so filling a space, that no other body can be in the same space with it, among its accidents: so that a body composed of organs and of large dimensions, may be not only all crowded within one wafer, but an entire distinct body may be in every separable part of this wafer; at least in every piece that carries in it the appearance of bread.

These, besides many other lesser subtilties, are the evident results of this doctrine: and it was a natural effect of its being received, that their philosophy should be so transformed as to agree to it, and to prepare men for it.

Now to apply this to the matter we are upon, we find none of these subtilties among the ancients. They seem to apprehend none of those difficulties, nor do they take any pains to solve or clear them. They had a philosophical genius, and shewed it in all other things: they disputed very nicely concerning the attributes of God, concerning his essence, and the Persons of the Trinity: they saw the difficulties concerning the incarnation of the Eternal Word, and Christ's being both God and man: they treat of original sin, of the power of grace, and of the decrees of God.

They explained the resurrection of our bodies, and the different states of the blessed and the damned.

They saw the difficulties in all these heads, and were very copious in their explanations of them: and they may be rather thought by some too full, than too sparing, in the canvassing of difficulties; but all those were mere speculative matters, in which the difficulty was not so soon seen as on this subject: yet they found these out, and pursued them with that subtilty that shewed they were not at all displeased, when occasions were offered them to shew their skill in answering difficulties: which, to name no more, appears very evidently to be St. Augustin's character. Yet neither he nor any of the other fathers seem to have been sensible of the difficulties in this matter.

They neither state them nor answer them; nor do they use those reserves when they speak of philosophical matters, that men must have used who were possessed of this doctrine: for a man cannot hold it without bringing himself to think and speak otherwise upon all natural things than the rest of mankind do.

They are so far from this, that, on the contrary, they deliver

ART.
XXVIII. themselves in a way that shews they had no such apprehensions of things.

They thought that all creatures were limited to one place: and from thence they argued against the heathens, who believed that their deities were in every one of those statues which they consecrated to them.

From this head they proved the divinity of the Holy Ghost; because he wrought in many different places at once: which he could not do if he were only a creature.

They affirm, that Christ can be no more on earth, since he is now in heaven, and that he can be but in one place.

They say, that which hath no bounds nor figure, and that can neither be touched nor seen, cannot be a body: that bodies are extended in some place, and cannot exist after the manner of spirits.

They argue against the eternity of matter, from this, that nothing could be produced, that had a being before it was produced; and on all occasions they appeal to the testimony of our senses as infallible.

They say, that to believe otherwise tended to reverse the whole state of life, and order of nature, and to reproach the providence of God; since it must be said, that he has given the knowledge of all his works to liars and deceivers, if our senses may be false: that we must doubt of our faith, if the testimony of hearing, seeing, and feeling, could deceive us.

And in their contests with the Marcionites and others, concerning the truth of Christ's body, they appeal always to the testimony of the senses as infallible; and even treating of the sacrament, they say, without limitation or exception, that it was bread, as their eyes witnessed, and true wine that Christ did consecrate to be the memorial of his body and blood; and they tell us in this very particular, that we ought not to doubt of the testimony of our senses.

Another presumptive proof, that the ancients knew nothing of this doctrine, is, that the heathens and the Jews, who charged them, and their doctrine, with every thing that they could invent to make both it and them odious and ridiculous, could never have passed over this, in which both sense and reason seemed to be so evidently on their side.

They reproach the Christians for believing a God that was born, a God of flesh that was crucified and buried: they laughed at their belief of a judgment to come, of endless flames, of a heavenly paradise, and of the resurrection of the body. Those who writ the first apologies for the Christian religion, Justin Martyr, Tertullian, Origen, Arnobius, and Minutius Felix, have given us a large account of the blasphemies both of Jews and Gentiles, against the doctrines of Christianity.

Cyril of Alexandria has given us Julian's objections in his

own words; who having been not only initiated into the Christian religion, but having read the scriptures in the churches, and being a philosophical and inquisitive man, must have been well instructed concerning the doctrine and the sacraments of this religion: and his relation to the emperor Constantine must have made the Christians concerned to take more than ordinary pains on him. When he made apostacy from the faith, he reproached the Christians with the doctrine of baptism, and laughed at them for thinking that there was an ablution and sanctification in it, conceiving it a thing impossible that water should wash or cleanse a soul: yet neither he nor Porphyry, nor Celsus before them, did charge this religion with the absurdities of transubstantiation.

ART. XXVIII.

It is reasonable to believe, that if the Christians of that time had any such doctrine among them, it must have been known. Every Christian must have known in what sense those words, 'This is my body,' and 'This is my blood,' were understood among them. All the apostates from Christianity must have known it, and must have published it, to excuse or hide the shame of their apostacy; since apostates are apt to spread lies of them whom they forsake, but not to conceal such truths as are to their prejudice. Julian must have known it; and if he had known it, his judgment was too true, and his malice to the Christian religion too quick, to overlook or neglect the advantages which this part of their doctrine gave him. Nor can this be carried off by saying, that the *eating of human flesh* and the *Thyestean suppers*, which were objected to the Christians, relate to this: when the fathers answer that, they tell the heathens that it was a downright calumny and lie: and do not offer any explanations or distinctions taken from their doctrine of the sacrament, to clear them from the mistake and malice of this calumny. The truth is, the execrable practices of the Gnostics, who were called Christians, gave the rise to those as well as to many other calumnies: but they were not at all founded on the doctrine of the eucharist, which is never once mentioned as the occasion of this accusation.

Another presumption, from which we conclude that the ancients knew nothing of this doctrine, is, that we find heresies and disputes arising concerning all the other points of religion: there were very few of the doctrines of the Christian religion, and not any of the mysteries of the faith, that did not fall under great objections: but there was not any one heresy raised upon this head: men were never so meek and tame as easily to believe things, when there appeared strong evidence, or at least great presumptions, against them. In these last eight or nine centuries, since this doctrine was received, there has been a perpetual opposition made to it, even in dark and unlearned ages; in which implicit faith and blind obedience have carried a great sway. And though the secular arm has been employed with great and unrelenting severities to extirpate all that have opposed it; yet all the while many have stood out against it, and have suffered much and long for their rejecting it. Now it is not to be imagined that such an opposition should have been made to this doctrine, during the nine hundred years last past, and that for the former eight hundred years there should have been no disputes at all concerning it: and that while all other things were so much questioned, that several fathers writ, and councils were called, to settle the belief of them, yet that for about eight hundred years, this was the single point that went down so easily, that no treatise was all that while writ to prove it, nor council held to establish it.

Certainly the reason of this will appear to be much rather, that since there have been contests upon this point these last nine ages, and that there were none the first eight, this doctrine was not known during those first ages; and that the great silence about it for so long a time, is a very strong presumption, that in all that time this doctrine was not thought of.

The last of those considerations that I shall offer, which are of the nature of presumptive proofs, is, that there are a great many rites and other practices, that have arisen out of this doctrine as its natural consequences, which were not thought of for a great many ages; but that have gone on by a perpetual progress, and have increased very fruitfully, ever since this doctrine was received. Such are the elevation, adoration, and processions, together with the doctrine of concomitance, and a vast number of rites and rubrics; the first occasions and beginnings of which are well known. These did all arise from this doctrine, it being natural, especially in the ages of ignorance and superstition, for men upon the supposition of Christ's being corporally present, to run out into all possible inventions of pomp and magnificence about this sacrament; and it is very reasonable to think, since these things are of so late and so certain a date, that the doctrine upon which they are founded is not much ancienter.

The great simplicity of the primitive forms, not only as they are reported by Justin Martyr and Tertullian in the ages of the poverty and persecutions of the church, but as they are represented to us in the fourth and fifth centuries by Cyril of Jerusalem, the Constitutions, and the pretended Areopagite, have nothing of that air that appears in the latter ages. The sacrament was then given in both kinds; it was put in the hands of the faithful; they reserved some portions of it: it was given to children for many ages: the laity and even boys were employed to carry it to dying penitents; what remained of it was burnt in some places, and consumed by the clergy, and by children in other places, the making cataplasms of it, the mixing the wine with ink, to sign the condemnation of heretics, are very clear presumptions that this doctrine was not then known.

ART. XXVIII.

But above all, their not adoring the sacrament, which is not done to this day in the Greek church, and of which there is no mention made by all those who writ of the offices of the church in the eighth and ninth centuries so copiously; this, I say, of their not adoring it, is perhaps more than a presumption, that this doctrine was not then thought on. But since it was established, all the old forms and rituals have been altered, and the adoring the sacrament is now become the main act of devotion and of religious worship, among them. One ancient form is indeed still continued, which is of the strongest kind of presumptions that this doctrine came in much later than some other superstitions which we condemn in that church. In the masses that are appointed on saints-days, there are some collects in which it is said, that the sacrifice is offered up in *honour to the saint;* and it is prayed, that it may become the *more valuable and acceptable, by the merits and intercessions of the saint.* Now when a practice will well agree with one opinion, but not at all with another, we have all possible reason to presume at least, that at first it came in under that opinion, with which it will agree, and not under another which cannot consist with it. Our opinion is, that the sacrament is a federal act of our Christianity, in which we offer up our highest devotions to God through Christ, and receive the largest returns from him: it is indeed a superstitious conceit to celebrate this to the honour of a saint; but howsoever upon the supposition of saints hearing our prayers, and interceding for us, there is still good sense in this: but if it is believed that Christ is corporally present, and that he is offered up in it, it is against all sense, and it approaches to blasphemy, to do this to the honour of a saint, and much more to desire that this, which is of infinite value, and is the foundation of all God's blessings to us, should receive any addition or increase in its value or acceptation from the *merits or intercession* of saints. So this, though a late practice, yet does fully evince, that the doctrine of the corporal presence was not yet thought on, when it was first brought into the office.

So far I have gone upon the presumptions that may be offered to prove that this doctrine was not known to the ancients. They are not only just and lawful presumptions, but they are so strong and violent, that when they are well considered, they force an assent to that which we infer from them. I go next to the more plain and direct proofs that we find of the opinion of the ancients in this matter.

They call the elements bread and wine after the consecration. Justin Martyr calls them *bread and wine, and a nourishment which nourished:* he indeed says it is not *common bread and wine;* which shews that he thought it was still so

Apolog. 2

ART. XXVIII.

in substance; and he illustrates the sanctification of the elements by the incarnation of Christ, in which the human nature did not lose or change its substance by its union with the divine: so the bread and the wine do not, according to that explanation, lose their proper *substance*, when they become the flesh and blood of Christ.

Lib. iv. de Hær. c. 34.

Irenæus calls it that *bread over which thanks are given*, and says, it is *no more common bread, but the eucharist consisting of two things, an earthly and a heavenly.*

Tertullian arguing against the Marcionites, who held two gods, and that the Creator of this earth was the bad god; but that Christ was contrary to him; urges against them this,

Lib. i. adv. Marcion. sect. 9.

that Christ made use of the creatures: and says, *he did not reject bread by which he represents his own body*: and in an-

Lib. iii. adv. Marcion. sect. 12.

other place he says, *Christ calls bread his body*, that from thence you may understand *that he gave the figure of his body to the bread.*

Lib. viii. contra Celsum.

Origen says, *We eat of the loaves that are set before us; which by prayer are become a certain holy body, that sanctifies those who use them with a sound purpose.*

Ep. 69.

St. Cyprian says, *Christ calls the bread that was compounded of many grains, his body; and the wine that is pressed out of many grapes, his blood, to shew the union of his people.* And

Ep. 63.

in another place, writing against those who used only water, but no wine, in the eucharist, he says, *We cannot see the blood by which we are redeemed, when wine is not in the chalice; by which the blood of Christ is shewed.*

In Anchoreto.

Epiphanius being to prove that man may be said to be made after the image of God, though he is not like him, urges this, *That the bread is not like Christ, neither in his invisible Deity, nor in his incarnate likeness, for it is round and without feeling as to its virtue.*

In orat. de Baptis. Christi.

Gregory Nyssen says, *The bread in the beginning is common; but after the mystery has consecrated it, it is said to be, and is, the body of Christ:* to this he compares the sanctification of the mystical oil, of the water in baptism, and the stones of an altar, or church, dedicated to God.

De Benedict. Patriarch. c. 9.

St. Ambrose calls it still bread; and says, this *bread is made the food of the saints.*

Hom. 24. in Ep. ad Cor.

St. Chrysostom on these words, *the bread that we break*, says, *What is the bread? The body of Christ: What are they made to be who take it? The body of Christ.* Which shews that he considered the bread as being so the body of Christ, as the worthy receivers became his body; which is done, not by a change of substance, but by a sanctification of their natures.

Comm. in Matt. c. 26.

St. Jerome says, *Christ took bread, that as Melchisedec had in the figure offered bread and wine, he might also represent the truth* (that is in opposition to the figure) *of his body and blood.*

St. Augustin does very largely compare the sacraments

being called the body and blood of Christ, with those other places in which the church is called his body, and all Christians are his members: which shews that he thought the one was to be understood mystically as well as the other. He calls the eucharist frequently our daily bread, and the sacrament of bread and wine. All these call the eucharist *bread and wine* in express words: but when they call it *Christ's body and blood*, they call it so *after a sort*, or that *it is said to be*, or with some other mollifying expression.

ART. XXVIII.

Cit. apud Fulgent. de Baptismo.

St. Augustin says this plainly, *After some sort the sacrament of the body of Christ is his body, and the sacrament of his blood is the blood of Christ; he carried himself in his own hands in some sort, when he said, This is my body.*

Aug. Ep. 23. ad Bonifac. Serm. 2. in Psal. 33.

St. Chrysostom says, *The bread is thought worthy to be called the body of our Lord:* and in another place, reckoning up the improper senses of the word *flesh*, he says, the scriptures used to call the *mysteries* (that is, the sacrament) *by the name of flesh, and sometimes the whole church is said to be the body of Christ.*

Chrys. Ep. ad Cæsar. et in Comm. in Ep. ad Gal. c. 5.

So Tertullian says, *Christ calls the bread his body, and names the bread by his body.*

Tertul. lib. iv. adv. Marc. sect. 60.

The fathers do not only call the consecrated elements bread and wine; they do also affirm, that they retain their proper nature and substance, and are the same thing as to their nature that they were before. And the occasion upon which the passages, that I go next to mention, are used by them, does prove this matter beyond contradiction.

Apollinaris did broach that heresy which was afterwards put in full form by Eutyches; and that had so great a party to support it, that as they had one general council (a pretended one at least) to favour them, so they were condemned by another. Their error was, that the human nature of Christ was swallowed up by the divine, if not while he was here on earth, yet at least after his ascension to heaven. This error was confuted by several writers who lived very wide one from another, and at a distance of above a hundred years one from another. St. Chrysostom at Constantinople, Theodoret in Asia, Ephrem patriarch of Antioch, and Gelasius bishop of Rome. All those write to prove that the human nature did still remain in Christ, not changed, nor swallowed up, but only sanctified by the divine nature that was united to it. They do all fall into one argument, which very probably those who came after St. Chrysostom took from him: so that though both Theodoret and Gelasius's words are much fuller, yet because the argument is the same with that which St. Chrysostom had urged against Apollinaris, I shall first set down his words. He brings an illustration from the doctrine of the sacrament, to shew that the human nature was not destroyed by its union with the divine; and has upon that these

Epist. ad Cæsarium.

ART. XXVIII.

words, As before the bread is sanctified, we call it bread; but when the divine grace has sanctified it by the means of the priest, it is freed from the name of bread, and is thought worthy of the name of the Lord's body, though the nature of bread remain in it: and yet it is not said there are two bodies, but one body of the Son: so the divine nature being joined to the body, both these make one Son and one Person.

In Phot. Bibl. Cod. 229.

Ephrem of Antioch says, *The body of Christ received by the faithful does not depart from its sensible substance: so baptism,* says he, *does not lose its own sensible substance, and does not lose that which it was before.*

Dial. 1. et 2. cont. Eutych.

Theodoret says, *Christ does honour the symbols with the name of his body and blood; not changing the nature, but adding grace to nature.* In another place pursuing the same argument, he says, *The mystical symbols after the sanctification do not depart from their own nature: for they continue in their former substance, figure, and form, and are visible and palpable as they were before; but they are understood to be that which they are made.*

Lib. de duabus nat. Christ.

Pope Gelasius says, *The sacraments of the body and blood of Christ are a divine thing; for which reason we become by them partakers of the divine nature: and yet the substance of bread and wine does not cease to exist: and the image and likeness of the body and blood of Christ are celebrated in holy mysteries.* Upon all these places being compared with the design with which they were written, which was to prove that Christ's human nature did still subsist, unchanged, and not swallowed up by its union with the divinity, some reflections are very obvious: first, if the corporal presence of Christ in the sacrament had been then received in the church, the natural and unavoidable argument in this matter, which must put an end to it, with all that believed such corporal presence, was this: Christ has certainly a natural body still, because the bread and the wine are turned to it; and they cannot be turned to that which is not. In their writings they argued against the possibility of a substantial change of a human nature into the divine; but that could not have been urged by men who believed a substantial mutation to be made in the sacrament; for then the Eutychians might have retorted the argument with great advantage upon them.

The Eutychians did make use of some expressions, that were used by some in the church, which seemed to import that they did argue from the sacrament, as Theodoret represents their objections. But to that he answers as we have seen, denying that any such substantial change was made. The design of those fathers was to prove, that things might be united together, and continue so united, without a change of their substances, and that this was true in the two natures in the person of Christ: and to make this more sensible, they bring in the matter of the sacrament, as a thing known and ART. confessed: for in their arguing upon it they do suppose it as XXVIII. a thing out of dispute.

Now, according to the Roman doctrine, this had been a very odd sort of an argument, to prove that Christ's human nature was not swallowed up of the divine; because the mysteries or elements in the sacrament are changed into the *substance of Christ's body, only they retain the outward appearances of bread and wine.*

To this an Eutychian might readily have answered, that then the human nature might be believed to be destroyed: and though Christ had appeared in that likeness, he retained only the accidents of human nature; but that the human nature itself was destroyed, as the *bread* and the *wine* were destroyed in the eucharist.

This had been a very absurd way of arguing in the fathers, and had indeed delivered up the cause to the Eutychians: whereas those fathers make it an argument against them, to prove, that notwithstanding an union of two beings, and such an union as did communicate a sanctification from the one to the other, yet the two *natures* might remain still distinguished; and that it was so in the *eucharist;* therefore it might be so in the person of Christ. This seems to be so evident an indication of the doctrine of the whole church in the fourth and fifth centuries, when so many of the most eminent writers of those ages do urge it so home as an argument in so great a point, that we can scarce think it possible for any man to consider it fully without being determined by it. And so far we have considered the authorities from the fathers, to shew that they believed that the substance of bread and wine did still remain in the sacrament.

Another head of proof is, that they affirm, that our bodies are nourished by the sacrament; which shews very plainly, that they had no notion of a change of substance made in it.

Justin Martyr calls the eucharist, *That food by which our* Apol. 1. *flesh and blood, through its transmutation into them, are nourished.*

Irenæus makes this an argument for the resurrection of our bodies, that they are fed by the body and blood of Christ: *When the cup and the bread receives the word of God, it be-* Lib. v. adv. *comes the eucharist of the body and blood of Christ, by which* Hæres. *the substance of our flesh is increased and subsists:* and he c. 4. adds, that *the flesh is nourished by the body and blood of Christ, and is made his member.*

Tertullian says, *The flesh is fed with the body and blood of* De Resur-*Christ.* rect. Carn. sect. 6.

Origen explains this very largely on those words of Christ, *It is not that which enters within a man, that defiles the man:* In Matt. c. he says, if every thing that goes into the belly is cast into the 15. draught, then *that food which is sanctified by the word of God,*

2 F

ART. XXVIII. and by prayer, goes also into the belly, as to that which is material in it, and goes from thence into the draught. And a little after he adds, *It is not the matter of the bread, but the word that is pronounced over it, which profits him that eats it, in such a way as is not unworthy of the Lord.*

16th Con. Tol. can. 6.

The bishops of Spain, in a council that sat at Toledo in the seventh century, condemned those that began to consecrate round wafers, and did not offer one entire loaf in the eucharist, and appointed, for so much of the bread as remained after the communion, that either it should be put in some bag, or if it was needful to eat it up, that *it might not oppress the belly of him that took it with an overcharging burden, and that it might not go into the digestion;* they fancying that a lesser quantity made no digestion, and produced no excrement.

In the ninth century both Rabanus Maurus and Heribald believed, that the sacrament was so digested, that some part of it turned to excrement, which was also held by divers writers of the Greek church, whom their adversaries called, by way of reproach, *stercoranists*. Others indeed of the ancients did think that no part of the sacrament became excrement, but that it was spread through the whole substance of the communicant, for the good of body and soul. Both Cyril of Jerusalem, St. Chrysostom, and John Damascene, fell into this conceit; but still they thought that it was changed into the substance of our bodies, and so nourished them without any excrement coming from any part of it.

Cyril. Catech. Myst. 5. Chrysost. Sermo de Pœnitent. et Eucharist. Damas. lib. iv. de Ortho. fide, c. 13.

The fathers do call the consecrated elements the *figures*, the *signs*, the *symbols*, the *types*, and *antitypes*, the *commemoration*, the *representation*, the *mysteries*, and the *sacraments*, of the body and blood; which does evidently demonstrate, that they could not think that they were the very substance of his body and blood. Tertullian, when he is proving that Christ had a true body, and was not a phantasm, argues thus, *He made bread to be his body, saying, This is my body; that is, the figure of my body*: from which he argues, that since his body had that for its *figure*, it was a true body; for an empty thing, such as a phantasm is, cannot have a *figure*. It is from hence clear, that it was not then believed that Christ's body was literally in the sacrament; for otherwise the argument would have been much clearer and shorter; Christ has a *true body*, because we believe that the sacrament is truly his *body*; than to go and prove it so far about, as to say a phantasm has no figure: but the sacrament is the figure of Christ's body, therefore it is no phantasm.

Lib. iv. adv. Marcion. sect. 60.

Ennarat. in Psal. iii.

St. Austin says, *He commended and gave to his disciples the figure of his body and blood.* And when the Manicheans objected to him, that *blood* is called in the Old Testament the *life* or *soul*, contrary to what is said in the New; he answers, that *blood* was not the *soul* or *life*, but only the sign of it;

and that the sign sometimes bears the name of that of which it is the sign: so says he, *Christ did not doubt to say, This is my body, when he was giving the sign of his body.* Now that had been a very bad argument, if the bread was truly the body of Christ; it had proved that the sign must be one with the thing signified.

ART XXVIII.
Lib. cont. Adimant. c. 12.

The whole ancient liturgies, and all the Greek fathers, do so frequently use the words *type, antitype, sign,* and *mystery,* that this is not so much as denied; it is their constant style. Now it is apparent that a thing cannot be the *type* and *symbol* of itself. And though they had more frequent occasions to speak of the eucharist, than either of baptism or the chrism; yet as they called the *water* and the *oil, types* and *mysteries,* so they bestowed the same descriptions on the elements in the eucharist; and as they have many strong expressions concerning the *water* and the *oil,* that cannot be literally understood: so upon the same grounds it will appear reasonable, to give the same exposition to some high expressions that they fell into concerning this sacrament. Facundus has some very full discourses to this purpose: he is proving that Christ may be called the *adopted Son of God,* as well as he is truly *his Son;* and that because he was baptized. *The sacrament of adoption, that is baptism, may be called baptism; as the sacrament of his body and blood, which is in the consecrated bread and cup, is called his body and blood: not that the bread is properly his body, or the cup properly his blood; but because they contain in them the mystery of his body and blood.* St. Austin says, *That sacraments must have some resemblance of those things of which they are the sacraments: so the sacrament of the body of Christ is after some manner his body; and the sacrament of his blood is after some manner his blood.* And speaking of the eucharist as a sacrifice of praise, he says, *The flesh and blood of this sacrifice was promised before the coming of Christ, by the sacrifices that were the types of it. In the passion the sacrifice was truly offered; and after his ascension it is celebrated by the sacrament of the remembrance of it.* And when he speaks of the murmuring of the Jews, upon our Saviour's speaking of giving his flesh to them, to eat it; he adds, *They foolishly and carnally thought, that he was to cut off some parcels of his body, to be given to them: but he shews that there was a sacrament hid there.* And he thus paraphrases that passage. *The words that I have spoken to you, they are spirit and life: understand spiritually that which I have said; for it is not this body which you see, that you are to eat, or to drink this blood which they shall shed, who crucify me. But I have recommended a sacrament to you, which being spiritually understood, shall quicken you: and though it be necessary that it be celebrated visibly, yet it must be understood invisibly.*

Defen. Conc. Chalced. l. 9. c. 5.

Ep. 23. ad Bonifac.

Lib. xx. con. Faust. c. 21.
Ennar. in Psal. xcviii. 5.

Primasius compares the sacrament to a pledge, which a dying man leaves to any one whom he loved. But that which

Comm. in 1 Ep. ad Cor.

ART. XXVIII.
Lib. iv. de Sacram. c. 5.

is more important than the quotation of any of the words of the fathers is, that the author of the books of the sacrament, which pass under the name of St. Ambrose, though it is generally agreed that those books were writ some ages after his death, gives us the prayer of consecration, as it was used in his time: he calls it the *heavenly words*, and sets it down. The offices of the church are a clearer evidence of the doctrine of that church than all the discourses that can be made by any doctor in it; the one is the language of the whole body, whereas the other are only the private reasonings of particular men: and, of all the parts of the office, the prayer of consecration is that which does most certainly set out to us the sense of that church that used it. But that which makes this remark the more important is, that the prayer, as set down by this pretended St. Ambrose, is very near the same with that which is now in the canon of the *mass*; only there is one very important variation, which will best appear by setting both down.

Ut supra. That of St. Ambrose is, *Fac nobis hanc oblationem, ascriptam, rationabilem, acceptabilem, quod est figura corporis et sanguinis Domini nostri Jesu Christi, qui pridie quam pateretur, &c.* That in the canon of the mass is, *Quam oblationem tu Deus in omnibus quæ sumus benedictam, ascriptam, ratam, rationabilem, acceptabilemque facere digneris: ut nobis corpus et sanguis fiat dilectissimi Filii tui Domini nostri Jesu Christi.*

We do plainly see so great a resemblance of the latter to the former of these two prayers, that we may well conclude, that the one was begun in the other; but at the same time we observe an essential difference. In the former this sacrifice is called the *figure of the body and blood of Christ*. Whereas in the latter it is prayed, that *it may become to us the body and blood of Christ*. As long as the former was the prayer of consecration, it is not possible for us to imagine, that the doctrine of the corporal presence could be received; for that which was believed to be the *true body and blood of Christ*, could not be called, especially in such a part of the office, *the figure of his body and blood*; and therefore the change that was made in this prayer was an evident proof of a change in the doctrine; and if we could tell in what age that was done, we might then upon greater certainty fix the time in which this change was made, or at least in which the inconsistency of that prayer with this doctrine was observed.

I have now set down a great variety of proofs reduced under different heads; from which it appears evidently that the fathers did not believe this doctrine, but that they did affirm the contrary very expressly. This sacrament continued to be so long considered as the figure or image of Christ's body, that the seventh general council, which met at Constantinople in the year 754, and consisted of above three hundred and thirty bishops, when it condemned the worship of images,

affirmed that this was the only *image* that we might lawfully ART.
have of Christ; and that he had appointed us to offer this XXVIII.
image of his body, to wit, the *substance of the bread*. That
was indeed contradicted with much confidence by the second
council of Nice, in which, in opposition to what appears to
this day in all the Greek liturgies, and the Greek fathers, they
do positively deny that the sacrament was ever called the
image of Christ: and they affirm it to be the *true body of
Christ*.

In conclusion, I shall next shew how this doctrine crept
into the church; for this seems plausible, that a doctrine of
this nature could never have got into the church in any age,
if those of the age that admitted it had not known that it had
been the doctrine of the former age, and so upwards to the
age of the apostles. It is not to be denied, but that very
early both Justin Martyr and Irenæus thought, that there was
such a sanctification of the elements, that there was a divine
virtue in them: and in those very passages which we have
urged from the arguings of the fathers against the Eutychians,
though they do plainly prove that they believed that the *substance of bread and wine* did still remain; yet they do suppose
an union of the elements to the body of Christ, like that of
the human nature's being united to the divine. Here a foundation was laid for all the superstructure that was afterwards
raised upon it. For though the liturgies and public offices
continued long in the first simplicity, yet the fathers, who did
very much study eloquence, chiefly the Greek fathers, carried
this matter very far in their sermons and homilies. They did
only apprehend the profanation of the sacrament, from the
unworthiness of those who came to it; and being much set
on the begetting a due reverence for so holy an action, and a
seriousness in the performance of it, they urged all the *topics*
that sublime figures or warm expressions could help them
with: and with this exalted eloquence of theirs we must
likewise observe the state that the world fell in in the fifth
century; vast swarms out of the north overrun the Roman
empire, and by a long continued succession of new invaders
all was sacked and ruined. In the west, the Goths were followed by the Vandals, the Alans, the Gepides, the Franks,
the Sweves, the Huns, and the Lombards, some of these
nations; and in the conclusion the Saracens and Turks in the
east made havoc of all that was polite or learned; by which
we lost the chief writings of the first and best times; but instead of these, many spurious ones were afterwards produced,
and they passed easily in dark and ignorant ages. All fell
under much oppression and misery, and Europe was so overrun with barbarity and ignorance, that it cannot be easily
apprehended, but by such as have been at the pains to go
through one of the ungratefullest pieces of study that can be
well imagined, and have read the productions of those ages.

ART. XXVIII. The understanding the scriptures, or languages, or history, was not so much as thought on. Some affected homilies or descantings on the rituals of the church, full of many very odd speculations about them, are among the best of the writings of those times. They were easily imposed on by any new forgery; witness the reception and authority that was given to the Decretal Epistles of the popes of the first three centuries; which for many ages maintained its credit, though it was plainly a forgery of the eighth century, and was contrived with so little art, that there is not in them colour enough to excuse the ignorance of those that were deceived by it. As it is an easy thing to mislead ignorant multitudes, so there is somewhat in incredible opinions and stories, that is suited to such a state of mankind: and as men are apt to fancy that they see sprights, especially in the night, so the more of darkness and unconceivableness that there is in an opinion, it is the more properly calculated for such times. The ages that succeeded were not only times of ignorance, but they were also times of much corruption. The writers of the fourth and fifth centuries give us dismal representations of the corruptions of their times; and the scandalous unconstancy of the councils of those ages, is too evident a proof of what we find said by the good men of those days: but things fell lower and lower in the succeeding ages. It is an amazing thing, that in the very office of consecrating bishops, examinations are ordered concerning those crimes, the very mention of which give horror; *De Coitu cum Masculo et cum Quadrupedibus.*

The popes more particularly were such a succession of men, that, as their own historians have described them, nothing in any history can be produced that is like them. The characters they give them are so monstrous, that nothing under the authority of unquestioned writers, and the evidence of the facts themselves, could make them credible.*

But that which makes the introduction of this doctrine appear the more probable is, that we plainly see the whole body of the clergy was every where so influenced by the management of the popes, that they generally entered into combinations to subject the temporalty to the spiritualty: and therefore every opinion that tended to render the persons of the clergy sacred, and to raise their character high, was sure to receive the best entertainment, and the greatest encouragement possible. Nothing could carry this so far as an opinion that represented the priest as having a character by which, with a few words, he could make a god. The opinion of *transubstantiation* was such an engine, that it being once set on foot, could not but meet with a favourable reception from those who were then seeking all possible

* See note, page 253.

colours to give credit to their authority, and to advance it. The numbers of the clergy were then so great, and their contrivances were so well suited to the credulity and superstition of those times, that, by visions and wonderful stories confidently vouched, they could easily infuse any thing into weak and giddy multitudes. Besides, that the genius of those times led them much to the love of pomp and show; they had lost the true power and beauty of religion, and were willing, by outward appearances, to balance and compensate for their great defects.

ART. XXVIII.

But besides all those general considerations, which such as are acquainted with the history of those ages know do belong to them in a much higher degree than is here set forth; there are some specialties that relate to this doctrine in particular, which will make the introduction of it appear the more practicable. This had never been condemned in any former age: for as none condemn errors by anticipation or prophecy; so the promoters of it had this advantage, that no formal decision had been made against them. It did also in the outward sound agree with the words of the institution, and the phrases generally used, of the elements being changed into the body and blood of Christ: outward sound and appearance was enough in ignorant ages to hide the change that was made. The step that is made from believing any thing in general, with an indistinct and confused apprehension, to a determined way of explaining it, is not hard to be brought about.

The people in general believed that Christ was in the sacrament, and that the elements were his body and blood, without troubling themselves to examine in what manner all this was done: so it was no great step in a dark age to put a particular explanation of this upon them: and this change being brought in without any visible alterations made in the worship, it must needs have passed with the world the more easily: for in all times visible rites are more minded by the people than speculative points, which they consider very little. No alterations were at first made in the worship; the adoration of the host, and the processions invented to honour it, came afterwards.

Honorius the IIId, who first appointed the adoration, does not pretend to found it on ancient practice: only he commands the priests to tell the people to do it: and he at first enjoined only an inclination of the head to the sacrament. But his successor, Gregory the IXth, did more resolutely command it, and ordered a bell to be rung at the consecration and elevation, to give notice of it, that so all those who heard it might kneel and join their hands, and so worship the host.

Greg. De cret. lib. iii. tit. 41. cap. 10.

The first controversy about the manner of the presence arose incidentally upon the controversy of images: the council at Constantinople decreed, that the sacrament was the *image of Christ, in which the substance of bread and wine remained.*

ART.
XXVIII. Those of Nice, how furiously soever they fell upon them for calling the sacrament the *image of Christ*, yet do no where blame them for saying that *the substance of bread and wine remained in it:* for indeed the opinion of Damascene, and of most of the Greek church, was, that *there was an assumption of the bread and wine into an union with the body of Christ.* The council of Constantinople brought in their decision occasionally, that being considered as the settled doctrine of the church; whereas those of Nice did visibly innovate and falsify the tradition: for they affirm, as Damascene had done before them, that the elements were called *antitypes of Christ's body*, only before they were consecrated, but not after it: which they say none of the fathers had done. This is so notoriously false, that no man can pretend now to justify them in it, since there are above twenty of the fathers that were before them, who in plain words call the elements after consecration, the *figure and antitype of Christ's body*: here then was the tradition and practice of the church falsified, which is no small prejudice against those that support the doctrine, as well as against the credit of that council.

About thirty years after that council, Paschase Radbert, abbot of Corby in France, did very plainly assert the corporal presence in the eucharist: he is acknowledged both by Bellarmine and Sirmondus to be the first writer that did on purpose advance and explain that doctrine: he himself values his pains in that matter; and as he laments the slowness of some in believing it, so he pretends that he had moved many to assent to it. But he confesses, that some blamed him for ascribing a sense to the words of Christ that was not consonant to truth. There was but one book writ in that age to second him; the name of the author was lost, till Mabillon discovered that it was writ by one Herigerus, abbot of Cob. But all the eminent men and the great writers of that time wrote plainly against this doctrine, and affirmed, that the bread and wine remained in the sacrament, and did nourish our bodies as other meats do. Those were Rabanus Maurus, archbishop of Mentz; Amalarius, archbishop of Triers; Heribald, bishop of Auxerre; Bertram, or Ratramne; John Scot Erigena; Walafridus Strabus; Florus, and Christian Druthmar. Three of these set themselves on purpose to refute Paschase.

Rabanus Maurus, in an epistle to abbot Egilon, wrote against Paschase for saying, that it was that body that was born of the Virgin, that was crucified and raised up again, which was daily offered up. And though that book is lost, yet as he himself refers his reader to it in his Penitential, so we have an account given of it by the anonymous defender of Paschase.

Ratramne was commanded by Charles the Bald, then emperor, to write upon that subject; which he in the beginning of his book promises to do, not trusting to his own sense, but following the steps of the holy fathers. He tells us, that there were different opinions about it: some believing that the body of Christ was there without a *figure;* others saying that it was there in a *figure,* or *mystery:* upon which he apprehended that a great schism must follow. His book is very short, and very plain: he asserts our doctrine as expressly as we ourselves can do: he delivers it in the same words, and proves it by many of the same arguments and authorities, that we bring.

ART. XXVIII.

Raban and Ratramne were, without dispute, reckoned among the first men of that age.

John Scot was also commanded by the same emperor to write on the same subject: he was one of the most learned and the most ingenious men of the age; and was in great esteem both with the emperor, and with our king Alfred. He was reckoned both a saint and a martyr. He did formerly refute Paschase's doctrine, and assert ours. His book is indeed lost; but a full account of it is given us by other writers of that time. And it is a great evidence, that his opinion in this matter was not then thought to be contrary to the general sense of the church in that age: for he having writ against St. Austin's doctrine concerning predestination, there was a very severe censure of him and of his writings published under the name of the church of Lyons: in which they do not once reflect on him for his opinions touching the eucharist. It appears from this, that their doctrine concerning the sacrament was then generally received; since both Ratramne and he, though they differed extremely in the point of predestination, yet both agreed in this. It is probable that the Saxon homily,* that was read in England on Easter-day, was taken from Scot's book; which does fully reject the corporal presence. This is enough to shew that Paschase's opinion was an innovation broached in the ninth century, and was opposed by all the great men of that age.

The tenth century was the blackest and most ignorant of all the ages of the church: there is not one writer in that age that gives us any clear account of the doctrine of the church: such remote hints as occur do still savour of Ratramne's doc-

* 'Throughout the whole of this Homily, the bread and wine are stated to be understood *ghostly* and *spiritually,* as the body and blood of Christ. Quoting 1 Cor. x. *They ate the same spiritual meat, and drank the same spiritual drink,* it is said, " Neither was that stone then from which the water ran *bodely Christ, but it* signified *Christ,* because that heavenly meat that fed them forty years, and that water which from the stone did flow, *had* SIGNIFICATION *of Christes bodye and his bloude,* that now be offered daylye in Godes church: it was the same which we now offer *not* BODELY *but* GHOSTLY. Moyses and Aaron saw that the heavenly meat was visible and corruptible; *and they understood it* SPIRITUALLY *and received it* SPIRITUALLY. The Saviour saith, *He that eateth my fleshe and drinketh my blood hath everlasting lyfe:* and He bade them eat, not that body which he was going about with, nor that blood to drink which he shed for us; *but he* MEANT *by that*

ART.
XXVIII.

trine. All men were then asleep, and so it was a fit time for the tares that Paschase had sown to grow up in it. The popes of that age were such a succession of monsters, that Baronius cannot forbear to make the saddest exclamations possible against their debaucheries, their cruelties, and their other vices. About the middle of the eleventh century, after this dispute had slept almost two hundred years, it was again revived.

Bruno bishop of Angiers, and Berengarius his archdeacon, maintained the doctrine of Ratramne. Little mention is made of the bishop; but the archdeacon is spoken of as a man of great piety; so that he passed for a saint, and was a man of such learning, that when he was brought before pope Nicolaus, no man could resist him. He writ against Paschase, and had many followers: the historians of that age tell us that his doctrine had overspread all France. The books writ against him by Lanfranc and others are filled with an impudent corrupting of all antiquity. Many councils were held upon this matter; and these, together with the terrors of burning, which was then beginning to be the common punishment of heresy, made him renounce his opinion: but he returned to it again; yet he afterwards renounced it: though Lanfranc reproached him, that it was not the love of truth, but the fear of death, that brought him to it. And his final retracting of that renouncing of his opinion is lately found in France, as I have been credibly informed. Thus this opinion, that in the ninth century was generally received, and was condemned by neither pope nor council, was become so odious in the eleventh century, that none durst own it: and he who had the courage to own it, yet was not resolute enough to stand to it: for about this time the doctrine of extirpating heretics, and of deposing such princes as were defective in that matter, was universally put in practice: great bodies of men began to separate from the Roman communion in the southern parts of France; and one of the chief points of their doctrine was their believing that Christ was not corporally present in the eucharist; and that he was there only in a *figure* or *mystery*. But now that the contrary doctrine

---

word the holy Eucharist, which SPIRITUALLY *is His body and His blood.* . . .
. . . . . In the old law faithful men offered God divers sacrifices that had for *signification* of Christes body; certainly this *Eucharist*, which we do now hallow at God's altar *is a* REMEMBRANCE *of Christ's body*, which he offered for us: *and of His blood which He shed for us.*"

For these extracts the Editor is indebted to Dr. Adam Clarke, who, in his 'Discourse on the nature and design of the Eucharist,' quotes them from a very rare work, intituled 'A Testimonie of Antiquitie, shewing the aunciente fayth in the Church of England, touching the Sacrament of the Body and Bloude of the Lorde here publikely preached, and also receaved in the Saxous' tyme, above 600 years ago. Imprinted at London, by John Day.' 18mo. without date, but known to have been printed in 1567. At the conclusion is an attestation signed by Matthew Parker, archbishop of Canterbury, Thomas archbishop of York, and thirteen other bishops.—[ED.]

was established, and that those who denied it were adjudged to be burnt, it is no wonder if it quickly gained ground, when on the one hand the priests saw their interest in promoting it, and all people felt the danger of denying it. The anathemas of the church, and the terrors of burning, were infallible things to silence contradiction at least, if not to gain assent.

ART. XXVIII.

Soon after this doctrine was received, the schoolmen began to refine upon it, as they did upon every thing else. The master of the sentences would not determine how Christ was present; whether formally or substantially, or some other way. Some schoolmen thought that the *matter* of bread was destroyed; but that the *form* remained, to be the *form* of Christ's body, that was the *matter* of it. Others thought that the *matter* of the elements remained, and that the *form* only was destroyed: but that to which many inclined, was the assumption of the elements into an union with the body of Christ, or a hypostatical union of the Eternal Word to them, by which they became as truly a body to Christ, as that which he has in heaven: yet it was not the same, but a different body.

Lib. iv. Dist. 11.

Stephen bishop of Autun was the first that fell on the word *transubstantiation*. Amalric, in the beginning of the thirteenth century, denied in express words the corporal presence: he was condemned in the fourth council of the Lateran as an heretic, and his body was ordered to be taken up and burnt: and in opposition to him transubstantiation was decreed. Yet the schoolmen continued to offer different explanations of this for a great while after that: but in conclusion all agreed to explain it as was formerly set forth. It appears, by the crude way in which it was at first explained, that it was a novelty; and that men did not know how to mould and frame it: but at last it was licked into shape; the whole philosophy being cast into such a mould as agreed with it. And therefore, in the present age, in which that philosophy has lost its credit, great pains are taken to suppress the new and freer way of philosophy, as that which cannot be so easily subdued to support this doctrine, as the old one was. And the arts, that those who go into the new philosophy take to reconcile their scheme to this doctrine, shew that there is nothing that subtile and unsincere men will not venture on: for, since they make *extension* to be of the *essence of matter*, and think that *accidents* are only the *modes of matter*, which have no proper being of themselves, it is evident, that a body cannot be without its *extension*, and that *accidents* cannot subsist without their subject; so that this can be in no sort reconciled to transubstantiation: and therefore they would willingly avoid this special manner of the presence, and only in general assert that Christ is corporally present. But the decrees of the Lateran and Trent councils make it evident, that *transubstantiation* is now a doctrine that is bound upon

De Sacram. Altaris, c. 13.

them by the authority of the church and of tradition; and that they are as much bound to believe it, as to believe the corporal presence itself. Thus the going off from the simplicity in which Christ did deliver the sacrament, and in which the church at first received it, into some sublime expressions about it, led men once out of the way, and they still went further and further from it. Pious and rhetorical figures, pursued far by men of heated imaginations and of inflamed affections, were followed with explanations invented by colder and more designing men afterwards, and so it increased till it grew by degrees to that to which at last it settled on.

But after all, if the doctrine of the corporal presence had rested only in a speculation, though we should have judged those who held it to be very bad philosophers, and no good critics; yet we could have endured it, if it had rested there, and had not gone on to be a matter of practice, by the adoration and processions, with every thing else of that kind, which followed upon it: for this corrupted the worship.

The Lutherans believe a consubstantiation, and that both Christ's body and blood, and the substance of the elements, are together in the sacrament: that some explain by an *ubiquity*, which they think is communicated to the human nature of Christ, by which his body is every where as well as in the sacrament: whereas others of them think, that since the words of Christ must needs be true in a literal sense, his body and blood is therefore in the sacrament, but *in*, *with*, and *under* the bread and wine. All this we think is ill grounded, and is neither agreeable to the words of the institution, nor to the nature of things. A great deal of that which was formerly set forth in defence of our doctrine falls likewise upon this. The *ubiquity* communicated to the human nature, as it seems a thing in itself impossible, so it gives no more to the sacrament than to every thing else. Christ's body may be said to be in every thing, or rather every thing may be said to be his *body* and *blood*, as well as the elements in the sacrament. The impossibility of a body's being without extension, or in more places at once, lies against this, as well as against *transubstantiation*. But yet, after all, this is only a point of speculation, nothing follows upon it in practice, no adoration is offered to the elements; and therefore we judge that speculative opinions may be borne with, when they neither fall upon the fundamentals of Christianity, to give us false ideas of the essential parts of our religion, nor affect our practice; and chiefly when the worship of God is maintained in its purity, for which we see God has expressed so particular a concern, giving it the word which of all others raises in us the most sensible and the strongest ideas, calling it *jealousy*; that we reckon we ought to watch over this with much caution. We can very well bear with some opinions, that we think ill grounded, as long as they are only matters

THE XXXIX ARTICLES. 445

of opinion, and have no influence neither on men's morals ART XXVIII nor their worship. We still hold communion with bodies of men, that, as we judge, think wrong, but yet do both live well, and maintain the purity of the worship of God. We know the great design of religion is to govern men's lives, and to give them right ideas of God, and of the ways of worshipping him. All opinions that do not break in upon these, are things in which great forbearance is to be used; large allowances are to be made for men's notions in all other things; and therefore we think that neither *consubstantiation* nor *transubstantiation*, how ill grounded soever we take both to be, ought to dissolve the union and communion of churches: but it is quite another thing, if under either of these opinions an adoration of the elements is taught and practised.*

This we believe is plain idolatry, when an insensible piece of matter, such as bread and wine, has divine honours paid it: when it is believed to be God, when it is called God, and is in all respects worshipped with the same adoration that is offered up to Almighty God. This we think is gross idolatry. Many writers of the church of Rome have acknowledged, that if *transubstantiation* is not true, their worship is a strain of idolatry beyond any that is practised among the most depraved of all the heathens.

The only excuse that is offered in this matter is, that since the declared object of worship is Jesus Christ, believed to be there *present*, then, whether he is *present* or *not*, the worship terminates in him; both the secret acts of the worshippers, and the professed doctrine of the church, do lodge it there. And therefore it may be said, that though he should not be actually present, yet the act of adoration being directed to him must be accepted of God, as right meant, and duly directed, even though there should happen to be a mistake in the outward application of it.†

---

* See note, pp. 417, 418.

† This vain pretence of worshipping on condition that the consecrated bread is Christ, is thus met and ably refuted by Bishop Taylor:—

'I will not censure the men that do it, or consider concerning the action whether it be *formal idolatry* or no. God is their judge and mine, and I beg he would be pleased to have mercy upon us all; but yet they that are interested, for their own particulars, ought to fear and consider these things. 1. That no man, without his own fault, can mistake a creature so far, as to suppose him to be a God. 2. That when the heathens worshipped the sun and moon, they did it upon their confidence that they were gods, and would not have given to them divine honours, if they had thought otherwise. 3. That the distinction of material and formal idolatry, though it have a place in philosophy, because the understanding can consider an act with its error, and yet separate the parts of the consideration; yet hath no place in divinity, because in things of so great concernment it cannot but be supposed highly agreeable to the goodness and justice of God, that every man be sufficiently instructed in his duty and convenient notices. 4. That no man in the world upon these grounds, except he that is malicious and spiteful, can be an idolater; for if he have an ignorance great enough to excuse him, he can be no idolater; if he have not, he is spiteful and malicious; and then all the heathen are also excused as well as they. 5. That if good intent and ignorance in such cases can take off

ART. XXVIII.

In answer to this, we do not pretend to determine how far this may be pardoned by God; whose mercies are infinite, and who does certainly consider chiefly the hearts of his creatures, and is merciful to their infirmities, and to such errors as arise out of their weakness, their hearts being sincere before him. We ought to consider this action as it is in itself, and not according to men's apprehensions and opinions about it. If the conceits that the ancient idolaters had both concerning their gods, and the idols that they worshipped, will excuse from idolatry, it will be very hard to say that there were ever any idolaters in the world. Those who worshipped the sun, thought that the great divinity was lodged there, as in a vehicle or temple; but yet they were not by reason of that misconception excused from being idolaters.

If a false opinion upon which a practice is founded, taken up without any good authority, will excuse men's sins, it will be easy for them to find apologies for every thing. If the worship of the elements had been commanded by God, then an opinion concerning it might excuse the carrying of that too far; but, there being no command for it, no hint given about it, nor any insinuation given of any such practice in the beginnings of Christianity, an opinion that men have taken up cannot justify a new practice, of which neither the first, nor a great many of the following ages knew any thing. An opinion cannot justify men's practice founded upon it, if that proves to be false. All the softening that can be given it is, that it is a sin of ignorance; but that does not change the nature of the action, how far soever it may go with relation to the judgments of God: if the opinion is rashly taken up

---

the crime, then the persecutors that killed the apostles, thinking they did God good service, and Saul in blaspheming the religion and persecuting the servants of Jesus, and the Jews themselves in crucifying the Lord of life, *who did it ignorantly as did also their rulers*, have met with the excuse upon the same account. And therefore it is not safe for the men of the Roman communion to take anodyne medicines and narcotics to make them insensible of the pain; for it will not cure their disease. Their doing it upon the cloak of error and ignorance, I hope will dispose them to receive a pardon; but yet also that supposes them criminal; and although I would not for all the world be their accuser, or the aggravator of the crime; yet I am not unwilling to be the remembrancer, that themselves may avoid the danger. For though Jacob was innocent in lying with Leah instead of Rachel, because he had no cause to suspect the deception, yet if Penelope, who had not seen Ulysses in twenty years, should see one come to her nothing like Ulysses, but saying he were her husband, she should give but a poor account of her chastity if she should actually admit him to her bed, only saying, if you be Ulysses, or on supposition that you are Ulysses, I admit you. For if she certainly admits him, of whom she is uncertain, she certainly is an adultress; because she having reason to doubt, ought first to be satisfied of her question. Since therefore besides the insuperable doubts of the main article itself, in the practice and particulars there are acknowledged so many ways of deception, and confessed that the actual failings are frequent, it will be but a weak excuse to say, I worship thee if thou be the Son of God; and I do not worship thee if thou beest not consecrated; *and, in the mean time, the Divine worship is actually exhibited to what is set before us.* At the best we may say to these men, as our blessed Saviour to the woman of Samaria, " ye worship ye know not what; but we know what to worship."'—[ED.]

and stiffly maintained, the worship that is introduced upon it ART.
is aggravated by the ill foundation that it is built upon. We XXVIII.
know God by his essence is every where; but this will not
justify our worshipping any material object upon this pretence,
because God is in it; we ought never to worship him towards
any visible object, unless he were evidently declaring his
glory in it; as he did to Moses in the flaming bush; to the
Israelites on mount Sinai, and in the cloud of glory; or to us
Christians in a sublimer manner in the human nature of Jesus
Christ.

But by this parity of reason, though we were sure that
Christ were in the elements, yet since he is there invisible, as
God is by his essence every where, we ought to direct no
adoration to the elements; we ought only to worship God,
and his Son Christ Jesus, in the grateful remembrance of his
sufferings for us; which are therein commemorated. We
ought not to suffer our worship to terminate on the visible
elements; because if Christ is in them, yet he does not manifest that visibly to us: since therefore the opinion of the
corporal presence, upon which this adoration is founded, is
false, and since no such worship is so much as mentioned,
much less commanded in scripture; and since there can scarce
be any idolatry in the world so gross, as that it shall not
excuse itself by some such doctrine, by which all the acts of
worship are made to terminate finally in God; we must conclude that this plea cannot excuse the church of Rome from
idolatry, even though their doctrine of the corporal presence
were true; but much less if it is false. We do therefore condemn this worship as idolatry, without taking upon us to
define the extent of the mercies of God towards all those who
are involved in it.

If all the premises are true, then it is needless to insist
longer on explaining the following paragraph of the Article;
that *Christ's body is received in the sacrament in a heavenly
and spiritual manner, and that the mean by which it is received
is faith;* for that is such a natural result of them, that it
appears evident of itself, as being the conclusion that arises
out of those premises.

The last paragraph is against the *reserving, carrying about,
the lifting up, or the worshipping, the sacrament.* The point
concerning the worship, which is the most essential of them,
has been already considered. As for the reserving or carrying
the sacrament about, it is very visible that the institution is,
'Take, eat,' and 'drink ye all of it;' which does import, that
the consuming the elements is a part of the institution, and,
by consequence, that they are a sacrament only as they are
distributed and received. It is true, the practice of *reserving*
or sending about the elements began very early; the state of
things at first made it almost unavoidable. When there
were yet but a few converted to Christianity, and when there

were but few priests to serve them, they neither could nor durst meet altogether, especially in the times of persecution; so some parts of the elements were sent to the absent, to those in prison, and particularly to the sick, as a symbol of their being parts of the body, and that they were in the peace and communion of the church. The bread was sent with the wine, and it was sent about by any person whatsoever; sometimes by boys; as appears in the famous story of Serapion in the third century. So that the condition of the Christians in that time made that necessary, to keep them all in the sense of their obligation to union and communion with the church; and that could not well be done in any other way. But we make a great difference between this practice, when taken up out of necessity, though not exactly conform to the first institution: and the continuing it out of superstition, when there is no need of it. Therefore instead of consecrating a larger portion of elements than is necessary for the occasion, and the reserving what is over and above; and the setting that out with great pomp on the altar, to be worshipped, or the carrying it about with a vast magnificence in a procession invented to put the more honour on it; or the sending it to the sick with solemnity; we choose rather to consecrate only so much as may be judged fit for the number of those who are to communicate. And when the sacrament is over, we do, in imitation of the practice of some of the ancients, consume what is left, that there may be no occasion given either to superstition or irreverence. And for the *sick*, or the *prisoners*, we think it is a greater mean to quicken their devotion, as well as it is a closer adhering to the words of the institution, to consecrate in their presence: for though we can bear with the practice of the Greek church, of reserving and sending about the eucharist, when there is no idolatry joined with it; yet we cannot but think that this is the continuance of a practice, which the state of the first ages introduced, and that was afterwards kept up, out of a too scrupulous imitation of that time; without considering that the difference of the state of the Christians, in the former and in the succeeding ages, made that what was at first innocently practised (since a real necessity may well excuse a want of exactness in some matters that are only positive) became afterwards an occasion of much superstition, and in conclusion ended in idolatry. Those ill effects that it had are more than is necessary to justify our practice in reducing this strictly to the first institution.

As for the lifting up of the eucharist, there is not a word of it in the gospel; nor is it mentioned by St. Paul: neither Justin Martyr nor Cyril of Jerusalem speak of it; there is nothing concerning it neither in the Constitutions, nor in the Areopagite. In those first ages all the elevation that is spoken of is, the lifting up of their hearts to God. The elevation of the sacrament began to be practised in the sixth century; for it is mentioned in the liturgy called St. Chrysostom's, but believed to be much later than his time. German, a writer of the Greek church of the thirteenth century, is the first that descants upon it: he speaks not of it as done in order to the adoration of it, but makes it to represent both Christ's being lifted up on the cross, and also his resurrection. Ivo of Chartres, who lived in the end of the eleventh century, is the first of all the Latins that speaks of it; but then it was not commonly practised; for the author of the Micrologus, though he writ at the same time, yet does not mention it, who yet is very minute upon all particulars relating to this sacrament. Nor does Ivo speak of it as done in order to adoration, but only as a form of shewing it to the people. Durand, a writer of the thirteenth century, is the first that speaks of the *elevation* as done in order to the *adoration*. So it appears that our church, by cutting off these abuses, has restored this sacrament to its primitive simplicity, according to the institution and the practice of the first ages.

ART. XXVIII.

Germ.
Const. in Theor.
Tit. 12.
Bibl. patr.
Ivo. Carn.
Ep-deSacr.
Missæ. t. ii.
Bibl. pat.

Dur. Rat.
div. Offic.
lib. iv. de sexta parte Can.

ARTICLE XXIX.

Of the wicked which eat not the Body of Christ in the use of the Lord's Supper.

𝕮𝖍𝖊 𝖂𝖎𝖈𝖐𝖊𝖉 𝖆𝖓𝖉 𝖘𝖚𝖈𝖍 𝖆𝖘 𝖇𝖊 𝖛𝖔𝖎𝖉 𝖔𝖋 𝖆 𝖑𝖎𝖛𝖊𝖑𝖞 𝖋𝖆𝖎𝖙𝖍, 𝖆𝖑𝖙𝖍𝖔𝖚𝖌𝖍 𝖙𝖍𝖊𝖞 𝖉𝖔 𝖈𝖆𝖗𝖓𝖆𝖑𝖑𝖞 𝖆𝖓𝖉 𝖛𝖎𝖘𝖎𝖇𝖑𝖞 𝖕𝖗𝖊𝖘𝖘 𝖜𝖎𝖙𝖍 𝖙𝖍𝖊𝖎𝖗 𝖙𝖊𝖊𝖙𝖍 (𝖆𝖘 𝕾𝖙. 𝕬𝖚𝖘𝖙𝖎𝖓 𝖘𝖆𝖎𝖙𝖍) 𝖙𝖍𝖊 𝕾𝖆𝖈𝖗𝖆𝖒𝖊𝖓𝖙 𝖔𝖋 𝖙𝖍𝖊 𝕭𝖔𝖉𝖞 𝖆𝖓𝖉 𝕭𝖑𝖔𝖔𝖉 𝖔𝖋 𝕮𝖍𝖗𝖎𝖘𝖙, 𝖞𝖊𝖙 𝖎𝖓 𝖓𝖔 𝖜𝖎𝖘𝖊 𝖆𝖗𝖊 𝖙𝖍𝖊𝖞 𝕻𝖆𝖗𝖙𝖆𝖐𝖊𝖗𝖘 𝖔𝖋 𝕮𝖍𝖗𝖎𝖘𝖙; 𝖇𝖚𝖙 𝖗𝖆𝖙𝖍𝖊𝖗, 𝖙𝖔 𝖙𝖍𝖊𝖎𝖗 𝖈𝖔𝖓𝖉𝖊𝖒𝖓𝖆𝖙𝖎𝖔𝖓, 𝖉𝖔 𝖊𝖆𝖙 𝖆𝖓𝖉 𝖉𝖗𝖎𝖓𝖐 𝖙𝖍𝖊 𝕾𝖎𝖌𝖓 𝖔𝖗 𝕾𝖆𝖈𝖗𝖆𝖒𝖊𝖓𝖙 𝖔𝖋 𝖘𝖔 𝖌𝖗𝖊𝖆𝖙 𝖆 𝕿𝖍𝖎𝖓𝖌.

THIS Article arises naturally out of the former, and depends upon it: for if Christ's body is corporally present in the sacrament, then all persons good or bad, who receive the sacrament, do also receive Christ: on the other hand, if Christ is present only in a *spiritual manner*, and if the mean that receives Christ is *faith*, then such as believe not, do not receive him. So that to prove that the wicked do not receive Christ's body and blood, is upon the matter the same thing with the proving that he is not corporally present; and it is a very considerable branch of our argument by which we prove that the fathers did not believe the corporal presence, because they do very often say, that the wicked do not receive Christ in the sacrament.

Here the same distinction is to be made that was mentioned upon the article of baptism. The sacraments are to be considered either as they are acts of church-communion, or as they are federal acts, by which we enter into covenant with God. With respect to the former, the visible profession that is made, and the action that is done, are all that can fall under human cognizance: so a sacrament must be held to be good and valid, when, as to outward appearance, all things are done according to the institution: but as to the internal effect and benefit of it; that turns upon the truth of the profession that is made, and the sincerity of those acts which do accompany it: for, if these are not seriously and sincerely performed, God is dishonoured, and his institution is profaned. Our Saviour has expressly said, that 'whosoever eats his flesh, and drinks his blood, has eternal life.' From thence we conclude, that no man does truly receive Christ, who does not at the same time receive with him both a right to eternal life, and likewise the beginnings and earnests of it. The sacrament being a federal act, he who dishonours God, and profanes this institution, by receiving it unworthily, becomes highly guilty before God, and draws down judgments upon himself: and as it is confessed on all hands, that the inward and spiritual effects of the sacrament depend upon the state and disposition of him that communicates, so we, who own no other presence but an inward and spiritual one, cannot conceive that the wicked, who believe not in Christ, do receive him.

In this point several of the fathers have delivered themselves very plainly.

Origen says, *Christ is the true food, whosoever eats him shall live for ever; of whom no wicked person can eat; for if it were possible that any who continues wicked should eat the Word that was made flesh, it had never been written, Whoso eats this bread shall live for ever.* This comes after a discourse of the sacrament, which he calls the typical and symbolical body, and so it can only belong to it. In another place he says, *The good eat the living bread, which came down from heaven; but the wicked eat dead bread, which is death.* [Comment. in Matth. c. 15.]

Zeno, bishop of Verona, who is believed to have lived near Origen's time, has these words: *There is cause to fear that he, in whom the Devil dwells, does not eat the flesh of our Lord, nor drink his blood; though he seems to communicate with the faithful; since our Lord has said, He that eats my flesh, and drinks my blood, dwells in me, and I in him.* [D'Achery. Spicilegium. Tom. ii.]

St. Jerome says, *They that are not holy in body and spirit, do neither eat the flesh of Jesus, nor drink his blood; of which he said, He that eats my flesh, and drinks my blood, hath eternal life.* [In cap. 66. Isaiæ.]

St. Augustin expresses himself in the very words that are cited in the Article, which he introduces with these words: *He that does not abide in Christ, and in whom Christ does not abide, certainly does not spiritually eat his flesh, nor drink his blood, though he may visibly and carnally press with his teeth the sacrament of the body and blood of Christ: but he rather eats and drinks the sacrament of so great a matter to his condemnation.* And in another place he says, *Neither are they* (speaking of vicious persons) *to be said to eat the body of Christ, because they are not his members:* to which he adds, *He that says, Whoso eats my flesh, and drinks my blood, abides in me, and I in him, shews what it is not only in a sacrament, but truly to eat the body of Christ, and to drink his blood.* He has upon another occasion those frequently cited words, speaking of the difference between the other disciples and Judas, in receiving this sacrament: *These did eat the bread that was the Lord (panem Dominum); but he the bread of the Lord against the Lord (panem Domini contra Dominum).* [Tract. 26. in Joan.] [Lib xxi. de Civ. Dei, c. 25.] [Tract. 54. in Joan.] To all this a great deal might be added, to shew that this was the doctrine of the Greek church, even after Damascene's opinion concerning the assumption of the elements into an union with the body of Christ, was received among them. But more needs not be said concerning this, since it will be readily granted, that, if we are in the right in the main point of denying the corporal presence, this will fall with it.

ARTICLE XXX.

Of both Kinds.

The Cup of the Lord is not to be denied to Lay People. For both Parts of the Sacrament, by Christ's Ordinance and Commandment, ought to be ministred to all Christian Men alike.

THERE is not any one of all the controversies that we have with the church of Rome, in which the decision seems more easy and shorter than this. The words of the institution are not only equally express and positive as to both kinds, but the diversity with which that part that relates to the *cup* is set down, seems to be as clear a demonstration for us, as can be had in a matter of this kind: and looks like a special direction given, to warn the church against any corruption that might arise upon this head. To all such as acknowledge the immediate union of the Eternal Word with the human nature of Christ, and the inspiration by which the apostles were conducted, it must be of great weight to find a specialty marked as to the chalice: of the cup it is said, 'Drink ye all of it;' whereas of the bread it is only said, 'Take, eat;' so we cannot think the word *all* was set down without design. It is also said of the cup, 'and they all drank of it;' which is not said of the bread: we think it no piece of trifling nicety to observe this specialty. The words added to the giving the cup are very particularly emphatical. 'Take, eat, This is my body which is given for you,' is not so full an expression as, 'Drink ye all of this, for this is my blood of the new testament which is shed for many, for the remission of sins.' If the surest way to judge of the extent of any precept, to which a reason is added, is to consider the extent of the reason, and to measure the extent of the precept by that; then since all that do communicate, need the remission of sins, and a share in the *new covenant*, the reason, that our Saviour joins to the distribution of the cup, proves that they ought all to receive it. And if that discourse in St. John concerning the eating Christ's flesh, and the drinking his blood, is to be understood of the sacrament, as most of the Roman church affirm, then the *drinking Christ's blood* is as necessary to *eternal life* as the *eating his flesh;* by consequence it is as necessary to receive the cup as the bread. And it is not easy to apprehend why it should still be necessary to consecrate in both kinds, and not likewise to receive in both kinds. It cannot be pretended, that since the apostles were all of the sacred order, therefore their receiving in both kinds is no precedent for giving the laity the cup; for Christ gave them both kinds, as they were sinners who were now to be admitted into covenant with God by the sacrifice of his body and blood. They were in that 'to shew forth his death,' and were to 'take, eat, and drink, in remembrance of him.' So that this institution was delivered to them as they were *sinners*, and not as they were *priests*. They were not constituted by Christ the pastors and governors of his Church, till after his resurrection, when 'he breathed on them, and laid his hands on them, and blessed them.' So that at this time they were only Christ's disciples and witnesses; who had been once sent out by him on an extraordinary commission; but had yet no stated character fixed upon them.

ART. XXX.

John xx. 22.

To this it is said, that Christ, by saying, 'Do this,' constituted them *priests ;* so that they were no more of the laity, when they received the cup. This is a new conceit taken up by the schoolmen unknown to all antiquity: there is no sort of tradition that supports this exposition; nor is there any reason to imagine, that 'Do this,' signifies any other than a precept to continue that institution as a memorial of Christ's death; and 'Do this,' takes in all that went before, the *taking*, the *giving*, as well as the *blessing*, and the *eating*, the bread; nor is there any reason to appropriate this to the blessing only, as if by this the consecrating and sacrificing power were conferred on the priests. From all which we conclude both that the apostles were only disciples at large, without any special characters conferred on them, when the eucharist was instituted, and that the eucharist was given to them only as disciples, that is, as laymen.

The mention that is made, in some places of the New Testament, only of 'breaking of bread,' can furnish them with no argument; for it is not certain that these do relate to the sacrament; or if they did, it is not certain that they are to be understood strictly; for, by a figure common to the eastern nations, *bread* stands for all that belongs to a meal; and if these places are applied to the sacrament, and ought to be strictly understood, they will prove too much, that the sacrament may be consecrated in one kind; and that the 'breaking of bread,' without the *cup*, may be understood to be a complete sacrament. But when St. Paul spoke of this sacrament, he does so distinctly mention the 'drinking the cup' as well as 'eating the bread,' that it is plain from him how the apostles understood the words and intent of Christ, and how this sacrament was received in that time.

From the institution and command, which are express and positive, we go next to consider the nature of sacramental actions. They have no virtue in them, as charms tied either to elements, or to words; they are only good because commanded. A different state of things may indeed justify an alteration as to circumstances: the danger of *dipping* in cold

ART.
XXX.

climates, may be a very good reason for changing the form of baptism to *sprinkling;* and if climates were inhabited by Christians to which wine could not be brought, we should not doubt but that whensoever God makes a real necessity of departing from any institution of his, he does thereby allow of such a change, as that necessity must draw after it: so we do not condemn the license that is said to have been granted by pope Innocent the Eighth to celebrate without wine in Norway; nor should we deny a man the sacrament who had a natural and unconquerable aversion to wine, or that communicated being near his last agonies, and that should have the like aversion to either of the elements. When those things are real, and not pretended, *mercy is better than sacrifice.* The punctual observance of a sacramental institution does only oblige us to the essential parts of it, and in ordinary cases: the pretence of what may be done, or has been done, upon extraordinary occasions, can never justify the deliberate and unnecessary alteration of an essential part of the sacrament. The whole institution shews very plainly, that our Saviour meant that the *cup* should be considered every whit as essential as *bread;* and therefore we cannot but conclude from the nature of things, that since the sacraments have only their effects from their institution, therefore so total a change of this sacrament does plainly evacuate the institution, and by consequence destroy the effect of it.

All reasoning upon this head is an arguing against the institution; as if Christ and his apostles had not well enough considered it; but that 1200 years after them, a consequence should be observed that till then had not been thought of, which made it reasonable to alter the manner of it.

The *concomitance* is the great thing that is here urged; since it is believed that Christ is entirely under each of the elements; and therefore it is not necessary that both should be received, because Christ is fully received in any one. But this subsists on the doctrine of *transubstantiation;* so if that is false, then here upon a controverted opinion, an uncontroverted piece of the institution is altered. And if *concomitance* is a certain consequence of the doctrine of *transubstantiation,* then it is a very strong argument against the antiquity of that doctrine, that the world was so long without the notion of *concomitance;* and therefore, if *transubstantiation* had been sooner received, the *concomitance* would have been more easily observed. The institution of the sacrament seems to be so laid down, as rather to make us consider the *body* and *blood* as in a state of separation, than of concomitance; the *body* being represented apart, and the *blood* apart; and the *body as broken,* and the *blood as shed.* Therefore we consider the design of the sacrament is, to represent Christ to us as dead, and in his *crucified,* but

THE XXXIX ARTICLES. 455

not in his *glorified* state. And if the opinion be true, that
the glorified bodies are of another texture than that of flesh
and blood which seems to be very plainly asserted by St.
Paul, in a discourse intended to describe the nature of the
glorified bodies, then this theory of concomitance will fail
upon that account. But whatsoever may be in that, an
institution of Christ's must not be altered or violated, upon
the account of an inference that is drawn to conclude it needless. He who instituted it knew best what was most fitting
and most reasonable; and we must choose rather te acquiesce
in his commands, than in our own reasonings.

ART. XXX.

If, next to the institution and the theory that arises from
the nature of a sacrament, we consider the practice of the
Christian church in all ages, there is not any one point in
which the tradition of the church is more express and more
universal than in this particular, for above a thousand years
after Christ. All the accounts that we have of the ancient
rituals, both in Justin Martyr, Cyril of Jerusalem, the Constitutions, and the pretended Areopagite, do expressly mention both kinds as given separately in the sacrament. All
the ancient liturgies, as well these that go under the names of
the apostles, as those which are ascribed to St. Basil and St.
Chrysostom, do mention this very expressly; all the offices
of the western church, both Roman and others; the missals
of the latter ages, I mean down to the twelfth century, even
the *Ordo Romanus*, believed by some to be a work of the
ninth, and by others of the eleventh century, are express in
mentioning the distribution of both kinds. All the fathers,
without excepting one, do speak of it very clearly, as the universal practice of their time. They do not so much as give a
hint of any difference about it. So that, from Ignatius down
to Thomas Aquinas, there is not any one writer that differs
from the rest in this point; and even Aquinas speaks of the
taking away the chalice as the practice only of some churches;
other writers of his time had not heard of any of these
churches; for they speak of *both kinds* as the universal
practice.

Apol. 2.
Catech.
Mis. 4 ta.
Const.
Apost. l. ii.
c. 57.
Eccles.
Hiera. c. 3.

Aquin.
Com. in
6. Johan. v.
53. InSum-
ma. par. 9.
quæst. 80.
art. 12.

But besides this general concurrence, there are some
specialties in this matter: in St. Cyprian's time some thought
it was not necessary to use *wine* in the sacrament; they
therefore used *water* only, and were from thence called
Aquarii. It seems they found that their morning assemblies
were smelled out by the *wine* used in the sacrament; and
Christians might be known by the smell of *wine* that was still
about them; they therefore intended to avoid this, and so
they had no wine among them, which was a much weightier
reason, than that of the wine sticking upon the beards of the
laity. Yet St. Cyprian condemned this very severely, in a
long epistle writ upon that occasion. He makes this the
main argument, and goes over it frequently, that we ought to

Cyp. Ep.
63. ad
Cecil.

ART. XXX.

follow Christ, and do what he did: and he has those memorable words, *If it be not lawful to loose any one of the least commands of Christ, how much more is it unlawful to break so great and so weighty a one; that does so very nearly relate to the sacrament of our Lord's passion, and of our redemption; or by any human institution to change it into that which is quite different from the divine institution.* This is so full, that we cannot express ourselves more plainly.

Among the other profanations of the Manicheans, this was one, that they came among the assemblies of the Christians, and did receive the bread, but they would not take any wine: this is mentioned by pope Leo in the fifth century; upon which pope Gelasius, hearing of it in his time, appointed that all persons should either communicate in the sacrament *entirely*, or be *entirely* excluded from it; for that such a dividing of one and the same sacrament might not be done without a heinous sacrilege.

Leo. Ser. 4.
in Quadrag.
Decret. de
Consecr.
dist. 2.

In the seventh century a practice was begun of *dipping* the *bread* in the *wine*, and so giving both kinds together. This was condemned by the council of Bracara, as plainly contrary to the gospel: *Christ gave his body and blood to his apostles distinctly, the bread by itself, and the chalice by itself.* This is, by a mistake of Gratian's, put in the canon-law, as a decree of pope Julius to the bishops of Egypt. It is probable, that it was thus given first to the sick, and to infants; but though this got among many of the eastern churches, and was, it seems, practised in some parts of the west; yet, in the end of the eleventh century, pope Urban in the council of Clermont decreed, that none should communicate without taking the body apart, and the blood apart, except upon necessity, and with caution; to which some copies add, and *that by reason of the heresy of Berengarius, that was lately condemned, which said that the figure was completed by one of the kinds.*

Decret. de
Consecr.
dist. 2.

Concil.
Claramont.
can. 28.

We need not examine the importance or truth of these last words; it is enough for us to observe the continued practice of communicating in both kinds till the twelfth century; and even then, when the opinion of the corporal presence begot a superstition towards the elements, that had not been known in former ages, so that some drops sticking to men's beards, and the spilling some of it, its freezing or becoming sour, grew to be more considered than the institution of Christ; yet for a while they used to suck it up through small quills or pipes (called *fistulæ*, in the *Ordo Romanus*), which answered the objection from the *beards*.

In the twelfth century, the bread grew to be given generally *dipt in wine*. The writers of that time, though they justify this practice, yet they acknowledge it to be contrary to the institution. Ivo of Chartres says, the people did communicate with *dipt bread, not by authority, but by necessity, for fear of spilling the blood of Christ.* Pope Innocent the Fourth said, that all might have the *chalice* who were so cautious that nothing of it should be spilt.

In the ancient church, the instance of Serapion is brought to shew that the bread alone was sent to the sick, which he that carried it was ordered to *moisten* before he gave it him. Justin Martyr does plainly insinuate that both kinds were sent to the absents; so some of the *wine* might be sent to Serapion with the bread; and it is much more reasonable to believe this, than that the bread was ordered to be dipt in *water;* there being no such instance in all history; whereas there are instances brought to shew that both kinds were carried to the sick. St. Ambrose received the bread, but expired before he received the cup: this proves nothing but the weakness of the cause that needs such supports. Nor can any argument be brought from some words concerning the communicating of the *sick,* or of *infants.* Rules are made from ordinary, and not from extraordinary practices. The small portions of the sacrament that some carried *home,* and reserved to other occasions, does not prove that they communicated only in one kind. They received in *both,* only they kept (out of too much superstition) some fragments of the *one,* which could be more easily, and with less observation, saved and preserved, than of the *other:* and yet there are instances that they carried off some portions of both kinds. The Greek church communicates during most of the days in Lent, in *bread dipt in wine;* and in the *Ordo Romanus* there is mention made of a particular communion on Good Friday; when some of the bread that had been formerly consecrated was put into a chalice with unconsecrated wine: this was a practice that was grounded on an opinion that the unconsecrated wine was sanctified and consecrated by the contact of the bread; and though they used not a formal consecration, yet they used other prayers, which was all that the primitive church thought was necessary even to consecration; it being thought, even so late as Gregory the Great's time, that the Lord's Prayer was at first the prayer of consecration.

These are all the colours which the studies and the subtilties of this age have been able to produce for justifying the decree of the council of Constance;* that does acknowledge,

ART. XXX.

Eus. Hist. l. vi. c. 44.

Just. Mart. Apol. 2.

Paulinus in vita Ambros.

Conc. Const. Sess. 13.

---

* The following is the decree of the council of Constance on the subject of half communion:—

'Cum in nonnullis mundi partibus, quidam temerarie asserere præsumant, populum Christianum debere sumere eucharistiæ sacramentum, sub utraque panis et vini specie suscipere, et non solum sub specie panis, sed etiam sub specie vini, populum laicum passim communicent, etiam post cœnam, vel alias non jejunum, &c. &c. hinc est, quod hoc presens concilium sacrum generale Constant. in spiritu sancto legitime congregatum, adversus hunc errorem saluti fidelium providere satagens, matura plurium doctorum, tam divini quam humani juris, deliberatione præhabita, declarat, decernit, et diffinit, quod licet Christus post cœnam instituerit,

ART.
XXX.

that *Christ did institute this sacrament in both kinds, and that the faithful in the primitive church did receive in both kinds: yet, a practice being reasonably brought in to avoid some dangers and scandals, they appoint the custom to continue, of consecrating in both kinds, and of giving to the laity only in one kind: since Christ was entire and truly under each kind.* They established this practice, and ordered that it should not be altered without the authority of the church. So late a practice and so late a decree cannot make void the command of Christ, nor be set in opposition to such a clear and universal practice to the contrary. The wars of Bohemia that followed upon that decree, and all that scene of cruelty which was acted upon John Huss and Jerom of Prague, at the first establishment of it, shews what opposition was made to it even in dark ages, and by men that did not deny transubstantiation. These prove that plain sense and clear authorities are so strong, even in dark and corrupt times, as not to be easily overcome. And this may be said concerning this matter, that as there is not any one point in which the church of Rome has acted more visibly contrary to the gospel than in this; so there is not any one thing that has raised higher prejudices against her, that has made more forsake her, and has possessed mankind more against her, than this. This has cost her dearer than any other.

et suis discipulis administraverit, sub utraque specie panis et vini, hoc venerabile sacramentum, tamen hoc non obstante, sacrorum canonum auctoritas laudabilis; et approbata consuetudo ecclesiæ servavit et servat, quod hujus modi sacramentum non debet confici post cœnam, neque a fidelibus recipi non jejunis, nisi in casu infirmitatis, alterius necessitatis, ajure vel ecclesia concesso vel admisso. Et sicut hæc consuetudo ad evitandum aliqua pericula et scandala est rationabiliter introducta, quod licet in primitiva ecclesia hujusmodi sacramentum reciperetur a fidelibus sub utraque specie, *postea* a conficientibus sub utraque, *et a laicis* tantummodo sub specie panis, suscipiatur, &c. Unde cum hujusmodi consuetudo ab ecclesia et sanctis patribus rationabiliter introducta, et diutissime observata sit, *habenda est pro lege, quam non licet reprobare,* aut sine ecclesiæ auctoritate pro libito mutare. Quapropter dicere, quod hanc consuetudinem aut *legem* observare, sit sacrilegum aut illicitum, censeri debet erroneum: et pertinaciter asserentes oppositum præmissorum, *tanquam hæretici arcendi sunt, et graviter puniendi* per diœcesanos locorum, seu officiales eorum, aut inquisitores hæreticæ pravitatis, in regnis seu provinciis, in quibus contra hoc decretum, aliquid fuerit forsan attentatum, aut præsumptum, juxta canonicas et legitimas sanctiones, in favorem catholicæ fidei, contra hæreticos et eorum fautores, salubriter adinventas.' *Labb.* and *Coss.* vol. xii. p. 99, &c. Par. 1672.

The above decree is thus confirmed by the council of Trent:—

' Si quis dixerit, sacram ecclesiam catholicam, non justis causis et rationibus, adductam fuisse, ut laicos atque etiam clericos non conficientes, sub panis tantummodo specie communicaret; aut in eo errasse; anathema sit!!!' *Sessio* xxi. canon 2.—[ED.]

ARTICLE XXXI.

Of the one Oblation of Christ finished upon the Cross.

The offering of Christ once made, is that perfect Redemption, Propitiation, and Satisfaction for all the Sins of the whole World, both Original and Actual: And there is none other Satisfaction for Sin, but that alone: Wherefore in the Sacrifices of Masses, in the which it was commonly said, that the Priest did offer Christ for the quick and the dead, to have Remission of Pain and Guilt, were blasphemous Fables and dangerous Deceits.

IT were a mere question of words to dispute concerning the term *sacrifice*, to consider the extent of that word, and the many various respects in which the eucharist may be called a sacrifice. In general, all acts of religious worship may be called *sacrifices:* because somewhat is in them offered up to God: 'Let my prayer be set forth before thee as incense, and the lifting up of my hands as the evening sacrifice. The sacrifices of God are a broken spirit: a broken and a contrite heart, O God, thou wilt not despise.' These shew how largely this word was used in the Old Testament: so in the New we are exhorted by him (that is, by Christ) ' to offer the sacrifice of praise to God continually, that is, the fruit of our lips, giving thanks to his name.' A Christian's dedicating himself to the service of God, is also expressed by the same word of ' presenting our bodies a living sacrifice, holy and acceptable to God.' All acts of charity are also called ' sacrifices, an odour of a sweet smell, a sacrifice acceptable, well-pleasing to God.' So in this large sense we do not deny that the *eucharist* is a ' sacrifice of praise and thanksgiving:' and our church calls it so in the office of the Communion. In two other respects it may be also more strictly called a *sacrifice*. One is, because there is an oblation of bread and wine made in it, which being sanctified are consumed in an act of religion. To this many passages in the writings of the fathers do relate. This was the oblation made at the altar by the people: and though at first the Christians were reproached, as having a strange sort of religion, in which they had neither *temples, altars,* nor *sacrifices*, because they had not those things in so gross a manner as the heathens had; yet both Clemens Romanus, Ignatius, and all the succeeding writers of the church, do frequently mention the oblations that they made: and in the ancient liturgies they did with particular prayers offer the bread and wine to God, as the great Creator of all things; those were called the gifts or offerings which were offered to God, in imitation of Abel, who offered the

Ps. cxli. 2.
Ps. li. 17.

Hebr. xiii. 15.

Rom. xii. 1.

Phil. iv. 18.

ART. fruits of the earth in a sacrifice to God. Both Justin
XXXI. Martyr, Irenæus, the Constitutions, and all the ancient
liturgies, have very express words relating to this. Another
respect, in which the *eucharist* is called a *sacrifice*, is, because
it is. a commemoration, and a representation to God of the
sacrifice that Christ offered for us on the cross: in which we
claim to that, as to our expiation, and feast upon it, as our
peace-offering, according to that ancient notion, that covenants were confirmed by a *sacrifice*, and were concluded in a
feast on the sacrifice. Upon these accounts we do not deny
but that the *eucharist* may be well called a *sacrifice:* but still
it is a commemorative *sacrifice*, and not propitiatory: that
is, we do not distinguish the *sacrifice* from the *sacrament;*
as if the priest's consecrating and consuming the elements,
were in an especial manner a *sacrifice* any other way, than as
the communicating of others with him is one: nor do we
think that the consecrating and consuming the elements is an
act that does reconcile God to the ' quick and the dead :'' we
consider it only as a federal act of professing our belief in the
death of Christ, and of renewing our baptismal covenant with
him. The virtue or effects of this are not general; they are
limited to those who go about this piece of worship sincerely
and devoutly; they, and they only, are concerned in it, who
go about it: and there is no special propitiation made by this
service. It is only an act of devotion and obedience in those
that ' eat and drink worthily;' and though in it they ought
to pray for the whole body of the church, yet those their
prayers do only prevail with God, as they are devout intercessions, but not by any peculiar virtue in this action.

On the other hand, the doctrine of the church of Rome is,
that the *eucharist* is the highest act of homage and honour
that creatures can offer up to the Creator, as being an oblation of the Son to the Father; so that whosoever procures
a mass to be said, procures a new piece of honour to be done
to God, with which he is highly pleased; and for the sake of
which he will be reconciled to all that are concerned in
the procuring such masses to be said; whether they be still on
earth, or if they are now in purgatory: and that the priest, in
offering and consuming this *sacrifice*, performs a true act of
priesthood by reconciling sinners to God. Somewhat was
already said of this on the head of purgatory.

It seems very plain, by the institution, that our Saviour, as
he blessed the sacrament, said, ' Take, eat :' St. Paul calls it
a ' communion of the body and blood of the Lord ;' and a
' partaking of the Lord's table :' and he, through his whole
discourse of it, speaks of it as an action of the church and of
all Christians; but does not so much as by a hint intimate
any thing peculiar to the priest: so that all that the scripture
has delivered to us concerning it, represents it as an action of
the whole body, in which the priest has no special share but

that of officiating. In the Epistle to the Hebrews there is a ART. very long discourse concerning *sacrifices* and *priests*, in order XXXI. to the explaining of Christ's being both *priest* and *sacrifice*. There a *priest* stands for a person called and consecrated to offer some living *sacrifice*, and to slay it, and to make reconciliation of sinners to God, by the shedding, offering, or sprinkling, the blood of the *sacrifice*. This was the notion that the Jews had of a priest; and the apostle, designing to prove that the death of Christ was a true *sacrifice*, brings this for an argument, that there was to be another priesthood after the *order of Melchisedec*. He begins the fifth chapter with settling the notion of a priest, according to the Jewish ideas: and then he goes on to prove that Christ was such a priest, 'called of God and consecrated.' But in this sense he appro- Heb. v. 10. priates the priesthood of the new dispensation singly to Christ, in opposition to the many priests of the Levitical law: 'and they truly were many priests,' because 'they were not ch. vii. 23, suffered to continue, by reason of death: but this man, 24. because he continueth ever, hath an unchangeable priesthood.'

It is clear from the whole thread of that discourse, that, in the strictest sense of the word, Christ himself is the only *Priest* under the gospel; and it is also no less evident that his death is the only *sacrifice*, in opposition to the many oblations that were under the Mosaical law, to take away sin; which appears very plain from these words, 'Who needeth ver. 27. not daily, as those high priests, to offer up sacrifice, first for his own sins, and then for the people; for this he did once, when he offered up himself.' He opposes that to the annual expiation made by the Jewish high priest, 'Christ entered in once to the holy place, having obtained redemption for us by his own blood:' and having laid down that general maxim, that 'without shedding of blood there was no remission,' he ch. ix. 12. says, 'Christ was offered once to bear the sins of many:' he 22. ver. 28. puts a question to shew that all *sacrifices* were now to cease; 'When the worshippers are once purged, then would not sa- Heb. x. 2. crifices cease to be offered?' and he ends with this, as a full conclusion to that part of his discourse: 'Every priest stands ver. 11,12. daily ministering and offering oftentimes the same sacrifices, which can never take away sin: but this man, after he had offered up one sacrifice for sins, for ever sat down on the right hand of God.' Here are not general words, ambiguous expressions, or remote hints, but a thread of a full and clear discourse, to shew that, in the strict sense of the words, we have but one *Priest*, and likewise but one *Sacrifice*, under the gospel;* therefore how largely soever those words of

* The Epistle to the Hebrews (ch. x. 14.) tells us, that 'Christ ought to be but once offered, because *by that one offering he has fully satisfied for our sins*, and *has perfected for ever them that are sanctified*. If therefore by that *first offering* he hath fully satisfied for our sins, then is there *no more need of any offering for sin* '

ART. XXXI.

priest or *sacrifice* may have been used; yet, according to the true idea of a propitiatory *sacrifice*, and of a *priest* that reconciles sinners to God, they cannot be applied to any acts of our worship, or to any order of men upon earth. Nor can the value and virtue of any instituted act of religion be carried, by any inferences or reasonings, beyond that which is put in them by the institution: and therefore since the institution of this sacrament has nothing in it that gives us this idea of it, we cannot set any such value upon it: and since the reconciling sinners to God, and the pardoning of sin, are free acts of his grace, it is therefore a high presumption in any man to imagine they can do this by any act of theirs, without powers and warrants for it from scripture. Nor can this be pretended to without assuming a most sacrilegious sort of power over the attributes of God: therefore all the virtue that can be in the sacrament is, that we do therein gratefully commemorate the *sacrifice* of Christ's death, and, by renewed acts of faith, present that to God as our *sacrifice*, in the memorial of it, which he himself has appointed: by so doing we renew our covenant with God, and share in the effects of that death which he suffered for us. All the ancient liturgies have this as a main part of the office, that being mindful of the death of Christ, or commemorating it, they offered up the gifts.

This is the language of Justin Martyr, Irenæus, Tertullian, Cyprian, and of all the following writers. They do compare this *sacrifice* to that of Melchisedec, who offered *bread and wine:* and though the text imports only his *giving bread and wine to Abraham* and his followers, yet they applied that generally to the oblation of *bread and wine* that was made on the altar: but this shews that they did not think of any sacrifice made by the offering up of Christ. It was the bread and the wine only which they thought the priests of the Christian religion did offer to God. And therefore it is remarkable, that when the fathers answer the reproach of the

---

If by that *first sacrifice he hath perfected for ever them that are sanctified*, the mass certainly must be altogether needless to make any addition to that which is already perfect. In a word, if the sacrifices of the law were therefore repeated, as this Epistle tells us, because they were *imperfect*; and had they been otherwise, they should have ceased to have been offered; what can we conclude, but the church of Rome then, in every mass she offers, does violence to the *cross of Christ*; and in more than one sense, *crucifies to herself the Lord of glory?*

'Lastly, the council of Trent declares, that because there is a new and proper *sacrifice* to be offered, it was necessary that our Saviour Christ should institute a new and proper *priesthood* to offer it. And so they say he did, after the *order of Melchisedec*, in opposition to that after the *order of Aaron* under the law. Now certainly nothing can be more contrary to this Epistle than such an assertion: both whose description of this priesthood shews it can agree only to our blessed Lord; and which indeed in express terms declares it to be peculiar to him. It calls it *an unchangeable priesthood*, that passes not to any other, as that of Aaron did from father to son, but continues in him only, because that he also himself continues for evermore.' *Wake.*—[ED.]

heathens, who charged them with irreligion and impiety for having no *sacrifices* among them, they never answer it by saying, that they offered up a *sacrifice* of inestimable value to God; which must have been the first answer that could have occurred to a man possessed with the ideas of the church of Rome. On the contrary, Justin Martyr, in his Apology, says, *They had no other sacrifices but prayers and praises:* and in his Dialogue with Trypho he confesses, that *Christians offer to God oblations, according to* Malachi's *prophecy, when they celebrate the eucharist, in which they commemorate the Lord's death.* Both Athenagoras and Minutius Felix justify the Christians for having no other sacrifices but pure hearts, clean consciences, and a steadfast faith. Origen and Tertullian refute the same objection in the same manner: they set the prayers of Christians in opposition to all the sacrifices that were among the heathens. Clemens of Alexandria and Arnobius write in the same strain; and they do all make use of one topic, to justify their offering no sacrifices, that God, who made all things, and to whom all things do belong, needs nothing from his creatures. To multiply no more quotations on this head, Julian in his time objected the same thing to the Christians, which shews that there was then no idea of a *sacrifice* among them; otherwise he, who knew their doctrine and rites, had either not denied so positively as he did their having sacrifices; or at least he had shewed how improperly the eucharist was called one. When Cyril of Alexandria, towards the middle of the fifth century, came to answer this, he insists only upon the inward and spiritual sacrifices that were offered by Christians; which were suitable to a pure and spiritual essence, such as the Divinity was, to take pleasure in; and therefore he sets that *in opposition to the sacrifices of beasts, birds, and of all other things whatsoever:* nor does he so much as mention, even in a hint, the sacrifice of the eucharist; which shews that he did not consider that as a sacrifice that was propitiatory.

ART. XXXI.

Apol. 2.

Leg. pro Christ. Minut. in Octav.
lib. viii. con. Celsum.
Tert. Apol. c. 30.
Clem. Strom. l. vii. Arnob. lib. vii.

Cyr. Al. lib. x. cont. Jul.

These things do so plainly set before us the ideas that the first ages had of this sacrament, that to one who considers them duly, they do not leave so much as a doubt in this matter. All that they may say in homilies, or treatises of piety, concerning the *pure-offering* that, according to Malachi, all Christians offered to God in the sacrament, concerning the sacrifice, and the unbloody sacrifice of Christians, must be understood to relate to the prayers and thanksgivings that accompanied it, to the commemoration that was made in it of the sacrifice offered once upon the cross, and finally to the oblation of the bread and wine, which they so often compare both to Abel's sacrifice, and to Melchisedec's offering bread and wine.

ART.
XXXI.

It were easy to enlarge further on this head, and from all the rituals of the ancients to shew, that they had none of those ideas that are now in the Roman church. They had but one *altar* in a church, and probably but one in a city: they had but one *communion* in a day at that *altar*: so far were they from the many *altars* in every church, and the many masses at every altar, that are now in the Roman church. They did not know what solitary masses were, without a communion. All the liturgies and all the writings of the ancients are as express in this matter as is possible. The whole constitution of their worship and discipline shews it. Their worship concluded always with the eucharist: such as were not capable of it, as the *catechumens*, and those who were doing public penance for their sins, assisted at the more general parts of the worship; and so much of it was called their *mass*, because they were dismissed at the conclusion of it. When that was done, then the faithful stayed, and did partake of the eucharist; and at the conclusion of it they were likewise dismissed; from whence it came to be called the *mass of the faithful*. The great rigour of penance was thought to consist chiefly in this, that such penitents might not stay with the faithful to communicate. And though this seems to be a practice begun in the third century, yet, both from Justin Martyr and Tertullian, it is evident that all the faithful did constantly communicate. There is a canon, among those which go under the name of the Apostles', against such as came and assisted in the other parts of the service, and did not partake of the eucharist; the same thing was decreed by the council of Antioch; and it appears by the Constitutions, that a deacon was appointed to see that no man should go out, and a subdeacon was to see that no woman should go out, during the oblation. The fathers do frequently allude to the word *communion*, to shew that the sacrament was to be common to all. It is true, in St. Chrysostom's time, the zeal that the Christians of the former ages had to communicate often, began to slacken; so that they had thin communions, and few communicants: against which that father raises himself with his pathetic eloquence, in words which do shew that he had no notion of solitary masses, or of the lawfulness of them: and it is very evident, that the neglect of the sacrament in those who came not to it, and the profanation of it by those who came unworthily, both which grew very scandalous at that time, set that holy and zealous bishop to many eloquent and sublime strains concerning it, which cannot be understood, without making those abatements that are due to a copious and Asiatic style, when much inflamed by devotion.

Can. 9.
Apost.

Con. Antioch. A.D.
341.can.2.
Const. Apost. l. viii.
cap. 11.
Hom. 3. in
Ep. ad
Eph. cap.i.

In the succeeding ages we find great care was taken to suffer none that did not communicate to stay in the church,

THE XXXIX ARTICLES.

and to see the mysteries. There is a rubric for this in the office mentioned by Gregory the Great. The writers of the ninth century go on in the same strain. It was decreed by the council of Mentz, in the end of Charles the Great's reign, that no priest should say mass alone; for how could he say, 'The Lord be with you,' or, 'Lift up your hearts,' if there was no other person there besides himself? This shews that the practice of solitary masses was then begun, but that it was disliked. Walafridus Strabus says, that to a lawful mass it was necessary that there should be a priest, together with one to answer, one to offer, and one to communicate. And the author of Micrologus, who is believed to have writ about the end of the eleventh century, does condemn solitary communions, as contrary both to the practice of the ancients, and to the several parts of the office: so that till the twelfth century it was never allowed of in the Roman church; as to this day it is not practised in any other communion.

^{ART.} XXXI.
Dialog.
Conc. Moguut. can. 43.

Walaf.
Strab. de Rebus Eccles. c. 22.

But then with the doctrine of purgatory and transubstantiation mixt together, the saying of masses for other persons, whether alive or dead, grew to be considered as a very meritorious thing, and of great efficacy; thereupon great endowments were made, and it became a trade. Masses were sold, and a small piece of money became their price; so that a profane sort of simony was set up, and the holiest of all the institutions of the Christian religion was exposed to sale. Therefore we, in cutting off all this, and in bringing the sacrament to be, according to its first institution, a communion, have followed the words of our Saviour, and the constant practice of the whole church for the first ten centuries.

So far all the articles that relate to this sacrament have been considered. The variety of the matter, and the importtant controversies that have arisen out of it, has made it necessary to enlarge with some copiousness upon the several branches of it. Next to the infallibility of the church, this is the dearest piece of the doctrine of the church of Rome; and is that in which both priests and people are better instructed than in any other point whatsoever; and therefore this ought to be studied on our side with a care proportioned to the importance of it: that so we may govern both ourselves and our people aright in a matter of such consequence, avoiding with great caution the extremes on both hands, both of excessive superstition on the one hand, and of profane neglect on the other. For the nature of man is so moulded, that it is not easy to avoid the one without falling into the other. We are now visibly under the extreme of neglect, and

ART.
XXXI.
therefore we ought to study by all means possible to inspire our people with a just respect for this holy institution, and to animate them to desire earnestly to partake often of it; and, in order to that, to prepare themselves seriously to set about it with the reverence and devotion, and with those holy purposes and solemn vows, that ought to accompany it.

ARTICLE XXXII.

Of the Marriage of Priests.

Bishops, Priests, and Deacons, are not commanded by God's Law either to vow the Estate of single Life, or to abstain from Marriage: Therefore it is lawful for them, as well as for all Christian Men, to marry at their own discretion, as they shall judge the same to serve better to Godliness.

THE first period of this Article to the word *Therefore*, was all that was published in king Edward's time. They were content to lay down the assertion, and left the inference to be made as a consequence that did naturally arise out of it. There was not any one point that was more severely examined at the time of the Reformation than this: for as the irregular practices and dissolute lives of both seculars and regulars had very much prejudiced the world against the celibate of the Roman clergy, which was considered as the occasion of all those disorders; so, on the other hand, the marriage of the clergy, and also of those of both sexes who had taken vows, gave great offence. They were represented as persons that could not master their appetites, but that indulged themselves in carnal pleasures and interests. Thus, as the scandals of the unmarried clergy had alienated the world much from them; so the marriage of most of the reformers was urged as an ill character both of them and of the Reformation; as a doctrine of libertinism, that made the clergy look too like the rest of the world, and involved them in the common pleasures, concerns, and passions, of human life.

The appearances of an austerity of habit, of a severity of life in watching and fasting, and of avoiding the common pleasures of sense, and the delights of life, that were on the other side, did strike the world, and inclined many to think, that what ill consequences soever *celibate* produced, yet that these were much more supportable, and more easy to be reformed, than the ill consequences of an unrestrained permission of the clergy to marry.

In treating this matter, we must first consider *celibate* with relation to the laws of Christ and the gospel; and then with relation to the laws of the church. It does not seem contrary to the purity of the worship of God, or of divine performances, that married persons should officiate in them; since, by the law of Moses, priests not only might marry, but the priesthood was tied to descend as an inheritance in a certain family. And even the high priest, who was to perform the great function of the annual atonement that was made for the sins

ART.
XXXII. of the whole Jewish nation, was to marry, and be derived to his descendants that sacred office. If there was so much as a remote unsuitableness between a married state and sacerdotal performances, we cannot imagine that God would by a law tie the priesthood to a family, which by consequence laid an obligation on the priests to marry. When Christ chose his twelve apostles, some of them were married men; we are sure, at least, that St. Peter was; so that he made no distinction, and gave no preference to the unmarried: our Saviour did no where charge them to forsake their wives; nor did he at all represent *celibate* as necessary to the 'kingdom of heaven,' or the dispensation of the gospel.* He speaks indeed

* 'In the Bible, we read that the priests, under the old dispensation, were married, and that the high priesthood passed from father to son. And in the New Testament, that St. Peter, whom you call your first pope (although you are not his successor in either doctrine or practice), was a married man; "And when Jesus was come into Peter's house, he saw his wife's mother laid, and sick of a fever," Matt. viii. 14; and Paul says, "Have we no power to lead about a sister, a wife, as well AS OTHER APOSTLES, and as the brethren of the Lord, and CEPHAS?" 1 Cor. ix. 5. I read, moreover, in the directions given by God to the bishops and deacons, these words, "A bishop must then be blameless, THE HUSBAND OF ONE WIFE, one that ruleth well his own house, having his children in subjection, with all gravity; for if a man know not how to rule his own house, how shall he take care of the church of God?" "Let the deacons be THE HUSBANDS OF ONE WIFE, ruling their children, and their own houses well." 1 Tim. iii. 2, 4, 5, 12. And in the Epistle to the Hebrews (xiii. 4.) it is written, "Marriage is honourable IN ALL, and the bed undefiled; but whoremongers and adulterers God will judge." But the word of God informs us, "that in the latter times, some shall depart from the faith," (as your church did, when it commanded pope Pius the IVth's creed to be taught and believed, as necessary to salvation,) that one of the marks by which this apostacy shall be known, is "forbidding to marry." 1 Tim. iv. 1, 3. Whether, then, this mark of the apostacy better fits us, who do marry, or you, who forbid and condemn marriage of the clergy, and have besides set up monasteries and nunneries, let the people judge.

'But I must give another instance of your church's contempt of God's word:— In 1 Tim. iii. 2. it is said, "a bishop then must be BLAMELESS, *the husband of one wife*;" and in Heb. xiii. 4. "Marriage is HONOURABLE *in all*." Why does the church of Rome condemn marriage of the clergy? Her own council of Lateran must speak—"Because it is UNWORTHY that they should be the slaves of CHAMBERING and UNCLEANNESS." I shall now give the decree in the words of Lateran, "Decernimus etiam ut ii, qui in ordine subdiaconatus, et supra, *uxores duxerint*, aut concubinas habuerint, officio, atq. ecclesiastico beneficio careant. Cum enim ipsi templum Dei, vasa Domini, sacrarium Spiritus Sancti debeant esse, et dici: INDIGNUM est, eos CUBILIBUS, et IMMUNDITIIS deservire." 2 Concil Lat. Labbei, vol. x. p. 1003, canon vi. Here then is Lateran against the word of God, and yet, according to you, the council of Lateran was infallible!!! Before this council, pope Gregory the VIIth had condemned the marriage of the clergy, in the 13th can. of the first Roman council, in A. D. 1074. (Labbei concil: vol. x. p. 326— 328.) Gregory had, besides, assembled councils or synods in other places, to condemn the marriage of the clergy. The English clergy opposed this in a very determined manner; and, when Gregory's decree was published in Germany, the clergy appealed to the word of God, and charged the pope with contradicting St. Paul. But Gregory was more than a match for them; and he, who deprived kings of their kingdoms, and trampled royalty under foot, easily prevailed, after some time, against the clergy.

'The public must now have a specimen of your church's *consistency*, contradiction, and extraordinary doctrine, on the subject of matrimony. The church of Rome calls marriage a sacrament!! (one of the five *new* sacraments she herself made;) and, according to the Trent doctrine, the sacraments confer grace, *justifying* grace. Luther maintained that "the sacraments of the new law do not confer *justifying* grace upon those who do not place a bar in the way." This is the first

of some that brought themselves to the state of eunuchs for the 'sake of the gospel;' but in that he left all men at full liberty, by saying, 'Let him receive it that is able to receive it;' so that in this every man must judge of himself by what he finds himself to be. That is equally recommended to all ranks of men, as they can bear it. St. Paul does affirm, that 'marriage is honourable in all;' and to avoid uncleanness, he says, 'It is better to marry than to burn;' and so gives it as a rule, that 'every man should have his own wife.' Among all the rules or qualifications of bishops or priests, that are given in the New Testament, particularly in the Epistles to Timothy and Titus, there is not a word of the celibate of the clergy, but plain intimations to the contrary, that they were and might be married. That of 'the husband of one wife' is repeated in different places: mention is also made of the *wives* and *children* of the clergy, rules being given concerning them: and not a word is so much as insinuated, importing, that this was only tolerated in the beginnings of Christianity, but that it was afterwards to cease. On the contrary, the 'forbidding to marry' is given as a character of the apostacy of the later times. We find Aquila, when he went about preaching the gospel, was not only married to Priscilla, but that he carried her about with him: not to insist on that privilege that St. Paul thought he might have claimed, of 'carrying about with him a sister and a wife, as well as the other apostles.' And thus the first point seems to be fully cleared, that by no law of God the clergy are debarred from marriage. There is not one word in the whole scriptures that does so much as hint at it; whereas there is a great deal to the contrary.

Marriage being then one of the rights of human nature, to which so many reasons of different sorts may carry both a wise and a good man, and there being no positive precept in the gospel that forbids it to the clergy; the next question is, Whether it is in the power of the church to make a perpetual law, restraining the clergy from marriage? It is certain that no age of the church can make a law to bind succeeding ages; for whatsoever power the church has, she is always in possession of it; and every age has as much power as any of the former ages had. Therefore if ony one age should by a law enjoin celibate to the clergy, any succeeding age may repeal and alter that law. For ever since the inspiration that conducted the apostles has ceased, every age of the church may make or change laws in all matters that are within their authority. So it seems very clear, that the church can make no perpetual law upon this subject.

---

of the "*plurimæ Lutheri hæreses*" condemned by pope Leo X. (Labb. and Coss. vol. xiv. 5 Conc. Lat. p. 392.) Marriage then, according to your doctrine, confers justifying grace. But what would this *sacrament* confer on you? Pollution and damnation !!! This is most excellent! " Doth a fountain send forth at the same place sweet water and bitter?" James iii. 11.' *Page's Letters to a Romish Priest.*—[ED.]

ART.
XXXII.

In the next place it may be justly doubted, whether the church can make a law that shall restrain all the clergy in any of those natural rights in which Christ has left them free. The adding a law upon this head to the laws of Christ, seems to assume an authority that he has not given the church. It looks like a pretending to a strain of purity beyond the rules set us in the gospel: and is plainly the laying a yoke upon us, which must be thought tyrannical, since the Author of this religion, who knew best what human nature is capable of, and what it may well bear, has not thought fit to lay it on those whom he sent upon a commission that required a much greater elevation of soul, and more freedom from the entanglements of worldly or domestic concerns, than can be pretended to be necessary for the standing and settled offices in the church. Therefore we conclude, that it were a great abuse of church power, and a high act of tyranny, for any church, or any age of the church, to bar men from the services in the church, because they either are married, or intend to keep themselves free to marry, or not, as they please: this does indeed bring the body of the clergy more into a combination among themselves; it does take them in a great measure off from having separated interests of their own; it takes them out of the civil society, in which they have less concern, when they give no pledges to it. And so in ages in which the papacy intended to engage the whole priesthood into its interests against the civil powers, as the immunity and exemptions of the clergy made them safe in their own persons, so it was necessary to free them from any such incumbrances or appendages by which they might be in the power or at the mercy of secular princes. This, joined with the belief of their *making God* with a few words, by the virtue of their character, and of their *forgiving sin*, was like armour of proof, by which they were invulnerable, and by consequence capable of undertaking any thing that might be committed to them. But this may well recommend such a rule to a crafty and designing body of men, in which it is not to be denied, that there is a deep and refined policy; yet we 'have not so learned Christ,' nor to 'handle the word of God,' or the authority that he has trusted to us, *deceitfully*.

As for the consequences of such laws, inconveniences are on both hands: as long as men are corrupt themselves, so long they will abuse all the liberties of human nature. If not only common lewdness in all the kinds of it, but even brutal and unnatural lusts, have been the visible consequences of the strict law of celibate; and if this appears so evident in history that it cannot be denied; we think it better to trust human nature with the lawful use of that in which God has not restrained it, than to venture on that which has given occasion to abominations that cannot be mentioned without horror. As for the temptation to covetousness, we think it is neither so great, nor so unavoidable, upon the one hand, as those monstrous ones are on the other. It is more reasonable to expect divine assistances to preserve men from temptations, when they are using those liberties which God has left free to them, than when, by pretending to a purity greater than that which he has commanded, they throw themselves into many snares. It is also very evident, that covetousness is an effect of men's tempers, rather than of their marriage; since the instances of a ravenous covetousness, and of a restless ambition, in behalf of men's kindred and families, hath appeared as often and as scandalously among the *unmarried* as among the *married clergy*.

ART. XXXII.

From these general considerations concerning the power that the church has to make either a perpetual or an universal law in a thing of this kind; I shall, in the next place, consider, in short, what the church has done in this matter. In the first ages of Christianity, Basilides and Saturninus, and after them, both Montanus and Novatus, and the sect of the Encratites, condemned marriage as a state of libertinism that was unbecoming the purity required of Christians. Against those we find the fathers asserted the lawfulness of marriage to all Christians, without making a difference between the clergy and the laity. It is true, the appearances that were in Montanus and his followers seem to have engaged the Christians of that age to strain beyond them in those things that gave them their reputation: many of Tertullian's writings, that critics do now see were writ after he was a Montanist, which seems not to have been observed in that age, carry the matter of celibate so high, that it is no wonder, if, considering the reputation that he had, a bias was given by these to the following ages in favour of celibate: yet it seemed to give great and just prejudices against the Christian religion, if such as had come into the service of the church should have forsaken their wives. It is visible how much scandal this might have given, and what matter of reproach it would have furnished their enemies with, if they could have charged them with this, that men, to get rid of their wives, and the care of their families, went into orders; that so, under a pretence of a higher degree of sanctity, they might abandon their families. Therefore great care was taken to prevent this. They were so far from requiring priests to forsake their wives, that such as did it, upon their entering into orders, were severely condemned by the canons that go under the name of the Apostles. They were also condemned by the council of Gangra in the fourth century, and by that of Trullo in the seventh age. There are some instances brought of bishops and priests, who are supposed to have married after they were ordained; but as there are only few of those, so perhaps they are not well proved. It must be acknowledged, that the general practice was, that men once in orders did not marry: but many bishops in the

ART.
XXXII.
best ages lived still with their wives. So did the fathers both of Gregory Nazianzen and of St. Basil. And among the works of Hilary of Poictiers, there is a letter writ by him in exile to his daughter Abra, in which he refers her to her mother's instruction in those things which she, by reason of her age, did not then understand; which shews that she was then very young, and so was probably born after he was a bishop.

Socr. Hist.
Eccl. lib. i.
c. 11.
Some proposed in the council of Nice, that the clergy should depart from their wives; but Paphnutius, though himself unmarried, opposed this, as the laying an unreasonably heavy yoke upon them. Heliodorus, a bishop, the author of the first of those love-fables that are now known by the name of *Romances*, being upon that account accused of too much levity, did, in order to the clearing himself of that imputation, move that clergymen should be obliged to live from their wives. Which the historian says they were not tied to before; for till then bishops lived with their wives. So that in those days the living in a married state was not thought unbecoming the purity of the sacred functions. A single marriage was never objected in bar to a man's being made bishop or priest. They did not indeed admit a man to orders that been *twice married*; but even for this there was a distinction: if a man had been once married before his baptism, and was once married after his baptism, that was reckoned only a single marriage; for what had been done when in heathenism went for nothing. And Jerome, speaking of bishops who had been twice married, but by this nicety were reckoned to be the *husbands of one wife*, says, 'the number of those of this sort in that time could not be reckoned; and that more such bishops might be found, than were at the council of Arimini.' Canons grew to be frequently made against the marriage of those in holy orders; but these were positive laws made chiefly in the Roman and African synods; and since those canons were so often renewed, we may from thence conclude that they were not well kept. When Synesius was ordained priest, he tells in an Epistle of his, that he declared openly, that he would not live secretly with his wife, as some did; but that he would dwell publicly with her, and wished that he might have many children by her. In the eastern church the priests are usually married before they are ordained, and continue afterwards to live with their wives, and to have children by them, without either censure or trouble. In the western church we find mention made, both in the Gallican and Spanish synods, of the wives both of bishops and priests; and they are called *episcopæ* and *presbyteræ*. In the Saxon times the clergy in most of the cathedrals of England were openly married: and when Dunstan, who had engaged king Edgar to favour the monks, in opposition to the married clergy, pressed them to forsake their wives, they refused to do it, and so were turned

out of their benefices, and monks came in their places. Nor was the celibate generally imposed on all the clergy before Gregory the Seventh's time, in the end of the eleventh century. He had great designs for subjecting all temporal princes to the papacy; and, in order to that, he intended to bring the clergy into an entire dependance upon himself; and to separate them wholly from all other interests but those of the ecclesiastical authority: and that he might load the married clergy with an odious name, he called them all Nicolaitans; though the accounts that the ancients give us of that sect say nothing that related to this matter: but a name of an ill sound goes a great way in an ignorant age. The writers that lived near that time condemned this severity against the married clergy, as a new and a rash thing, and contrary to the mind of the holy fathers; and they tax his rigour in turning them all out. Yet Lanfranc among us did not impose the celibate generally on all the clergy, but only on those that lived at cathedrals and in towns; he connived at those who served in villages. Anselm carried it further, and imposed it on all the clergy without exception: yet he himself laments that unnatural lusts were become then both common and public; of which Petrus Damiani made great complaints in Gregory the Seventh's time. Bernard, in a sermon preached to the clergy of France, says it was common in his time, and then even *bishops* with *bishops* lived in it. The observation that abbot Panormitan made of the progress of that horrid sin, led him to wish that it might be left free to the clergy to marry as they pleased. Pius the Second said, that there might have been good reasons for imposing the celibate on the clergy; but he believed there were far better reasons for leaving them to their liberty. As a remedy to these more enormous crimes, dispensations for concubinate became so common, that, instead of giving scandal by them, they were rather considered as the characters of modesty and temperance; in such concubinary priests the world judged themselves safe from practices on their own families.

When we consider those effects that followed on the imposing the celibate on the clergy, we cannot but look on them as much greater evils than those that can follow on the leaving it free to them to marry. It is not to be denied but that, on the other hand, the effects of a freedom to marry may be likewise bad: that state does naturally involve men in the cares of life, in domestic concerns, and it brings with it temptations both to luxury and covetousness. It carries with it too great a disposition to heap up wealth, and to raise families; and, in a word, it makes the clergy both look too like, and live too like, the rest of the world. But when things of this kind are duly balanced, ill effects will appear on both hands: those arise out of the general corruption of human nature, which does so spread itself, that it will corrupt us in the

ART. XXXII.

most innocent, and in the most necessary practices. There are excesses committed in eating, drinking, and sleeping. Our depraved inclinations will insinuate themselves into us in our best actions: even the public worship of God and all devotion receive a taint from them. But we must not take away those liberties in which God has left human nature free, and engage men to rules and methods that put a violence upon mankind: this is the less excusable, when we see, in fact, what the consequences of such restraints have been for many ages.

Yet after all, though they who 'marry, do well;' yet those 'who marry not, do better,' provided they live chaste, and do not *burn*. That man, who subdues his body by fasting and prayer, by labour and study, and that separates himself from the concerns of a family, that 'he may give himself wholly to the ministry of the word, and to prayer,' that lives at a distance from the levities of the world, and in a course of native modesty and unaffected severity, is certainly a burning and shining light: he is above the world, free from cares and designs, from aspirings, and all those restless projects which have so long given the world so much scandal: and therefore those, who allow themselves the liberty of marriage, according to the laws of God and the church, are indeed engaged in a state of many temptations, to which if they give way, they lay themselves open to many censures, and they bring a scandal on the Reformation for allowing them this liberty, if they abuse it.

Acts vi. 4.

It remains only to consider how far this matter is altered by vows; how far it is lawful to make them; and how far they bind when they are made. It seems very unreasonable and tyrannical to put vows on any, in matters in which it may not be in their power to keep them without sin. No vows ought to be made, but in things that are either absolutely in our power, or in things in which we may procure to ourselves those assistances that may enable us to perform them. We have a federal right to the promises that Christ has made us, of inward assistances to enable us to perform those conditions that he has laid on us; and therefore we may vow to observe them, because we may do that which may procure us aids sufficient for the execution of them. But if men will take up resolutions, that are not within those necessary conditions, they have no reason to promise themselves such assistances: and if they are not so absolutely masters of themselves, as to be able to stand to them without those helps, and yet are not sure that they shall be given them, then they ought to make no vow in a matter which they cannot keep by their own natural strength, and in which they have not any promise in the gospel that assures them of divine assistances to enable them to keep it. This is, therefore, a tempting of God, when men pretend to serve him by assuming a stricter course of life than either he has commanded, or they are able to go through with. And it may ART. prove a great snare to them, when by such rash vows they XXXII. are engaged into such a state of life, in which they live in constant temptations to sin, without either command or promise, on which they can rest as to the execution of them.

This is to 'lead themselves into temptation,' in opposition to that which our Saviour has made a petition of that prayer which he himself has taught us. Out of this, great distractions of mind, and a variety of different temptations, may, and probably will, arise; and that the rather, because the vow is made; there being somewhat in our natures that will always struggle the harder because they are restrained. It is certain that every man, who dedicates himself to the service of God, ought to try if he can dedicate himself so entirely to it, as to live out of all the concerns and entanglements of life. If he can maintain his purity in it, he will be enabled thereby to labour the more effectually, and may expect both the greater success here, and a fuller reward hereafter. But because both his temper and his circumstances may so change, that what is an advantage to him in one part of his life may be a snare and an encumbrance to him in another part of it, he ought therefore to keep this matter still in his own power, and to continue in that *liberty*, in which God has left him *free*, that so he may do as he shall find it to be most expedient for himself, and for the work of the gospel.

Therefore it is to be concluded, that it is unlawful either to impose or to make such vows. And, supposing that any have been engaged in them, more, perhaps, out of the importunity or authority of others, than their own choice; then though it is certainly a character of a man that shall dwell in God's holy hill, that though 'he swears to his own hurt, yet he changes Psal. xv. 4. not;' he is to consider, whether he can keep such a vow, without breaking the commandments of God, or not: if he can, then, certainly, he ought to have that regard to the name of God, that was called upon in the vow, and to the solemnities of it, and to the scandals that may follow upon his breaking it, that if he can continue in that state, without sinning against God, he ought to do it, and to endeavour all he can to keep his vow, and preserve his purity. But if, after he has used both fasting and prayer, he still finds that the obligation of his vow is a snare to him, and that he cannot both keep it, and also keep the commandments of God; then the two obligations, that of the law of God, and that of his vow, happening to stand in one another's way, certainly the lesser must give place to the greater. Herod's oath was ill and rashly made, but worse kept, when, 'for his oath's sake,' Matt. xiv. he ordered the head of John the Baptist to be cut off. Our 9. xv. 5. Saviour condemns that practice among the Jews, of vowing that to the *corban* or treasure of the temple, which they ought to have given to their parents; and imagining that, by

ART.
XXXII.
such means, they were not obliged to take care of them, or to supply them. The obligation to keep the commandments of God is indispensable, and antecedent to any act or vow of ours, and therefore it cannot be made void by any vow that we may take upon us: and if we are under a vow, which exposes us to temptations that do often prevail, and that probably will prevail long upon us, then we ought to repent of our rashness in making any such vow, but must not continue in the observation of it, if it proves to us like the taking fire into our bosom, or the handling of pitch. A vow that draws many temptations upon us, that are above our strength to resist them, is, certainly, much better broken and repented of, than kept. So that, to conclude, celibate is not a matter fit to be the subject either of a law or a vow; every man must consider himself, and what he is able to receive: 'He that marries does well, but he that marries not does better.'

ARTICLE XXXIII.

Of Excommunicate Persons, how they are to be avoided.

That Person which, by open Denunciation of the Church, is rightly cut off from the Unity of the Church, and Excommunicate, ought to be taken of the whole Multitude of the Faithful as a Heathen and a Publican: Until he be openly reconciled by Penance, and be received into the Church by a Judge that hath Authority thereunto.

ALL Christians are obliged to a strict purity and holiness of life: and every private man is bound to avoid all unnecessary familiarities with bad and vicious men; both because he may be insensibly corrupted by these, and because the world will be from thence disposed to think, that he takes pleasure in such persons, and in their vices. What every single Christian ought to set as a rule to himself, ought to be likewise made the rule of all Christians, as they are constituted in a body under guides and pastors. And as, in general, severe denunciations ought to be often made of the wrath and judgments of God against sinners; so if any that is called a *brother*, that is, a Christian, lives in a course of sin and scandal, they ought to give warning of such a person to all the other Christians, that they may not so much 'as eat with him,' but may *separate* themselves from him. 1 Cor. v. 11.

In this, private persons ought to avoid the moroseness and affectation of saying, 'Stand by, for I am holier than thou:' Isai. lxv. 5. 'if one is overtaken in a fault, then those who are spiritual Gal. vi. 1. ought to restore such an one in the spirit of meekness:' every one considering himself, 'lest he be also tempted.' Excessive rigour will be always suspected of hypocrisy, and may drive those on whom it falls either into despair on the one hand, or into an unmanageable licentiousness on the other.

The nature of all societies must import this, that they have a power to maintain themselves according to the design and rules of their society. A combination of men, made upon any bottom whatsoever, must be supposed to have a right to exclude out of their number such as may be a reproach to it, or a mean to dissolve it: and it must be a main part of the office and duty of the pastors of the church, to separate the good from the bad, to warn the unruly, and to put from among them wicked persons. There are several considerations that shew not only the lawfulness, but the necessity, of such a practice.

First, that the contagion of an ill example and of bad prac-

ART. XXXIII.
1 Cor. xv. 33.
2 Tim. ii. 17.
2 Thess. iii. 14.

tices may not spread too far to the corrupting of others: 'Evil communications corrupt good manners.' Their 'doctrines will eat and spread as a gangrene:' and therefore, in order to the preserving the purity of those who are not yet corrupted, it may be necessary to *note* such persons, and to 'have no company with them.'

Jude 23.
1 Cor. v. 2, 5, 7.
2 Cor. ii. 1, 2, 3.

A second reason relates to the persons themselves, that are so separated, that they may be *ashamed;* that they may be thus 'pulled out of the fire,' by the terror of such a proceeding, which ought to be done by *mourning* over them, lamenting their sins and praying for them.

1 Tim. i. 20.

The apostles made use even of those extraordinary powers that were given to them for this end. St. Paul delivered Hymenæus and Alexander unto Satan, 'that they might learn not to blaspheme.' And he ordered that the incestuous person at Corinth 'should be delivered to Satan for the destruction of the flesh, that the spirit might be saved in the day of the Lord Jesus.' Certainly a vicious indulgence to sinners is an encouragement to them to live in sin; whereas when others about them try all methods for their recovery, and mourn for those sins in which they do perhaps glory, and do upon that withdraw themselves from all communication with them, both in spirituals, and as much as may be in temporals likewise; this is one of the last means that can be used in order to the reclaiming of them.

Gal. v. 12.

Another consideration is the peace and the honour of the society. St. Paul wished that 'they were cut off that troubled the churches:' great care ought to be taken, that 'the name of God and his doctrine be not blasphemed,' and to give no occasion to the enemies of our faith to reproach us; as if we designed to make parties, to promote our own interests, and to turn religion to a faction; excusing such as adhere to us in other things, though they should break out into the most scandalous violations of the greatest of all the commandments of God. Such a behaviour towards excommunicated persons would also have this further good effect; it would give great authority to that sentence, and fill men's minds with the awe of it, which must be taken off, when it is observed that men converse familiarly with those that are under it.

These rules are all founded upon the principles of societies, which, as they associate upon some common designs, so, in order to the pursuing those, must have a power to separate themselves from those who depart from them.

Gal. i. 8, 9.
1 Cor. xvi. 22.

In this matter there are extremes of both hands to be avoided: some have thought, that because the apostles have, in general, declared such persons to be *accursed,* or under an 'anathema, who preach another gospel,' and 'such as love not the Lord Jesus, to be Anathema Maran-atha,' which is generally understood to be a total cutting off, never to be admitted till 'the Lord comes;' that therefore the church may still put men under an *anathema*, for holding such unsound doctrines, as, they think, make the gospel to become another, in part at least, if not in whole; and that she may thereupon, in imitation of another practice of the apostles, deliver them over *unto Satan*, casting them out of the protection of Christ, and abandoning them to the Devil: reckoning that the 'cutting them off' from the body of Christ is really the exposing them to the Devil, who goes about as a roaring lion, seeking whom he may devour. But with what authority soever the apostles might, upon so great a matter as the ' changing the gospel,' or the ' not loving the Lord Jesus,' denounce an *anathema*, yet the applying this which they used so seldom, and upon such great occasions, to every opinion, after a decision is made in it, as it has carried on the notion of the infallibility of the church, so it has laid a foundation for much uncharitableness, and many animosities: it has widened breaches, and made them incurable. And, unless it is certain that the church which has so decreed cannot err, it is a bold assuming of an authority to which no fallible body of men can have a right. That ' delivery unto Satan' was visibly an act of a miraculous power lodged with the apostles: for as they struck some *blind* or *dead*, so they had an authority of letting loose evil spirits on some to haunt and terrify, or to punish and plague them, that a desperate evil might be cured by an extreme remedy. And therefore the apostles never reckon this among the standing functions of the church; nor do they give any charge or directions about it. They used it themselves, and but seldom. It is true, that St. Paul being carried by a just zeal against the scandal, which the incestuous person at Corinth had cast upon the Christian religion, did adjudge him to this severe degree of censure: but he *judged* it, and did only order the Corinthians to publish it, as coming from him, ' with the power of our Lord Jesus Christ:' that so the thing might become the more public, and that the effects of it might be the more conspicuous. The primitive church, that being nearest the fountain, did best understand the nature of church-power, and the effects of her censures, thought of nothing, in this matter, but of denying to suffer apostates, or rather scandalous persons, to mix with the rest in the sacrament, or in the other parts of worship. They admitted them upon the profession of their repentance, by an imposition of hands, to share in some of the more general parts of the worship; and even in these they stood by themselves, and at a distance from the rest: and when they had passed through several degrees in that state of mourning, they were by steps received back again to the communion of the church. This agrees well with all that was said formerly concerning the nature and the ends of church-power; ' which was given for edification, and not for destruction.' This is suitable to the designs of the gospel,

ART. XXXIII.

2 Cor. x. 8

ART. XXXIII. both for preserving the society pure, and for reclaiming those who are otherwise like to be carried away by the ' Devil in his snare.' This is to *admonish* sinners as *brethren*, and not to use them as enemies; whereas the other method looks like a power that designs *destruction*, rather than *edification*, especially when the secular arm is called in, and that princes are required, under the penalties of deposition, and losing their dominions, to extirpate and destroy, and that by the cruelest sort of death, all those whom the church doth so anathematize.

We do not deny but that the form of denouncing or declaring *anathemas* against heresies and heretics is very ancient. It grew to be a form expressing horror, and was applied to the dead as well as to the living. It was understood to be a *cutting* such persons off from the communion of the church: if they were still alive, they were not admitted to any act of worship; if they were dead, their names were not to be read at the altar among those who were then commemorated. But as heat about opinions increased, and some lesser matters grew to be more valued than the weightier things both of law and gospel, so the adding *anathemas* to every point, in which men differed from one another, grew to be a common practice, and swelled up at last to such a pitch, that, in the council of Trent, a whole body of divinity was put into canons, and an *anathema* was fastened to every one of them. The *delivering to Satan* was made the common form of excommunication; an act of apostolical authority being made a precedent for the standing practice of the church. Great subtilties were also set on foot concerning the force and effect of church-censures: the straining this matter too high, has given occasion to extremes on the other hand. If a man is condemned as an heretic, for that which is no heresy, but is an article founded on the word of God, his conscience is not at all concerned in any such censure: great modesty and decency ought indeed to be shewed by private persons, when they dispute against public decisions: but unless the church is infallible, none can be bound to implicit faith, or blind submission. Therefore an *anathema*, ill founded, cannot hurt him against whom it is thundered. If the doctrine, upon which the censures and denunciations of the church are grounded, is true, and if it appears so to him that sets himself against it, he who thus *despises* the pastors of the church *despises* Christ; in whose name, and by whose authority, they are acting. But if he is still under convictions of his being in the right, when he is indeed in the wrong, then he is in a state of ignorance, and his sins are sins of ignorance, and they will be judged by that God, who knows the sincerity of all men's hearts, and sees into their secretest thoughts, how far the ignorance is wilful and affected, and how far it is sincere and invincible.

And as for those censures that are founded upon the proofs that are made of certain facts that are scandalous, either the person on whom they are charged knows himself to be really guilty of them, or that he is wronged, either by the witnesses, or the pastors and judges: if he is indeed guilty, he ought to consider such censures as the medicinal provisions of the church against sin: he ought to submit to them, and to such rebukes and admonitions, to such public confessions, and other acts of self-abasement, by which he may be recovered out of 'the snare of the Devil;' and may repair the public scandal that he has brought upon the profession of Christianity, and recover the honour of it, which he has blemished, as far as lies in him.

ART XXXIII.

2 Tim. ii. 26

This is the 'submitting to those that are over him, and the obeying them as those that watch for his soul, and that must give an account of it.' But if, on the other hand, any such person is run down by falsehood and calumny, he must submit to that dispensation of God's providence, that has suffered such a load to be laid upon him: he must not betray his integrity; he ought to commit his way to God, and to bear his burden patiently. Such a censure ought not at all to give him too deep an inward concern: for he is sure it is ill founded, and therefore it can have no effect upon his conscience. God, who knows his innocence, will acquit him, though all the world should condemn him. He must indeed submit to that separation from the body of Christians: but he is safe in his secret appeals to God, who sees not as man sees, but judges righteous judgment: and such a censure as this cannot be bound in heaven.

Heb. xiii. 17.

In the pronouncing the censures of the church, great care and tenderness ought to be used; for men are not to be rashly *cut off* from the body of Christ; nothing but a wilful obstinacy in sin, and a deliberate contempt of the rules and orders of the church, can justify this extremity. Scandalous sinners may be brought under the medicinal cure of the church, and the offender may be denied all the privileges of Christians, till he has repaired the offence that he has given. Here another extreme has been run into by men, who, being jealous of the tyranny of the church of Rome, have thought that the world could not be safe from that, unless all church-power were destroyed: they have thought that the ecclesiastical order is a body of men bound by their office to preach the gospel, and to offer the sacraments, to all Christians; but that as the gospel is a doctrine equally offered to all, in which every man must take the particular application of the promises, the comforts, and the terrors of it to himself, as he will answer it to God; so they imagine that the sacraments are in the same promiscuous manner to be offered to all persons; and that every man is to *try and examine himself*, and so to partake of them; but that the clergy have no authority to deny them to any person, or to put marks of distinction or of infamy on men: and that therefore the ancient discipline of the church did arise out of a mutual compromise of Christians, who, in times of misery and persecution, submitted to such rules as seemed necessary in that state of things; but that now all the authority that the church hath, is founded only on the law of the land, and is still subject to it. So that what changes or alterations are appointed by the civil authority must take place, in bar to any laws and customs of the church, how ancient or how universal soever they may be.

In answer to this, it is not to be denied, but that the degrees and extent of this authority, the methods and the management of it, were at first framed by common consent: in the times of persecution, the laity, who embraced the Christian religion, were to the church instead of the magistrate. The whole concerns of religion were supported and protected by them; and this gave them a natural right to be consulted with in all the decisions of the church. The *brethren* were called to join with the *apostles* and *elders* in that great debate concerning the circumcision of the Gentiles, which was settled at Jerusalem; and of such practices we find frequent mention in St. Cyprian's Epistles: the more eminent among the laity were then naturally the patrons of the churches; but when the church came under the protection of Christian princes and magistrates, then the patronage and protection of it fell to them, upon whom the peace and order of the world depended. Yet though all this is acknowledged, we see plainly, that in the New Testament there are many general rules given, for the government and order of the church. Timothy and Titus were appointed to *ordain*, to *admonish*, and *rebuke*, and that *before all*. The body of the Christians is required to *submit* themselves to them, and to *obey* them; which is not to be carried to an indefinite and boundless degree, but must be limited to that doctrine which they were to teach, and to such things as depended upon it, or tended to its establishment and propagation. From these general heads we see just grounds to assert such a power in the pastors of the church as is for *edification*, but not for *destruction;* and, therefore, here is a foundation of power laid down; though it is not to be denied but that, in the application of it, such prudence and discretion ought to be used, as may make it most likely to attain those ends for which it is given.

A general consent, in time of persecution, was necessary; otherwise too indiscreet a rigour might have pulled down that which ought to have been built up. If in a broken state of things a common consent ought to be much endeavoured and stayed for, this is much more necessary in a regular and settled time, with relation to the civil authority, under whom the whole society is put, according to its constitution. But it can never be supposed that the authority of the *pastors of the church* is no other than that of a lawyer or a physician to their clients, who are still at their liberty, and are in no sort bound to follow their directions. In particular advices, with relation to their private concerns, where no general rules are agreed on, an authority is not pretended to; and these may be compared to all other advices, only with this difference, that the *pastors* of the church 'watch over the souls of their people, and must give an account of them.' But when things are grown into method, and general rules are settled, there the consideration of edification and unity, and of maintaining peace and order, are such sacred obligations on every one that has a true regard to religion, that such as despise all this may be well looked on as *heathens* and *publicans*; and they are so much worse than they, as a secret and well-disguised traitor is much more dangerous than an open, professed enemy. And though these words of our Saviour, of 'telling the church,' may, perhaps, not be so strictly applicable to this matter, in their primary sense, as our Saviour first spoke them; yet the nature of things, and the parity of reason, may well lead us to conclude, that though those words did immediately relate to the composing of private differences, and of delating intractable persons to the synagogues, yet they may be well extended to all those public offences, which are injuries to the whole body; and may be now applied to the Christian church, and to the pastors and guides of it, though they related to the synagogue when they were first spoken.

ART. XXXIII.

Matt. xviii. 17.

It is therefore highly congruous both to the whole design of the Christian religion, and to many passages in the New Testament, that there should be rules set for censuring offenders, that so they may be reclaimed, or at least ashamed, and that others may fear: and as the final sentence of every authority whatsoever, must be the cutting off from the body all such as continue in a wilful disobedience to the laws of the society; so if any, who call themselves Christians, will live so as to be a reproach to that which they profess, they must be cut off, and cast out; for if there is any sort of power in the church, it must terminate in this. This is the last and highest act of their authority; it is like death or banishment by the civil power, which are not proceeded to but upon great occasions, in which milder censures will not prevail, and where the general good of the society requires it: so *casting out* being the last act of church-power, like a parent's disinheriting a child, it ought to be proceeded in with that slowness, and upon such considerations, as may well justify the rigour of it. A wilful contempt of order and authority carries virtually in it every other irregularity; because it dissolves the union of the body, and destroys that respect, by which all the other ends of religion are to be attained; and, when this is deliberate and fixed, there is no other way of proceeding, but by *cutting off* those who are so refractory, and who set so ill an example to others.

If the execution of this should happen to fall under great

ART.
XXXIII.

disorders, so that many scandalous persons are not censured, and a promiscuous multitude is suffered to break in upon the most sacred performances, this cannot justify private persons, who upon that do withdraw from the communion of the church: for after all that has been said, the divine precept is to every man to 'try and examine himself,' and not to *try* and censure others. All order and government are destroyed, if private persons take upon them to judge and censure others; or to separate from any body, because there are abuses in the use of this authority.

Private confession in the church of Rome had quite destroyed the government of the church, and superseded all the ancient penitentiary canons; and the tyranny of the church of Rome had set many ingenious men on many subtle contrivances, either to evade the force of those canons, to which some regard was still preserved, or to maintain the order of the church, in opposition to the appeals that were made to Rome: and while some pretended to subject all things to the papal authority, others studied to keep up the ancient rules. The encroachments that the temporal and spiritual courts were making upon one another occasioned many disputes: which being managed by such subtle men as the civilians and canonists were, all this brought in a great variety of cases and rules into the courts of the church: so that, instead of the first simplicity, which was evident in the constitution of the church, not only for the first three centuries, but for a great many more that came afterwards, there grew to be so much practice, and so many subterfuges in the rules and manner of proceeding of those courts, that the church has long groaned under it, and has wished to see that effected which was designed in the beginnings of the Reformation. The draught of a reformation of those courts is still extant; that so instead of the intricacies, delays, and other disorders, that have arisen from the canon law, we might have another short and plain body of rules; which might be managed, as anciently, by bishops, with the assistance of their clergy. But though this is not yet done, and that, by reason of it, *the tares grow up with the wheat*, we ought to *let them grow together* till the great harvest comes, or at least, till a proper *harvest* may be given to the church by the providence of God; in which the good may be distinguished and separated from the bad, without endangering the ruin of all; which must certainly be the effect of people's falling indiscreetly to this before the time.

ARTICLE XXXIV.

Of the Traditions of the Church.

It is not necessary that Traditions and Ceremonies be in all Places one, or utterly like; for at all times they have been diverse, and may be changed according to the diversity of Countries and Men's Manners, so that nothing be ordained against God's Word. Whosoever through his private Judgment, willingly and purposely doth openly break the Traditions and Ceremonies of the Church, which be not repugnant to the Word of God, and be ordained and approved by common Authority, ought to be rebuked openly (that others may fear to do the like) as one that offendeth against the common Order of the Church, and hurteth the Authority of the Magistrate, and woundeth the Consciences of weak Brethren.

Every particular or national Church hath Authority to ordain, change, and abolish Ceremonies or Rites of the Church, ordained only by men's Authority; so that all things be done to edifying.

This Article consists of two branches: the first is, that the church hath power to appoint such rites and ceremonies as are not contrary to the word of God; and that private persons are bound to conform themselves to their orders. The second is, that it is not necessary that the whole church should meet to determine such matters; the power of doing that being in every national church, which is fully empowered to take care of itself; and no rule made in such matters is to be held unalterable, but may be changed upon occasion.

As to the first, it hath been already considered, when the first words of the twentieth Article were explained. There the authority of the church in matters indifferent was stated and proved. It remains now only to prove, that private persons are bound to conform themselves to such ceremonies, especially when they are also enacted by the civil authority. It is to be considered, that the Christian religion was chiefly designed to raise and purify the nature of man, and to make human society perfect: now brotherly love and charity does this more than any one virtue whatsoever: it raises a man to the likeness of God; it gives him a divine and heavenly temper within himself, and creates the tenderest union and firmest happiness possible among all the societies of men: our Saviour has so enlarged the obligation to it, as to make it, by the extent he has given it, 'a great and new commandment,' by which all the world may be able to know and distinguish his followers from the rest of mankind: and as all John xiii. 34, 35. xv. 12, 17.

the apostles insist much upon this in every one of their Epistles, not excepting the shortest of them; so St. John, who writ last of them, has dwelt more fully upon it than upon any other duty whatsoever. Our Saviour did particularly intend that his followers should be associated into one body, and joined together, in order to their keeping up and inflaming their mutual love; and therefore he delivered his prayer to them *all* in the plural, to shew that he intended that they should use it in a body: he appointed baptism as the way of receiving men into *this body*, and the eucharist as a joint memorial that the *body* was to keep up that of his death. For this end he appointed pastors to teach and keep his followers in a body: and in his last and longest prayer to the Father, he repeats this, that 'they might be one;' that 'they might be kept in one (body), and made perfect in one,' in five several expressions; which shews both how necessary a part of his religion he meant this should be, and likewise intimates to us the danger that he foresaw, of his followers departing from it; which made him intercede so earnestly for it. One expression that he has of this union, shews how entire and tender he intended that it should be; for he prayed that the union might be such as that between *the Father and himself* was. The apostles use the figure of a *body* frequently, to express this union; than which nothing can be imagined that is more firmly knit together, and in which all the parts do more tenderly sympathise with one another.

Upon all these considerations we may very certainly gather, that the dissolving this union, the dislocating this body, and the doing any thing that may extinguish the love and charity by which Christians are to be made so happy in themselves, and so useful to one another, and by which the body of Christians grows much the firmer and stronger, and shines more in the world; that, I say, the doing this upon slight grounds, must be a sin of a very high nature. Nothing can be a just reason either to carry men to it, or to justify them in it, but the imposing on them unlawful terms of communion; for in that case it is certain, that 'we must obey God rather than man;' that we must 'seek truth and peace' together; and that the rule of 'keeping a good conscience in all things,' is laid thus, to do it first 'towards God, and then towards man.' So that a schism that is occasioned by any church's imposing unlawful terms of communion, lies at their door who impose them, and the guilt is wholly theirs.* But without such a necessity, it is certainly, both in its own nature, and in its consequences, one of the greatest of sins, to create needless disturbances in the church, and to give occasion to all that alienation of mind, all those rash censures, and unjust judgments, that do arise from such divisions. This receives a

---

* See note, page 100.

very great aggravation, if the civil authority has concurred by ART.
a law to enjoin the observance of such indifferent things; for XXXIV.
to all their lawful commands we owe an obedience, 'not only
for fear, but for conscience sake;' since the authority of the Rom.xiii.5.
magistrate is chiefly to be employed in such matters. As to
things that are either commanded or forbidden of God, the
magistrate has only the execution of these in his hands; so
that in those, his laws are only the sanctions and penalties of
the laws of God. The subject matter of his authority is about
things which are of their own nature indifferent; but that may
be made fit and proper means for the maintaining of order,
union, and decency, in the society: and therefore such laws as
are made by him in those things, do certainly bind the conscience, and oblige the subjects to obedience. Disobedience
does also give scandal to the weak. *Scandal* is a *block* or
trap laid in the way of another, by which he is made to
stumble and fall. So this figure of giving scandal, or the
laying a stumbling-block in our brother's way, is applied to
our doing of such actions as may prove the occasions of sin
to others. Every man, according to the influence that his
example or authority may have over others, who do too easily
and implicitly follow him, becomes thereby the more capable
of giving them *scandal*: that is, of drawing them after him to
commit many sins: and since men are under fetters, according to the persuasions that they have of things, he who thinks
a thing sinful, does sin if he does it, as long as he is under
that apprehension; because he deliberately ventures on that Rom. xiv.
which he thinks offends God; even while 'he doubts of it,' 23.
or makes a *distinction* between meats, (for the word rendered
doubts, signifies also the *making a difference*,) 'he is damned'
(that is, self-condemned, as acting against his own sense of
things) if he does it. Another man, that has larger thoughts
and clearer ideas, may see that there is no sin in an action,
about which others may be still in doubt, and so upon his
own account he may certainly do it: but if he has reason to
believe that his doing that may draw others, who have not
such clear notions, to do it after his example, they being still
in doubt as to the lawfulness of it, then he gives *scandal*, that
is, he lays a stumbling-block in their way, if he does it, unless
he lies under an obligation from some of the laws of God, or
of the society to which he belongs, to do it. In that case he
is bound to obey; and he must not then consider the consequences of his actions; of which he is only bound to take
care, when he is left to himself, and is at full liberty to do, or
not to do, as he pleases.

This explains the notion of *scandal*, as it is used in the
Epistles: for there being several doubts raised at that time,
concerning the lawfulness or obligation of observing the
Mosaical law, and concerning the lawfulness of eating meats
offered to idols, no general decision was made, that went

ART. XXXIV.

Rom. xiv. 13.

through that matter; the apostles having only decreed, that the Mosaical law was not to be imposed on the Gentiles; but not having condemned such as might of their own accord have observed some parts of that law, scruples arose about this; and so here they gave great caution against the laying a *stumbling-block* in the way of their brethren. But it is visible from this, that the fear of giving scandal does only take place where matters are free, and may be done or not done. But when laws are made, and an order is settled, the fear of giving scandal lies all on the side of obedience; for a man of weight and authority, when he does not obey, gives scruples and jealousies to others, who will be apt to collect from his practice that the thing is unlawful: he who does not conform himself to settled orders gives occasion to others, who see and observe him, to imitate him in it; and thus he lays a scandal or stumbling-block in their way; and all the sins which they commit through their excessive respect to him, and imitation of him, are in a very high degree to be put to his account, who gave them such occasion of falling.

The second branch of this Article is against the unalterableness of laws made in matters indifferent; and it asserts the right of every national church to take care of itself. That the laws of any one age of the church cannot bind another, is very evident from this, that all legislature is still entire in the hands of those who have it. The laws of God do bind all men at all times; but the laws of the church, as well as the laws of every state, are only provisions made upon the present state of things, from the fitness or unfitness that appears to be in them for the great ends of religion, or for the good of mankind. All these things are subject to alteration, therefore the power of the church is in every age entire, and is as great as it was in any one age since the days in which she was under the conduct of men immediately inspired. So there can be no unalterable laws in matters indifferent. In this there neither is nor can be any controversy.

An obstinate adhering to things, only because they are ancient, when all the ends for which they were at first introduced do cease, is the limiting the church in a point in which she ought still to preserve her liberty: she ought still to pursue those great rules in all her orders, of doing all things to *edification*, with *decency*, and *for peace*. The only question that can be made in this matter is, whether such general laws as have been made by greater bodies, by general councils for instance, or by those synods whose canons were received into the body of the canons of the catholic church; whether these, I say, may be altered by national churches; or whether the body of Christians is so to be reckoned one body, that all the parts of it are bound to submit, in matters indifferent, to the decrees of the body in general? It is certain, that all the parts of the catholic church ought to hold a communion one with another, and mutual commerce and correspondence together: but this difference is to be observed between the Christian and the Jewish religion, that the one was tied to one nation, and to one place, whereas the Christian religion is universal, to be spread to all nations, among people of different climates and languages, and of different customs and tempers: and therefore, since the power in indifferent matters is given the church only in order to edification, every nation must be the proper judge of that within itself. The Roman empire, though a great body, yet was all under one government; and therefore all the councils that were held while that empire stood, are to be considered only as national synods, under one civil policy. The Christians of Persia, India, or Ethiopia, were not subject to the canons made by them, but were at full liberty to make rules and canons for themselves. And in the primitive times we see a vast diversity in their rules and rituals. They were so far from imposing general rules on all, that they left the churches at full liberty: even the council of Nice made very few rules: that of Constantinople and Ephesus made fewer: and though the abuses that were growing in the fifth century gave occasion to the council of Chalcedon to make more canons, yet the number of these is but small: so that the tyranny of subjecting particular churches to laws that might be inconvenient for them, was not then brought into the church.

The corruptions that did afterwards overspread the church, together with the papal usurpations, and the new *canon law* that the popes brought in, which was totally different from the old one, had worn out the remembrance of all the ancient canons; so it is not to be wondered at, if they were not much regarded at the Reformation. They were quite out of practice, and were then scarce known. And as for the subordination of churches and sees, together with the privileges and exemptions of them, these did all flow from the divisions of the Roman empire into dioceses and provinces, out of which the dignity and the dependences of their cities did arise.

But now that the Roman empire is gone, and that all the laws which they made are at an end, with the authority that made them; it is a vain thing to pretend to keep up the ancient dignities of *sees;* since the foundation upon which that was built is sunk and gone. Every empire, kingdom, or state, is an entire body within itself. The magistrate has that authority over all his subjects, that he may keep them all at home, and hinder them from entering into any consultations or combinations but such as shall be under his direction: he may require the pastors of the church under him to consult together about the best methods for carrying on the ends of religion; but neither he nor they can be bound to stay for the concurrence of other churches. In the way of managing this, every body of men has somewhat peculiar to itself: and

ART. XXXIV.

ART.
XXXIV.
the pastors of that body are the properest judges in that matter. We know that the several churches, even while under one empire, had great varieties in their forms, as appears in the different practices of the eastern and western churches: and as soon as the Roman empire was broken, we see this variety did increase. The Gallican churches had their missals different from the Roman: and some churches of Italy followed the Ambrosian. But Charles the Great, in compliance with the desires of the pope, got the Gallican churches to depart from their own missals, and to receive the Roman; which he might the rather do, intending to have raised a new empire; to which a conformity of rites might have been a great step. Even in this church there was a great variety of usages, which perhaps were begun under the Heptarchy, when the nation was subdivided into several kingdoms.

It is therefore suitable to the nature of things, to the authority of the magistrate, and to the obligations of the pastoral care, that every church should act within herself as an entire and independent body. The churches owe not only a friendly and brotherly correspondence to one another; but they owe to their own body government and direction, and such provisions and methods as are most likely to promote the great ends of religion, and to preserve the peace of the society both in church and state. Therefore we are no other way bound by ancient canons, but as the same reason still subsisting, we may see the same cause to continue them, that there was at first to make them.

Of all the bodies of the world, the church of Rome has the worst grace to reproach us for departing in some particulars from the ancient canons, since it was her ill conduct that had brought them all into desuetude: and it is not easy to revive again antiquated rules, even though there may be good reason for it, when they fall under that tacit abrogation, which arises out of a long and general disuse of them.

ARTICLE XXXV.

Of Homilies.

The Second Book of Homilies, the several Titles whereof we have joined under this Article, doth contain a godly and wholesome Doctrine, and necessary for these Times; as doth the former Book of Homilies, which were set forth in the Time of Edward the Sixth; and therefore we judge them to be read in Churches by the Ministers, diligently and distinctly, that they may be understanded of the People.

The Names of the Homilies.

1. *Of the right Use of the Church.*
2. *Against Peril of Idolatry.*
3. *Of repairing and keeping clean of Churches.*
4. *Of good Works. First, of Fasting.*
5. *Against Gluttony and Drunkenness.*
6. *Against Excess of Apparel.*
7. *Of Prayer.*
8. *Of the Place and Time of Prayer.*
9. *That Common Prayers and Sacraments ought to be ministered in a known Tongue.*
10. *Of the reverent Estimation of God's Word.*
11. *Of Alms-doing.*
12. *Of the Nativity of Christ.*
13. *Of the Passion of Christ.*
14. *Of the Resurrection of Christ.*
15. *Of the worthy receiving of the Sacrament of the Body and Blood of Christ.*
16. *Of the Gifts of the Holy Ghost.*
17. *For the Rogation-Days.*
18. *Of the State of Matrimony.*
19. *Of Repentance.*
20. *Against Idleness.*
21. *Against Rebellion.*

AT the time of the Reformation, as there could not be found at first a sufficient number of preachers to instruct the whole nation; so those that did comply with the changes which were then made, were not all well-affected to them; so that it was not safe to trust this matter to the capacity of the one side, and to the integrity of others; therefore, to supply the defects of some, and to oblige the rest to teach according to the *form of sound doctrine,* there were two books of Homilies prepared; the first was published in king Edward's time; the second was not finished till about the time of his death; so it was not published before queen Elizabeth's time. The design of them was to mix speculative points with practical matters; some explain the doctrine, and others enforce the rules of life and manners. These are plain and short discourses, chiefly calculated to possess the nation with a sense of the purity of the gospel, in opposition to the corruptions of popery; and to reform it from those crying sins that had been so much connived at under popery, while men knew the price of them, how to compensate for them, and to redeem themselves from the guilt of them, by masses and sacraments, by indulgences and absolutions.

In these Homilies the scriptures are often applied as they were then understood; not so critically as they have been explained since that time. But by this approbation of the two books of Homilies, it is not meant that every passage of scripture, or argument that is made use of in them, is always convincing, or that every expression is so severely worded, that it may not need a little correction or explanation: all that we profess about them, is only that they *contain a godly and wholesome doctrine.* This rather relates to the main importance and design of them, than to every passage in them. Though this may be said concerning them, that considering the age they were written in, the imperfection of our language, and some lesser defects, they are two very extraordinary books. Some of them are better writ than others, and are equal to any thing that has been writ upon those subjects since that time. Upon the whole matter, every one who subscribes the Articles, ought to read them, otherwise he subscribes a blank; he approves a book implicitly, and binds himself to read it, as he may be required, without knowing any thing concerning it. This approbation is not to be stretched so far, as to carry in it a special assent to every particular in that whole volume; but a man must be persuaded of the main of the doctrine that is taught in them.

To instance this in one particular; since there are so many of the Homilies that charge the church of Rome with *idolatry,* and that from so many different topics, no man who thinks that church is not guilty of *idolatry,* can with a good conscience subscribe this Article, that the Homilies *contain a good and wholesome doctrine, and necessary for these times;* for according to his sense they contain a false and an uncharitable charge of *idolatry* against a church that they think is not guilty of it; and he will be apt to think that this was done to heighten the aversion of the nation to it: therefore any who have such favourable thoughts of the church of Rome, are bound, by the force of that persuasion of theirs, not to sign this Article, but to declare against it, as the authorizing of an accusation against a church, which they think is ill grounded, and is by consequence both unjust and uncharitable.

By *necessary for these times,* is not to be meant that this was a book fit to serve a turn; but only that this book was necessary at that time to instruct the nation aright, and so was of great use then: but though the doctrine in it, if once true, must be always true, yet it will not be always of the same necessity to the people. As for instance; there are many discourses in the Epistles of the apostles that relate to the controversies then on foot with the Judaizers, to the engagements the Christians then lived in with the heathens, and to those corrupters of Christianity that were in those days. Those doctrines were necessary for that time; but though they are now as true as they were then, yet, since we have no commerce either with Jews or Gentiles, we cannot say that it is as necessary for the present time to dwell much on those matters, as it was for that time to explain them once well. If the nation should come to be quite out of the danger of falling back into popery, it would not be so necessary to insist upon many of the subjects of the Homilies, as it was when they were first prepared.

ARTICLE XXXVI.

Of Consecration of Bishops and Ministers.

The Book of Consecration of Archbishops and Bishops, and Ordering of Priests and Deacons, lately set forth in the Time of Edward the Sixth, and confirmed at the same Time by Authority of Parliament, doth contain all Things necessary to such Consecration and Ordering; neither hath it any Thing that of itself is superstitious and ungodly. And therefore whosoever are Consecrated and Ordered according to the Rites of that Book since the Second Year of the aforenamed King Edward unto this Time, or hereafter shall be Consecrated or Ordered according to the same Rites, we decree all such to be rightly, orderly, and lawfully Consecrated and Ordered.

As to the most essential parts of this Article, they were already examined, when the pretended sacrament of orders was explained; where it was proved, that *prayer* and *imposition* of hands was all that was necessary to the giving of orders; and that the forms added in the Roman Pontifical are new, and cannot be held to be necessary, since the church had subsisted for many ages before those were thought on. So that either our ordinations without those additions are good: or the church of God was for many ages without true orders. There seems to be here insinuated a ratification of orders that were given before this Article was made; which being done (as the lawyers phrase it) *ex post facto*, it seems these orders were unlawful when given, and that error was intended to be corrected by this Article. The opening a part of the history of that time will clear this matter.

There was a new form of ordinations agreed on by the bishops in the third year of king Edward; and when the book of Common-Prayer, with the last corrections of it, was authorized by act of parliament in the fifth year of that reign, the new book of Ordinations was also enacted, and was appointed to be a part of the Common-Prayer-Book. In queen Mary's time these acts were repealed, and those books were condemned by name. When queen Elizabeth came to the crown, king Edward's Common-Prayer-Book was of new enacted, and queen Mary's act was repealed. But the book of Ordination was not expressly named, it being considered as a part of the Common-Prayer-Book, as it had been made in king Edward's time; so it was thought no more necessary to mention that *office* by name, than to mention all the other offices that are in the book. Bishop Bonner set on foot a nicety, that since the book of Ordinations was by name condemned in queen Mary's time, and was not by name received in queen Elizabeth's time, that therefore it was still condemned by law, and that by consequence ordinations performed according to this book were not legal. But it is visible, that whatsoever might be made out of this, according to the niceties of our law, it has no relation to the validity of ordinations, as they are sacred performances, but only as they are legal actions, with relation to our constitution. Therefore a declaration was made in a subsequent parliament, that the book of Ordination was considered as a part of the Book of Common-Prayer: and, to clear all scruples or disputes that might arise upon that matter, they by a retrospect declared them to be good; and from that retrospect in the act of parliament the like clause was put in the Article.

The chief exception that can be made to the form of giving orders amongst us, is to those words, 'Receive ye the Holy Ghost;' which as it is no ancient form, it not being above five hundred years old, so it is taken from words of our Saviour's, that the church in her best times thought were not to be applied to this. It was proper to him to use them, who had the 'fulness of the Spirit' to give it at pleasure: he made use of it in constituting his apostles the governors of his church in his own stead; and therefore it seems to have a sound in it that is too bold and assuming, as if we could convey the Holy Ghost. To this it is to be answered, that the churches both in the east and west have so often changed the forms of ordination, that our church may well claim the same power of appointing new forms, that others have done. And since the several functions and administrations that are in the church are by the apostle said to flow 'from one and the same Spirit,' all of them from the *apostles* down to the *pastors* and *teachers*, we may then reckon that the *Holy Ghost*, though in a much lower degree, is given to those who are inwardly moved of God to undertake that holy office. So that though that extraordinary effusion that was poured out upon the apostles, was in them in a much higher degree, and was accompanied with most amazing characters; yet still such as do sincerely offer themselves up, on a divine motion, to this service, receive a lower portion of this Spirit. That being laid down, these words, 'Receive the Holy Ghost,' may be understood to be of the nature of a wish and prayer; as if it were said, 'May thou receive the Holy Ghost;' and so it will better agree with what follows, 'And be thou a faithful dispenser of the word and sacraments.' Or it may be observed, that in those sacred missions the church and churchmen consider themselves as acting in the *name* and *person* of Christ. In baptism it is expressly said, 'I baptize in the name of the Father,' &c. In the eucharist we repeat the words of Christ,

ART.
XXXVI.
and apply them to the elements, as said by him. So we consider such as deserve to be admitted to those holy functions, as persons called and sent of God; and therefore the church in the name of Christ sends them; and because he gives a portion of his Spirit to those whom he sends, therefore the church in his name says, 'Receive the Holy Ghost.' And in this sense, and with this respect, the use of these words may be well justified.

THE XXXIX ARTICLES.

ARTICLE XXXVII.

Of Civil Magistrates.

The Queen's Majesty hath the chief Power in this Realm of England, and other her Dominions, under whom the chief Government of all Estates of this Realm, whether they be Ecclesiastical or Civil, in all Causes doth appertain, and is not, nor ought to be, subject to any Foreign Jurisdiction.

Where we attribute to the Queen's Majesty the chief Government, by which Titles we understand the Minds of some slanderous Folks to be offended: We give not to our Princes the ministering either of God's Word or of the Sacraments; the which thing the Injunctions also lately set forth by Elizabeth our Queen do most plainly testify; but that only Prerogative which we see to have been given always to all godly Princes in Holy Scriptures by God himself, that is, That they should rule all Estates and Degrees committed to their charge by God, whether they be Ecclesiastical or Temporal, and restrain with the Civil Sword the stubborn and evil-doers.

The Bishop of Rome hath no Jurisdiction in this Realm of England.

The Laws of the Realm may punish Christian Men with Death for heinous and grievous Offences.

It is lawful for Christian Men, at the Commandment of the Magistrate, to wear weapons, and serve in the Wars.

THIS Article was much shorter as it was published in king Edward's time, and did run thus: *The king of England is supreme head in earth, next under Christ, of the church of England and Ireland.* Then followed the paragraph against the pope's jurisdiction, worded as it is now: to which these words were subjoined, *The civil magistrate is ordained and allowed of God; wherefore we must obey him, not only for fear of punishment, but also for conscience sake.* In queen Elizabeth's time it was thought fitting to take away those prejudices that the papists were generally infusing into the minds of the people against the term *head;* which seemed to be the more incongruous, because a woman did then reign; therefore that was left out, and instead of it the words *chief power* and *chief government* were made use of, which do signify the same thing.

The queen did also by her Injunctions offer an explanation of this matter; for whereas it was given out by those who had complied with every thing that had been done both in her father's and in her brother's time, but that resolved now

ART.
XXXVII.
to set themselves in opposition to her, that she was assuming a much greater authority than they had pretended to: she upon that ordered that explanation which is referred to in the Article, and is in these words: 'For certainly her majesty neither doth nor ever will challenge any authority, other than that was challenged and lately used by the said noble kings of famous memory, king Henry the Eighth, and king Edward the Sixth, which is and was of ancient time due to the imperial crown of this realm; that is, under God to have the sovereignty and rule over all manner of persons born within these her realms, dominions, and countries, of what estate, either ecclesiastical or temporal, soever they be: so as no other foreign power shall or ought to have any superiority over them. And if any person that hath conceived any other sense of the said oath, shall accept the same oath with this interpretation, sense, or meaning, her majesty is well pleased to accept every such in that behalf, as her good and obedient subjects; and shall acquit them of all manner of penalties, contained in the said act, against such as shall peremptorily and obstinately refuse to take the same oath.'

Thus this matter is opened, as it is both in the Article and in the Injunctions. In order to the treating regularly of this Article, it is, first, to be proved that the pope hath no jurisdiction in these kingdoms. 2dly, That our kings or queens have it. And, 3dly, The nature and measures of this power and government are to be stated.

As for the pope's authority, though it is now connected with infallibility, yet it was pretended to, and was advanced for many ages before *infallibility* was so much as thought on. Nor was the doctrine of their infallibility ever so universally received and submitted to in these *western* parts as was that of their universal jurisdiction. They were in possession of it: appeals were made to them: they sent legates and bulls every where: they granted exemptions from the ordinary jurisdiction; and took bishops bound to them by oaths, that were penned in the form of oaths of *fealty* or homage. This was the first point that our reformers did begin with, both here and every where else; that so they might remove that which was an insuperable obstruction, till it was first taken out of the way, to every step that could be made toward a reformation. They laid down therefore this for their foundation, that all bishops were by their office and character equal; and that every one of them had the same authority that any other had over that flock which was committed to his care: and therefore they said, that the *bishops of Rome* had no authority, according to the constitution in which the churches were settled by the apostles, but over the city of *Rome:* and that any further jurisdiction that any ancient popes might have had, did arise from the dignity of the *city*, and the customs and laws of the *empire*.* As for their deriving that authority from St. Peter, it is very plain that the apostles were all made equal to him; and that they never understood our Saviour's words to him, as importing any authority that was given to him over the rest; since they continued to the last, while our Saviour was among them, 'disputing which of them should be the greatest.' The proposition that the mother of James and John made, in which it is evident that they likewise concurred with her, shews that they did not apprehend that Christ had made any declaration in favour of St. Peter, as by our Saviour's answer it appears that he had not done; otherwise he would have referred them to what he had already said upon that occasion. By the whole history of the Acts of the Apostles, it appears that the apostles acted and consulted in common, without considering St. Peter as having any superiority over them. He was called to give an account of his baptizing Cornelius; and he delivered his opinion in the council of Jerusalem, without any strain of authority over the rest. St. Paul does expressly deny, that the other apostles had any superiority or jurisdiction over him; and he says in plain words, that 'he was the apostle of the uncircumcision, as St. Peter was the apostle of the circumcision;' and in that does rather claim an advantage over him; since his was certainly the much wider province. He withstood St. Peter to his face, when he thought that he deserved to be blamed; and he speaks of his own *line* and *share*, as being subordinate in it to none: and by his saying, that 'he did not stretch himself beyond his own measure,' he plainly insinuates, that within his own province he was only accountable to Him that had called and sent him. This was also the sense of the primitive church, that all bishops were *brethren, colleagues*, and *fellow-bishops*: and though the dignity of that city, which was the head of the empire, and the opinion of that church's being founded by St. Peter and St. Paul, created a great respect to the bishops of that see, which was supported and increased by the eminent worth, as well as the frequent martyrdoms, of their bishops; yet St. Cyprian in his time, as he was against the suffering of any causes to be carried in the way of a complaint for redress to Rome, so he does in plain words say, that 'all the apostles were equal in power; and that all bishops were also equal; since the whole office and episcopate was one entire thing, of which every bishop had a complete and equal share.' It is true, he speaks of the *unity* of the Roman church, and of the union of other churches with it; but those words were occasioned by a schism that Novatian had made then at Rome; he being elected in opposition to the rightful bishop: so that St. Cyprian does not insinuate any thing concerning an authority of the see of Rome over other sees, but

ART XXXVII.

Mark ix. 33, 35.
Luke xxii. 24, 27.
Matt. xx. 21, 24, 26.

Acts xi. 2, 3.
Acts xv. 7, 14, 19.
Gal. ii. 7, 8, 11.

2 Cor. x. 14.

De Unit. Eccles.

* The reader ought to study Barrow's 'Treatise of the Pope's Supremacy,' in which that great writer has exhausted this subject.—[ED.]

ART. XXXVII.

speaks only of their union under one bishop; and of the other churches holding a brotherly communion with that bishop. Through his whole epistles he treats the bishops of Rome as his equals, with the titles of *brother* and *colleague*.

Conc. Nic. can. 6.

In the first general council, the authority of the bishops of the great sees is stated as *equal*. The bishops of Alexandria and Antioch are declared to have, *according to custom*, the same authority over the churches subordinate to them, that the bishops of Rome had over those that lay about that city. This authority is pretended to be derived only from *custom*, and is considered as under the limitations and decisions of a

Ep. x. ad Greg.

general council. Soon after that, the Arian heresy was so spread over the *east*, that those who adhered to the Nicene faith, were not safe in their numbers; and the *western* churches being free from that contagion, (though St. Basil laments that they neither understood their matters, nor were much concerned about them, but were swelled up with pride,) Athanasius and other oppressed bishops fled to the bishops of Rome, as well as to the other bishops of the *west;* it being natural for the oppressed to seek protection wheresoever they can find it: and so a sort of appeals was begun, and they were

Con. Sard. can. 3. et 7. Con. Constant. can. 3.

authorized by the council of Sardica. But the ill effects of this, if it should become a precedent, were apprehended by the second general council; in which it was decreed, that *every province should be governed by its own synod;* and that all bishops should be at first judged by the *bishops of their own province;* and from them an appeal was allowed to the bishops of the *diocese;* whereas by the canons of Nice no appeal lay from the bishops of the *province*. But though this canon of Constantinople allows of an appeal to the bishops of every such division of the Roman empire as was known by the name of *diocese;* yet there is an express prohibition of any other or further appeal; which is a plain repealing of the canon at Sardica. And in that same council it appears upon what the dignity of the see of Rome was then believed to be founded; for Constantinople being made the seat of the empire, and called *new Rome*, the bishops of that see had the same privileges given them, that the bishops of *old Rome* had; except only the point of *rank*, which was preserved to *old Rome*, because of the dignity of the city.

Con. Chalced. can. 28.
Labb. and Coss. vol. iv. p. 1691.

This was also confirmed at Chalcedon in the middle of the fifth century. This shews, that the authority and privileges of the bishops of Rome were then considered as arising out of the dignity of that city, and that the order of them was subject to the authority of a general council.

Conc. Afric. cap. 101. et 105. Epist. ad Bonifac. et Celest. Labb. and

The African churches in that time knew nothing of any superiority that the bishops of Rome had over them: they condemned the making of appeals to them, and appointed that such as made them should be excommunicated. The popes, who laid that matter much to heart, did not pretend to an universal jurisdiction as St. Peter's successors by a divine right: they only pleaded a canon of the council of Nice; but the Africans had heard of no such canon, and so they justified their independence on the see of Rome. Great search was made after this canon, and it was found to be an imposture. So early did the see of Rome aspire to this universal authority, and did not stick at forgery in order to the compassing of it. In the sixth century, when the emperor Mauritius continued a practice begun by some former emperors, to give the bishop of Constantinople the title of universal bishop; Pelage, and after him Gregory the Great, broke out into the most pathetical expressions that could be invented against it; he compared it to the pride of Lucifer; and said, that *he who assumed it was the forerunner of antichrist;* and as he renounced all claim to it, so he affirmed that none of his predecessors had ever aspired to such a power.

ART. XXXVII.
Coss. vol. iii. p. 528
532.

Greg. Ep. lib. iv. Ep. 32, 34, 36, 38, 39.
lib. vi. Ep. 24, 28, 30, 31.
lib. vii. Ep. 69.

This is the more remarkable, because the Saxons being converted to the Christian religion under this pope's direction, we have reason to believe that this doctrine was infused into this church at the first conversion of the Saxons: yet pope Gregory's successor made no exceptions to the giving himself that title, against which his predecessor had declaimed so much: but then the confusions of Italy gave the popes great advantages to make all new invaders or pretenders enlarge their privileges; since it was a great accession of strength to any party to have them of their side. The kings of the Lombards began to lie heavy on them; but they called in the kings of a new conquering family from France, who were ready enough to make new conquests; and when the nomination of the popes was given to the kings of that race, it was natural for them to raise the greatness of one who was to be their creature; so they promoted their authority; which was not a little confirmed by an impudent forgery of that time of the Decretal Epistles of the first popes; in which they were represented as governing the world with an universal and unbounded authority. This book was a little disputed at first, but was quickly submitted to; and the popes went on upon that foundation, still enlarging their pretensions. Soon after that was submitted to, it quickly appeared that the pretensions of that see were endless.

They went on to claim a power over princes and their dominions; and that first with relation to spiritual matters. They deposed them, if they were either heretics themselves, or if they favoured heresy, at least so far as not to extirpate it. From deposing they went to the disposing of their dominions to others; and at last Boniface the Eighth completed their claim; for he decreed, that *it was necessary for every man to be subject to the pope's authority:* and he asserted a direct dominion over princes as to their temporals, that they

ART.
XXXVII.

were all subject to him, and held their dominions under him, and at his courtesy. As for the jurisdiction that they claimed over the spiritualty, they exercised it with that rigour, with such heavy taxes and impositions, such exemptions and dispensations, and such a violation of all the ancient canons, that as it grew insupportably grievous, so the management was grossly scandalous, for every thing was openly set to sale. By these practices they disposed the world to examine the grounds of that authority, which was managed with so much tyranny and corruption. It was so ill founded, that it could not be defended but by force and artifices. Thus it appears, that there is no authority at all in the scripture for this extent of jurisdiction that the popes assumed: that it was not thought on in the first ages: that a vigorous opposition was made to every step of the progress that it made: and that forgery and violence were used to bring the world under it. So that there is no reason now to submit to it.

As for the patriarchal authority, which that see had over a great part of the Roman empire, that was only a regulation made conform to the constitution of that empire: so that the empire being now dissolved into many different sovereignties, the new princes are under no sort of obligation to have any regard to the Roman constitution: nor does a nation's receiving the faith by the ministry of men sent from any see, subject them to that see; for then all must be subject to Jerusalem, since the gospel came to all the churches from thence. There was a decision made in the third general council in the case of the Cypriotic churches, which pretended that they had been always complete churches within themselves and independent; therefore they stood upon this privilege, not to be subject to appeals to any patriarchal see. The council judged in their favour. So since the Britannic churches were converted long before they had any commerce with Rome, they were originally *independent;* which could not be lost by any thing that was afterwards done among the Saxons, by men sent over from Rome. This is enough to prove the first point, that the bishops of Rome had no lawful jurisdiction here among us.

The second is, that kings or queens have an authority over their subjects in matters ecclesiastical. In the Old Testament, the kings of Israel intermeddled in all matters of religion:

1 Sam. xv. 30. xxii. 14.

Samuel acknowledged Saul's authority; and Abimelech, though the high priest, when called before Saul, appeared and answered to some things that were objected to him that related to the worship of God. Samuel said in express words

xv. 17.

to Saul, that 'he was made the head of all the tribes;' and one of these was the *tribe of Levi.* David made many laws about sacred matters, such as the orders of the courses of the priests, and the time of their attendance at the public service. When he died, and was informing Solomon of the extent of his authority, he told him, that 'the courses of the priests and all the people were to be wholly at his commandment.' Pursuant to which, Solomon did appoint them their charges in the service of God; and 'both the priests and Levites departed not from his commandment in any matter.' He turned out Abiathar from the high priest's office, and yet no complaint was made upon it, as if he had assumed an authority that did not belong to him. It is true, both David and Solomon were men that were particularly inspired as to some things; but it does not appear that they acted in those matters by virtue of any such inspiration. They were acts of regal power, and they did them in that capacity. Jehoshaphat, Hezekiah, and Josiah, gave many directions and orders in sacred matters: but though the priests withstood Uzziah when he was going to offer incense in the holy place, yet they did not pretend privilege, or make opposition to those orders that were issued out by their kings. Mordecai appointed the feast of *Purim*, by virtue of the authority that king Ahasuerus gave him: and both Ezra and Nehemiah, by virtue of commissions from the kings of Persia, made many reformations and gave many orders in sacred matters.

ART. XXXVII.
1 Chron. xxiii. 6.
xxviii. 21. 2 Chron. viii. 14, 15.

2 Chron. xvii. 8, 9. ch. x. 8, to the end. xxvi. 16—19.

Under the New Testament, Christ, by saying, 'Render to Cæsar the things which are Cæsar's,' did plainly shew, that he did not intend that his religion should in any sort lessen the temporal authority. The apostles writ to the churches to 'obey magistrates, to submit to them, and to pay taxes:' they enjoined obedience, 'whether to the king as supreme, or to others that were sent by him:' 'every soul,' without exception, is charged 'to be subject to the higher powers.' The magistrate is ordained of God, and 'is his minister to encourage them that do well, and to punish the evil doers.' If these passages of scripture are to be interpreted according to the common consent of the fathers, churchmen are included within them, as well as other persons. There was not indeed great occasion to consider this matter before Constantine's coming to the empire; for till then the emperors did not consider the Christians otherwise than either as enemies, or at best as their subjects at large: and therefore, though the Christians made an address to Aurelian in the matter of Samosatenus, and obtained a favourable and just answer to it; yet in Constantine's time, the protection that he gave to the Christian religion led him and his successors to make many laws in ecclesiastical matters, concerning the *age*, the *qualifications*, and the *duties*, of the clergy. Many of these are to be found in Theodosius and Justinian's code: Justinian added many more in his Novels. Appeals were made to the emperors against the injustice of synods: they received them, and appointed such bishops to hear and try those causes as happened to be then about their courts. In the council of Nice many complaints were given to the emperor by the

Rom. xiii. 6.
Ver. 1.
1 Pet. ii. 13, 14.

ART.
XXXVII.

bishops against one another. The emperors called general councils by their summons; they sate in them, and confirmed their decrees. This was the constant practice of the Roman emperors, both in the east and in the west: when the church came to fall under many lesser sovereignties, those princes continued still to make laws, to name bishops, to give investitures into benefices, to call synods, and to do every thing that appeared necessary to them, for the good government of the church in their dominions.

When Charles the Great was restoring those things that had fallen under much disorder in a course of some ignorant and barbarous ages, and was reviving both learning and good government, he published many Capitulars, a great part of them relating to ecclesiastical matters; nor was any exception taken to that in those ages: the synods that were then held were for the greatest part mixed assemblies, in which the *temporalty* and the *spiritualty* sate together, and judged and decreed of all matters in common. And it is certain, that such was the *sanhedrim* among the Jews in our Saviour's time; it was the supreme court both for spirituals and temporals.

In England our princes began early, and continued long, to maintain this part of their authority. The letters that are pretended to have passed between king Lucius and pope Eleutherius are very probably forgeries; but they are ancient ones, and did for many ages pass for true. Now a forgery is generally calculated to the sense of the age in which it is made. In the pope's letter, the King is called *God's vicar in his kingdoms;* and it is said to *belong to his office, to bring his subjects to the holy church, and to maintain, protect, and govern them in it.* Both Saxon and Danish kings made a great many laws about ecclesiastical matters; and after the conquest, when the nation grew into a more united body, and came to a more settled constitution, many laws were made concerning these matters, particularly in opposition to those practices that favoured the authority that the popes were then assuming; such as appeals to Rome, or bishops going out of the kingdom without the king's leave. King Alfred's laws were a sort of a text for a great while; they contain many laws about sacred matters. The exempting of monasteries from episcopal jurisdiction was granted by some of our kings at first. William the Conqueror, to perpetuate the memory of his victory over Harold, and to endear himself to the clergy, founded an abbey in the field where the battle was fought, called *Battle-Abbey:* and in the charter of the foundation, in imitation of what former kings had done in their endowments, this clause was put; *It shall be also free and quiet for ever from all subjection to bishops, or the dominion of any other persons.* This is an act that does as immediately relate to the authority of the church, as any one that we can imagine. The Constitutions of Clarendon were asserted by both king and parliament, and by the whole body of the clergy, as *the ancient customs of the kingdom*. These relate to the clergy, and were submitted to by them all, Becket himself not excepted, though he quickly went off from it.

It is true, the papacy got generally the better of the temporal authority in a course of several ages; but at last the popes living long at Avignon, together with the great schism that followed upon their return to Rome, did very much sink in their credit, and that stopped the progress they had made before that time: which had probably subdued all, if it had not been for those accidents. Then the councils began to take heart, and resolved to assert the freedom of the church from the papal tyranny. *Pragmatic sanctions* were made in several nations to assert their liberty. That in France was made with great solemnity: in these the bishops did not only assert their own jurisdiction, independent in a great measure of the papacy, but they likewise carried it so far as to make themselves independent on the civil authority, particularly in the point of elections. This disposed princes generally to enter into agreements with the popes; by which the matter was so transacted, that the popes and they made a division between them of all the rights and pretensions of the church. Princes yielded a great deal to the popes, to be protected by them in that which they got to be reserved to themselves. Great restraints were laid both on the clergy, and likewise on the see of Rome, by the appeals that were brought into the secular courts, from the ordinary judgments of the ecclesiastical courts, or from the bulls or powers that legates brought with them. A distinction was found that seemed to save the ecclesiastical authority, at the same time that the secular court was made the judge of it. The *appeal* did lie upon a pretence that the ecclesiastical judge had committed some *abuse* in the way of proceeding, or in his sentence. So the *appeal* was from that *abuse*, and the secular court was to examine the matter according to the rules and laws of the church, and not according to the principles or rules of any other law: but upon that they did either confirm or reverse the sentence. And even those princes that acknowledge the papal authority, have found out distinctions to put such stops to it as they please; and so to make it an engine to govern their people by, as far as they think fit to give way to it; and to damn such bulls, or void such powers, as they are afraid of.

Thus it is evident, that both according to scripture, and the practice of all ages and countries, the princes of Christendom have an authority over their subjects in matters ecclesiastical. The reason of things makes also for this; for if any rank of men are exempted from their jurisdiction, they must thereby cease to be subjects: and if any sort of causes, spiritual ones in particular, were put out of their authority, it were an easy

ART. XXXVII. thing to reduce almost every thing to such a relation to *spirituals*, that if this principle were once received, their authority would be very precarious and feeble. Nothing could give princes stronger and juster prejudices against the Christian religion, than if they saw that the effect of their receiving it must be the withdrawing so great a part of their subjects from their authority; and the putting as many checks upon it as those that had the management of this religion should think fit to restrain it by. In a word, all mankind must be under one obedience and one authority. It remains that the measures and the extent of this power be rightly stated.

It is certain, first, that this power does not depend upon the prince's religion; whether he is a Christian, or not; or whether he is of a true or a false religion: or is a good or a bad man. By the same tenure that he holds his sovereignty, he holds this likewise. Artaxerxes had it as well as either David or Solomon, when the Jews were once lawfully his subjects; and the Christians owed the same duty to the emperors while heathen, that they paid them when Christian. The relations of nature, such as that of a *parent* and *child*, *husband* and *wife*, continue the same that they were, whatsoever men's persuasions in matters of religion may be: so do also civil relations, *master* and *servant*, *prince* and *subject*: they are neither increased nor diminished by the truth of their sentiments concerning religion. All persons are subject to the prince's authority, and liable to such punishments as their crimes fall under by law. 'Every soul is subject to the higher powers:' neither is *treason* less *treason*, because spoke in a pulpit or in a sermon: it may be more treason for that than otherwise it would be, because it is so public and deliberate, and is delivered in the way in which it may probably have the worst effect. So that, as to persons, no great difficulty can lie in this, since 'every soul' is declared to be 'subject to the higher powers.'

As to ecclesiastical causes, it is certain, that as the magistrate cannot make void the laws of nature, such as the authority of parents over their children, or of husbands over their wives, so neither can he make void the law of God: that is from a superior authority, and cannot be dissolved by him. Where a thing is positively commanded or forbid by God, the magistrate has no other authority but that of executing the laws of God, of adding his sanctions to them, and of using his utmost industry to procure obedience to them. He cannot alter any part of the doctrine, and make it to be either truer or falser than it is in itself; nor can he either take away or alter the sacraments, or break any of those rules that are given in the New Testament about them; because in all these the authority of God is express, and is certainly superior to his. The only question that can be made, is concerning indifferent things: for instance, in the canons or

other rules of the church, how far they are in the magistrate's ART.
power, and in what cases the body of Christians, and of the XXXVII.
pastors of the church, may maintain their union among themselves, and act in opposition to his laws. It seems very clear,
that in all matters that are indifferent, and are determined by
no law of God, the magistrate's authority must take place,
and is to be obeyed. The church has no authority that she
can maintain in opposition to the magistrate, but in the executing the laws of God and the rules of the gospel: in all
other things, as she acts under his protection, so it is by his
permission. But here a great distinction is to be made between two cases that may happen: the one is, when the
magistrate acts like one that intends to preserve religion, but
commits errors and acts of injustice in his management; the
other is, when he acts like one that intends to destroy religion, and to divide and distract those that profess it. In the
former case, every thing that is not sinful of itself, is to be
done in compliance with his authority; not to give him umbrage, nor provoke him to withdraw his protection, and to
become, instead of a nursing father, a persecutor of the
church. But on the other hand, when he declares, or it is
visible, that his design is to destroy the faith, less regard is to
be had to his actions. The people may adhere to their pastors, and to every method that may fortify them in their
religion, even in opposition to his invasion. Upon the whole
matter, the power of the king in ecclesiastical matters among
us is expressed in this Article under those reserves, and with
that moderation, that no just scruple can lie against it; and it
is that which all the kings, even of the Roman communion,
do assume, and in some places with a much more unlimited
authority. The methods of managing it may differ a little;
yet the power is the same, and is built upon the same foundations. And though the term *head* is left out by the Article,
yet even that is founded on an expression of Samuel's to
Saul, as was formerly cited. It is a figure, and all figures
may be used either more loosely or more strictly. In the
strictest sense, as the *head* communicates vital influences to
the whole body, Christ is the only head of his church: he
only ought to be in all things obeyed, submitted to, and depended on; and from him all the functions and offices of the
church derive their usefulness and virtue. But as *head* may
in a figure stand for the fountain of order and government, of
protection and conduct, the king or queen may well be called
the head of the church.

The next paragraph in this Article is concerning the lawfulness of capital punishments in Christian societies. It has
an appearance of compassion and charity, to think that men
ought not to be put to death for their crimes, but to be kept
alive, that they may repent of them. Some, both ancients
and moderns, have thought that there was a cruelty in all

ART. XXXVII. capital punishments that was inconsistent with the gentleness of the gospel; but when we consider that God, in that law which he himself delivered to the Jews by the hand of Moses, did appoint so many capital punishments, even for offences against positive precepts, we cannot think that these are contrary to justice or true goodness; since they were dictated by God himself, who is eternally the same, unalterable in his perfections. This shews that God, who knows most perfectly our frame and disposition, knows that the love of life is planted so deep in our natures, and that it has such a root there, that nothing can work so powerfully on us, to govern and restrain us, as the fear of death. And therefore, since the main thing that is to be considered in government is the good of the whole body; and since a feeble indulgence and impunity may set mankind loose into great disorders, from which the terror of severer laws, together with such examples as are made on the incorrigible, will naturally restrain them; it seems necessary, for the preservation of mankind and of society, to have recourse sometimes to capital punishments.

The precedent that God set in the Mosaical law seems a full justification of such punishments under the gospel. The charity, which the gospel prescribes, does not take away the rules of justice and equity, by which we may maintain our possessions, or recover them out of the hands of violent aggressors: only it obliges us to do that in a soft and gentle manner, without rigour or resentment. The same charity, though it obliges us, as Christians, not to keep up hatred or anger in our hearts, but to pardon, as to our own parts, the wrongs that are done us; yet it does not oblige us to throw up the order and peace of mankind, and abandon it to the injustice and violence of wicked men. We owe to human society, and to the safety and order of the world, our endeavours to put a stop to the wickedness of men; which a good man may do with great inward tenderness to the souls of those whom he prosecutes. It is highly probable, that as nothing besides such a method could stop the progress of injustice and wickedness, so nothing is so likely a mean to bring the criminal to repent of his sins, and to fit him to die as a Christian, as to condemn him to die for his crimes; if any thing can awaken his conscience, and strike terror in him, that will do it. Therefore, as capital punishments are necessary to human society, so they are often real blessings to those on whom they fall; and it may be affirmed very positively, that a man who can harden himself against the terrors of death, when they come upon him so solemnly, so slowly, and so certainly, he being in full health, and well able to reflect on the consequences of it, is not like to be wrought on by a longer continuance of life, or by the methods of a natural death.

It is not possible to fix rules, to which capital punishments ought to be proportioned. It is certain, that, in a full equality, *life* only can be set against *life:* but there may be many other crimes, that must end in the ruin of society, and in the dissolution of all order, and all the commerce that ought to be among men, if they go unpunished. In this all princes and states must judge according to the real exigencies and necessities that appear to them. Nor can any general rule be made, save only this, that since man was made after the image of God, and that the life of man is precious, and when once extinguished it ceases for evermore; therefore all due care and tenderness ought to be had in preserving it; and since the end of government is the preservation of mankind, therefore the lives of men ought not to be too lightly taken, except as it appears to be necessary for the preservation and safety of the society.

ART. XXXVII.

Under the Gospel, as well as under the Law, the magistrate is the 'minister of God,' and has the sword put in his hand; which ' he beareth not in vain,' for he is appointed to be ' a revenger, to execute wrath on him that doeth evil.' The natural signification of his carrying the sword is, that he has an authority for punishing capitally; since it is upon those occasions only that he can be said to use the sword as a revenger. Nor can Christian charity oblige a man, whom the law has made to be the avenger of blood, or of other crimes, to refuse to comply with that obligation which is laid upon him by the constitution under which he is born; he can only forgive that of which he is the master, but the other is a debt which he owes the society; and his private forgiving of the wrong done himself, does not reach to that other obligation, which is not in his own power to give away.

Rom. xiii. 4.

The last paragraph in this Article is concerning the lawfulness of wars. Some have thought all wars to be contrary to Christian charity, to be inhuman and barbarous; and that therefore men ought, according to the rule set us by our Saviour, ' not to resist evil ;' but when one injury is done, not only to bear it, but to shew a readiness rather to receive new ones; ' turning the other cheek to him that smites us on the one; going two miles with him that shall compel us to go one with him; and giving our cloak to him that shall take away our coat.' It seems just, that, by a parity of reason, societies should be under the same obligations to bear from other societies, that single persons are under to other single persons. This must be acknowledged to be a very great difficulty; for as, on the one hand, the words of our Saviour seem to be very express and full; so, on the other hand, if they are to be understood literally, they must cast the world loose, and expose it to the injustice and insolence of wicked persons, who would not fail to take advantages from such a compliance and submission. Therefore these words must be considered, first, as addressed to private persons; then, as

Matt.v.39.

Ver. 40.

relating to smaller injuries, which can more easily be borne; and, finally, as phrases and forms of speech, that are not to be carried to the utmost extent, but to be construed with that softening that is to be allowed to the use of a phrase. So that the meaning of that section of our Saviour's sermon is to be taken thus; that private persons ought to be so far from pursuing injuries, to the equal retaliation of an 'eye for an eye, or a tooth for a tooth,' that they ought in many cases to bear injuries, without either resisting them, or making returns of evil for evil; shewing a patience to bear even repeated injuries, when the matter is small and the wrong tolerable.

Under all this, secret conditions are to be understood, such as when by such our patience we may hope 'to overcome evil with good;' or at least to shew to the world the power that religion has over us, to check and subdue our resentments. In this case certainly we ought to sacrifice our just rights, either of defence, or of seeking reparation, to the honour of religion, and to the gaining of men by such an heroical instance of virtue. But it cannot be supposed that our Saviour meant that good men should deliver themselves up to be a prey to be devoured by bad men: or to oblige his followers to renounce their claims to the protection and reparations of law and justice.

In this St. Paul gives us a clear commentary on our Saviour's words: he reproves the Corinthians 'for going to law with one another, and that before unbelievers;' when it was so great a scandal to the Christian religion in its first infancy. He says, 'Why do not ye take wrong? Why do not ye suffer yourselves to be defrauded?' Yet he does not deny, but that they might claim their rights, and seek for redress; therefore he proposes their doing it by arbitration among themselves, and only urges the scandal of suing before heathen magistrates; so that his reproof did not fall on their suing one another, but on the scandalous manner of doing it. Therefore men are not bound up by the gospel from seeking relief before a Christian judge, and, by consequence, those words of our Saviour's are not to be urged in the utmost extent of which they are capable. If private persons may seek reparation of one another, they may also seek reparations of the wrongs that are done by those who are under another obedience; and every prince owes a protection to his people in such cases; for 'he beareth not the sword in vain;' he is their *avenger*. He may demand reparation by such forms as are agreed on among nations; and, when that is not granted, he may take such reparation from any that are under that obedience, as may oblige the whole body to repair the injury. Much more may he use the sword to protect his subjects, if any other comes to invade them. For this end chiefly he has both the sword given him, and those taxes paid him, that may enable him to support the charge, to which the use of it may put him. And as a private man owes, by the ties of humanity, assistance to a man whom he sees in the hands of thieves and murderers; so princes may assist such other princes as are unjustly fallen upon, both out of humanity to him who is so ill used, and to repress the insolence of an unjust aggressor, and also to secure the whole neighbourhood from the effects of success in such unlawful conquests. Upon all these accounts we do not doubt but that wars, which are thus originally, as to the first occasion of them, *defensive*, though in the progress of them they must be often *offensive*, may be lawful.

God allowed of wars in that policy which he himself constituted; in which we are to make a great difference between those things that were permitted by reason of the hardness of their hearts, and those things which were expressly commanded of God. These last can never be supposed to be immoral since commanded by God, whose precepts and judgments are altogether righteous. When the soldiers came to be baptized of St. John, he did not charge them to relinquish that course of life, but only to 'do violence to no man, to accuse no man falsely, and to be content with their wages.' Nor did St. Peter charge Cornelius to forsake his post when he baptized him. The primitive Christians thought they might continue in military employments, in which they preserved the purity of their religion entire; as appears both from Tertullian's works, and from the history of Julian's short reign. But though wars, that are in their own nature only defensive, are lawful, and a part of the protection that princes owe their people; yet unjust wars, designed for making conquests, for the enlargement of empire, and the raising the glory of princes, are certainly public robberies, and the highest acts of injustice and violence possible; in which men sacrifice to their pride or humour the peace of the world, and the lives of all those that die in the quarrel, whose blood God will require at their hands. Such princes become accountable to God, in the highest degree imaginable, for all the rapine and bloodshed that is occasioned by their pride and injustice.

When it is visible that a war is unjust, certainly no man of conscience can serve in it, unless it be in the defensive part: for though no man can owe that to his prince to go and murder other persons at his command, yet he may owe it to his country to assist towards its preservation, from being overrun even by those whom his prince has provoked by making war on them unjustly. For even in such a war, though it is unlawful to serve in the attacks that are made on others, it is still lawful for the people of every nation to defend themselves against foreigners.

There is no cause of war more unjust, than the propagating the true religion, or the destroying a false one. That is to be

ART. XXXVII. left to the providence of God, who can change the hearts of men, and bring them to the knowledge of the truth, when he will. Ambition, and the desire of empire, must never pretend to carry on God's work. 'The wrath of man worketh not out the righteousness of God.' And it were better barefacedly to own that men are set on by carnal motives, than to profane religion, and the name of God, by making it the pretence.

ARTICLE XXXVIII.

Of Christian Men's Goods, which are not common.

The Riches and Goods of Christians are not common, as touching the Right, Title, and Possession of the same; as certain Anabaptists do falsely boast. Notwithstanding, every Man ought of such Things as he possesseth, liberally to give Alms to the Poor, according to his Ability.

THERE is no great difficulty in this Article, as there is no danger to be apprehended that the opinion condemned by it is like to spread. Those may be for it, who find it for them. The poor may lay claim to it, but few of the rich will ever go into it. The whole charge that is given in the scripture for charity and almsgiving; all the rules that are given to the *rich*, and to *masters*, to whom their servants were then properties and slaves, do clearly demonstrate that the gospel was not designed to introduce a community of goods. And even that fellowship or community, which was practised in the first beginnings of it, was the effect of particular men's charity, and not of any law that was laid on them. 'Barnabus having land, sold it, and laid the price of it at the apostles' feet.' And when St. Peter chid Ananias for having vowed to give in the whole price of his land to that distribution, and then withdrawing a part of it, and, by a lie, pretending that he had brought it all in; he affirmed that the right was still in him, till he by a vow had put it out of his power. When God fed his people by miracle with the manna, there was an equal distribution made; yet, when he brought them into the promised land, every man had his property. The equal division of the land was the foundation of that constitution; but still every man had a property, and might improve it by his industry, either to the increasing of his stock, the purchasing houses in towns, or buying of estates, till the redemption at the jubilee.

It can never be thought a just and equitable thing, that the sober and industrious should be bound to share the fruits of their labour with the idle and luxurious. This would be such an encouragement to those whom all wise governments ought to discourage, and would so discourage those who ought to be encouraged, that all the order of the world must be dissolved, if so extravagant a conceit should be entertained. Both the rich and the poor have rules given them, and there are virtues suitable to each state of life. The rich ought to be sober and thankful, modest and humble, bountiful and charitable, out of the abundance that God has given them, and not to set their hearts upon uncertain riches, but to trust in

Acts iv. 36, 37.

Acts v. 3, 4.

the living God, and to make the best use of them that they can. The poor ought to be patient and industrious, to submit to the providence of God, and to study to make sure of a better portion in another state, than God has thought fit to give them in this world.

It will be much easier to persuade the world of the truth of the first part of this Article, than to bring them up to the practice of the second branch of it. We see what particular care God took of the poor in the old dispensation, and what variety of provision was made for them; all which must certainly be carried as much higher among Christians, as the laws of love and charity are raised to a higher degree in the gospel. Christ represents the essay that he gives of the day of judgment, in this article of charity, and expresses it in the most emphatical words possible; as if what is given to the poor were to be reckoned for as if it had been given personally to Christ himself; and in a great variety of other passages this matter is so often insisted on, that no man can resist it who reads them, and acknowledges the authority of the New Testament.

It is not possible to fix a determined quota, as was done under the Law, in which every family had their peculiar allotment, which had a certain charge specified in the Law, that was laid upon it. But under the Gospel, as men may be under greater inequalities of fortune than they could have been under the old dispensation; so that vast variety of men's circumstances makes that such proportions as would be intolerable burdens upon some, would be too light and disproportioned to the wealth of others. Those words of our Saviour come pretty near the marking out every man's measure. 'These have of their abundance cast into the offerings of God; but she of her penury hath cast in all the living that she had.' *Abundance* is superfluity in the Greek, which imports that which is over and above the 'food that is convenient;' that which one can well spare and lay aside. Now, by our Saviour's design, it plainly appears, that this is a low degree of charity, when men give only out of this: though, God knows, it is far beyond what is done by the greater part of Christians. Whereas that which is so peculiarly acceptable to God is when men give out of their *penury*, that is, out of what is necessary to them; when they are ready, especially upon great and crying occasions, even to pinch nature, and straiten themselves within what upon other occasions they may allow themselves; that so they may distribute to the necessities of others, who are more pinched, and are in great extremities. By this every man ought to judge himself, as knowing that he must give a most particular account to God, of that which God hath reserved to himself, and ordered the distribution of it to the poor, out of all that *abundance* with which he has blessed some far beyond others.

ARTICLE XXXIX.

Of a Christian Man's Oath.

As we confess that vain and rash Swearing is forbidden Christian Men by our Lord Jesus Christ, and James his Apostle; so we judge that Christian Religion doth not prohibit, but that a Man may swear when the Magistrate requireth, in a Cause of Faith and Charity, so it be done according to the Prophet's teaching, in Justice, Judgment, and Truth.

An oath is an appeal to God, either upon a testimony that is given, or a promise that is made, confirming the truth of the one, and the fidelity of the other. It is an appeal to God, who knows all things, and will judge all men: so it is an act that acknowledges both his omniscience, and his being the Governor of this world, who will judge all at the last day according to their deeds, and must be supposed to have a more immediate regard to such acts, in which men made him a party. An appeal truly made, is a committing the matter to God: a false one is an act of open defiance, which must either suppose a denial of his knowing all things, or a belief that he has forsaken the earth, and has no regard to the actions of mortals: or, finally, it is a bold venturing on the justice and wrath of God, for the serving some present end, or the gaining of some present advantage: and which of these soever gives a man that brutal confidence of adventuring on a false oath, we must conclude it to be a very crying sin; which must be expiated with a very severe repentance, or will bring down very terrible judgments on those who are guilty of it.

Thus, if we consider the matter upon the principles of natural religion, an oath is an act of worship and homage done to God; and is a very powerful mean for preserving the justice and order of the world. All decisions in justice must be founded upon evidence; two must be believed rather than one; therefore the more terror that is struck into the minds of men, either when they give their testimony, or when they bind themselves by promises, and the deeper that this goes, it will both oblige them to the greater caution in what they say, and to the greater strictness in what they promise. Since therefore truth and fidelity are so necessary to the security and commerce of the world, and since an appeal to God is the greatest mean that can be thought on to bind men to an exactness and strictness in every thing with which that appeal is joined; therefore the use of an oath is fully justified upon the principles of natural religion. This has spread itself so universally through the world, and began so

ART.
XXXIX.

Gen. xxi. 23.

xxvi. 28.

xxxi. 53.

Josh. ix. 15, 19, & 2 Sam. xxi. 1.

Lev. v. 1.

Judg. xvii. 2.

1 Sam. xiv. 24, 28, 44.

Matt. xxvi. 63, 64.

early, that it may well be reckoned a branch of the law and light of nature.

We find this was practised by the patriarchs; Abimelech reckoned that he was safe, if he could persuade Abraham to swear to him by God, that he would not deal falsely with him; and Abraham consented so to swear. Either the same Abimelech, or another of that name, desired that an oath might be between Isaac and him; and 'they sware one to another.' Jacob did also swear to Laban. Thus we find the patriarchs practising this before the Mosaical Law. Under that Law we find many covenants sealed by an oath; and that was a sacred bond, as appears from the story of the Gibeonites. There was also a special constitution in the Jewish religion, by which one in authority might put others under an *oath*, and *adjure* them either to do somewhat, or to declare some truth. The law was, that 'when any soul (i.e. man) sinned, and heard the voice of swearing (adjuration), and was a witness whether he hath seen it, or known it, if he do not utter it, then he shall bear his iniquity;' that is, he shall be guilty of perjury. So the form then was, the judge or the parents did adjure all persons to declare their knowledge of any particular. They charged this upon them with an oath or curse, and all persons were then bound by that oath to tell the truth. So Micah came and confessed, upon his mother's adjuration, that he had the eleven hundred shekels, for which he heard her put all under a curse: and upon that she blessed him. Saul, when he was pursuing the Philistines, put the people under a curse, if they should eat any food till night; and this was thought to be so obligatory, that the violation of it was capital, and Jonathan was put in hazard of his life upon it. Thus the high priest put our Saviour under the oath of *cursing*, when he required him to tell, whether he was the Messias or not? Upon which our Saviour was, according to that law, upon his oath; and though he had continued silent till then, as long as it was free to him to speak or not, at his pleasure; yet then he was bound to speak, and so he did speak, and owned himself to be what he truly was.

This was the form of that constitution: but if, by practice, it were found that men's pronouncing the words of the oath themselves, when required by a person in authority to do it; and that such actions, as their lifting up their hand to heaven, or their laying it on a Bible, as importing their sense of the terrors contained in that book, were like to make a deeper impresssion on them, than barely the judge's charging them with the *oath* or *curse;* it seems to be within the compass of human authority, to change the rites and manner of this oath, and to put it in such a method as might probably work most on the minds of those who were to take it. The institution in general is plain, and the making of such alterations seems to be clearly in the power of any state, or society of men.

In the New Testament we find St. Paul prosecuting a discourse concerning the *oath*, which God sware to Abraham, 'who, not having a greater to swear by, swore by himself;' and to enforce the importance of that, it is added, 'an oath for confirmation (that is, for the affirming or assuring of any thing) is the end of all controversy.' Which plainly shews us what notion the author of that Epistle had of an oath; he did not consider it as an impiety or profanation of the name of God.

ART. XXXIX.
Heb. vi. 13, 14, 15.
Ver. 16.

In St. John's visions an angel is represented as 'lifting up his hand, and swearing by him that liveth for ever and ever:' and the apostles, even in their Epistles, that are acknowledged to be writ by divine inspiration, do frequently appeal to God in these words, 'God is witness;' which contain the whole essence of an oath. Once St. Paul carries the expression to a form of imprecation, when he calls 'God to record upon (or against) his soul.'

Rev. x. 5, 6.
Rom. i. 9.
Gal. i. 20.
2 Cor. i. 23.

These seem to be authorities beyond exception, justifying the use of an oath upon a great occasion, or before a competent authority; according to that prophecy quoted in the Article, which is thought to relate to the times of the Messias: 'And thou shalt swear, The Lord liveth, in truth, in judgment, and in righteousness; and the nations shall bless themselves in him, and in him shall they glory.' These last words seem evidently to relate to the days of the Messiah: so here an oath religiously taken is represented as a part of that worship, which all nations shall offer up to God under the new dispensation.

Jer. iv. 2.

Against all this the great objection is, that when Christ is correcting the glosses that the Pharisees put upon the law, whereas they only taught that men 'should not forswear themselves, but perform their oaths unto the Lord;' our Saviour says, 'Swear not at all; neither by the heaven, nor the earth, nor by Jerusalem, nor by the head; but let your communication be yea, yea, and nay, nay; for whatsoever is more than these, cometh of evil.' And St. James, speaking of the enduring afflictions, and of the patience of Job, adds, 'But above all things, my brethren, swear not; neither by the heaven, neither by the earth, neither by any other oath; but let your yea be yea, and your nay, nay; lest ye fall into condemnation.' It must be confessed that these words seem to be so express and positive, that great regard is to be had to a scruple that is founded on an authority that seems to be so full. But according to what was formerly observed of the manner of the judiciary oaths among the Jews, these words cannot belong to them. Those oaths were bound upon the party by the authority of the judge; in which he was passive, and so could not help his being put under an oath: whereas our Saviour's words relate only to those oaths which a man took voluntarily on himself, but not to those

Matt. v. 34—37.
Jam. v. 12.

ART.
XXXIX.

under which he was bound, according to the law of God. If our Saviour had intended to have forbidden all judiciary oaths, he must have annulled that part of the authority of magistrates and parents, and have forbid them to put others under oaths. The word *communication*, that comes afterwards, seems to be a key to our Saviour's words, to shew that they ought only to be applied to their communication or commerce; to those discourses that pass among men, in which it is but too customary to give oaths a very large share. Or since the words that went before, concerning the performing of vows, seem to limit the discourse to them, the meaning of 'swear not at all,' may be this; Be not ready, as the Jews were, to make vows on all occasions, to devote themselves or others: instead of those, he requires them to use a greater simplicity in their communication. And St. James's words may be also very fitly applied to this, since men in their afflictions are apt to make very indiscreet vows, without considering whether they either can, or probably will, pay them; as if they would pretend by such profuse vows to overcome or corrupt God.

This sense will well agree both to our Saviour's words and to St. James's; and it seems most reasonable to believe that this is their true sense, for it agrees with every thing else; whereas, if we understand them in that strict sense of condemning all oaths, we cannot tell what to make of those oaths which occur in several passages of St. Paul's Epistles: and least of all, what to say to our Saviour's own answering upon oath, when adjured. Therefore all rash and vain swearing, all swearing in the communication or intercourse of mankind, is certainly condemned, as well as all imprecatory vows. But since we have so great authorities from the scriptures in both Testaments for other oaths; and since that agrees so evidently with the principles of natural religion, we may conclude with the Article, that a man may swear when the magistrate requireth it. It is added, *in a cause of faith and charity;* for certainly, in trifling matters, such reverence is due to the holy name of God, that swearing ought to be avoided: but when it is necessary, it ought to be set about with those regards that are due to the great God, who is appealed to. A gravity of deportment, and an exactness of weighing the truth of what we say, are highly necessary here: certainly, our words ought to be few, and our hearts full of the apprehensions of the majesty of that God, with whom we have to do, before whom we stand, and to whom we appeal, who knows all things, 'and will bring every work to judgment, with every secret thing, whether it be good, or whether it be evil.'

APPENDIX.

No. 1.

THE AUGSBURG CONFESSION.

To the short account of this confession already given,* the Editor is induced to add the following particulars.†

'The Augsburg confession was prepared for the twofold purpose of rebutting the slanders of the papists, and of publishing to Europe the doctrines of the reformers. The emperor Charles V., in order to terminate the disputes between the pope and the princes who favoured the Reformation, which tended to distract his empire by civil discord, and threw a formidable barrier into the way of his ambitious projects, had ordered the convention of a Diet, at Augsburg, and promised his personal attendance. The pope, also, who had long been pressing on the emperor the adoption of violent measures to suppress the obstinate heretics, as the holy father termed them, cherished the flattering expectation that this diet would give a death-blow to the Protestant cause. Encouraged by the promise of impartial audience from the emperor, the elector of Saxony charged Luther, Melancthon, Bugenhagen, and Jonas, to make a sketch of their doctrines to be used at the diet. Such a summary was written by Luther in seventeen sections, termed the Torgan Articles. The emperor, however, instead of reaching Augsburg on the 8th of April, according to promise, did not arrive until the 15th of June. Melancthon, in the mean time, expanded these Torgan Articles into what is now denominated the Augsburg Confession. This enlarged work was then submitted to Luther at Coburg, and received his cordial sanction. On the 25th of June, therefore, at 3 o'clock, P. M. this memorable confession was publicly pronounced in the presence of the emperor, his brother king Ferdinand, the electors John of Saxony, with his son John Frederick, George of Brandenburg, Francis and Ernest, dukes of Luneburg and Brunswick, Philip landgrave of Hesse, Wolfgang, prince of Anhalt, and about two hundred other princes and divines. The chancellors of the Elector, Baier and Pontanus arose, the former holding in his hand the German copy, and the latter the Latin original. The emperor desired

---

* See note, page 5.

† For these remarks, together with the translation of the Twenty-one Articles, the Editor is indebted to a work entitled 'Elements of Popular Theology, with special reference to the Doctrines of the Reformation, as avowed before the Diet at Augsburg, in 1530. By S. S. Schmucker, D. D., Professor of Christian Theology in the Theological Seminary of the general Synod of the Lutheran church, Gettysburg, Pa. Andover, 1834.'—[ED.]

the Latin to be read; but the Elector remonstrated, alleging, that as the diet was assembled on German ground, it ought to use the German language. The emperor having assented, Dr. Baier read the German copy, and, it is said, pronounced it with such an emphasis and so powerful a voice, that every syllable was heard, not only by all in the hall, but also by the vast multitudes who had crowded around the doors and windows of the spacious edifice. This confession, although it did not change the predetermined purpose of the politic Charles, exerted a prodigious influence in favour of the reformers in the minds of the numerous princes, divines, and literary men, who had assembled from a distance on this memorable occasion. It was soon after disseminated throughout Europe, and has been translated into the Hebrew, Greek, Spanish, Belgic, Italian, Slavonic, French, and English languages. The version found in this work, was made by the writer from the original Latin. This remark may not be superfluous, as most of the English versions which he has seen were made from the German copy; which though entirely coincident in sense differs occasionally in its phraseology. This Confession, which is justly styled the mother-symbol of the Reformation, has been adopted by the major part of all Protestant Europe, and has for about three centuries past been the standing symbol of Lutherism in the following kingdoms:

Germany, including Prussia, part of Hungary, small part of France... 17,000,000
Denmark, in which the king must profess the Augsburg Confession 1,000,000
Norway, including Iceland 746,000
Sweden 2,800,000

Lapland and Finland also contain numerous churches of the Augsburg Confession. The United Brethren or Moravians, though peculiar in their church government, have always retained the Augsburg Confession as their symbol, and yet adhere to it more strictly than most other portions of the Lutheran church. The whole number of Christians in Europe who profess the Augsburg Confession has been rated by good authors at 27,000,000, but certainly is upward of 20,000,000, and embraces in it seventeen reigning sovereigns.'

APPENDIX. 521

CONFESSIO AUGUSTANA.

I. DE DEO.

ECCLESIÆ magno consensu apud nos docent, decretum Nicenæ synodi, de unitate essentiæ Divinæ, et de tribus personis, verum et sine ulla dubitatione credendum esse. Videlicet, quòd sit una essentia Divina, quæ et appellatur et est Deus, æternus, incorporeus, impartibilis, immensa potentia, sapientia, bonitate, Creator et Conservator omnium rerum visibilium et invisibilium, et tamen tres sint personæ, ejusdem essentiæ et potentiæ, et coæternæ, Pater, Filius, et Spiritus Sanctus. Et nomine personæ utuntur ea significatione, qua usi sunt in hac causa scriptores ecclesiastici, ut significet non partem aut qualitatem in alio, sed quod propriè subsistit.

Damnant omnes hæreses, contra hunc articulum exortas, ut Manichæos, qui duo principia ponebant, bonum et malum. Item Valentinianos, Arianos, Eunomianos, Mahometistas, et omnes horum similes. Damnant et Samosatenos, veteres et neotericos, qui, cùm tantùm unam personam esse contendant, de Verbo et de Spiritu Sancto astutè et impiè rhetoricantur, quòd non sint personæ distinctæ, sed quod Verbum significet verbum vocale et Spiritus motum in rebus creatum.

II. DE PECCATO ORIGINIS.

Item docent, quòd, post lapsum Adæ, omnes homines secundum naturam propagati nascantur, cum peccato, hoc est, sine metu Dei, sine fiducia, erga Deum, et cum concupiscentia quodque hic morbus, seu vitium originis verè sit peccatum, damnans et afferens nunc

THE AUGSBURG CONFESSION.

ARTICLE I.
OF GOD.

OUR churches with one accord teach, that the decree of the council of Nice, concerning the unity of the Divine essence, and concerning the three persons, is true, and ought to be confidently believed, viz. that there is one Divine essence, which is called and is God, eternal, incorporeal, indivisible, infinite in power, wisdom and goodness, the Creator and Preserver of all things visible and invisible: and yet that there are three persons, who are of the same essence and power, and are co-eternal, the Father, the Son, and the Holy Spirit. And the term person they use in the same sense, in which it is employed by ecclesiastical writers on this subject; to signify not a part or quality of something else, but that which exists of itself.

[They condemn all heresies which have sprung up against this Article, such as that of the Manichæans, who maintained two principles, a bad and a good one. Likewise the Valentinians, Arians, Eunomians, Mahometans, and all such like. They condemn also the followers of Samosatenus, the older and later ones, who, when they contend that there is only one Person, subtilely and impiously discourse of the Word and Holy Spirit, that they are not distinct persons, but that the Word signifies the vocal word, and the Spirit the motion created in things.*]

ARTICLE II.
OF NATURAL DEPRAVITY.

Our churches likewise teach, that since the fall of Adam, all men who are naturally engendered, are born with a depraved nature, that is, without the fear of God or confidence towards him, but with sinful propensities: and that this disease, or natural depravity, is really

---

* The passages included within these marks [ ], having been omitted in the Author's translation, are supplied by the Editor.

quoque æternam mortem his, qui non renascuntur per baptismum et Spiritum Sanctum.

Damnant Pelagianos, et alios, qui vitium originis negant esse peccatum, et ut extenuent gloriam meriti et beneficiorum Christi, disputant hominem propriis viribus rationis coram Deo justificari posse.

sin, and still condemns and causes eternal death to those, who are not born again by baptism and the Holy Spirit.

[They condemn the Pelagians and others who deny that original corruption is sin, and who, that they may diminish the glory of the merits and benefits of Christ, allege that man may, by the proper operation of reason, be justified before God.]

III. De Filio Dei.

Item docent, quòd Verbum, hoc est, Filius Dei, assumserit humanam naturam in utero beatæ Mariæ Virginis, ut sint duæ naturæ, divina et humana, in unitate personæ inseparabiliter conjunctæ, unus Christus, vere Deus, et vere homo, natus ex virgine Mariâ, vere passus, crucifixus, mortuus et sepultus, ut reconciliaret nobis Patrem, et hostia esset non tantùm pro culpa originis, sed etiam pro omnibus actualibus hominum peccatis. Idem descendit ad inferos, et verè resurrexit tertia die, deinde ascendit ad cœlos, ut sedeat ad dexteram Patris, et perpetuò regnet et dominetur omnibus creaturis, sanctificet credentes in ipsum, misso in corda eorum Spiritu Sancto, qui regat, consoletur ac vivificet eos, ac defendat adversus diabolum, et vim peccati. Idem Christus palam est rediturus, ut judicet vivos et mortuos, etc., juxta Symbolum Apostolorum.

ARTICLE III.

Of the Son of God and his Mediatorial Work.

They likewise teach, that the Word, that is, the Son of God, assumed human nature, in the womb of the blessed Virgin Mary, so that the two natures, human and divine, inseparably united in one person, constitute one Christ, who is true God and man, born of the Virgin Mary; who truly suffered, was crucified, died and was buried, that he might reconcile the Father to us, and be a sacrifice not only for original sin, but also for all the actual sins of men. He likewise descended into hell, and truly arose on the third day; and then ascended to heaven, that he might sit at the right hand of the Father, might perpetually reign over all creatures, and might sanctify those who believe in him, by sending into their hearts the Holy Spirit, who governs, consoles, quickens, and defends them against the devil and the power of sin. The same Christ will return again openly, that he may judge the living and the dead, &c., according to the Apostolic Creed.

IV. De Justificatione.

Idem docent, quod homines non possint justificari coram Deo propriis viribus, meritis aut operibus, sed gratis justificentur propter Christum per fidem, cùm credunt se in gratiam recipi, et peccata remitti propter Christum, qui sua morte pro nostris peccatis satisfecit. Hanc fidem imputat Deus pro justitia coram ipso, Rom. 3. et 4.

ARTICLE IV.

Of Justification.

They in like manner teach, that men cannot be justified before God by their own strength, merits, or works; but that they are justified gratuitously for Christ's sake, through faith; when they believe, that they are received into favour, and that their sins are remitted on account of Christ, who made satisfaction for our transgressions by his death. This faith God imputes to us as righteousness.

APPENDIX.

V. De Ministerio Eccles.

Ut hanc fidem consequamur, institutum est ministerium docendi Evangelii et porrigendi sacramenta. Nam per verbum et sacramenta, tanquam per instrumenta donatur Spiritus Sanctus, qui fidem efficit, ubi et quando visum est Deo, in iis, qui audiunt Evangelium, scilicet, quòd Deus non propter nostra merita, sed propter Christum justificet hos, qui credunt, se propter Christum in gratiam recipi. Damnant Anabaptistas, et alios, qui sentiunt Spiritum Sanctum contingere sine verbo externo hominibus per ipsorum præparationes et opera.

ARTICLE V.
Of the Ministerial Office (and Means of Grace).

In order that we may obtain this faith, the ministerial office has been instituted, whose members are to preach the gospel, and administer the sacraments. For through the instrumentality of the word and sacraments, as means of grace, the Holy Spirit is given, who, in his own time and place, produces faith in those who hearken to the gospel message, namely, that God, for Christ's sake, and not on account of any merit in us, justifies those who believe in Christ.

[They condemn the Anabaptists and others, who think that the Holy Spirit comes upon men by their own preparations and works, without the external word.]

VI. De Nova Obedientia.

Item docent, quod fides illa debeat bonos fructus parere, et quòd oporteat bona opera, mandata à Deo, facere, propter voluntatem Dei, non ut confidamus per ea opera justificationem coram Deo mereri. Nam remissio peccatorum et justificatio fide apprehenditur, sicut testatur et vox Christi. Cùm feceritis hæc omnia, dicite, servi inutiles sumus. Idem docent et veteres scriptores ecclesiastici; Ambrosius enim inquit: Hoc constitutum est a Deo, ut qui credit in Christum, salvus sit, sine opere, solâ fide gratis accipiens remissionem peccatorum.

ARTICLE VI.
Concerning new Obedience (or a Christian Life).

They likewise teach, that this faith must bring forth good fruits; and that it is our duty to perform those good works which God has commanded, because he has enjoined them, and not in the expectation of thereby meriting justification before him. For, remission of sins and justification are secured by faith; as the declaration of Christ himself implies: 'When ye shall have done all those things, say, we are unprofitable servants.'

[The same thing is taught by the ancient ecclesiastical writers: for Ambrose says, 'this has been ordained by God, that he who believes in Christ is saved without works, receiving remission of sins freely through faith alone.']

VII. De Ecclesia.

Item docent, quod una sancta ecclesia perpetuò mansura sit: Est autem ecclesia congregatio sanctorum, in qua evangelium rectè docetur, et rectè administrantur sacramenta. Et ad veram unitatem ecclesiæ, satis est consentire de doctrinâ evangelii et administratione sacramentorum. Nec necesse est ubi-

ARTICLE VII.
Of the Church.

They likewise teach, that there will always be one holy church. The church is the congregation of the saints, in which the gospel is correctly taught, and the sacraments are properly administered. And for the true unity of the church nothing more is required, than agreement concerning the doctrines of

que esse similes traditiones humanas, seu ritus aut ceremonias, ab hominibus institutas. Sicut inquit Paulus: Una fides, unum baptisma, unus Deus et Pater omnium, &c.

the gospel, and the administration of the sacraments. Nor is it necessary, that the same human traditions, that is, rites and ceremonies instituted by men, should be every where observed. As Paul says: 'One faith, one baptism, one God and Father of all,' &c.

VIII. QUID SIT ECCLESIA.

Quanquam ecclesia propriè sit congregatio sanctorum, et verè credentium; tamen, cùm in hac vita multi hypocritæ et mali admixti sint, licet uti sacramentis, quæ per malos administrantur, juxta vocem Christi. Sedent scribæ et pharisæi in cathedra Moysis, &c. Et sacramenta et verbum propter ordinationem et mandatum Christi sunt efficacia, etiamsi per malos exhibeantur. Damnant Donatistas et similes, qui negabant licere uti ministerio malorum in ecclesia, et sentiebant, ministerium malorum inutile et inefficax esse.

ARTICLE VIII.

WHAT THE CHURCH IS.

Although the church is properly a congregation of saints and true believers; yet as, in the present life, many hypocrites and wicked men are mingled with them, it is lawful for us also to receive the sacraments, when administered by unconverted men, agreeably to the declaration of our Saviour, 'that the scribes and pharisees sit in Moses' seat,' &c.

[They condemn the Donatists and such like who denied that it is lawful to make use of the ministry of wicked men in the church, and who thought the ministry of such useless and without efficacy.]

IX. DE BAPTISMO.

De baptismo docent, quòd sit necessarius ad salutem, quodque per baptismum offeratur gratia Dei. Et quòd pueri sint baptizandi, qui per baptismum oblati Deo, recipiantur in gratiam Dei. Damnant Anabaptistas, qui improbant baptismum puerorum et affirmant pueros sine baptismo salvos fieri.

ARTICLE IX.

OF BAPTISM.

Concerning baptism our churches teach, that it is a necessary ordinance, that it is a means of grace, and ought to be administered also to children, who are thereby dedicated to God, and received into his favour.

[They condemn the Anabaptists who reject the baptism of children; and who affirm that infants may be saved without baptism.]

X. DE CŒNA DOMINI.

De cœna Domini docent, quòd corpus et sanguis Christi verè adsint, et distribuantur vescentibus in cœnâ Domini et improbant secus docentes.

ARTICLE X.

OF THE LORD'S SUPPER.

In regard to the Lord's supper they teach, that the body and blood of Christ are actually present under the emblems of bread and wine; and are dispensed to the communicants.

XI. DE CONFESSIONE.

De confessione docent quòd absolutio privata in ecclesiis retinenda sit quanquam in confessione non sit necessaria omnium delictorum enumeratio. Est

ARTICLE XI.

OF CONFESSION.

In regard to confession they teach, that private absolution ought to be retained in the churches; but that an enumeration of all our transgressions is not

enim impossibilis juxta Psalmum xix. 12. 'Delicta quis intelligit?' requisite in confession. For this is an impossibility, according to the declaration of the Psalmist: 'Who can understand his errors?'

XII. DE PŒNITENTIA.

De pœnitentia docent, quòd lapsis post baptismum contingere possit remissio peccatorum quocunque tempore, cùm convertuntur. Et quòd ecclesia talibus redeuntibus ad pœnitentiam absolutionem impertiri debeat. Constat autem pœnitentia propriè his duabus partibus: altera est, contritio seu terrores incussi conscientiæ agnito peccato. Altera est, fides, quæ concipitur ex evangelio, seu absolutione, et credit propter Christum remitti peccata, et consolatur conscientiam, et ex terroribus liberat. Deinde sequi debent bona opera, quæ sunt fructus pœnitentiæ. Damnant Anabaptistas, qui negant semel justificatos posse amittere Spiritum Sanctum. Item, qui contendunt, quibusdam tantam perfectionem in hac vita contingere, ut peccare non possint. Damnantur et Novatiani, qui nolebant absolvere lapsos post baptismum redeuntes ad pœnitentiam. Rejiciuntur et isti, qui non docent remissionem peccatorum per fidem contingere, sed jubent nos mereri gratiam per satisfactiones nostras.

ARTICLE XII.
OF REPENTANCE.

Concerning repentance they teach, that those who have relapsed into sin after baptism, may at any time obtain pardon, when they repent: and that the church ought to grant absolution (restore to church-privileges) to such as manifest repentance. But repentance properly consists of two parts. The one is contrition or dread on account of acknowledged sin. The other is faith, which is produced by the gospel, or by means of absolution: which believes that pardon for sin is bestowed for Christ's sake; which tranquillizes the conscience, and liberates it from fear. Such repentance must be succeeded by good works as its fruits. They condemn the doctrine of such as deny, that those who have once been justified, may lose the Holy Spirit. In like manner those who contend, that some persons attain so high a degree of perfection in this life, that they cannot sin. They reject also those, who are unwilling to absolve (restore to church-privileges) such as have backslidden after baptism, even if they repent: as also those who teach, that remission of sins is not obtained through faith; but require us to merit grace by our good works.

XIII. DE USU SACRAMENTORUM.

De usu sacramentorum docent, quòd sacramenta instituta sint, non modò ut sint notæ professionis inter homines, sed magis ut sint signa et testimonia voluntatis Dei erga nos, ad excitandam et confirmandam fidem in his, qui utuntur, proposita. Itaque utendum est sacramentis, ita ut fides accedat, quæ credat promissionibus, quæ per sacramenta exhibentur et ostenduntur. Damnant igitur illos, qui docent, quod sacramenta ex opere operato justificent, nec docent

ARTICLE XIII.
OF THE USE OF THE SACRAMENTS.

Concerning the use of the sacraments our churches teach, that they were instituted not only as marks of a Christian profession amongst men; but rather as signs and evidences of the divine disposition towards us, tendered for the purpose of exciting and confirming the faith of those who use them. Hence the sacraments ought to be received with faith in the promises which are exhibited and proposed by them. They therefore condemn those who maintain, that the sa-

fidem requiri in usu sacramentorum, quæ credat remitti peccata.

craments produce justification in their recipients as a matter of course (ex opere operato), and who do not teach that faith is necessary, in the reception of the sacraments, to the remission of sins.

XIV. DE ORDINE ECCLESIASTICO.

De ordine ecclesiastico docent, quòd nemo debeat in ecclesia publicè docere, aut sacramenta administrare, nisi ritè vocatus.

ARTICLE XIV.
OF CHURCH ORDERS.

Concerning church orders they teach, that no person ought publicly to teach in the church, or to administer the sacraments, without a regular call.

XV. DE RITIBUS ECCLESIASTICIS.

De ritibus ecclesiasticis docent, quòd ritus illi servandi sint, qui sine peccato servari possunt, et prosunt ad tranquillitatem et bonum ordinem in ecclesia, sicut certæ feriæ, festa et similia. De talibus rebus tamen admonentur homines, ne conscientiæ onerentur, tanquam talis cultus ad salutem necessarius sit. Admonentur etiam, quod traditiones humanæ institutæ ad placandum Deum, ad promerendam gratiam, et satisfaciendum pro peccatis, adversentur evangelio et doctrinæ fidei. Quare vota et traditiones de cibis et diebus, &c., institutæ ad promerendam gratiam, et satisfaciendum pro peccatis, inutiles sint et contra evangelium.

ARTICLE XV.
OF RELIGIOUS CEREMONIES.

Concerning ecclesiastical ceremonies they teach, that those ceremonies ought to be observed, which can be attended to without sin, and which promote peace and good order in the church, such as certain holy-days, festivals, &c. Concerning matters of this kind, however, caution should be observed, lest the consciences of men be burdened, as though such observances were necessary to salvation. Men should also be apprised, that human traditionary observances, instituted with a view to appease God, to merit his favour, and make satisfaction for sins, are contrary to the gospel and the doctrine of faith. Wherefore vows and traditionary observances concerning meats, days, &c. instituted to merit grace and make satisfaction for sins, are useless, and contrary to the gospel.

XVI. DE REBUS CIVILIBUS.

De rebus civilibus docent, quòd legitimæ ordinationes civiles sint bona opera Dei, quòd Christianis liceat gerere magistratus, exercere judicia, judicare res ex Imperatoriis et aliis præsentibus legibus, supplicia jure constituare, jure bellare, militare, lege contrahere, tenere proprium, jusjurandum postulantibus magistratibus dare, ducere exorum, nubere. Damnant Anabaptistas, qui interdicunt hæc civilia officia Christianis. Damnant et illos, qui evangelicam perfectionem non collocant in timore Dei et fidei, sed in deserendis civilibus officiis, quia evangelium tradit justitiam æternam cordis. Interim non dissipat Politiani aut œconomiam, sed

ARTICLE XVI.
OF POLITICAL AFFAIRS.

In regard to political affairs our churches teach, that legitimate political enactments are good works of God; that it is lawful for Christians to hold civil offices, to pronounce judgment and decide cases according to the imperial and other existing laws; to inflict just punishment, wage just wars, and serve in them; to make lawful contracts; hold property; to make oath when required by the magistrate, to marry and be married. They condemn the Anabaptists, who interdict to Christians the performance of these civil duties. They also condemn those who make evangelical perfection consist not in the fear of God and in faith, but in the abandon-

APPENDIX. 527

maximè postulat conservare tanquam ordinationes Dei, et in talibus ordinationibus exercere caritatem. Itaque necessariò debent Christiani obedire magistratibus suis et legibus. Nisi cùm jubent peccare, tunc enim magis debent obedire Deo, quam hominibus, Actor. 5. v. 29.

ment of all civil duties: because the gospel teaches the necessity of ceaseless righteousness of heart, whilst it does not reject the duties of civil and domestic life, but directs them to be observed as of divine appointment, and performed in the spirit of Christian benevolence. Hence Christians ought necessarily to yield obedience to the civil officers and laws of the land; unless they should command something sinful; in which case it is a duty to obey God rather than man. Acts v. 29.

XVII. DE CHRISTI REDITU AD JUDICIUM.

Item docent, quòd Christus apparebit in consummatione mundi adjudicandum, et mortuos omnes resuscitabit, piis et electis dabit vitam æternam et perpetua gaudia, impios autem homines ac diabolos condemnabit, ut sine fine crucientur. Damnant Anabaptistas, qui sentiunt, hominibus damnatis ac diabolis finem pœnarum futurum esse. Damnant et alios, qui nunc spargunt Judiacas opiniones, quòd ante resurrectionem mortuorum, pii regnum mundi occupaturi sint, ubique oppressis impiis.

ARTICLE XVII.
OF CHRIST'S RETURN TO JUDGMENT.

Our churches also teach, that at the end of the world, Christ will appear for judgment; that he will raise all the dead; that he will give to the pious and elect eternal life and endless joys, but will condemn wicked men and devils to be punished without end. They reject the opinions of the Anabaptists, who maintain, that the punishment of devils and condemned men will have an end: in like manner they condemn those, who circulate the Judaizing notion, that, prior to the resurrection of the dead, the pious will engross the government of the world, and the wicked be every where oppressed. [German: The pious will establish a separate temporal government, and all the wicked be exterminated.]

XVIII. DE LIBERO ARBITRIO.

De libero arbitrio docent, quòd humana voluntas habeat aliquam libertatem ad efficiendam civilem justitiam, et diligendas res ratione subjectas. Sed non habet vim sine Spiritu Sancto efficiendæ justitiæ Dei, seu justitiæ spiritualis, quia animalis homo non percipit ea, quæ sunt Spiritus Dei; sed hæc fit in cordibus, cum per verbum Spiritus Sanctus concipitur. Hæc totidem verbis dicit Augustinus lib. 3. Hypognosticon. Esse fatemur liberum arbitrium omnibus hominibus, habens quidem judicium rationis, non per quod sit idoneum in iis, quæ ad Deum pertinent, sine Deo aut inchoare aut certè peragere, sed tantum in operibus vitæ præsentis tam bonis, quam etiam malis; Bonis dico, quæ de bono naturæ oriuntur, i. e. velle laborare in agro, velle manducare et bibere, velle

ARTICLE XVIII.
OF FREE WILL.

Concerning free will our churches teach, that the human will possesses some liberty for the performance of civil duties, and for the choice of those things lying within the control of reason. But it does not possess the power, without the influence of the Holy Spirit, of being just before God, or yielding spiritual obedience: for the natural man receiveth not the things which are of the Spirit of God: but this is accomplished in the heart, when the Holy Spirit is received through the word.

[The same is declared by Augustin in similar words: 'We confess that the will of man is free, having indeed the judgment of reason, not by which it may, in those things that pertain to God, be able, without Him, either to begin or accomplish any thing; but only in actions, good

habere amicum, velle habere indumenta, velle fabricare domum, uxorem velle ducere, pecora nutrire, artem discere diversarum rerum bonarum, velle quicquid bonum ad præsentem pertinet vitam. Quæ omnia non sine divino gubernaculo subsistunt, imò ex ipso et per ipsum sunt et esse cœperant. Malis verò dico, ut est: velle idolum colere, velle homicidium, etc. Damnant Pelagianos, et alios, qui docent, quòd sine Spiritu Sancto, solis naturæ viribus, possimus Deum super omnia diligere, item præcepta Dei facere, quoad substantiam actuum. Quanquam enim externa opera aliquo modo efficere natura possit: potest enim continere manus a furto, a cæde; tamen interiores motus non potest efficere, ut timorem Dei, fiduciam erga Deum, castitatem, patientiam, etc.

as well as evil, of this present life. By good, I mean those which arise from the good of nature; for instance, the desire to labour, to eat and drink, to have a friend, have clothing, build a house, marry a wife, feed cattle, learn the arts of all useful things, to choose any thing which concerns this present life; all which, however, do not subsist independently of the Divine government; nay, rather, they are of, and owe their being to, Him. But by evil, I mean, the desire to worship an idol, conceive murder,' &c. &c. They condemn the Pelagians, and others, who teach that it is possible, by the sole power of reason, without the aid of the Holy Spirit, to love God above all things, and to do his commands. For, although nature may be able to do, after a certain manner, external actions, as to keep one's hands from theft, from murder, &c.; yet it cannot perform the inner motions, such as, the fear of God, faith in God, chastity, patience, &c.]

XIX. DE CAUSA PECCATI.

De causa peccati docent, quòd tametsi Deus creat et conservat naturam, tamen causa peccati est voluntas malorum, videlicet, diaboli et impiorum, quæ non adjuvante Deo, avertit se a Deo, sicut Christus ait Joh. 8. Cùm loquitur mendacium, ex seipso loquitur.

ARTICLE XIX.
OF THE AUTHOR OF SIN.

On this subject they teach, that although God is the Creator and Preserver of universal nature; the cause of sin must be sought in the depraved will of the devil and wicked men, which, when destitute of divine aid, turns itself away from God: agreeably to the declaration of Christ, ' When he speaketh a lie, he speaketh of his own.' John viii. 44.

XX. DE BONIS OPERIBUS.

Falso accusantur nostri, quòd bona opera prohibeant. Nam scripta eorum, quæ extant de decem præceptis, et alia simili argumento testantur, quòd utiliter docuerint de omnibus vitæ generibus et officiis, quæ genera vitæ, quæ opera in qualibet vocatione Deo placeant. De quibus rebus olim parum docebant Concionatores, tantum puerilia et non necessaria opera urgebant, ut certas ferias, certa jejunia, fraternitates, peregrinationes, cultus sanctorum, rosaria, monachatum et similia. Hæc adversarii nostri admoniti non dediscunt, nec perinde prædicant hæc inutilia opera, ut olim. Præterea incipiunt fidei mentionem facere, de qua olim mirum erat silentium. Docent, nos non tantùm operibus justifi-

ARTICLE XX.
OF GOOD WORKS.

Our writers are falsely accused of prohibiting good works. Their publications on the ten commandments, and other similar subjects, shew, that they gave good instructions concerning all the different stations and duties of life, and explained what course of conduct, in any particular calling, is pleasing to God. Concerning these things preachers formerly said very little, but urged the necessity of puerile and useless works, such as certain holy-days, fasts, brotherhoods, pilgrimages, worship of saints, rosaries, monastic vows,&c. These useless things, our adversaries, having been admonished, no longer teach as formerly. Moreover, they now begin to make mention of faith, about which they formerly observed a marvellous si-

APPENDIX. 529

cari, sed conjungunt fidem et opera, et dicunt, nos fide et operibus justificari. Quæ doctrina tolerabilior est priore, et plus affere potest consolationis, quàm vetus ipsorum doctrina. Cùm igitur doctrina de fide, quam oportet in ecclesia præcipuam esse, tam diu jacuerit ignota, quemadmodum fateri omnes necesse est, de fidei justitia altissimum silentium fuisse in concionibus, tantùm doctrinam operum versatam esse in Ecclesiis, nostri de fide sic admonuerunt Ecclesias. Principio, quod opera nostra non possint reconciliare Deum, aut merere remissionem peccatorum, et gratiam, et justificationem, sed hanc tantùm fide consequimur, credentes quòd propter Christum recipiamur in gratiam, qui solus positus est mediator et propitiatorium, per quam reconcilietur pater. Itaque qui confidit, operibus se mereri gratiam, is aspernatur Christi meritum et gratiam, et quærit sine Christo humanis viribus viam ad Deum, cum Christus de se dixerit: Ego sum via, veritas et vita. Hæc doctrina de fide ubique in Paulo tractatur, (Eph. 2.) 'Gratia salvi facti estis per fidem, et hoc non ex vobis. Dei donum est non ex operibus,' etc. Et ne quis cavilletur, a nobis novam Pauli interpretationem excogitari, tota hæc. causa habet testimonia Patrum. Nam Augustinus multis voluminibus defendit gratiam et justitiam fidei contra merita operum. Et similia docet Ambrosius de vocatione Gentium, et alibi. Sic enim inquit de vocatione gentium: Vilesceret redemtio sanguinis Christi, nec misericordiæ Dei humanorum operum prærogativa succumberet, si justificatio quæ fit per gratiam, merites præcedentibus deberetur, ut non munus largientis, sed merces esset operantis. Quanquam autem hæc doctrina contemnitur ab imperitis, tamen experiuntur piæ ac pavidæ conscientiæ, plurimum eam consolationis afferre, quia conscientiæ non possunt reddi tranquillæ per ulla opera, sed tantùm fide, cùm certo statuunt, quòd propter Christum habeant placatum Deum. Quemadmodum Paulus docet, (Rom. v.) 'Justificati per fidem, pacem habemus apud Deum.' Tota hæc doctrina ad illud certamen perterrefactæ conscientiæ referenda est, nec sine illo

lence. They now teach, that we are not justified by works alone, but join faith to works, and maintain that we are justified by faith and works. This doctrine is more tolerable than their former belief, and is calculated to impart more consolation to the mind. Inasmuch, then, as the doctrine concerning faith, which should be regarded as a principal one by the church, had so long been unknown; for all must confess, that concerning the righteousness of faith, the most profound silence reigned in their sermons, and the doctrine concerning works alone was discussed in the churches; our divines have admonished the churches as follows:—First, that our works cannot reconcile us to God, or merit the remission of sins, or grace, or justification; but this we can attain only by faith, when we believe that we are accepted by grace, for Christ's sake, who alone is appointed our mediator and propitiatory sacrifice, by which the Father is reconciled. He, therefore, who expects to merit grace by his works, casts contempt on the merits of Christ, and is seeking the way to God, in his own strength, without the Saviour; who nevertheless has told us, 'I am the way, the truth, and the life.' This doctrine concerning faith, is incessantly inculcated by the apostle Paul, (Ephes. ii.) 'Ye are saved by grace, through faith, and that not of yourselves, it is the gift of God,' &c. And lest any one should cavil at our interpretation, and charge it with novelty, we state that this whole matter is supported by the testimony of the fathers. For Augustin devotes several volumes to the defence of grace, and the righteousness of faith, in opposition to the merit of good works. And Ambrosius, on the calling of the Gentiles, &c. inculcates the same doctrine. But although this doctrine is despised by the ignorant; the consciences of the pious and timid find it a source of much consolation, for they cannot attain tranquillity in any works, but in faith alone, when they entertain the confident belief that, for Christ's sake, God is reconciled to them. Thus Paul teaches us, Rom. v. 'Being justified by faith, we have peace with God.'

certamine intelligi potest. Quare malè judicant de ea re homines imperiti et prophani, qui Christianam justitiam nihil esse somniant, nisi civilem et philosophicam justitiam. Olim vexabantur conscientiæ doctrina operum non audiebant ex evangelio consolationem. Quosdam conscientia expulit in desertum, in monasteria, sperantes ibi se gratiam merituros esse per vitam monasticam. Alii alia excogitaverunt opera, ad promerendam gratiam et satisfaciendum pro peccatis. Ideo magnoperè fuit opus, hanc doctrinam de fide in Christum tradere, et renovare, ne deesset consolatio pavidis conscientiis, sed scirent, fide in Christum apprehendi gratiam et remissionem peccatorum et justificationem. Admonentur etiam homines, quòd hic nomen fidei non significet tantùm historiæ notitiam, qualis est in impiis et diabolo, sed significet fidem, quæ credit non tantum historiam, sed etiam effectum historiæ, videlicet hunc articulum, Remissionem peccatorum, quòd videlicet per Christum habeamus gratiam, justitiam et remissionem peccatorum. Jam qui scit, se per Christum habere propitium Patrem, is verè novit Deum, scit se ei curæ esse, invocat eum; Denique non est sine Deo sicut gentis. Nam diaboli et impii non possunt hunc articulum credere, Remissionem peccatorum. Ideo Deum tanquam hostem oderunt, non invocant eum, nihil boni ab eo expectant. Augustinus etiam de fidei nomine hoc modo admonet lectorem et docet, in scripturis nomen fidei accipi, non pro notitia, qualis est in impiis, sed pro fiducia, quæ consolatur et erigit perterrefactas mentes. Præterea docent nostri, quòd necesse sit bona opera facere, non ut confidamus per ea gratiam mereri, sed propter voluntatem Dei. Tantùm fide apprehenditur remissio peccatorum ac gratia. Et quia per fidem accipitur Spiritus Sanctus, jam corda renovantur, et induunt novus affectus, ut parere bona opera possint. Sic enim ait Ambrosius: Fides bonæ voluntatis, et justæ actionis genetrix est. Nam humanæ vires, sine Spiritu Sancto, plenæ sunt impiis affectibus, et sunt imbecilliores, quàm ut bona opera possint efficere coram Deo. Adhæc, sunt in potestate diaboli, qui impellit hominis

This whole doctrine must be referred to the conflict in the conscience of the alarmed sinner, nor can it be otherwise understood. Hence the ignorant and worldly-minded are much mistaken, who vainly imagine that the righteousness of the Christian is nothing else than what in common life and in the language of philosophy is termed morality. Formerly the consciences of men were harassed by the doctrine of works, nor did they receive any consolation from the gospel. Some followed the dictates of conscience into deserts, and into monasteries; hoping there to merit the divine favour by a monastic life. Others invented different kinds of works, to merit grace, and make satisfaction for their sins. There was therefore the utmost necessity, that this doctrine concerning faith in Christ should be inculcated anew; in order that timid minds might find consolation, and know that justification and the remission of sins are obtained by faith in the Saviour. The people are also now instructed, that faith does not signify a mere historical belief, such as wicked men and devils have; but that in addition to a historical belief, it includes an acquaintance with the consequences of the history, such as remission of sins, by grace through Christ, righteousness, &c. &c. Now he who knows that the Father is reconciled to him through the Son, possesses a true acquaintance with God, confides in his providence, and calls upon his name: and is therefore not without God as are the Gentiles. For the devil and wicked men cannot believe the article concerning the remission of sins. But they hate God as an enemy, do not call upon his name, nor expect any thing good at his hands. Augustin, in speaking of the word faith, admonishes the reader that in scripture this word does not signify mere knowledge, such as wicked men possess, but that confidence or trust by which alarmed sinners are comforted and lifted up. We moreover teach, that the performance of good works is necessary, because it is commanded of God, and not because we expect to merit grace by them. Pardon of sins and grace are obtained only by faith. And because

ad varia peccata, ad impias opiniones, ad manifesta scelera. Quemadmodum est videre in philosophis qui et ipsi conati honestè vivere, tamen id non potuerunt efficere, sed contaminati sunt multis manifestis sceleribus. Talis est imbecilitas hominis, cum est sine fide et sine Spiritu Sancto, et tantum humanis viribus se gubernat. Hinc facilè apparet, hanc doctrinam non esse accusandam, quòd bona opera prohibeat, sed multò magis laudandam, quòd ostendit, quomodo bona opera facere possimus. Nam sine fide nullo modo potest humana natura primi aut secundi præcepti opera facere. Sine fide non invocat Deum, à Deo nihil expectat, non tolerat crucem, sed quærit humana præsidia, confidit humanis præsidiis. Ita regnant in corde omnes cupiditates, et humana concilia, cùm abest fides et fiducia erga Deum. Quare et Christus dixit: Sine me nihil potestis facere, Joh. 15. Et Ecclesia canit: Sine tuo numine, nihil est in homine, nihil est innoxium.

the Holy Spirit is received by faith, the heart of man is renovated, and new affections produced, that he may be able to perform good works. Accordingly Ambrosius states, faith is the source of holy volitions and an upright life. For the faculties of man, unaided by the Holy Spirit, are replete with sinful propensities, and too feeble to perform works that are good in the sight of God. They are moreover under the influence of Satan, who urges men to various crimes, and impious opinions, and manifest offences; as may be seen in the examples of the philosophers who, though they endeavoured to lead perfectly moral lives, failed to accomplish their design, and were guilty of many notorious crimes. Such is the imbecility of man, when he undertakes to govern himself by his own strength without faith and the Holy Spirit. From all this it is manifest, that our doctrine, instead of deserving censure for the prohibition of good works, ought much rather to be applauded, for teaching the manner in which truly good works can be performed. For without faith, human nature is incapable of performing the duties either of the first or second table. Without it, man does not call upon God, nor expect any thing from him, but seeks refuge amongst men, and reposes on human aid. Hence when faith and confidence in God are wanting, all evil desires and human schemes reign in the heart; as Christ says, 'without me ye can do nothing,' John xv.; and the church responds, Without thy favour there is nothing good in man.

XXI. DE CULTU SANCTORUM.

De cultu sanctorum docent, quòd memoria sanctorum proponi potest, ut imitemur fidem eorum, et bona opera juxta vocationem; Ut Cæsar imitari potest exemplum Davidis in bello gerendo ad depellendos Turcas à patria. Nam uterque rex est. Sed scriptura non docet invocare sanctos, seu petere auxilium à sanctis. Quia unum Christum nobis proponit mediatorem, propitiatorium, Pontificem et intercessorem. Hic invocandus est, et promisit, se exaudi-

ARTICLE XXI.

OF THE INVOCATION OF SAINTS.

Concerning the invocation of saints our churches teach, that the saints ought to be held in remembrance, in order that we may, each in his own calling, imitate their faith and good works; that the emperor may imitate the example of David, in carrying on war to expel the Turks from our country; for both are kings. But the sacred volume does not teach us to invoke saints or to seek aid from them. For it proposes Christ to us as our

turum esse preces nostras, et hunc cultum maximè probat, videlicet ut invocetur in omnibus aflictionibus, 1 Joh. ii. Si quis peccat, habemus advocatum apud Deum, etc. Hæc ferè summa est doctrinæ apud nos, in qua cerni potest, nihil inesse, quod discrepit à scripturis, vel ab Ecclesia Catholica, vel ab Ecclesia Romana quatenus ex scriptoribus nota est. Quod cùm ita sit, inclementer judicant isti, qui nostras pro hæreticis haberi postulant, sed dissensio est de quibusdam abusibus, qui sine certa auctoritate in Ecclesias irrepserunt, in quibus etiam, si qua esset dissimilitudo, tamen decebat hæc lenitas Episcopos, ut propter confessionem, quam modò recensuimus, tolerarent nostros, quia ne canones quidem tàm duri sunt, ut eosdem ritus ubique esse postulent, neque similes unquam omnium Ecclesiarum ritus fuerunt. Quanquam apud nos magna exparte veteres ritus diligenter servantur. Falsa enim calumnia est, quòd omnes ceremoniæ, omnia vetera instituta in Ecclesiis nostris aboleantur. Verùm publica querela fuit, abusus quosdam, in vulgaribus ritibus hærere. Hi quia non poterant bona conscientia probari, aliqua ex parte correcti sunt.

only mediator, propitiation, high priest, and intercessor. On his name we are to call, and he promises, that he will hear our prayers, and highly approves of this worship, viz.; that he should be called upon in every affliction, 1 John ii. : ' If any one sin, we have an advocate with the Father,' &c. This is the substance of our doctrines, from which it is evident, that they contain nothing inconsistent with the scriptures, or opposed either to the catholic (universal) or to the Roman church, so far as they accord with scripture. Under these circumstances, those certainly judge harshly, who would have us regarded as heretics. But the difference of opinion between us relates to certain abuses, which have crept into the churches without any good authority; in regard to which, if we do differ, the bishops ought to treat with lenity and tolerate us, on account of the confession, which we have just made. For, even the canons of the church are not so rigid, as to require every where a uniformity of rites; nor have the rites of all the churches ever been the same. Nevertheless, the ancient rites of the church we have in general carefully retained. For it is a slanderous charge, that all the ancient customs and institutions are abolished in our churches. But there was a general complaint, that some abuses had crept into the customary rites; and these, because we could not with a good conscience retain them, we have in part corrected.

'THE CORRUPTIONS IN THE CATHOLIC CHURCH WHICH THE REFORMERS CORRECTED.*

In addition to the preceding confession of their faith, the confessors also submitted to the Diet a list of the corruptions which had crept into the Roman church, and which had been corrected by them. As this list of abuses corrected, is seldom found annexed to the modern editions of the confessions, and will moreover not be entirely superfluous at the present day, we here present them to the reader, from the authentic German edition of Dr. Baumgarten.'

CHAPTER I.
OF COMMUNION IN ONE KIND.

As there is nothing contained in the doctrines of our churches, inconsistent with scripture, or with the catholic church; and as we have merely rejected certain abuses,

* The Translation of these chapters, on the abuses which crept into the church, is from the work of Dr. Schmucker, already referred to, with the exception of co. iii. iv. and vii., which having been very much abridged or omitted by Dr. S., the Editor has supplied.

some of which had in the course of time crept into the church, whilst others were forcibly introduced into it; necessity demands that we should give some account of them, and assign the reasons which induced us to admit the alterations, in order that your imperial majesty may perceive that nothing was done in this matter in an unchristian or presumptuous manner, but that we were compelled to admit these alterations by the word of God, which is justly to be held in higher regard than any customs of the church. In our churches, communion is administered to the laity in both kinds, because we regard this as a manifest command and precept of Christ, Matt. xxvi. 27. 'Drink ye all of it.' In this passage Christ teaches, in the plainest terms, that they should all drink out of the cup. And in order that no one may be able to cavil at these words, and explain them as referring to the clergy alone, Paul informs us, that the entire church at Corinth received the sacrament in both kinds, 1 Cor. xi. 26. And this custom was retained in the church, as is proved by history and the writings of the fathers. Cyprian frequently mentions the fact that in his day, the cup was given to the laity. St. Jerome also says, the priests who administer the sacrament, dispense the blood of Christ to the people. And pope Gelasius himself commanded, that the sacrament should not be divided. (Distinct. 2. de Consecrat. cap. Comperimus.) There is no canon extant which commands that one kind alone should be received. Nor can it be ascertained when, or by whom, the custom of receiving bread alone was introduced, although cardinal Cusanus mentions the time when it was approved. Now it is evident, that such a custom, introduced contrary to the divine command, and also in opposition to the ancient canons, is wrong. It was therefore improper to coerce and oppress the conscience of those who wished to receive the sacrament, agreeably to the appointment of Christ, and compel them to violate the institution of our Lord. And inasmuch as the dividing of the sacrament is contrary to its institution by Christ, the host is not carried about in procession amongst us.

CHAPTER II.
THE CELIBACY OF THE PRIESTS.

There has been general complaint among persons of every rank on account of the scandalous licentiousness and lawless lives of the priests; who were guilty of lewdness, and whose excesses had risen to the highest pitch. In order to put an end to such odious conduct, to adultery, and other lewd practices, several of our ministers have entered the matrimonial state. They themselves declare, that in taking this step they were influenced by the dictates of conscience, and a sacred regard for the holy volume, which expressly informs us, that marriage was appointed of God to prevent licentiousness: as Paul says, (1 Cor. vii. 2.) ' To avoid fornication, let every man have his own wife.' Again, ' It is better to marry than to burn;' (1 Cor. vii. 9.) and according to the declaration of Christ, that not all men can receive this word, (Matt. xix. 12.) In this passage Christ himself, who well knew what was in man, declares that few persons are qualified to live in celibacy: for 'God created us male and female,' (Gen. i. 27.) And experience has abundantly proved how vain is the attempt to alter the nature or meliorate the character of God's creatures by mere human purposes or vows, without a peculiar gift or grace of God. It is notorious that the effort has been prejudicial to purity of morals; and in how many cases it has occasioned distress of mind, and the most terrific apprehensions of conscience, is known by the confessions of numerous individuals. Since then the word and law of God cannot be altered by human vows or enactments, the priests for this and other reasons have entered into the conjugal state. It is moreover evident from the testimony of history and the writings of the fathers, that it was customary in former ages for priests and deacons to be married. Hence the injunction of Paul to Timothy, (1 Tim. iii. 2.) ' A bishop then must be blameless, *the husband of one wife*.' It is but four hundred years since the clergy in Germany were compelled by force to abandon the matrimonial life, and submit to a vow of celibacy; and so generally and resolutely did they resist this tyranny, that the archbishop of Mayence, who published this papal edict, was well nigh losing his life in a commotion excited by the measure. And in so precipitate and arbitrary a manner was that decree executed, that the pope not only prohibited all future marriages of the priests, but even cruelly rent asunder the social ties of those who had long been living in the bonds of lawful wedlock, thus violating alike not only the laws of God, and the natural and civil rights of the citizen, but even the canons which the popes themselves made, and the decrees of the most celebrated councils! It is the deliberate and well-known opinion of many distinguished, pious, and judicious men, that this compulsory celibacy and prohibition of matrimony (which God himself instituted and left optional), has been productive of no good, but is the prolific source of numerous and abominable vices. Yea, even one of the popes, Pius II., himself declared, as history informs us, that though there may be several reasons why the marriage of priests should be prohibited, there are many more and weightier ones why it should not. And doubtless this was the deliberate declaration of Pius, who was a sensible and wise man. We would therefore confidently trust, that your majesty, as a Christian emperor, will graciously reflect, that in these latter days, to which reference is made in the sacred volume, the world has become still more degenerate, and mankind more frail and liable to temptation. It will be well to beware, lest, by the prohibition of marriage, licentiousness and vice be promoted in the German States. For on this subject no man can devise better or more salutary laws than those enacted by God, who himself instituted marriage for the promotion of virtue amongst men. The ancient canons also enjoin that the rigour of human enactments must on some subjects be accommodated to the infirmities of human nature, in order to avoid greater evils. Such a course would in this case be necessary and Christian: for what injury could result to the church, from the marriage of the clergy, and others who are to serve in the church? yea, it is probable that the church will be but imperfectly supplied with ministers, should this rigorous prohibition of marriage be continued. If therefore it is evident from the divine word and command, that matrimony is lawful in ministers, and history teaches that their practice formerly was conformed to this precept; if it is evident that the vow of celibacy has been productive of the most scandalous and unchristian conduct, of adultery, unheard-of licentiousness, and other abominable crimes, among the clergy, as some of the dignitaries at Rome have themselves often confessed and lamented, it is a lamentable thing that the Christian estate of matrimony has not only been presumptuously forbidden, but in some places speedy punishment been inflicted as though it were a heinous crime! Matrimony is moreover declared a lawful and honourable estate, by the laws of your imperial majesty, and by the code of every empire in which justice and law prevailed. Of late, however, innocent subjects, and especially ministers, are cruelly tormented on account of their marriage. Nor is such conduct a violation of the divine laws alone; it is equally opposed to the canons of the church. The apostle Paul denominates that a doctrine of devils which forbids marriage, (1 Tim. iv. 1, 3.) And Christ says, (John viii. 44.) 'The devil is a murderer from the beginning.' For that may well be regarded as a doctrine of devils which forbids marriage and enforces the prohibition by the shedding of blood. But as no human law can abrogate or change a command of God, neither can any vows produce this effect. Therefore Cyprian also admonishes, that if any woman do not observe the vow of chastity, it is better for her to be married: (Lib. i.) and all the canons observe more lenity and justice toward those who assumed the vow of celibacy in youth, as is generally the case with priests and monks.

CHAPTER III.
Of the Mass.

Our churches are falsely accused that they abolish the mass; for the mass is retained by us, and is celebrated with high reverence. Also almost all the usual ceremonies are observed, except that in some places German are mixed with the Latin songs, which are added for the purpose of teaching the people; for ceremonies serve to teach the inexperienced. And not only Paul commandeth to use in the church a tongue which the people understand; but also it is constituted and ordained by the law of man.

The people are accustomed to use the sacrament together, if any be prepared for it; and that also doth increase the reverence and the religion of public ceremonies; for none are admitted and allowed to receive the sacrament, but such as are first examined. They are also admonished of the dignity and use of the sacrament, how great comfort it brings to fearful and trembling consciences, to the intent that they may learn to believe God, and ask and look for all good things from him.

This honour delights God; such use of the sacraments nourishes piety towards God. Therefore it does not appear that the mass is celebrated with more reverence among our adversaries than with us. It is undoubtedly and evidently known also that this hath been a common and very grievous complaint of all good men of a long season, that the masses have been shamefully abused and applied to lucre; and every man sees how wide this abuse doth appear in all temples, and by what sort of men masses are said, only for reward or stipend; how many celebrate contrary to the injunctions of the canons. But Paul grievously threatens those who treat the sacrament unworthily, when he says, 'whoso eateth this bread and drinketh this cup of the Lord unworthily, shall be guilty of the body and blood of the Lord.' Therefore when our priests were admonished of that sin, private masses ceased with us, because almost all private masses were done for lucre and advantage. And the bishops knew of these abuses well, and if they had corrected them in time, there would have been less dissension than there now is. Before, by reason of their dissimulation and unwillingness to hear and see what was amiss, they suffered many vices to creep into the church. Now they begin, when too late, to complain of the calamities and miseries of the church, when indeed all this tumult has arisen from no other source than these abuses, which were so manifest that they could be endured no longer. There are now great dissensions touching the mass and sacrament; and peradventure the world is punished for so long profaning and abusing masses, which the bishops have suffered for so many ages in the churches, when they both could and ought to have amended them: for it is written in the decalogue, that he that abuseth the name of God shall not be unpunished. But since the world began, nothing that God ever ordained hath been so abused and turned to filthy lucre as the mass has been. An opinion came in which increased private masses above measure: viz. that Christ by his passion did satisfy for original sin, but did institute and ordain the mass that it should be an oblation for daily sins, both mortal and venial. From this sprung a common opinion that the mass is a work that taketh away the sins of the quick and dead, by reason of the work wrought. Then arose the dispute whether one mass for many were as much worth as if for each individual a separate mass had been said. This disputation brought forth an infinite multitude of masses. Of these opinions our preachers and learned men gave warning that they dissented from holy scripture, and tarnished the glory of the passion of Christ. For the passion of Christ was an oblation and satisfaction not only for original sin, but also for all other sins; as it is written in the Hebrews, 'We are sanctified by the offering of the body of Jesus Christ once for all;' also ' by one oblation he hath perfected for ever them that are sanctified.' Also the scripture teaches, that we are justified before God by faith in Christ, when we believe that our sins are forgiven us for Christ's sake. Now if the mass takes away the sins of the quick and dead even by its own proper virtue, their justification is the work of masses and not of faith; which thing scripture denies. But Christ commands to do it in remembrance of him. Wherefore the mass was instituted, that faith in them that use the sacrament should remember what benefits it receives by Christ, and so should raise up and comfort the trembling and fearful conscience. For to remember Christ is to remember the benefits of Christ, and to think that, truly and in very deed, they are exhibited to us. Neither is it enough for us to remember the history; for this wicked men and Jews may remember. Wherefore the mass is to be celebrated that the sacrament may be administered to those who have need of comfort. Ambrose said, 'because I always sin, I ought always to take medicine.' Now forasmuch as the mass is such a communication of the sacrament, one common mass is kept by us every holy day; and also on other days, if any desire the sacrament, it is given to them that ask it. And this manner is not new in the church. For the old fathers before Gregory speak nothing of the private, but very much of the common, mass. Chrysostom says, 'That the priest standeth daily at the altar, and some he calls to communion, and others he keeps away.' And it appears by the old canons that some one priest did celebrate the mass, and from him all the other priests and deacons received the body of the Lord; for so are the words of the canon of Nice, Let deacons in order after the priests receive communion from the bishop or priests. And Paul, speaking of the communion, commands, that one should tarry for another that there may be a common participation. Forasmuch then as the mass, according to us, has the example of the church taken out of the holy scriptures and fathers, we trust that it cannot be improved; especially since the common and public ceremonies are, for the most part, kept in the usual way, only the number of masses is unlike; which, for great and manifest abuses, it were profitable at least to moderate. For in times past mass was not celebrated every day, not even in great congregations, and where most people assembled together, as the Tripartite history, lib. ix. cap. 38. testifies. Again, in Alexandria scriptures are read on Wednesdays and Fridays, and doctors expound them, and all things are done without the solemn custom of the oblation.

CHAPTER IV.
Of Confession.

Confession is not done away in our churches; for the body of the Lord is not delivered to any except they are first examined and absolved. And the people are most diligently instructed in the faith of absolution: of which before this time there was little mention. The people are taught to hold the absolution in great esteem; because it is the voice of God, and pronounced by His command. The power of the keys is highly extolled, by shewing how much comfort it brings to troubled consciences; and that God requires faith that we should give credence to that absolution as to a voice sounding from heaven; and that faith in Christ truly obtains and receives remission of sins.

Before this, satisfactions were too much magnified, but there was no mention of faith and the merits of Christ, and of the righteousness of faith; wherefore in this our churches are not to be blamed. For even our adversaries are compelled to admit, that the doctrine of penance is most diligently treated and opened by our divines. But concerning confession they teach that the enumeration of sins is not necessary; and that consciences are not to be charged with the care of reckoning up all faults, for it is impossible to rehearse all sins, as the prophet records, saying, 'Who can understand his errors?' Jeremiah also says, 'The heart of man is deceitful above all things, and desperately wicked.' Wherefore if no sins should be forgiven but those which can be rehearsed, consciences could never be quieted; for many sins they neither see nor remember. Also, old writers witness that the numbering of sins is not necessary, for, in the decrees, Chrysostom is cited speaking thus: 'I say not to thee that thou shew thyself openly, nor ac use thyself before others, but I wish thee to obey the prophet, saying, 'declare thy way before God;' therefore confess thy sins, with prayer, unto God the true judge. Lay open the sins not with the tongue, but with the memory of thy conscience,' &c. &c. And the gloss concerning penance acknowledges that confession is of human authority.

CHAPTER V.

OF DIVERSITY OF MEATS.

The doctrine was formerly inculcated, that the diversity of meats and other human traditions were useful in order to merit grace and make satisfaction for sin. Hence new fasts, new ceremonies, and new orders, were daily invented, and strenuously insisted on as necessary parts of worship, the neglect of which was attended with heinous guilt. Thus occasion was given to many scandalous corruptions in the church. In the first place, the grace of Christ and the doctrine concerning faith are thereby obscured. Yet these doctrines are inculcated in the gospel with great solemnity, the merits of Christ are represented as of the utmost importance, and faith in the Redeemer is placed far above all human merits. Hence the apostle Paul inveighs bitterly against the observance of the Mosaic ritual and human traditions, in order to teach us that we acquire righteousness and grace not by our own works, but by faith in Christ. This doctrine was however entirely obscured by the notion that grace must be merited by legal observances, fasts, diversities of meats, habits, &c. *Secondly*, such traditions were calculated to obscure the divine law; for these traditions are elevated far above the word of God. No one was regarded as leading a Christian life, who did not observe these holy days, and pray, and fast, and dress, in this peculiar manner. Truly good works were regarded as mere worldly matter, such as fulfilling the duties of our calling, the labours of a father to support his family and educate them in the fear of the Lord, that mothers should take charge of their children, that the government should rule the country, &c. Such works which God has commanded, were pronounced worldly and imperfect, but these traditions had the credit of being the only holy and perfect works. For these reasons, to the making of such traditions there was no end. *Thirdly*, these traditions became extremely burdensome to the consciences of men. For it was not possible to observe them all, and yet the people were taught to regard them as necessary parts of worship. Gerson asserts that many were thus driven to despair, and some put an end to their own existence, because they heard of no consolation in the grace of Christ. How much the consciences of men were perplexed on these subjects, is evident from the writings of those divines (summistis) who undertook to compile these traditions, and point out what was just and proper. So complicated an undertaking did they find it, that in the mean time the salutary doctrines of the gospel on more important subjects, such as faith and consolation in affliction, and others of like import, were totally neglected. Accordingly many pious men of those times complained that these traditions served only to excite contention and prevent devout souls from attaining the true knowledge of Christ. Gerson and several others uttered bitter complaints on this subject. And Augustin also complains, that the consciences of men ought not to be burdened with these numerous and useless traditions. Our divines were therefore compelled by necessity, and not by contempt of their spiritual superiors, to correct the erroneous views which had grown out of the misapprehension of these traditions. For the gospel absolutely requires that the doctrine of faith be steadily inculcated in the churches; but this doctrine cannot be rightly understood by those who expect to merit grace by works of their own appointment. We therefore teach that the observance of these human traditions cannot merit grace, or atone for sins, or reconcile us unto God; and ought therefore not to be represented as a necessary part of Christian duty. The proofs of this position are derived from scripture. Christ excuses his apostles for not observing the traditions, saying, 'In vain do they worship me, teaching for doctrines the commandments of men.' As He calls this a vain service, it cannot be a necessary one. And, again, 'Not that which goeth into the mouth defileth a man.' (Matth. xv. 3, 9, 11.) Again, Paul says, 'The kingdom of God is not meat and drink.' (Rom. xiv. 17.) 'Let no man therefore judge you in meat or in drink.' (Col. ii. 16.) Peter says, 'Why tempt ye God to put a yoke upon the neck of the disciples which

APPENDIX.

neither our fathers nor we were able able to bear? But we believe that through the grace of our Lord Jesus Christ we shall be saved.' (Acts xv. 10, 11.) Here Peter expressly forbids that the consciences of men should be burdened with mere external ceremonies, either those of the Mosaic ritual or others. And Paul calls those prohibitions which forbid meats and to be married, 'doctrines of devils.' (1 Tim. iv. 1, 3.) For it is diametrically contrary to the gospel either to institute or perform such works with a view to merit pardon of sin, or under the impression that no one can be a Christian who does not observe them. The charge, however, that we forbid the mortification of our sinful propensities, as Jovian asserts, is groundless. For our writers have always given instruction concerning the cross which it is the duty of Christians to bear. We moreover teach, that it is the duty of every one, by fasting and other exercises, to avoid giving any occasion to sin, but not to merit grace by such works. But this watchfulness over our body is to be observed always, not on particular days only. On this subject Christ says, ' Take heed to yourselves lest at any time your hearts be overcharged with surfeiting.' (Luke xxi. 34.) Again, ' The devils are not cast out but by fasting and prayer. (Matth. xvii. 21.) And Paul says, ' I keep under my body, and bring it into subjection.' (1 Cor. ix. 27.) By which he wishes to estimate, that this bodily discipline is not designed to merit grace, but to keep the body in a suitable condition for the several duties of our calling. We do not therefore object to fasting itself, but to the fact that it is represented as a necessary duty, and that specific days have been fixed for its performance.

CHAPTER VI.

OF MONASTIC VOWS.

In speaking of Monasticism it will be requisite to consider the light in which it has been viewed, the disorders which have occurred in monasteries, and the fact that many things are yet daily done in them contrary both to the word of God and the papal directions. In the time of St. Augustin the monastic life was optional; subsequently, when the doctrine and the discipline of monasteries were corrupted, vows were invented, in order that the evil might be remedied as it were by a species of incarceration. In addition to these monastic vows, other burdens were invented, by which persons were oppressed even during their minority. Many adopted this mode of life through ignorance, who, though of riper years, were fully acquainted with their infirmity. All these, in whatever way they may have been enticed or coerced into these vows, are compelled to remain, although even the papal regulations would liberate many of them. This severity has frequently been censured by many pious persons in former times; for they well knew that both boys and girls were often thrust into these monasteries merely for the purpose of being supported. They saw also the deplorable consequences of this course, and many have complained that the canons have been so grossly violated. Monastic vows were also represented in a very improper light. They were represented as equal to baptism, and as a method of deserving pardon and justification before God, yea as being not only a meritorious righteousness, but also the fulfilment of the commands and counsels of the gospel. They also taught that the monastic life was more meritorious than all the professions which God appointed : such as that of minister, civil officers, &c. as their own books will prove, and they cannot deny. In short, he that has been enticed into a monastery, will learn but little of Christ. Formerly schools were kept in monasteries, in which the scriptures and other things were taught, so that ministers and bishops could be selected from them. Now they pretend that the monastic life is so meritorious in the sight of God, as to be a state of perfection far superior to those modes of life which God himself has commanded. In opposition to all this we teach, that all who do not feel inclined to a life of celibacy, have the power and right to marry. Their vows to the contrary cannot annul the command of God : nevertheless, to avoid fornication, ' let every man have his own wife, and let every woman have her own husband.' (1 Cor. vii. 2.) To this course we are urged and compelled, both by the divine precepts, and the general nature of man, agreeably to the declaration of God himself; ' It is not good for man to be alone, I will make him an help meet for him.' (Gen. ii. 18.) Although the divine precept concerning marriage already absolves many from their monastic vows, our writers assign many other reasons to demonstrate that they are not binding. Every species of worship invented by men, without a divine precept, in order to merit justification and grace, is contrary to the gospel and the will of God. As Christ himself says, ' But in vain do they worship me, teaching for doctrines the commandments of men.' (Matt. xv. 9.) Coincident with this is the doctrine of Paul, that we should not seek our righteousness in our own services, invented by men; that true righteousness in the sight of God must be sought in faith, and in our confidence in the mercy of God through Christ, his only Son. But it is notorious, that the monks represent their fictitious righteousness as amply sufficient to merit the pardon of sin and divine grace. But what is this else than to rob the merits of Christ of their glory, and to deny the righteousness of faith? Hence it follows, that these vows were unjust and a false worship, and of course not binding. For a vow to do any thing contrary to the divine command, that is an 'oath improper in itself, is not obligatory, as even the canons declare; for an oath cannot bind us to sin.' St. Paul says to the Galatians, 'Christ is become of no effect unto you, whosoever of you are justified by the law; ye are fallen from grace.' (Gal. v. 4.) Those therefore who would be justified by their vows, have abandoned the grace of God through Christ; for they rob Christ of his glory, who alone can justify us, and transfer this glory to their vows and monastic life. It is moreover a corruption of the divine law and of true worship, to hold up the monastic life to the people as the only perfect one. For Christian perfection consists in this, that we love and fear God with all our heart, and yet combine with it sincere reliance and faith in him through Christ: that it is our privilege and duty to supplicate the throne of grace for such things as we need in all our trials, and in our respective callings; and to give diligence in the performance of good works. It is in this that true perfection consists, and the true worship of God, but not in begging, or in a black or a white cap. This extravagant praise of celibacy, is calculated to disseminate among the people erroneous views on the sanctity of the married life. Examples are on record, of persons who abandoned their wives and children, and business, and shut themselves up in a monastery, under the vain impression that thus they came out from the world, and led a holier life. They forgot that we ought to serve God according to his own directions, and not the inventions of men.

CHAPTER VII.
OF THE POWER OF THE CHURCH.

There have been great disputes respecting the power of bishops, in which many men have injuriously mingled together the power of the church and the power of the sword. From this confusion the greatest wars and commotions have proceeded; while the pontiffs, relying upon the power of the keys, have not only instituted new modes of worship—have not only, with reservation of cases, and with violent communications, burdened consciences; but have also attempted to transfer the kingdoms of the world, and to take away the empire from emperors. Well disposed and learned men have long since reproved these vices in the church. Therefore our preachers, for the comforting of consciences, have been compelled to shew the difference between the ecclesiastical power, and the power of the sword; and have taught that both of them are, because of God's commandment, to be had in great reverence and honour as the highest benefits of God upon earth. And thus our learned men think that the power of the keys, or the power of the bishop, is, according to the gospel, a power to preach the gospel, to remit and retain sins, and to minister the sacraments. For with this commandment Christ sent forth his apostles, saying, 'As my Father hath sent me, even so I send you.' 'Receive ye the Holy Ghost; whose sins ye remit, they are remitted unto them, and whose sins ye retain, they are retained.' (John xx.) Also, in the gospel according to Mark, he says, 'Go, preach the gospel to every creature,' &c. (Mark xvi.)

This power is to be exercised only in teaching or preaching the word, and by administering the sacraments either to many or few, as the case may be; for here are granted, not corporal things but eternal things, as eternal righteousness, the Holy Ghost, eternal life. These things cannot come but by the ministration of the word and sacraments. As Paul saith, 'The gospel is the power of God unto salvation, to every one that believeth,' (Rom. i.) Therefore, since the power of the church granteth eternal things, and is exercised only by the ministration of the word, it does not interfere with civil administration, just as the art of singing hinders not civil or political administration; for political administration is occupied about other things than the gospel. For the magistrate does not defend minds, but bodies and corporal things, against manifest injuries, and restrains men with the sword and corporal punishment, for the maintenance of justice and peace. Therefore the power of the church and the civil power should not be mixed and confounded together: the ecclesiastical has its own commandments to teach the gospel and to administer the sacraments. Let it not therefore break into another's office—let it not transfer the kingdoms of the world—let it not abrogate the laws of princes—let it not take away lawful obedience—let it not interrupt judgments in any civil ordinances or contracts—let it not prescribe laws to governors concerning the form of the commonwealth; since Christ said, 'My kingdom is not of this world,' (John xviii.) Also, in another place, he saith, 'Who made me a judge or a divider over you?' (Luke xii.) And Paul saith to the Philippians, 'Our conversation is in heaven,' (Phil. iii.) And to the Corinthians, 'The weapons of our warfare are not carnal, but mighty through God to the pulling down of thoughts,' &c. (2 Cor. x.) In like manner, our teachers distinguish the offices of both these powers, and teach to honour them both, and to acknowledge that each of them is a gift and benefit of God.

If bishops have any power of the sword, that power they have not as bishops by the commandment of the gospel, but by the law of man, bestowed upon them by kings and emperors, for the civil administration of their own goods. So that this is different from that of the administration of the gospel. Therefore, whensoever any question is made of the jurisdiction of bishops, the temporal power ought to be separated from the ecclesiastical jurisdiction. Undoubtedly, according to the gospel, and as they say, *de jure divino*, no power belongs to the bishops as bishops, that is, to those to whom is committed the ministration of the word and sacraments, save only this power to remit sins, also to judge of doctrines, and to reject a doctrine contrary to the gospel, and to exclude from the communion of the church wicked men whose wickedness is known, and this by the word, without the secular arm. In this the churches are bound by the law of God to render obedience, according to that, 'He that heareth you, heareth me,' (Luke x.)

But when they teach any thing against the gospel, then the churches have a commandment of God prohibiting obedience, as this, 'Beware of false prophets;' (Matt. vii.) and Paul to the Galatians, 'If an angel from heaven preach any other gospel, let him be accursed,' (Gal. i.) Also to the Corinthians, 'We can do nothing against the truth, but for the truth,' (2 Cor. xiii.) Also, in another place he saith, 'Power is given to us for edification, and not for destruction.' So also do the canon laws command, 2 *q.* 7 *cap. Sacerdotes, et cap. oves*. And St. Austin, in reply to the epistle of Petilia, says, 'If catholic bishops be deceived any where by chance, and think any thing against the canonical scriptures of God, we ought not to consent to them.' If bishops have any other power, or jurisdiction, in determining of certain causes, as of matrimony or of tithes, they have it by man's law; where, when the ordinaries fail in the discharge of their duties, because of their subjects, for the continuance of peace among them, princes are bound, whether they will or not, to see the law administered. Moreover, it is disputed, whether bishops or pastors have the right to ordain ceremonies in the churches, and to make laws of meats, of holy days, and degrees of ministers or orders, &c. Those that suppose that power is vested in bishops, allege this testimony: 'I have yet many things to say unto you, but ye cannot bear them now, but when the Spirit of truth is come, he shall teach you all truth,' (John xvi.) They allege also the example of the apostles, who made a prohibition that the people should abstain from blood and things strangled; (Acts xv.) They allege the Sabbath changed into Sunday, the Lord's day, contrary to the Decalogue, as it appears; neither is there any example more boasted of than the changing of the Sabbath-day. Great, say they, is the power and authority of the church, since it dispensed with one of the ten commandments.

But as touching this question our divines thus teach, that bishops have no power to decree and ordain any thing against the gospel, as is shewed above. The canon laws teach the same thing, (ix. dist.) Moreover, it is contrary to scripture to make traditions, or to exact obedience to them, that by that observance we may satisfy for sin, or deserve grace or righteousness. For thus the glory of the merit of Christ is injured, when by such observances we go about to deserve justification. Now it is evident, that because of this persuasion, traditions have grown almost to an infinite number in the church; and the doctrine of faith, and righteousness of faith, in the mean while, hath been oppressed. For still more holy days were made, and fasting days commanded; new ceremonies, and new honourings of saints, were instituted. For the devisers and actors of such things thought to get remission of sins and justification by these works. So formerly penitential canons increased, or which we still see some remains in these satisfactions. Likewise the authors of traditions act contrary to the command of God, when they place sin in meats, days, and such like things; and burden the church with the bondage of the law, as if there ought to be among Christians, for the meriting of righteousness, a worship of God like unto that of which we read in Leviticus, the ordering whereof God committed, as they say, to the apostles and bishops. And the pontiffs appear to be deceived by the example of Moses's law: hence those burdens, that certain meats defile and pollute the conscience, and that it is deadly sin to omit and leave unsaid canonical hours; that fastings deserve remission of sins, and that they are necessary to the righteousness of the New Testament; that sin, in a case reserved, cannot be forgiven without the authority of the reserver, where, indeed, the canons themselves speak only of the reservation of the canonical penalty, and not of the reservation of sin. From whence and of whom have the bishops the power and authority to impose these traditions upon the church, to wound consciences? For there are clear testimonies which prohibit the making of such traditions either to deserve remission of sins, or as necessary to the righteousness of the New Testament, or to salvation. For Paul to the Colossians saith, ' Let no man therefore judge you in meat, or in drink, or in respect of an holy day,' &c. Also, ' if ye be dead with Christ from the rudiments of the world, why, as though living in the world, are ye subject to ordinances, (touch not, taste not, &c.) after the commandments and doctrines of men?' Also to Titus he openly prohibited traditions, warning, ' that they should not give heed to Jewish fables, and commandments of men, that turn from the truth;' and Christ, speaking of them that enforce traditions, says in this wise, ' Let them alone, they are blind, leaders of the blind;' and he reproves such modes of worship, saying, ' Every plant which my heavenly Father hath not planted, shall be rooted up.'

If bishops have the power of lading churches with infinite traditions, and grieving consciences, why doth scripture so often prohibit the making and following traditions? —and why doth it call them doctrines of devils?—did the Holy Ghost forewarn us of these things in vain? Wherefore it must needs follow, that since ordinances, instituted as things necessary, or with an opinion to deserve remission of sin, are contrary to the gospel: that it is not lawful for any bishop to institute such. For it is necessary that the doctrine of Christian liberty be kept still in the churches, which is, that the bondage of the law is not necessary to justification, as it is written in the Epistle to the Galatians, 'Be not entangled again with the yoke of bondage.' The pre-eminence of the gospel must still be retained, which declares, that we obtain remission of sins and justification freely by faith in Christ, and not for certain observations or rites devised by men. What shall we think then of the Lord's day, and the like rites of the temples? To this our learned men respond, that it is lawful for bishops or pastors to make ordinances, that things be done orderly in the church; not that we should purchase by them remission of sins, or that we can satisfy for sins, or that consciences are bound to judge them necessary, or to think that they sin, who, without offending others, break them. So Paul ordains that in the congregation women should cover their heads, and that interpreters and teachers be heard in order in the church. It is convenient that the churches should keep such ordinances for the sake of charity and tranquillity, that so one should not offend another, that all things may be done in the churches in order, and without tumult, but yet so that the conscience be not charged, as to think that they are necessary to salvation, or to judge that they sin, who, without hurting others, break them. As that no one should say that a woman sins, who goeth abroad bareheaded, offending none. Even such is the observation of the Lord's day, of Easter, of Pentecost, and the like holy days and rites. For they that judge that by the authority of the church the observing of Sunday, instead of the Sabbath-day, was ordained as a thing necessary, do greatly err. The scripture permits and grants that the keeping of the Sabbath-day is now free, for it teaches that the ceremonies of Moses's law, since the revelation of the gospel, are not necessary. And yet because it was needful to ordain a certain day, that the people might know when they ought to come together, it appears that the church did appoint Sunday, which day, as it appears, pleased them rather than the Sabbath-day, even for this cause, that men might have an example of Christian liberty, and might know that the keeping and observance of either Saturday, or of any other day, is not necessary. There are wonderful disputations concerning the changing of the law—the ceremonies of the new law—the changing of the Sabbath-day,—which all have sprung from a false persuasion and belief of men, who thought that there must needs be in the church an honouring of God, like the Levitical law, and that Christ committed to the apostles, and bishops, authority to invent and find out ceremonies necessary to salvation. These errors crept into the church when the righteousness of faith was not clearly taught. Some dispute that the keeping of the Sunday is not fully, but only in a certain manner, the ordinance of God. They prescribe of holy days, how far it is lawful to work. Such manner of disputations, whatever else they be, are but snares of consciences. For although they busy themselves to modify and qualify their traditions, tempering the rigour of them with favourable declarations; yet notwithstanding as long as the opinion that they are necessary doth remain (which must needs remain where righteousness of faith and Christian liberty are not known), this equity and favour can never be perceived nor known. The apostles commanded to abstain from blood; who doth now observe and keep it? And yet they that do not keep it, sin not; for undoubtedly the apostles would not burden the conscience with such bondage, but they prohibited it for a time, for avoiding of slander; for the perpetual will and mind of the gospel is to be considered in a decree. Scarcely any canons are diligently kept, and many daily go out of use, even with those who defend traditions. Neither can consciences be assisted or consulted, unless this equity is observed, that is, that we know that canons and decrees are to be kept without the opinion of necessity, and that consciences are not hurt, though traditions be forgotten and be utterly set aside. Certainly bishops might easily preserve lawful obedience, if they would not compel men to keep traditions, which cannot be kept with a good conscience. They command priests to live unmarried; they receive none, unless they swear in effect that they will not teach the pure doctrine of the gospel. Our churches do not require that bishops should repair and re-establish concord at the expense of their honour (and yet it would become good pastors so to do), but they only require that they would release unjust burdens which are novelties, being received contrary to the custom of the catholic church. We will not deny, but that in the beginning some constitutions were grounded upon reasonable and probable causes, which yet are not now agreeable nor suited to later times. It appears, also, that some were wrongfully received; wherefore it might please the gentleness of the pontificate now to mitigate and release them, since such change would not break the unity of the church. For many traditions have, in process of time, been changed, as the canons themselves testify. But if it cannot be obtained that those observations should be released which cannot, without sin, be complied with; we must needs follow the rule of the apostles, which commands rather to obey God than men. Peter forbids bishops to be lords and emperors over the church. Now, it is not intended by us to take away jurisdiction from the bishops, but this one thing we require of them, that they would suffer the gospel to be purely taught, and that they would release a few certain ordinances, which cannot be observed without sin. But if they will not remit or release any thing, let them look to their charge how they shall render their accounts to God, in that they, by reason of their obstinacy, are the cause of this schism.

Conclusion.

The foregoing are the principal subjects of dispute between us. It were indeed easy to enumerate many other abuses and errors, but for the sake of brevity we have omitted them. Much complaint, for example, has existed concerning indulgences, pilgrimages, and the abuse of excommunication. The clergy have also had endless disputes with the monks about confession and numberless other subjects. These things we have omitted, in order that those of greater importance may be the more carefully weighed.

   (Signed) JOHN, the Elector of Saxony.
          GEORGE, Earl of Brandenburg.
         ERNEST, Duke of Luneberg.
         PHILIP, Landgrave of Hesse.
         JOHN FREDERICK, Duke of Saxony.
         FRANCIS, Duke of Luneberg.
         WOLFGANG, Prince of Anhalt.
         The Senate and Magistracy of Nuremberg.
         The Senate of Reutlingen.

No. II.

BULLA PII QUARTI
Super formâ Juramenti professionis fidei.
Datum Romæ, Anno 1564.

Apostolicas et ecclesiasticas traditiones, reliquasq. ejusdem Ecclesiæ observationes et constitutiones firmissimé admitto, et amplector. Item sacram scripturam juxta eum sensum, quem tenuit et tenet sancta mater Ecclesia, cujus est judicare de vero sensu, et interpretatione sacrarum scripturarum, admitto: nec eam unquam, nisi juxta unanimem consensum Patrum accipiam, et interpretabor. Profiteor quoque septem esse veré et proprié sacramenta novæ legis a Jesu Christo, Domino nostro, instituta, atque ad salutem humani generis, licet non omnia singulis necessaria, scilicet Baptismum, Confirmationem, Eucharistiam, Pœnitentiam, Extremam Unctionem, Ordinem et Matrimonium: Illaque gratiam conferre: et ex his baptismum, confirmationem, et ordinem, sine sacrilegio reiterari non posse. Receptos quoque et approbatos Ecclesiæ Catholicæ ritus, in suprædictorum omnium sacramentorum solemni administratione recipio et admitto. Omnia et singula, quæ de peccato originali, et de justificatione in sacrosancta Tridentina Synodo definita et declarata fuerunt, amplector et recipio. Profiteor pariter in missa offerri Deo verum, proprium et propitiatorium sacrificium, pro vivis et defunctis: atque in sanctissimo Eucharistiæ sacramento esse verè, realitèr, et substantialitèr corpus et sanguinem, unâ cum anima et divinitate Domini nostri Jesu Christi, fierique conversionem totius substantiæ panis, in corpus, et totius substantiæ vini, in sanguinem: quam conversionem Catholica Ecclesia transubstantiationem appellat. Fateor etiam sub altera tantum specie, totum atque integrum Christum, verumque sacramentum sumi. Con-

THE NEW CREED OF THE CHURCH OF ROME.*

1. The apostolic and ecclesiastical traditions, and other observances and constitutions of the church, do I firmly admit and embrace.

2. Also the sacred scripture, according to that sense which our holy mother the church hath holden and doth hold (whose office it is to judge of the true sense and interpretation of holy scriptures) do I admit, neither will I ever receive and expound it but according to the uniform consent of the fathers.

3. I do also profess that there are truly and properly seven sacraments of the new law, instituted by our Lord Jesus Christ and necessary to the salvation of mankind, though all be not necessary for every man: that is to say, baptism, confirmation, the eucharist, penance, extreme unction, orders, and marriage: and that they confer grace, and that among these, baptism, confirmation, and orders, cannot be reiterated without sacrilege. Also the received and approved rites of the Catholic church used in the solemn administration of all the aforesaid sacraments, I receive and admit.

4. All and every the things which, concerning original sin and justification, were defined and declared in the holy council of Trent, I embrace and receive.

5. Also I confess that in the mass is offered to God a true, proper, and propitiatory sacrifice for the quick and the dead. And that in the most holy eucharist is truly, really, and substantially the body and blood, with the soul and divinity, of our Lord Jesus Christ: and that there is made a conversion of the whole substance of the bread into his body, and of the whole substance of the wine into his blood, which conversion

---

* As this new creed is of great importance in our controversy with the papal church, the original, copied *verbatim et literatim* from the authorised document, is likewise given.

APPENDIX. 545

stantèr teneo purgatorium esse, animasque ibi detentas fidelium suffragiis juvari: Similitèr et sanctos unà cum Christo regnantes, venerandos, atque invocandos esse, eosque orationes Deo pro nobis offerre, atque eorum reliquias esse venerandas. Firmissimè assero, imagines Christi ac Deiparæ semper Virginis, necnon aliorum sanctorum, habendas et retinendas esse: atq. eis debitum honorem, ac venerationem impertiendam. Indulgentiarum etiam potestatem à Christo in Ecclesia relictam fuisse, illarúmque usum Christiano populo maximè salutarem esse affirmo. Sanctam Catholicam, et Apostolicam Romanam Ecclesiam, omnium Ecclesiarum matrem et magistram agnosco: Romanoq. Pontifici, B. Petri, Apostolorum principis, successori, ac Jesu Christi Vicario veram obedientiam spondeo ac juro: cætera item omnia à sacris canonibus, et œcumenicis conciliis, ac præcipuè à sacrosancta Tridentina Synodo tradita, definita, et declarata, indubitantèr recipio, atque profiteor, simulque contraria omnia, atque hæreses quascunque ab Ecclesia damnatas, rejectas, et anathematizatas, ego pariter damno, rejicio et anathematizo. Hanc veram Catholicam fidem, (extra quam nemo salvus esse potest) quam in præsenti sponte profiteor, et veraciter teneo, eandem integram et inviolatam, usque ad extremum vitæ spiritum, constantissimè (Deo adjuvante) retinere et confiteri, atque à meis subditis, vel illis quorum cura ad me in munere meo spectabit, teneri, doceri, et prædicari, quantum in me erit, curaturum. Ego idem N. spondeo, voveo, ac juro. Sic me Deus adjuvet, et hæc sancta Dei Evangelia.

Volumus autem, quod præsentes literæ, in cancelleria nostra Apostolica, de more, legantur. Et ut omnibus faciliùs pateant, in ejus Quinterno describantur ac etiam imprimantur. Nulli ergo omnino hominum liceat hanc paginam nostræ voluntatis et mandati infringere, vel ei ausu temerario contraire. Si quis autem hoc attentare præsumserit, indignationem omnipotentis Dei, ac beatorum Petri et Pauli, Apostolorum ejus, se noverit incursurum.

the catholic church calls transubstantiation.

6. I confess also, that under one kind only, all and whole Christ, and the true sacrament, is received.

7. I do constantly hold that there is a purgatory, and that the souls detained there are holpen by the suffrages of the faithful.

8. And likewise that the saints reigning with Christ, are to be worshipped and prayed unto. And that they offer their prayers unto God for us: and that their relics are to be worshipped.

9. And most firmly I avouch, that the images of Christ, and of the mother of God, always a virgin, and of other saints, are to be had and retained, and that to them due honour and veneration is to be given.

10. Also, that the power of indulgencies was left by Christ in the church; and I affirm the use thereof to be most wholesome to Christ's people.

11. That the holy, catholic and apostolic Roman church is the mother and mistress of all churches, I acknowledge; and I vow and swear true obedience to the bishop of Rome, the successor of St. Peter, the prince of the apostles, and the vicar of Jesus Christ.

12. And all other things likewise do I undoubtedly receive and confess, which are delivered, defined, and declared by the sacred canons, and general councils, and especially the holy council of Trent: and withal, I condemn, reject, and accurse, all things that are contrary hereunto, and all heresies whatsoever, condemned, rejected, and accursed by the church: and I will be careful that this true Catholic faith (out of which no man can be saved, which at this time I willingly profess and truly hold) be constantly (with God's help) retained and confessed, whole and inviolate, to the last gasp; and by those that are under me, or such as I shall have charge over in my calling, holden, taught, and preached to the uttermost of my power: I the said N. promise, vow, and swear, so God help me, and his holy gospels.

Our pleasure is, that these present letters, according to custom, be read in

Datum Romæ, apud sanctum Petrum, anno Incarnationis Dominicæ Millicemo Quingantesimo sexagesimo quarto Idibus Novem. Pontificatus nostri anno quinto.

FED. CARDINALIS CÆSIUS
CÆ. GLORIERIUS.

our Apostolic chancery: and that they may be the more easily known unto all men, that they be there copied and imprinted.

It shall not be lawful, therefore, for any man to infringe this our will and commandment, or by audacious boldness to contradict the same.

Which if any man shall presume to attempt: let him know that he shall incur the indignation of Almighty God, and of Saint Peter and Saint Paul, his blessed apostles. Dated at Rome in the year of the incarnation of our Lord 1564. Id. November; the 5th year of our papacy.

APPENDIX. 547

No. III.

SESSIO 22. CAPUT 9.
Prolegomenon Canonum Sequentium.

Quia vero adversus veterem hanc, in sacrosancto evangelio Apostolorum traditionibus, sanctorumque patrum doctrina fundatam fidem, hoc tempore multo disseminati sunt errores, multaque a multis docentur et disputantur; sacrosancta synodus post multos, gravesque his de rebus maturè habitos tractatus, unanimi patrum omnium consensu, quæ huic purissimæ fidei sacræque doctrinæ adversantur, damnare, et a sancta ecclesia eliminare, per subjectos hos canones constituit.

De Sacrificio Missæ.

CANON I.

Si quis dixerit in missa non offerri Deo verum et proprium sacrificium; aut quod offerri non sit aliud, quam nobis Christum ad manducandum dari; anathema sit.

CANON II.

Si quis dixerit, illis verbis, 'Hoc facite in meam commemorationem;' Christum non instituisse Apostolos sacerdotes; aut non ordinasse, ut ipsi, aliique sacerdotes offerrent corpus, et sanguinem suum; anathema sit.

CANON III.

Si quis dixerit, missæ sacrificium tantum esse laudis, et gratiarum actionis, aut nudam commemorationem sacrificii in cruce peracti, non autem propitiatorium; vel soli prodesse sumenti; neque pro vivis et defunctis pro peccatis, pœnis satisfactionibus et aliis, necessitatibus offerri debere; anathema sit.

CANON IV.

Si quis dixerit, blasphemiam irrogari sanctissimo Christi sacrificio, in cruce peracto, per missæ sacrificium; aut illi per hoc derogari; anathema sit.

CANON V.

Si quis dixerit, imposturam esse, missas celebrare in honorem sanctorum et pro illorum intercessione, apud Deum obtinenda, sicut ecclesia intendit; anathema sit.

CANON VI.

Si quis dixerit, canonem missæ errores continere, ideoque abrogandum esse; anathema sit.

CANON VII.

Si quis dixerit, cœremonias, vestes, et externa signa, quibus in missarum celebratione ecclesia catholica utitur, irritabula impietatis esse, magis quam officia pietatis; anathema sit.

CANON VIII.

Si quis dixerit, missas, in quibus solus sacerdos sacramentaliter communicat, illicitas esse ideoque abrogandas; anathema sit.

CANON IX.

Si quis dixerit, ecclesiæ Romanæ ritum, quo summissa voce pars canonis et verba consecrationis proferuntur, damnandum esse; aut lingua tantum vulgari missam celebrari debere; aut aquam non miscendam esse vino in calice offerendo, eo quod sit contra Christi institutionem; anathema sit.

Conc. Trident. Sessio xxii. *cap.* ix. *de Sacrificio Missæ.*

No. IV.

MISSALE ROMANUM, EX DECRETO SACROSANCTI CONCILII TRIDENTINI RESTITUTUM. S. PII V. JUSSU EDITUM, CLEMENTIS VIII., ET URBANI PAPÆ OCTAVI AUCTORITATE RECOGNITUM.

DE DEFECTIBUS IN CELEBRATIONE MISSARUM OCCURRENTIBUS.

Sacerdos celebraturus, omnem adhibeat diligentiam, ne desit aliquid ex requisitis ad Sacramentum Eucharistiæ conficiendum. Potest autem defectus contingere ex parte materiæ consecrandæ, et ex parte formæ adhibendæ, et ex parte ministri conficientis. Quidquid enim horum deficit, scilicet materia debita, forma cum intentione, et Ordo Sacerdotalis in conficiente, non conficitur Sacramentum. Et his existentibus, quibuscumque aliis deficientibus, veritas adest Sacramenti. Alii verò sunt defectus, qui in Missæ celebratione occurrentes, et si veritatem Sacramenti non impediant; possunt tamen aut cum peccato, aut cum scandalo contingere.

II. DE DEFECTIBUS MATERIÆ.

Defectus ex parte materiæ possunt contingere, si aliquid desit ex iis, quæ ad ipsam requiruntur. Requiritur enim ut sit panis triticeus, et vinum de vite; et ut hujusmodi materia consecranda in actu consecrationis sit coram Sacerdote.

III. DE DEFECTU PANIS.

Si panis non sit triticeus, vel si triticeus, admixtus sit granis alterius generis in tanta quantitate, ut non maneat panis triticeus, vel si alioqui corruptus, non conficitur Sacramentum.

2. Si sit confectus de aqua rosacea, vel alterius distillationis, dubium est an conficiatur.

7. Si Hostia consecrata dispareat, vel casu aliquo, ut vento, aut miraculo, vel ab aliquo animali accepta, et nequeat reperiri; tunc altera consecretur.

IV. DE DEFECTU VINI.

Si vinum sit factum penitus acetum, vel penitus putridum, vel de uvis acerbis, seu non maturis expressum, vel ei admixtum tantum aquæ, et vinum sit corruptum; non conficitur Sacramentum.

6. Si quis percipiat ante consecrationem, vel post consecrationem, totum vinum esse acetum, vel aliàs corruptum, idem servetur quod suprà, ac si deprehenderet non esse positum vinum, vel solam aquam fuisse appositam in Calice.

8. Si materia quæ esset apponenda, ratione defectus vel panis, vel vini, non posset ullo modo haberi, si id sit ante consecrationem Corporis, ulteriùs procedi non debet · si post consecrationem Corporis, aut etiam vini, deprehenditur defectus alterius speciei, altera jam consecrata: tunc si nullo modo haberi possit, procedendum erit, et Missa absolvenda, ita tamen ut prætermittantur verba, et signa, quæ pertinent ad speciem deficientem. Quód si expectando aliquamdiu haberi possit, expectandum erit, ne sacrificium remaneat imperfectum.

V. DE DEFECTIBUS FORMÆ.

Defectus ex parte formæ possunt contingere, si aliquid desit ex iis, quæ ad integritatem verborum in ipsa consecratione requiruntur.

VI. DE DEFECTIBUS MINISTRI.

Defectus ex parte Ministri possunt contingere quoad ea, quæ in ipso requiruntur. Hæc autem sunt: In primis intentio, deinde dispositio animæ, dispositio corporis, dispositio vestimentorum, dispositio in ministerio ipso, quoad ea, quæ in ipso possunt occurrere.

APPENDIX.

VII. DE DEFECTU INTENTIONIS.

Si quis non intendit conficere, sed delusoriè aliquid agere. Item si aliquæ Hostiæ ex oblivione remaneant in Altari, vel aliqua pars vini, vel aliqua. Hostia lateat, cùm non intendat consecrare nisi quas videt. Item si quis habeat coram se undecim Hostias, et intendat consecrare solùm decem, non determinans quas decem intendit, in his casibus non consecrat, quia requiritur intentio.

IX. DE DEFECTIBUS DISPOSITIONIS CORPORIS.

Si quis non est jejunus post mediam noctem etiam post sumptionem solius aquæ, vel alterius potus, aut cibi, per modum etiam medicinæ, et in quantumcumque parva quantitate, non potest communicare, nec celebrare.

2. Si autem ante mediam noctem cibum, aut potum sumpserit, etiam si postmodum non dormierit, nec sit digestus, non peccat: sed ob perturbationem mentis, ex qua devotio tollitur, consulitur aliquando abstinendum.

3. Si reliquiæ cibi remanentes in ore transglutiantur, non impediunt Communionem, cùm non transglutiantur per modum cibi, sed per modum salivæ. Idem dicendum si lavando os deglutiatur stilla aquæ præter intentionem.

5. Si præcesserit pollutio nocturna, quæ causata fuerit ex præcedenti cogitatione, quæ sit peccatum mortale, vel evenerit propter nimiam crapulam, abstinendum est à communione, et celebratione, nisi aliud Confessario videatur.

X. DE DEFECTIBUS IN MINISTERIO IPSO OCCURRENTIBUS.

Possunt etiam defectus occurrere in ministerio ipso, si aliquid ex requisitis ad illud desit: ut si celebretur in loco non sacro, vel non deputato ab Episcopo, vel in Altari non consecrato, vel tribus mappis non cooperto; si non adsint luminaria cerea; si non sit tempus debitum celebrandi, quod est ab aurora usque ad meridiem communiter: si celebrans; saltem Matutinum cum Laudibus non dixerit; si omittat aliquid ex vestibus sacerdotalibus: si vestes sacerdotales, et mappæ non sint ab Episcopo, vel ab alio hanc habente potestatem benedictæ: si non adsit clericus, vel alius deserviens in Missa, vel adsit, qui deservire non debet, ut mulier: si non adsit Calix cum Patena conveniens, cujus cuppa debet esse aurea, vel argentea, vel stannea; non ærea, vel vitrea: si Corporalia non sint munda, quæ debent esse ex lino, nec serico in medio ornata, et ab Episcopo vel ab alio hanc habente potestatem benedicta, ut etiam superiùs dictum est; si celebret capite cooperto sine dispensatione; si non adsit Missale licèt memoriter sciret Missam, quam intendit dicere.

5. Si musca, vel aranea, vel aliquid aliud ceciderit in Calicem ante consecrationem, projiciat vinum in locum decentem et aliud ponat in Calice, misceat parum aquæ, offerat, ut suprà, et prosequatur Missam: si post consecrationem ceciderit musca, aut aliquid ejusmodi, et fiat nausea sacerdoti, extrahat eam, et lavet cum vino, finita Missa comburat, et combustio ac lotio hujusmodi in sacrarium projiciatur. Si autem non fuerit ei nausea, nec ullum periculum timeat, sumat cum sanguine.

6. Si aliquid venenosum ceciderit in Calicem, vel quo provocaret vomitum, vinum consecratum reponendum est in alio Calice, et aliud vinum cum aqua apponendum denuò consecrandum, et finita Missa sanguis repositus in panno lineo, vel stuppa tamdiù servatur, donec species vini fuerint desiccatæ, et tunc stuppa comburatur, et combustio sacrarium projiciatur.

7. Si aliquod venenatum contigerit Hostiam consecratam, tunc alteram consecret, et sumat modo quo dictum est: et illa servetur in tabernaculo loco separato donec species corrumpantur et corruptæ deinde mittantur in sacrarium.

8. Si sumendo sanguinem particula remanserit in Calice, digito ad labium Calicis eam adducat, et sumat ante purificationem, vel infundat vinum, et sumat.

9. Si Hostia ante consecrationem inveniatur fracta, nisi populo evidenter appareat, talis Hostia consecretur; si autem scandalum populo esse possit, alia accipiatur, et offeratur: quod si illius Hostiæ jam erat facta oblatio, eam post ablutionem

sumat. Quod si ante oblationem Hostia appareat confracta, accipiatur altera integra, si citra scandalum, aut longam moram fieri poterit.

10. Si propter frigus, vel negligentiam, Hostia consecrata dilabatur in Calicem propterea nihil est reiterandum, sed Sacerdos Missam prosequatur, faciendo cæremonias, et signa consueta cum residua parte Hostiæ, quæ non est madefacta sanguine, si commodè potest. Si verò tota fuerit madefacta, non extrahat eam, sed omnia dicat omittendo signa, et sumat pariter Corpus, et sanguinem, signans se cum Calice, dicens: *Corpus et Sanguis Domini nostri*, &c.

11. Si in hieme sanguis congletur in Calice, involvatur Calix pannis calefactis : si id non proficeret, ponatur in ferventi aqua prope Altare, dummodo in Calicem non intret, donec liquefiat.

12. Si per negligentiam aliquid de Sanguine Christi reciderit, si quidem super terram, seu super tabulam, lingua lambatur, et locus ipse radatur quantum satis est, et abrasio comburatur; cinis verò in sacrarium recondatur. Si verò super lapidem altaris ceciderit, sorbeat sacerdos stillam, et locus benè abluatur, et ablutio in sacrarium projiciatur. Si super linteum Altaris, et ad aliud linteum stilla pervenerit: si usque ad tertium, linteamini ter abluantur ubi stilla ceciderit, Calice supposito, et aqua ablutionis in sacrarium projiciatur.

13. At si contingat totum Sanguinem post consecrationem effundi, si quidem aliquid vel parum remansit, illud sumatur, et de effuso reliquo sanguine fiat ut dictum est. Si verò nihil omnino remansit, ponat iterùm vinum, et quam, et conseret ab eo loco. *Simili modo postquam cœnatum est*, facta priùs tamen Calicis oblatione, ut suprà.

14. Si Sacerdos evomat Eucharistiam, si species integræ appareant, reverenter sumantur, nisi nausea, fiat; tunc enim species consecratæ cautè separentur, et in aliquo loco sacro reponantur, donec corrumpantur, et postea in sacrarium projiciantur. Quòd si species non appareant, comburatur vomitus, et cineres in sacrarium mittantur.

15. Si Hostia consecrata, vel aliqua ejus particula dilabatur in terram, reverenter accipiatur, et locus, ubi cecidit mundetur, et aliquantulum abradatur, et pulvis, seu abrasio hujusmodi in sacrarium immittatur. Si ceciderit extra Corporale in mappam, seu alio quovis modo in aliquod linteum, mappa vel linteum, hujusmodi diligenter lavetur, et lotio ipsa in sacrarium effundatur.

16. Possunt etiam defectus in ministerio ipso occurrere, si Sacerdos ignoret ritus, et cæremonias ipsas in eo servandas : de quibus omnibus in superioribus Rubricis, copiosè dictum est.

INDEX.

ABRAHAM, the possibility of a tradition from Adam to him, 93. the occasion and design of a revelation to him, ib.
Absolute decrees. See Decrees.
Absolution, in what sense it ought to be pronounced, 356. the bad effects of the hasty absolutions of the church of Rome, 369. as used in the church of England, is only declaratory, 370. this agreeable to the practice of the primitive church, 371. a prayer used in the church of Rome after absolution, ib. this does not mend it, ib. when this practice was introduced, ib.
Abstinence. See Fasting.
Action, whether God is the first and immediate cause of every action, 38. what it is that denominates an action good or bad, 174. distinction between those that are universally binding on all, and such as bind only some sort of men, 179. the judgments to be made of them from appearances, ib.
Acts of the Apostles, when and by whom wrote, 74.
Acts, no successive acts in God, 30.
Adam, wherein the image of God, in which he was created, consisted, 143, 144. whether the death he was threatened with was only natural, 141, 145. whether by covenant he was constituted to represent all his posterity, 147. of the propagation of his sin, 148. See Original Sin.
Adoration, God only the proper object of it, 57. what it is, ib. Christ proposed in the New Testament as the object of it, ib. ought not to be given to any creature, 58. See Host.
Adultery, on the part of the wife, dissolves marriage, 377. this agreeable both to the law of nature and the gospel, ib. and to the practice of the primitive church, ib. the contrary doctrine of a modern date, 378.
Agobard, bishop of Lyons, wrote with great vehemence against the worship of images, 310.
Ahab, his feigned humiliation rewarded, 174.
Air, greatly improved by the industry of man, 36.
Almsgiving, a main part of charity, 370. See Charity.
Altar, but one in a church among the primitive Christians, 464.
Amalric expressly denied the corporal presence, 443. is condemned by the Lateran council, and his body raised and burnt on that account, ib.
Ambassador, his extensive power, 359.
Ambrose, the variation of that prayer of consecration, which goes under his name, from that used in the mass, 436.
Ananias, wherein the guilt of his sin lay, 513.
Anathemas, the form of denouncing them against heretics very ancient, 480. what was meant by them, ib. a great number of them denounced by the council of Trent, ib. those ill-founded cannot hurt, ib. See Censures.
Angels, good or bad, are capable of doing many things beyond our reach, 78. are perfect moral agents, and yet cannot sin, 153. worshipping them expressly forbid in the New Testament, 322. invocation of them disclaimed in the first ages of Christianity, 323.
Animal spirits, their subtile nature, 40. their influence on our managing matter, 78. receive their quality from that of the blood, 144. are the immediate organs of thought and subtiler parts of the blood, 154. a conjecture how they may excite thought, 156.

INDEX.

Annihilation only in the power of God, 35. a common mistake about it rectified, ib. created beings have not a tendency to it, ib.

Antiquity, not a note of the true church, 240.

Apocrypha, the Christian churches were for some ages strangers to these books, 113. were first mentioned by Athanasius, 114. where and by whom wrote, ib. were left out of the canon by the council of Laodicea, ib. were first received into it by that of Trent, ib. were always denied to be a part of it by the best and most learned writers, ib. See Maccabees.

Apostles were not the authors of the Creed which goes by their name, 2. 137. how far they complied with Judaism, 8, 268. the difficulties they met with in propagating Christianity, 76. could not be impostors, ib. nor imposed on, 78. their being endowed with extraordinary inspiration, no argument for a succession of infallibility, 281. of the powers with which our Saviour sent them, 333. were not constituted priests by our Saviour's words, 'Do this,' in the sacrament, 453. did not derive their authority from St. Peter, being all equal to him, 499.

Apparitions, there are many histories of them well attested, 41. to disbelieve all unreasonable, ib.

Apollinarian heresy, what it was, 431. was confuted by many great men of different ages, ib.

Aquarii, those who used water instead of wine in the sacrament, 455. their reason for so doing, ib. are severely condemned by St. Cyprian, ib.

Aquinas, Thomas, his notion of providence and free-will, 198. his distinction to avoid making God the author of sin, 199. his doctrine concerning image-worship, 312.

Arians, their opinion that Christ is a creature of a spiritual nature, 61. councils decree differently concerning this, 276.

Arminians, their opinions of free-will and predestination, 195. were condemned by the synod of Dort, 204. the occasion of their becoming the distinction of a party instead of doctrinal points, ib. See Remonstrants.

Artemon held the same opinion of Christ as the Socinians, 61.

Articles of the Church of England, objections against them, 1. reasons for their descending to so many particulars, 5. the fundamental Article of the Reformation, 6. how or by whom the Articles were prepared, ib. what the sanction of public authority to them implies, 7. whether they are Articles of peace only, or of doctrine, ib. to the laity, only Articles of church-communion, 8. distinction between articles of faith and articles of doctrine, ib. what the clergy are bound to by their subscriptions, 9. a royal declaration to end disputes about this matter, 10. may have different senses, ib. this illustrated by the third Article, ib. care taken to settle the true reading of them, 11. collations of them with MSS., 11—18. difficulty arising from the various readings cleared, 19. express words of scripture for each Article not necessary, 97. several differences of the present from those published in king Edward's reign, 69, 115, 116, 341, 467. the latitude of the articles, 9, 226, 338. fundamental Articles ought not to be too strictly determined, 242. the moderation of the Articles, 10, 151, 152, 226, 398, 507.

Assistance, the doctrine of inward assistances proved from scripture, 155. how they are conveyed to us, 156. the effect of them, ib.

Athanasius, his account of the books of the Old Testament, 113. and those of the Apocrypha, 114. was not author of the Creed which goes by his name, 136. the condemnatory clauses of it explained, ib.

Atheists, their objections to the argument, from the consent of mankind, for the being of God answered, 20. their arguments for the eternity of the world considered, 22. that for its being made by chance answered, 23. their objections to miracles answered, 25. the notion that the world is a body to God, the foundation of Atheism, 29.

INDEX. 553

Attrition, an imperfect contrition, 366. the doctrine of the church of Rome concerning it, ib. See Contrition.

Augsburg Confession of faith, on what occasion it was prepared, 5.

Augustin, or Austin, his doctrine of original sin, 147. and of reprobation, ib. hated Pelagianism, 197. wherein he differed from the Sublapsarians, 198. speaks very doubtfully concerning the state of the soul after death, 294. a famous passage about his mother Monica referred to, 295. his extraordinary relations of miracles not to be credited, 318. his declaration against invocation of saints, 325. thought that all who were baptized were regenerated, 396. his rule concerning figurative expressions, 423.

Auricular Confession. See Confession.

Authority of the books of the Old Testament, 95, 105. that of the New, 101, 102. that of the Apocrypha disproved, 113. that of the church in religious matters not absolute, 234. in relation to ceremonies, 264. distinction between that which is founded on infallibility and an authority of order, 268. lawful authority in the church, what it is, 337. is subject to the law of the land, 482. the highest act of their authority, 483. that of the pope, 498, 499. of the king in ecclesiastical matters, 502, 506. See Pope, King, Church.

B.

Baitulia, the least ensnaring of all idols, 303.

Baptism, what it is, 44. the danger of delaying it till death, 190. what gave rise to this practice, ib. what necessary to make it true and valid, 242. that by laics and by women not null, though irregular, 244. the obligation baptism brings us under, 245. baptism no new thing among the Jews in our Saviour's time, 391. its institution as a federal act was by Christ, 392. wherein the Christian differs from that of St. John, 393. what meant by being born of water and of the Spirit, ib. it is a precept, but not a mean necessary to salvation, 394. the ends and purposes of it, 395. the bad consequences of maintaining the absolute necessity of it, 396. how it becomes effectual to salvation, 397. wherein it agrees with circumcision, 399. baptism of infants most agreeable to the institution of Christ, 400. and to the practice of circumcision under the Old Testament, ib. why the office for baptizing infants is the same with that for persons of riper age, 401. reasonableness of changing the form to sprinkling, 454.

Basil, St. his opinion of the souls of the martyrs, 319.

Beasts are not mere machines, 40. may have spirits of an inferior order, ib.

Begetting, the natural meaning of it, 51. what understood by it when spoken of the Son of God is beyond our present comprehension, ib.

Beginning, what meant by it in the first of St. John's Gospel, 52.

Begotten and born of God, the meaning of these expressions, 189, 191.

Berengarius, his character, 442. opposed the doctrine of the corporal presence, ib. had many followers, ib.

Binding and loosing, that power granted equally to all the apostles, 261. what the Jewish writers meant by it, ib.

Bishops, the declaration of their faith was at first in very general terms, 2. which they sent round them, ib. what obliged them afterwards to make fuller declarations, 3. a succession of them no certain note of a true church, 241. why confirmation was in the earliest ages reserved for the bishop only, 352. no instructions for celibacy given them in the New Testament. 469. many of them in the best ages were married, 471. of their consecration, 494. are all equal by their office and character, 498. authority of those in great sees only from custom, 500. See Pope.

Blood, a probable conjecture about the natural state of it, 143. its influence on the animal spirits, 144.

Body, of the state of our Saviour's body from his death to his resurrection, 80, 81. whether it put on a new form in his ascension, ib. glorified bodies are of a different texture from those of flesh and blood, 455. See Resurrection.

INDEX.

Boniface VIII. pope, claimed a feudatory power in temporals over princes, 254.

Brain, the influence of its disorder upon the mind, 40. our thoughts are governed by impressions made on it, 154.

Bread in the sacrament in what sense the body of Christ, 404. when dipping it in the wine became a practice, 456. this condemned by the council of Bracara, ib.

C.

Calf, golden, what intention the Israelites had in making it, 304. the design of those calves set up by Jeroboam, ib. See Idolatry.

Calvinists, how far they agree with St. Austin about predestination, 198. the peculiar advantages and disadvantages of their opinions on this subject, 222. See Supralapsarians.

Canon. See Scriptures.

Canons of the church, what respect due to them for antiquity, 488. the new canon law different from the old, 489. ancient canons little regarded by the reformers, 490. were brought into desuetude by the church of Rome, ib.

Cassian, his doctrine concerning predestination, 197. is opposed and defended by several, ib. his collations were in great esteem, 198.

Catholic, not a note of the true church, 239.

Celibacy of the clergy, no rule for it in the gospel, 468. not in the power of the church to order it, 469. the political advantages of it, 470. when and by whom it was first introduced, 471. the practice of the church not uniform in it, ib. was not imposed on all the clergy till the end of the eleventh century, 473. the good and bad consequences of it, 470, 473. vows not lawful in this matter, 474. and are not binding, though made, 475. See Oath.

Censures of the church, how to behave under them, 481. what right the laity have to be consulted in them, 482. are agreeable to the design of Christianity, 483. defects in them no just cause of separation, 484. popery introduced a great variety of rules concerning them, ib. a further reformation in these still wanted, ib.

Century, the great ignorance that prevailed in the tenth century, 441.

Ceremonial law, was not designed to be perpetual, 122. the design of its institution, 128. is now abolished, as become useless and impossible, 129.

Ceremonies, the church has power to appoint them, 264. the practice of the Jewish church in this matter, ib. changes in them sometimes necessary, 265. the practice of the apostles, 266. when appointed, ought to be observed, if lawful, 267, 485. cautions to be observed in appointing them, 267. unity among Christians, a great reason for observing them, 485.

Cerinthus denied the divinity of Christ in the earliest age of Christianity, 53.

Chalice. See Cup.

Chance, the absurdity of maintaining that the world was made by it, 24. an argument for this opinion answered, ib.

Charity and brotherly love, their great usefulness in the Christian religion, 485. charity to the poor, of the extent of it, 178. what renders it acceptable to God, 370. is more particularly recommended by the gospel, 514. our Saviour's rule concerning the measure of it, ib.

Charles the Great, a council in his time, and books published in his name, against image-worship, 310. introduced the Roman Missal into the Gallican church, 490. published many Capitulars concerning ecclesiastical matters, 504.

Cherubims that were in the holiest of all, no argument for image-worship, 314.

Children, of their parents' power over them, 399. in what sense they are said to be holy, ib.

Chinese, their alleged antiquity without foundation, 23.

Chrism, used by the church of Rome in confirmation, what it is, 353. might only be consecrated by the bishop, 354. was applied by presbyters in the Greek church, ib. great disputes about it, 355.

Christ, in two respects the Son of God, 51. in what sense of one substance with the Father, ib. proofs of his di-

INDEX. 555

vinity, 52—62. this was early denied by Ebion and Cerinthus, 53. was the Creator of all things, 52. has all the names, operations, and attributes, of God given him, 56. is proposed in the New Testament as the object of divine worship, 58. this not charged as idolatry by the Jews at that time, ib. the Jews understood this part of our religion in a manner consistent with their former ideas, ib. what those were, 59. the Arian and Socinian hypothesis concerning him, 60. is not to be worshipped as an angel or prophet, but as truly God, 61. took on him the nature of man, 62. the two natures united in one person, ib. the design of using the term Person, 64. that there shall be an end to his mediatorial office, ib. but not to his personal glory, ib. of the certainty and design of his death, 65. it was not merely in confirmation of his doctrine, and a pattern of suffering, 66. atoned for more than Adam's sin, 67. in what sense his death is said to be our sacrifice, ib. his agony explained, ib. the reconciliation made by his death not absolute, and without conditions, 68. of his descent into hell, 69. when and by whom this article was introduced, ib. several different opinions about this, 70, 71. what seems to be the true meaning of it, 72. proof of his resurrection depends on the authority of the New Testament, 73. several circumstances concurring to prove it, 73—80. his ascension not capable of so full a proof, 80. this depends chiefly on the testimony of the apostles and effusion of the Holy Ghost, ib. his resurrection was brought about by a miracle, ib. curiosity about the manner of it taxed, 81. how it may be said he was three days in the grave, ib. the intention of his staying forty days after on earth, ib. of the manner of his ascension, ib. the great authority with which he is vested, 82. of his glorious appearance at the last day, ib. whether he was the mediator of the old, as well as the new dispensation, 124. his death applied to those who are incapable of expressly laying hold of it, 128. his death the only cause of our justification, 167. Christ alone was without sin, 184. of the efficacy and extent of his death, 169, 208, 209. is our only mediator in point of intercession as well as redemption, 323. why he chose to suffer at the time of the passover, 404. he is the only Priest, and his death the only sacrifice under the gospel, 461.

Christianity gives much purer ideas of God than the Mosaic dispensation, 57. the foundation of, 167. does not lessen the temporal authority, 503. raises the laws of love and charity to a high degree, 514. does not condemn all oaths, 517.

Christians are not exempt from capital punishment for great crimes, 508. in what case may engage in war, 509. or go to law, 510. are not obliged to have their goods in common, 513. may swear on important occasions, 517.

Chronology, the diversity of it no sufficient objection to the authority of the scriptures, 109.

Chrysostom, St. mentions nothing of relics, 319. denies that any miracles were wrought in his time, ib. condemns auricular confession, 363.

Church ought to proportion her rules of communion and censure to those of the gospel, 190. of its authority to establish doctrines, 233. what a true church is, 243, 247, 248. may be visible, though not infallible, 247. of her power in appointing ceremonies, 264, 265. and in matters of faith, 268. can make no new terms of salvation, 269. the meaning of Christ's words, 'Tell the church,' &c., 280. how the church is the pillar and ground of truth, ib. there was to be an authority in the church, 334. what it is, 337. the order settled by the apostles was for succeeding ages, 335. every church an independent body, 490. the respect due from one church to another, ib. wherein her authority in opposition to the civil magistrate consists, 506.

Church of Rome owns the positive doctrines of the church of England, 5. its tyranny in imposing its doctrines, 8. their opinion concerning the scriptures and traditions confuted, 90.

INDEX.

leave the second commandment out of their Catechism, 133. maintain that original sin is quite taken away by baptism, 145. the consequence of this, 146. their doctrine concerning the remission of sins, 164. the use of the sacraments, ib. and the sufficiency of inherent holiness for justification, 166. what they call a good work, 172. what they teach concerning the love of God, 176. their doctrine of supererogation confuted, 180. their distinction of mortal and venial sin, 187. just prejudices against its infallibility, 234—262. their notes of a true church, 239. these do not agree to their church, 240. have erred not only in their living and ceremonies, but in matters of faith also, 249. the influence of the popes on the canons, ceremonies, and government, of the church, 250. is guilty of a circle, 239, 270. the absurdity of this, ib. their doctrine concerning purgatory, 285. See Purgatory. concerning pardons, 298. of indulgences, 299. of image-worship, 301. of worshipping of relics, 315. of the invocation of saints and angels, 322. of worship in an unknown tongue, 344. of their five additional sacraments, 351. of the intention of the priest being necessary to the essence of a sacrament, 388. of transubstantiation, 415. of withholding the cup from the laity, 452. of the sacrifice of the mass, 460. of the celibacy of the clergy, 461.

Church of England and Rome, wherein they agree, and wherein of different opinions, 139. answer to the question, Where was your church before Henry VIII.? 248. See Articles, Authority.

Circumcision, why not necessary to be continued, 123. of infants under the Old Testament an argument for infant baptism under the New, 400.

Claud of Turin wrote with vehemence against image-worship, 310.

Clergy, the import of their subscription to the Articles, 9. their marriage made an argument against the Reformation, 467. this not contrary to the purity of divine performances, ib. those in England were married in the Saxon times, 472. are subject to their princes in ecclesiastical matters, 502. See Celibacy, Councils.

Commandments, or moral law, the nature of it, 130. the two first against idolatry, 131. the morality of them, ib. the third against not only vain and idle, but false swearing, 132. the morality of this, ib. the fourth, in what sense moral and reasonable, ib. the rigour of it abated by our Saviour, 133. these four distinct commandments, ib. why this division is preferred to that of the church of Rome, ib. the order of the second table, ib. the fifth and tenth, how they are the fences of the intermediate four, 134. in what sense the last is moral, ib. of the obligation of this law upon Christians, ib.

Communion of the body and blood of Christ, the meaning of it explained, 404.

Concomitance, no sufficient argument for communion only in one kind, 454.

Confession of sins, the scripture account of it, 357. auricular confession not necessary, 361. no authority for it in scripture, ib. nor from the practice of the primitive Christians, 362. the first occasion and progress of it, 363. gave great scandal at Constantinople, ib. how far the power of the church extends in this matter, 365. the good and bad effects of it, ib. ought to be no law of the church, because not a law of God, 366. the bad effects of it in the church of Rome, 366, 484.

Confession of adversaries, not a note of the true church, 240.

Confirmation a very ancient practice, and justifiable as used in the church of England, 352. reasons why it is no sacrament, 353. the form of it in the church of Rome, ib. whether the bishop only should confirm, 354. great disputes about this, 355.

Consecration, the effect of it in the eucharist, according to the doctrine of the church of Rome, 416. the virtue of it depends on the intention of the priest, 417. by whom a bell was ordered to be rung at the consecration, 439. it was an opinion that the Lord's Prayer was at first the prayer of consecration, 457.

INDEX. 557

Consequences of opinions ought not to be charged as tenets, 423, 424.

Constance, council of, its decree for withholding the cup from the laity, 458. the absurdity of it, and cruelty used to establish it, ib.

Constantia, the legend concerning her great respect for Hilarion's body, 318.

Constantinople, council, made no new additions to the Creed, 3. said that the Holy Ghost proceeded from the Father only, 89. condemned image-worship, 309.

Consubstantiation, what the Lutherans mean by it, 444. their doctrine confuted, ib. ought not to dissolve the union of churches where adoration is not joined with it, 445.

Contrition, the definition of it, 366. wherein the church of Rome make it differ from attrition, ib. their doctrine concerning it liable to great abuse, 367.

Corporal presence, how the doctrine concerning it came into the church, 437. the progress of it, 437—444. See Transubstantiation.

Covenant, whether God made one with Adam for his posterity, 147. the tenor of the new covenant, 190.

Covetousness, the precept against it not moral in the strictest sense, 133. not a crime more peculiar to the married than the unmarried clergy, 470.

Councils, cannot be called without the consent of princes, 272. popes were not always consulted, 273. have assumed the power of censuring, depriving, and making popes, 274. what makes a council to be general, 275. the numbers necessary, and how cited, ib. not of divine institution, because no rules in scripture concerning them, 275. several arguments against their infallibility, 275—283. they have been contrary to one another, 276. disorders and intrigues in councils, ib. no general councils pretended in the first three centuries, 279. no prospect of another general council, ib. of the decree of the council of Jerusalem, 281. some general councils have erred, 282. doctrines are not to be believed on their authority, 283.

Creation imports infinite power, 35, 52. the nearest approach to a true idea of it, ib. is ascribed to Christ in the New Testament, 56.

Creeds were at first conceived in general terms, 2. that which goes by the name of the Apostles' not made by them, 2, 137. what probably was the first, 2. the occasion of their being enlarged, 3. those of Nice and Constantinople, ib. none of the three Creeds named with exactness, 135. that of Nice is the Constantinopolitan, ib. that of Athanasius not made by him, 136. that said to be the Apostles' of no great antiquity, 138.

Cross, a prayer used in the consecration of a cross, 313.

Crucifixion of Christ, and his death, owned by all Christians, 64. denied by the Docetæ and Mahomet, ib.

Cup, or chalice, in the sacrament, ought to be given to the laity, 452. this particularly enjoined in the words of institution, ib. not to the clergy only, as priests, 453. this the practice for above a thousand years, 455. the insufficiency of concomitance and other arguments advanced against it, 454—456.

Cyprian owned not the infallibility of pope Stephen, 251. made the effect of a sacrament to depend on the good state of the administrator, 386.

D.

Damnation, to eat and drink their own damnation explained, 411. damnation sometimes means temporary punishments, ib.

Daniel, his prophecy of the LXX. weeks explained, 121.

Death might have been the natural consequence of Adam's fall, 147. this not to be restrained to a natural death, ib. how this might be transmitted to his posterity, 145. prayers for the dead, an early practice in the church, 294. what gave rise to it, ib. Tertullian's opinion about it, 295. the absurdity of masses for the dead, 296. the method of commemorating eminent saints in the primitive times, ib.

Death-bed repentance, the trusting to it a fatal error, 190, 368, 369.

Decrees of God have been the subject

INDEX.

of many disputes, 9, 140. the foundation of the doctrine of absolute decrees, 147. this seems contrary to the nature of God, 148. and exposes the Christian religion, 149. upon what views God formed his decrees concerning mankind, 194. four opinions concerning them, 195, 196.

Decretal Epistles of the first popes, with what view published, 252. are universally held spurious, ib. was a forgery of the eighth century, contrived with little art, 438.

Delivery unto Satan, an effect of the extraordinary power of the apostles, 478, 479.

Dipping in baptism, the danger of it in cold climates, a good reason for sprinkling, 454. the custom of dipping the bread in the wine in the Lord's supper, when introduced, 456. was condemned by the council of Bracara, ib.

Discipline in the church, the nature and necessity of it, 389, 477. that of the primitive church lay heaviest on the clergy, 389. moderation ought to be observed in it, 477.

Divorce lawful in case of adultery, 377. our Saviour's rule in this case, ib. this agreeable to the opinion of the fathers, ib. the contrary was not established till the council of Trent, 378.

Docetæ, a sect that denied the death of Christ, 64.

Doctrine, the difference between Articles of faith, and those of doctrine, 8. the tyranny of imposing doctrines, ib. conformity of doctrines with former times, not a note of a true church, 240.

Donatists, their notions concerning the sacraments, 386.

Dulia and Hyperdulia, degrees of worship paid to images in the church of Rome, 313.

Durandus was censured by the church of Rome for his opinion of image-worship, 311.

E.

Earth is greatly improved by man's industry, 36. the influence of the wind upon it, ib. See World.

Eating and drinking their own damnation, the meaning of the phrase, 411. opinions of several fathers concerning eating and drinking Christ's body and blood, 451.

Ebion denied the divinity of Christ very early, 53.

Edward VI., differences of the Articles in his reign from the present, 115, 116, 284, 341, 346, 402, 467, 494, 497.

Egyptians, their alleged antiquity without foundation, 23.

Elders, who they were at the council of Jerusalem, 281.

Election, of election and predestination, 198. See Predestination.

Elevation of the host not known in the first ages, 428, 448. what gave rise to it, 449. was not done at first, in order to adoration, ib. who first mentions it with that view, ib.

Eliberis, council of, condemned pictures on the walls of churches, 306. forbid the lighting candles about the tombs of martyrs in day-light, 319, 328.

Elizabeth, queen, gives authority to require subscriptions to the Articles, 9. a royal declaration for taking them in the literal sense, ib. her injunctions concerning supremacy, 497.

Elohim, the meaning of it in the Old Testament, 43.

Emperors, their authority in ecclesiastical affairs, 503.

Endowments were procured by impostors in the church of Rome, 297. by what means the profuseness of them was restrained, ib. when they are to be held sacred, ib. the violation of them, when founded on false opinions, no sacrilege, 298.

Enthusiasts, an extravagant sort of them at the Reformation, 123.

Ephesus, council, their decree concerning the Holy Ghost, 86.

Epicureans set all things at liberty, and denied Providence, 196.

Epiphanius, his zeal against pictures in churches, 308. is severe upon the Collyridians for worshipping the blessed Virgin, 328.

Epistles, why the general ones were not so early and universally received, as the rest of the New Testament, 103.

INDEX. 559

Erudition, a book published, called the Necessary Erudition, a preliminary to compiling the Articles, 6.

Eternity, in a succession of determinate durations impossible, 22. of the world disproved, 23. See World.

Eucharist, in what sense it may be called a sacrifice, 459. the virtue of it, to whom limited, 460. the doctrine of the church of Rome concerning it, ib. wherein the virtue of it consists, 462. the importance of the controversy concerning it, 465. See Lord's Supper.

Eugenius, pope, does not mention bishops as belonging to the sacrament of orders, 374.

Evil, whether God is the author of it, 38. the being of it in the world, how accounted for by the Remonstrants, 213. liberty cannot be asserted without it, 223.

Evil spirits, what sort of miracles they can perform, 78.

Eunapius, his spiteful representation of the primitive martyrs, 320.

Eutychian heresy was condemned by the Athanasian Creed, 136. what it was, 431. was confuted by several ancient writers, ib. the force of their argument explained, 432.

Excommunication, the nature of it, and its necessity in some cases, 477—483. ought not to be done rashly, 483.

Extreme unction no sacrament, 378. a passage in St. James, which seems to favour it, explained, 379. the design and effects of the anointing by the apostles and elders, 380. the matter and form of it used in the church of Rome, 381. was not reckoned a sacrament in the first ages of Christianity, 383. when and by whom decreed to be one, ib. argument for it answered, 384.

F.

Fabri Honoratus, the doctrines of the church of Rome examined in this book, chiefly taken from him, 375. his character, ib.

Faith, the scriptures the only and complete rule of it, 89. no articles of it to be allowed, but what are proved from scripture, 96. an objection against this answered, 97. what is meant by it in the New Testament, 162. how it justifies, 167. is indispensably necessary to salvation, 168, 394. the nature of justifying faith, 168.

Fall of Adam, of its consequences to him, and his posterity, 140, 149, 150. See Sin.

Fasting, times of fasting, appointing them in the power of the church, 265. when joined with prayer, its efficacy, 369. in what cases of no avail, 370. the absurdity of pretending to expiate sins by it, ib.

Fate, the Stoics put all things, even the gods themselves, under it, 196. this downright atheism, ib. was maintained by the Essens, ib. is a prevailing opinion among the Mahometans, ib.

Figures in scripture, how to be explained, 112. were frequently made use of by Christ, 409. Augustine's rule for explaining them, 423.

Fire of purgatory, the proof alleged for it examined, 293.

Forgiving injuries, the necessity and extent of it, 190.

Forms were settled very early in most churches, 2. these not all in the same words, ib. See Creed.

Francfurt, council, condemned the Nicene council, together with the worship of images, 309.

Free-will, wherein it consists, 152. See Liberty.

Frumentius preached to the Indians before he was ordained, 340.

Future state was looked for under the Old Testament, 126. but is brought to a much clearer light by the gospel, 127.

G.

Gehenna, hell known by that name among the Jews, 72.

Gelasius, pope, condemns the communicating in one kind, only as sacrilege, 456.

General Council. See Council.

Gentiles, their prejudices against Christianity, 76.

German and Lupus reform Britain from Pelagianism, 197. a legendary miracle said to be wrought by them, ib.

INDEX.

Gnostics pretended to traditions from the apostles, 96. their opinion concerning the soul, 196. were detested by all Christians for idolatry, 307.

God, his existence proved from the universal consent of mankind, 20. objections that some nations do not believe a Deity, and that it is not the same belief amongst them all, answered, ib. the visible world, and history of nations, prove a Deity, 21—25. whence the notion of a plurality of gods might take its rise, 21. the argument from miracles considered, 25. and from the idea of God, ib. this not the most conclusive, 26. must be eternal, and necessarily exists, ib. his existence ought not to be proved from scripture, 27. his unity proved from the order of the world, and from the idea of infinite perfection, 27. from the scriptures, ib. is without body or parts, 28. the origin of the notion of a good and bad god, 29. the world not a body to God, ib. the outward manifestations and bodily parts ascribed to God in scripture, how to be understood, 30. no successive acts in God, 31, 33. question concerning his immanent acts, 31. is without passions, ib. the meaning of scriptures, which ascribe these to him, ib. is of infinite power, 32. objections to this answered, ib. wherein his wisdom consists, and a twofold distinction of it, ib. true ideas of his goodness of great importance, 33. wherein it consists, ib. and how limited, 34. has a power of creating and annihilating, 32, 35. is the preserver of all things, 35. this a consequence of his being infinitely perfect, 37. objection against his providence answered, 38. whether he does immediately produce all things, ib. or is the author of evil, 39. all agree that the Father is truly God, 48. just notions of him the fundamental article of all religion, 48, 131. the best manner of framing an idea of him, 48. is the only proper object of adoration, 56. in what sense called the God of Abraham, &c. long after they were dead, 126. image of God in which man was created, wherein it consisted, 143. distinction between the methods of his goodness and the strictness of his justice, 174. the doctrine of the church of Rome concerning our love of God, 177. his view in forming his decrees, 194. what meant by his hardening Pharaoh's heart, 219. the impiety of speaking too boldly of him, 223.

Goods, the unreasonableness of a community of them, 513.

Good Works. See Works.

Gospel condemns all idolatry, 57. the design of it, 76. refines upon the law of Moses, 132.

Government was settled in the church by the apostles, 334. the necessity of church government, 335.

Grace, assisting and preventing grace, asserted and proved from scripture, 155—159. a probable conjecture concerning the conveyance of actual grace, 156. the efficacy and extent of it, 158, 206, 209, 220.

Greek church, wherein they differed from the Latins, 86.

Gregory I., pope, condemns worshipping of images, 309. the IId declares for them, ib. the IXth first ordered the adoration of the Host as now practised, 439. Gregory the Great, his violent opposition to the title of Universal Bishop, 501.

H.

Head of the church, in what sense Christ is the only head of the church, 507. and in what sense the king is called the head, ib.

Hebrews, why the authority of the Epistle to them was doubted, 102. proofs of its authority, 103.

Heliodorus, a bishop, author of the first romance, 472. proposed that clergymen should live from their wives, ib.

Hell, three different senses of it, 10. of Christ's descent into hell, 69. See Christ. The gates of hell shall not prevail against the church, the meaning of this, 260.

Henry VIII. several steps towards reformation, and the foundation of the Articles were laid in his time, 6.

Heresies occasioned the enlargement of Creeds, 4.

Heretics, several of them pretended to traditions from the apostles, 96. when

INDEX.

the doctrine of extirpating them took place, 442.

Hezekiah commended for breaking the brazen serpent, 317.

Hilarion, a fabulous story of his body and tomb, 318.

Hobbes grafted fate and absolute necessity on the Supralapsarian hypothesis, 204.

Holiness of life, not a note of the church, 240. a twofold sense of holiness in scripture, 400.

Holy Ghost, or Holy Spirit, what meant by it in the Old and New Testament, 84. is properly a distinct person in the Trinity, 85. curiosities about his procession to be avoided, ib. decrees of several churches and councils about it, 86. the doctrine of the church of England concerning it, ib. is truly God, 87. his testimony not a sufficient argument to prove the canon of the scriptures, 101. of the sin against the Holy Ghost, 188, 190. 'It seemed good to the Holy Ghost, and to us,' the meaning of this, 281. of the form, 'Receive ye the Holy Ghost,' in ordination, 495.

Homilies of the Church of England, their names, 491. when and on what account they were composed, ib. the meaning of the approbation of them, 492. ought to be read by all who subscribe them, ib. the meaning of their being said to be *necessary for these times*, ib.

Honorius, pope, was condemned as a Monothelite, 251, 252. the IIId first appointed the adoration of the Host, 439.

Host, adoration of it, by whom first introduced, 439. is plain idolatry, 445. argument for it answered, 446. reserving, carrying it about, and the elevation of it, without foundation in scripture or primitive practice, 447, 448.

Huss, John, met with great cruelty from the church of Rome, 458.

I.

James I., king, his declaration concerning the subscription of the Articles, 9.

Jansenius published a system of St.

Austin's doctrine, 201. on what account his book was condemned at Rome, 202.

Iberians were converted by their king before he was baptized, 340.

Idolatry, the necessity of guarding against it at the establishment of Christianity, 4. what makes it a great sin, 34, 131. the Jews were particularly jealous of every thing that savoured of it, 53. the design both of the Jewish and Christian religion to banish it, 57. by what means the seed of Abraham were preserved from it, 93. the nature and immorality of it, 131, 302. general rules concerning it, 301. several kinds of it among the heathens, 302. was very strictly prohibited among the Jews, 303. this owing chiefly to the Egyptian idolatry, ib. the expostulations of the prophets against it, ib. how practised by the Israelites, 304. is contrary to the nature and perfections of God, 306. St. Paul condemns the idolatry of the Greeks and Romans, ib. the refined notions of the Athenians concerning it, ib. was much condemned by the writers of the first four centuries, 307.

Idols, enchantment in sacrifices offered to them, 413. Christians not to partake of them, 414.

Jehu rewarded, though acting with a bad design, 174.

Jerome, St. once admired, but afterwards opposed, Origen's doctrine, 197. maintained that no Christian would finally perish, 292. set a high value on relics, 316. but disclaims the worshipping of them, ib. said that the souls of the saints might be in several places at once, 320.

Jerom of Prague suffered cruelly by the Roman catholics, 458.

Jesuits, wherein they differed from the Semipelagians, 199. what gave them great merit at Rome, 200.

Jews, their aversion to idolatry and Christianity, 52. did not charge Christianity with idolatry, 58. their notions of God, 59. their notion of the state of the soul after death, 71, 291. expected the Messias to be a conqueror, 76, 95. were always rebellious, 106. wherein the Jewish and Christian re-

INDEX.

ligions differed from those of the heathen, 108. their objections against the authority of the New Testament, 122. looked for more than transitory promises, 126. believed that some sins cannot be expiated by sacrifices, ib. of their ceremonial, judiciary, and moral laws, 128, 129. imagined that the souls of all mankind were in Adam's body, 149. the distinguishing point of the Jewish from the Christian religion, 211. their religion had a period fixed to it, 248. had many rites not mentioned in the Old Testament, 265. fell into great errors, though the keepers of the oracles of God, 270. believe that every Jew shall have a share in the world to come, 291. they prayed only to God, 322. of the office of their high priest, 339. had their worship in a known tongue, 342. their authority over their children, 398. were strictly prohibited the eating of blood, 405. their objections to Christianity, 426

Images, the worshipping even the true God by them expressly forbidden, 304. in churches when introduced, 308. great debates about them, 309. foundation of image-worship laid by the council of Nice, ib. is carried much further by the modern church of Rome, 310. those of the Egyptians and Chineses less scandalous, 311. the decision of the council of Trent in this matter, 313. reason for enlarging on this subject, ib. the argument in favour of them drawn from the Cherubims answered, 314. the sum of the arguments against them, ib. the corruptions occasioned by worshipping them, 315.

Immaterial substance, proof of its being in us, 39. its nature and operations, ib. objections against it answered, 40. there may be other intellectual substances which have no bodies, 41. these beings were created by God, and are not rays of his essence, ib.

Imposition of hands, a necessary rite in giving orders, 372.

Indulgences, the doctrine and practice of the church of Rome concerning them, 298. when introduced and established, 299. the abuse of them gave rise to the Reformation, ib. the pretences for them examined, 300. no foundation for them in scripture or in the first ten centuries, ib. the natural ill tendency of them, 301. See Pardons.

Industry of man, of great advantage to the earth and air, 36.

Infallibility, proofs of it ought to be very express, 234. is not to be inferred from the necessity of it, ib. general considerations against it, 235. miracles, though necessary, not pretended to support it, 236. the Jewish had a better claim to it than the Roman church, ib. reasons why it cannot be proved from scripture, 238. a circle not to be admitted, 239. notes of the church no proof of it, ib. argument against the infallibility both of popes and general councils, 255. proofs from scripture answered, 258. the importance of this controversy, 262. no determination where it is fixed, 277.

Infants are by the law of nature and nations in the power of their parents, 399. argument from circumcision for infant baptism, ib. this agreeable to the institution of Christ, 400, 401.

Infinite, time nor number cannot be infinite, 22. difference betwixt an infinite succession of time, and composition of matter, 23.

Injuries, our Saviour's words concerning them explained, 509.

Innocent I., pope, his Epistle advanced to favour the chrism, does not prove it, 382. the VIIIth granted license to celebrate the Lord's supper without wine in Norway, 454. the IVth said that all might have the cup who were cautious that none of it was spilt, 457.

Insects, the argument for chance from the production of them considered, 24.

Inspiration, a general notion of it, 110. several kinds and degrees of it, ib. different styles in those degrees, 111. distinguished from enthusiasm and imposture by miracles and prophecy, ib. of individual words, or strict order of time, not necessary, ib.

John, St. the passage concerning the Trinity in his first Epistle doubtful, 46. the beginning of his Gospel ex-

INDEX. 563

plained, 52. this confirmed by the state of the world at that time, 53.
Jonas of Orleans wrote against image-worship, 310.
Josephus, his account of the books of the Old Testament, 113.
Josias, what those books of the law were which were discovered in his time, 108.
Irenæus, his care to prove the authority of the Gospel, 102.
Judgment, private, ought to be allowed in religious matters, 246.
Julian the Apostate, though he reproaches the Christians for baptism, does not charge them with the absurdities of transubstantiation, 427. objected that the Christians had no sacrifices, 463.
Just, or justified, two senses of these words, 160.
Justification, several mistaken notions of it, 123. whence they proceeded, ib. the law of Moses not sufficient to justify, 160. the condition of our justification, 161, 164. the difference between St. Paul and St. James on this subject explained, 162, 163. inherent holiness not the cause of justification, 166. what we ought to believe concerning it, and the proper use to be made of this doctrine, 169.

K.

Keys, of the power of them committed to St. Peter, 260.
Kingdom of heaven, what meant by it in the gospel, 260.
Kings, their authority, founded on scripture, 502. and practice of the primitive church, 503. this does not depend on their religion, 506. cannot make void the laws of God, ib.
King of England declared head of the church, 497. this claimed very early by them, 504.
Kiss of Peace, a practice of the apostolic times, why let fall, 265.

L.

Laity, were of great use to the church in times of persecution, 482. had a right to be consulted in the decisions of the primitive church, ib. how far required to submit to the clergy, 482, 483.
Languages, the gift of them to the apostles, a strong proof of Christianity, 75.
Laodicea council, their catalogue of the canonical books, 114. why the book of the Revelation was not in it, ib. condemned those who invocated angels, 324.
Latria, a degree of religious worship, the doctrine and practice of the church of Rome concerning it, 311, 312, 313.
Laud, archbishop, falsely accused with corrupting the doctrine of the church, 18, 19. espoused the Arminian tenets, 204.
Law, not binding the consciences of those of a different persuasion, 6, 7. in what sense the laws of the Jews are said to be statutes for ever, 122. why not always observed, 123. errors that flowed from mistaking the word Law in the New Testament, ib. the design of the ceremonial law, 128. it is now abrogated, 129. judiciary laws of the Jews belonged only to them, ib. what is meant by the moral law, 130. laws of the church in matters indifferent are not unalterable, 488.
Lay administrations in the church not lawful, 333—336. lay baptism, how introduced, 396.
Liberius, pope, condemned Athanasius, and subscribed to Semi-Arianism, 251.
Liberty, several opinions about it, 152, 153. wherein it consists, 153. the notions of the Stoics, Epicureans, Philosophers, and Jews, concerning it, 195, 196. that of the Fathers, 196, 197. what coaction is consistent with it, 210. the Remonstrants' notion of it, 214. several advantages and temptations that attend the different opinions, 222. See Predestination.
Limbus Infantum, a supposed partition in hell for children that die without baptism, 147.
Limbus Patrum, what, 71. without foundation in scripture, ib.
Lombard, Peter, the first that reckons seven sacraments, 351.
Lord's supper, the change made in the

2 o 2

Article concerning it in queen Elizabeth's reign, 402, 403. the importance of the controversy with the church of Rome concerning it, 403, 415. the words of the institution explained, 403—408. the design of it, 410. who are unworthy receivers of it, 411. the danger of this, 411, 450. of the good effects of worthy receiving, 412. what meant by the communion of the body and blood of Christ, ib. of receiving it in both kinds, 452.

Lucifer, the common notion of his sin, 55.

Lucretius owns that the world had a beginning, 23. his argument for chance from the production of insects, answered, 24.

Luther, what determined him to embrace St. Austin's opinions, 199. whether he asserted free-will, 202.

Lutherans have universally gone into the Semipelagian opinions, 202. their doctrine of consubstantiation, 444. wherein it differs from transubstantiation, ib.

Lie, what is the lowest, and what the highest, act of that kind, 301.

M.

Maccabees, the first book commended, 291. the second of little authority, ib. the argument in favour of purgatory taken from this book confuted, 292.

Macedonians denied the divinity of the Holy Ghost, 86. this heresy condemned by the Athanasian Creed, 135, 136.

Mahomet denied the death of Christ, 64.

Mahometans, one sect assert liberty, but the generality fate, 196. maintain that men of all religions are equally acceptable to God, 228.

Magistrate, the extent of his authority in sacred things, 485.

Man, though all resemble one another, yet each have their peculiar difference, 24.

Manichees denied the authority of the Gospels, 102. scarce deserved the name of Christians, 104. their absurd opinions, ib. concerning the Old and New Testament, 116. of original sin, 142. did not use wine in the sacrament, 456.

Marcionites, their opinions, 102, 196. are opposed by Origen, 196.

Marriage, in what degrees, and why, unlawful, 130. why it ought to be for life, ib. the meaning of that passage, ' Such as marry do well, but such as marry not do better,' 179, 474. is no sacrament, 374. in what sense a mystery, ib. the bad consequences of the Romish doctrine on this subject, 375. is dissolved by adultery, 377. the practice of the church in this matter, ib. whether a Christian may marry an infidel, 399. that of the clergy lawful, 467. is recommended equally to all ranks of men, 468. is one of the rights of human nature, 469. several of the apostles and fathers of the primitive church were married, ib.

Martyrs, the regard due to their bodies, 315. this being carried too far degenerates into superstition, 316.

Mass, the absurdity of saying masses for the dead, 296. this was the occasion of great endowments, 297. as practised in the church of Rome not known in the primitive ages, 464. what was understood by it in the primitive church, ib. solitary masses not known to them, ib. the bad effects of them, 297, 465.

Matter, of the divisibility of it, 22. a difference between the succession of time, and the divisibility of matter, 23. is a passive principle, 25, 49. is not capable of thought, 39. objections to this answered, 40. how the mind acts on it, we cannot distinctly conceive, ib. had its first motion from the Eternal Mind, 49. the great influence of the animal spirits on it, 78.

St. Matthew's and St. Mark's Gospel, Papias, his account of them, 102.

Maurus Rabanus wrote against the corporal presence, 440.

Mean, what meant by it, 394.

Melito, bishop of Sardis, his account of the books of the Old Testament, 113.

Memories of the martyrs, what, 318, 319.

Merit of congruity, what meant by it, 175. there is no such merit, ib. See Works.

INDEX. 565

Messias, the revelation those before and under the law had of one, 117. Jews have long had, and still have, an expectation of him, ib. proofs of the Messias from the Old Testament, 117—121. Daniel very express in this matter, 121. the proofs summed up, 122. the objections of the Jews answered, ib.

Metaphor, no good foundation for argument, 280, 288.

Middle knowledge, what meant by it, 32, 33, 200.

Millennium, an account of it, 290.

Mind. See Soul.

Ministers, their unworthiness hinders not the effect of the sacraments, 386. their intention not necessary to the essence of a sacrament, 387. ought to be censured for their faults, 389.

Miracles well attested a proof of the being of a God, 25. a distinct idea of them, 49. the nature and design of them, 77, 422. how to know if they are performed by good or evil spirits, 77, 78. of those wrought by Moses, 106. the spiteful construction put upon those of our Saviour by the Jews, 188. are necessary to prove infallibility, 234. the instruments of them not to be superstitiously used, 317. were not to be attempted without an inward impulse, 380. are an appeal to our senses, 420. those that are contrary to our senses not to be believed, ib. the absurdity of those pretended in the church of Rome, 415, 423.

Missals, those of the Gallican church different from the Roman, 490.

Molina and Fonseca invented the middle or mean science, 200. what meant by it, ib.

Moral evil, how reconciled with providence, 38. the occasion of physical evil, ib.

Moral Law. See Commandments.

Morality, the sources of it, 130. two orders of moral precepts, ib. religion the foundation of it, 131.

Moses, the design of the Mosaical religion, 57. God's design in ordering him to put things in writing, 93, 94. his miracles a proof of his divine mission, 106. the design and authority of his writings, ib. his laws not unalterable, 123. of the covenant he made between God and the Israelites, 124. the several things he supposed known, ib. the Jews had better reason to invoke him, than Christians have any saint under the gospel, 322.

Mysteries that contradict reason are not to be believed, 421.

N.

Natalitia, the day of a saint's death, so called, 295.

Nature, though we cannot fix the bounds of it, we can know what goes beyond it, 77.

Nazianzen, his complaints of councils, 276.

Necessary, whether God's acts are so, 30.

Necessary Erudition, the title of a book, published at the beginning of the Reformation, 6.

Necessary existence must belong to God, 26.

Necessity justifies the breaking through the rules of worship, 339.

Nectarius, bishop of Constantinople, what occasioned him to forbid confession, 363.

Negative, why to be maintained in points of faith, and not in matters of fact, or theories of nature, 6.

Nestorius, his doctrine concerning the person of Christ, 63, 64. concerning the Blessed Virgin, 320. his heresies are condemned in the Athanasian Creed, 135, 136.

Nice, council, composed their Creed out of many former ones, 3. what they determined concerning the Trinity, 47. asserted the worship of images, 309. was rejected in England on that account, 310. the history and acts of that council give a bad opinion of them, ib. the nature of that worship they allowed to images, 311.

Nicene Creed, an account of it, 135.

Nicolaitans, a name of reproach given to the married clergy, 473.

Notes, the pretended ones of the true church examined, 239.

Novatians opposed the receiving the lapsed into the church, 189, 362.

INDEX.

O.

Oaths, ill and rashly made, ought not to be kept, 475. what an oath is, 515. a false one, what, ib. oaths were very early used, 516. are lawful among Christians, 517. objections against them answered, ib. all vain and rash swearing condemned, 518. when and in what manner they ought to be taken, ib.

Oil began very early to be used in sacred rites, 353, 381. what probably introduced it, ib. that used by the apostles was attended with a miraculous effect, 378, 379. the form of applying it in the church of Rome, 381. this is of a modern date, 382. argument from the fitness of it answered, 384.

Old Testament. See Scriptures.

Opinions, a rule to be observed in representing different opinions, 151. in what case opinion is no excuse for sin, 446.

Opus Operatum, or the act of receiving the sacraments not sufficient to convey grace, 347.

Orders, the different ranks of them in the church, 371. no sacrament, ib. what the essentials of them are, 372. validity of those of the church of England, 494. See Pastors.

Ordination by laymen valid, 340. the form of it in the Greek church, 372. in the church of Rome, 373. several regulations about them, 494. the phrase, ' Receive ye the Holy Ghost,' which is used in them, explained and vindicated, 495.

Origen, his care in settling the canon of the New Testament, 102. his opinion of the soul, free-will, and providence, 196. his doctrine was much followed, ib.

Original sin, various opinions about it, 140—142. what the scriptures teach concerning it, 142. how it may be conveyed, 143, 144. the consequences of it more than a natural death, 144. the effects of it not quite taken away by baptism, 146.

Overal, bishop, espoused the Arminian tenets, 204.

P.

Pagans not excused from idolatry, because they worshipped the true God under their idols, 446.

Papias, who conversed with the apostles, his account of the Gospels of St. Matthew and St. Mark, 102.

Papists. See Church of Rome.

Parable, consequences to be drawn from the scope of them, and not from particular phrases, 288.

Paradise, what notion the Jews had of it, 72.

Pardon of sin, the conditions of it, 33. the doctrine of the church of Rome concerning pardons, 299. the abuse and bad consequences of it, 182, 298. this gave rise to the Reformation, 299. the pretence of their being only an exemption from penance examined, 300. is without foundation in scripture or antiquity, ib.

Parents, their authority over their children by the Jewish constitution, 398. this agreeable to Christianity and the law of nature, 399. their obligation more particularly to take care of their souls, 400, 401.

Paris council condemned image-worship, 310.

Passion defined, 31. in what sense ascribed to God, ib. its influence, 153.

Passover, the original and design of its institution, 403. a type of our deliverance by the Messias, 404.

Pastors, a succession of them ought to be in the church, 333. this to continue till the end of the world, 334. and did not belong to the infancy of Christianity only, 335. the danger of taking this office, without a due vocation, 335, 336. who are lawfully called, 336. lawful authority, what, 337. where the jurisdiction is fixed in the church of Rome, 339. what may be done in cases of necessity, ib. instances of lay preachers, ib.

Patriarchal authority of the see of Rome is dissolved with that empire, 502.

Pelagius, his opinion of original sin, 140. objections against it, ib. his opinion of liberty, 154, 197. his character, 197. is opposed by several learned men, ib. had many followers in Britain, ib.

INDEX. 567

Penance, a long one imposed on sinners in the primitive times, 182. whence the word is derived, 355. the several acts of it, ib. no characters of a sacrament in it, 357. the doctrine of the church of Rome concerning it, ib. no sacrament, because of a modern date, ib. many canons about it, 363. the ancient discipline slackened, ib. whether penance is to be performed before absolution, 368. the absurdity of the doctrine of the church of Rome on this subject, ib. what is the true penance enjoined by the gospel, 369.

Perfection, no councils of perfection in the New Testament, 177. a passage in the nineteenth of St. Matthew, which seems to imply this, explained, 178. in what sense we are called to be perfect as God and Christ, 185. the scripture represents the best of men as imperfect, ib. this is no encouragement to live in sin, ib.

Perseverance, a necessary consequence of absolute decrees, 211.

Person, resulting from the conjunction of two natures, what, 62. what meant by Christ's having one person, 64. of the personality of the Holy Ghost, 86.

St. Peter, of the authority committed to him, 259. had no superiority, 499. was withstood by St. Paul, ib.

Pharisees, asserted free-will and providence, 196.

Philosophers, their opinion of matter, 29. despised revelation, secret assistances, and miracles, 76. their account of original sin, and the pre-existence of souls, 142. were puzzled about free-will and providence, 196. were not so gross idolaters as the vulgar among the heathens, 302.

Philosophy was new modelled to explain transubstantiation, 424.

Photinus, his opinion of Christ, 61.

Pictures in churches condemned by the council of Eliberis, 308. soon led to idolatry, 309.

Plato, his opinion of the soul after death, 291. was probably the source of purgatory, ib.

Polycarp, a remarkable passage concerning his body, 317.

Popes, when they took the full power of indulgences to themselves, 182. have been condemned for heresy, 251, 252. their ambition, forgeries, and cruelties, 252. of their pretended power over princes, 253. arguments against their infallibility, 250, 254. alleged proofs of it answered, 259. several absurdities in asserting it, ib. were not much consulted in calling some councils, 273. of the pardons and indulgences granted by them, 298. have been the most wicked succession of men history has produced, 438. their authority was pretended to long before their infallibility, 498. their jurisdiction founded on a forgery, 501. the extent of their claim, and by whom completed, ib. See church of Rome.

Prayer, what outward gestures proper for it, 57. prayers for the dead, an early practice in the church, 294. what gave occasion to it, ib. Tertullian's opinion of them, 295. why not practised in the church of England, ib. prayers in an unknown tongue. See Worship. the great efficacy of prayer with right dispositions, 370. the absurdity of appointing prayers as a task, ib.

Preaching of the apostles, the nature of it, and wherein it differed from that of their successors, 398.

Precepts, wherein they differ from the means of salvation, 394.

Predestination, the controversy about it reduced to a single point, 193. three main questions that arise out of it, ib. various opinions about it, 194. history of the controversy concerning it both in ancient and modern times, 195—204. general reflections on the subject, 221. the advantages and disadvantages of the several opinions, 222. points in which all are agreed, 224. how far the Article has determined in this controversy, 225. the design of the cautions added to it, 226. passages in the Liturgy concerning it explained, 226, 227. the impartiality observed in treating this subject, 227.

Prescience, the notions of the Supralapsarians concerning it, 205. those of the Sublapsarians, 212. the certainty of it is not causal, but eventual, 217. a conditionate prescience agreeable to scripture, ib.

Presence, real, the meaning of it as taught by the church of England, 414. the doctrine of the church of Rome concerning it, 415. the mystical presence is acknowledged by them, 423. whence the controversy about the matter of the presence took its rise, 439.

Preventing grace, proof of it, 157. of the efficacy and extent of it, 158. See Grace.

Priest, the rules concerning the high priest of the Jews dispensed with in cases of necessity, 339. the Jewish notion of a priest, 461. Christ was both a Priest and Sacrifice, ib.

Primasius, his comparison of the eucharist, 435.

Private judgment, objections against it answered, 245, 246. is allowed by the church of Rome, 246.

Procession of the Holy Ghost, we can have no explicit idea of it, 85. yet ought to be believed, 86.

Promises, whether any other than temporary under the old dispensation, 124. those that were national only temporary, ib. particular persons had a prospect of a future state, 125. proofs of this, 125, 126.

Prophecy, not a mark of the true church, 240. of those relating to the Messias, 117—122.

Prophetical writings, why dark and obscure, 110, 111.

Providence, wherein it consists, 36, 37. how the difficulty of conceiving it may be removed, 37. objections against it considered, 38. the necessity of it, ib. was denied by the Epicureans and Sadducees, 196. how the great designs of it are carried on, 218.

Punishments, the temporal ones of good men, no argument for the reserve of others in another state, 287. the lawfulness and necessity of capital punishments, 507. the measure and extent of them, 508, 509.

Purgatory, the doctrine of the church of Rome concerning it, 284. no foundation for it in scripture, 286. arguments for it considered, 287, 288. reasons for rejecting it, 289. a middle state not warranted from scripture, ib. different opinions about the state after death, 290. the sources of this doctrine, 291. argument from Maccabees examined, ib. a passage from the New Testament alleged in favour of it, considered, 293. not known for the first six hundred years, 294. was never received by the Greek church, ib. is a remnant of paganism, ib. the great abuses of this doctrine, 297. political reasons are not sufficient to support it, 298.

R.

Radbert, Paschase, the first who asserted and explained the corporal presence, 440. was opposed by all the eminent men of his time, ib.

Ratramne, his account of the real presence, 440.

Real presence, the meaning of it in the doctrine of the church of England, 414. the absurdity of the Romish doctrine on this head, 415—424. See Transubstantiation.

Reconciliation by the death of Christ is not absolute and without conditions, 68.

Redemption, the Remonstrants' notion of its extent, 218.

Reformation, why many wild sects sprang up with it, 4. the fundamental article on which it depends, 6. the main ground upon which it is justified, 100. what occasioned the first beginnings and progress of it, 299.

Reformed, their different opinions concerning free-will and predestination, 202.

Reformers, reasons for their descending into so many particulars, 5. put Christianity on its right foundation, 167. those in England were Sublapsarians, 202.

Regeneration, how it may be explained, 156.

Relics, whence a superstitious regard for them took its rise, 316. the consequence of enshrining of them, ib. were appointed to be venerated by the council of Trent, ib. have no countenance from scripture, 317. nor from the practice of the first Christians, ib. no use made of them in the times of persecution, when most necessary, 318. fables and forgeries invented to support them, 318, 321. the novelty of the worship of them, 320.

Religion, just notions of God the basis of it, 34, 48, 131. the assistance that revealed religion can receive from philosophy, 144. the design of natural and revealed religion, 154, 332. the truths of religion are impressed by a divine direction, 156. Alcoran asserts that all religions are equally acceptable to God, 228. Hobbes makes religion and law to be the same, ib. the hypothesis of those who would accommodate their religion to their secular interest, ib. these opinions condemned, 229—231. all religions are not alike, 232. a true notion of it, 369.

Remission of sins, the notion of it under the old dispensation, 126, 127. not previous to justification, 163. is an act of God's favour, 166, 167. the nature of it in the gospel, 286. of the power of it committed to the apostles, 357, 358. in what sense it is continued by their successors, 261, 262.

Remonstrants, their opinions concerning free-will and predestination, 195, 213. their arguments, 213—221. difficulties obviated by their doctrine, 218. the advantages and disadvantages of it, 222, 223.

Repentance, not the valuable consideration, but the condition of justification, 168. the true notion of it, 356, 368. the danger of trusting to a death-bed repentance, ib.

Reprobation, the Supralapsarians' notion of it, 212. is a doctrine hard to be digested, 224.

Resurrection, the possibility of it, 42. of the nature of the body after it, ib. was denied by the Sadducees, 94. was believed under the Old Testament, 124—127. completes the happiness of a future state, 290.

Resurrection of Christ. See Christ.

Revelation, what it is, and the design of it, 154, 332. that which destroys the evidence of our senses is not to be believed, 420. See Scripture.

Revelation of St. John its authority proved, 104. why not mentioned in the catalogue of the council of Laodicea, 114.

Righteousness, the doctrine of the church of Rome concerning it, 166, 167. that of the reformed, 167.

Rites. See Ceremonies.

Rock of the church, what meant by it, 259, 260.

Roman catholic. See Church of Rome.

Ruffin was the first who mentioned the article of Christ's descent into hell, 69.

S.

Sabbath is not moral in the highest sense, 132. the reasonableness of it, ib. of the change of it, 133. works of necessity or charity may be done on it, 179.

Sacramental actions, the nature of them considered, 453. may be altered as to circumstances, ib.

Sacraments, the doctrine of the church of Rome concerning them, 164, 347. its bad consequences, ib. of the essentials of them, 244. are to be measured only by the institution, 296. are more than mere ritual acts, 347, 348. do not justify by the *Opus Operatum*, 349. a sacrament defined, ib. matter is of the essence of it, 350. must be instituted by Christ, ib. Protestants acknowledge only two, ib. Lombard the first who mentioned seven of them, 351. reasons for rejecting the five additional sacraments, 384. sacraments are ordained to be used, and not to be gazed on and carried about, ib. their effect depends on the worthy receiving, and not on the intention of him that dispenses them, 386.

Sacraments considered as acts of church-communion, or as federal acts, 450.

Sacrifices, expiatory ones, the nature of them, 65. how the death of Christ may be said to be our sacrifice, 67. in a general sense all religious worship may be so called, 459. but one Priest and one Sacrifice in the Christian religion, 461. answer of the fathers to the heathens, who charged them with having no sacrifices, 463.

Sadducees denied the resurrection 94.

from whom sprung, and what gave rise to their opinions, 123. our Saviour's answer to their puzzling question, 125. asserted liberty free from all restraints, 196.

Saints were not invocated under the Old Testament, 322. more rational foundation for this under the old than under the new dispensation, ib. Christ the only mediator and intercessor, 323. this superstition derived from the heathens, ib when it was introduced, 325. its progress, ib. the absurdity of it, 326. scandalous offices of this kind in the church of Rome, ib. what they found this practice upon, 327. arguments for it examined, 327—331.

Salvation, whether eternal salvation was promised under the Old Testament, 124. is to be obtained only by the name of Christ, 228. of those who never heard of the Christian religion, 230. curiosity in this not to be indulged, 231. how far the Article has determined in it, 232. difference between the means of salvation, and commanded precepts, 336.

Samosatenus, his opinion of Christ, 61.

Sanctification, what it is, and wherein it differs from justification, 164. is not perfected in this life, 189.

Scandal, the true notion of it, 487. the fear of giving scandal no warrant to break established laws, 488.

Schism in the church, the making it a great sin, 486.

Schoolmen, their vain attempt to explain the Trinity, 85. their many subtilties in the doctrine of the eucharist, 418. their explanation of the real presence, 443.

Scot, John, his character, 441. wrote against the doctrine of the corporal presence, ib.

Scotus, Erigena, wrote against St. Austin's doctrine of predestination, 198.

Scriptures, the being of God ought not to be proved from them, 27. his unity frequently asserted in them, ib. their style suited to the capacities of those for whom they were writ, 29, 30. their meaning to be taken from the scope of them, 39. New Testament, when wrote, 74. was early received, 75. the names and number of the canonical books, 88. are the only complete rule of faith, 90. Old Testament was always appealed to by Christ and his apostles, 94, 95, 105. the care taken to preserve them, 96. just consequences from them are to be believed, 97. contain all that is necessary to salvation, 98. are no sure guard against error, 99. ought not to be read carelessly, ib. proofs of the canon of the New Testament, 101—105. their authority is not founded on the judgment of the church, 104. that of the Old, 105—112. why divided into three volumes, 111. why they were called canonical, 115.

Sees, whence their privileges and exemptions rose, 489. the vanity of keeping up their ancient dignity, ib.

Semipelagians, their notion of assisting grace and free-will, 155, 197.

Senses, their influence on the mind, 315. the importance of their evidence, 420. they determine our judgment of miracles, ib. the foundation of our belief of them, 421. were appealed to by the fathers as infallible, 426.

Septuagint was highly esteemed in our Saviour's time, 106. when, and at whose charge, it was wrote, 107, 108. how it may be reconciled to the Hebrew, 109.

Serenus, bishop of Marseilles, his zeal against image-worship, 309.

Serpent, brazen, the breaking it when it came to be superstitiously used, vindicated, 317.

Severity ought not to be affected, 191.

Sin, Adam's sin said to be personal by the Pelagians and Socinians, 140. our being liable to death and the miseries of mortality thought by some to be original sin, 141. experience and scripture teach an universal corruption, 142. how this came about, 143. God's justice vindicated in the imputation of Adam's sin, 143. whether it deserves damnation, 144. church of Rome believe original sin is taken away by baptism, 145. St. Austin's doctrine concerning it, 146, 147. the manner of its propagation not easy to be explained, 147. reasons why many are of a different opinion, 148. how they explain the passages of scripture, and the Article concerning it, 150. what meant by deadly and venial sin, 187. the sin against the Holy Ghost explained, 188. none capable of this sin since miracles have ceased, 189. of the pardon of sin after baptism, ib. is pardoned according to the sincerity of our repentance, 190. what meant by the sin unto death, 191. difference to be made between deliberate sins and sins of infirmity, ib. sins once pardoned not liable to after punishment, 286. unless with temporal chastisements, 287. of the apostles' power of remitting sins, 358. whether this be continued in the church, ib.

Socinians, their notion of the death of Christ, 66. of Adam's sin, 140. objections against it, ib. their doctrine concerning predestination, 195. their opinion of prescience and contingencies, ib. how far they agree with the Remonstrants and Calvinists, 221.

Soldania, a most degenerate nation said to deny the being of a God, 20.

Son of God. See Christ.

Soul is distinct from matter, 39. what perceptions we have of its nature and operation, ib. of the souls of beasts, 40. the soul is not the same with the animal spirits, ib. how it acts on matter, inconceivable to us, ib. in some places of scripture stands for a dead body, 70. philosophers' notion of its pre-existence, 142. how defiled by Adam's sin, 145. conjectures about its state after death, 289. various opinions concerning this, 289—295.

Spirits, animal, their nature and use, 40, 154. are the immediate organs of thought, ib.

Spirits, invisible, the probability of their existence, and conjectures about their nature, 41. are not emanations or rays of the Divine Essence, ib. what meant by the spirits in prison, 70, 71. of the power of evil spirits, 77. See Soul.

Stephen, St. worshipped Christ in his last moments, 58. no other care taken of his body, but to bury it, 317. no mention made of worshipping him, 324.

Stephen, pope, his infallibility denied by Cyprian and Firmilian, 251.

Stephen, bishop of Autun, the first who introduced the word transubstantiation, 443.

Stoics, made all sins alike, 187. put all things under a fate, 196.

Sublapsarians, their doctrine concerning predestination, 212. avoid answering the Supralapsarians, and seem in effect not to differ from them, ib.

Subscription, what the clergy are bound to by their subscription of the Articles, 9. does import an assent to them, 11. different persons may subscribe to them in different senses, ib.

Suetonius, his account of Christ, 74.

Supererogation. See Works.

Superstition, the danger of its being suffered to mix with religion, 316.

Supralapsarians, the chief basis of their doctrine concerning predestination, 204. their arguments from the absurdity of the contrary opinion, 205.

Supremacy of the pope disproved, 498—502. that of kings or queens asserted, 502—506.

Swearing. See Oath.

Symbols, federal, the nature of them, 413.

T.

Temple, how the glory of the second exceeded the first, 119.

Thought different from matter and motion, 39. has no parts, 39, 40. whether beasts have thought, 40. is governed by impressions made on the brain, 154. is influenced by the animal spirits, 156.

Time cannot be eternal, 22. is not divisible to infinity, as matter is, 23.

Timothy and Titus, rules given them concerning church government, 334.

Tradition, oral, the regard due to it, 91, 92. the doctrine of the church of Rome concerning it, ib. no rule in matters of faith, ib. the scriptures intended to prevent the impostures of it, 92. no certain way of conveying the articles of religion, 94. was objected against on many occasions by our Saviour, ib. the occasion of great errors and ruin of the Jews, 94, 95. the apostles laid no stress on them, 95. arguments of Irenæus and Tertullian against them, 96. objection from the darkness of scripture an-

swered, 97. the difference between a settled canon of scripture and oral tradition, 104. traditions concerning image-worship departed from, 310.
Transubstantiation, a paragraph against it in the Articles in Edward the VIth's reign, 402. why it was afterwards suppressed, 402, 403. the doctrine of the church of Rome concerning it, 415. the consequences of it, 416. the grounds on which it was believed, 418. is contrary to our faculties both of sense and reason, 419. it was not received in the first and best ages, 424. several presumptive proofs of this, 424—429. the fathers believed the elements continued to be bread and wine after consecration, 429—431. by whom it was formed and broached, 431. several arguments against it, 433—451. how this doctrine crept into the church, 437. by whom the term was first introduced, 443.
Tree of knowledge of good and evil, and the tree of life, conjectures about them, 141, 144.
Trent council, the disappointments of it, a great probability there will never be another, 279. first received the Apocrypha into the canon, 114. their decree concerning good works, 170. declined to give a clear decision about image-worship, 312. reasons of this, 313. did not determine positively about relics, 316. did not decree the office of a bishop an order, or a sacrament, 374. was the first that decreed the indissolubleness of marriage, even for adultery, 378. decreed extreme unction to be a sacrament, 383.
Trinity is not to be proved by reason, 42. tradition of it very ancient, ib. not to be proved by the Old Testament without the New, 43. what meant by one substance, and what by three persons, in explaining it, ib. the difficulties in it no sufficient reason for not believing it, ib. different methods of explaining it, ib. several proofs of it, 44—46. from whence the errors in this doctrine took their rise, 48.
Tully, his account of the notion the heathens had of their images, 305.
Twisse, carried it high to the Supralapsarian hypothesis, 204.

V.

Valentinians pretended to traditions from the apostles, 96.
Various readings of the scriptures, whence they arose, 109. are inconsiderable, and affect not our faith or morals, ib.
Ubiquity of human nature impossible, 444.
Vigilantius complains of the worshipping of relics, 316, 320. and of saints and angels, 328.
Virgin, blessed, was reprimanded by our Saviour, 185. why she was not taken notice of in the first age of superstition, 319. has the preference to God and Christ in the worship of the church of Rome, 326.
Virgins, parable of ten virgins contradicts supererogation, 181.
Visible church, what it is, 233.
Understanding is as free as the will, 247.
Union of the church among themselves, and with their head, is not a note of the true church, 240.
Unity of the Godhead, proofs of it, 27. is a chief article of the Christian religion, 28.
Unity among Christians, the advantages of it, 486. the great sin of dissolving it, ib.
Vows of celibacy unlawful, 475. of the obligation of them, ib. See Oath.
Usher, archbishop, his explanation of Daniel's seventy weeks, 121.

W.

War, in what cases lawful, 511. and when unlawful, ib.
Water in baptism, what it is an emblem of, 391.
Will, whether it is always determined by the understanding, 153. wherein our liberty consists, ib. the opinions of the Pelagians and Semipelagians concerning it, 154, 155. See Liberty.
Winds, their great influence on the earth, 36. are under a particular direction of Providence, ib.
Wisdom of God, wherein it consists, 32.
Women are not allowed to teach, 334.
Works, what is meant by good works, 163. they are indispensably necessary to salvation, 170. the doctrine of the church of Rome concerning them,

172. none absolutely perfect, ib. this the opinion of the best men in all ages, ib. the absurdity of asserting the merit of good works, ib. the use to be made of the doctrine of the imperfection of good works, 173. whether any good works can be performed without divine assistance, 174. works of supererogation, the foundation of that doctrine destroyed, 180. its bad consequences, 183.

World is not eternal, because time nor number cannot be eternal or infinite, 22. the novelty of history, a further proof of this, 23. not made by chance, 24. objection from the production of insects answered, ib. is not a body to God, 29. is preserved by a constant Providence, 36. many changes made in it by the industry of man, ib. shall be destroyed by fire, 82.

Worship of God, what it is, 341. the design of the various acts of it, ib. the philosophers' notion that the varieties of worship were acceptable to God, 228. that it should not be in an unknown tongue proved from reason, scripture, and the practice of the primitive church, 341—344. when the present practice of the church of Rome was introduced, 344. arguments for it answered, 344, 345.

INDEX

OF THE

TEXTS OF SCRIPTURE,

AND OF THE APOCRYPHA,

REFERRED TO IN THE WORK.

Those marked thus (*) have been added in this edition.

GENESIS.

	Page
i. 26,* note	42
27.	143
27, 28.	143
iii. 15.	117
22.	141
vi. 5.	142, 172
viii. 21.	142
xii. 1.*	93
3.	117
xv. 6.	160
xxi. 23.	516
xxii. 18.	117
xxvi. 24.	117
28.	516
xxviii. 14.	117
xxxi. 19.* 30.*	93
53.	516
xlix. 10.	117

EXODUS.

	Page
i. 21.	172
iii. 1.	132
6.	125
iv. 21.	212
vii. 22.	219
viii. 15, 19, 32.	219
x. 20.	212
xi. 10.	212
xii. 3—14.	403
xiv. 8.	212
xvii. 14.*	92
xx. 4,* 5.* note	249
4, 5.*	302
17,	133
xxiii. 20.	59
21.*	59
xxiv. 4.*	92
12.*	94
xxv. 22.*	94
xxix. 42.*	94

	Page
xxxii. 1, 4, 5.	304
10, and through the whole Old Testament	150
32.	322
xxxiv. 6.	213

LEVITICUS.

	Page
i. 3, 4.	93
v. 1.	516
vii. 26, 27.	405
x. 3.	389
xiii. 3,* 6,* &c. note	359
xiv. 11,* note	359
xvi.* note*	65
xvii. 14. 405,* note,	406
xix. 12.	132
xxvi. 1.	303

NUMBERS.

	Page
xvi. 38.	297
xxiv. 17.	117

DEUTERONOMY.

	Page
iv. 13, 15, 17, 23.	303
v. 21.	133
vi. 3.*	97
4.	27
4,* note	27
6—9.*	97
vii. 7, 8.*	207
viii. 3*	81
ix. 4—6.*	207
x. 15,* 16.*	207
xi. 18—21.*	97
xii. 30.	303
xvi. 22.	303
xvii. 12,* note	236

	Page
xviii. 15.	117
xxvi. 16, to end of Deut.	107
xxvii. 8.*	92
36, to the end	107
xxxi. 9,* 19,* 22,* 24—26.*	92
xxxi. 11—13.*	97
xxxiv. 6.	316

JOSHUA.

	Page
vii.	292
viii. 32, 35.*	97
ix. 15, 19.*	516
xxiv. 2, 3.*	93
26.*	92

JUDGES.

	Page
xvii. 2.	516

1 SAMUEL.

	Page
iii. 11.	389
xiv. 24, 28, 44.	516
xv. 30.	502
17.	502
xxii. 14.	502
xxiii. 11, 12.	217
9—12.*	94

2 SAMUEL.

	Page
xxi. 1.*	516

1 KINGS.

	Page
viii. 46.	142
xii. 27—33.	304
xvi. 31.	304
xxi. 29.	174

INDEX OF TEXTS.

2 KINGS.	Page
x. 30, 3	174
28, 29	304
xiii. 21.	317
xvii. 28, 32, 41.	305
xviii. 4.	317
xxiii. 2,* 21,* 24.*	98

1 CHRONICLES.	
xxiii. 6.	503
xxxviii. 21.	503

2 CHRONICLES.	
viii. 14, 15.	503
x. 8, to the end	503
xvii. 8, 9.	503
16—19.	503
xxviii. from 36 to the end	107
xxx. 18, 19.	172
xxxiv. 14.	107

EZRA.	
iii. 12,* note	120

NEHEMIAH.	
viii. 1—8.*	98
8.	342
18.*	98
ix. 5.	342

PSALMS.	
i. 15.	322
xv. 4.	475
xvi. 10.*	70
11.	71
10.*	81
11.	125
xvii. 14, 15.	125
xxxiii. 11.	208
xxxvi. 9.	210
xlix. 7.	181
14, 15	125
l. 15.	322
li. 1, 2, 16, 17.	126
4.	217
10, 11.	155
17.	459
lxv. 2.	331
lxxiii. 24.	71
lxxxiv. 11.	125
lxxxvii. 6.	125
xc. 17.	125
xcvi. 13.	125
xcviii. 5.	435
xcix. 8.	287
5, 9.	314
cvi. 19, 20.	304

	Page
cx. 3.	209
cxvi.	405
cxix. 18, 27, 32, 35.	155
18, 35.	246
cxxx. 3, 4.	172
cxli. 2.	381, 459

PROVERBS.	
ii. 6.*	155
iii. 6, 34.*	155
xvi. 4.	212
xxiv. 16.	142
xxx. 8.	179, 514

ECCLESIASTES.	
vii. 29.	142
ix. 11.	241
xi. 9.	125
xii. 14.	125

ISAIAH.	
i. 18.	126
v. 4.	208, 220
vi. 1,* 3,* 9,* 10.*	63
vii. 14.	118
viii. 1.*	92
20.*	98
xi. 1, 2, 10.	118
xii. 3.	409
xxv. 8.	125
xxvi. 19.	125
xxix. 13.*	178
xxx. 8.	92
xxxiv. 16.*	98
xxxv. 5, 6.	117
xl. 26, 28.*	52
18—27	303
xlii. 1—4.	117
8.	331
xliv. 6, 8.	28
6,* note	28
9—21.	303
24.*	52
xlv. 5.*	52
xlviii. 12,* 13.*	52
li. 12,* 13.*	52
liii.	127, 118
10.*	67
liv. 13.*	246
lvii. 2.	71
lxi.	118
1.	71
lxv. 1.	158
5.*	477

JEREMIAH.	
i. 9, 10,* note	359
iv. 2.	517
x. 1—17.	303
1—16.*	52

	Page
xvii. 9.	142
xxiii. 5.	119
xxxi. 29, 30.	148
31—34.	119
33, 34.	155
33, 34.	209
xxxi. 34.	286
33, 34.*	246
xxxvi. 2, 26—32.*	92

EZEKIEL.	
xviii. 20.	148
24.	220
32.	214
xxxiii. 11.	220, 214
xxxvi. 25, &c.	119
26, 27.	155
26, 27.	210

DANIEL.	
vii. 9.*	82
10.*	82
ix.	127
24—27.	121
xii. 2.*	83
2.	125

HOSEA.	
vi. 6.	265
viii. 4, 5.	304
xiv. 2.	331
xiii. 9.	220

JOEL.	
ii. 28, &c.	119

MICAH.	
v. 2.	119

HABAKKUK.	
i. 13.	213
ii. 2.*	93
18—20.	303

HAGGAI.	
ii. 9.	59
3,* note	120
6—9.	119

ZECHARIAH.	
ix. 9.	120

MALACHI.	
iii. 1—3.	120
iv. 5, 6.	121

INDEX OF TEXTS.

1 MACCABEES.
i. 56. — 108

2 MACCABEES.
xii. 40. — 291

MATTHEW.
ii. 4—6.* — 98
4. — 81
iii. 2. — 260, 391
6. — 357
7. — 150
15.* — 392
iv. 4.* — 81
10. — 28, 53
10.* — 57
17. — 260
v. 12, 15 — 140
17, 18. — 134
17,* note — 406
26. — 287
32. — 377
33. — 132
34—37. — 517
39, 40. — 509
48. — 150, 185
vii. 22, 23. — 387
viii. 14,* note — 468
ix. 6. — 56
x. 15. — 217
41, 42. — 171
xi. 21. — 217
21—23. — 208
25, 26. — 207
27. — 56
xii. 7. — 265
24, 31. — 188
25, 26. — 78
32. — 288
xiii. 11,* 19,* 24*—
48.* — 260
xiv. 9. — 475
xv. — 433
3, 6, 9. — 94
5. — 475
7—9.* — 178
xvi. 15. — 281
16, 18, 19. — 259
16,* 18,* 19,* note 259
18. — 248
xviii. 17,* note — 236
17. — 280, 483
19. — 45
35. — 190
xix. 9. — 377
10, 11, 12. — 469
13, 14. — 401
16, 17, 20, 21. — 178
xx. 16. — 211
20, 24. — 185
21, 24, 26. — 499
28. — 66
xxi. 21. — 380
xxii. 21. — 266

xxii 29. — 125
31, 32. — 125
36—40. — 177
xxiii. 23. — 265
37. — 219
xxv. 9. — 181
31.* — 82
31.*—46. — 83
46.* — 83
xxvi. 26. — 404
26, 27. — 351
37, 39.* — 184
41.* — 146
63, 64. — 516
xxviii. 19. — 45, 350
19, 20. — 392
20. — 248, 281
40. — 392

MARK.
ii. 27. — 133
vi. 13. — 379
viii. 38. — 229
ix. 33,* 35. — 499
x. 11. — 377
xi. 17. — 182, 297
xiv. 22. — 404
xvi. 15. — 209, 281
16. — 349, 394

LUKE.
i. 3, 4.* — 93
4. — 96
6. — 185
20. — 185
ii. 49. — 185
iii. 14. — 511
iv. 16—21.* — 98
vii. 19—23.* — 98
ix. 26. — 82
xi. 13. — 84, 155
52. — 261
xii. 33. — 179
xiii. 3,* note — 360
xvi. 18. — 377
25.* — 289
xvii. 4. — 190
10. — 177
xxi. 4. — 514
xxii. 19. — 404
24—27.* — 499
32. — 262
xxiii. 40. — 150
43. — 289
43, 46. — 72
xxiv. 25—27.* — 98
25—27.* — 105
44. — 105
47. 168, 288, 393
52. — 57

JOHN.
i. 1, 2, 3. — 52
12. — 158
14. — 63

i. 25. — 391
29. — 66, 404
36,* note — 162
ii. 4. — 185
25. — 56
iii. 3, 5. — 147, 349
3, 5, 6. — 84, 393
6. — 143
6, 9. — 185
8. — 157
18. — 160, 168
19. — 231
25. — 56
iv. 22,* note — 446
23, 24. — 341
34. — 184
v. 25, 26. — 56
39.* — 94
40. — 144, 220
vi. 44.* — 158
32, 33. — 407
56, 63. — 408
39, 40. — 56
47, 48, 51. — 407
53, 54, 55. — 408
viii. 10, 11. — 150
xi. 51. — 339
xii. 41.* — 63
xiii. 1. — 211
34, 35.* — 485
xiv. 1. — 323
2.* — 82
2. — 155
13. — 56, 380
16, 26. — 85
16, 26.* — 87
26. — 87
xv. 5, 16. — 158
12, 17.* — 485
26. — 56, 87
xvi. 8—13. — 85
13.* — 87
13. — 280
xvii. 3. — 28
6.* — 209
9, 10. — 209
11, 12.* — 211
11, 21—23. — 486
12. — 219
xviii. 8, 9.* — 211
22, 23. — 339
xx. 21. — 333
22. — 453
23. — 358
31.* — 93
31. — 96, 144
xxi. 15—17. — 262

ACTS.
i. 11. — 80
ii. 23.* — 67
27, 31.* — 70
31. — 71
38. — 168
39. — 399

INDEX OF TEXTS.

	Page		Page		Page
iii. 12, 16.	80	iii. 24, 25.	128	v. 5.	190
iv. 12.	230	25.	66	7.	404
24, 25.*	52	28.	162	11.	357, 477
36, 37.	513	iv. 2.	158	vi. 6, 7.	510
v. 3, 4.	513	3, 22.	160	11.	164
3, 9.	358	v. 1.	286	19.	316
29.	266	5.	156	20.	178
34.	87	12, to the end	67	vii. 6, 12.	281
vi. 4.	474	12, 15.	140	9.	469
vii. 41.	304	12.	148	14.	400
51.	211, 219	18.	219	25.	282
59, 60.	58	vi.		38.	179
viii. 12, 14, 17.	352	3—5.	392	40.	282
23.	358	17.	2	viii. 5, 6.	28
26, to the end	398	23.	144	ix. 5,* note	468
x.	511	23.*	187	5.	469
25, 26.*	53	vii. 7.	134	18.	180
28.*	400	11, 12, 13, 14, 16,		19—23.	266
34, 35.	230	17, 18, 21, 23, 24,		20, 21, 22.	328
38.*	184	25.	175	x.* note	441
44, 47, 48.	394	viii. 6.	144	2.	391
xi. 2, 3.	499	7, 8.	143	16.	348, 410
2—18.*	257	13.	146	16, 17.	351
xiii. 48.	212, 219	18.	289	16.*	412
xiv. 14, 15.*	53	26.	85	18.	414
15.*	57	26.*	87	18, 20.	413
22.	289	29, 30.	211	xi. 1.	185
23.	335	34.*	82	16.	266
xv.*	128	ix. 11.	207	23.	404
6.*	268	11, 13.	211	23, 27.	351
9.	282	17, 18.	211	27, 29.	411
7, 14, 19.	499	18.	219	29.	150
7,* note	260	19.	208	xii. 4, 8, 9, 11, 13.	85
19.*	257	20.	211	12—26.*	486
28	274, 281	21.	210	13.	395
29.* note	406	22.	212	28.	334
39.	185	x. 9, 10.	229	xiii. 1, 2, 3.	370
xvi. 14.	158	14,	223, 230	2.	380
31—33.	398	xi. 20.	158	4,* note	249
xvii. 2, 3.*	98	29.*	211	4,* note	468
11.	95	xii. 1.	459	xiv.* note	468
16, 24, 29.	305	6, 7, 8.	334	14, 15, 16, 17, 26.	343
29.	57	xiii. 1.	272, 503	40.	264
xviii. 28.*	98	2.	150	xv. 24*—28.*	64
xix. 2—5.	393	5.	487	27.	82
xx. 28.	56	6.	503	28.	82
28.*	63	14.	393	21, 22.	142
34.	180	xiv. 10, 11, 12.*	83	22.*	127
xxiv. 16.	486	13.	487, 488	33.*	478
xxviii. 23.*	98	19.	264	40.	82
		23.	150, 487	41.	290
		xvi. 20, 24.	45	49.	141
ROMANS.				50.	82
passim	142	1 CORINTHIANS.		xvi. 22.	478
i. 7.	45			23.	45
9.	517	i. 3.	45		
20—32.	306	17.	397	2 CORINTHIANS.	
18, 24, 26.	247	26, 27, 29.	158		
25.	327	ii. 4.	77	i. 2.	45
26, 28.	212	10.	85	21, 22.	353
ii. 12.	163	10, 11.*	87	23.	517
12, 14, 15.	230	iii. 7.	219	ii. 1, 2, 3.	478
iii. 2.	105, 270	10—15.	293	7.	190
4.	509	10—15,* note	293	iii. 17, 18.*	87
22, 29, 30.	211	iv. 7.	158, 219	iv. 4.	71
24.	161	v. 2, 5, 7.	478	17.	171, 289

2 P

INDEX OF TEXTS.

	Page
v. 1, 2.	290
6, 8.	290
10.*	83
17.	142, 209
21.	66
21,* note	166
vi. 16, 156.	281
vii. 1.	173, 177
3.	150
x. 5.	403
8.	479
14.	499
xii. 8, 9.	58
9.	156
13.	45, 180
xiii. 14.	45, 413

GALATIANS.

i. 1,* 12,* 17.*	257
3.	45
8,* note	263
8, 9.*	478
20.	517
ii. 4.	264
7, 8, 11.	499
11—14.	185, 257*
16.	162
21.	209
iii. 10.	187
iv. 4.*	392
4.*	406
9.	264
v. 1.	264
3.	398
6.	168
12.	390, 478
17.	143, 146
vi. 18.	45
1.	191, 477

EPHESIANS.

i. 2.	45
3—6. 9—11.*	207
7.	66
13, 14.*	82
13, 14.*	156
17—19.	210
18.	247
ii. 1—9.*	207
2.	71
2, 3, 12.	157
15, 16, 20, 21.	376
10.	209
20.	260
22.*	156
iii. 9.	413
17.	156, 247
iv. 4, 5, 6.	28
9.	69
11—13, 16.	334
22, 24.	143
30.	85, 211
v. 32.	374
vi. 23.	45

PHILIPPIANS.

	Page
i. 2.	46
23.	290
ii. 1.	413
6, 7, 8, 9, 10, 11.	54
6.	63
10.	58
12.	173, 181
12, 13.	219
13.	158, 209
iii. 10.	413
13, 14.	172
iv. 18.	459
23.	45

COLOSSIANS.

i. 2.	4
14, 20—22.	66
16.*	52
16.	63
16, 17.	56
19.*	82
24.	181
ii. 8,* 18.*	291
9.*	82
9, 10.	324
12.	392, 395
18, 8—10.	178, 323
18.*	53
iii. 1.	392
9, 10.	393
17.	173

1 THESSALONIANS.

i. 1.	46
9.	57
ii. 16.	150
iv. 17.*	83
v. 28.	45

2 THESSALONIANS.

i. 2.	45
ii. 11.	247
iii. 6, 14, 15.	192
14.	357, 478
18.	45

1 TIMOTHY.

i. 2.	45
20.	478
ii. 1—3.	333
5.	323
iii.	334
2, 4, 5, 12,* note	468
2, 4, 5, 12.	469
15.	280, 334
iv. 1, 3,* note	468
3.	469
6.	2
v. 1, 3, 17, 19, 22.	334
1, 19, 20.	389
20.	357

	Page
vi. 3.	2
3, 4, 5.	389
20.	334, 350

2 TIMOTHY.

i. 2.	45
9.*	212
13.	2, 333
18.*	295
ii. 2.	333
15.	334
17.	478
19.	170
26.	481
iii. 15.*	105
15—17.	95
iv. 2.	191
2, 5.	334
8.	290

TITUS.

i. 4.	45
5, 9, 13.	324
9.	268
13.	191
ii. 13.	56
14.	168
iii. 5.	349, 295*
10.	268, 334

PHILEMON.

3.	45
25.	45

HEBREWS.

i. 3.	63
4, 5.	61
6.	58
6, 7, 8, 10, 12, 13, 14.	61
13.	213
ii. 5.	288
16.	62
iii. 1.	62
iv. 16.	156
v. 4.	334
10.	461
vi.	220
2.	352
4—6.	189
6.	191
13, 14, 15, 16.	517
vii. 23, 24.	461
26.	184
27.	461
viii. 12.	286
ix. 3, 5, 7.	314
11, 12, 13, 14.	66
12.*	461
20.	405
22.*	127
22, 28.	461
26.	66
28.	66

INDEX OF TEXTS.

	Page
x.*	129
2.	461
10, 12, 14, 19, 29.*	66
11, 12.	461
14,* note	461
25.	266
28.	126
38.	220
xi. 10.	290
xiii. 4.	469
4,* note	468
5.	211, 281
7.	324
7, 17.	335
12.	66
15.	459
17.	481
20.	66

JAMES.

	Page
i. 5.	156
17, 18.	211
ii. 1.	56
10, 11.	187
24.	163
iii. 2.	172, 180
11,* note	469
v. 12.	517
14, 15.	379
15, 16.	191
15,* note	381
16.	355, 361

1 PETER.

	Page
i. 15.	185
15, 16.	150
i. 19.	66, 184
ii. 13, 14.	503
22.*	184
24.	66
iii.	348
iii. 18.	66
19.	70
21.	242, 351, 396
iv. 17.	150, 411
v. 2, 3.	335

2 PETER.

	Page
i. 15, 16.*	93
15.	96
17.	258
19.	128
ii. 1.	219
iii. 9.	213
10, 12.*	82

1 JOHN.

	Page
i. 9.	355
ii. 2.	66, 219
20, 27.	353
iii. 6, 9, 18.	189
9.	156
11,* 23.*	486
16.	56
iv. 21.*	486
v. 7.	46
16.	191
18.	189
20.	56

2 JOHN.

	Page
i. 3.	45
8.	290

JUDE.

	Page
4.*	212
23.	478

REVELATIONS.

	Page
i. 4, 5.	46
7.*	82
8, *11—18,* note	28
i. 8.	56
11, 19.*	93
11, 12, 13, 17, 18.*	28
ii. & iii.	220
iii. 5.	212
7.	261
v. 8, to the end of chap.	58
13.	64
x. 5, 6.	517
xiii. 8.	67,* 212
xiv. 13.	290
xix. 10.	53,* 323
10.*	57
16.	56
xx. 12.	212
xxi. 5.*	93
14.	260
27.	212
xxii. 8, 9.*	53
9.	323
12, 13, 16,* note	28
12,* note	104

INDEX

OF THE

MATTER CONTAINED IN THE EDITOR'S NOTES.

ABSOLUTION, canon of Trent pronouncing absolution to be a judicial and not a declaratory act, 358. the doctrine of the church of England on the same in her Liturgy explained and vindicated, 358, 359. in the papal church supplies the place of contrition, 360.

Apocryphal, derivation, 89.

Arius, character of, enters the field of controversy; opinions, condemnation, excommunication, death, 60.

Arminius, account of, 202. his five points, 203. opinions condemned in synod of Dort, 203.

Attrition, what, considered *with absolution* equal to contrition, 360.

Augsburg, Confession of, presentation to the emperor, 5. effect upon the Diet, ib., see also 519—532.

B.

Buchannan, Dr. Claudius, relates instances of the doctrine of a Trinity, &c. &c., among the Hindoos, 42.

C.

Cassian, founder of Semipelagianism, his doctrine attacked by the followers of Augustin, leading principles of his disciples, 152.

Catechism of council of Trent teaches worship of the Virgin Mary, 326. maintains that purgatory is a fire, 286. teaches the doctrine of supererogation, 171.

Cerinthus, opinions of, avoided by St. John, 54.

Chalcedon, council of, decree concerning the nature of Christ, 136.

Christ, titles of the Godhead given to, 28.

Church, various senses of the word, 233. Notes of the Church, by Bellarmine, confuted, 239. whether Rome be a true church, 242, 243. whether visibility be necessary to its being, 248. where before Luther, 248—250. 'Hear the Church,' &c., 280.

Communion, half-, decree of council of Constance concerning, 457, 458. confirmed by council of Trent, 458.

Confession, church of England on the same, 356. decrees of councils of Lateran and Trent, ib.

Contrition, *necessary, according to the church of Rome,* when the priestly absolution cannot be had, 360.

Council of
Antioch, condemned Paul of Samoseta, 47.
Carthage, condemned Pelagius, 139. Second at ditto, ditto, 140.
Chalcedon, condemned Eutyches, 136.
Constantinople, condemned the heresy of Macedonius, 135.
Constance, called to heal the papal schism, 273.
Constance, decree on half-communion, 457, 458.
Diospolis, acquits Pelagius, 140.
Dort, synod of, condemned Arminius, 203.
Ephesus, condemned Nestorius, 64. decreed against enlarging creeds, 263.
Another at Ephesus, called Conventus Latronum, took part with Eutyches, 136.
Florence, decree concerning purgatory, 285.
Jerusalem, acquitted Pelagius, 140.
Laodicea, decree against invocation of angels, 324.

IN THE EDITOR'S NOTES. 581

Lateran, 2d council, decree against marriage of the clergy, 468.
Ditto, against prayers in an unknown tongue, 344.
Milevum, condemned Pelagius, 140.
Nice, 1st council, condemned Arius, 60.
Nice, 2d council, decree concerning image worship, 311, 312.
Trent, makes a new canon of scripture, 88, 89. teaches that sacraments confer grace, 164.
— canons respecting merit of good works, 171.
— concerning relics and images, 312, 313.
— appeals to council of Nice on same, 313.
— decree and canons respecting extreme unction, 378, 379.
— decree on half-communion, 458.
— doctrine and canon respecting adoration of the eucharist, 417.
— decree making absolution a judicial act, 358.
— decree making attrition with absolution equal to contrition, 360.
— decrees the Vulgate the authentic edition of the Bible, 257.
— decrees concerning purgatory, 285, 286.
— indulgences, 299.
— saint worship, 322.
— doctrine of intention, 388.
— decree in favour of worship in an unknown tongue, 344.
— decree establishing five new sacraments, 351.
— decree concerning auricular confession, 356.
— makes *words* the *matter* of the sacrament of penance, 356.

D.

Deuteronomy vi. 4, much stress laid on, by the Jews, 27, 28.
Dort, synod of, condemned Arminius, 203.

E.

Ebionites, origin, opinions of, 53, 54.
Eucharist, adoration of, decreed by council of Trent, 417. novelty and danger of, 417, 418. vain pretence of adoring conditionally, 445, 446.
Eutyches, founder of a heresy, the cause

of a council being summoned at Constantinople; there delivers his doctrine; degraded; condemned at Chalcedon, 136.
Extreme unction, doctrine and canons of council of Trent concerning, and time of administering, 378, 379. not mentioned in James v. 14; 381.

G.

Godhead, unity of, the Lord our God one Jehovah—much stress laid on by the Jews, 27, 28.
Gregory XVI. (present pontiff) teaches invocation of the Virgin Mary, 326.

H.

Homily, Saxon, rejects the doctrine of the corporal presence, 441, 442. of Church of England on Justification, 161, 162.

I.

Images, canon of Trent, 312. decreed to be worshipped by second council of Nice, 311, 312. of heathen original, 308.
Indulgences, account of their origin, 298. gave occasion to the procedure of Luther, ib. decree of Trent on them, 299.
Infallibility, as founded on the supposed necessity for it, confuted, 234, 235. considered in reference to the Jewish church, 236, 237. confuted, 256. and considered in connection with Sixtus Vth and Clement VIIIth's editions of Vulgate, 257, 258. the precise seat of it unknown and not agreed on among themselves, 256. the power of the keys, examined by Whitby, 260, 261. 'Thou art Peter,' considered by Jewell, 259. 'Hear the Church,' &c., examined, 280.
Intention, doctrine of, 388.
Invocation of saints and angels, catechism of Trent, 326. letters of present pontiff (Gregory XVI.), 326. decree of council of Laodicea against same, 324.

J.

Jansenius, of Ypres, his work 'Augustinus,' account of, Mosheim's statement of it, effect of it on the controversy concerning grace, condemnation of five propositions in it by Innocent the Xth, controversy arising therefrom respecting papal infallibility as to matters of fact, 200, 201.

Justification, through faith, Hooker's judgments thereon, 161. and distinction between England and Rome as to the same, 165, 166. homily of church of England, 161, 162. by gifts received from God, 161.

K.

Keys, power of, considered, 260. Tertullian on, 261. 'Thou art Peter,' &c., primitive interpretation, Jewell, 259. 'Hear the church,' &c. explained, 280.

M.

Macedonius, founder of a heretical sect, elected bishop of Constantinople by the Arians, removed, again took possession of the see, persecutes the orthodox, his opinions, condemned at Constantinople, 135.

Marriage, lawful in ecclesiastics, forbidden by second council of Lateran, condemned by Gregory VII., pleaded for in England and Germany, a sacrament in the papal church, therefore confers grace on the laity, and yet brings pollution and damnation on the clergy, 468, 469.

Mass, sacrifice of, contrary to Hebrews x. 14; 461, 462.

N.

Nestorius, character of, appointed to the see of Constantinople, persecutes the Arians, espouses the cause of Anastasius, cited to the council of Ephesus, broaches his heresy, afterwards prevaricates, deposed, banished, death, 63, 64.

O.

Orders, opinions of Mason, Taylor, Milbourn, referred to thereon, 333.

P.

Pelagianism, vide Pelagius.

Pelagius, character, his heresy, propagates it first privately, condemned at council of Carthage, goes into the East, supported by the bishop of Jerusalem, assumes more boldness, accused before a council at Jerusalem, afterwards acquitted by the council of Diospolis, appeals successfully to the bishop of Rome, opposed by the African church, condemned by the same bishop of Rome who had acquitted him, afterwards publicly condemned at Ephesus and other places, the heresy crushed in the bud by the influence of Augustin, 139, 140.

Prayers, in an unknown tongue, contradictory decrees of councils of Lateran and Trent, 344.

Priesthood of Christ, passes not to another, therefore no new order of priests to offer sacrifice, 462.

Purgatory, decreed at Florence and Trent, canon of Trent, 285. a fire, according to Catechism of Trent, 286. 1 Cor. iii. 10, examined, 293. of heathen original, Meagher's opinion thereon, 182. Bishop Taylor thereon, ib.

R.

Relics, canon of Trent respecting, 312. Eusebius misquoted thereon by Dr. Milner, 318. other fathers similarly corrupted according to Dr. James, 319.

Revelation, book of, citation by Clemens of Rome, 104.

Rome, her fearful corruptions according to Baronius and others, 253. has added new articles to the creed of the church, 263. her question as to 'Where was protestantism before Luther?' answered and retorted, 248—250. a true church in one sense, though not in another, 242, 243.

Ruffinus, character, contests with Jerome, first published the Apostles' creed, 69.

S.

Sacraments, seven in church of Rome, canon of Trent respecting them, 351. creed of pope Pius, on same, Appendix. are justificatory, according to Trent, 164. confer grace *ex opere operato*, according to Trent, 468. this asserted by Leo X., 469.

Samosatenus, Paulus, his character, opinions, condemnation, and expulsion, 47.

Scape-goat, ceremony not a distinct one, parts of the same sacrifice, meaning, 65.

Schism, scandalous, in the popedom, suppressed by council of Constance, 273, 274. vide Separation.

Scripture, canon of, published at the council of Trent, 88, 89. confirmed by the creed of pope Pius IV. 89. church of Rome differs in this canon from itself in former ages, 90. current of antiquity against their canon, true state of this question, 90, 91. not the judge of controversies, but the rule whereby to judge them, 91, 92. the only rule by which to determine the notes of the church, 92. a sufficient rule for all who believe them to be the word of God, 92.

Separation, from papal church, true grounds of—what constitutes schism—papal church guilty of schism—therefore the cause of the separation, 100, 101.

Semipelagianism, vide Cassian.

Socinianism, vide Socinus.

Socinus, Lælius and Faustus, founders of the sect of Socinians, their characters, title of Socinian used sometimes in an unlimited sense, sum of their theology, 60, 61.

Spalato, archbishop of, visits England, renounces popery, embraces it again, imprisonment and death, Preface ix, x.

Supererogation, doctrine of, taught in Catechism of council of Trent, 171.

T.

Temple, second, how more glorious than the first, 120.

Transubstantiation, makes Christ a transgressor of the Levitical law, 406. rejected in the Saxon Homily, 441, 442.

Trent, council of, defined and determined new articles of faith, not previously defined or determined, 284,285. Stillingfleet's views and arguments thereon, ib. canon on seven sacraments, 351. on absolution, 358. on confession, 356. on indulgences, 299. on works, 171. on efficacy of sacraments, *ex opere operato*, 164. on purgatory, 285, 286. on relics, 312. on images, ib. on Latin prayers, 344.

Trinity, traces of the doctrine amongst the Hindoos, 42.

U.

Unction, vide Extreme.

W.

Works, inefficient for justification, judgment of the church in her Homily, 161. judgment of Hooker, 165. canon of Trent on the same—catechism of Trent asserts that they can satisfy both for a man's own sins and those of others, 171.

NAMES AND WORKS

OF

AUTHORS REFERRED TO, OR QUOTED,

IN

THE EDITOR'S NOTES.

Name and Designation.	Centuries in which they flourished.	Works quoted.
Allport, Rev. Josiah, Minister of St. James, Birmingham,		Translation of Davenant on the Colossians.
Bagster,		Comprehensive Bible.
Barrow, Isaac, D.D., Master of Trinity College, Cambridge,	17th	Treatise of the Pope's Supremacy, and a Discourse concerning the Unity of the Church.
Buchannan, Claudius, D.D. Vice-Provost of the College of Fort William, Bengal,	18th and 19th	Christian Researches in Asia.
Chillingworth, William, A.M.	17th	Religion of Protestants, a safe way to Salvation.
Clarke, Adam, LL.D.,	19th	Sermons.
Clemens, bishop of Rome,	1st	Epistle to the Corinthians.
Cosin, John, D.D. Bishop of Durham,	17th	A Scholastical History of the Canon of Scripture.
Cossart, vide Labbe.		
Davenant, John, D.D., bishop of Sarum,	17th	Letter to Bishop Hall.
Evagrius Scholasticus, of Antioch,	6th	Ecclesiastical History.
Eusebius, Pamphilus, bishop of Cæsarea,	4th	Ecclesiastical History.
Gibson, Edmund, bishop of London,	17th and 18th	Preservative against Popery.
Gregory XVI. pope,		Encyclical Letter.
Homilies of the church of England.	16th	
Hooker, Richard,	16th	Sermon on Justification.
Horne, Thos. Hartwell, B.D.		Introduction to the Critical Study and Knowledge of the Holy Scriptures.
Hume, David,	18th	History of England.
James, Thomas, keeper of the Bodleian Library,	16th and 17th	Bellum Papale, and Treatise of the Corruption of Scripture, Councils, and Fathers, &c. &c., for Maintenance of Popery.

Name and designation.	Centuries in which they flourished.	Works quoted.
Jewell, John, D.D., bishop of Sarum,	16th	A Replie unto M. Hardinge's Answeare.
Labbe and Cossart,	17th	Edition of the Councils.
Lynde, Sir H.,	17th	Via Tuta and Via Devia.
Maclaine, Archibald, D. D.,	18th	Translation of Mosheim.
Magee, William, D. D., archbishop of Dublin,	19th	Discourses on the Scripture Doctrine of Atonement and Sacrifice.
Mason, Francis, B. D., Fellow of Merton College, Oxford,	16th	Of the Consecration of the Bishops in the Church of England.
Milner, John, D. D., bishop of the Roman church,	19th	The End of Religious Controversy.
Milbourn, Rev. Luke,	17th	A Legacy to the Church of England.
Meagher, Andrew, Doctor of the Sorbonne,	18th	The Popish Mass.
Mosheim, Laurence, D. D., Chancellor of the University of Gottingen,	18th	Ecclesiastical History.
Morney, Philip, Lord du Plessis,	16th and 17th	Mystery of Iniquity, the History of the Papacy.
Page, James R., A. M.,		Letters to a Romish Priest.
Pearson, John, D.D. bishop of Chester,	17th	Exposition of the Creed.
Sixtus V., pope,	16th	Preface to edition of the Vulgate.
Socrates Scholasticus, of Constantinople,	4th	Ecclesiastical History.
Stillingfleet, Edward, D. D., bishop of Worcester,	17th	A Rational Account of the Grounds of Protestant Religion.
Taylor, Jeremy, D. D., bishop of Down and Connor,	17th	Polemical Discourses.
Wake, William, D. D., archbishop of Canterbury,	17th and 18th	Exposition of the Doctrine of the Church of England, in Reply to Bossuet, bishop of Meaux.
Whitby, Daniel, D. D., Prebendary of Sarum,	16th and 17th	Paraphrase of the New Testament, and Romish Doctrines not from the Beginning.

www.ingramcontent.com/pod-product-compliance
Lightning Source LLC
Chambersburg PA
CBHW020629230426
43665CB00008B/97